CA Proficiency 2

Taxation 2 (NI)

2019–2020

Published in 2019 by
Chartered Accountants Ireland
Chartered Accountants House
47–49 Pearse Street
Dublin 2
www.charteredaccountants.ie

ISBN: 978-1-912350-27-8

Typeset by Deanta Global Publishing Services
Printed by CPI Group (UK) Ltd, Croydon, CR0 4YY

Contents

PART FOUR STAMP TAXES AND VAT ON PROPERTY

Chartered Accountants Ireland *Code of Ethics*

Chartered Accountants Ireland's *Code of Ethics* applies to all aspects of a Chartered Accountant's professional life, including dealing with corporation tax issues, capital gains tax issues, inheritance tax issues and stamp duty issues. The *Code of Ethics* outlines the principles that should guide a Chartered Accountant, namely:

- Integrity
- Objectivity
- Professional Competence and Due Care
- Confidentiality
- Professional Behaviour.

As a Chartered Accountant, you will have to ensure that your dealings with the tax aspects of your professional life are in compliance with these fundamental principles. Set out in **Appendix 2** is further information regarding these principles and their importance in guiding you on how to deal with issues which may arise throughout your professional life, including giving tax advice and preparing tax computations.

Part One

Corporation Tax

1

Introduction and General Principles of Corporation Tax

Learning Objectives

After studying this chapter you will understand:

- Companies are liable to corporation tax on the different types of profit that they earn, with each source of income and chargeable gain computed separately.
- The computation of taxable profits is based on the profits per the financial statements, with certain tax adjustments.
- The computation of a company's chargeable gains/(losses).
- The principles for determining when an accounting period for corporation tax purposes begins and ends.
- The rate of corporation tax applying to taxable total profits.
- Residence principles for corporation tax.
- Administrative aspects of paying corporation tax and filing corporation tax returns.
- An awareness of the failure to notify penalties for corporation tax.
- An awareness of the legislation in regard to senior accounting officers and their duties.
- Corporation tax enquiry procedures.
- Record-keeping requirements for companies.
- The penalty regime for errors in returns.
- Details of the HMRC initiative, Managing Serious Defaulters.
- Details of the rules for publishing deliberate tax defaulters.
- An awareness of the legislation that requires certain large companies to publish their tax strategies.
- An awareness of 'country-by-country' reporting.

Chartered Accountants Ireland's *Code of Ethics* applies to all aspects of a Chartered Accountant's professional life, including dealing with corporation tax issues. Further information regarding the principles in the *Code of Ethics* is set out in **Appendix 2**.

In addition, **Appendix 3** examines the distinction between tax planning, tax avoidance and tax evasion, which can arise in relation to all taxes, including corporation tax.

1.1 The UK Corporation Tax Regime

Corporation tax chargeable is calculated by applying the relevant corporation tax rate to the company's taxable total profits (TTP). The financial year (FY) for corporation tax commences on 1 April every year, so the FY 2019 commenced on 1 April 2019. The main rate of corporation tax for the FY 2019 is 19% (FY 2018: 19%).

Payment of corporation tax depends on the size of the company (see **Section 1.5**).

1.2 Overview – Application and Accounting Periods

A company is defined as "any body corporate or unincorporated association". Therefore, unincorporated societies, trade and voluntary associations, members' clubs and certain charities may find themselves within the corporation tax regime. Partnerships are specifically excluded from the definition of a "body corporate" (although a limited liability partnership (LLP) is classed as a body corporate. The taxation of LLPs is beyond the scope of this textbook).

Corporation tax is levied on the profits of companies, as defined, and is payable by the company. For companies, all transactions should be included in the financial statements. Therefore, the computation of corporation tax requires the analysis of those profits between the various sources of income and chargeable gains. The types of profit that are chargeable to corporation tax consist of trading income, chargeable gains, property income, miscellaneous income and surplus non-trade loan relationship credits. A dividend payment is not an expense of the company and therefore does not attract tax relief per se. A company's income and gains are generally calculated using income tax and CGT principles and the rules for the various types of income apply, in the main, to the UK corporation tax regime albeit with some differences.

The FY for corporation tax purposes commences each year on 1 April and ends on the following 31 March, with corporation tax rates fixed for financial years.

Directors of UK companies are required to prepare and file statutory accounts with Companies Registry (or Companies House) for every 12-month accounting period. At the end of an accounting period, HM Revenue & Customs (HMRC) will issue a notice (Form CT603) specifying the 12-month period for which HMRC consider that a corporation tax return (Form CT600 (2019) Version 3) is due. While the corporation tax accounting period would normally follow the statutory accounting period, there are specific rules that determine the date of commencement and cessation of a corporation tax accounting period.

1.2.1 Accounting Periods

Corporation tax is assessed on the profits arising in the company's accounting period. The term "accounting period" is given a special meaning for corporation tax purposes. Ordinarily it is the period for which the company makes up its accounts ("period of account"), **but an accounting period for corporation tax cannot exceed 12 months**.

1.2.2 The Beginning of the Accounting Period

For corporation tax purposes, the first accounting period of a company begins whenever the company comes within the charge to UK corporation tax. A company may come within the charge to UK corporation tax in one of several ways:

1. A company not resident in the UK, which is carrying on a trade outside the UK, may become resident in the UK. Its first accounting period will start on the day it becomes UK resident.
2. A company may acquire for the first time a source of income chargeable to corporation tax. For example, a non-resident company may be within the charge to to UK corporation tax on certain of its income streams (see **Chapter 8, Section 8.2** for more details).
3. A new company may be created and acquire a source of income.
4. An unincorporated partnership or sole trade may become incorporated.

1.2.3 The End of the Accounting Period

An accounting period runs for a maximum of 12 months from its start. It will end earlier if the company's own accounting date (i.e. its period of account) is less than 12 months. A new accounting period starts immediately after the end of the previous accounting period, unless the accounting period ended because the company ceased altogether to be within the charge to corporation tax.

An accounting period ends when any one of the following happens:

- the expiry of 12 months from the beginning of the accounting period;
- the accounting date of the company, that is the date to which it makes up its accounts;
- the end of a period for which a company does not make up accounts;
- the company begins to trade;
- the company comes within the charge to corporation tax in respect of its trade or, if it carries on more than one trade, of all its trades;
- the company ceases to trade;
- the company ceases to be within the charge to corporation tax in respect of its trade or, if it carries on more than one trade, of all its trades;
- the company begins to be resident in the UK;
- the company ceases to be resident in the UK;
- the company ceases to be within the charge to corporation tax; or
- the commencement of the winding up of the company.

Example 1.1
Start Ltd was incorporated on 1 June 2019. The money subscribed for share capital was put on deposit. The company commenced to trade on 1 September 2019. It prepared its first set of financial statements for the period ended 31 December 2019 and intends to prepare annual financial statements to 31 December each year thereafter.

As Start Ltd acquired a source of income on 1 June, an accounting period commenced. As it commenced to trade on 1 September, an accounting period is deemed to end, even though no actual set of financial statements are prepared. Therefore, Start Ltd has an accounting period of three months, ending on 31 August 2019. Its next accounting period is from 1 September to 31 December 2019. Thereafter it will have accounting periods ending on 31 December each year.

1.2.4 Companies that Prepare Accounts for a Period of Less Than 12 Months

For accounting periods of less than 12 months that have resulted from a change in the normal annual accounting date of the company, HMRC has no special powers. For example, if a company has prepared a 12-month set of accounts to 31 December 2018, then an eight-month set of accounts to 31 August 2019 followed by a 12-month set of accounts to 31 August 2019, corporation tax is simply payable for each of the three accounting periods. However, when seeking to amend the accounting periods of a company, the relevant company law conditions must be met. Broadly, a company may not extend accounting periods more than once in five years unless it falls into some very specific categories.

1.2.5 Companies that Prepare Accounts for a Period Exceeding 12 Months

As the maximum length of an accounting period is 12 months, where a company prepares a set of accounts for a period exceeding 12 months, this "period of account" must be broken down into tranches, each a maximum of 12 months long.

> ***Example 1.2***
> X Ltd, a trading company, prepared a set of accounts for 18 months ending on 30 June 2020. In these circumstances corporation tax is payable for the following "accounting periods":
>
> 1. 12-month accounting period to 31 December 2019.
> 2. Six-month accounting period to 30 June 2020 (remember an accounting period is terminated automatically by reference to the date to which a set of accounts is prepared).

As you can see from this example, **if the period of account is longer than 12 months, the first accounting period will always be at least 12 months long.**

In the above example, the statement of profit or loss was 18 months long, meaning a tax-adjusted trading profits computation would have to be prepared. This would involve adjusting for the various normal add-backs and deductions to produce a tax-adjusted trading profits computation corresponding to an 18-month period. One would then **time-apportion** the tax-adjusted trading profits for this 18-month period to arrive at the relevant tax-adjusted trading income for each of the accounting periods mentioned above. Capital allowances are then computed separately for each of the two accounting periods. In this situation, therefore, capital allowances are not allowed as a trading expense until after the trading income has been time-apportioned.

It should be particularly noted that, as a general rule, the profits should be apportioned on a time basis according to the number of days in the accounting period. However, HMRC reserves the right to divide and apportion profits in a different fashion if they believe, and can demonstrate, that it was a "more accurate and fairer estimate". Notwithstanding this, chargeable gains are **always** allocated to the period in which they occurred. For example, if there was only one capital disposal in the 18-month period, say on 1 May 2020, then the adjusted chargeable gain would be assessed and brought into the computation for the six-month accounting period ending on 30 June 2020. In addition, qualifying charitable donations (see **Chapter 3**) are split between the two chargeable accounting periods, based on the date that the donation is actually paid. Finally, dividends that represent franked investment income are split between the two chargeable accounting periods, based on the date of receipt of the dividend (rather than being time-apportioned).

Each of the split periods will require the preparation of a separate company tax return, and have separate due dates for the payment of corporation tax. There is only one filing deadline, however, which is normally 12 months after the end of the second period of account.

1.2.6 Corporation Tax Self-assessment

As each company has its own accounting period end, the law relates payment of tax and filing of returns to that period end, split if necessary, as discussed above. Companies report their liability to corporation tax to HMRC via the self-assessment procedures and each company must calculate its own liability. Thus companies are required to prepare a corporation tax computation, setting out the liability due, and to submit this to HMRC in conjunction with the corporation tax return (Form CT600, to include any relevant supplementary pages) and a copy of their statutory accounts, which are the accounts the company must file at Companies House/Companies Registry or that the organisation must prepare under its constitution. This includes directors' and auditors' reports. However, if the company files abbreviated accounts at Companies House/Companies Registry, it **must** file full accounts as part of its company tax return. Accounts can be prepared under IFRS or UK GAAP. See **Section 1.10** for more on corporation tax self-assessment.

1.2.7 UK GAAP

For the avoidance of doubt, UK GAAP includes accounts of companies prepared under International Accounting Standards, International Financial Reporting Standards and under Financial Reporting Standards, including FRS 102 *The Financial Reporting Standard applicable in the UK and Republic of Ireland*. Students should note that the adoption of FRS 102 may result in the need for transitional adjustments for tax purposes, which are beyond the scope of this book.

1.3 The Charge to Corporation Tax

Corporation tax is assessed on the profits of companies for accounting periods. Accordingly the concept of basis periods in the income tax code is not carried into the corporation tax system.

The question of whether, and how, a company is to be charged to corporation tax depends on whether or not it is resident in the UK. A company is resident in the UK if it is incorporated in the UK. If it is not incorporated in the UK, it will still be deemed resident in the UK (for corporation tax purposes) if it is centrally managed and controlled in the UK.

In the case of a **company resident in the UK**, the charge to corporation tax is imposed on **all its income** wherever arising and **its chargeable gains** wherever the assets were situated. In a situation where a company is UK resident and a source of income is taxed both in the UK and in another country, double taxation relief should be considered (see **Chapter 8**). However, section 18A of the Corporation Tax Act 2009 (CTA 2009) does allow a UK-resident company to exempt all of its foreign branches permanently from UK corporation tax (see **Chapter 8, Section 8.1.1**).

Chapter 8, Section 8.2 sets out the scenarios where a non-resident company is chargeable to UK corporation tax.

There are four special rules in the corporation tax code which should be noted at this stage:

1. The taxation of dividends received by UK companies provides various exemptions for dividends received (see **Chapter 5**).
2. A paying company is, generally, not required to withhold income tax from annual interest, royalties or annuities if the recipient is also a company resident in the UK. If interest is being paid by a UK company to a company not resident in the UK, basic rate income tax at 20% must be deducted and the CT61 procedure followed. Non-resident companies can apply to HMRC to have the interest paid gross without deduction of tax (see **Chapter 3**).
3. Companies may receive income that has suffered income tax at source. Corporation tax is charged on the gross amount of any payments received by a company under deduction of income tax (see **Chapter 3**).
4. No deduction is allowed for dividends paid by a company (or any item treated as a distribution of profits under tax rules) when computing taxable profits. Nor, indeed, is any deduction allowed for the corporation tax payment itself.

1.4 Rates of Corporation Tax

Rate	Name	As From	Taxable total profits (TTP)
19%	Main rate	FY 2018	All profits, irrespective of size
19%	Main rate	FY 2019	All profits, irrespective of size
17%	Main rate	FY 2020	All profits, irrespective of size

The above rates are applicable for single companies with a full 12-month accounting period.

1.4.1 Main Rate of Corporation Tax

The main rate of corporation tax for the 2018 financial year, i.e. the FY that commenced on 1 April 2018, was 19%. The main rate for FY 2019 is 19%, and will fall to 17% for FY 2020 commencing on 1 April 2020.

A separate corporation tax regime is due to come into operation in Northern Ireland at a currently undetermined date. From that date, qualifying profits of certain qualifying companies may be subject to a 12.5% rate of corporation tax. The detailed provisions of this regime are beyond the scope of this textbook.

> ***Example 1.3***
> Mary Ltd had taxable total profits (TTP) from selling clothes of £200,000 in the year ended 31 March 2020.
>
> Corporation tax payable by Mary Ltd is £38,000 (£200,000 × 19%).

1.4.2 Short Accounting Periods

If a company produces accounts for a period of less than 12 months, taxable total profits are still taxed at the main rate applicable to the relevant financial year(s).

1.4.3 Accounting Period Straddles Two Financial Years

Where a company's accounting period straddles two financial years, and the rate of corporation tax for each year is not the same, its taxable total profits must be apportioned on a time basis for each of the two financial years and then charged to corporation tax at the rates applicable for each financial year.

Once again, HMRC reserve the right to amend this general rule if a more accurate and fairer estimate can be applied to the split between the financial years.

> ***Example 1.4***
> For the year ended 30 September 2020, Starlight Ltd had TTP of £400,000. The corporation tax payable by the company is as follows:

FY 2019: 1 October 2019–31 March 2020	
£400,000 × 6/12 = £200,000 × 19%	£38,000
FY 2020: 1 April 2020–30 September 2020	
£400,000 × 6/12 = £200,000 × 17%	£34,000
Total liability	£72,000

1.5 Dates of Payment of Corporation Tax

1.5.1 Overview

A small or medium-sized company's corporation tax is due and payable nine months and one day after the end of the accounting period. However, "large" companies are required to pay their corporation tax liabilities in up to four quarterly instalments. The number of quarterly instalment payments a company needs to make depends on the length of the accounting period and the number of related 51% group companies at the end of the previous accounting period. A company is deemed to be "large" if its augmented profits exceed the upper relevant maximum amount, currently £1,500,000, as adjusted for the number of related 51% group companies at the end of the previous accounting period. However, the company will not be required to pay by instalments in an accounting period where the "augmented profits" for that period do not exceed £10 million **and** it was not "large" in the previous period. Also, a company is not treated as "large" for an accounting period if its corporation tax liability does not exceed £10,000.

Augmented profits are taxable total profits (TTP) plus non-group franked investment income (FII). FII is any dividend received irrespective of location of the paying company. Only non-group FII is included, i.e. dividends received from shareholdings less than 51%.

However, while augmented profits are measured against the above limits to establish if instalment payments are required, the actual instalment payments are only calculated on the basis of TTP. This is because, often, any non-group FII received will meet one of the dividend exemptions outlined in **Chapter 5**.

1.5.2 Related 51% Group Companies

The above limits (of £10 million and £1.5 million) are reduced where the company has related 51% group companies at the end of the previous accounting period and where the accounting period is less than 12 months. The number of related 51% group companies to be taken into account for the purpose of these limits are those in existence **on the last day of the previous accounting period**.

For the purpose of the corporation tax instalment payment rules, a company is classed as a related 51% group company if it is a member of a 51% group. A "group" of companies, for this purpose, means a group headed by a company. So if, for example, an individual shareholder and their family were to directly own the shares in a number of companies, the companies would not be related 51% group companies.

If, instead, an individual shareholder and their family were to own a company, which in turn owned at least 51% of the share capital of three subsidiaries, then the four companies would be related 51% group companies. In this situation, the upper relevant maximum amount would be divided by four to determine whether each company was or was not liable to pay corporation tax in instalments, assuming each company was a related 51% group company at the end of the previous accounting period.

A related 51% holding is either a direct or indirect holding of at least 51% of the issued share capital or voting power or being entitled to at least 51% of the distributable income or net assets on a winding up. The residence of a company is irrelevant.

Importantly, companies that have only been related 51% group companies for part of any accounting period are deemed to have been related 51% group companies for the whole of the accounting period.

However, a related 51% group company is ignored if it has not carried on any trade or business at any time in the accounting period (or for the part of the period during which it was a related 51% group company); generally this applies to dormant companies.

Finally, a holding company is considered as not carrying on a trade or business (and thus is not included in the number of related 51% group companies for the purposes of the instalment payment rules) provided that:

1. its only assets are shares in subsidiaries;
2. it is not entitled to deduct any outgoings as charges or management expenses; and
3. its only profits are dividends from subsidiaries and these are distributed in full to its shareholders.

All of the above conditions must be satisfied.

The related 51% group company rules therefore play an important part in determining if a company is required to pay corporation tax in instalments.

Example 1.5

A Ltd (which prepares accounts to March each year) has five related 51% group companies (all wholly-owned subsidiaries) at the end of the year ended 31 March 2019. A Ltd then acquires a new subsidiary in September 2019, but also disposes of two of its subsidiaries in September 2019. A Ltd has augmented profits for the accounting period ended 31 March 2020 of £425,000. A Ltd was not "large" in 2019.

To determine if the company was "large" in 2020, the number of related 51% group companies at the end of the previous accounting period is used. Therefore, £1.5 million would be divided by six – being five related 51% group companies plus the company itself. The threshold would be £250,000. Having established that the company is "large" in 2020 (because it has augmented profits of £425,000, which is clearly in excess of £250,000) we then need to determine if it is subject to the quarterly instalment regime.

As A Ltd was not "large" in the prior year (i.e. in 2019), the £10 million threshold is used for the purposes of assessing whether instalments are required in the 2020 period. We divide this by the number of related 51% group companies at the end of the 2019 period (i.e. six – being five related 51% group companies plus the company itself).

The limit for A Ltd is thus £1,666,667 (£10,000,000/6). Therefore A Ltd will not pay in instalments for the accounting period ended 31 March 2020 and its corporation tax will fall due on 1 January 2021. The acquisition of a new subsidiary in 2019 and the disposal of two of the existing subsidiaries does not impact on the number of related 51% group companies because it is the number of related 51% group companies at the end of the previous accounting period, for both the £1,500,000 and £10,000,000 limits, that is used.

However, when assessing whether instalments will be required in 2021, the number of related 51% group companies will be six (and the limits will be divided by seven, being A Ltd plus six related 51% group companies). The acquisition is counted, but the two disposals are not – because a company is treated as a related 51% group company for the whole period if it is one even for a single day.

1.5.3 Due Date and Calculation of Instalments

Unless the "large" company is also classed as "very large" (see **Section 1.5.4**), the first of the maximum four quarterly instalments falls due six months and 13 days after the start of the accounting period, the second after a further three months, the third after a further three months with the fourth and final instalment due three months and 14 days after the end of the accounting period. In essence, for a company with a 12-month accounting period, the instalments are due on the 14th day of the seventh and tenth months during the accounting period and the first and fourth months after the end of the accounting period.

Where the accounting period is less than 12 months, the final instalment remains due on the normal date, three months and 14 days after the end of the accounting period. In this scenario, earlier instalments only fall due if their due date is prior to the date of the final instalment.

The liability due at each instalment is calculated using the following formula, namely:

$$\frac{3 \times \text{company's total liability}}{\text{No. of months in accounting period}}$$

For example, for an eight-month period, the first instalment would be 3/8ths of the total tax liability, then the second instalment would be another 3/8ths, and a final instalment of 2/8ths of the total tax liability for the period. Interest is charged on instalments paid late at the late instalment rate as set by HMRC (3.25% from 21 August 2018; 3% between 21 November 2017 and 20 August 2018).

Example 1.6
Trust Limited is a large company with an accounting year end of 31 December. Its instalments of corporation tax will fall due for payment on:

(a) 14 July and 14 October in the accounting period; and
(b) 14 January and 14 April after the accounting period.

Example 1.7
Syracuse Limited had a corporation liability for the year ended 31 March 2020 of £1,000,000. The amount of each instalment is 3 × (1,000,000/12) = £250,000 and these payments will fall due on: 14 October 2019, 14 January 2020, 14 April 2020 and 14 July 2020.

Example 1.8
Andes Limited has a corporation tax liability of £990,000 for the nine-month period ended 31 October 2019. The instalment amount is calculated initially by applying the above formula, giving a figure of £330,000 (namely 3 × (£990,000/9)). The instalments and due dates are thus:

- £330,000 on 14 August 2019,
- £330,000 on 14 November 2019 and
- £330,000 on 14 February 2020.

The first instalment is always due six months and 13 days after the first day of the accounting period, i.e. 14 August 2019 which is six months and 13 days after 1 February 2019. The final instalment is always due three months and 14 days after the end of the accounting period.

As noted above, the instalments are based on the estimated corporation tax liability for the current period. Thus it is very important that companies accurately forecast their potential corporation tax liabilities to avoid incurring significant interest charges. This will invariably entail the company reviewing its estimates each quarter and adjusting payments already made and still to be made accordingly.

1.5.4 Very Large Companies

The Corporation Tax (Instalment Payments) (Amendment) Regulations 2017 implemented changes to the due date of instalments for "very large" companies. The rules apply to accounting periods beginning on or after 1 April 2019 and require "very large" companies to make payments earlier than "large" companies.

A "very large" company is one whose augmented profits exceed £20 million. Again, this threshold is adjusted for the number of related 51% group companies at the end of the previous accounting period and if the company has an accounting period less than 12 months. A company is not treated as "very large" for an accounting period if its corporation tax liability does not exceed £10,000.

When a company is first classed as "very large" no grace period is given, i.e. the earlier due dates will immediately apply to that accounting period.

Where the accounting period is 12 months, the first payment will be due two months and 13 days after the beginning of the accounting period. The second, third and fourth payments will be due three months after the previous payment, i.e. the second payment three months after the first, the third three months after the second and so on. This will be the 14th day of months three, six, nine and 12 of the accounting period.

Where the accounting period is less than 12 months, the final instalment will remain due on the normal date, i.e. on the 14th day of the last month of the accounting period. Once again, earlier instalments only fall due if their due date is prior to the date of the final instalment.

The calculation of each instalment is unchanged and the £10,000 rule (adjusted if necessary for accounting periods of less than 12 months) equally applies.

Example 1.9

Design Ltd has a 12-month accounting period ended 31 March 2020. It is a "very large" company with a projected corporation tax liability of £5,000,000.

Each corporation tax instalment is:

$$\frac{(3 \times £5{,}000{,}000)}{12} = £1{,}250{,}000$$

The due date of each instalment is:

1. First instalment: £1,250,000 due 14 June 2019 (two months and 13 days from the beginning of the accounting period).
2. Second instalment: £1,250,000 due 14 September 2019 (three months after the first instalment).
3. Third instalment: £1,250,000 due 14 December 2019 (three months after the second instalment).
4. Fourth instalment: £1,250,000 due 14 March 2020 (three months after the third).

Design Ltd will therefore pay its entire corporation tax liability for 2020 before the end of the period.

Example 1.10

Tidal Ltd has an eight-month accounting period ended 30 November 2019. It is a "very large" company with a projected corporation tax liability of £6,000,000.

Each corporation tax instalment is:

$$\frac{(3 \times £6{,}000{,}000)}{8} = £2{,}250{,}000$$

The due date of each is as follows:

1. First instalment: £2,250,000 due 14 June 2019 (two months and 13 days from the beginning of the accounting period).
2. Second instalment: £2,250,000 due 14 September 2019 (three months after the first instalment).
3. Third instalment: £1,500,000 due 14 November 2019 (as the last instalment falls due before the deadline for the third instalment, the third instalment also falls due on this date).

Again, the company will have paid its entire corporation tax liability for the accounting period in question before the period has ended.

1.5.5 Interest

If a company pays its corporation tax liability after the due date, then it will be charged late payment interest, calculated from the day after the normal due date until the effective date of payment. For companies required to pay in instalments, the position is considered after the due date for each instalment (where applicable) on a cumulative basis and the interest position is calculated by HMRC after the company submits its corporation tax return.

If a company has overpaid corporation tax, it may make a repayment claim and it will also be entitled to interest on the repayment. The repayment interest runs from the "material date" to the date when the repayment was issued. Interest paid/received on late payments or overpayments of corporation tax are treated as interest paid/received on a non-trading loan relationship and included in the calculation of the net loan relationship debit or credit. The effect of this is that interest paid is deductible for corporation tax and any interest received is taxable.

Example 1.11

Wright Limited, a large company, has always prepared accounts to 31 March. It had paid the following instalments in respect of the accounting period ending 31 March 2020:

£2.5 million on 14 October 2019, £6.5 million on 14 January 2020, £3 million on 14 April 2020 and £3 million on 14 July 2020, a total of £15 million.

On submission of its corporation tax return, the company's tax liability was actually £16 million, and the balance of £1 million was paid on 1 January 2021.

Thus the £16 million should have been paid in instalments of £4 million each (3 × (£16 million/12)) and the schedule below sets out the under/over payments:

Date	**Paid**	**Actually Due**	**Under/(over)**	**Cumulative**
	£	£	£	£
14 October 2019	2.5m	4m	1.5m	1.5m
14 January 2020	6.5m	4m	(2.5m)	(1m)
14 April 2020	3m	4m	1m	Nil
14 July 2020	3m	4m	1m	1m

Interest would thus be charged/(received) as follows:

- Charged on £1.5 million from 14 October 2019 until 13 January 2020.
- Received on £1 million from 14 January 2020 until 13 April 2020.
- Charged on £1 million from 14 July 2020 until 31 December 2020.

1.5.6 Penalties

In order to dissuade companies from deliberately understating their instalments, HMRC reserve the right to impose penalties (on top of the above interest charges) where they find no justifiable reasons for inadequate instalment payments. This would normally involve consideration of the contemporaneous records of the company and a request for the company's explanation of why their estimates were incorrect.

A penalty can arise where:

- a company, or person acting on its behalf, deliberately or recklessly fails to pay the right amount on a particular instalment date; or

- a company, or person acting on its behalf, fraudulently or negligently makes a claim for repayment under the Instalment Regulations.

The penalty is an amount not exceeding twice the amount of interest charged on any unpaid amount in respect of the total liability of the company for its accounting period. Any penalties paid are not deductible for corporation tax purposes.

1.5.7 Group Payment Arrangements

Given the potential uncertainties over the tax liabilities of individual group members and, until such time as all relevant group relief and other claims have been determined after the end of the accounting period, HMRC permits arrangements whereby instalments can be paid by one nominated company in the group and subsequently allocated amongst the group in line with their eventual individual final liabilities. This is particularily efficient from an interest perspective as often the final liabilities in groups are dependent on group relief allocations.

1.5.8 Overview of Instalment Payment Rules

To summarise, the following steps should be taken:

1. Determine if the company is "large" in the current period (i.e. divide the £1.5 million limit by the number of related 51% group companies on the last day of the previous accounting period). The company is "large" if augmented profits (TTP plus FII) are greater than this threshold.
2. If the company is "large" in this period (but was not in the previous period), the £10 million threshold is used to assess whether quarterly instalments are required. (Note, this test only affects whether the tax liability is due to be paid in instalments; it does not affect the initial test to determine whether the company is "large" in the period). The £10 million threshold is divided by the number of related 51% group companies at the **end of the previous period.**
3. If the threshold in 2. is not exceeded, instalment payments are not required. If this threshold is exceeded and the company has a corporation tax liability in excess of £10,000 (adjusted if necessary), calculate the instalment payments using the following formula:

$$\frac{3 \times \text{corporation tax liability}}{\text{No. of months in accounting period}}$$

4. If the company is required to make instalment payments in the period, set out the due dates of each instalment. Remember that "very large" companies have different instalment deadlines. A "very large" company is one whose augmented profits exceed £20 million (in any accounting period beginning on or after 1 April 2019) adjusted for the number of related 51% group companies at the end of the previous accounting period and if the company has an accounting period of less than 12 months.

1.6 Computation of Income

The basic rule for the calculation of taxable income is that, apart from certain special provisions relevant only to companies, it is computed in accordance with income tax principles.

The income tax scheme of capital allowances and balancing charges is brought into the corporation tax system. However, **capital allowances** due to trading companies are **treated as**

trading expenses for corporation tax purposes and not as a deduction from the assessable income as in the case of income tax.

For the purposes of computing the tax-adjusted profits of a company from its statement of profit or loss for an accounting period, the following particular points of difference should be noted:

- Bona fide directors' salaries, fees, benefits payable for directors, etc. are deductible, unlike the drawings/salary of a self-employed person.
- Where a director has a company car available for private use, there is no adjustment for the "personal element" for corporation tax purposes, unlike the personal element of a self-employed person.

> ***Example 1.12***
> Joe and Ann jointly own Deduction Ltd and are both directors on the board of the company. Deduction Ltd pays all the motor expenses incurred in running Joe's car. Only 75% of the expenses are incurred in respect of the business. The balance of 25% is personal.
>
> Deduction Ltd will be entitled to a full deduction for all the motor expenses, even though some of the expense is personal; however Joe will be liable to income tax on the benefit in kind arising on the personal motor expenses paid by the company.

- Dividend payments by a company are not deductible for corporation tax purposes as they are treated as appropriations of profit. In most cases, however, dividends paid by a company will not form part of the 'profit or loss before tax' result and will be deducted after.
- Interest and related costs on borrowings, which are used for trading purposes (e.g. financing of stock, debtors and fixed assets used for the purpose of the trade), are fully allowable on the **accruals** basis. If, on the other hand, a company has borrowed money and applies the funds for non-trading purposes, say, for the purchase of shares in a subsidiary or as other investments, then such interest charges are not deductible against trading income. However, these would generally qualify as non-trade deficits under the loan relationship rules (see **Chapter 3**). It should be noted, however, that the tax deduction a company receives for interest and related costs on borrowings (irrespective of its purpose) may be subject to a restriction as a result of the corporate interest restriction legislation (see **Chapter 9, Section 9.5**)

A pro forma corporation tax computation, together with notes on important adjustments, is set out in **Chapter 2**.

1.7 Computation of Investment Income

A company's investment income would, in the main, include property income and income from non-trading loan relationships. Companies that include investment business can claim a deduction for management expenses (see **Chapter 2**).

1.7.1 Property Income (Income from Land and Buildings)

Companies are charged corporation tax on income arising from the letting of land and property, wherever situated. Income generated from land and property in the UK is aggregated into one "UK property business". Income from all land and property outside the UK is combined into the company's "overseas property business".

Property business profits/(losses) are computed in accordance with generally accepted accounting principles and the types of income assessable under this schedule would include payments for a licence to occupy, exercise or use of a right over land, income from furnished lettings (to include furnished holiday lettings), ground rents and other annual payments in respect of land and so forth.

Landlords of residential property can deduct the actual costs incurred on replacing furnishings in the company's accounting period. This relief is available for domestic items, including furnishings, appliances and kitchenware provided for the use of a lessee in a dwelling-house. Fixtures are excluded. The old item must no longer be available for use in the dwelling-house. The expenditure must be of a capital nature and incurred "wholly and exclusively" for the purposes of the property business. Furthermore, no deduction is available if the dwelling-house qualifies as furnished holiday accommodation. The amount of the deduction is the expenditure incurred on the replacement item.

Interest is excluded from a property income computation and is dealt with as a non-trading "debit" under the loan relationship rules (see **Section 2.5.3** and **Chapter 3**). Unlike for individuals, relief for finance costs in respect of residential properties is not restricted.

Basis of Assessment

Tax is charged on the income arising during the accounting period. The rent taken into account is the amount receivable whether or not it is actually received, i.e. on an accruals rather than a cash basis. The cash basis for property income that applies to individuals and partners, does **not** apply to companies.

1.7.2 Premiums on Short Leases

Calculation of Taxable Portion of Premium

Where a company receives a premium on the creation of a "short lease" (i.e. the duration of the lease does not exceed 50 years), the premium will be treated partly as a disposal for CGT purposes (outside the scope of this text) and partly as income.

The latter is treated as property income in the year in which the lease is granted (in addition to any actual rent for that period). This is computed as the amount of the premium less 2% for each complete year of the lease except the first (or by the formula $P \times (50 - Y)/50$, where P is the premium and Y is the number of complete years in the term of the lease excluding the first). This was covered in detail on the CA Proficiency 1 course and should be revisited. The tenant paying the premium is entitled to a deduction for the element of the premium taxed on the landlord as income, however this is split over the term of the lease and a full, up-front deduction is not received.

Allowable Deductions Incurred in Calculating Property Income

The following amounts may be deducted from the gross rents:

1. Rent payable.
2. Rates (if any), property insurance, etc.
3. Cost of goods or services which the landlord is obliged to provide and for which he receives no separate consideration, e.g. gas, electricity, waste disposal.
4. Cost of repairs (excluding improvements and items treated as capital expenditure).

Examples of common repairs that are normally deductible in computing rental business profits include:

- exterior and interior painting and decorating;
- stone cleaning;
- damp and rot treatment;
- mending broken windows, doors, furniture and machines such as cookers or lifts;
- re-pointing; and
- replacing roof slates, flashing and gutters.

5. Accountancy fees incurred in drawing up rental accounts and keeping rental records.
6. The actual cost incurred on replacing furnishings in the company's accounting period – see **Section 1.7.1.**
7. Legal fees of a revenue nature wholly and exclusively incurred in connection with the rental business. Legal costs involved with the first letting of a property for more than one year are deemed to be of a capital nature and are not allowable. However, legal and professional costs incurred in respect of the renewal of short-term leases (a lease of less than 50 years) are allowable, though not the payment of a premium. Finally, legal costs incurred in acquiring or adding to a property and those involved with the change of use of a property in vacant periods between lets are disallowable.

Allowable expenses are normally deducted on an accruals basis rather than on a paid basis. Expenses incurred in respect of a property before a lease commences in respect of that property are, in the main, not deductible. In the case of interest and rent, no deduction is allowed for either interest or rent payable in respect of a period before the property is first **occupied** by a lessee. However, relief may be available under the legislative provisions for pre-trading expenditure.

Expenses incurred after the termination of a lease are not deductible. However, expenses incurred after the termination of one lease and before the commencement of another lease of the property are deductible, provided the following three conditions are satisfied:

1. the expenses would otherwise be deductible;
2. the person who was the lessor of the property does not occupy the premises during the period when the property is not let; and
3. the property is let by the same lessor at the end of the period.

Example 1.13

A company purchased a rental property on 1 April 2019. Between the date of purchase and 31 May 2019 the company spent £25,000 refurbishing the property. On 1 June 2019 the property was leased for £800 per month payable in advance.

The following expenses were incurred up to 31 May 2019:

	£
Auctioneers/advertising fees for first tenants	800
Repairs and maintenance	600
Light and heat	300
Security and insurance	500
Interest on loan	1,200

continued overleaf

The following expenses were incurred in the period 1 June 2019 to 31 March 2020:

	£
Water charges	600
Light and heat	350
Security	400
Interest	2,250
Repairs/maintenance of a revenue nature	870

Calculate the taxable rental profits for the year ended 31 March 2020.

Solution

	£	£
Gross rents receivable (£800 × 10)		8,000
Less: qualifying expenses		
Auctioneers/advertising for first tenants	800	
Water charges	600	
Light and heat	650	
Security and insurance	900	
Repairs/maintenance	870	(3,820)
Property income		4,180

Note: expenses incurred prior to letting the property are allowable as pre-letting expenditure. The interest incurred on the property loan is not a property-deductible expense. Instead, this is an allowable non-trade loan relationship deficit (see **Chapter 3**).

1.7.3 Property Income Losses

If a property company, carried on commercially, incurs losses in an accounting period on its rental business, these losses can be set against the company's total profits for the same accounting period. The treatment of property income losses is dealt with in more detail in **Chapter 4.**

1.7.4 Letting of Surplus Accommodation

Under section 44 CTA 2009, the letting of surplus business accommodation (not land held as trading stock and not part of a building of which another part is used to carry on the trade) on a short-term basis is taxed as trading income, rather than as property income.

Accommodation is deemed to be surplus to requirements only if it has been used in the last three years to carry on the trade (or was acquired in the last three years), the trader intends to use it for the trade at a later date and the letting is for a term of not more than three years. If accommodation is temporarily surplus to requirements at the beginning of an accounting period, it continues to be temporarily surplus to requirements until the end of that period.

1.8 Miscellaneous Income

Sections 979–981 of CTA 2009 charge corporation tax on the income of a company that is not already taxable under other corporation tax provisions. Income treated as miscellaneous income includes, but is not limited to:

- any payment for a service where there is an agreement that the service would be provided for a reward;
- any income that is not otherwise taxable and which is received under an agreement or arrangement;

- any payment for the use of money that is not interest or is not within the loan relationships legislation (see **Chapter 3**).

This list is not exhaustive.

1.9 Computation of Chargeable Gains

Where a chargeable gain accrues to a company in an accounting period on the disposal of a chargeable asset under the chargeable gains regime, or on a gain transferred to the company under section 171A Taxation of Chargeable Gains Act 1992 (TCGA 1992) by another capital gains group member (see **Chapter 10**), the chargeable gain is included in the company's taxable total profits. The gain calculated is after deducting both allowable capital losses in the current accounting period and those brought forward from previous years.

Since company chargeable gains are included within the company's taxable total profits, they fall to be taxed at the same rate as trading profits and other income. Note that companies are generally not liable to CGT, but instead pay corporation tax on their chargeable gains.

1.9.1 Disposals

It is important to note that the disposal of intangible assets may come within the intangible assets regime, while the disposal of loan stock is dealt with under the loan relationship rules. Thus the main category of disposals that will be relevant to companies will be the disposal of land and property, goodwill (acquired or created before 1 April 2002) and shareholdings, i.e. assets which give rise to chargeable gains or losses. Companies may also dispose of assets that fall under the chattels rules (see **Chapter 15**).

The basic calculation is broadly computed in accordance with normal CGT principles, with two important exceptions. First, a company does receive the CGT annual exemption. Secondly, companies are able to avail of the indexation allowance up to 31 December 2017 only.

1.9.2 Basic Computation

The basic chargeable gains computation considers the difference between the net selling price of the asset being disposed of, compared with its original cost (or March 1982 value, if relevant and higher) coupled with any further allowable items of expenditure, including enhancement expenditure. As money values are being compared over different time periods, as set out earlier, HMRC allows companies to apply indexation to the historical costs of the item being disposed of, but only up to December 2017 for disposals on or after 1 January 2018.

The gross sales proceeds are reduced by the incidental costs of sale, which could include such items as legal fees, estate agent fees, valuation fees, etc. The costs associated with the purchase are added to the actual purchase cost (or March 1982 valuation) and these items will attract indexation from the relevant date up to the date of disposal, but only up to December 2017 for disposals on or after 1 January 2018 of assets acquired before that date.

The indexation factor is calculated by taking the movement in the Retail Price Index (RPI) between the date of acquisition of the asset and the date of sale.

The indexation factor is computed using the following formula:

$$\frac{(\text{RPI at sale} - \text{RPI at acquisition})}{\text{RPI at acquisition}}$$

The result is rounded to three decimal places and is then applied to the relevant cost items to arrive at the indexation allowance. This is deducted in the computation. It should be noted that a non-resident company subject to corporation tax on the disposal of certain chargeable assets (see **Chapter 8, Section 8.2**) is also able to avail of indexation allowance, if relevant.

Indexation allowance can reduce a chargeable gain to nil; however, it cannot either create or increase a capital loss. In the final CA Proficiency 2 examination you are provided with the Retail Prices Indices needed to calculate indexation allowance (see also **Appendix 2**).

1.9.3 Capital Losses

The above basic calculation could result in a capital loss, although note that the indexation allowance cannot create or increase a loss. If the company has other chargeable gains in the same period, this loss is first set against such chargeable gains. If unutilised, the capital loss is carried forward to set against future chargeable gains of subsequent accounting periods. A capital loss on a disposal by a company to a connected person can only be offset against chargeable gains on disposals to the same connected person, either in the period that the capital loss arises or in a future accounting period.

There are no provisions for the carry back of capital losses by a company. Nor are there any provisions for the surrender of capital losses between group members or, in the main, for setting capital losses against taxable profits of the company or another member of the same loss-relief group. However, it is possible to transfer transactions that generate chargeable gains or capital losses, either wholly or partially, within a capital gains group under section 171A TCGA 1992 (see **Chapter 10**). Where a capital loss arises on the disposal, this effectively transfers the capital loss to the recipient group company, either wholly or partially.

Note: as set out earlier, in a situation where a company has an accounting period exceeding 12 months, the chargeable gains are allocated to the period in which the disposal took place (and are not time-apportioned).

Example 1.14

X Ltd prepares accounts to 31 March. In the year ended 31 March 2020, the tax-adjusted trading profit was £20,000. On 30 November 2019 the company sold a chargeable asset for £16,000, incurring incidental costs of sale of £1,000. It had purchased the asset for £10,000 some three years previously and the indexation factor was 0.105 up to 31 December 2017.

X Ltd – Year ended 31 March 2020

	£
Trading income	20,000
Chargeable gain (Note)	3,950
	23,950
Corporation tax due: £23,950 @ 19%	4,551
Note – chargeable gain	
Gross sales proceeds	16,000
Less: incidental costs of sale	(1,000)
	15,000
Purchase cost	(10,000)
	5,000
Indexation allowance: £10,000 × 0.105	(1,050)
Indexed chargeable gain	3,950

Example 1.15

Lauren Ltd prepares accounts to 31 March each year.

In February 2003 the company bought an asset for £12.6m. The costs of acquisition were £0.7m. In April 2004, enhancement capital expenditure of £1.8m was incurred on this asset. Lauren Ltd disposed of this asset in July 2019 for £37.9m, having incurred £1.1m on incidental costs of sale. Set out the chargeable gain to be included within the corporation tax computation of the above company for the year ended 31 March 2020.

Assume the following Retail Price Index (RPI) figures:

December 2017	278.1
February 2003	179.3
April 2004	185.7

Solution

	£ 000	£ 000
Gross sales proceeds		37,900
Less: incidental costs of sale		(1,100)
Net sales proceeds		36,800
Acquisition costs	12,600	
Incidental costs of acquisition	700	
Enhancement expenditure	1,800	
		(15,100)
Unindexed gain		21,700
Indexation allowance:		
Acquisition cost (£12.6m × 0.551)	6,443	
Incidental costs of acquisition (£0.7m × 0.551)	386	
Enhancement (£1.8m × 0.498)	896	
		(7,768)
Chargeable gain		13,932

Indexation factor

Cost	(278.1 – 179.3)/179.3 = 0.551
Enhancement	(278.1 – 185.7)/185.7 = 0.498

Notes

In the corporation tax computation, the chargeable gain amount is included immediately after the total income has been ascertained as follows:

	£
Trading income	X
Net credit from loan relationships	X
Miscellaneous income	X
Property income	X
Chargeable gains	X
Taxable total profits (TTP)	X

1.9.4 Substantial Shareholdings Exemption (SSE)

The substantial shareholdings exemption (SSE), subject to all of the relevant conditions being fulfilled, will result in there being no chargeable gain on the disposal of shares or an interest in shares held by a company in another company. As such, it should always be considered where a company disposes of shares.

SSE is an important exemption and is dealt with in detail in **Chapter 10**. Gains on the disposal of shares that do not qualify for SSE should be included in the corporation tax computation and are subject to corporation tax in the usual way.

1.10 Residence of Companies

1.10.1 The Incorporation Test

The most important factor in determining a company's liability to corporation tax (or other UK taxes) is the company's **residence**. The starting point for determining if the company is UK resident is the "incorporation test". However, if a company is not UK resident under this test it may still be UK resident under the "central management and control test".

1.10.2 The Central Management and Control Test

The concept of central management and control in relation to the residence of a company has evolved from case law. The earliest case that dealt with company tax residence is *Calcutta Jute Mills Co. Ltd v. Nicholson*. This case established that residence is located where a company's centre of control is located. The most important subsequent case is *de Beers Consolidated Mines v. Howe* (1906). In this case it was held that a company's residence is where its real business is carried on, and that place is where the central management and control actually abides.

The central management and control test was further endorsed in *Bullock v. Unit Construction Co. Ltd* (1959). This case emphasised the point that central management and control is a question of fact and is not necessarily located where it appears to be located, e.g. where the board of directors hold their meetings. These principles were reaffirmed by the Court of Appeal in 2006 in the case of *Wood v. Holden*.

A 2009 case, *Laerstate BV v. HMRC*, also examined this concept and provides a useful indication of factors a court will look at to determine residence:

- Whether the board meets regularly on strategy/policy?
- Is documentation tabled?
- Are there minutes accurately reflecting the discussions?
- Are all meetings held and documents signed outside the UK?

These and other UK court decisions determined that one of the key factors in determining where a company is resident is where it is **managed and controlled**. The following are the factors which have been taken into account by the UK courts in determining the centre of the company's management and control and, therefore, its place of residence:

- Where are the questions of important policy determined?
- Where are the directors' meetings held?
- Where do the majority of the directors reside?

- Where are the shareholders' meetings held?
- Where is the negotiation of major contracts undertaken?
- Where is the head office of the company?
- Where are the books of account and the company books (minute book, share register, etc.) kept?
- Where are the company's bank accounts?

As you can see, control is generally determined by reference to where the directors hold their meetings and **whether real decisions affecting the company are taken at those meetings**. In each case, one needs to look at the facts to determine where the company is actually managed and controlled.

In summary, a company is resident in the UK if it is incorporated in the UK, i.e it has a UK Companies House/Companies Registry number. If it is not incorporated in the UK it will be resident in the UK if it is centrally managed and controlled in the UK.

1.10.3 Implications of UK Residence

A company resident in the UK is chargeable to corporation tax on all its profits wherever the income arises. This includes the results of foreign branches, although double taxation relief will be available for any corporation tax or equivalent paid in another jurisdiction. A company can however elect into the foreign branch exemption regime to exempt the results of all of its branches from UK corporation tax (see **Chapter 8**.) Corporation tax is also payable on the disposal of chargeable assets irrespective of where the asset was situated and whether or not the proceeds were received or transmitted to the UK. Again, double taxation relief will be a consideration.

1.10.4 Non-resident Companies

A non-resident company is chargeable to corporation tax if it carries on a trade in the UK through a permanent establishment (PE). If it has a PE, then it will be chargeable on its trading income, income from property and on any chargeable gains arising on the disposal of assets situated in the UK and which are used for the purposes of the PE trade. A company is deemed to have a PE in a particular country if it has a fixed place of business (or a dependent agent) there through which the company carries out, either wholly or partly, its business.

From 6 April 2020, profits of UK property businesses, other UK property income and profits of loan relationships that the non-resident company is a party to for the purpose of the property business or generating the income will be subject to UK corporation tax at the relevant rate for the accounting period.

It should be noted that a non-resident company which does not carry on a trade in the UK through a PE remains chargeable to income tax at the basic rate (currently 20%) on any other UK income that it may have. See **Chapter 8, Section 8.2** for more on the taxation of non-resident companies.

1.10.5 Dual Resident Companies

It is sometimes the case that a former non-resident company, having become UK resident, may be deemed, under the domestic law of the foreign jurisdiction, to continue to be resident in that jurisdiction. In this scenario, the company has dual residence and the terms of the relevant double taxation treaty have to be examined. Double taxation treaties will generally contain a "tie-breaker" clause which will be applied to determine if the company is "treaty resident" in the UK or the foreign jurisdiction for tax purposes. These tie-breaker clauses are beyond the scope of this text.

1.11 Self-assessment and Administration

1.11.1 Filing of Company Tax Return

Companies are obliged to notify and report their liability to corporation tax to HMRC under the Corporation Tax Self-Assessment (CTSA) regime.

The resultant company tax return must include a declaration by the person making the return that, to the best of their knowledge and belief, the return is correct and complete.

A complete company tax return should include:

1. completed form CT600;
2. any appropriate supplementary pages;
3. a copy of the relevant statutory accounts, generally including the statement of profit or loss;
4. a tax computation showing how the figures on the CT600 have been derived from the statutory accounts.

If the company files abbreviated accounts at Companies House/Companies Registry, it must file full accounts as part of its company tax return. A company tax return is due for filing online with HMRC by the due date (in response to a "notice to deliver" sent by HMRC on form CT603). The due date is the last day of whichever of the following periods is the last to end:

1. Within 12 months of the end of the accounting period.
2. If the company's statutory accounting period lies between 12 and 18 months, then 12 months from the end of the accounting period.
3. If the company's statutory accounts are for a period longer than 18 months, then 30 months from the beginning of that period.
4. Within three months of receiving a notice to deliver (where the notice has been forwarded late to the company).

All companies and organisations are required to file their company tax return online in iXBRL format. This means that data within the accounts and computations must be XBRL tagged. XBRL (Extensible Business Reporting Language) is an XML-based computer language for the electronic transmission of business and financial data. Companies and organisations are also required to pay any corporation tax and related payments due electronically (for example by direct debit).

It is always the responsibility of the company to inform HMRC, in writing, within three months from when it comes within the charge to corporation tax; this is normally satisfied by completing and submitting form CT41G. However, in many cases, Companies Registry will have informed HMRC of the formation of the new company. HMRC would then write to the company (sending them form CT41G) requesting all the relevant information and details relating to the new company.

While HMRC will generally write to the new company (provided they have been supplied with the relevant details), the responsibility for notification always rests with the company. If a company fails to notify HMRC, then it will assume that the first accounting period will run for 12 months from the date of incorporation, which may or may not be the actual position. It is therefore imperative that the company keep HMRC appraised of any relevant changes in the company's details (address, accounting period, directors, etc.).

Penalties for failure to notify are contained within UK taxes legislation and are applicable to most taxes. However, in respect of corporation tax, these generally mean that a company that has not received a company tax return or notice to file must inform HMRC if it becomes chargeable to tax within 12 months from the end of the relevant accounting period.

Different companies can have different accounting dates, so the time limit for notifying HMRC will differ accordingly. If a company's accounting date is 30 June 2020 and it is liable to corporation tax for that period, notification of chargeability must be given to HMRC by 30 June 2021.

Penalties for failure to notify are calculated based on the potential lost revenue to HMRC that could have arisen due to failure to notify (so this could be calculated on the basis of the corporation tax liability in the first accounting period).

The level of penalty will depend on how the failure to notify arose, and how HMRC became aware of it (see **Table 1.1**). Students should note that Table 1.1 is **not** included in the Tax Reference Material provided in the final examination. No penalty will be charged if the company has a reasonable excuse for failure to notify.

Table 1.1: HMRC Penalties – Failure to Notify

Type of failure to notify	Unprompted disclosure	Prompted disclosure
Non-deliberate – notified within 12 months	0%–30%	10%–30%
Non-deliberate – notified after 12 months	10%–30%	20%–30%
Deliberate but not concealed	20%–70%	35%–70%
Deliberate and concealed	30%–100%	50%–100%

Example 1.16
An example of "deliberate and concealed" failure to notify would be as follows:

Ferdinand Ltd has never submitted tax returns. The company bought a property in 2011 from which it has been receiving rental income. When questioned by HMRC about the source of funds to purchase the property, Ferdinand, the sole shareholder and director, says the money was lent to the company by overseas family members. HMRC later find that Ferdinand Ltd owned a number of rental properties prior to 2011 and that the money actually came from the sale of one of those properties. For the earlier years when asked to explain the source of the company's funds, Ferdinand took active steps to conceal the company's liability. For those years the failure is deliberate and concealed. There may also be a failure to notify penalty on the company for the chargeable gain on the sale of the property.

The act of concealment can include:

- creating false stock records;
- creating false evidence of a non-taxable source to explain undisclosed taxable income;
- creating false invoices to support inaccurate figures of turnover;
- back-dating or post-dating invoices or contracts;
- deliberately destroying records so that they are no longer available;
- creating sales records that deliberately understate the value of the goods sold.

1.11.2 Company Records

A company must keep all business records and accounts, including contracts and receipts, until the latest of:

1. six years from the end of the relevant accounting period;
2. the date that any enquiries are completed; or
3. the date after which enquiries may not be commenced.

If a return is demanded more than six years after the end of the accounting period, any records that the company still has must be retained until the later of the end of the enquiry or the expiry of the right to start an enquiry.

The maximum penalty for failing to preserve records is £3,000 per chargeable accounting period. However, there is no penalty for failing to keep or preserve records which might have been needed only for the purposes of claims, elections or notices not included in the return.

1.11.3 Company Tax Return and Amendments

Directors of UK companies are required to file statutory accounts with Companies Registry for every 12-month accounting period. In general, the corporation tax accounting period follows the statutory accounting period but, for corporation tax purposes, there are specific dates at which an accounting period will begin or end and, as discussed earlier, these can differ from those for the statutory accounts.

If the statutory period of account is greater than 12 months, it is divided for corporation tax purposes into 12-month tranches and a residue period. For example, if A Ltd prepared accounts for the 18-month period ending 31 December 2020, it would be required to submit company tax returns for the 12 months ended 30 June 2020 and for the six-month period ended 31 December 2020. The filing date for both returns is 31 December 2020, being 12 months after the end of the period of accounts. However, there will be two deadlines for payment of corporation tax, providing the instalment payment rules do not apply.

A company can amend its return at any time within 12 months of the return's filing deadline. This time limit is not extended if a return is delivered late.

If a return is delivered more than 12 months late, no amendment to the return can be made.

Penalties

If the company's tax return is not filed within three months of the due date, it will incur a flat rate penalty of £100. The penalty rises to £200 after this and is increased to £500 and £1,000 where the failure occurs for a third successive time.

While the above penalties are not tax-related, if a company fails to deliver a return within 18 months of the end of an accounting period (or a later filing date, if applicable), then the penalty becomes 10% of the unpaid tax at that date if it remains undelivered within two years of the due date, rising to 20% thereafter. The latter tax-related penalties are in addition to the flat rate penalties above.

1.11.4 Enquiries

The time span for which HMRC may give notice that it is enquiring into a stand-alone company tax return is 12 months from the date that the return was filed or, if the return was delivered late, 12 months from after the next quarter dates (31 January, 30 April, 31 July and 31 October) following the date on which the return was actually delivered. Where a company is a member of a group that is not small (as defined), the relevant time span is that the enquiry must be opened within 12 months from the statutory filing date. Broadly, a group will be a 'small group' if it satisfies at least two of the following conditions:

1. aggregate turnover is not more than £6.5 million net (or £7.8 million gross);
2. aggregate balance sheet total is not more than £3.26 million net (or £3.9 million gross);
3. aggregate number of employees is not more than 50.

'Net' is the aggregate after any set-offs or other adjustments to eliminate inter-group transactions; 'gross' is without those set-offs or other adjustments.

Normally HMRC would conduct its enquiries under procedures set out in its enquiry manual. With many UK companies being family owned and run, it would not be unusual to find that HMRC would open an enquiry into the tax affairs of the directors/working shareholders at the same time. During the course of the enquiry, the company and/or its professional advisors will be asked to supply various documents and details relating to the queries raised by HMRC. In some circumstances a meeting may take place. Minutes of all such meetings would be taken and HMRC would normally request that the company would sign a copy of these minutes as a verification of their content.

The enquiry would be complete when HMRC issues a closure notice. However, HMRC can issue a Partial Closure Notice (PCN) ahead of the final closure of an enquiry. HMRC tend to issue PCNs in enquiries where a taxpayer's tax affairs are complex or where there is avoidance or large amounts of tax at risk. If HMRC believes that the original company tax return requires amendment, it notifies the company in writing. Any additional corporation tax which is deemed to be now due will attract interest and will most likely include a penalty for the relevant error. HMRC will make an offer to the company to encompass all outstanding liabilities. If the company is dissatisfied, it has the right to appeal and must lodge its appeal with the First-tier Tribunal within 30 days from the date that an assessment was received.

1.11.5 The Appeals Process

If either the company or HMRC disagree with the decision of the First-tier Tribunal, they can ask for a review by the Upper Tribunal. If the company or HMRC remain dissatisfied, the decision can be appealed to the Court of Appeal, but only on points of law, and not in respect of findings of fact by the Upper Tribunal.

Tax cases appealed from the Upper Tribunal now skip the High Court and go straight to the Court of Appeal. From a commercial point of view, companies must be mindful of the potentially huge costs involved in such a course of action and these must be weighed against the tax at stake.

Penalties

The penalty regime set out in **Section 1.11.6** covers income tax, CGT, corporation tax, stamp taxes, VAT on property and inheritance tax and applies where an error has been made in a relevant return.

1.11.6 Taxpayer's Behaviour

The penalty regime for incorrect returns focuses on the behaviour of the taxpayer. For corporation tax purposes, the taxpayer is the company acting through its directors and officers. Where a company has made a mistake in a return submitted to HMRC, but has taken reasonable care in the preparation of that return, no penalty will be applied by HMRC.

In its *Compliance Handbook*, HMRC states that appointing a tax advisor does not automatically mean that the company has taken reasonable care in the preparation of a return. The tax advisor should be competent and qualified, nevertheless the company still bears responsibility for the return and the director is expected, within his ability and competence, to make sure that the return being signed is correct.

The categories of behaviour where penalties will be imposed are:

1. Careless (failure to take reasonable care).
2. Deliberate but not concealed (the inaccuracy is deliberate but there are no arrangements to conceal it).
3. Deliberate and concealed (the inaccuracy is deliberate and there are arrangements to conceal it).

Once HMRC has categorised the "behaviour" of the taxpayer, the potential lost revenue (PLR) will be computed. The penalty imposed is based on a percentage of the PLR, which is the additional amount of tax due or payable as a result of correcting the inaccuracy.

However, HMRC may apply reductions to the proposed penalty where the company has disclosed the inaccuracy. Disclosure is split into two types (unprompted and prompted), with greater reductions being given where the company makes a disclosure which has not been prompted by HMRC.

A disclosure is unprompted if it is made when the person has no reason to believe that HMRC has discovered or is about to discover the inaccuracy or under-assessment.

The ranges of percentage penalties that will be applied by HMRC to the PLR, based on the behaviour of the taxpayer and the extent of the disclosure, are summarised in **Table 1.2**. Students should note that Table 1.2 is **not** included in the Tax Reference Material provided in the final examination.

Table 1.2: HMRC Penalties – Categories of Behaviour

Behaviour	Careless	Deliberate but not concealed	Deliberate and concealed
Minimum penalty with unprompted disclosure	0%	20%	30%
Minimum penalty with prompted disclosure	15%	35%	50%
Maximum penalty	30%	70%	100%

Example 1.17

HMRC discovers an arithmetical error in Peony Ltd's tax return for the year ended 31 March 2020. The PLR is calculated to be £5,000. The return had been prepared by the company's financial controller and signed by its sole director, Dee. She had not checked the tax return before signing it and so was not aware of the error.

The company has been careless in the preparation of its tax return and was not able to disclose the error to HMRC before it was discovered. As the error was arithmetical, it was within Dee's competence and ability to find it. HMRC may impose a penalty of 30% of £5,000, i.e. £1,500, in addition to charging interest for late payment, although the penalty may be mitigated to 15% if a prompted disclosure is made. An umprompted disclosure is not possible as HMRC have already discovered the error.

A company has the usual rights, including appeal to the First-tier Tribunal against the imposition of the penalty, its amount and/or the conditions of the penalty (it will also be able to appeal the non-suspension of a penalty).

In the case of deliberate inaccuracy that is found to be attributable to an officer (to include a director, secretary or shadow director) of the company, both the company and the officer are liable for the penalty.

1.11.7 Compliance Checks

HMRC has a suite of powers at its disposal to carry out compliance checks covering all the taxes for which it is responsible.

The relevant legislation includes:

1. one set of powers to visit businesses to inspect premises, assets and records and ask taxpayers and third parties for information and documents;
2. important safeguards for taxpayers;
3. flexibility in setting record-keeping requirements; and
4. specific time limits for assessments and claims.

1.11.8 Publishing Details of Deliberate Tax Defaulters

In addition to recovering underpaid tax due, any interest thereon and a penalty tied to the potential lost revenue, legislation allows HMRC to publish the details of certain taxpayers, including companies, caught deliberately evading more than £25,000 in tax.

Deliberate tax defaults are: incorrect returns, failures to notify and certain VAT and excise duty wrongdoings. This measure does not, however, apply to late filing or late payment penalties.

Details of the Scheme

For HMRC to consider publication of a person's (including company's) name and details, the following conditions must apply:

- a relevant penalty of the type set out above must be incurred;
- the taxpayers must be penalised for one or more deliberate or deliberate and concealed defaults; and
- the amount of tax evaded must be greater than £25,000. In working out whether this threshold is reached, all tax which has been subject to a penalty for deliberate errors will be added together.

HMRC will not publish details where a full disclosure is made, either unprompted or prompted, and the taxpayer co-operates fully with HMRC, thereby receiving the maximum penalty reduction available.

Publication Rules

Publication follows a strict set of rules:

- All the penalty decisions which underpin the scheme can be appealed to an independent tribunal.
- No publication is possible until all appeals are concluded or opportunities to appeal have expired.
- The publication process is not part of the enquiry process.
- HMRC must publish within 12 months of the penalty becoming final and cease publishing that information 12 months thereafter.

A list of defaulters is published quarterly on www.gov.uk.

HMRC will publish if the criteria are met, unless there are exceptional circumstances. HMRC are unlikely to decide not to publish because of a possible impact on the person's reputation, business interests or creditworthiness.

Taxpayers should thus be encouraged to make a qualifying disclosure where possible, not only to achieve full penalty mitigation but also to avoid having their details published under this measure.

1.11.9 Managing Serious Defaulters Programme

HMRC's Managing Serious Defaulters (MSD) programme is aimed at closely monitoring the tax affairs of individuals and businesses, including companies, classed as "deliberate defaulters", i.e. where a "deliberate" or "deliberate with concealment" penalty has been charged. The key objective of the programme is to ensure taxpayers in the programme are compliant with their tax obligations and demonstrate a permanent change in their behaviour.

The programme is not voluntary – HMRC will decide whether the deliberate defaulter's tax affairs warrant closer monitoring. It will advise the taxpayer in writing of their inclusion in the programme at the end of the relevant compliance check. Where a full unprompted disclosure has been made, the defaulter will not be placed into the MSD programme, subject to having been given the maximum penalty reduction for deliberate behaviour.

The MSD programme applies to businesses and individual taxpayers who have been found to have made a deliberate understatement of any size, and applies the enhanced monitoring to all the defaulter's tax affairs rather than just the area(s) from which the initiating behaviour originated.

In addition to the penalty for the original offence, for up to a five-year period afterwards, the taxpayer may be subject to additional monitoring, with the level and term of monitoring depending on the seriousness of the offence.

HMRC will continue to check that returns are filed on time and that any tax due is paid on time, but there will also be regular reviews of the deliberate defaulter's tax affairs to check that any errors or failings have been rectified. There are a variety of measures HMRC may use to monitor a deliberate defaulter's tax affairs, which are beyond the scope of this textbook. The MSD programme is in addition to the publishing of details of deliberate defaulters.

1.12 Tax Transparency and Accountability Measures

The area of tax continues to attract attention globally, with public and media interest in the tax position of large multinationals of particular interest as 'tax transparency' and accountability moves up the agenda of many governments. Over the last 10 years, the UK has introduced specific measures focusing on tax transparency and accountability – senior accounting officer's responsibilities, publication of large businesses' tax strategy and country-by-country reporting.

1.12.1 Duties of Senior Accounting Officers of Qualifying Companies

The senior accounting officer (SAO) legislation applies to certain large companies and is a measure targeted at the tax accountability of large businesses. Although all companies have an obligation to deliver correct and complete tax returns, compliance with this obligation can be compromised if the company's tax accounting arrangements are not fit for purpose. These arrangements range from how a company accounts for its business transactions, to how it works out its final tax liability. The SAO provisions apply to the tax accounting arrangements in place for the calculation of various taxes including, but not limited to, corporation tax, VAT, PAYE and stamp taxes.

The legislation addresses the potential "accountability gap" by making the SAO of a qualifying company responsible for ensuring that appropriate tax accounting arrangements are in place. In many cases the SAO will be the chief financial officer of the company or group.

This measure applies to qualifying companies, which are generally UK incorporated companies, with either:

- turnover of more than £200 million, or
- a relevant balance sheet total of more than £2 billion

in the preceding financial year, either alone or when its results are aggregated with other UK companies in the same group.

The SAO is the director or officer with overall responsibility, as appropriately delegated, for the company's financial accounting arrangements. The company will judge who best fits this definition, and in most cases this will be evident from the established governance arrangements.

This requires the SAO of a qualifying company to take reasonable steps to ensure that the company establishes and maintains appropriate tax accounting arrangements.

The SAO of a qualifying company must also provide HMRC with a certificate stating whether the company has appropriate tax accounting arrangements or, where it does not, provide an explanation. The certificate must be submitted no later than the end of the period for filing the accounts for the financial year.

Penalties may arise for failure to comply with this legislation, as follows:

- a penalty of £5,000, assessable on the SAO, for failure to comply with the main duty of taking reasonable steps to ensure that the company establishes and maintains appropriate tax accounting arrangements;
- a penalty of £5,000, again assessable on the SAO, for failure to provide a certificate or providing an incorrect certificate; or
- a penalty where a company fails to notify HMRC of the name(s) of the person who was the SAO throughout the financial year.

1.12.2 Large Businesses' Tax Strategy

The requirement for certain large companies to publish their tax strategies online and free of charge to the public is a measure targeted at the tax transparency of large businesses.

The legislation applies to "qualifying companies", which are defined as:

- UK-registered companies, partnerships and permanent establishments of groups with turnover of £200 million or more, or gross assets of £2 billion or more, on the last day of the previous financial year; or
- multinational businesses with any operations (regardless of size) carried out through UK companies or permanent establishments that have consolidated turnover of €750 million or more.

For the purpose of this measure, a qualifying group comprises two or more relevant bodies, where one or more relevant body in the group is the 51% subsidiary of another relevant body in the group.

The legislation affects stand-alone companies, partnerships and groups. Companies that are part of a UK group or a UK sub-group at the end of that group's previous financial year are not considered qualifying companies.

Minimum Information Requirements

The legislation requires the company to prepare and sign-off the company's UK tax strategy. HMRC's view is that board-level approval is likely to be required to satisfy this requirement. It must then be published on the internet, available to the public free of charge for a year. Where a company is a qualifying company, the minimum information that must be made publicly available in respect of UK tax is:

1. The company's approach to risk management and governance arrangements in relation to UK tax.
2. The company's attitude towards UK tax planning so far as it affects UK tax.
3. The level of risk that a company is prepared to accept in relation to UK tax.
4. The company's approach towards its dealings with HMRC.

There is no requirement for publication of the amounts of taxes paid, although this is a requirement for qualifying companies under the country-by-country reporting rules (see **Section 1.12.3**).

Publication Requirements

A company's tax strategy should be published for the first time before the end of the first financial year commencing after 15 September 2016. For example, for a company with a December year-end, the first year caught by these new rules was 31 December 2017.

If the company was a qualifying company in the previous financial year it must publish its tax strategy before the end of the current financial year and not more than 15 months after the day on which its previous tax strategy was published. Once published, the strategy must remain there until replaced with the following year's version.

It can be published as a separate document or a self-contained part of a wider document and does not need to be called a "strategy" but can be referred to as a "policy". It must remain accessible to the public, free of charge for the period until the next year's strategy is published. The responsibility to ensure preparation and publication rests with the head of the group or sub-group.

If there are any 'stand-alone' UK subsidiaries of a foreign group, these are treated as separate sub-groups, i.e. that company would need to publish its own tax strategy.

Penalties

Penalties apply to the entity or group for failure to:

- publish a tax strategy within the prescribed period that meets the legislative requirements;
- ensure that the tax strategy remains accessible on the internet for the prescribed period.

Penalties are assessed on the head of the group or sub-group. The following penalties for non-compliance are contained in the legislation:

- Up to a maximum of £7,500 where the strategy is not published before the end of the accounting period or not publicly available for at least a year from publication.

  A warning notice will be issued for non-publication on or after the first day of non-publication. This allows 30 calendar days for publication; therefore a penalty will apply from day 31 onwards.
- A further penalty of up to £7,500 if the strategy remains unpublished six months after the end of the accounting period.
- A further £7,500 per month thereafter until the strategy is published.

The above penalties are subject to the normal appeals process. No penalty will arise if a business has a reasonable explanation for the failure to publish and if it remedies that failure without unreasonable delay.

In addition to the above potential penalties, companies affected should not discount the reputational risk that could result for not complying with the legislation. Reputational damage could have a greater financial impact than any penalty imposed by the legislation.

1.12.3 Country-by-country Reporting

Country-by-country (CbC) reporting was introduced as part of the OECD's Base Erosion and Profit Shifting (BEPS) project to provide participating tax authorities, including the UK, with an overall picture of the worldwide position on the profit and tax paid by multinational enterprises (MNEs) operating in their jurisdiction. This legislation is another measure aimed at tax transparency.

Information reported under the UK's CbC legislation is designed to enable HMRC to make a more informed assessment of where tax risks lie. HMRC has stated that it intends to use CbC reports as part of its risk-assessment process for cross-border transactions, principally between members of a multinational group.

Qualifying Entities

An entity is required to submit a CbC report for any period, if it is part of an MNE group, and the MNE group passes the following two tests:

1. it has two or more enterprises that are resident for tax purposes in different jurisdictions; and
2. it had consolidated group revenue of €750 million in the previous period.

In the UK, where an MNE group meets these criteria, the CbC obligations are imposed on the UK ultimate parent entity (UPE). If there is no UK UPE, the obligations fall on the highest entity in the group that is UK resident for tax purposes or has a permanent establishment in the UK. This is referred to as the UK entity (UKE).

Filing a CbC Report

A UK UPE must file a CbC report in respect of every period it is in scope. A UKE must file a CbC report when:

- "the UPE of the group is resident for tax purposes in a country that does not require it to file a CbC report; or
- the UPE of the group is resident for tax purposes in a country that either has entered into an international agreement which allows for exchange of information (like the Multilateral Convention for Mutual Administrative Assistance in Tax Matters), but has not entered into specific arrangements to exchange CbC reports; or
- HMRC has notified the UK entity that exchange arrangements with the country in which the UPE is tax resident are not operating effectively".

UPEs and UKEs are required to notify HMRC for each period covered by a CbC report. The deadline for notification is the end of the period to which the report relates.

Exceptions to the Need to Report

An exception to the need to report can be granted if the information the UKE would be required to file has already been filed, either in a CbC report already received by HMRC or one that has been filed with a jurisdiction that will exchange the report with HMRC.

The exception to report must be applied for by the UKE. When applying, the UKE must inform HMRC, by the filing deadline, which entity in the MNE group has filed the CbC report and the date the report was filed.

Report Content

A CbC report must be filed in XML format, which allows it to be validated and provides a common medium for exchange between the countries adopting CbC reporting rules.

For each country (i.e. tax jurisdiction) in which the MNE group carries on its business, the report must show:

- the amount of revenue, profit before income tax and income tax paid and accrued; and
- the total employment, capital, retained earnings and tangible assets.

Administration and Penalties

The deadline for filing CbC reports is 12 months after the end of the period to which the CbC report relates. CbC reports must be filed online through the secure HMRC portal, and the MNE will need to register online to do so.

The reporting and notification requirements are supported by a penalty regime in the event that an entity does not provide its CbC report or notification on time without a reasonable excuse for the failure, or knowingly supplies incorrect information.

An initial penalty of £300 can be charged for failure to comply with the filing obligation. Following notification of this initial penalty, if the failure continues a further penalty of £60 can arise for each subsequent day. A £3,000 penalty can be charged for an inaccuracy in a CbC report.

Questions

Review Questions

(See Suggested Solutions to Review Questions at the end of this textbook.)

Question 1.1

A long-standing client comes into your office to discuss their future business plans. Peter Dorman and his wife, Angela, are the directors and shareholders of Gourmet Ltd, a UK company specialising in producing gourmet ready-meals.

They have carried out some market research and as a result are planning to expand into an overseas market by setting up a new company. This company will purchase the plant and premises in the overseas country for production of the company's products, which will then be sold in that country.

The shares in the new company will still be owned by Peter and Angela, who will be the only directors. They will appoint a local manager to operate the plant, appoint suppliers and recruit staff. However, Peter and Angela will be wholly responsible for any strategic decisions such as those involving finance, investment and marketing strategy. They will make these decisions from the UK.

Requirement

Explain, with supporting analysis, whether the new company will be considered resident in the UK for corporation tax purposes. If you consider the new company will be UK resident, state the deadline for informing HM Revenue & Customs that the company is within the charge to corporation tax.

Question 1.2

Venus Ltd

Venus Ltd prepares accounts to 31 December each year. It owns shares in the following companies:

Company	% shareholding*	Date acquired
Solar Ltd	59	31/03/2006
Saturn Ltd	40	15/08/2010
Mars Ltd	71	29/12/2012
Neptune Ltd	60	01/03/2020

* The remaining shares are held by entirely unconnected third parties.

Taxable total profits of the company in the year ended 31 December 2019 are £550,000. Projected taxable profits are £425,000 for 31 December 2020. The company also expects to receive a dividend from Saturn Ltd of £80,000 in the 31 December 2020 accounting period. No dividend was received in 2019.

Energy Ltd

Energy Ltd has no related 51% group companies. Recently it changed its accounting date from 31 March to 31 December.

Recent results of the company are as follows:

	£
Year ended 31 March 2020	1,200,000
Nine months ended 31 December 2020 (projected)	1,200,000

Requirement

Explain whether Venus Ltd and Energy Ltd are required to pay their corporation tax liability in instalments for the accounting period ended 31 December 2020. If instalment payments are required, you are **not** required to calculate these.

Venus Ltd and Energy Ltd are entirely unconnected companies.

2

Computation of Corporation Tax

Learning Objectives

After studying this chapter you will understand:

- The format of a corporation tax computation – as you work through the other corporation tax chapters, make sure that you understand how they fit into the pro forma corporation tax computation.
- That there are many items in the financial statements that are required to be adjusted in moving from profit per the accounts to taxable total profits; the competence to make these adjustments resulting in the ability to calculate the liability to corporation tax is a critical skill.
- That additional tax relief for expenditure on R&D may be claimed by companies of all sizes.
- How the corporation intangibles regime applies to intangible assets acquired, created or enhanced on or after 1 April 2002.
- The taxation of investment companies and how surplus management expenses of such companies can be used.

2.1 Pro Forma Corporation Tax Computation

TYPICAL COMPANY LIMITED

Corporation Tax Computation for the 12-month accounting period to 31 March 2020

	Notes	£	£
Trading income:			
Tax-adjusted trading profits	2	X	
Losses forward under section 45 CTA 2010 (see **Chapter 4**)		(X)	
			X
Property income (see **Chapter 1, Section 1.7**)			X
Miscellaneous income (see **Chapter 1, Section 1.8**)			X
Loan relationships:			
Surplus non-trade loan relationship credits	3		X
Chargeable gains	4		X
"Total profits"			X

continued overleaf

Deduct: management expenses/surplus management expenses carried forward	5	(X)
Deduct: surplus non-trade loan relationship debits	3	(X)
Deduct: qualifying charitable donations	6	(X)
Deduct: losses carried forward under section 45A CTA 2010		(X)
Taxable total profits (TTP)	7	X

Notes

1. The computation should always have the name of the company at the top and an appropriate heading, i.e. "corporation tax computation for the 12-month accounting period to...".
   Remember: it is possible for a corporation tax accounting period to be less than 12 months but it can never exceed 12 months. This is discussed in detail in **Chapter 1**.
2. The tax-adjusted trading profits are arrived at after making a number of adjustments. It should be particularly noted that the tax-adjusted trading profits represent the final trading income figure **after** capital allowances have been deducted, but **before** relief for unutilised trading losses carried forward from the **same trade**.
3. The income to be included here is income receivable during the accounting period, *without* deduction of UK income tax. For example, deposit interest earned by a **company** on deposits with a UK bank or building society is normally **paid gross**. However, any interest paid with tax deducted should be grossed up.
   Interest relating to non-trading loan relationships is taxed as investment income on an accruals basis. A company will have a non-trading loan relationship if it is not a party to that loan relationship for the purposes of its trade. Any debits and credits that are not brought into account as trading income and expenses are termed non-trading profits and deficits.
   Non-trading credits and debits that have been deducted and added back in the adjustment of trading profits calculation are then pooled, i.e. added together, to arrive at the net amount to be brought into account. If the net amount is a debit this is deducted from total profits. See **Chapter 5**.
4. A corporation tax computation also includes chargeable gains by companies. The computation method for arriving at the appropriate chargeable gains to include in the corporation tax computation was dealt with in detail in **Chapter 1**. See also **Chapter 10** for more information on chargeable gains in the context of companies.
5. Management expenses/surplus management expenses carried forward are the first deduction from total profits (see **Section 2.6**).
6. Qualifying charitable donations (QCDs) made by a company are allowed as deductions from the company's total profits in calculating the corporation tax chargeable for an accounting period. They are deducted from the company's total profits for the period after any other relief from corporation tax other than group relief. See more on QCDs in **Chapter 3**.
7. When adding back expenses or making deductions, include an explanation of the tax treatment separately in the computation.

2.2 Adjustments in Arriving at the Trading Result

The starting point when calculating the adjusted trading result is always the profit/(loss) before tax as calculated in the financial statements. In arriving at the adjusted trading profit/(loss) the following steps should **always** be considered:

1. Look out for receipts or income that are not taxable.
2. Deduct non-trading income and gains taxed under other rules.
3. Add back any expenses not properly associated with the trading activities.

2.2.1 Add-back of Expenses not Properly Associated with Trading Activities

When an expense falls to be disallowed, it is added back in the adjustment of trading result computation.

Summary of Expenses Commonly Disallowed

1. Expenses or losses of a capital nature:

   - Depreciation.
   - Loss on sale of fixed assets (if a chargeable asset, remember to compute the chargeable gain/loss position as discussed in **Chapters 1** and **10**).
   - Improvements to premises.
   - Purchase of fixed assets.
   - Losses on sale of non-trading intangibles.
   - Amortisation of goodwill (classed as a corporate intangible) – see **Section 2.5.1** for when the amortisation of goodwill may be allowable and is not required to be added back.
   - Amortisation of other intangibles (not classed as corporate intangibles).

2. Expenses not wholly and exclusively laid out for the purposes of the trade or business:

   - Rental expenses (may be allowable against property income).
   - Political donations – never allowed.
   - Qualifying charitable donations should be added back and then allowed later as a deduction from total profits.
   - Fines, defaults, surcharges, penalties and interest on tax (however, interest on late corporation tax is added back but later allowed as a non-trade debit to be deducted from non-trade loan relationship credits or deducted from total profits).

Treatment of Certain Specific Items

(a) Bad debts

Under UK generally accepted accounting principles (GAAP), a company may have general and specific bad debts provisions. Under general tax principles, general provisions are not deductible. Therefore, if there are any movements on the general bad debts provision account, an adjustment must be made, i.e.:

- Increase in a general provision for bad debts – not allowable; therefore, add this back.
- Decrease in a general provision for bad debts – not taxable; therefore, deduct this amount.

As there is no difference between the tax and accounting rules in relation to any other movements on bad debts, there is no adjustment required for the following items:

- Specific bad debts written off – deducted in the statement of profit or loss and also allowed for tax purposes.
- Specific bad debts recovered – credited to the statement of profit or loss and therefore taxable.
- Increase in a specific provision for bad debts – deducted in the statement of profit or loss and therefore allowed for tax purposes.
- Decrease in a specific provision for bad debts – credited to the statement of profit or loss and therefore taxable.

Under IFRS, the manner of calculating a provision for doubtful debts is more specific than under UK GAAP. As a result, increases in bad debt provisions are treated as deductible for tax purposes, provided that they are properly calculated in accordance with these standards.

(b) Entertainment Expenses

General entertainment expenses incurred are completely disallowed. Entertainment includes the provision of accommodation, food, drink or any other form of hospitality, including the provision of gifts.

Expenditure on bona fide staff entertainment is allowable, provided its provision is not incidental to the provision of entertainment to third parties (such as customers, suppliers or other business contacts). Entertaining for and gifts to employees are normally deductible for the company except for excessive amounts. Gifts to customers not costing more than £50 per donee per year are allowable if they carry a conspicuous advertisement for the business and are not food, drink or tobacco. In looking at whether the £50 limit has been breached it is necessary to take into account the cost of all such gifts carrying a conspicuous advertisement (excluding any gifts already disallowed) given to the same person in the same accounting period.

(c) Legal Expenses

Legal expenses associated with the following are **allowable**:

- debt recovery, if it relates to the company's trading income;
- renewal of short leases, i.e. those less than 50 years;
- product liability claims and employee actions, unless the company has been found to be in breach of legislation by a court or tribunal, etc.; and
- maintaining existing trading rights and assets.

The following legal expenses are not allowable:

- legal costs incurred in the acquisition of assets, as they are considered capital, including any abortive expenditure; and
- fines or penalties for breaches in legislation, e.g. health and safety.

(d) Repairs

Replacement of items, redecoration and repairs not involving material improvements – expenditure is allowable.

(e) Motor Vehicle Hire

Where a car is held on an operating lease, the deduction available for the lease hire charges depends on the CO_2 emissions of the car.

Where the CO_2 emissions exceed 110g/km, 15% of the lease hire charge will be disallowed. This 15% restriction does not apply to commercial vehicles. Any maintenance or insurance element included therein is fully allowable. Prior to 1 April 2018, the threshold was 130g/km for leases entered into before that date.

Example 2.1

A company, which prepares annual accounts to 31 December, leased a new car on 1 June 2019. The car's CO_2 emissions are 143g/km.

In the annual accounts to 31 December 2019 lease hire charges of £10,000 were incurred.
Disallowable: £10,000 × 15% = £1,500

From 1 January 2019, companies reporting under IFRS must apply IFRS 16 *Leases* and will be required to change the accounting treatment of operating leases, which effectively moves operating leases to the statement of financial position. This means that operating lease rentals will no longer be charged to the company's statement of profit or loss, which will now instead reflect both a depreciation charge and an interest charge.

From a tax perspective, the operating lease rentals are still treated as revenue costs for the use of the asset over the period of the lease. These should be allocated to the periods of account for which the asset is leased in accordance with the accruals concept. Therefore, lessees applying IFRS 16 are required to make an adjustment in their tax computation to ensure that relief is obtained for the full amount of the rental payments accrued in each period. This will mean that any depreciation and interest charge should be added back.

An alternative tax treatment is permitted, which allows a deduction for operating lease rentals equal to the amount shown in the accounts in respect of the interest charge and the depreciation of the asset. This is an equally acceptable way of achieving relief from a tax perspective.

The UK Government has therefore broadly retained the existing tax treatment for operating leases as a result of IFRS 16. Therefore, both lessors and lessees applying FRS 102 will continue to apply the existing tax rules for operating leases.

The operating lease rentals are still treated as revenue costs for the use of the asset over the period of the lease. These should be allocated to the periods of account for which the asset is leased in accordance with the accruals concept. Therefore, lessees applying IFRS 16 are required to make an adjustment in their tax computation to ensure that relief is obtained for the full amount of the rental payments accrued in each period. This will mean that any depreciation and interest charge should be added back.

As a result of IFRS 16, there are a number of transitional changes to the tax treatment of such leases, which are beyond the scope of this textbook.

(f) Interest on Late Payment of Tax

Interest on late payment of any tax (including VAT, PAYE, etc.) is not allowed in computing tax-adjusted profits; neither are any penalties arising from VAT, PAYE or any other tax, including corporation tax. However, interest on late payment of corporation tax should be added back and then treated as a non-trade debit – meaning that it is allowable. Any interest received on overpaid corporation tax is thus taxable as a non-trading loan relationship credit.

(g) Accountancy/Taxation Fees

- Normal routine accounting, auditing and taxation compliance costs are allowable.
- Special costs associated with Tribunal/Appeal hearings or HMRC enquiries or inspections are likely to be disallowed. However, if no additional tax results from the hearing, enquiry or inspection, there is a possible argument that the costs should be allowed.
- Fee protection insurance charges to cover the risk of incurring additional costs are only allowable if the additional costs are of a revenue nature.

(h) Pre-trading Expenses

Pre-trading expenses, as their name indicates, are incurred before the trade has commenced. Relief for such expenses is given in the accounting period in which the trade commences in respect of those revenue items which satisfy the relevant test.

Qualifying expenses are those:

- incurred in the seven years prior to the commencement, and
- that would be allowed as a deduction in calculating trading profits if they had been incurred after trading commenced.

Examples of qualifying pre-trading expenses include: accountancy fees, market research, feasibility studies, salaries, advertising, preparing business plans and rent paid.

These pre-trading expenses are deductible against income of the trade if they were incurred in the seven-year period prior to commencement. If these expenses exceed the company's trading income, resulting in a loss, this loss **can** be offset against other profits of the company, and it can be group-relieved. It can also be carried forward against future income of the same trade. It cannot be carried back as the company was not trading in its previous period.

Qualifying charitable donations incurred in the seven years before a trade commences are treated as paid when the trade commences, i.e. they are deductible from total profits as qualifying charitable donations in the first year of trading.

Any interest that a company incurs in the seven years before trading commences is classified as a non-trade debit under the loan relationship rules. As non-trade debits carried forward can only be set-off against future non-trade income, the company has a choice to elect that the pre-trading non-trade debits be treated as a trading expense of the year when it commences trading.

Example 2.2
Ray Ltd commenced to trade on 1 July 2019. It incurred the following pre-trading expenditure:

		£
December 2011	Market research	8,000
December 2018	Director's salary	30,000
January 2019	Business entertainment	5,000
May 2019	Marketing expenditure	17,000

Notes: The market research expenditure is not deductible as it was not incurred within seven years before the trade commenced. The business entertainment expenditure is never allowable. The expenditure on the director's salary and marketing are allowable. Therefore, Ray Ltd incurs deductible expenses of £47,000 on 1 July 2019. These are fully deductible in calculating trading income of the first accounting period.

(i) Expenditure on Research and Development (R&D)
For R&D purposes, a company claiming under the small and medium-sized (SME) company R&D regime will qualify for an enhanced deduction from its trading profits of 130% of its qualifying R&D expenditure. The tax relief is obtained by adjusting the trading income computation and, as the expenditure is already allowed for corporation tax purposes, this brings the total tax relief obtained on this expenditure to 230%.

A company claiming under the large R&D regime receives a 12% taxable R&D expenditure credit (RDEC) on qualifying expenditure. See **Section 2.4** below for more on these regimes for companies, including the rules that apply where the company incurs a trading loss and makes a claim for R&D relief under either regime.

(j) Payments for Intangible Assets
From 1 April 2002, the corporate intangibles regime provides companies with tax relief on certain intangible assets (see **Section 2.5**). The definition of intangible asset for these purposes is that "it has the same meaning it has for accounting purposes". For taxation purposes, intellectual property includes both UK and overseas rights.

Intangible asset is defined for accounting purposes in IAS 38 as "an identifiable non-monetary asset without physical substance". An asset is a resource that is controlled by the entity as a result of past events (for example, purchase or self-creation) and from which future economic benefits (inflows of cash or other assets) are expected." Included within intangible assets, therefore, are items such as patents, trademarks, registered designs, brand names, copyrights, goodwill, know-how agreements and publishing copyright.

Accounting gains and accounting losses relating to intangible assets used in a company's business are translated into credits and debits for tax purposes. Although all the credits and debits are brought into account as revenue items, different rules govern how they enter the calculation depending on the nature of the business activity for which the intangible fixed asset is held, e.g. whether the assets are held for trading purposes, a property business or for non-trading purposes. Expenditure is a "debit", whereas income is a "credit". The corporate intangibles regime is examined in more detail at **Section 2.5**.

(k) Redundancy Payments

The following rules apply if a company, as an employer, makes a redundancy payment (statutory) or an approved contractual payment to an employee and the payment is in respect of the employee's employment in the employer's trade. An approved "contractual payment" means a payment which, under an agreement, an employer is liable to make to an employee on the termination of the employee's contract of employment.

Statutory redundancy payments are specifically allowable as are approved contractual payments up to the statutory limit. On cessation of the trade, a redundancy expense is not incurred "wholly and exclusively" for the purpose of the trade. However, UK tax legislation allows a deduction for statutory redundancy payments made to members of staff on cessation of trade. If the business wants to be more generous and pay amounts in excess of statutory redundancy levels, a deduction is available under section 79 Income Tax (Trading and Other Income) Act 2005. However, relief is limited to three times the statutory redundancy level. Therefore when a business is ceasing, it can (in total) obtain a deduction for termination payments up to four times the statutory payment – once under section 77, and three more times under section 79.

The deduction is allowed for the accounting period in which the payment is made unless the trade has permanently ceased in which case it is treated as made on the last day of the trade.

For any voluntary payments in excess of the statutory (or approved) payments, these additional voluntary payments are allowable only if the sole reason for their disallowance is the cessation of the trade or part of the trade.

(l) Subscriptions

Political subscriptions and donations are not allowable. Subscriptions to a relevant professional body or to trade magazines are generally allowable.

(m) Lease Payments for Assets Capitalised in the Statement of Financial Position

In accordance with IFRS 16 *Leases*, where a finance-leased asset is capitalised in the statement of financial position the amounts expensed in the statement of profit or loss are the interest expense and depreciation. The lease payment is not expensed to the statement of profit or loss. Where the burden of the wear and tear of the asset is borne by the lessor, the lessee is not entitled to capital allowances. Rather, the accounts depreciation charge will be deductible for tax purposes, provided it is based on normal commercial accounting principles. This means, in effect, that no tax adjustment needs to be made in respect of finance-leased assets. If the finance lease depreciation relates to a motor vehicle the deduction available for the depreciation on the finance lease depends on the CO_2 emissions of the car. The rules for finance-leased motor vehicles are identical to those outlined at (e) above for motor vehicle hire.

Example 2.3

A company, which prepares annual accounts to 31 March, purchased a new car under finance lease for £26,775 on 1 October 2019. The car's CO_2 emissions are 120g/km.

In the annual accounts to 31 March 2020 depreciation of £2,678 has been charged. Disallowable: £2,768 ×15% = £415.

(n) Pension Contributions

"Wholly and exclusively" Rule

Where an employer's payments to a pension scheme meet the "wholly and exclusively for the purposes of the trade" test and are of a revenue nature, they will be an allowable deduction from profits on a **paid** basis. This rule applies to employer contributions only. Given the large number of owner-managed companies, HMRC would be anxious to establish that contributions in respect of controlling directors (or the wider family circle) meet the "wholly and exclusively for the purposes of the trade" test. HMRC is also likely to enquire into the deductibility of the pension contributions paid in connection with the sale or transfer of shares, or shortly before such a transaction. Thus, the amount included within the statement of profit or loss may well require adjustment in the trading income computation if it includes accrued employer contributions or contributions not deemed wholly and exclusive. Accrued contributions deducted from the salary of employees are not subject to the 'paid' rule or the "wholly and exclusively" rule and are allowable even if accrued.

Thus, ordinary annual contributions by an employer to a registered pension scheme for the benefit of his employees are **generally** allowable for tax purposes in the year in which they are paid if the company is carrying on a trade, or as management expenses if the company has an investment business (see **Section 2.6**).

HMRC also consider contributions made to preserve the reputation and morale of staff as allowable deductions.

Spreading Provisions

Pension contributions, although allowable, may have to be spread forward where they exceed certain limits. An initial comparison is made with the **total contributions** of the previous chargeable period; where the current-year contributions are greater than 210% of the previous period, 'spreading' may have to take place. This rule does not apply to the first accounting period in which employer contributions are made, as there is no previous year to compare to.

In this situation, HMRC considers the excess of the current year's payment over 110% of the previous year. Where this excess is:

- less than £500,000 there is no forward spreading of the contributions;
- between £500,000 and less than £1 million, half of the excess is spread into the following year;
- between £1 million and £2 million, one-third of the excess is spread into each of the next two accounting periods;
- £2 million or more, one-quarter of the excess is spread over the next three accounting periods.

Example 2.4
An employer makes the following pension contributions for the two years ended 31 December 2019:

	£
31 December 2018	200,000
31 December 2019	1,420,000

As the 2019 contribution is greater than 210% of that of 2018, HMRC will calculate the potential amount, if any, to be spread forward.

The excess is found by comparing the current year (2019) contribution with 110% of that of the previous period, namely £220,000. The resultant excess is thus £1,200,000. Since this figure lies between £1 million and £2 million, one-third of the excess is spread over each of the next two accounting periods. The £220,000 not treated as excess is fully deductible in 2019, in addition to £400,000 of the £1,200,000 excess. Therefore £800,000 would be added back in 2019.

Relief for the £1,420,000 paid in 2019 would thus be available to the company as follows:

	£
31 December 2019	620,000
31 December 2020	400,000
31 December 2021	400,000

(o) Keyman Insurance

Generally premiums paid under loss of profits insurance policies are tax deductible, therefore any sums received from the insurance company if the policy pays out are taxable as trading receipts.

Policies which provide indemnity for loss or damage to fixed or intangible assets, trading stock and trade debts are allowable if they are deemed to be wholly and exclusively for the purpose of the trade.

Keyman insurance is insurance taken out by a company in its own favour against the death or critical illness of key employees (the keyman) whose services are vital to the success of the employer's business. Such premiums are, generally, allowable and the proceeds of any such policies are taxable as trading receipts. However, there is a potential argument that, if the key person is also the sole/majority shareholder, HMRC may seek to argue that there is a dual purpose to the premiums, i.e. that they seek to protect the value of the shares of the company and thus that there is also a private benefit to the payment of the premiums. This could result in the premiums not being allowable for tax but, potentially, if the policy did pay out, they may still seek to argue for taxing the payout.

Note: in cases where there is a personal benefit to the policy and the premiums are paid on behalf of a participator or an associate of a participator of a close company (see **Chapters 6** and **7**), the amounts are disallowed for corporation tax and will result in the participator being taxed on the premiums paid as a distribution i.e. a dividend (see **Chapter 7**). If the participator, or their associate on whose behalf the premiums are paid, is an employee or director of the company, then the premiums will be allowable for corporation tax as they will be taxed on the individual personally as a benefit in kind.

(p) Delayed Payment of Royalties to a Related Party

A special rule applies where a royalty:

- is payable by a company to, or for the benefit of, a 'related party' and is accrued in the accounting period; and

- it is not paid within 12 months of the end of the accounting period in which it is accrued; and
- its receipt is not at some time fully taxable on the recipient.

In such circumstances, the royalty will only count as a deductible debit when it is actually paid and should therefore be added back in the corporation tax computation for the period in which it is accrued.

Section 835 CTA 2009 sets out four cases in which A (a natural person or a legal entity, including a company) is a related party of B (a company). The four cases are:

1. where A is a company and either A or B controls/has a major interest in the other; or
2. where A is a company and both companies are under the control of the same person; or
3. where B is a close company and A is either a participator/an associate of a participator in B or is a participator in a company that has control of B (see **Chapters 6** and **7**); or
4. where A and B are companies within the same group (see **Chapter 9**).

2.2.2 Deduction of Non-trading Income and Gains

Deduct	**Then tax instead as follows:**
▪ Interest received	Generally taxed under the loan relationship rules. If miscellaneous income, then tax gross amount with credit for any tax deducted (if applicable).
▪ Rents	Property income, deduct related expenses and any expenditure incurred on replacing furnishings in residential property. See **Section 1.7.1**.
▪ Dividends received from other UK companies	Should be exempt from UK corporation tax provided one of the exemptions is met. See **Chapter 5**.
▪ Foreign dividends received	Should be exempt from UK corporation tax provided one of the exemptions is met. See **Chapter 5**.
▪ Profits on disposal of assets	If a chargeable asset, then compute chargeable gain as described in **Chapters 1** and **10**.

2.2.3 Provisions made under IAS 37/FRS 102

Provisions made under IAS 37 *Provisions, Contingent Liabilities and Contingent Assets* and FRS 102 *The Financial Reporting Standard applicable in the UK and Republic of Ireland* are generally allowable for tax purposes, provided that the provision would be allowable under general rules if it were an expense, e.g. a provision in relation to a capital item would not be deductible.

2.2.4 Interest

Interest, and any related expenditure, is deductible on an accruals basis if it is **trade-related**, i.e. it is treated the same as in the financial statements and, therefore, no adjustment is required. This is the case even if the money is borrowed to buy capital assets. However, these assets must be used in the trade and must not be used for investment purposes.

Other interest, which is not trade-related, must be disallowed in calculating trading income and may then be relievable as a non-trade debit (see Chapter 3).

Overall, interest from both trade and non-trade sources is also subject to the corporate interest restriction rules (see **Chapter 9, Section 9.5**).

2.2.5 Transfer Pricing Adjustments

Adjustments may be required to the adjustment of trading results calculation as a result of the transfer pricing rules (see **Chapter 11**).

Note that transfer pricing adjustments may also arise in other elements of the computation of taxable total profits as the rules apply to all transactions between connected parties, not just the sale of goods. Thus, transfer pricing adjustments may also need to be made in relation to royalties and loan relationships.

2.2.6 Employee Share Schemes

Many companies use employee share schemes as a way of attracting, rewarding and retaining staff. Some schemes are open to all employees. Others may only apply to key employees and directors. In some cases there may not be a formal scheme at all, just arrangements for individual employees; for example, under the terms of a service agreement or their contract of employment.

UK tax legislation has a number of approved share schemes that can attract favourable tax treatment. These, together with unapproved schemes and their tax treatment, were covered on the CA Proficiency 1 course and should be revisited.

A company may incur costs in setting up and running shares schemes – the question is if these costs are deductible for corporation tax purposes. The costs of setting up employee share schemes and employee share ownership trusts are capital expenditure and, therefore, would not be an allowable deduction in computing taxable profits under ordinary principles. This would include any initial amount settled to bring a trust into existence. However, specific statutory deductions are given for the costs of setting up the following approved schemes:

- share incentive plans;
- savings-related share option schemes; and
- company share option plans.

These specific statutory deductions are given for the accounting period in which the expenditure is incurred, except where the scheme is approved more than nine months after the end of that period. In that case, the expenditure should be disallowed for the period of payment, and allowed instead in the period in which the scheme is finally approved.

If a scheme has been used to grant options or transfer shares before the date of approval, the costs of setting up the scheme are not allowable.

An employer's expenditure in meeting the incidental costs of running an employee share scheme for the benefit of its employees is revenue expenditure and therefore is allowable as a deduction in calculating taxable trading profits.

A company is also entitled to claim a corporation tax deduction on an employee's share option when the employee exercises it. The deduction claimable is the value of the shares under option at the date of exercise less the exercise price.

If the relevant accounts contain a share-based payment calculated in accordance with UK GAAP, this therefore does not qualify for a corporation tax deduction and should be added back.

2.2.7 Payments to Directors and Other Employees

Bona fide directors' salaries, fees, and benefits payable for directors, etc. are deductible for corporation tax purposes. Such income is, of course, assessable in the hands of the individual director as employment income. Where a director has a company car available for private use, there is no disallowance for the inevitable "personal element" for corporation tax purposes. Again, a director with the use of a company car for private purposes will, of course, suffer tax under the benefit in kind regime. See **Chapter 12** for more on the taxation of directors.

Any salary or bonus accrued in the company's accounts is deductible in the period in which it is accrued, subject to the accrual being paid within nine months of the end of the accounting period.

2.3 Capital Allowances

The computation of capital allowances is beyond the scope of this textbook. However, remember to deduct capital allowances from trading income to arrive at tax-adjusted trading profits.

2.4 Research and Development

2.4.1 Overview

Relief is available for capital research and development (R&D) expenditure incurred by a company via the capital allowances regime and for revenue R&D expenditure through the various tax reliefs available. The definition of R&D for tax purposes follows its definition under UK GAAP.

Capital Expenditure
For capital expenditure, relief may be claimed on providing facilities to carry out research and development. This includes buildings used for R&D purposes, but not any land element. As noted above, the computation of capital allowances is beyond the scope of this textbook and relevant figures for capital allowances are provided in the examples and questions contained in this textbook and in your final examination.

Revenue Expenditure
Enhanced tax relief for revenue R&D can only be claimed on "relevant" R&D, i.e. R&D related to the trade carried on by the company or from which it is intended that a trade be carried on.

2.4.2 Qualifying Company

Tax relief for qualifying expenditure on R&D may be claimed by companies of all sizes. There is no minimum level of qualifying expenditure in order for relief to be available.

2.4.3 Qualifying R&D Revenue Expenditure

While the definition of R&D follows that under UK GAAP (and specifically IAS 38 *Intangible Assets*), HMRC recommend that the Department for Business, Energy & Industrial Strategy guidance tests must also be applied. In essence, a project will qualify as an R&D project if it is carried on in the field of science or technology, and it is undertaken to extend knowledge and to address scientific or technological uncertainties.

Qualifying revenue expenditure is similar (but not identical) under the SME and large companies R&D tax relief regimes. However, under **both** regimes, the expenditure must meet the following conditions and, *inter alia*:

1. must not be capital in nature – however, expenditure of a capital nature may qualify for 100% R&D capital allowances instead;
2. must be attributable to relevant R&D that is either directly undertaken by the company or on its behalf; and

3. must be incurred on staffing costs (to include salaries and wages (but not redundancy payments), employer's NIC, employer's pension fund contributions (but not non-cash benefits in kind), consumable or transformable materials, software, externally provided workers, utilities (such as power, water and fuel), subcontracted R&D expenditure and on payments to participants in clinical trials.

Where R&D activity results in goods or services sold in the normal course of a company's business, the cost of consumable items reflected in those goods or services does not qualify for relief. Qualifying expenditure on consumable items is limited to the cost of only those items fully used up or expended by the R&D activity itself and which do not go on to be sold as part of a commercial product e.g. a prototype.

One difference between the SME and large company R&D regimes is the ability, under the SME relief regime, to claim the enhanced deduction on 65% of qualifying subcontracted R&D costs, but only where the company and the subcontractor are not connected (or where an election has not been made under section 1135 CTA 2009 to treat the company and the subcontractor as connected). If the company is connected to the subcontractor or an election to be treated as connected is made, the company can claim SME R&D tax relief on the lower of:

- the payment that it makes to the subcontractor; **or**
- the relevant expenditure of the subcontractor, as long as the whole amount of the subcontract payment is brought into account in determining the subcontractor's profit in accounts drawn up under GAAP within 12 months of the end of the claimant company's accounting period for which the relief is claimed.

"Connected" has the meaning given by section 1122 CTA 2010. Broadly, a company is connected with another company if:

- the same person has control of both; or
- a person has control of one company and a person connected with them has control of the other; or
- a group of two or more persons has control of each company, and the groups consist of the same persons.

For a large company, the expenditure on R&D contracted to other persons is generally not allowable. However, it can be qualifying expenditure if it is revenue expenditure on relevant R&D and the company contracts for work to be directly undertaken by a qualifying body (generally a non-taxable body such as an educational establishment or a charity) or an individual or a partnership (each member of which is an individual).

R&D tax relief claims (including claims for the payable tax credit) should be made by the company in its corporation tax return for the relevant accounting period. A company has a two-year time limit from the end of the relevant accounting period to make an R&D claim.

2.4.4 R&D Tax Relief: Small and Medium-sized Companies

A small or medium-sized company (SME) is defined in accordance with EU guidelines as a company that has either:

- turnover of €100 million or less; or
- a balance sheet total of €86 million or less;

and has fewer than 500 employees. (Note that the turnover and net assets limit are correctly denoted in euro.)

Calculation of Enhanced Deduction

An SME, as defined, can qualify for a total deduction from its trading profits of 230% of its qualifying R&D expenditure. The qualifying expenditure must be such that it would have been allowable as a deduction in computing the taxable profits of a trade carried on by the company.

Where the company has a trading loss in an accounting period in which it also claims relief under the SME R&D tax relief regime, the company may (instead of any loss relief that it may be entitled to) surrender the loss for a cash payment of 14.5% of the surrenderable loss for the chargeable period.

The tax relief is claimed as an adjustment to the trading income computation. The qualifying expenditure is first added back and then the enhanced deduction later made at 230%. The SME regime has an upper limit of €7.5 million per R&D project. Should qualifying costs exceed that amount, the excess may be claimed under the R&D regime for large companies.

> ***Example 2.5***
> Tiny Ltd spends £165,000 on qualifying R&D in its accounting period ended 31 March 2020.
>
> In calculating taxable trade profits for the year to 31 March 2020 the total deduction for R&D will be:
>
> £165,000 × 230% = £379,500
>
> If the £165,000 has already been deducted in arriving at the company's adjusted trading result, an additional deduction of £214,500 should be deducted for corporation tax purposes.

Impact of Grants Received

Often an SME company may claim and receive grant aid in relation to an R&D project. This can affect whether an R&D claim is possible under the regime for SMEs or that for large companies, even if the company meets the R&D SME definition.

If the grant received towards the project is notified State aid, then a claim is not possible under the SME regime. This is because State aid would then be obtained twice on the same expenditure. Instead, the company would be required to claim under the large company regime (see **Section 2.4.5**). In such a case, the grant aid received is **not** deducted from the expenditure qualifying for relief under the large company regime.

If the grant received towards the project does not constitute notified State aid, then a claim is still possible under the SME regime providing the remaining conditions are met. In this case the grant received **is** required to be deducted from the qualifying expenditure, with 230% relief available on the net amount.

Calculation of Payable Tax Credit for Loss-making Companies

As noted earlier, if a company makes a claim for R&D tax relief under the SME regime and has a trading loss, then the company may claim a payable tax credit. The company effectively surrenders the whole or part of this loss in return for the payable tax credit. Should the company choose to claim the payable tax credit instead of relief for the trading loss in the usual way (see **Chapters 4** and **9**), the surrenderable loss is the lower of:

1. the unrelieved trading loss; or
2. 230% of the qualifying R&D expenditure.

The payable tax credit is calculated as 14.5% of the surrenderable loss for the period.

Example 2.6

Innova Ltd has been trading for several years and recently completed the period of account ending on 31 March 2020. The company's draft corporation tax computation currently denotes an adjusted tax loss of £1,742,000 before a claim for R&D tax relief. You review the R&D expenditure incurred and note that £800,000 qualifies under the legislation and that Innova Ltd is an SME.

Prepare the adjusted corporation tax computation and outline how relief is obtained by a company incurring a loss and also making a claim for R&D relief.

Solution

Innova Ltd – corporation tax computation for the accounting period ended 31 March 2020

	£
Adjusted tax loss before R&D relief	(1,742,000)
Add: qualifying R&D expenditure	800,000
Deduct: claim for R&D relief £800,000 @ 230%	(1,840,000)
Adjusted tax loss	(2,782,000)

Innova Ltd has made a trading loss of £2,782,000 in its accounting period ended 31 March 2020.

This loss is available to carry back against total profits under section 37(3)(b) CTA 2010, or to carry forward under section 45A CTA 2010, for use against the company's future profits arising from the same trade. Alternatively, the company may surrender the lower of its unrelieved trading loss of £2,782,000 and 230% of qualifying R&D expenditure (£1,840,000) for a repayable R&D tax credit. The level of tax credit claimable would therefore be £266,800 (14.5% x £1,840,000).

Losses available for carry back, for offset in the current year against other income or for carry forward would be as follows:

	£
Loss (as above)	2,782,000
Less: surrendered	(1,840,000)
Remaining losses	£942,000

The decision whether to surrender £1,840,000 of the loss and claim the R&D payable credit, or to not surrender the losses, should be discussed with the company directors – particularly considering that the difference in the rate of relief for the losses surrendered of £1,840,000 is 4.5% (i.e. main corporation tax rate of 19% – 14.5% rate of relief for tax credit).

2.4.5 R&D Tax Relief: Large Companies

A company not meeting the definition of an SME for R&D purposes, or one meeting the SME definition but in receipt of State aid, or one meeting the SME definition but having exceeded the SME €7.5 million upper limit for a project can instead claim under the R&D tax relief rules for large companies.

Arriving at the costs of what qualifies as R&D expenditure for large companies is almost identical to that for SMEs, except where sub-contracted costs are concerned (see **Section 2.4.3**).

Large companies receive an R&D expenditure credit (RDEC) on qualifying costs incurred.

The RDEC is **treated as a taxable receipt** in calculating the adjusted trading result of the trade for the accounting period, which is why it is sometimes called the 'above the line credit'. The company will also receive a **credit against its tax liability** of the same amount. This credit is equal to 12% of the company's **qualifying R&D expenditure** incurred.

If the company's corporation tax liability is **lower** than the RDEC or, if the company claiming the RDEC **incurs a trading loss** in the period, the company is entitled to claim a payable credit (subject to a number of adjustments, which are beyond the scope of this textbook).

Example 2.7

Conan Limited is a large company with the following results for the year to 31 December 2019.

	£
Turnover	7,500,000
R&D expenditure	(750,000)
Other expenditure	(5,750,000)
Net profit	1,000,000

Demonstrate how the corporation tax charge is calculated for a company claiming R&D tax relief under the large company regime, assuming the R&D expenditure qualifies for tax relief. It should be assumed that the company's net profit represents fully taxable profits for corporation tax purposes.

Solution

	£	£
Turnover		7,500,000
R&D activity	(750,000)	
12% RDEC (£750,000 × 12%)	90,000	(660,000)
Other expenditure		(5,750,000)
Taxable total profits		1,090,000
Corporation tax @ 19% (Note)		117,100
Profit after tax		972,900
Note: Corporation tax calculation		
Taxable total profits		1,090,000
Corporation tax @ 19%		207,100
Deduct: RDEC		(90,000)
Net corporation tax payable		117,100

2.5 The Corporate Intangibles Regime

As noted at **Section 2.2.2(j)**, a special corporation tax regime has been in place since 1 April 2002 that applies to a company's expenditure in respect of intangible fixed assets (IFAs). IFAs are a company's "intellectual property" and include such things as patents, copyrights, trademarks and goodwill. Patent royalties are also within the scope of this regime and fall to be taxed on the accruals basis.

The rules apply to expenditure on the creation, acquisition and enhancement of IFAs (including abortive expenditure), as well as expenditure on their preservation and maintenance, on or after 1 April 2002.

Companies generally obtain tax relief on expenditure on IFAs created or acquired after 1 April 2002 through their amortisation policy, as long as this is in accordance with UK GAAP. The company can, if it chooses, apply instead a fixed irrevocable rate allowance of 4% per annum, effectively writing-off the IFA over 25 years. A company would generally only elect to do so where the 4% election would accelerate relief, e.g. the amortisation policy under the relevant accounting standard is to write-off the IFA over a period of time in excess of 25 years. Or, where no accounting amortisation is available, a company can choose the 4% election.

In this regime, the loss or gain on the disposal of an IFA asset created or acquired on or after 1 April 2002 is either taxable (for income and profits on disposal) or deductible (for expenses (including amortisation) and losses on disposal). There is also a form of rollover relief available in the situation where an IFA is disposed of for more than the original cost and the disposal proceeds are reinvested in newly-acquired IFAs. The amount by which the disposal proceeds exceed **the original cost** may be rolled over against the cost of the new IFA assets. However, the clawed back amortisation cannot be rolled over, only the profit on the original cost of the goodwill.

Example 2.8

Dapper Limited purchased a business inclusive of a trading copyright on 1 April 2014. The copyright element cost £400,000 and is being amortised over 10 years. The company's accounting period end is 31 March.

During the 31 March 2020 period the company sells the business and copyright. The copyright element is sold for £850,000. Any income profit on the sale of the copyright could be rolled over against reinvestment in new intangible assets. However, the clawed back amortisation cannot be rolled over, only the profit on the original cost of the copyright.

To date the company has received corporation tax relief on the copyright totalling £200,000 in its last five accounting periods (as the company is not entitled to claim amortisation in the period of disposal). The tax written down value, which also equates to its accounting value, is £200,000. Therefore the taxable receipt on the copyright is £650,000 (£850,000 – £200,000). However, the amount on which rollover relief can be claimed is £450,000 (£850,000 – £400,000). The company will be taxed on the clawed back £200,000 amortisation as a trading receipt.

Under the regime, gains and losses relating to intangible assets used in a company's business are generally taxed as revenue items. Expenditure is a "debit" and income a "credit". The actual tax treatment of these debits and credits depends on whether the assets are held for trading purposes, a property business or a non-trading purpose.

2.5.1 Treatment of Goodwill

Relief is potentially available for goodwill in one of two ways.

Goodwill Acquired before 8 July 2015

Relief is available for amortisations of relevant assets, including certain goodwill (see definition later), acquired before 8 July 2015, but only where the relevant asset was not received from a related party individual or partnership. For the purposes of this rule, the term "related party" is defined as a participator or associate of a participator in a close company (see **Chapters 6** and **7**). This rule applies to transfers to both UK close limited companies and to non-UK resident companies that would be categorised as a close company if they were resident in the UK.

Overall, this measure prevents corporation tax relief being available for goodwill where a company acquires internally generated goodwill and customer-related IFAs from related individuals on the incorporation of a business.

For the purpose of this provision, relevant assets include the following assets acquired before 8 July 2015:

1. goodwill;
2. an IFA consisting of information relating to customers, or potential customers, of a business;

3. an IFA consisting of a relationship (whether contractual or not) between someone carrying on a business and one or more customers of that business;
4. an unregistered trade mark or sign used in the course of a business; or
5. a licence or other right that relates to an asset within items 1 to 4.

Goodwill Acquired on or after 1 April 2019

Companies that acquire goodwill (and certain other customer-related intangible assets) on or after 1 April 2019 only receive relief where:

- they acquire the goodwill (or customer-related assets) as part of a business; and
- other qualifying intellectual property (IP) is also acquired as part of the acquisition.

The categories of qualifying IP assets include patents, registered designs, copyright and design rights.

Relief is given at a fixed rate of 6.5% per annum (restricted for periods of less than 12 months) on the lower of:

- the cost of the goodwill (or customer-related assets); or
- six times the amount of the qualifying IP.

If no qualifying IP assets are acquired as part of the transaction, no relief is available for the relevant assets, including any goodwill. This measure is therefore targeted at IP-intensive acquisitions by companies.

Again, relief is not available for internally generated goodwill and customer-related IFAs in a related party incorporation.

Goodwill acquired prior to 1 April 2019 continues to be subject to the tax treatment prevailing at the time it was acquired.

Example 2.9

On 1 July 2019, Innovate Ltd purchased a business from an unconnected third party. The purchase included copyright (£50,000), design rights (£75,000) and goodwill (£800,000). The intangible assets acquired are each being amortised in the company's accounts over 10 years in accordance with IAS 38 *Intangible Assets*. The company's accounting period end is 31 March.

Set out the tax relief available for the intangible assets acquired as part of this transaction in respect of the accounting period ended 31 March 2020.

Copyright

£50,000/10 × 9/12 = £3,750 amortisation in the company accounts. No adjustment is required to the company's corporation tax computation in 2020 as the company obtains relief via its amortisation policy. The company will therefore obtain a deduction for the full £3,750 amortised in the 2020 period.

Patent

£75,000/10 × 9/12 = £5,625 amortisation in the company accounts. No adjustment is required to the company's corporation tax computation in 2020 as the company obtains relief via its amortisation policy. The company will therefore obtain a deduction for the full £5,625 amortised in the 2020 period.

Goodwill

£800,000/10 × 9/12 = £60,000 amortisation in the company accounts. Add-back of £60,000 required in the company's corporation tax computation in 2020 and relief to be calculated in accordance with the rules for relevant assets acquired on or after 1 April 2019.

continued overleaf

Relief is given at a fixed rate of 6.5% on the lower of:

- the amount of the relevant asset, i.e. £800,000; or
- six times the amount of the qualifying IP, i.e. £50,000 patent + £75,000 design rights = £125,000 × 6 = £750,000

Therefore the maximum goodwill that qualifies as a relevant asset is £750,000.

In 2020, the company should obtain a corporation tax deduction of £750,000 × 6.5% × 9/12 = £36,563. This should be deducted in its calculation of trading profits.

Debits and credits on the disposal of relevant assets (including goodwill) that do not qualify for corporation tax relief as set out in this section are deemed to be a non-trading debit or credit and dealt with in accordance with the loan relationship rules (see **Chapter 3**).

2.5.2 Trading Debits and Credits

Debits and credits in respect of assets held for the purposes of a trade are dealt with in the normal trading income computation as expenses and receipts of that particular trade. If they relate to a property business, then they are dealt with as property income.

2.5.3 Non-trading Debits and Credits

Non-trading debits and credits on intangible assets are initially grouped together and netted-off against each other. If there is a resultant net gain, then it is assessable under the catch-all "miscellaneous income" provisions (see **Chapter 1, Section 1.8**).

If there is a net "loss", then the company has a choice about how it wishes to relieve this loss, i.e. either to group-relieve the loss or to set it against the company's total profits of that accounting period. Any unutilised loss is carried forward to the next accounting period and treated as if it were a non-trading debit of that period.

Gains or losses on the disposal of IFAs not within the corporate intangibles regime continue to be dealt with under the CGT regime and will either be chargeable gains or allowable capital losses.

2.5.4 Rollover Relief for IFAs

As previously mentioned, there is a form of rollover relief available in the situation where an IFA within the corporate intangibles regime is disposed of for more than the original cost and the disposal proceeds are reinvested in newly-acquired IFAs. The amount by which the disposal proceeds exceed the **original cost** (not the tax written down value) may be rolled over against the cost of the new IFA. In this situation, the company is taxed as if the disposal proceeds of the old IFA and the cost of the newly acquired IFAs are both reduced by this excess. Relief is further restricted where not all of the net proceeds from the IFA are reinvested.

The reinvestment must occur in the period 12 months before to three years after the time the old IFA is realised. Claims for the relief must be made within four years after the later of either the end of the accounting period of disposal of the old IFA, or the acquisition of the new IFA.

Relief is also available where the reinvestment occurs in a group company (see **Section 2.5.5**).

> ***Example 2.10***
> Taking **Example 2.8**, assume Dapper Limited thereafter purchases a business with a trading copyright costing £900,000 during the 2021 period. This qualifies for IFA rollover relief as the entire proceeds were reinvested. The rollover relief which can be claimed is £450,000 (£850,000 – £400,000). Therefore, the £450,000 trading profit in the corporation tax computation is not subject to corporation tax and should be deducted. The company will still be subject to corporation tax on the clawed-back £200,000 amortisation as a trading receipt.
>
> The £450,000 is rolled over against the base cost of the new IFA, which is reduced for tax relief amortisation purposes to £450,000 (£900,000 purchase price less £450,000 rollover relief).

2.5.5 Groups

A company may be part of an IFA group for the purposes of the corporate intangibles regime. This can give important benefits to the companies within the group, namely that IFAs can be transferred from one group company to another without triggering a taxable receipt, i.e. on a no gain/no loss basis. In addition, taxable receipts on disposal of IFAs can also be rolled over inter-group. The definition of an IFA group mirrors that of a capital gains tax group (see **Chapter 10** for examples).

Companies are in an IFA group where:

1. at each level, there is a 75% direct holding; and
2. the top company has an effective interest of at least 51% in the group companies.

A company can only be a member of one IFA group.

Assets classified as IFAs under the corporate intangibles regime can be transferred between members of the IFA group on a tax-neutral basis. This is similar to the rule that applies under section 171 TCGA 1992 for chargeable assets taxed under the capital gains tax regime, where the companies are part of a capital gains tax group.

In particular, this means the transferee inherits the transferor's tax written down value for the IFA, and all such debits and credits that have been brought into account are treated for this purpose as though they had been brought into account by the transferee.

> ***Example 2.11***
> Again, taking **Example 2.8**, assume that Dapper Limited instead of selling the copyright for its market value of £850,000, that it transferred this inter-group to its 100% subsidiary.
>
> This is transferred on a tax-neutral basis. The tax written down value of the copyright at that point is £200,000. The recipient company can claim tax relief on the remaining amortisation. It is treated, for all intents and purposes, as if it had always owned the copyright.

> ***Example 2.12***
> Now assume that Dapper Limited has a 100% subsidiary that reinvests in a patent at a cost of £900,000 in 2021.
>
> As the entire proceeds were reinvested inter-group, the rollover relief that can be claimed is £450,000 (£850,000 – £400,000). This is rolled over against the base cost of the new intangible owned by the subsidiary, which is reduced for tax relief amortisation purposes to £450,000. That is, the gain on an IFA disposed of by Dapper is rolled over against the purchase of the IFA made by its subsidiary, the companies being together in a corporate intangibles group.
>
> Therefore the £450,000 trading profit in the corporation tax computation is not subject to corporation tax and should be deducted. Dapper Limited will still be subject to corporation tax on the clawed-back £200,000 amortisation as a trading receipt.

2.5.6 Degrouping Charges on IFAs

A degrouping IFA charge may arise where a company leaves a group and there has been an earlier transfer to it of an IFA within the corporate intangibles regime on a tax-neutral basis in the previous six years. The rules are modelled on the capital gains degrouping rules, as they are aimed at the same potential problem.

The broad effect is to recognise a gain or loss deferred on an earlier tax-neutral disposal if the IFA in question leaves the group other than by a direct disposal of the IFA. The company leaving the group makes a deemed disposal and reacquisition of the IFA at market value immediately after the time it acquired the IFA from another group company at the date of the original transfer.

The event that triggers a degrouping adjustment is a company ceasing to be a member of a group; but the amount of the gain or loss is determined by reference to the previous tax-neutral transfer in the previous six years. Although the calculation of any gain or loss on disposal is calculated by reference to the market value of the IFA at the time immediately following the disposal by a group member to the transferee company, the taxable credit or deductible debit resulting is treated as though it arose immediately prior to the transferee company leaving the group.

However, like the rules for degrouping charges on chargeable assets (see **Chapter 10**), where a company leaves the group as a result of a disposal of shares by another group company, any degrouping charge is made by way of an adjustment to the consideration taken into account for calculating the gain or loss on the disposal of shares. A consequence of this is that if the substantial shareholdings exemption (SSE) (see **Chapter 10**) applies to the share disposal, it will also apply to the degrouping intangibles charge.

In such circumstances, the assets that would have been subject to a degrouping charge will remain at their tax written down value and continue to attract relief as they did prior to degrouping.

Should the SSE not be available on the share disposal, the degrouping charge remains taxable on the company leaving the group. In this scenario, the amortisation deduction for the period that the company leaves the group will also need to be adjusted to reflect an acquisition cost based instead on market value at the time of the original transfer.

If two or more related 51% group companies that would form a group by themselves leave the main group at the same time, the degrouping adjustment does not apply to any IFA transfers that have taken place between those related 51% group companies. However, if one of these companies subsequently leaves the sub-group, there may be a degrouping adjustment on that occasion, again subject to the potential for the SSE to be available. Full or partial reallocation of the taxable credit is possible between group members. In addition, the departing company may of course invest in new IFAs and defer the gain via a claim for rollover relief.

Example 2.13
Following on from the scenario in **Example 2.11**, Dapper Limited sells the shares in its subsidiary in the 2021 accounting period. The subsidiary is deemed to have realised and reacquired the IFA for its 2020 market value of £850,000. That gives rise to a taxable credit of £650,000, representing the excess of the market value at the time of the transfer (£850,000) over the tax written down value at that time (£200,000).

However, no taxable trading debit will arise if Dapper Limited is able to meet the conditions for the SSE on the disposal of the shares. Instead, the subsidiary leaving the group continues to receive tax relief on the intangible as it did prior to degrouping and there is no change to the tax written down value at that time.

2.6 Investment Companies

A company that is in the business of holding and managing investments is taxed as an "investment company". The key feature is that, for tax purposes, allowable expenses in respect of investment activity are limited to those required for investment management. These are known as management expenses.

An investment company is defined in the legislation as "any company whose business consists **wholly** or **partly** in the making of investments." The meaning of business is taken from case law, but broadly there must be some active behaviour carried on by the company in relation to the investments. Therefore, a company that carries on a substantial trading activity and a small investment business will still be able to claim relief for management expenses.

2.6.1 Management Expenses

Management expenses include all expenses relating to the management of a company's investment business. Expenses that are directly related to a particular source of income must be deducted from that income source, e.g. letting expenses are deductible against property income, and costs associated with financing will be deductible as trade or non-trade deficits. If a company carries on both an investment business and a trading activity within the same entity, the expenses must be allocated on a just and reasonable basis.

Items of a capital nature cannot be claimed as management expenses.

Investments are not held for a business or other commercial purposes if they are held directly/indirectly in consequence of, or in connection with, any arrangements for securing a tax advantage. In addition, no deduction is allowed in so far as the expenses are otherwise deductible from total profits, or in calculating any component of total profits.

Expenditure on appraising and investigating investments will, in general, be revenue in nature. However, the process of appraisal will eventually reach the stage where the company will decide which, if any, companies it is seeking to acquire. Expenditure up to the point at which a decision is made to acquire a particular investment will generally be non-capital. Similar considerations apply where it is a disposal rather than an acquisition that is being considered.

Once it has been decided to purchase/dispose of an investment, any costs incurred after that point will be costs of the acquisition/disposal and therefore capital. An abortive acquisition or disposal is no different, in terms of the nature of expenditure, from a successful acquisition/disposal.

The following table shows types of expenditure that are either allowable or disallowable as management expenses.

Allowable expenditure	Disallowable expenditure
Costs, such as keeping the investment company share register, printing annual accounts and holding annual shareholder meetings.	Professional fees in respect of land held as investments (fees for managing/protecting such assets would be allowable).
Costs incurred in respect of stock exchange quotations.	Cost of appraising investments (a general appraisal of the market would not be disallowed, and work on a potential new investment would not be disallowed until such point as a firm decision to acquire the investment is made).

continued overleaf

Maintenance and repair costs in respect of premises used by the investment company.	Brokerage, commissions and stamp duty in respect of investments.
Directors' and employee remuneration (subject to being a reasonable expense of managing investments and the 9-month rule for accruals).	Costs of raising capital (but will qualify as a non-trade loan relationship deficit).
Payments in respect of an HMRC-approved retirement scheme.	Capital expenditure.

An investment company is also subject to the self-assessment regime for corporation tax and is subject to the same administrative rules.

2.6.2 *Utilisation of Management Expenses*

Management expenses are first deducted against a company's total income. Therefore it does not matter if the company also carries on trading activity as relief for management expenses is not restricted to investment or non-trading activity. The deduction is **mandatory** and must be made before **any** other deductions from total profits.

Where management expenses cannot be fully utilised against a company's total profits (known as 'excess management expenses'), they can be surrendered as group relief or carried forward and treated as having been incurred in the next period until such time as they are fully utilised. Any surplus carried forward is also deducted from total profits of the next period. In cases where management expenses are group relieved, there is a requirement for the surrendering company to use these against its own income sources first (i.e. only excess management expenses can be group relieved).

Companies with investment business that have excess qualifying charitable donations can carry those excess charitable donations forward as management expenses (see **Chapter 4**).

2.6.3 *Capital Allowances*

Capital allowances are available in respect of capital expenditure incurred for the purpose of the company's investment business. The computation of capital allowances is beyond the scope of this textbook.

Questions

Review Questions

(See Suggested Solutions to Review Questions at the end of this textbook.)

Question 2.1

Telestar Ltd, a company which commenced to trade many years ago, makes up its accounts each year to 31 March. It has no related 51% group companies.

The statement of profit or loss to 31 March 2020 is as follows:

		£	£
Gross profit			239,800
Grant for extension of premises			10,000
Employment grant			1,000
Patent royalty received from individual (net of 20%) (Note 1)			1,600
Discount received			3,300
Dividends from a UK company received on 10 May 2019 (Telestar Ltd qualifies as small and the shareholding is 40%)			1,300
Profit on sale of van (Note 2)			1,000
Profit on sale of shares (Note 3)			3,000
Bank deposit interest (paid gross)			600
			261,600
Less:	Discount given	3,000	
	Goods stolen	3,000	
	Business overdraft interest	5,800	
	Depreciation	15,389	
	Van expense	3,400	
	Motor expenses	2,400	
	Bad debts	2,300	
	Obsolete stock – written off	2,600	
	Salaries and wages	100,000	
	Telephone	311	
	Entertainment (Note 4)	2,700	
	Depreciation on finance leases (Note 5)	1,300	
	Legal fees (Note 6)	2,400	144,600
Profit before tax			117,000

Notes

1. The patent royalty was received in December 2019 and relates to the company's non-trading activities. The patent was granted in 2001.
2. Profit on sale of van – the van was acquired second-hand on 03/02/2005 for £12,000. It was sold on 05/05/2019 for £4,000. The net book value of the van at 31/03/2019 was £3,000. To date, capital allowances of £12,000 have been obtained thereon.
3. Profit on sale of shares – these shares in Video Plc were acquired on 31/03/2005 for £3,000 and sold on 30/04/2019 for £6,000. Indexation factor up to 31 December 2017 is 0.456. The shares represented 0.25% of Video Plc's share capital and the company owns no other shares in Video Plc.

4. The charge for entertainment is made up as follows:

	£
Prizes for top salespersons of the year	900
Christmas party for staff	750
Christmas gifts for suppliers (hampers)	150
Reimbursement of managing director for costs incurred entertaining customers at home	350
General customer entertainment	550
	2,700

5. Finance lease depreciation – this relates to a machine leased in 2014, the cost of which is capitalised in the company's accounts.
6. The legal fees relate to the extension of the premises.
7. Capital allowances for the year are £7,272.

Requirement
Calculate the corporation tax liability for the year ended 31 March 2020 and show the dates on which the tax is payable.

Question 2.2

The statement of profit or loss of Zaco Ltd for the year ended 30 September 2019 is as follows:

STATEMENT OF PROFIT OR LOSS

	£		£
Salaries and wages	62,500	Gross profit	489,250
Rent and rates	5,400	Dividends (Note 6)	3,600
Repairs (Note 1)	16,100	Bad debts	300
Insurance	1,720	Profit on sale of fixed assets (Note 7)	15,200
Professional fees (Note 2)	1,600	Bank interest receivable	1,200
Depreciation	13,000	Property income	4,300
Audit fees	1,000		
Subscriptions (Note 3)	2,400		
Entertainment (Note 4)	600		
Staff award (Note 5)	1,000		
Discount allowed	320		
Bank interest	7,060		
Light and heat	21,250		
Profit	379,900		
	513,850		513,850

Zaco Ltd has no related 51% group companies.

Notes

1. Repairs – includes improvements to offices of £5,200.
2. Professional fees – includes debt collection fees of £200, architect's fees re. office improvements of £300.
3. Subscriptions – includes political donations of £750 and staff race sponsorship of £1,000.
4. Entertainment – this is made up as follows:

	£
Customer entertainment	450
Supplier entertainment	150
	600

5. Staff award – a special award of £1,000 was made to an employee who achieved first place in Ireland in his engineering examinations during the year.
6. Dividends – foreign dividends (net of 20% withholding tax) £3,600. Received on 31 August 2019 and meets one of the dividend exemptions.
7. Profit on sale – indexation factor 0.035 up to 31 December 2017

Building	£
Cost June 2008	200,000
Proceeds July 2019	215,200
Profit on sale	15,200

8. The capital allowances (including balancing allowances and charges) are £9,846.
9. There are capital losses brought forward of £10,000.

Requirement
Calculate the company's corporation tax liability for the year.

Question 2.3

From the following information you are required to calculate the corporation tax liability of Alpha Ltd for the year ended 31 March 2020. Alpha Ltd has had two wholly-owned subsidiaries since 2010.

Statement of Profit or Loss

	£		£
Salaries and wages (Note 1)	71,300	Gross profit	600,000
Rent and rates (Note 2)	7,600	UK dividends (Note 14)	4,500
Repairs (Note 3)	18,500	Gain on sale of fixed assets (Note 15)	1,000
Insurance (Note 4)	1,350	Amortisation of grant (Note 16)	240
Loss on sale of investments (Note 5)	600	Interest on tax overpaid	475
Legal expenses (Note 6)	2,700	Royalties received (net of 20% tax) (Note 17)	2,500
Commissions	9,209	Rent received	6,000
Depreciation	13,260	Deposit interest (received gross)	1,500
Audit fees	1,550	Bad debts recovered	50

Subscriptions (Note 7)	3,400	
Discounts allowed	900	
Bank interest (Note 8)	3,300	
Other interest (Note 9)	7,000	
Light and heat	11,234	
Motor expenses (Note 10)	33,126	
Sundry (Note 11)	3,740	
Entertainment		
Expenses (Note 12)	1,191	
Finance lease depreciation (Note 13)	1,700	
Net profit	424,605	–
	616,265	616,265

Notes

1. Salaries and wages include £25,000 in respect of staff bonuses relating to the year ended 31 March 2020 which were paid in full by 31 March 2020.
2. Rent and rates include an amount of £1,000 received by the company which relates to part of the company's premises which has been let to a sub-tenant on a short-term basis.
3. Repairs include an amount of £15,000 for an extension to the factory premises.
4. Insurance includes an amount of £350 relating to the let premises.
5. Loss on sale of investments (2% shareholding):

	£
UK shares purchased 2005:	
Cost	10,000
Proceeds (01/07/2019)	(9,400)
	600

6. Legal expenses:

	£
Debt collection	700
Extension to factory	2,000
	2,700

7. Subscriptions:

	£
Chamber of Commerce	450
Trade association	1,135
Political	1,815
	3,400

8. Bank interest – bank interest includes an amount of £1,500 relating to borrowings taken out to finance the extension to the factory premises.
9. Other interest is deemed to be from a trading loan relationship £7,000.
10. Motor expenses – the company leased six new motor cars on 1 April 2017. All of the cars had CO_2 emissions of 145g/km.

The motor expenses can be analysed as follows:

	£
Leasing charges on leased cars	21,126
Running costs of leased cars	12,000
	33,126

11. Sundry:

	£
Interest on late payments of VAT	1,630
Parking fines	30
Christmas party	500
Gifts to customers (hampers)	541
General office expenses	1,039
	3,740

12. Entertainment includes an amount of £1,191 for hotel and accommodation for overseas customers
13. Finance lease depreciation relates to new machinery leased in 2013, the cost of which is capitalised in the company's accounts.
14. UK dividends:

	£
Dividend on Bank of Ireland shares received 1 December 2019	1,800
Dividend from subsidiary received 1 April 2019	2,700
	4,500

15. Sale of fixed asset:

	£
Cost (July 2007)	4,000
Proceeds (January 2020)	5,000
Profit on sale	1,000

The asset is not a chargeable asset for capital gains tax.

16. A grant of £1,200 was received on 2 April 2019 in respect of the factory extension. This is being amortised over a five-year period.
17. Royalties were received from non-trading activities.
18. Capital allowances for the accounting period are £26,006.
19. The company has a trading loss of £20,000 carried forward from the year ended 31 March 2017.
20. There is a capital loss carried forward of £189 from year ended 31 March 2019.

Question 2.4

It is January 2021, and you are the newly appointed financial controller of a UK stand-alone company. When recruited, it was made clear to you that some of your duties would involve tax compliance in order to minimise the cost of taking professional advice. One of your first projects is to review the draft corporation tax computation for the year ended 31 March 2020 which was prepared by your predecessor.

The company, Comtech Limited, has its own R&D department and, when reviewing the draft corporation tax computation, you noted that no claims for R&D tax relief have been made. You mention this in passing to the finance director who asks you to prepare a memo outlining the key aspects of the UK R&D tax relief scheme and the potential amounts that the company could claim tax relief on for the 2020 period only, including providing explanations of your calculations and the overall tax saving available.

Comtech's turnover for the year ended 31 March 2020 was £34.6 million (which equates to roughly €40 million) and it has 55 employees. Its balance sheet total was £48 million (roughly €55 million).

You have reviewed the draft computation and are satisfied that, aside from any potential claim for relief on R&D expenditure, no other adjustments to the draft taxable total profits figure of £1,828,925 is required.

The R&D team is tasked with developing new and innovative products for the company to bring to market, so its work directly links to the trade of the company and, in its particular field, Comtech is considered a 'blue skies' industry leader.

At a meeting with the head of the R&D department, it is established that the revenue costs of running the R&D department in 2020 were as follows:

	£
Gross wages	212,567
Redundancy payments	4,250
Employer's NIC	27,209
Pension scheme contributions	15,000
Company car benefit in kind	7,825
Consumable items (used up as part of R&D process)	22,425
Power, water and fuel	8,762
Software	4,933
Rates	25,655
Professional fees*	12,250
	340,876

* During the period, the R&D department sub-contracted some of its work to a specialist laboratory nearby, at a cost of £12,250. The laboratory is not connected to the company.

Having reviewed all of the above costs you do not identify any tax disallowable items therein.

Requirement

Prepare a memo to the finance director in which you:

(a) Outline the UK R&D regime including details of the amount of relief potentially available to companies and the conditions for claiming the relief.

(b) Assuming the activities of the R&D department qualify as R&D as defined by tax legislation, calculate the maximum amount of tax relief available to the company under the UK R&D regime. Outline for the finance director the tax saving to be achieved by making the R&D claim and any other relevant recommendations.

Question 2.5

Investco Ltd is a small company under the dividend exemption rules. It reported the following results for the accounting period ended 31 March 2020 in its management accounts:

Investment income	**£**
UK dividend income	25,000
Bank interest (received gross)	3,000
Rental income	12,000
Total income	40,000

Expenses	**£**
Directors' remuneration	12,000
Appraisal costs of identified target	1,750
Shareholder meeting costs	2,240
Rent of office	3,000
Repairs to office door	500
Total expenses	(19,490)
Net profit per management accounts	20,510

The company also had a chargeable gain of £5,000 that has not yet been reflected in its accounts.

Requirement
Calculate the corporation tax payable for Investco Ltd for the accounting period ended 31 March 2020.

Question 2.6

Paul Morrisey, a relatively new client of your practice, called you in early February for some advice in relation to his company, Classic Engineering Consultancy Ltd, which provides consultancy services to local engineering businesses. The company is not a client of your practice and the tax compliance work is carried out by a small 'one man band' in the local area who is not a Chartered Accountant.

It is now early July 2021 and only yesterday Paul received a letter from HMRC informing him it had opened an enquiry into the company tax return for 31 March 2020, which had been filed online by the local accountant on 10 June 2021. The Inspector of Taxes has asked for detailed analysis of a number of items. The computation filed for that period is reproduced at Appendix 1.

Paul knows the return was late, but said he had been told there would be no penalty as this was the first time this had happened. His words were, "This letter that I have received – has the company anything to worry about? I assume every company receives a letter like this now and again." Paul is an additional rate taxpayer.

APPENDIX 1

Classic Engineering Consultancy Ltd

Corporation tax computation for the accounting period ended 31 March 2020

Trading Profits Computation

	Notes	£	£
Net profit per accounts			1,610,622
Add:			
Profit on sale of machine		11,400	
Disallowed repairs and renewals	1	–	
Disallowed advertising and promotion	2	1,450	
Disallowed legal fees	3	–	
Depreciation	4	22,900	
Disallowed motor expenses	5	–	
Disallowed travel expenses	6	–	
Disallowed donation	7	500	
Disallowed entertainment	8	1,200	
			37,450
Adjusted profit			1,648,072
Less: capital allowances			49,744
Tax-adjusted trading profits			1,598,328
Corporation tax payable @ 18%*			287,699

*Paid in full on 1 January 2021.

Taxable profits in 2019 were noted as £1,423,333.
Net profit per company accounts (agreed to final company accounts) = £1,610,622.

Notes:
Extracts from accounts analysis/supporting notes to tax computation:

1. Repairs and renewals comprises:

	£
Painting the exterior of the existing workshop	12,750
Repairs and maintenance of equipment	11,267
Extension to workshop	50,400
Total	74,417

(Reviewed and all allowable.)

2. Advertising and promotion comprises:

	£
Christmas gifts to regular customers (gourmet hampers – disallowed)	1,450
Promotional literature	12,000
Business advertising in newspaper and trade magazines	9,200
Total	22,650

3. Legal fees comprises:

	£
Planning appeal costs for planning application denied for workshop in new location	11,725
Renewal of lease on parts store for another 10 years	2,500
Accounting fees incurred in inquiry by HMRC into personal tax return of Paul (no additional tax was payable as a result)	1,500
Total	15,725

(Reviewed and all allowable.)

4. Depreciation comprises:

	£
Depreciation on motor vehicles	6,744
Depreciation on building	2,000
Depreciation on machinery: hire purchase*	28,289
: non-hire purchase	14,156
Total	51,189

* Treated as an allowable deduction in the computation.

5. Motor expenses comprises:

	£
Fuel, road tax and insurance	5,222
Parking fines incurred by staff visiting other sites	240
Parking fines incurred by Paul	400
Contract hire costs of new vans (all 175g/km)	4,765
Contract hire costs of car leased in 2019 (90g/km)	3,000
Total	13,627

6. Travel expenses comprise:

	£
Air fares and hotel expenses incurred on business trips to trade fairs	1,750
Meals with potential new suppliers/customers	900
Expenses incurred sending trainee engineers on courses	1,400
Total	4,050

7. Subscriptions and donations comprise:

	£
Subscription to *Engineering Monthly*	448
Donation to political party – disallowed	500
Total	948

8. Entertainment comprises:

	£
Staff Christmas party	500
Entertaining potential clients and their family in restaurant – disallowed	1,200
Total	1,700

9. General expenses comprise:

	£
Write-off of loan to Paul on 31 December 2019*	50,000
Miscellaneous small allowable items	566
Total	50,566

* Write-off of loan to Paul is allowable for corporation tax as long as the company forgoes the section 455 tax (which was 25% at that time) it originally paid on this loan when it was taken out in January 2005. The company has not therefore submitted a claim for this.

Requirement
Write a letter to Paul dealing with the following:

(a) Review, check, comment on and adjust (if necessary) the corporation tax computation for the accounting period ended 31 March 2020. You should assess if the correct corporation tax liability has been paid. All relevant information to do so is provided in Appendix 1 above. Assume that capital allowances have been calculated correctly and that the company has no related 51% group companies.

(b) If the correct liability has not been paid, outline the implications for the company of any under/overpayment arising including calculating the potential penalty (if any).

(c) Advise the company what action should be taken in the context of the letter from HMRC and the outcome of your work in (a) and (b) above. Assess if it is correct that no late filing penalty will be payable for the late submission of the 2020 corporation tax return.

3

Income Tax on Annual Payments, Qualifying Charitable Donations and Loan Relationships

Learning Objectives

After studying this chapter you will understand the following:

- Some of the different types of annual payments a company can make or receive and their tax treatment.
- What a qualifying charitable donation is and how a company obtains tax relief on them.
- The treatment of income, profits, losses and expenses from non-trading loan relationships and how these are treated for corporation tax purposes.

3.1 Annual Payments

3.1.1 Relevant Payments

A company must deduct 20% basic rate income tax when making certain relevant payments. Such payments include but are not limited to:

- Patent royalties, where the recipient is not a UK company or where payment is to an individual.
- Annual interest and other annual payments, where the recipient is not a UK company or where payment is to an individual.
- Rents paid to non-residents in respect of UK property.
- Royalties paid to non-residents.

The following annual interest may be paid without deduction of tax:

- Interest paid to a bank or building society in the UK and to other UK companies that carry on a trade of lending that satisfy certain conditions.
- Interest paid to a resident of a country with which the UK has a tax treaty that provides for withholding tax to be reduced to nil, provided that clearance has been received from HMRC to make payments gross.
- Annual payments made by a member of the group to another member of the same group.
- Interest on loans for fixed periods of less than one year, known as 'short interest'.

Royalties Paid to Non-residents

Additional obligations to deduct income tax at source from royalties paid to non-resident persons apply (these are beyond the scope of this textbook). The deduction of income tax by the company must follow the CT61 process outlined below.

3.1.2 Payment of Tax Deducted from Annual Payments

Banks, building societies, etc. are not required to deduct income tax from interest paid, hence this source of income is paid gross.

Income tax at the basic rate of 20% must be deducted from relevant annual payments and paid over to HMRC. Any amounts so deducted must be paid online using form CT61. The form must, potentially, be completed a maximum of five times during an accounting period, namely on four defined quarter dates as well as the date coinciding with the end of the accounting period. Thus, for a company with a year ended 31 March 2020, it could potentially have to complete CT61 forms for the quarters ending 30 June 2019, 30 September 2019, 31 December 2019 and 31 March 2020. If the company has a year ended 31 January, then as well as the above four quarter dates, it would also potentially have to complete a form for the period ending 31 January for any relevant payments made in that month. The return for each period and any tax is due 14 days after the end of the return period. For example, the return for the quarter to 30 June 2019 would be due by 14 July 2019.

3.1.3 Credit for Tax Suffered on Annual Payments Received

Where, in an accounting period, a company receives a payment from which UK income tax has been deducted, the grossed-up amount is included within the company's corporation tax computation. For example, if patent royalties used in the company's trade were paid net of tax, the grossed-up figure would be included within the trading income computation.

Where a company both makes and receives payments from which it deducted income tax and had it deducted, respectively, then as well as completing the relevant CT61 form for the period in which the various payments were made, the company must also consider the net income tax position at the end of the accounting period. If the tax suffered on income exceeds the tax deducted from amounts paid net, then this excess is reclaimed by subtracting it from the company's corporation tax liability.

If a company receives a payment from which foreign tax (including withholding tax) has been deducted, again the grossed-up amount is included within the company's corporation tax computation. Later in the computation the company may be entitled to double tax relief for the foreign tax paid. Note that double tax relief is not available for any foreign tax paid on dividends that are exempt from corporation tax.

3.2 Qualifying Charitable Donations

A payment made to a charity by a company may be a qualifying charitable donation (QCD) if certain conditions are met (these conditions are beyond the scope of this textbook). QCDs include:

- cash donations to charity (these are always paid gross by a company);
- gifts of shares quoted on a recognised stock exchange (including the AIM) to a charity, and
- gifts of UK land or buildings to charity.

QCDs incurred before a trade commences are treated as paid when the trade commences, i.e. they are deductible from total profits as qualifying charitable donations in the first year of trading.

For cash donations, the amount paid to charity is first added back in the adjustment of trading profits and then deducted from total profits in arriving at taxable total profits for the chargeable accounting period in which the donation is made.

For gifts of shares or UK land/buildings, it is the market value at the date of the gift (plus any costs of transfer) that is treated as a QCD. Again, these are first added back and then later deducted from total profits.

Under section 1300(5) CTA 2009, QCDs made by a company are deducted from the company's total profits for the period **after** any other relief from corporation tax, other than group relief.

The amount of the deduction is limited to the amount that reduces the company's taxable total profits for the period to nil. Reliefs, such as trading losses carried back, are given **prior** to any deduction of QCDs. This may result in the company's QCDs being wasted as it is not possible to choose how much of a loss is to be carried back and partial claims are not possible. Any surplus is not available to carry forward and relief is effectively lost (e.g. if a company has a trading loss or no total profits, it will not receive any relief for QCDs). However if the company has an investment business, excess QCDs can be carried forward as management expenses (see **Chapter 2**, **Section 2.6**). It may be possible for group companies to relieve excess QCDs (see **Chapter 9**).

In addition, where the company has a long period of account, QCDs are split between the two chargeable accounting periods, based on the date that the donation is actually paid (see **Chapter 1**, **Section 1.2.5**).

3.3 Loan Relationships

3.3.1 General

A loan relationship arises when a company lends or borrows money, including issuing or investing in debentures or buying gilts. This can either be:

1. a creditor relationship (where the company lends or invests money); or
2. a debtor relationship (where the company borrows money or issues securities).

The following types of debt (not exhaustive) have always been included within loan relationships: bank loans and deposits, advances, mortgages, overdrafts, debentures and government stock.

A normal trade debt is however **not** a loan relationship, nor are, *inter alia*, finance leases, hire purchase agreements or loan guarantees.

From a corporation tax standpoint, it is imperative to distinguish whether a loan relationship is trading or non-trading. In addition, the corporate interest restriction rules (see **Chapter 9**, **Section 9.5**) can also impact on the deductibility of trade and non-trade interest paid by a company.

3.3.2 Treatment of Trading Loan Relationships

In making any distinction between trade or non-trade loan relationships, accounts must have been prepared in accordance with the appropriate accounting standards and methods. This approach means that all credits and debits (both capital and revenue) have been brought into account in the corporation tax computation under the accruals basis.

In essence, where a company either owes or is due monies for the purposes of its trade (other than those items mentioned above), then it is within the trading loan relationship rules. In this situation, any resultant credits and debits are included as trading receipts and expenses within the trading income computation and no adjustments are required. When the company is the lender, it is very difficult for it to fall within the "trading loan relationship" regime unless the loans were entered into in the course of activities forming an integral part of its trade. The latter situation is only likely to be the case for companies in the financial sector.

3.3.3 Treatment of Non-trading Loan Relationships

If a loan relationship does not have a trading purpose it will be a non-trading loan relationship. In such cases, any non-trade finance costs paid must first be added back in the adjustment of trading profits. Any non-trade finance income received must also be deducted in the adjustment of trading profits. This is followed by a separate 'pooling' exercise where non-trade credits and debits are grouped together, i.e. non-trading loan relationship debits and credits are combined to result in a net deficit or surplus. If a surplus results, the surplus is taxable as "surplus non-trade loan relationship credits". If a deficit results, relief may be available (see **Section 3.3.4**). For many companies, their only source of non-trading income will be bank interest receivable from investment of surplus funds.

Neither a UK nor an overseas property business of a company is deemed to be "trading" for loan relationship rules. This would mean, for example, that a property rental business that has interest payable does not get a deduction for the interest payable as a property rental expense or as a trading expense (because property rental does not constitute a trade), but may be able to obtain relief for the interest as a non-trading loan relationship debit. Such interest and related costs would therefore be added back, firstly in the adjustment of trading profits computation.

Some examples of non-trade loan relationships are:

- interest and other costs on monies borrowed for a property generating property income;
- interest and other costs on monies borrowed to lend to or invest in another company.

3.3.4 Relief for Non-trading Deficits

If the result of the pooling exercise (outlined above) is that a surplus credit arises on non-trading loan relationships, this income must be included in the calculation of total profits for corporation tax purposes.

If the result is that a surplus net deficit on non-trading loan relationships arise from the loan relationship pooling exercise, the company has a choice as to how it uses this. Relief can be given by:

1. offset in the current year against total profits of the company of the same accounting period, before QCDs and in preference to trading and property losses, but after management expenses (see **Chapter 2, Section 2.6.1**);
2. carry back against surplus non-trading loan relationship credits (if any) for the previous 12 months (an 'all or nothing' claim, and can be carried back even if a current-year claim has not been made);
3. surrendered as group relief (see **Chapter 9**); or
4. carry forward and offset against total profits in future accounting periods of the company or another group company. This is subject to the loss restriction rule that applies only to losses carried forward (see **Chapter 4, Section 4.1.1**).

The company must make a claim to utilise the surplus deficit. In the case of points 1, 2 and 4 above, the claim must be made within two years of the end of the accounting period; while for 3, the claim must be made at any time up to the first anniversary of the filing date for the corporation tax return.

Two important points to bear in mind are:

1. unlike the rules for normal trading losses (see **Chapter 4**), a company can make partial current year claims (e.g. to preserve foreign tax that may have been suffered), i.e. the in-year set-off does not have to be automatically and fully applied.
2. the carried forward deficit can be set against the company's (or another group company's) total profits in the following years. Again, the company can disclaim sufficient of the carried forward deficit to preserve income that may have suffered a foreign tax credit.

3.3.5 Costs of Finance

Many costs associated with obtaining loan finance are allowable debits (i.e. expenses) in the case of both trading and non-trading loan relationships. Examples of such costs include arrangement fees with banks, legal fees on the transfer of a security and pursuing bad debts, and brokers' fees related to transactions in existing securities.

It is also worthwhile noting that the cost of abortive expenditure incurred in trying to bring a loan relationship into existence is also potentially allowable, provided the expense would have been allowable if the loan had been raised.

As the accounting treatment for certain costs of finance may dictate that the interest is capitalised, perhaps incorporated within fixed assets, relief is obtained by adjusting the corporation tax computation for such items not charged through the statement of profit or loss. Care must be taken not to double-count such relief when the underlying asset is eventually sold and/or during its life written off (through amortisation). Note that this treatment does **not** apply to interest charged to work in progress, as it will have already been included within the movement in this asset, year on year.

Questions

Review Questions

(See Suggested Solutions to Review Questions at the end of this textbook.)

Question 3.1

Spider Ltd has the following income/payments during the year to 31 March 2020:

	£
Accounting profits (after charging depreciation of £5,000)	96,000
Property income	17,000
Payment to British Red Cross	8,000

Requirement

Calculate the company's taxable total profits for the year ended 31 March 2020.

Question 3.2

During the year ended 31 December 2019, Venus Ltd had the following loan relationship transactions:

- Interest received from a bank deposit account: £15,000.
- A bank loan of £75,000, which at the bank's instigation of an early repayment agreement, was fully settled for £55,000 by 31 December 2019.
- Legal fees of £1,500 were incurred in connection with the above bank loan settlement.

Requirement
Calculate Venus Ltd's net non-trading loan relationship credit/deficit for the year ended 31 December 2019.

Question 3.3

Special rules apply to a company's 'loan relationships' for corporation tax purposes.

(a) Explain the term "loan relationship".
(b) Give examples of loan relationships.
(c) Briefly explain how the amount to be included in the corporation tax computation is calculated.

Question 3.4

During the year ended 31 March 2020, a manufacturing company had the following transactions in interest receivable and payable:

	£
Interest receivable:	
Customers charged interest for paying late	724
Bank deposit interest	6,233
Bond held with local council	775
Interest payable:	
Bank overdraft	4,210
Mortgage on rental property	3,178
Bank loan for purchase of trading equipment	7,500
Bank loan to acquire shares in unconnected companies	555

Requirement
Calculate the amount of interest that should be included under non-trading loan relationships in the company's corporation tax computation for the 31 March 2020 accounting period end.

Question 3.5

Cleanoff Ltd is an office cleaning company. During the year ended 31 March 2020, the following transactions took place:

- The company paid interest of £475 to HMRC in respect of corporation tax paid late.
- The company took out a loan to finance the purchase of new equipment. Loan interest paid during the year totalled £2,000, with a further £200 owed at 31 March 2020.
- The company arranged a mortgage to purchase new office premises. The interest payable on this mortgage in the period to 31 March 2020 was £4,500, all of which was paid during the period.

Requirement
Explain how the above interest expenditure should be treated in the corporation tax computation of the company for the year ended 31 March 2020.

Question 3.6

Graham Ltd paid and received the following amounts during the year ended 31 March 2020.

- Interest on a loan to buy a property in which two of the four floors are used in the trade of the company, the remaining two floors are rented to an unconnected company – £12,000.
- Incidental costs of obtaining the loan finance to purchase the above property – £2,500.
- Bank overdraft interest payable – £4,300.
- Debenture interest receivable – £7,000.

Requirement
Calculate the amount assessable as a non-trading loan relationship credit/(debit) for the year ended 31 March 2020.

4

Corporation Tax Loss Relief

Learning Objectives

After studying this chapter you will understand:

- How relief is obtained for the different types of losses a company can incur.
- The special type of loss relief available when a company ceases to trade.
- How a company obtains relief for pre-trading expenditure.
- The anti-avoidance legislation that can apply when there is a change in the ownership of a company.
- The order of loss reliefs.
- The factors to consider when deciding upon the most tax-efficient form of loss relief for a company.

4.1 Relief for Trading Losses in a Single Company

Trading losses are computed in the same way as trading income, and the company must prepare its corporation tax computation in the normal way and forward its completed form CT600 (recording chargeable profits as "Nil"), statutory accounts and associated computations to HMRC, in iXBRL format, similar to that required if the company had made a trading profit. Trading losses can be relieved in a number of different ways. Trading losses may also be available for group relief, subject to the group relief rules (see **Chapter 9**).

There are a number of options available to relieve trading losses in a single company:

1. carry forward and offset against first available trading profits arising from the same trade (**only applies to trading losses incurred pre-1 April 2017**), subject to the carry-forward loss restriction rule (section 45 CTA 2010; see **Section 4.1.3**);
2. carry forward and offset against first available total profits, subject to the carry-forward loss restriction rule (section 45A CTA 2010; see **Section 4.1.3**);
3. offset against total profits in the current chargeable accounting period (section 37(3)(a) CTA 2010; see **Section 4.1.4**); and then
4. any excess may be carried back and offset against total profits in the preceding 12 months (section 37(3)(b) CTA 2010 – see **Section 4.1.5**).

In options 2–4, 'total profits' refers to income and gains before deducting qualifying charitable donations (QCDs). For options 2, 3 and 4, a formal claim is required within two years of the end of the accounting period in which the loss occurs.

CTA 2010 requires a formal claim to be made for items 2–4 above, and claims must be made within two years of the end of the accounting period in which the loss occurs.

4.1.1 Loss Restriction Rule – Losses Carried Forward

Companies with profits in excess of the relevant "deductions allowance" are not able to reduce profits wholly to nil by using relief for carried-forward losses. This rule applies to several different types of losses carried forward, including trading losses, surplus non-trading loan relationship deficits, non-trading losses on intangible fixed assets, excess management expenses and UK property business losses. Qualifying charitable donations cannot be carried forward.

In addition, because relief for certain types of carried-forward losses can only be set against particular types of profit (pre-1 April 2017 trading losses can only be set against future trading profits under section 45 CTA 2010), the relevant maximum must, in cases using such losses, be computed separately for trading profits and non-trading profits. The company may decide how its deductions allowance should be allocated between trading and non-trading profits.

A company that is not a member of a group has a deductions allowance for each accounting period of £5 million. If, however, the accounting period is less than 12 months, this amount is reduced proportionately. A company that is a member of a group may have a different deductions allowance, however it will never be more than £5 million (see **Chapter 9**).

Where a company's taxable profits exceed £5 million, only 50% of the profits above this threshold can be sheltered by carried-forward losses.

Example 4.1

Artic Limited is a stand-alone company. In its accounting period ending 31 March 2020 the company has £18 million of profits remaining after in-year reliefs. The company has trading losses carried forward from the accounting period ended 31 March 2019 of £20 million and wishes to claim relief for the maximum possible in 2020.

The company will pay corporation tax in 2020 as follows:

	£
Profit	18,000,000
Less: trading loss carried forward	(11,500,000)
(£5 million deductions allowance plus	
50% of the remaining £13,000,000)	
Taxable total profits	6,500,000
Corporation tax @ 19%	1,235,000

Loss Memo	£
Loss brought forward	20,000,000
Utilised via section 45A claim	(11,500,000)
Loss carried forward	8,500,000

A company that has carried-forward losses must specify the amount of the deductions allowance available in its corporation tax return for the period in which relief is claimed. This will normally be £5 million per 12-month accounting period. If the losses are to be set against different types of profit, the company will need to specify how it has divided its deductions allowance between its trading and non-trading profits.

4.1.2 Carry Forward of Trading Losses arising post-1 April 2017

Trading losses arising after 1 April 2017 can be carried forward, under section 45A CTA 2010, for set-off against **future total profits (of any type)**. As this is a carry-forward relief, the loss restriction rule may apply.

Any profits or losses of a company with an accounting period straddling 1 April 2017 may need to be allocated into notional periods falling before and after 1 April 2017 on a time-apportioned basis or, if this does not give a just and reasonable result, on a more just and reasonable basis.

Where a company has a trading loss carried forward under section 45A, it will only be relieved if the company makes a claim under section 45A(5). It is not necessary for the loss to be used to the full extent possible; the company can specify the amount of the loss it wants to relieve. Any remainder will be carried forward to the subsequent period.

4.1.3 Carry Forward of Trading Losses arising pre-1 April 2017

Trading losses arising before 1 April 2017 can only be carried forward, under section 45 CTA 2010, for set-off against **future trading profits of the same trade** only.

Again, the results of a company with an accounting period straddling 1 April 2017 may need to be allocated into notional periods falling before and after 1 April 2017, as previously outlined.

While no formal claim is required to carry forward pre-1 April 2017 trading losses (as this relief is given automatically), the company must state the amount of the loss to be carried forward in its corporation tax return. As this is also a carry-forward relief, the loss restriction rule may apply. However, a company can claim to prevent automatic relief in this manner where the losses carried forward would be offset against profits arising post-1 April 2017.

Pre-1 April 2017 carry-forward losses are set against the first available trading profits from the same trade. If there are not sufficient profits to use up the total losses, the excess is further carried forward to be offset against the next available trading profits.

In a scenario where a company has unused trading losses irrespective of the date they were incurred, this could create an issue if the company ceases to trade. This means there would be no future profits/trading profits against which to offset the carried-forward losses. Any balance of carried-forward trading losses would thus be wasted.

There is, however, a special type of relief for trading losses incurred in the last 12 months of trading. Losses in this period are known as 'terminal losses', and can potentially be relieved (see **Section 4.2**).

Example 4.2

ABC Ltd, a UK company with no subsidiaries, has the following results for the year ended 31 March 2020.

	£
Trading income (as adjusted for tax purposes)	55,000
Net credit from loan relationships	2,000
Property income	3,200
Chargeable gains	25,000
Qualifying charitable donations	(3,000)
Trading losses (of same trade) brought forward under section 45 CTA 2010	(70,000)

Solution

Corporation tax computation for ABC Ltd for the year ended 31 March 2020

	£	£
Trading income	55,000	
Less: trading losses c/fwd	(55,000)	

continued overleaf

	0
Net credit from loan relationships	2,000
Property Income	3,200
Chargeable gains	25,000
Total profits	30,200
Qualifying charitable donations	(3,000)
Taxable total profits (TTP)	27,200
Corporation tax payable:	
£27,200 @ 19%	5,168

As ABC Ltd does not have augmented profits in excess of £1.5 million, the corporation tax will be due on or before 1 January 2021.

Loss Memo

Trading losses brought forward	70,000
Utilised (y/e 31/03/2020)	(55,000)
Carried forward (to offset against future trading profits of the same trade)	15,000

If the trading profits of ABC Limited had been greater than £70,000 for the year ended 31 March 2020, all of the losses brought forward would have been utilised.

If ABC Ltd had made no trading profit (i.e. it either broke even or made a loss), then the brought forward trading losses would have been carried forward to the year ended 31 March 2021 to be set against any potential trading profits of that year, provided the same trade was being carried on. This process would be continued until either all of the losses had been utilised or the company ceased trading.

4.1.4 Relief by Set-off against Total Profits of the same Accounting Period

Before carrying forward the trading loss of an accounting period, a company with other sources of income can choose to set a current-period trading loss against the total profits of the same accounting period, under section 37(3)(a) CTA 2010. Offset of a trading loss in the current period against other income is **not** subject to the loss restriction rule. In addition, a current-year offset can result in qualifying charitable donations (QCDs) being wasted as these cannot be carried back or forward.

The claim must be for the lower of the available loss or the available profit. In other words, no partial claims are allowed – the claim must either use all of the loss or eliminate all of the available profits.

Example 4.3
Jones Ltd has the following results for the year ended 31 March 2020. Jones Ltd does not have any related 51% group companies.

	£
Trading loss	(17,500)
Net credit from loan relationships	5,000
Property income	4,300
Chargeable gains	7,200
Qualifying charitable donations	(2,500)

Solution

	£
Net credit from loan relationships	5,000
Property income	4,300
Chargeable gains	7,200

continued overleaf

Total profits	16,500
Less: trading loss of same accounting period (under section 37(3)(a))	(16,500)
Taxable total profits (TTP)	Nil
Corporation tax payable	Nil

As the company's trading loss of £17,500 is greater than its total profits, the QCDs of £2,500 cannot be offset and are wasted. The company's remaining loss in 2020 of £1,000 can either be carried forward under section 45A or carried back.

4.1.5 Relief by Set-off against Total Profits of the same Accounting Period followed by Carry-back against Total Profits of the previous 12 Months

Where a company has incurred a trading loss that exceeds the total profits of the same accounting period, and it has made a claim against these total profits under section 37(3)(a) CTA 2010, the company can then elect to carry the "excess" back to set against the total chargeable profits of the previous 12 months (under section 37(3)(b) CTA 2010). To obtain this relief the company must have carried on the same trade in the previous 12 months. The relief for the trading loss must be taken in this strict order (i.e. against total profits of the same accounting period first). Any excess losses after in-year offset can either be carried back or forward (as previously described). Offset of a trading loss in the previous 12 months is also **not** subject to the loss restriction rule.

Once again, there is no facility to make a partial claim of the trade losses incurred. If there are no profits in the current period, then it is not possible to make a current-year section 37(3)(a) claim. However, this does not prevent a carry back. Remember that the carry back of a loss is for a full 12-month period. If the previous accounting period is less than 12 months, you can carry back to the period before that one by applying time apportionment to the total profits of the previous period.

Example 4.4

Apple Ltd, a single company, has the following results for the accounting periods ended 31 March 2018 through to 31 March 2020. It has carried on the same trade throughout and there has been no change of ownership.

Year ended	31 March 2018	31 March 2019	31 March 2020
	£	£	£
Trading income	10,000	(16,500)	7,600
Property income	4,000	2,700	3,850
Chargeable gains	6,750	8,300	–

Outline the various options that are open to Apple Ltd to utilise its trading losses of £16,500 for the accounting period ended 31 March 2019.

Solution

(a) It can first utilise as much of the loss as possible (£11,000) against the company's total profits of the same period and then either carry the balance (£5,500) back to the previous 12-month period to set against the total profits of that period (namely the £20,750 in the year ended 31 March 2018);

or

(b) it could elect to carry forward the remaining £5,500 to set against the future total profits (i.e. the £7,600 in the year ended 31 March 2020) by not choosing to carry back. As the losses being carried forward arose post-1 April 2017, they can be relieved against total profits of any

continued overleaf

type, rather than future profits of the same trade. There is no restriction here as profits are well below the company's £5 million deductions allowance.

The company could also choose to carry forward the entire loss to the next accounting period. However, it is unlikely to do this as that would trigger a corporation tax liability in 2019. The company's method of choice will depend on the specifics of the original assessable profits. In commercial terms, the company may more than likely adopt the carry-back option – because the results of the future period may not be known for some considerable time and corporation tax rates may fall in the future. A carry-back would secure a refund of corporation tax with obvious cash flow benefits. It is important to be aware of all potential options available to the company.

A carry-back of trading losses to the previous 12-month period could, in some circumstances, substantially reduce the company's corporation tax liability for that period, and possibly even wipe it out completely. In this situation, a company may decide not to make any payment for that year. However, the company will still be charged **interest** on the unpaid liability from its normal due date until the due date of the loss period.

Example 4.5

Zanny Limited had an accounting year end of 30 September. Its taxable total profits for the year ended 30 September 2019 were £125,000, and it had a corporation tax liability of £23,750. In the first four months of 2019, the company suffered a major downturn in trading activity and it had projected trading losses for the following year to 30 September 2020 of £180,000. The company had no other income and decided that it would thus not need to make the payment of £23,750 on 1 July 2020.
In due course, the company carried back its 2020 trading losses and wiped out the 2019 profits of £125,000. However, HMRC will still charge interest on the corporation tax liability from 1 July 2020 to 1 July 2021 – the effective date of the loss carry-back.

4.2 Relief for Losses on Cessation (Terminal Losses)

4.2.1 Section 39 CTA 2010 – Relief for Trading Losses in the Final 12 Months

It is possible that a company may have to cease trading as a result of a downturn in its trading activities. Thus, a company may have unused trading losses, and it will obviously not have any future profits against which to set any such losses. It is also unlikely that a company will cease trading exactly on its former accounting year end.

The trading losses available for relief on cessation are known as 'terminal losses' and may qualify for terminal loss relief.

A terminal loss is the loss relevant to the last 12 months of trading. Where the date of cessation coincides with the company's year end, the terminal loss will be the whole of that period's loss. Where the cessation date is not coterminous with the company's accounting date, the 12-month period will be the last period (if less than 12 months) plus the relevant proportion of the preceding accounting period. Thus, if a company that has always had 30 September as its accounting year-end ceased on 31 March 2020, then the terminal loss would comprise the loss of the six months to 31 March 2020, plus 6/12ths of the loss (if any) of the accounting year ended 30 September 2019.

Instead of the normal carry-back period of 12 months, terminal losses can be carried back for 36 months, provided the same trade was being carried on during that time. The terminal loss can be carried back in full without tailoring against **total** profits arising in the previous 36 months, starting with the later periods first. For example, if a terminal loss arose in the year to 31 December 2019, it could be carried back against profits of the year to 31 December 2018, then to 31 December 2017 and finally to 31 December 2016.

4.2.2 Section 45F CTA 2010 – Relief for Trading Losses Carried Forward

When a trade ceases, the company may also be able to claim terminal loss relief under section 45F CTA 2010 for carried-forward losses of that trade which were not relieved in previous years due to the loss restriction rule. This only applies for trade losses carried forward to the period of cessation under section 45 or section 45A CTA 2010.

Where certain conditions are met, section 45F relief allows these losses to be set against profits of the three years **ending** with the end of the period of cessation without being subject to the loss restriction. For example, if a trade ceases in the period ending on 31 March 2020, relief will be available under section 45F against the profits of the three years from 1 April 2017 to 31 March 2020. Therefore the three-year period used for relief under section 45F is not the same as the three-year period for relief under section 39 CTA 2010.

The extent to which losses can be relieved depends on whether they were previously carried forward under section 45 or section 45A.

- Losses carried forward to the period of cessation under section 45A that can be set against total profits can be relieved against total profits in the previous 36 months.
- Losses carried forward to the period of cessation under section 45 can be relieved against profits of the same trade only in the previous 36 months.

Other non-trading losses carried forward cannot be relieved.

Relief is only available for periods beginning on or after 1 April 2017. In addition, relief under section 45F is not available against profits of:

- the period in which the loss to be used was originally sustained; or
- any preceding periods.

That is, relief is only available in periods subsequent to the original loss-making period. Losses relieved under section 45F should always be deducted from profits of a later period first, to the full extent possible, before they are deducted from profits of any earlier periods.

Profits of the period of cessation itself should therefore be given priority and relieved to the full amount possible before any profits of the preceding period are relieved. Terminal loss relief for losses pre-1 April 2017 is beyond the scope of this textbook.

4.3 Anti-avoidance – Trading Losses

The availability of unused trading losses is potentially valuable. If a company makes profits from its trade or has other sources of income against which the trading loss can be used under section 45A CTA 2010, it will not pay corporation tax until all the trading losses carried forward are utilised. Therefore a company with unused trading losses could be an attractive target for takeover by another company – the intention being to ensure that the loss-making company's trade is made profitable by the new shareholders (e.g. by transferring existing business to the loss-maker) and utilising the trading losses to offset against these newfound trading profits, thus reducing or eliminating its tax liability. This is called 'loss buying' or 'loss shopping'.

4.3.1 Anti-avoidance Test

Anti-avoidance rules are in place to limit the ability to do this type of planning. There are provisions to disallow the carry forward of trading losses incurred before **a change in ownership of a company's shares**. A change in ownership occurs when another company acquires more than half of a company's ordinary share capital. Only direct ownership changes are considered for this rule.

However, direct changes of ownership of more than 50% are ignored if the company concerned was a 75% subsidiary of the same parent company both before and after the change. The legislation is contained in sections 673–675 CTA 2010. The disallowance will apply if there is a change in the ownership of a company and either:

1. there is a "major change in the nature or conduct of a trade" carried on by the company within any period of five years (beginning no more than three years before the change in ownership) in which the change of ownership occurs (i.e. three years before or up to five years after the date of the change in ownership); or
2. at **any** time after the change in ownership, the scale of the activities in a trade carried on by the company has become small or negligible (and before any significant revival of the trade).

The provisions are designed to discourage the practice of purchasing shares in a company to obtain the benefit of accumulated trading losses carried forward.

In applying the provisions to the accounting period in which the change of ownership occurs, the part of the period occurring before the change of ownership and the part occurring after the change are treated as separate accounting periods. Apportionments are to be made on a time basis except where, to HMRC, it appears that that method would work unreasonably or unjustly.

A company that newly joins a corporation tax group for group relief purposes (see **Chapter 9**) is also treated as a change in ownership. However, for this rule to apply, neither 1. nor 2. above are required. Under this rule, any pre-acquisition trading losses cannot be surrendered as group relief for offset against group profits for a period of five years after the change in ownership.

4.3.2 Major Change in the Nature or Conduct of a Trade

A "major change in the nature or conduct of a trade" includes:

"(a) a major change in the type of property dealt in, or services or facilities provided in, the trade, or
(b) a major change in customers, outlets or markets of the trade."

Such a change will be regarded as occurring even if the change is the result of a gradual process that began outside the three-year period.

There have been a number of cases that have dealt with the meaning of a "major change in the nature or conduct of a trade" that provide some guidance on how these rules are to be interpreted and applied in practice.

Cases where it was held that there had been **no major change** in the nature or conduct of the trade, include:

1. A company that had sold its products directly to customers, mainly wholesalers, then commenced to do the same through distribution companies.
2. A company ceased to slaughter pigs and manufacture meat products and, for a temporary period of 16 months, distributed the same products manufactured by its parent company. After the 16-month period, it recommenced slaughtering and manufacturing meat products.
3. A company operating a dealership in one make of vehicle switched to operating a dealership in another make which served the same market.

Cases where it was held that there had been a **major change** in the nature or conduct of the trade, include:

1. A company that carried on a business of minting coins and medallions from precious metals purchased its principal supplier's entire stock of gold and then purchased gold directly from wholesalers. This resulted in substantial increases in stock levels.

2. A company that operated a retail chain of shops, changed its promotional policy by discontinuing the issue of trading stamps and reducing prices. The change resulted in a substantial increase in turnover.
3. A company that changed from providing a service to being instead a primary producer.

In addition, HMRC's Statement of Practice 10/91 also provides useful guidance.

4.4 Pre-trading Expenditure Resulting in a Loss

If allowable pre-trading expenditure expenses exceed the company's trading income, resulting in a loss, this loss can be used in the usual ways already covered in this chapter. See **Chapter 2, Section 2.2.1(h)** for more on pre-trading expenditure.

4.5 Relief for Qualifying Charitable Donations

As set out in **Chapter 3**, qualifying charitable donations (QCDs) are allowed as a deduction from a company's total profits and are deducted **after** any other relief from corporation tax, other than group relief. Any excess cannot be relieved by carry-back or carry-forward, unless the company is a company with investment business, in which case excess QCDs can be carried forward as management expenses (see **Chapter 2, Section 2.6**). QCDs may be available for group relief, subject to the group relief rules (which are dealt with in more detail in **Chapter 9**).

Reliefs, such as trading losses carried back, are given **prior** to any deduction of QCDs, which may result in the company's QCDs being wasted as it is not possible to choose how much of a loss is to be carried back and partial claims are not possible.

4.6 Property Losses

The income from the letting of UK land and property is taxed on companies as property income.

If the company has property losses, the utilisation of such losses is not ring-fenced. Property losses must first be set against the company's total profits for the same accounting period, before qualifying charitable donations and in preference to trading losses. Any excess is then carried forward and deemed to be a property loss of the next accounting period and is thus available for set-off against total profits. However, the property trade must still be carried on in the next accounting period. This process is continued until either:

- the property loss is used up; or
- the property business ceases.

Losses from a property business are very flexible. However, they **cannot** be carried back. Property losses may be available for group relief, subject to the group relief rules (see **Chapter 9**).

If a loss still remains after the cessation of the property business, the residue is deemed to be management expenses and carried forward for future relief as excess management expenses, but only if the investment business continues (see **Chapter 2, Section 2.6**).

Losses on furnished holiday lets can only be set-off against income from the same furnished holiday letting (FHL) business. UK losses can relieve UK FHL income only; likewise with EEA losses. Group relief of FHL losses is never available.

4.7 Non-trading Losses

A company can incur non-trading losses in any of the following situations.

4.7.1 Losses from Miscellaneous Income

Such losses are first relieved against other miscellaneous income of the same accounting period, and then against the miscellaneous income of future periods; hence, their use is quite restrictive.

4.7.2 Non-trading Losses on Intangible Fixed Assets

A company which incurs a non-trading loss on intangible fixed assets in an accounting period may claim all or part of the loss against the company's total profits for that period, or it might group-relieve the loss (see **Chapter 9**). It is only **excess** non-trading losses on IFAs that can be group-relieved. Any part that is not utilised is carried forward and treated as non-trading expenditure of the next accounting period, which can also be set against total profits.

4.7.3 Net Debits on Non-trading Loan Relationships

If a company incurs a deficit on its non-trading loan relationships, then it can be relieved by:

(a) set-off against the total profits of the company in the same accounting period, before QCDs and in preference to property and trading losses;
(b) carry back against surplus non-trading loan relationship credits (if any) for the previous 12 months (an 'all or nothing' claim, and can be carried back even if a current-year claim has not been made);
(c) carry forward and set against total profits in future accounting periods of the company or another group company.

Surplus non-trade loan relationship deficits may also be available for group relief, subject to the group relief rules (see **Chapter 9**).

4.7.4 Management Expenses

Companies with an investment business can deduct their management expenses from their total profits. The deduction must be made **before** any other deductions from total profits.

Excess management expenses can be carried forward to the next accounting period and deducted from total profits of that period. Companies with investment business that have excess qualifying charitable donations can carry those excess charitable donations forward as management expenses. Excess management expenses can also be group-relieved (see **Chapter 9**). See **Chapter 2, Section 2.6** for the taxation of investment companies.

4.8 Capital Losses

As noted in **Chapter 1**, a company is charged to corporation tax on its chargeable gains. The quantum of chargeable gains is reduced by any capital losses of the same period, as well as any unrelieved capital losses brought forward. Capital losses can only be set against chargeable gains of the current period or carried forward to set against future chargeable gains. It is not possible to carry back capital losses or to set such losses against other income, except in certain circumstances.

Capital losses **cannot** be group-relieved. However, a group can achieve a similar result by netting-off its gains and losses by utilising the election in section 171A TCGA 1992 (dealt with in **Chapter 10**).

Where a share disposal by an investing company meets the conditions for substantial shareholdings exemption (SSE), the disposal of such shares is deemed **not to be a chargeable gain**. Thus, in the circumstances where a capital loss would otherwise arise, no capital loss is created for the investing company because the entire transaction is exempt from corporation tax. In this scenario, a capital loss can be created by breaking one of the conditions for the exemption which applies automatically when its conditions are satisfied.

4.9 Choices regarding Loss Relief and Order of Loss Reliefs

4.9.1 Loss Relief – Considerations

If a company incurs a trading loss, it will have a variety of choices as to how best to relieve this loss. The choice of which loss relief to avail of will depend on a variety of factors including, *inter alia*:

1. the likelihood that the company will have future profits in the same trade and the quantum thereof;
2. for trading losses arising **before** 1 April 2017, the possibility that any offset against future trading profits will be subject to the restriction on the amount of profit that can be relieved by carried-forward losses;
3. for losses arising **after** 1 April 2017, the possibility that relief for these losses against future profits may be subject to the restriction on the amount of profit that can be relieved by carried-forward losses.
4. the rates of corporation tax of the different accounting periods involved;
5. the possibility that QCDs may be unrelieved;
6. the company's cash flow position;
7. the company's overriding desire to maximise the tax saved as a result of the loss claim;
8. the possibility of group-relieving losses to avoid a group company being unnecessarily exposed to corporation tax instalment payments (see **Chapter 9**); and
9. the level of future projected income of the company/group members.

Rates of corporation tax (both known and potential) should be factored into any decision in respect of how losses should be utilised.

4.9.2 Order of Loss Reliefs

Certain losses arising in the accounting period can be set-off against other profits of the company, either in the current period or in a future period; this is sometimes known as 'sideways relief'. However, there are specific rules as to the order in which these losses can be utilised. This applies to current-period trading losses and trading losses carried forward pre- and post-1 April 2017 (which may be restricted by the relevant deductions allowance outlined earlier).

Where a company makes a trading loss in the current accounting period, 'sideways relief' for that loss is given **after** relief for:

- management expenses (for companies with investment business – see **Section 2.6**);
- surplus non-trade debits brought forward (against total profits);
- losses from a UK property business; and
- surplus non-trade debits in the current year;

but **before**:

- relief for surplus non-trade debits carried back;
- relief for qualifying charitable donations; and
- losses claimed as group relief – both current-year and carried-forward losses (see **Chapter 9**).

4.10 Summary of Loss Reliefs

The table overleaf summarises the various loss reliefs discussed in this chapter.

SUMMARY OF LOSS RELIEFS

Type of Loss	Current Year	Carry Back	Carry Forward*	
			Pre-1 April 2017	Post-1 April 2017
Trading loss	• Set off against profits before QCDs. • 'All or nothing' claim – partial claims not permitted.	• Carried back against total profits of the previous 12 months before QCDs. • A current-year claim must be made before the excess trading loss is carried back. • 'All or nothing' claim.	Carried forward against future trading profits of the same trade in the same company.	Carried forward against total profits in the company/any group company.*
Non-trade loan relationship deficits	Set off against profits before QCDs in preference to trading and property losses – **can be tailored**, hence a partial claim is possible.	• Carried back against non-trade loan relationship surpluses of previous 12 months. • 'All or nothing' claim. • Losses can be carried back even if a current-year claim not made.	[Beyond scope of this textbook.]	Carried forward against total profits of the company/any group company.*
UK property losses	Mandatory set off against profits before QCDs in preference to trading losses – **cannot be tailored**, hence a partial claim is not possible.	Cannot be carried back.	[Beyond scope of this textbook.]	Carried forward against total profits of the company/any group company.*
Management expenses	Mandatory set off against profits before QCDs in preference to all other losses – **cannot be tailored**, hence a partial claim is not possible.	Cannot be carried back.	[Beyond scope of this textbook.]	Carried forward against total profits in the company/any group company.*

* The use of losses carried forward is subject to the relevant deductions allowance of £5 million (adjusted if necessary for periods of less than 12 months). Note that the deductions allowance that applies to the offset of carried-forward losses is a group-wide threshold (see **Chapter 9** for further detail on group relief).

Questions

Review Questions

(See Suggested Solutions to Review Questions at the end of this textbook.)

Question 4.1

Using the figures given below for Enya Ltd, show how the property income and trade losses may be used. Enya Ltd is not a member of a group.

		Property income	Trading profits/(losses)	Income from loan relationships
		£	£	£
y/e	31/03/2017	50,000	600,000	100,000
y/e	31/03/2018	(40,000)	700,000	50,000
y/e	31/03/2019	60,000	(1,300,000)	100,000
y/e	31/03/2020	80,000	100,000	35,000

Requirement
Calculate the taxable total profits for each year, showing the loss relief claimed and a loss memorandum showing the loss carried forward at 1 April 2020.

Question 4.2

Hells Bells Ltd shows the following results:

	Year ended 31 March 2020	Nine months ended 31 December 2020
	£	£
Trading profit/(loss)	167,000	(190,000)
Rents	4,000	(4,000)
Chargeable gains/(losses)	(19,000)	10,000
Net credit from loan relationships	10,000	20,000

Requirement
Calculate the corporation tax payable for each accounting period claiming the earliest possible relief for losses.

Question 4.3

Monk Ltd, a manufacturing company, prepares annual accounts to 31 March each year. Recent results were as follows:

	Year Ended 31 March	
	2020	2021
	£	£
Adjusted trading profit/(loss) (Note 1):		
(before capital allowances)	360,000	(310,000)
Capital allowances	20,000	90,000
Bank deposit interest	5,000	30,000
Property income	15,000	20,000
Chargeable gains	12,000	126,000

The following additional information is available:

1. Monk Ltd has an agreed unutilised trading loss forward from the year ended 31/03/2017 of £20,000.
2. The company wishes to claim the loss reliefs available so as to maximise the benefit of the losses.

Requirement

Compute the corporation tax payable for each of the above years and indicate the amount (if any) of unutilised losses available for carry forward to year ending 31 March 2022.

5

Distributions

Learning Objectives

After studying this chapter you will understand:

- The corporation tax treatment of dividends paid.
- The corporation tax treatment of dividends received from UK and non-UK companies.

5.1 Distributions

5.1.1 Distributions Paid by UK Companies

For corporation tax purposes, no deduction is allowed in computing income from any source for dividends or other distributions paid by a company. When doing a computation for a trading company, always start with 'profit (or loss) before taxation' so that there is no need to adjust for dividends as they will, generally, not have been deducted at that stage.

Other distributions may have been made by the company, such as certain interest and benefits paid to, or on behalf of, participators/associates of participators by close companies (see **Chapters 6** and **7**), will have been included in the statement of profit or loss and will therefore have to be added back.

In addition, dividends paid on preference shares are treated, for accounting purposes, as "share interest" and will already have been deducted from the profit or loss before tax, so must always be added back.

For corporation tax purposes, the distribution rules also apply whenever cash or assets are passed to the company's members. However, where the payment relates to a member who is an employee or director of a close company, the payment is taxed as employment income and is thus deductible for corporation tax.

Distributions can take a variety of forms and include:

1. Dividends paid by a company, including a capital dividend.
2. Redemption of bonus securities or redeemable shares.
3. Any distribution out of assets in respect of shares (except any part of which represents a repayment of capital).
4. Sale/transfer of assets by a close company at undervalue, or purchase of assets by a company at overvalue, from a shareholder. However, if the payee is a director or an employee, the transaction will be treated as employment income and assessed under those rules.

5. A bonus issue subsequent to a repayment of share capital (other than fully paid preference shares).
6. Interest payments in excess of a normal commercial rate of return, which may be treated as a dividend (see **Chapter 7**).
7. Certain expenses incurred by a close company in the provision of benefits for a non-working participator or a non-working associate of a participator will be treated as a distribution (see **Chapter 7**).

5.1.2 Distributions Received by UK Companies

The rules on the taxation of dividends and other distributions **received** by UK companies follow the **basic principle** that all dividends and other income distributions received by UK companies are **taxable**, regardless of the residence of the payer of the dividend.

However, due to a wide range of exemptions, **in practice** both UK and non-UK dividends received are **exempt** from corporation tax.

Note that this means dividends received from non-group companies (whether resident in the UK or not) are franked investment income (FII). The concept of FII is only relevant when calculating augmented profits for the purpose of the instalment payment rules for corporation tax (see **Chapter 1**).

The dividend exemption rules, and how they work, depend on whether the recipient company is a "small company" (section 931B CTA 2009) or a "large company", but companies can always elect for exempt dividends to be taxable on a receipt-by-receipt basis. This can sometimes reduce the rate of withholding tax under double taxation treaties, and may be beneficial if the recipient company has tax losses to set against the dividend such that no UK corporation tax liability arises.

Small Company

The definition of a "small company", for the purpose of the dividend exemption rules, is that the company receiving the dividend:

- has no more than 50 employees; and either
- has an annual turnover of less than €10 million; or
- gross assets of less than €10 million.

All companies that are not small companies are "large companies" for the purposes of the dividend exemption.

There are a number of other conditions for the small company exemption, but which are beyond the scope of this textbook.

Large Company

The large company exemption applies to dividends that fall into one of five classes, is not re-categorised interest and where no deduction is allowed outside the UK. The five classes of exempt dividend are:

1. Where the recipient controls the payer (subject to detailed rules) – section 931E CTA 2009.
2. Distributions in respect of non-redeemable ordinary shares – section 931F CTA 2009.
3. Distributions in respect of portfolio holdings (broadly, where the recipient controls less than 10% of the payer) – section 931G CTA 2009.
4. Distributions from transactions not designed to reduce tax – section 931H CTA 2009.
5. Dividends from shares accounted for as liabilities – section 931I CTA 2009.

5.2 Exempt Distributions

Some transactions, mainly dealing with situations where a company is being reorganised, have a different tax treatment from the overall distribution rules. These include:

1. Company purchase of its own shares – if the conditions for the capital treatment are not met, this will be treated as an income distribution (see **Chapter 20**).
2. Certain demergers.

Questions

Review Questions

(See Suggested Solutions to Review Questions at the end of this textbook.)

Question 5.1

Ice Sculptors Ltd received £475,000 of dividend income from Ice Sculptors Ireland Ltd, a non-UK tax resident company, net of overseas withholding tax of 10%. The dividend was received in September 2020, as part of its 31 December 2020 accounting period end. Ice Sculptors Ltd is not a small company for the purpose of the dividend exemption rules.

Ice Sculptors Ltd is a UK resident company and is able to secure control by virtue of powers conferred by the Articles of Association, so that the affairs of Ice Sculptors Ireland Ltd are conducted in accordance with its wishes.

Requirement
Advise your client whether the receipt of the above dividend is subject to UK corporation tax during the accounting period ended 31 December 2020.

Question 5.2

Outline in detail the UK dividend exemption rules.

Question 5.3

Distributions paid by a company can take many forms. Name the types of company transaction that are regarded as distributions.

Question 5.4

Dragger Ltd, a UK resident company, owns 30% of the ordinary share capital of Dragger GmbH, a company resident in Germany. During the year to 31 December 2020, Dragger Ltd received a dividend from Dragger GmbH of £48,000, after deduction of withholding tax at 20%. Dragger GmbH paid tax on the profits out of which the dividend was paid. Dragger GmbH has 20 employees and gross assets of €5 million.

Requirement
Explain the tax treatment of the dividend in Dragger Ltd. Ignore the effect of any double taxation treaty.

6

Close Companies

Learning Objectives

After studying this chapter you will understand:

- The definition of a close company.
- An overview of the tax rules that apply to close companies and their shareholders.

6.1 Meaning of Close Company

A close company is a UK resident company that is under the control of:

- five or fewer participators; or
- any number of participators who are also directors.

A company will not be a close company if it is non-UK resident. Control is the ability to exercise, or entitlement to acquire, direct or indirect control over the company's affairs, including the ownership of over 50% of the company's share capital, voting rights and distributable income or assets in the event of the winding up of the company.

Many UK private companies are close companies, whereas publicly quoted companies tend not to be close companies. As many private companies are close companies, the specific tax provisions that relate to close companies must be considered. Certain companies that under the above definitions would be regarded as close companies are not actually considered close companies (these are beyond the scope of this textbook).

6.2 Definitions

These definitions are based on those in Part 10 CTA 2010.

6.2.1 "Participator"

A "participator" is any person having a share or interest in the capital or income of the company and also includes:

1. a person who possesses, or who is entitled to acquire, share capital or voting rights in the company;
2. a "loan creditor" of the company (this is a creditor to the company because of money lent to the company or a capital asset sold to the company. A normal bank would not, however, be regarded as a loan creditor);

3. any person who has a right, or is entitled to acquire a right, to a share in the distributions of the company including any amounts payable to loan creditors by way of premium on redemption; and
4. any person who is entitled to secure that income or assets, either at present or in the future, will be applied directly or indirectly for his benefit.

Future entitlement includes anything which the person is entitled to do at a future date, or will at a future date be entitled to do.

6.2.2 "Control"

A person is regarded as having control of a company if he exercises, is able to exercise, or is entitled to acquire, direct or indirect control over the company's affairs and, in particular, if the person possesses or is entitled to acquire:

1. more than 50% of the company's issued share capital;
2. more than 50% of the company's voting share capital;
3. more than 50% of the company's income if it were distributed (excluding rights as a loan creditor); or
4. more than 50% of the company's assets in a winding up.

Importantly, if two or more persons together satisfy any of the conditions, they are deemed to have control. Therefore, in determining if an individual satisfies any of the above tests, the rights and powers of his associates and any company over which he, or he and his associates, have control, are attributed to him.

6.2.3 "Associate"

An "associate" of a participator means:

1. A relative of the participator (i.e. spouse or civil partner, parents or grandparents, child or grandchild, brother or sister).
2. A partner of the participator.
3. A trustee of a settlement established by the participator or a relative.
4. If the participator has an interest in any shares or obligations of a company which are subject to any trust, the trustees of any settlement concerned.

6.2.4 "Director"

In order to be regarded as a director, a person need not actually have the title director. A "director" includes a person:

1. occupying the position of director by whatever name called; or
2. in accordance with whose directions or instructions the directors are accustomed to act; or
3. who is a manager of the company or otherwise concerned in the management of the company's trade or business and who, as beneficial owner, is able to control at least 20% of the company's ordinary share capital (either directly or indirectly).

Example 6.1
Shares in Alphabet Ltd, a UK resident company, are held as follows:

	Status	Shareholding
Mr A	Director	10%
Mrs A		2%
Mrs C (Mr A's aunt)		2%
Mrs B		10%
B Ltd (Shares in B Ltd held 50% each by Mr and Mrs B)		5%
Mr J (Mrs B's cousin)		4%
Mr D	Director	10%
Mrs D		2%
Ms D (Mr and Mrs D's daughter)		2%
Mrs E (Mr D's sister)		2%
Mr F		6%
Mr G		5%
Other shareholdings (unrelated parties all holding < 5%)		40%
		100%

Is Alphabet Ltd under the control of five or fewer participators?

Shares held by Mr A:		
Mr A	10%	
Mrs A	2%	12%
Shares held by Mrs B:		
Mrs B	10%	
B Ltd	5%	15%
Shares held by Mr D:		
Mr D	10%	
Mrs D	2%	
Ms D	2%	
Mrs E	2%	16%
Mr F		6%
Mr G		5%
		54%

In determining the shares controlled by each participator, shares held by associates are included. While spouses, children, siblings and parents are included as associates, shares held by cousins or aunts are not included.

Alphabet Ltd is under the control of five or fewer participators and is, therefore, a close company.

6.3 Consequences of Close Company Status

A company controlled by a small group of persons can arrange its affairs to enable those persons to avoid income tax. The rationale for the special tax rules for close companies is to deal with the fact that closely held companies can, generally, take decisions in such a way as to minimise tax. These would not be feasible for a publicly quoted company.

Without the close company rules, it is likely that more individuals would incorporate, although incorporation has become more attractive given the recent reductions in the rate of corporation tax. The top income tax rate is currently 45% (plus either employee's NIC or self-employed Class 2 and Class 4 NIC), while the corporation tax rate for the financial year 2019 is 19%. Therefore, incorporation could possibly save money. However, the close company status provisions may make incorporation significantly less attractive, as they:

- extend the meaning of "distributions" to encompass certain benefits, excessive interest and transfers at undervalue that may be disguised distributions of profit to the shareholders or their families; and
- impose tax in respect of certain loans made to shareholders that would otherwise represent the extraction of profits without the payment of tax by the shareholders (section 455 being the legislative basis of the rule).

The detailed operation of these negative consequences is set out in **Chapter 7**.

Questions

Review Questions

(See Suggested Solutions to Review Questions at the end of this textbook.)

Question 6.1

X Ltd has 1,000 issued shares of £1, held as below:

Trustees of A's settlement	449
Mrs A (settlor)	60
Ten other shareholders	491
Total issued ordinary shares	1,000

The ten shareholders are not associated with each other or with A or Mrs A and none of them hold more than 50 shares.

Requirement
Determine if X Ltd is a close company.

Question 6.2

In a trading company, issued ordinary shares carry one vote each but 'A' ordinary shares do not confer any voting rights. The shareholders are as below:

	Ordinary shares	'A' ordinary shares
A	280	
Wife of A	100	
B (brother of A)	10	

Trustees of A's settlement	40	
Company X (controlled by A)	80	
	510	
Mrs C (daughter of B)	20	
10 other equal holdings	470	500
Total issued shares	1,000	500

The shares carry equal rights to dividend.

Requirement
Determine if the company is a close company.

Question 6.3

The authorised and issued share capital of Company Y is £1,000 in the form of 1,000 ordinary shares of £1 each, held as below.

A	200
B	100
C	50
D	50
E	40
Company Z	99
Other shareholders	461
Total issued ordinary shares	1,000

A, B and C are directors.

The issued capital of Company Z is £100 in the form of 100 ordinary shares of £1 each, held by:

F (son of E)	60
G	40
Total issued shares	100

The shareholders in Company Y, other than Company Z, are all individuals and none are related or otherwise associated. No 'other shareholder' holds more than 50 shares.

Requirement
Determine if the company is a close company.

7

Close Companies: Disadvantages

Learning Objectives

After studying this chapter you will understand the following:

- The holistic tax implications of expenses, excessive interest and loans made to participators (and their associates), by close companies.
- The holistic tax implications of transfers at undervalue made by a close company.

7.1 Disadvantages of Close Company Status

The disadvantages of close company status are as follows:

1. Certain **expenses** paid by a close company on behalf of participators/associates of participators are treated as distributions.
2. **Interest** payments made by the company to participators/associates of participators that are in excess of a normal commercial rate of return may be treated as a dividend.
3. There is a potential tax payable by close companies when making **loans** to participators or their associates.
4. Loans to participators or their associates that are subsequently **written off** will be assessable to income tax in the hands of the individuals.
5. Transfers at undervalue by close companies can result in the capital gains tax base cost of the share of shareholders in a close company being adjusted; or the undervalue charged as a distribution on participators or as employment income on employees.

There are also inheritance tax implications where a close company makes a transfer of value (see **Chapter 27**).

7.2 Certain Expenses for Participators and their Associates

Any expenses incurred by a close company in providing benefits or facilities of any kind for a non-working participator, or a non-working associate of the participator, are treated as a distribution. Where an item is treated as a distribution, the expense is disallowed in the company's corporation tax computation.

The following expense payments are not treated as distributions:

1. Any expense made good to the company by the participator/associate of a participator.
2. Any expense incurred in providing benefits or facilities to working directors or employees as such expenses are already assessable as benefits in kind.
3. Any expense incurred in connection with the provision for the spouse, children or dependants of any director or employee of any pension, annuity, lump sum or gratuity to be given on his death or retirement.

> ***Example 7.1***
> Mr A holds 2% of the ordinary share capital of X Ltd, a close company. Mr A is not an employee or director of X Ltd.
>
> X Ltd pays the rent on Mr A's house of £3,000 per annum. The amount is charged each year in X Ltd's accounts under rental expenses.
>
> As X Ltd is a close company and Mr A is a participator, the expense will be treated as a distribution. Accordingly, the £3,000 will be disallowed to X Ltd in arriving at its taxable total profits and will also be treated as a distribution in the hands of Mr A (i.e. Mr A will be treated as receiving a dividend of £3,000. This will be taxed accordingly).

7.3 Excessive Interest

A participator, or an associate of a participator, may lend money to the close company and charge interest on that loan. Interest payments made by a close company to non-working participators/associates that are in excess of a normal commercial rate of return may be treated as a dividend. Any excess is thus not deductible for corporation tax. If the payment is to an employee or director of the company, the interest is deductible for corporation tax purposes and is instead taxed on the employee's/director's employment income as a benefit in kind.

The allowable element of the interest paid by the company is subject to a late payment rule that prevents a corporation deduction being obtained where the interest is accrued and paid more than 12 months from the end of the relevant accounting period.

Any allowable element of the interest paid to the participator/associate (who is not an employee or director) is taxable on them under the income tax rules for savings income.

Interest payments by participators/associates to companies on overdrawn loan accounts that are below the normal commercial rate may be classed as a distribution or as a benefit in kind and taxable as employment income, depending on the status of the recipient. However, at all times the employment income treatment takes precedence over the distribution treatment.

> ***Example 7.2***
> Mr X owns 100% of X Ltd and has lent the company £100,000. He charges the company 10% interest annually. The amount is charged each year in X Ltd's accounts under 'Interest paid'. The commercial rate of interest on such a loan would be 5%.
>
> As X Ltd is a close company and Mr X is a participator, the excess interest of £5,000 will be treated as a distribution. Accordingly, the £5,000 will be disallowed to X Ltd in arriving at its taxable total profits. It will also be treated as a distribution in the hands of Mr X (i.e. Mr X will be treated as receiving a dividend of £5,000 for income tax purposes). When paying the interest to Mr X, X Ltd will be required to deduct 20% basic rate income tax and follow the CT61 procedure (see **Chapter 3**).

7.4 Loans to Participators and their Associates

Where a close company makes a loan to an **individual** who is a participator or an associate of a participator, the company will be required to pay tax in respect of the amount of the loan at the rate of 32.5% (section 455 CTA 2010). The section 455 tax is due for payment on the lower of:

- the loan balance outstanding at the end of the accounting period; or
- the loan balance outstanding nine months and one day from the end of the accounting period.

Any section 455 tax forms part of the company's corporation tax liability for the period and is due on the relevant date.

There are **three exceptions** to the above, that are **not** treated as loans to participators:

1. Where the business of the company is or includes the lending of money and the loan is made in the ordinary course of that business.
2. Where a debt is incurred for the supply of goods or services in the ordinary course of the business of the close company, unless the credit given exceeds six months or is longer than the period normally given to the company's customers.
3. Loans made to directors or employees of the company if:
   (a) the amount of the loan, together with all other loans outstanding made by the company to the borrower (or his spouse), does not exceed £15,000; **and**
   (b) the borrower works full time for the company; **and**
   (c) the borrower does not have a "material interest" in the company (broadly defined as more than 5% of ordinary share capital). If the borrower subsequently acquires a material interest, the company is required to pay corporation tax in respect of all the loans outstanding from the borrower at that time.

When the loan, or part of the loan, is repaid by the participator /associate or if it is released or written off, the section 455 tax, or a proportionate part of it, is refunded to the company provided a claim is made within four years of the end of the accounting period in which the repayment is made or the release or writing-off occurs. However, the tax is not refunded with interest. A refund of section 455 tax cannot be reclaimed until nine months and one day after the end of the accounting period in which the loan is repaid (or partially repaid), released or written off.

Depending on the timing of the repayment, the company can either:

- complete an amended return for the accounting period in which the loan was made (provided the amended return is submitted within the 12-month period); or
- write to HMRC with the appropriate details, or complete HMRC's iForm for claiming the repayment.

Example 7.3

ABC Ltd, a close company, made interest-free loans to the following shareholders in the accounting period to 31 March 2020. The company does not pay corporation tax in instalments. Assume the loans are still outstanding on 1 January 2021.

	£
Mr A (director owning 10% of the share capital)	
Loan made 29 June 2019	16,000
Mr B (director owning 4% of the share capital)	
Loan made 31 October 2019	10,000
Mr C (director owning 20% of the share capital)	
Loan made 31 December 2019	8,000

continued overleaf

What are the tax consequences for the company, assuming that no other loans had been made to the three individuals in the past? You may also assume that Mr A and Mr B work full time for the company.

Solution

The company will be required to pay corporation tax in respect of the loans to Mr A and Mr C at 32.5% of the outstanding amount, calculated as follows:

	£
Mr A	16,000
Mr C	8,000
	24,000 × 32.5% = £7,800

The loan to Mr B is not subject to this provision as Mr B:

1. is a director who works full time, and
2. does not have a "material interest" in the company, and
3. the loan is less than £15,000.

This tax of £7,800 must be paid over to HMRC on or before 1 January 2021 (nine months and one day after the accounting period end). The tax will be repaid (or partially repaid) by HMRC nine months and one day after the end of the accounting period in which the loans have been repaid (or partially repaid) by the shareholders.

7.4.1 "Bed and Breakfast" Rule

In the past, HMRC perceived avoidance behaviour to be taking place by participators and close companies seeking to exploit the legislation by what was known colloquially as the "bed and breakfasting" of loans to participators. Loans would be repaid by the accounting period end date, or in the nine months between the end of the accounting period, to prevent the section 455 charge becoming due and payable. The participator would then, very shortly after the repayment, redraw the money (or a greater amount). The participator had therefore only lost the use of the money for a very short period – and in many cases never intended the repayment to be lasting. In addition, other loans may be repaid after the section 455 tax has been paid on them, so that a section 455 repayment relief claim can be made. Again, the participator very shortly afterwards would have redrawn the money with the same result, i.e. the participator still had the funds but had also reclaimed the tax.

To tackle such behaviour, the '30-day rule' was introduced. This provision is a mechanical rule that applies where, within any 30-day period:

- repayments totalling £5,000 or more are made (before or after the end of the accounting period); and
- new loans totalling £5,000 or more are made (after the end of the first accounting period).

In this situation, the repayments are matched to repaying the new loans (rather than any earlier loans) to the extent that the repayment does not exceed the new loan.

Example 7.4

Mr Alf Bett owns 100% of the shares in ABC Limited. The company's accounting period ends on 31 March and it does not pay corporation tax in instalments.

On 25 May 2019 the company lends Mr Bett £6,000; on 29 March 2020 he repays the loan. On 3 April 2020, during the new accounting period, the company makes a new loan to him of £6,000. This is still outstanding at 1 January 2021.

continued overleaf

Solution
The legislation matches the repayment of £6,000 in March 2020 against the new loan. Therefore the loan made on 25 May 2019 is still treated as outstanding and section 455 tax of £1,950 (£6,000 × 32.5%) will therefore be due on 1 January 2021.

7.5 Write-off of Loans to Participators

Where a company makes a loan to a participator and subsequently releases or writes it off, the shareholder is deemed to receive a distribution, i.e. a dividend, at the time of writing off the loan as a debt is released. The participator will be treated as though their total income for the year in which the release, or writing off, occurs is increased by the amount released or written off. In other words, it is treated as a dividend in his or her hands. If the individual is an employee, this is instead taxed as employment income. The company is never entitled to a corporation tax deduction for the loan balance released or written off to its statement of profit or loss, irrespective of its treatment in the hands of the individual.

In addition, the section 455 tax already paid by the company is not available for offset against any additional tax arising in the hands of the individual. The company can, however, reclaim the section 455 tax paid, subject to the procedure, conditions and time limits for same already outlined.

Example 7.5
Assume that in Example 7.3 Mr A repays his loan of £16,000 on 1 February 2021 and at the same time the company writes off the loan to Mr C.

What are the tax consequences for the company and the shareholders?

Company

The company will be repaid the tax on Mr A's loan, i.e. £5,200 (32.5% × £16,000) but only after 1 January 2022, i.e. nine months and one day after the end of the accounting period in which repayment occurred (being 31 March 2021).

Shareholders:

There are no tax consequences for Mr A.

Mr C, however, will be assessed as receiving gross distribution income of £8,000. This amount will be subject to income tax at the dividend rate, and this charge will take precedence over any employment income tax charge. Tax will also be repaid on Mr C's loan. The company will also not be entitled to a corporation tax deduction for the £8,000 written off to the statement of profit or loss.

7.6 Transfers at Undervalue by Close Companies

7.6.1 Corporation Tax Implications for the Company

Where a company transfers an asset to any person other than by way of a bargain made at arm's length, section 17 TCGA 1992 treats them as having sold the asset at market value and, therefore, corporation tax will arise on any chargeable gain on the basis of deemed market value being substituted for the undervalue proceeds. A capital loss can arise on the basis of market value, which can be used in the usual way (see **Chapter 10**). HMRC are likely to very carefully scrutinise the market value utilised in such transactions.

The transferee of the asset is treated as having acquired the asset at market value. If the transfer took place at undervalue, the transferee will have a capital gains tax base cost that is higher than the amount they paid for the asset. However, generally speaking, such transfers are only likely to occur between persons connected to the company as the company is unlikely to be willing to suffer a chargeable gain or to forego a capital loss to give a third party a tax benefit.

7.6.2 CGT Implications for the Participator

A transfer at undervalue by a company to another company or individual, be they connected to the company or not, will also reduce the value of the company's shares. Put simply: if a company with assets worth £100,000 sells them for £20,000, the value of a 100% shareholding will be reduced by £80,000; the value of a 75% shareholding would be reduced by £60,000.

Section 125(1) TCGA 1992 restricts the advantage a shareholder may have gained if a close company transfers assets at undervalue in a bargain made other than at arm's length. The acquisition cost of the shares is reduced by an appropriate proportion of the difference between the market value of the asset and any consideration paid for it. The appropriate proportion is calculated by allocating the difference between the shareholders in proportion to their shareholding in the company. If the apportioned undervalue is greater than the shareholder's acquisition cost, the acquisition cost is reduced to nil. In situations where the transferee is a company and the transfer of the asset is covered by section 171 TCGA 1992 (see **Section 10.5**) then section 125 does not apply. In addition, a transfer at undervalue is also likely to be a transfer of value for inheritance tax purposes if the company is a close company (see **Section 27.1**).

7.6.3 Exceptions for Transfers at Undervalue by Participators

There are exceptions built into the legislation to ensure a taxpayer is not taxed twice on transfers of an asset at undervalue where the transferee is a participator/associate of a participator in the company, or where they are an employee (including a director).

Distribution Exception

Under section 125(4) TCGA 1992 Case 2, if the transferee is a participator or an associate of a participator in the company and the transfer is treated as a distribution under the close company rules, then section 125(1) does not apply and the base cost of the shares is not adjusted.

Employment Income Exception

Under section 125(4) Case 3, if the transferee is an employee of the company and the undervalue is treated as their employment income, then section 125(1) does not apply and the base cost of the shares is not adjusted. The undervalue is thus taxed under income tax as employment income, resulting in both income tax and NIC liabilities. Note that this treatment takes precedence where the transfer at undervalue is made to a participator who is also an employee or director.

Example 7.6

In March 2005, Mrs Donnelly buys 5,000 out of the 50,000 shares issued in Happy Holidays Ltd, a close company, for £50,000. In September 2012, Happy Holidays Ltd sells a caravan site with a market value of £800,000 to an unconnected person at a price of £500,000. In December 2019, Mrs Holland sells her 5,000 shares for £300,000. She is not an employee of the company. What are the consequences of these transactions?

The acquisition cost of Mrs Holland's shares is reduced by a proportionate part of the transfer at undervalue. Mrs Holland owns 5,000 out of the 50,000 issued shares. The undervalue is £300,000 (market value of £800,000 less the consideration paid of £500,000), thus the proportion by which the base cost of her shares is reduced is 10% of the undervalue, being £30,000. The revised base cost of her shares is therefore £20,000 (£50,000 less £30,000, the proportion of the undervalue), meaning she will have a chargeable gain on the disposal of her shares in December 2019 of £280,000 (£300,000 less the revised base cost of £20,000) and not £250,000.

continued overleaf

> If the company had sold the caravan to Mrs Donnelly for the above amount, as she is a participator in the company the base cost of her shares would not have been adjusted (in accordance with section 125(4) Case 2). Instead, she would have been taxed on her £30,000 share as a distribution, paying income tax at a maximum rate of 38.1%.
>
> If Mrs Donnelly had been a participator and an employee/director of the company, again the base cost of her shares would not have been adjusted, this time under section 125(4) Case 3. Instead, as an employee of the company, the employment income rules would take precedence and the £30,000 would be taxed on her as employment income instead of as a distribution at a maximum rate of 47%.

Questions

Review Questions

(See Suggested Solutions to Review Questions at the end of this textbook.)

Question 7.1

(a) State the tax effect on a close company arising out of a loan made to a participator in that company. Indicate the circumstances in which the loan would have no tax consequences for the company.

(b) Size Ltd is a close company and has the following adjusted profits for the year ended 31 March 2020:

	£
Property income	30,000
Trading income	100,000
Deposit interest	3,000
	133,000

Calculate Size Ltd's corporation tax liability for the year ended 31 March 2020.

Question 7.2

Close Ltd is a family-owned distribution company. Results to 31 March 2020 are as follows:

	£	£
Gross profit	50,000	
Other income (Note 1)	10,000	
		60,000
Depreciation	15,000	
Salaries	10,000	
Rent and rates	1,000	
Sundry (Note 2)	1,100	(27,100)
Net profit		32,900

Notes

1. Other income:

	£
Bank interest	8,500
Capital grants	1,500
	10,000

2. Sundry:

	£
Miscellaneous office expenses	300
Expenses of majority shareholder's brother Y who does not work for Close Ltd paid to him on 01/07/2019	800
	1,100

Capital allowances due are £4,000.

Requirement

(a) Compute the corporation tax payable.

(b) Explain the tax treatment of the expenses paid for Y.

Question 7.3

Maxi Ltd, a family-owned company, deals in farm machinery. The results for the year ended 31 March 2020 were as follows:

		£	£
Sales			6,300,000
Opening stock		1,100,000	
Purchases		5,650,000	
		6,750,000	
Closing stock		1,450,000	
			(5,300,000)
			1,000,000
Less:	Expenses		
	Administration	220,000	
	Financial	200,000	
	Distribution and sales (Note 1)	270,000	
	Depreciation	100,000	(790,000)
Trading profit			210,000
Loss on sale of plant (Note 4)		(20,000)	
Profit on sale of building (Note 2)		1,480,000	
Rents (Note 3)		200,000	
			1,660,000
Net profit			1,870,000

The directors have a policy of not paying dividends.

Notes

1. The following items were included in distribution and sales:

Entertainment	£
Entertaining customers	6,000
Entertaining suppliers	5,000

Staff Christmas party	10,000
Christmas gifts for suppliers	900
Cost of MD attending trade fair in London	850
	22,750

2. The building, which was sold in October 2019, had been acquired in 1970 for £2,000. It was valued at £50,000 on 31 March 1982. The building was located on a site on which planning permission had been granted for the construction of a shopping centre. Proceeds received for the building were £1.5 million. Legal fees of £18,000 were incurred in connection with the disposal. Indexation allowance from March 1982 to 31 December 2017 was 110%.
3. On 1 June 2019, the company re-let its investment property under a 20-year lease. A premium of £50,000 was received on the sub letting. This premium is included in property income in the statement of profit or loss.
4. Total capital allowances for the year were agreed at £50,000.

Additional information

In June 2019 the managing director (and principal shareholder) borrowed £550,000 from the proceeds from the sale of the building to purchase a new residence for himself in his own name.

Maxi Ltd has £210,000 of trading losses forward at 31 March 2017.

Requirement

Calculate the corporation tax payable by Maxi Ltd. The CGT consequences arising from the granting of the lease may be ignored.

Question 7.4

Servisco Ltd, a closely held firm of management consultants, had the following income for the year ended 31 March 2020:

	£
Professional income	430,000
Property income	100,000
Bank deposit interest	50,000
Chargeable gains before adjustment	86,400

The company had a loss forward of £9,000 on its professional activities from the year ended 31 March 2017.

The company received dividends of £17,500. £10,000 of these dividends were from another UK company in which Servisco has a minor shareholding. The remaining £7,500 gross dividend was from a company resident in the Republic of Ireland, in which Servisco Ltd holds 7.5% of the shares, and was received on 1 April 2019.

Requirement

Compute the company's corporation tax liability for the year ended 31 March 2020.

Question 7.5

Machinery Ltd was incorporated in the UK on 1 June 1970 and since that date has been engaged in providing machinery to companies.

The founder members of the company were Mr Vincent Duffy and his wife Julie and the company was formed to take over their existing business which they previously conducted in partnership. Mr and Mrs Duffy have actively encouraged members of their immediate family and other relatives to take up employment within the company and have endeavoured to ensure that the control of the company remains, as far as possible, within the family.

The company's statement of profit or loss for the year ended 31 March 2020 showed the following results:

		£	£
Sales			1,660,000
Stocks at 31/03/2020		450,000	
Stocks at 01/04/2019		(360,000)	(90,000)
			1,750,000
Purchases			(805,000)
Gross profit			945,000
Less:	Depreciation	59,790	
	Rent	79,710	
	Light and heat	17,500	
	Distribution costs	39,000	
	Bank and loan interest	65,000	
	Motor expenses (all vans)	44,300	
	Sundry expenses	13,000	(318,000)
	Net profit from trading		626,700
Add:	Bank deposit interest	10,000	
	Rents from let property (after allowable deductions)	50,000	60,000
	Profit for year		686,700

The shareholdings and loans made to the company as at 31 March 2020 were:

	Ordinary £1 shares	**Loans made (@ interest rate)**	**Interest paid £**
V. Duffy (director)	3,000	£4,000 @ 15%	600
Mrs J. Duffy (director)	1,250	£5,000 @ 12%	600
Trustees of settlement made by V. Duffy	2,900	£5,000 @ 15%	750
Executors of the will of J. Duffy deceased (father of V. Duffy)	2,000	£5,000 @ 15%	750
D. O'Connell (director)	2,750	£5,000 @ 15%	750
Mrs K. Moran (aunt of V. Duffy)	500	–	–
L. T. Smith (director)	2,100	£10,000 @ 13.21%	1,321
Louise Hare (company secretary)	3,000	£3,000 @ 5.5%	165
Paul Hare (husband of V. Duffy's sister)	2,500	£3,000 @ 6%	180
	20,000		5,410

Notes

1. V. Duffy is an executor of his father's will.
2. The loan interest was paid in addition to bank interest of £59,590, thus reconciling with the amount shown in the statement of profit or loss.
3. For the accounting period ended 31 March 2020, capital allowances were £10,700.
4. None of the shareholders are related except as shown above.
5. The share capital at 1 April 2019 was the same as at 31 March 2020.
6. The commercial rate of return is deemed to be 6%.

Requirement

Compute the corporation tax liability of the company for the accounting year ended 31 March 2020.

Question 7.6

Tax Advisors Ltd, a professional services company, had the following sources of income and charges for the year ended 31 March 2020:

	£
Trading income	100,000
Interest income	100,000
Qualifying charitable donations paid	(60,000)

Requirement

Calculate the corporation tax payable by Tax Advisors Ltd in respect of the above figures.

8

Non-resident Companies

Learning Objectives

After studying this chapter you will understand:

- The residence rules for companies resident in the UK.
- The tax treatment of a non-resident company.
- The principles of double tax relief.
- The UK's controlled foreign company (CFC) rules.

8.1 Introduction

You will recall from **Chapter 1** that a company incorporated in the UK is automatically UK tax resident. In addition, a company centrally managed and controlled in the UK is also regarded as resident in the UK. Most companies in the UK are UK resident and are therefore liable to UK corporation tax on all their profits, irrespective of where the income arises or wherever the assets (classed as chargeable gains) are situated. This is known as the worldwide basis of taxation. The remittance basis of taxation is not available to companies or branches of companies and is only available to individuals (see **Chapter 14**).

If a non-UK resident company were to move its central management and control to the UK, it would thus become UK resident. However, the jurisdiction of its incorporation may determine that it also remains resident in that other country. In this situation, the company becomes a dual-resident company, and the relevant double taxation treaty and any specific tiebreaker clause needs to be examined in such situations.

A company that is regarded as resident in another country under the terms of a double taxation treaty may, therefore, have its income exempt from UK corporation tax. See **Section 8.2** for the UK tax position of non-resident companies

8.1.1 UK Companies Trading Overseas

A UK company may trade overseas through a variety of different structures, each with differing tax implications.

Overseas Subsidiaries

Where a UK company expands into international markets, it may establish a separate subsidiary company in the foreign country. Often the foreign subsidiary is managed and controlled in that foreign country and is, therefore, not UK resident. Such foreign subsidiaries of UK companies are non-resident in the UK and are only liable to UK corporation tax as a non-resident company, as detailed later. Foreign subsidiaries typically do not generate UK profits (as they are established to generate foreign profits) and, therefore, in most cases no UK tax is payable by the foreign subsidiary. Foreign tax is likely to arise in the overseas jurisdiction. However, the UK parent may be subject to UK corporation tax on the income profits of the foreign subsidiary under the controlled foreign companies legislation (see **Section 8.6**).

Overseas Branches

Alternatively, the UK company may establish a branch in the foreign country. The profits of the foreign branch will be included with the year end results for the UK company and are chargeable to UK corporation tax as a UK resident company is subject to corporation tax on the worldwide basis as set out earlier. The foreign branch profits may or may not be assessed to tax in the foreign country, depending on the taxation rules in the foreign country. Where foreign tax is payable, this will normally be available for deduction by credit relief against the element of the UK corporation tax assessed on the branch profits, thereby providing double taxation relief.

UK corporation tax legislation allows companies with overseas branches to exempt the results (both profits and losses) of all of its overseas branches from UK corporation tax. This would mean that no double tax relief would be available as branch profits would not be subject to UK corporation tax. Companies are able to opt into this exemption regime, and any such election is irrevocable. This election amendment has effect from the start of the next accounting period after the election is submitted.

This election should be considered if additional UK corporation tax arises when branch profits are subject to additional UK corporation tax. The most relevant scenario for Northern Ireland companies is those who have a branch presence in the Republic of Ireland. Such branch companies pay only 12.5% Irish corporation tax on their Irish branch trading profits. However, an additional 6.5% (19% UK rate –12.5% Irish rate) corporation tax arises in the UK because those branch profits are also taxable in the UK despite full double taxation relief being available.

In this scenario, the additional UK corporation would be saved by entering into the foreign branch exemption election.

In a scenario where the Irish branch is loss-making, an additional saving of 6.5% arises on branch losses relievable in the UK. In loss-making scenarios where additional relief is available in the UK, the foreign branch exemption would be resisted.

8.1.2 Foreign Investment into the UK

Where a foreign company establishes an operation (e.g. factory in the UK), the operation may be run by a company in the group. This company may be a UK-resident company established specifically to run the UK operation. Sometimes, for international tax planning reasons, a non-resident company is used (see **Section 8.2**). Alternatively, a UK branch operation may instead be set up as part of the non-resident company structure.

8.2 Non-resident Companies Charge to Tax

A non-resident company is chargeable to UK corporation tax if it carries on a trade in the UK through a permanent establishment (PE). A PE is a fixed place of business through which the business of the company is wholly or partly carried on; **or** it can be where an agent has, and exercises, authority to do business on behalf of the company. Examples of a fixed place of business include a branch, workshop, factory or office.

If the non-resident company does carry on a trade in the UK through a PE, corporation tax will be charged on:

1. any trading income arising directly or indirectly through or from that PE;
2. any income, wherever arising, from property or rights used by, or held by or for that PE, e.g. income from patent rights held by the branch;
3. chargeable gains accruing on assets situated in the UK used for the purpose of the trade of the PE; and
4. from 6 April 2020, profits of UK property businesses, other UK property income and profits of loan relationships that the non-resident company is a party to for the purpose of the property business or generating the income.

Income from sources *within* the UK that are not subject to corporation tax (as set out above) are instead subject to **income tax** at the basic rate (currently 20%) on any UK income. If tax has been deducted at source from such income, the tax payable is limited to that amount.

Therefore the difference between a non-resident and a resident company is that any profits not attributable to the UK branch, e.g. foreign interest and foreign trading income, are not liable to UK tax. In addition, a non-resident company is not generally entitled to double tax relief in the UK for any foreign tax paid, as it is not UK resident.

Non-UK resident companies that have a permanent establishment in the UK can, however, claim credit relief for foreign taxes paid on income that is taxable on the permanent establishment. The non-UK resident company must show that all steps have been taken to minimise foreign tax suffered.
Note: profits are either liable or not liable.

8.3 Double Taxation Relief

As we have seen, UK resident companies are liable to UK corporation tax on worldwide income. Due to domestic tax laws, the company may, on occasion, be taxed in two countries on the same income:

- in the country where the income arises; and, also,
- in the country where the company is resident.

To eliminate this double tax charge, double taxation relief may be given in the country of residence. Relief can be obtained in one of three ways:

1. under the provisions of a double taxation treaty;
2. as credit relief (also known as 'unilateral relief') under a double taxation treaty or in its own right (i.e. via UK domestic legislation); or
3. as deduction relief.

8.3.1 Double Taxation Treaties

Relief can be provided under a double taxation treaty (DTT) in two main ways:

1. **Exemption relief** – where income is only taxable in the country of residence.
2. **Credit relief** – which reduces the UK corporation tax by the amount of overseas tax paid.

The maximum relief obtained cannot exceed the UK corporation tax on the same income.

8.3.2 Unilateral Relief

Where there is no DTT in place, relief for double taxation may be given as unilateral relief. This relief is the lower of:

- the overseas tax paid; or
- the UK corporation tax on that source of income.

The relief available is calculated on a source-by-source basis. The basic rule is that the relief available is the lower of the UK corporation tax due on that source of income and the foreign tax suffered. Note that overseas taxable income is always included gross in a corporation tax computation, i.e. inclusive of any foreign tax paid.

Double taxation relief will not be a consideration where a foreign dividend is received that meets one of the dividend exemption tests (see **Chapter 5**), or where the profits of a foreign branch are not subject to UK corporation tax due to the foreign branch exemption.

If an overseas dividend is not exempt (see **Chapter 5**), relief for foreign tax paid can be claimed. Overseas dividends received by a UK resident company may have suffered withholding tax. Withholding tax is generally recoverable (subject to the limit for unilateral relief) but not in cases where the dividend is exempt from UK corporation tax.

In addition, as dividends are paid out of post-tax profits, the dividend will also have suffered what is called 'underlying tax'. A credit for underlying tax can only be claimed when a company holds directly, or indirectly, at least 10% of the voting power of the company paying the dividend, or is a subsidiary of such a company. Where a dividend is paid by a non-resident company to a UK resident company, there is a cap for the underlying tax. The calculations of this cap and relief for underlying tax are beyond the scope of this textbook.

8.3.3 Surplus Foreign Tax

Generally there is no relief in a scenario where the foreign tax paid is greater than the UK corporation tax liability on that income. However, where surplus foreign tax arises on the profits of a non-exempt foreign branch whose profits of the overseas permanent establishment are subject to corporation tax in the UK, surplus unrelieved foreign tax (after double tax relief) may be **carried forward** to the next accounting period or **carried back** to accounting periods beginning in the previous **three years**.

The carry forward is indefinite, (unless the permanent establishment ceases to exist), though the surplus unrelieved foreign tax can only be set against corporation tax due on profits from the same permanent establishment.

The carry back is on a **LIFO basis**, starting with later years first. The time limit for a claim is **four years** from the end of the accounting period in which the surplus unrelieved foreign tax arose or, if later, one year after the foreign tax was paid.

8.4 The Controlled Foreign Company (CFC) Rules

As mentioned earlier, UK companies may decide to set up a non-resident subsidiary company. This may be in a low-tax territory with the aim of saving UK corporation tax.

The controlled foreign company (CFC) rules are designed to prevent companies shifting what are effectively UK profits to a foreign country where the tax paid is significantly lower than the amount that would have to be paid in the UK.

The CFC rules are based on the principle that overseas activities are not taxed in the UK unless there is an artificial reduction of the UK tax base. Also, should a company come within the regime, the legislation addresses only those profits that have been artificially diverted from the UK. Where there has been an artificial diversion of profits from the UK, the CFC rules can effectively subject the profits that have been artificially diverted from the UK to UK corporation tax.

A CFC is a company that:

1. is resident outside the UK; and
2. is controlled by persons resident in the UK. Control is established if the foreign resident company is controlled by more than 50% from the UK, or by more than 40% from the UK with any non-resident holding at least 40% but less than 55%.

The following are the key features of the legislation.

1. There are a number of entity-based exemptions for CFCs, such that no CFC charge is imposed in relation to any of its profits. The exemptions are:
   (a) Exempt-period exemption – for foreign companies becoming CFCs for the first time. This exemption applies for the first 12 months after a CFC comes under UK control, provided any necessary restructuring is undertaken to ensure no CFC charge arises in the subsequent accounting period.
   (b) Excluded territories exemption – for CFCs resident in certain territories, subject to conditions. HMRC provides a list of excluded territories. The Republic of Ireland is not an excluded territory.
   (c) Low profit exemption – for CFCs with low levels of profit. This exemption applies if the total accounting or taxable profits of the CFC are less than £50,000, or if total accounting or taxable profits are less than £500,000 and non-trading income therein is less than £50,000.
   (d) Low profit margin exemption – for CFCs whose profit is no more than 10% of operating expenditure.
   (e) Tax exemption – for CFCs that pay at least 75% of the tax that they would have paid in the UK.
2. "Gateway tests", which define chargeable profits that have been artificially diverted from the UK and that are subject to a CFC charge. The business profits of a foreign subsidiary are within the scope of the CFC regime if they pass through a "gateway". These gateways seek to address instances where there is a significant distortion between business activities undertaken in the UK and the profits arising from those activities being allocated outside the UK.
3. "Safe harbours" for the gateway tests are provided, covering general commercial business, incidental finance income and some sector-specific rules. A foreign subsidiary can rely on these safe harbours to show that some or all of its profits do not pass through the gateway and as such are outside the regime's scope and there is no CFC charge.

The entity-based exemptions should be examined first, followed by the gateway tests. If profits pass through a gateway test and do not satisfy the conditions for the relevant safe harbour, the UK company (which must hold 25% or more in the CFC) will pay the CFC charge.

The relevant profits passing through the gateway test are apportioned to the UK resident company. These are then subject to corporation tax in the UK with a credit given for any foreign tax paid. The due date for payment of the CFC charge is the same as the usual due date for payment of the company's corporation tax liability for the relevant accounting period.

The existence of a CFC and details of the CFC charge must be reported to HMRC in the company's corporation tax return under the self-assessment regime.

The CFC rules also apply to foreign branches of UK companies where the foreign branch is exempt from UK corporation tax under the foreign branch exemption.

Questions

Review Questions

(See Suggested Solutions to Review Questions at the end of this textbook.)

Question 8.1

In July 2019 Medtech Ltd, a UK resident company with a 30 June accounting period end, entered into a joint venture in Cyprus by purchasing a 48% holding in MedAssist Ltd, a company involved in the wholesale and distribution of pharmaceutical products. MedAssist also has a 30 June accounting period end.

One of the reasons Medtech invested in MedAssist was the low rate of corporation tax in Cyprus (10%). The other 52% of the shares in MedAssist are held by Medservices SA, a Portuguese company. Medtech has used MedAssist for the distribution of their own products in the past, which is how they became aware of this investment opportunity.

Requirement

Outline the rationale for the controlled foreign company (CFC) rules, assess if MedAssist Ltd is a CFC and consider if a CFC charge will arise on the basis of the above information. (Cyprus is not on the list of excluded territories.)

Question 8.2

Hulk Ltd, a UK resident company, owns 46% of the ordinary share capital of Black Widow Co. Black Widow Co. is resident in Germany. The remaining 54% shares in Black Widow Co. are held by a French resident company, Hawk Eye Srl.

For the year ended 31 March 2020, Black Widow Co. has profits, calculated in accordance with UK tax rules, of £1,500,000, of which 75% is regarded as having been artificially diverted from the UK. None of the controlled foreign company exemptions are available to Black Widow Co.

Black Widow Co. has suffered tax in its country of residence of £150,000. Hulk Ltd's accounting period end is also 31 March.

Requirement

(a) Determine if Black Widow Co. is a CFC.

(b) Calculate the CFC charge for the year ended 31 March 2020 on the basis of the above information. Who is responsible for paying the charge and how is it reported to HMRC?

Question 8.3

Shed-It Limited is a manufacturing company based in Newry and a client of your practice. Shed-It does not pay corporation tax in instalments. Stephanie Adams, the finance director, telephones you requiring advice on a possible expansion of Shed-It's activities.

Shed-It wants to expand into the Republic of Ireland as it believes there is a market for the company's products there. The Board is undecided if these activities should be operated through a branch of Shed-It or a 100%-owned Irish resident subsidiary company, Shed-It (Ireland) Ltd. The Board is aware that the rate of corporation tax in the ROI is much lower (12.5%) and is keen to keep its overall corporation tax liability as low as possible. However, projections prepared show that this Irish trading activity is likely to be loss-making, at least initially.

Shed-It is also the 56% owner of shares in a joint venture company in Cyprus, Shed-It Cyprus Inc. Having already established that Shed-It Cyprus Inc. is a controlled foreign company (CFC) and that a CFC charge is payable by Shed-It, you are provided with the following information in relation to the accounting period ended 31 March 2020 for Shed-It Cyprus Inc.:

- taxable profits are £1,822,650;
- 60% of those profits are caught by the CFC legislation; and
- the corporation tax rate in Cyprus is 10%.

Requirement
Write a letter to the finance director of Shed-It advising her on each of the following:

(a) Outline the exposure to UK corporation tax and any other relevant tax factors if Shed-It:

  (i) establishes a branch in the Republic of Ireland; or
  (ii) sets up a 100% wholly-owned subsidiary in the Republic of Ireland.

  Ignore any potential controlled foreign company implications.

(b) Stephanie is new to the role of finance director and, having never heard of the CFC legislation before, she asks you for some information. Define what a CFC is and outline, in general, the taxation implications of CFCs.

(c) Calculate the CFC charge payable by Shed-It for the accounting period ended 31 March 2020 in respect of Shed-It Cyprus Inc. **and** advise when this should be paid and how it is to be reported to HMRC.

Question 8.4

Prudent Limited, a UK resident company has the following income for the year ended 31 March 2020:

	£
Adjusted trading profits from UK business	1,400,000
Profits from an overseas branch	450,000
Taxable total profits	1,850,000
Withholding tax on overseas branch profits (@ 15%)	

Requirement
Calculate the UK corporation tax payable, with or without an irrevocable election that profits from all of its overseas branches are exempt from UK corporation tax.

9

Group Relief and Consortia Relief

Learning Objectives

After studying this chapter you will understand:

- The distinction between related 51% group companies, 75% subsidiaries, consortia and capital gains tax groups.
- That if one company in a group has a loss, it can be utilised by another group member either in the same accounting period or a future accounting period.
- The types of losses that may be group-relieved or relieved via consortium relief.
- How group relief is calculated.
- How consortium relief is calculated.
- When overseas losses may be surrendered to a UK parent company.
- The tax treatment of intragroup payments.
- The corporate interest restriction rules, which can restrict the deduction of interest by UK companies and groups.

9.1 Introduction

For corporation tax purposes, the percentage shareholding that one company has in another often determines the taxation consequences.

The main types of relationship for tax purposes (based on the degree of share ownership) are:

1. Related 51% group companies
2. 75% subsidiaries
3. Consortia
4. Capital gains groups (see **Chapter 10**).

9.1.1 Related 51% Group Companies

For corporation tax purposes, two companies are related 51% group companies only if they are members of a "51% group". A "group" of companies for this purpose means a group headed by a company, irrespective of where it is resident. Dormant companies are not counted.

As outlined in **Chapter 1**, the number of related 51% group companies can determine the limits to be applied for determining if a company is required to pay corporation tax in instalments.

A 51% relationship exists where there is an entitlement to at least 51% of the share capital, voting rights, income or net assets on a winding up.

A company is another company's related 51% group company in an accounting period if it is a related 51% group company for **any part** of the accounting period. This rule applies to each of two or more related 51% group companies even if they are related 51% group companies for different parts of the accounting period.

9.1.2 Group Relief

While related 51% group companies are based on more than 50% shareholding/control, special rules apply to situations where the share ownership reaches 75%.

For corporation tax purposes, two companies are members of a "group" for group relief purposes where one is a 75% subsidiary of the other, or both are 75% subsidiaries of a third company. In this context, for one company to be a 75% subsidiary of another, the holding company must have at least 75% of the ordinary share capital. However, if the company is not also entitled to at least 75% of the distributable income of the subsidiary **and** entitled to at least 75% of the net assets of the subsidiary on a winding up, group relief may be denied when there are unusual financing structures in a subsidiary so that, for example, the parent is entitled to less than 75% of profits.

For two companies to be in a group, there has to be a 75% effective interest. Hence, if company H owns 90% of company A, which in turn owns 80% of company B, then B **is not** in a group with H as H only has an effective interest of 72% of B (being 90% of 80%). Nevertheless, A and B **are** in a group for group relief purposes as they have a 75% relationship. Note that a company can be a member of more than one group for 75%-group relief purposes.

However, it should be noted that the group relief rules **cannot** be circumvented by trying to use company A as a conduit. For example, if B transfers losses to A, these cannot in turn be transferred by A to H.

A group-relief group may include non UK-resident companies. Furthermore, while losses may generally only be surrendered between UK-resident companies, group relief can, in certain circumstances, be available to UK branches or permanent establishments of overseas non-UK companies or to UK holding companies of overseas non-resident subsidiaries.

In addition, from 6 April 2020, a non-UK resident company that does not have a UK branch or UK permanent establishment but which is carrying on a UK property business that comes within the charge to corporation tax can also be regarded as a UK member of a group of companies for group relief purposes. This means that both profits and losses of such non-resident companies can be group-relieved to other members of the group. This is, however, dependent on whether or not relief has already been claimed elsewhere for the same loss.

9.1.3 Consortium Relief

A company is owned by a consortium if:

1. at least 75% of its ordinary share capital is owned by companies (known as members of the consortium), none of whose shareholding is less than 5%, and each member of the consortium is entitled to at least 5% of any profits available for distribution and at least 5% of any assets on a winding up; **or**
2. if a trading company is a 90% subsidiary of a holding company and is not a 75% subsidiary of any company apart from the holding company and, as a result of 1, the holding company is owned by a consortium, then that trading company is also owned by the consortium.

Although a consortium can be established with non-UK resident companies, losses generally cannot be surrendered to or from a non-UK resident company under the connsortium relief rules.

9.1.4 Capital Gains Groups

Companies are in a capital gains group if, at each level, there is a 75% holding and the top company has an effective interest of at least 51% in the group companies. Compare this with the effective 75% interest required for "group-relief groups".

Thus, if company S holds 80% of company T, which in turn holds 80% of U, which in turn holds 80% of V, which in turn holds 80% of W, then:

- S, T, U and V are in a capital gains group (since S has an effective 51.2% interest in V, being 80% × 80% × 80%);
- but S only has a 40.96% effective interest in W (80% × 80% × 80% × 80%), so W is not part of this capital gains group.

In contrast with the position for group relief outlined above, it is only possible to be part of one group for capital gains group. See **Chapter 10** for more on capital gains groups.

9.2 Intragroup Payments

Certain payments made by companies are generally required to be made under deduction of income tax at the standard rate (see **Chapter 3**).

A UK company is not required to deduct tax at source from intragroup interest and royalty payments where the other company is either:

1. UK resident; or
2. if non-resident, the company operates a UK permanent establishment (though see **Chapter 3, Section 3.1** for the rules for royalty payments to non-residents).

Inter-company interest can be accrued in the year to obtain tax relief, unless it is paid to a company resident in a territory with which the UK does not have a double taxation treaty that contains a non-discrimination article.

If interest is being paid by a UK company to a company not resident in the UK and without a UK permanent establishment, basic rate income tax (currently 20%) must be deducted and the CT61 procedure outlined in **Section 3.1.2** followed. However, the recipient company can apply to HMRC to have the interest paid gross without deduction of tax. See **Chapter 3** for more details.

9.3 Group Relief for Losses

9.3.1 Introduction

The group relief provisions mean that companies within a 75% group (see **Section 9.3.6**) can transfer current-period and most carry-forward losses to other group companies within the group. They can then be offset against taxable profits to reduce the group's overall corporation tax liability.

Generally, losses may only be surrendered between UK-resident companies. In certain circumstances group relief is available to UK branches of overseas companies (see **Section 9.3.9**) and losses of EEA overseas subsidiaries may be group-relieved to its UK holding company (see **Section 9.3.8**).

9.3.2 Current-period Losses

The type of eligible losses that can be group-relieved include:

1. trading losses; or
2. surplus non-trade loan relationship deficits.

The total amount of these losses may be surrendered by the surrendering company, even if it has other taxable profits against which these losses could be set.

Furthermore, the surrendering company may also surrender, in the following order:

3. excess qualifying charitable donations;
4. excess UK property business losses;
5. excess management expenses; and
6. excess non-trading losses on intangibles.

The amount of "excess" available for group relief in categories 3–6 inclusive refers to amounts in excess of a profit-related tax threshold. This threshold is the surrendering company's taxable profits before any losses are set off (including brought forward losses).

The surrendering company surrenders to the claimant company/companies (i.e. the profit-making companies), which must set the losses against taxable total profits of the same chargeable accounting period.

Any losses claimed under group relief cannot be carried back, carried forward or given to another group member.

The offset against taxable total profits is made after qualifying charitable donations and any current-year or brought-forward losses. However, the offset is made before losses brought back from a future period, i.e. losses carried back do not displace group relief already claimed.

Where the surrendering company's and claimant company's accounting periods are not coterminous, **both** the profits and losses must be apportioned so that only the results of the **overlap** period are relevant. The apportionment is generally calculated on a time basis, unless another method provides a more "just and reasonable" result.

9.3.3 Carry-forward Losses

Most losses carried forward (see **Chapter 4**), with the exception of pre-1 April 2017 losses, can also be surrendered to other group members. However, in such cases the loss restriction rule (see **Section 4.1**) should be considered. As a result, companies with profits in excess of the relevant deductions allowance are not able to reduce profits wholly to nil by using relief for carried-forward losses. Where a company is a member of a group, the £5 million deductions allowance is shared (on a pro-rata basis if necessary) amongst the group members as they see fit.

In addition, the deductions allowance that may be used by a group member is restricted so that where a company is a member of one group and an 'ultimate parent' of another, it is only able to use a share of the allowance from the group of which it is a member. This is designed to prevent groups from acquiring new members to increase the amount of the deductions allowance available.

Group surrender of carry-forward losses is denied to the extent that the company carrying the loss forward has the capacity to use the losses carried forward against its own profits. Relief is also denied where the surrendering company has no assets capable of producing income at the end of the period.

For the purpose of the deductions allowance, a group means two or more companies where:

- one company is the "ultimate parent" of each of the other companies; and
- is not the "ultimate parent" of any other company.

A company is the ultimate parent of another if it is the parent of that other company and no company is the parent of both companies.

A company is the parent of another company if:

- that other company is its 75% subsidiary; and
- it is beneficially entitled to at least 75% of any profits available for distribution to equity of that other company; or
- it would be beneficially entitled to at least 75% of assets in the event of a winding up of that other company.

Example 9.1: Definition of group for deductions allowance

Company A owns 100% of the shares in Company B, and Company B owns 100% shares in Company C.

Here, A is the ultimate parent; B is a 75% direct subsidiary; and C is a 75% indirect subsidiary. The "group" therefore comprises companies A, B and C for the purposes of the deductions allowance.

A and B cannot form a separate group because, while A is the ultimate parent of B, it is also the ultimate parent of C.

B and C cannot form a separate group because, while B is the parent of C, it cannot be the ultimate parent as A is the parent of both B and C.

It follows that there will be a single group deductions allowance to be shared amongst A, B and C.

The deductions allowance is allocated to companies that are members of the group by a nominated company. The nomination must be made by all the companies in the group that are within the charge to corporation tax and must state the date the nomination takes effect. The nomination must be signed by an "appropriate person" on behalf of each company. An "appropriate person" is a proper officer of the company or another person who has the authority of the company to act on its behalf.

Nominations cease to have effect when:

- a new group allowance nomination takes effect; or
- the nomination is revoked in writing by an appropriate person of a group company, or
- the nominated company ceases to be a company within the charge to UK corporation tax or ceases to be a member of the group.

The nominated company is responsible for submitting a group deductions allowance allocation statement for each of its accounting periods for which it is the nominated company. This statement must be received by HMRC before the first anniversary of the filing date of the nominated company's corporation tax return for the accounting period to which the statement relates.

A revised group allowance allocation statement can be submitted for an accounting period of a company that is or was the nominated company.

Example 9.2

Parker Ltd is a member of a large group and had trading profits of £10 million in the year ended 31 March 2020. A deductions allowance of £1 million has been allocated to Parker Ltd for the accounting period.

Advise Parker Ltd of the maximum value of losses that can be claimed from the group.

Parker Ltd can claim up to £5.5 million of losses, being:

Deductions allowance	£1 million
50% × (profits (£10 million) – deductions allowance (£1 million))	£4.5 million
Maximum group relief claim	£5.5 million

> ***Example 9.3: Deadline for submitting group allowance statement***
> Company A is a member of a group and prepares accounts to 31 March every year. In its accounting period ended 31 March 2020 it is nominated by all the other companies that are members of the group and the nomination takes effect from 1 October 2019.
>
> Company A must submit a group allowance allocation statement for its accounting period ended 31 March 2020 (the nominee's accounting period).This must be done before 31 March 2022.

9.3.4 Method of Relief

The maximum relief that can flow from one company to another is the lower of:

1. the available loss of the surrendering company (after deducting any prior surrenders for the overlapping period); or
2. the available total profits of the claimant company (after deducting any prior claims for the overlapping period).

A detailed illustration of the calculation of the relief is given in **Example 9.4** below.

The surrendering company is given some flexibility as regards both the method of relief and the amount to be relieved. To this extent, it may surrender current-period trading losses and surplus non-trading loan relationship deficits **before** setting them against its other profits for the period of the loss **and** it can choose the quantum of its losses that it wishes to surrender. As set out in **Section 9.3.2**, only the excess of the remaining types of loss for which group relief is available can be surrendered. Carry-forward losses can only be group-relieved after the surrendering company has made all possible current-year claims for those carry-forward losses This is also subject to the group's relevant deductions allowance.

The aim of group relief is to ensure that no company in the group is unnecessarily exposed to making payments of corporation tax in instalments. Overall the quantum of corporation tax across the group will remain the same irrespective of how the group loss is relieved, as each company is subject to a 19% rate of corporation tax in FY 2019.

Claimant Company

A company's 'available total profits' are its total profits after all possible deductions for the current period **except** amounts carried back from later periods **less** the amount of previously claimed group relief for that period.

The claimant company may claim maximum relief or part of the surrendering company's surrenderable amounts. The claimant company is therefore assumed to use its own current year losses or losses brought forward to determine the maximum amount of group relief it may claim. This is a theoretical calculation as HMRC is effectively restricting the availability of the losses to be claimed.

So, the profits available for offsetting group-relieved losses are calculated **after all other reliefs for the current period are claimed**, including surplus non-trade deficits on loan relationships. However, group relief is given **before** relief for any amounts brought back from later periods. It should also be remembered that if a company has qualifying charitable donations (QCDs), these are allowed as deductions from the company's total profits – but only after group relief.

Example 9.4
The following companies are in a group:

Company	Accounting period	
A	12 months to 31/12/2020	Profit £72,000
B	6 months to 30/06/2020	Profit £5,000
C	12 months to 30/09/2020	Current-year trading loss £120,000

Company B claims from company C, which has not previously surrendered any of its losses.

C's "available loss for the overlapping period" is the same as its loss for the overlapping period. This is because there have been no prior surrenders of C's losses. It is:

$$6/12 \times £120{,}000 = £60{,}000$$

B's "unrelieved available profits for the overlapping period" is also the same as its "available profits for the overlapping period". This is because it has made no prior claims. It is:

$$6/6 \times £5{,}000 = £5{,}000$$

The amount that can be surrendered/claimed is the lower of these. It is £5,000.
A then claims from company C, which has made a prior surrender. The calculations are as follows:
The overlapping period is nine months ended 30 September 2020.
C's "loss for the overlapping period" is:

$$9/12 \times £120{,}000 = £90{,}000$$

C's "available loss for the overlapping period" is this amount less the "amount of any prior surrenders attributable to the overlapping period".

Step 1

B's claim from C involves part of C's surrenderable amount for the accounting period ended 30 September 2020.

Step 2

The amount of B's claim, £5,000, is treated as being for the overlapping period in that claim, which is six months ended 30 June 2020.

The common period of the overlapping periods in B's claim and A's claim is six months ended 30 June 2020. The whole of the £5,000 is apportioned to that common period.

Step 3

The total, £5,000, is the "amount of any prior surrenders attributable to the overlapping period".

So C's "available loss for the overlapping period" is £90,000 less £5,000 which is £85,000.

A's "unrelieved available profits for the overlapping period" is the same as its "available for the overlapping period". This is because it has made no prior claims. It is:

$$9/12 \times £72{,}000 = £54{,}000$$

If there was another company in the group and A had already claimed group relief from this company for the same overlapping period, the amount of this would have to be deducted from the £54,000.

However, there have been no prior claims and, therefore, the amount that can be surrendered/claimed is the smaller of £85,000 and £54,000, which is £54,000.

Method of Claim

A claim for group relief is generally made on the claimant company's tax return, but there must also be a notice of consent given by the surrendering company. In order to amend a claim, the claimant company must withdraw the original and submit a new claim. All such claims must be made no later than:

1. the first anniversary of the filing date for the accounting period of the claim; or
2. 30 days after either the completion of an enquiry into the return, the amendment of a self-assessment or settlement of an appeal against an amendment.

There is also the facility for group-wide claims/surrenders to be made. It should be noted that no payment is required by the claimant company to the surrendering company in respect of the group relief transferred. However, any such payment, up to the level of the actual loss surrendered, is ignored for corporation tax purposes.

9.3.5 Examples

Example 9.5

A Ltd owns 80% of B Ltd. The following are the results for the year ended 31 December 2020:

	A Ltd	B Ltd
	£	£
Relevant trading profit/(loss)	10,000	(25,000)
Net credit on loan relationships	8,000	6,400

Calculate the corporation tax payable by each company.

	£	£
B Ltd		
Trading income		–
Net credit on loan relationships		6,400
Loss relief (section 37(3)(a) CTA 2010)		(6,400)
Taxable total profits (TTP)		NIL
A Ltd		
Trading income	10,000	
Net credit on loan relationships	8,000	
Total	18,000	
Group relief (section 99 CTA 2010)	(18,000)	
TTP	NIL	

Loss Memo	£
Relevant trading loss for y/e 31/12/2020	25,000
Utilised by way of:	
section 37(3)(a) against B Ltd	(6,400)
section 99 against profits of A Ltd	(18,000)
Losses to be carried forward under section 45A	600

Example 9.6

C Ltd owns 90% of D Ltd and 90% of E Ltd. The following are the results for the year ended 31 March 2020. Both C Ltd and D Ltd were "large" for instalment purposes in the previous accounting period. The companies have been in a group since 31 March 2000.

	C Ltd	D Ltd	E Ltd*
	£	£	£
Relevant trading profit	500,000	90,000	200,000
Net credit on loan relationships	6,000	12,000	23,000
Property income	30,000	10,000	18,000
Chargeable gain	110,000	–	–
Qualifying charitable donation	(5,000)		

* E Ltd has a trading loss of £594,000, which was carried forward from the accounting period ended 31 March 2019.

continued overleaf

Calculate the corporation tax payable by each company after maximum utilisation of any group relief available.

Solution

In questions of this type, one should begin by looking at the position in the absence of any group relief.

	C Ltd	**D Ltd**	**E Ltd**
	£	£	£
Trading profit/(loss)	500,000	90,000	200,000
Net credit on loan relationships	6,000	12,000	23,000
Property income	30,000	10,000	18,000
Chargeable gain	110,000	–	–
Qualifying charitable donations	(5,000)		
TTP	641,000	112,000	241,000
Corporation tax rate	19%	19%	19%

	C Ltd	**D Ltd**	**E Ltd**
	£	£	£
TTP (before group relief)	641,000	112,000	241,000
Less: section 45A CTA 2010			(241,000)
Less: section 99 CTA 2010	(353,000)	(12,000)	
TTP after group relief	288,000	100,000	-
Corporation tax rate × 19%	54,720	19,000	-

The limit for quarterly instalments must be calculated first. There are three related 51% group companies in the group; therefore the limit is £1,500,000/3, i.e. £500,000. It is important to note that a company can only surrender carried-forward losses that it is unable to deduct from its own profits during that accounting period. This means that E Ltd must first use the carried-forward losses against its own taxable profits before surrendering any remaining losses to C Ltd or D Ltd. It would appear that the losses of E Ltd can be surrendered in any manner as each company is paying corporation tax at 19%. However, because the instalment payments limit is £500,000, C Ltd Ltd would be required to pay its corporation tax in instalments as its augmented profits before any group relief is greater than £500,000. Therefore it will be critical to reduce the level of its TTP to at least £500,000.

In this example, because profits do not exceed £5 million, relief for the trading loss carried forward by E Ltd is not restricted by virtue of the deductions allowance.

Example 9.7: Corresponding accounting period

F Ltd owns 100% of G Ltd. F Ltd's results for the year ended 31 August 2020 show a trading loss of £12,000 and it has no other income.

G Ltd has had the following results for the two years ended 30 November 2019 and 2020:

	Year ended	
	30 Nov 2019	**30 Nov 2020**
	£	£
Trading income	16,000	10,000

Solution

For the year ended 30 November 2019, the overlap period would be 01 September 2019 to 30 November 2019 (although technically apportionment should be in days, we shall work in months for simplicity).

continued overleaf

	£
G Ltd (profits 3/12 of £16,000)	4,000
F Ltd (losses 3/12 of £12,000)	(3,000)

Thus G Ltd could make a group relief claim for £3,000 against its profits.

For the year ended 30 November 2020, the overlap period would be 01 December 2019 to 31 August 2020.

	£
G Ltd (profits 9/12 of £10,000)	7,500
F Ltd (losses 9/12 of £12,000)	(9,000)

Thus G Ltd could make a group relief claim for £7,500 against its profits.

The unutilised loss of £1,500 (£12,000 – £3,000 – £7,500) is available for relief in the normal way (either carry back/carry forward, etc.). The deductions allowance does not need to be considered in this example as the loss being utilised is not a loss carried forward.

9.3.6 Qualifying Group

To avail of group relief in the relevant accounting period, the profit-maker must be in the same "75% group" as the loss-maker. This condition is satisfied in relation to two companies if one company holds, directly or indirectly, not less than 75% of the ordinary share capital of that company, or if the companies are 75% subsidiaries of another company. Groups can include all companies whether UK resident or not. However, under general rules, the loss of a foreign company cannot be transferred and relieved in the UK, and vice versa, except as set out in **Sections 9.1.2, 9.3.8** and **9.3.9**.

A company may establish the 75% holding by aggregating any ordinary shares held directly in that company and also those held indirectly through the medium of a third company. This is illustrated further in the following examples of qualifying loss groups.

Examples of Qualifying 75% Loss Group for UK Group Surrenders

1. Where the loss-maker is a 75% subsidiary of the profit-maker, or vice versa:

2. Where both are 75% subsidiaries of a third company:

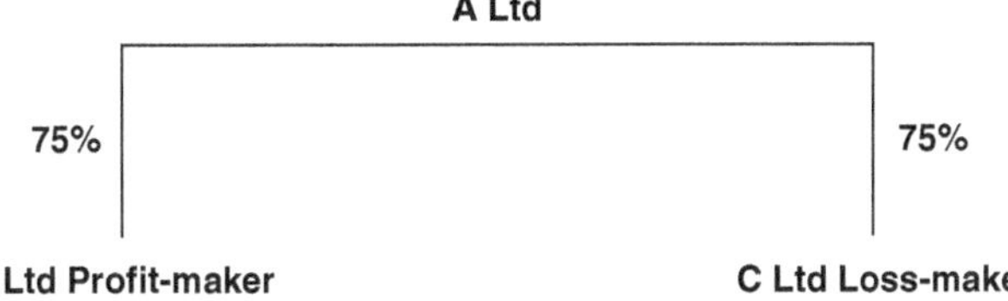

3. By establishing a 75% relationship through the medium of a third company – A Ltd owns 100% of C Ltd and 50% of B Ltd and C Ltd also owns 30% of B Ltd.

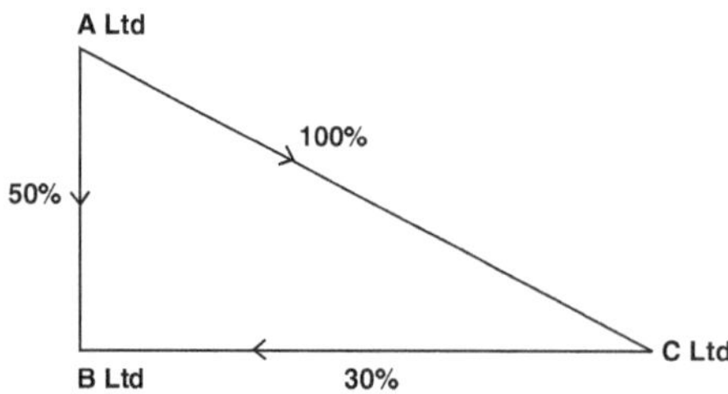

A Ltd, B Ltd and C Ltd are all members of the same 75% loss group.

9.3.7 General Considerations

1. In a qualifying group, relief may be passed upwards, downwards or sideways.
2. It is permissible for two or more profit-makers to avail of relief from any one loss-maker.
3. It is not necessary for the profit-maker to make a claim for the full amount of the loss-maker's loss, i.e. the claim may be tailored to suit the individual company's needs. It is not necessary for the profit-maker to make a payment to the surrendering company when claiming group relief.
4. Even if the relationship between the companies is less than 100% all of the loss may be grouped.
5. The rule in group relief that requires that losses of the surrendering company must first be applied in reducing other profits arising in the accounting period of the loss, only applies to carry-forward losses. The surrendering company may, for current-period losses only, choose to be liable to corporation tax on any trading or non-trading loan relationship profits of the period, while surrendering the full amount of the loss sustained in the period. However, losses in categories 3–6 in **Section 9.3.2** must be set first against any current-period income sources the company may have. Therefore it is only the excess, unused amounts of these losses that are available for surrender.
6. It is vital to remember that, before availing of group relief, the profit-maker concerned must claim all other reliefs, except set-off of losses for a subsequent accounting period and terminal relief.
7. Group relief is only available where the accounting period of both the loss-maker and profit-maker corresponds wholly or partly. Where they correspond partly (overlap period), the relief is restricted on a time-apportionment basis.
8. Generally, group relief claims must be made no later than the first anniversary of the filing date for the accounting period of the claim.
9. The loss-maker must give formal consent for the surrender of the loss.
10. Payments to the loss-maker by the profit-maker for availing of the losses are ignored for corporation tax purposes, provided they do not exceed the amount of the loss surrendered, i.e. no tax deduction is available to the profit-maker in respect of the payment and the receipt by the loss-maker is not taxable.
11. The group deductions allowance and the allocation of group relief should be done in the most tax-efficient manner. This will generally mean ensuring no company in the group is unnecessarily exposed to instalment payments of corporation tax.

9.3.8 Worldwide Groups

Groups can be established by including companies not resident in the UK. However, generally, the losses of a foreign company cannot be group relieved in the UK; nor can a UK company surrender losses to a non-resident company.

Example 9.8

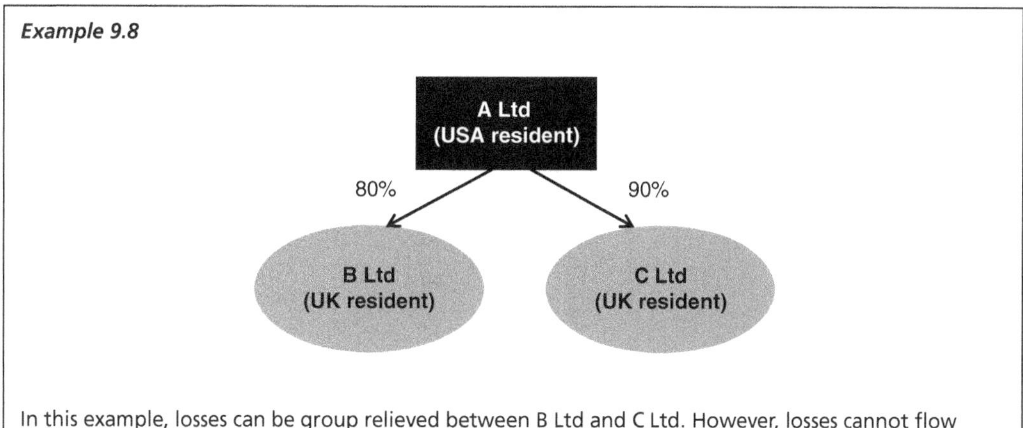

In this example, losses can be group relieved between B Ltd and C Ltd. However, losses cannot flow between A Ltd and either B Ltd or C Ltd. A Ltd establishes who the group members are, but it cannot claim or surrender group relief.

9.3.9 Overseas Losses of EEA Resident Subsidiaries

Following the Court of Justice of the European Union (CJEU) decision in *Marks & Spencer v. Halsey* (2005), a "qualifying overseas loss" may be surrendered for group relief purposes to the UK parent company if the losses are incurred by European Economic Area (EEA) subsidiaries and certain conditions are met. The EEA comprises all EU Member States plus Iceland, Liechtenstein, and Norway.

Anti-avoidance legislation prevents relief for such losses where the amount would not qualify for group relief but for any relevant arrangements, or the amount would not have arisen to the non-resident company but for any relevant arrangements and the main purpose, or one of the main purposes, of the relevant arrangements was to secure group relief.

To qualify for the relief, the surrendering company must be chargeable to tax under the law of an EEA state. Relief is available where either:

1. the surrendering company is a 75% subsidiary of the claimant company and the claimant company is resident in the UK; or
2. both the surrendering company and the claimant company are 75% subsidiaries of a third company that is resident in the UK.

The losses to be surrendered must meet the following conditions:

- the equivalence condition – the loss is a type of loss eligible for group relief;
- the EEA tax loss condition – the loss arises under the laws of the EEA state;
- the qualifying loss condition – the loss has not been, or cannot be, used in the current accounting period, or has not been carried back or carried forward by the company or a third party; and
- the precedence condition – the loss cannot be relieved in an intermediate holding company that is not resident in the UK, nor in the same territory as that in which the surrendering company is resident.

The qualifying loss condition essentially makes sure that relief is only available in the UK for only the surplus unused EEA loss.

Once it has been established that a loss exists under the above conditions it must be recalculated using UK rules. The maximum loss that can be surrendered is the recalculated EEA loss. The usual group relief rules for coterminous accounting periods and the amount that the claimant company can claim then apply.

Example 9.9

X Ltd is resident in France. It's corporation tax computation for the accounting period ended 31 March 2020 includes the following components:

	£
Trading loss	425,000
Non-trade interest paid	175,000
Property income	100,000
Unrelieved EEA loss	500,000

UK recalculation:

Trading loss	425,000
Surplus non-trade loan relationship debit	175,000
Potential loss available for group relief	600,000
Property income	100,000

The UK recalculation shows that, potentially, all £600,000 could be surrendered as group relief, leaving the £100,000 property income subject to corporation tax in France. However, under the rules a loss only meets the qualifying loss condition to the extent that relief cannot be given for any period.

In the EEA, £100,000 of either the foreign trading loss or the foreign surplus non-trade loan relationship debit is relieved against the foreign property income. This amount does not meet the qualifying loss condition. Therefore the amount available for relief in the UK is £500,000, although it would still need to be shown that the loss has not been used in the current accounting period, or carried back or carried forward by the company or a third party before it can qualify.

9.3.10 UK Permanent Establishments of Non-resident Companies

Losses may be transferred to a UK permanent establishment (PE) of a non-resident company by a UK group member (and vice versa) if the following conditions are satisfied:

- if a profit had arisen in the UK PE it would have been subject to UK corporation tax (and would not be exempt under a double tax treaty); and
- no part of the loss is relievable or allowable, in any period, against non-UK profits of any person for the purposes of any foreign tax.

The effect of such surrenders is that the loss of the UK PE is treated as relievable in the foreign territory in preference to relief in the UK.

If the non-resident company is established in the EEA, losses of its UK PE may be surrendered provided that they are not actually used against the non-UK profits of any person in any period. If the losses are subsequently used against non-UK profits, any UK group relief claimed is withdrawn.

9.4 Consortium Relief for Losses

9.4.1 Definition of a Consortium

If it is the case that a company is not a group member because it fails the 75% test (meaning group surrenders are not possible to or from that company), it should instead be considered if a consortium exists, which can provide consortium relief for losses.

As set out earlier, a consortium company is:

- a company that is **not** a 75% subsidiary of any company; and
- **at least** 75% of its ordinary shares are owned by companies, **each** of which owns **at least** 5%.

This is known as '**consortium condition 1**'. The company owned by the consortium members is referred to as a consortium-owned company; the companies holding the shares are known as consortium members. 'Consortium condition 2' scenarios are outlined in **Section 9.4.3**. A consortium can also be established by "link" companies, but these provisions are beyond the scope of this textbook.

9.4.2 Consortium Relief

Consortium relief is a variation of group relief where losses of a UK consortium-owned company can be surrendered to UK consortium members and vice versa. A surrender is also possible from a non-UK resident company carrying on a trade in the UK through a PE where a consortium relationship exists.

The surrender of losses for consortium relief is different to group relief because it is in proportion to the consortium member's interest in the consortium company. Remember, for group relief purposes once the group members have been established, potentially all the loss can be surrendered (subject to certain conditions being satisfied).

Note that the group relief rules outlined in **Section 9.3.8**, which allow relief for losses of overseas EEA subsidiaries, do not apply to consortium situations.

Example 9.10

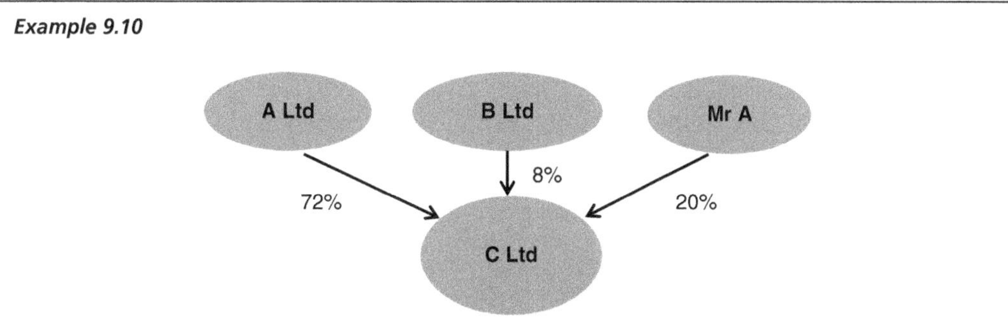

Assume that A Ltd is UK resident and B Ltd is resident in Ireland.

In this example, C Ltd is a consortium-owned company as at least 75% (in this case 80%) of its shares are owned by companies A Ltd and B Ltd, the consortium members. In addition, no single company owns 75% of the shares (as that would make the companies group members) and no single company holds less than 5% of the shares. It is irrelevant that the remaining 20% of the shares are held by an individual, Mr A.

The effect of consortium relief is that a loss of C Ltd is available to the UK resident consortium members. 72% of that loss could be transferred to A Ltd. No losses can be transferred to B Ltd because it is not UK resident; and no losses can be transferred to Mr A because he is an individual. And finally, losses cannot be transferred between A Ltd, B Ltd and Mr A.

C Ltd is owned, to the extent of 72%, by one UK resident company, which owns at least 5%. However, to determine whether a consortium exists we include the shares owned by B Ltd, even though B Ltd cannot receive or surrender losses under the consortium relief rules.

9.4.3 Consortium Condition 2

Consortium relief may also be available if 'consortium condition 2' applies, that is where:

- there is a consortium holding company; and
- that holding company has a 90% trading subsidiary that is not a 75% subsidiary of any company apart from the holding company; and
- as a result of 'consortium condition 1', the holding company is owned by a consortium.

When a consortium-owned company is a holding company in this way, losses can flow directly between the 90% trading subsidiary/subsidiaries and the consortium members, based on the amount of the 90% trading subsidiary's loss, multiplied by the consortium member's interest in the consortium-owned company.

A consortium member's interest is taken as the lowest percentage of the following factors:

- ownership of ordinary share capital;
- entitlement to profits available for distribution to equity holders;
- entitlement to assets distributable to equity holders on a winding up; or
- the proportion of the voting power that is directly possessed by the consortium member.

Losses can flow to or from the consortium members and the holding company. Again, all of the companies must be UK resident. A surrender is also possible from a non-UK resident company carrying on a trade in the UK through a PE.

Under consortium condition 2, the consortium-owned holding company and the consortium-owned trading company also form their own group for group relief purposes. Where there is a possibility of a group surrender and a consortium relief surrender, group relief takes priority. It is therefore deemed that any group relief claims that the consortium-owned holding company or 90% trading company could make within that group have been made. Therefore it is the net loss that may be surrendered to the consortium members in the relevant proportions.

Example 9.11

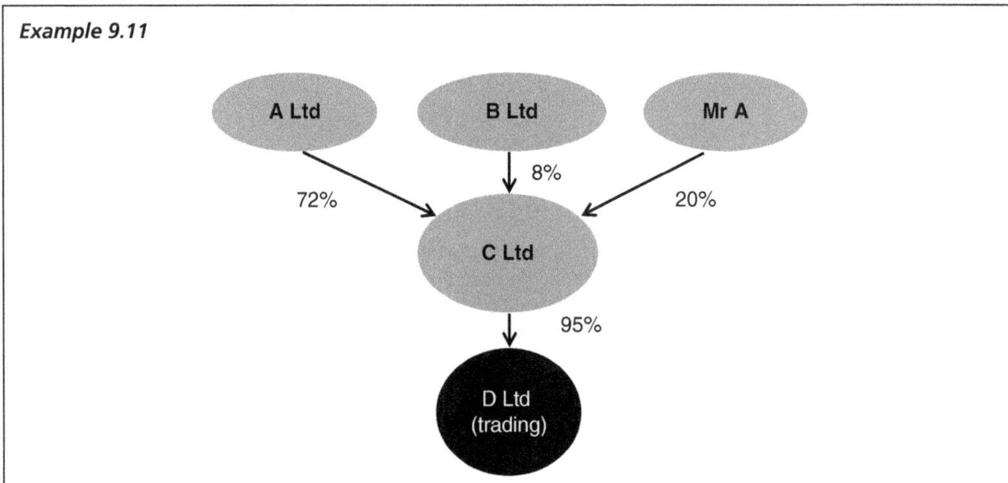

If, for example, D Ltd had a trading loss of £100,000 and C Ltd had no taxable total profits, 72% of D Ltd's loss (i.e. £72,000) could be surrendered to A Ltd. Note that it is the consortium member's interest in the holding company (C Ltd) that is relevant here – the loss is not further apportioned based on the holding company's interest in the trading subsidiary.

If C Ltd had other income of £50,000, a deemed group relief surrender from D Ltd to C Ltd of £50,000 would be made. Of the remaining £50,000, 72% (i.e. £36,000) could be surrendered to A Ltd.

9.4.4 Deemed Current-year Claim

Where a consortium-owned company has a loss and has other income, it is also deemed that a current-year section 37(3)(a) CTA 2010 loss relief claim is made first by the company **before** consortium relief is computed. Note that this differs to group relief, which does not require the surrendering company to make a current-year claim first in respect of either trading losses or surplus non-trade loan relationship deficits. It is therefore the consortium-owned companies' net loss after any current-year claim that is available to the consortium members. The current-year claim is only a notional claim – while it does restrict the maximum loss available under consortium relief, it does not actually have to be made by the company.

9.4.5 Available Amounts

Consortium Condition 1

If the consortium-owned company is loss-making, the maximum consortium relief available is the lower of:

- the consortium-owned company's loss, multiplied by the consortium member's interest in that consortium; or
- the consortium member's available profit.

Consortium Condition 2

If the 90% trading subsidiary of a consortium-owned holding company is loss-making, the maximum consortium relief available is the lower of:

- the consortium-owned 90% trading subsidiary's loss, multiplied by the consortium member's interest in that consortium; or
- the consortium member's available profit.

If the claimant company is a consortium-owned company, the maximum consortium relief available is the lower of:

- the consortium-owned company's profit, multiplied by the consortium member's interest in that consortium; or
- the consortium member's available loss.

The same rule applies to consortium condition 2 scenarios.

The consortium relief rules also contain provisions that mirror the group relief rules where the claimant company and surrendering company do not have coterminous accounting periods and where companies have recently become consortium-owned or consortium members part-way through an accounting period.

The types of losses that can be surrendered as group relief and the rules and restrictions that apply to them also apply to consortium relief.

9.4.6 Administrative Aspects

The group relief administration rules and time limits also apply to consortium relief claims.

Example 9.12

H Ltd owns 65% of K Ltd, I Ltd owns 25% of K Ltd and J Ltd owns 10% of K Ltd. Thus K Ltd is a consortium-owned company whose consortium members are H Ltd, I Ltd and J Ltd.

The results for the year ended 31 March 2020 were as follows:

	H Ltd	**I Ltd**	**J Ltd**	**K Ltd**
	£	£	£	£
Trading profit/(loss)	780,000	80,000	1,000	(63,000)
Net credit on loan relationships				13,000

H Ltd paid corporation tax in instalments in prior years.

Calculate the corporation tax liability for all four companies, assuming that it would be more efficient to relieve as much as possible of the loss in K Ltd to H Ltd. Assume H Ltd's only related 51% group company is K Ltd.

Solution

It would be more efficient for H Ltd to claim consortium relief of 65% on the £63,000 loss as this would reduce its taxable total profits to below £750,000, the limit at which it must make instalment payments of corporation tax. However, for consortium relief purposes, the amount available for surrender **must** be reduced by the potential current year claim by K Ltd against its other income sources.

Therefore the consortium relief that may be claimed by H Ltd, I Ltd and J Ltd is:

H Ltd	The lower of: (£63,000 − £13,000) × 65% = £32,500	
	£780,000	£32,500
I Ltd	The lower of: (£63,000 − £13,000) × 25% = £12,500	
	£80,000	£12,500
J Ltd	The lower of: (£63,000 − £13,000) × 10% = £5,000	
	£1,000	£1,000

So, the consortium members' corporation tax liabilities are:

H Ltd – Corporation Tax	£
Profits	780,000
Consortium relief	(32,500)
Taxable total profits (TTP)	747,500
Corporation tax: £747,500 @ 19%	142,025
Liability (due on or before 1 January 2021)	

I Ltd – Corporation Tax	£
Profits	80,000
Consortium relief	(12,500)
TTP	67,500

continued overleaf

Corporation tax: £67,500 @ 19% (due on or before 1 January 2021)	12,825
J Ltd – Corporation Tax	
Profits	1,000
Consortium relief	(1,000)
TTP	Nil

K Ltd has unused losses to use in the current period and then carry-forward of £17,000 (being £63,000 – £32,500 – £12,500 – £1,000).

9.5 The Corporate Interest Restriction Regime

The OECD's Base Erosion and Profit Shifting (BEPS) project is an initiative to tackle the issue of multinational enterprises 'shifting' profits between companies, often in groups, to minimise tax liabilities resulting in the erosion of a countries tax base. The Corporate Interest Restriction (CIR) legislation implements BEPS Action 4 recommendations to limit excessive tax relief for net interest and related costs. Ultimately, the aim is that a company only obtains a corporation tax deduction for finance costs commensurate with the extent to which its activities are subject to corporation tax in the UK.

The CIR applies to accounting periods starting on or after 1 April 2017 for all companies liable to corporation tax. However, groups with less than £2 million of net interest expense and other financing costs per annum are not be subject to the restriction and have no reporting requirements. This £2 million *de minimis* limit is adjusted for periods of less than 12 months.

9.5.1 Operation of the CIR

The CIR potentially applies where there is a 'worldwide group' (based on IFRS consolidation rules) (see **Section 9.3.8**), consisting of an 'ultimate parent' company and any consolidated subsidiaries. An ultimate parent with no consolidated subsidiaries is referred to as a "single-company worldwide group". In most cases the ultimate parent will have at least one consolidated subsidiary and is referred to as a "multi-company worldwide group". It is the ultimate parent's accounting period that is considered when calculating the CIR. However, groups can nominate one company (the reporting company) to file the CIR return for the whole group.

The aim of the legislation is to restrict a group's deductions of **net** interest and similar financing costs (its 'tax-interest') to an amount relative to the group's activities that are already taxed in the UK. In calculating this amount, any borrowings from third parties are taken into account.

The Steps for Calculating the CIR

There are two methods for calculating the interest allowance (the restriction) of a group's tax-interest deductions:

1. the fixed ratio method – limits the tax-interest deduction to 30% of the **UK** group companies' tax-EBITDA (i.e. taxable earnings before tax, interest, depreciation and amortisation); or
2. the group ratio method – limits the tax-interest deductions by calculating the proportion of net group interest expense (excluding interest on related party debt) as a percentage of the tax-EBITDA of **all** group companies.

The fixed ratio method is the default method; the group ratio method must be elected for (although this election can be revoked).

The group ratio method can potentially result in a higher restriction limit, i.e. higher than the 30% fixed rate, but it is capped at 100%. Similarly, if the calculation results in a negative result or if group EBITDA is zero, it is also set to 100%.

Once the method for calculating the interest allowance is decided upon, the modified debt cap must then be considered. This debt cap is a further potential restriction, capping the interest or debt allowance at the level of the group's 'net group-interest expense', i.e. its worldwide net debt costs **excluding** any inter-company finance costs. The UK companies in the group will therefore suffer a disallowance of tax-interest deductions where the **aggregate UK net tax interest expense** (ANTIE) in the accounting period exceeds its **interest capacity** for the period. This excess is referred to as the 'total disallowed amount', which can be allocated to the UK companies in any way (generally so that a company can avoid having to pay corporation tax instalments).

The interest capacity is calculated as the greater of:

- the interest allowance for accounting period; or
- £2 million (on a pro-rata basis if necessary).

Any unused interest allowance can be carried forward for up to five years. This means that disallowed interest can be "reactivated" if there is sufficient interest allowance in a subsequent period.

Example 9.13

An overseas parent company has a £10 billion loan from an external unconnected source on which it pays interest of £200 million. The overseas parent lends £200 million to its 100% UK subsidiary company, which pays £50 million in interest to its overseas parent. The UK subsidiary company itself hold 100% of the shares in a non-UK trading company.

The tax-EBIDTA of each company is:

	£m
Overseas parent	350
UK company	100
Non-UK trading company	100
Total group tax-EBIDTA	550

The group is a worldwide group and as the UK holding company has net interest expenses of over £2 million (being £50 million) it is subject to the CIR rules.

Using the fixed ratio method, the interest allowance is 30% of the UK company's tax-EBITDA, i.e. 30% × £100 million = £30 million.

Using the group ratio method, the interest allowance is:

$$\frac{\text{Group net qualifying interest expense}}{\text{Group tax} - \text{EBITDA}} \times 100$$

$$\frac{\text{£200 million}}{\text{£550 million}} \times 100 = 36.36\%$$

Therefore the group would elect to use the group ratio method as this gives a higher allowance. The modified debt cap would then need to be considered. As this is £200 million in this case, the interest allowance is not further restricted and remains at 36.36% of £100 million.

The UK company's interest capacity for the period is 36.36% × £100 million = £36,360,000 Therefore the excess of £13,640,000 would be disallowed.

9.5.2 *Administration*

The CIR rules contain special filing requirements that are in addition to the company's usual obligations under the corporation tax self-assessment regime. If a group is not subject to an interest restriction, there is no filing obligation. However, if a group is subject to an interest restriction in a period of account or it wishes to apply any unused interest allowance from a previous year in a later period, it must:

- appoint a reporting company; and
- file an interest restriction return for the period within 12 months of the period end.

An amended interest restriction return can be filed up to 36 months after the end of the relevant period of account. The filing responsibility for the interest restriction return falls on the reporting company which will normally be appointed by the group. The CIR regime has its own set of penalty rules for late filing and errors in returns etc.

Questions

Review Questions

(See Suggested Solutions to Review Questions at the end of this textbook.)

Question 9.1

B Ltd has the following results for year ended 31 March 2020:

	£
Tax-adjusted trading profits (i.e. after current year capital allowance claim)	170,000
Bank deposit interest	4,000
Property income	20,000

Unutilised trading losses brought forward from the year ended 31 March 2017 amount to £16,000. Z Ltd is a 100% trading subsidiary of B Ltd. During the year ended 31 March 2020, it incurred tax-adjusted trading losses of £96,000. It also had taxable interest income of £20,000.

Requirement
Compute B Ltd's corporation tax liability for the year ended 31 March 2020 after allowing for any group relief for losses of Z Ltd.

Question 9.2

A Ltd owns 80% of B Ltd's issued share capital and 75% of C Ltd's issued share capital. Results for year ended 31 March 2020 were:

	A Ltd	B Ltd	C Ltd
	£	£	£
Trading profit/(loss)	(90,000)	56,000	48,000
Net credit from loan relationships	1,000	2,000	3,000
Property income	20,000	25,000	2,000
Trading losses forward (from the accounting period ended 31 March 2017)	(4,000)	–	(26,000)

Requirement
Calculate the corporation tax payable by each company for the year ended 31 March 2020.

Question 9.3

Queen Ltd has two wholly-owned subsidiaries, Pawn Ltd and Rook Ltd. All three are trading companies. Accounts for the year to 31 March 2020 show the following results:

	Queen Ltd	Pawn Ltd	Rook Ltd
	£	£	£
Gross operating profit	297,463	81,000	47,437
Less: depreciation	12,000	10,000	16,000
Entertaining (customers)	1,350	1,200	1,650
Administration	73,650	61,110	107,373
Interest	11,150	10,720	3,000
	98,150	83,030	128,023
Net profit/(loss) before investment income	199,313	(2,030)	(80,586)

Notes

1. Rook Ltd was incorporated and commenced to trade on 1 April 2019.
2. (i) Interest is analysed as follows:

	Queen Ltd	Pawn Ltd	Rook Ltd
	£	£	£
Accrued 1 April 2019	(1,250)	–	–
Paid	10,000	9,000	2,750
Accrued 31 March 2020	2,000	1,720	250
Interest on overdue PAYE	400	–	–
	11,150	10,720	3,000

   (ii) Pawn Ltd has used its loan to purchase 7% of the share capital of Bridge Ltd, whose income consists mainly of property income from commercial properties. The interest paid by Queen and Rook is trade-related, unless otherwise identified.

3. (i) On 1 September 2019, Queen Ltd received a dividend of £9,000 from a French company in which it has a 20% shareholding. This dividend has not been included in the profit figures above.

   (ii) Queen Ltd also received deposit interest gross of £23,846, which is not included in the profit figures above.

4. Capital allowances

Queen Ltd	Pawn Ltd	Rook Ltd
£	£	£
7,375	3,000	5,627

5. Pawn Ltd had trade losses brought forward of £80,000 from the accouting period ended 31 March 2019. Queen Ltd intends to pay a dividend of £10,000 on 9 June 2020.

Requirement

(a) Compute the corporation tax liabilities (if any) of each of the three companies for the year ended 31 March 2020, on the assumption that all available reliefs are claimed to the benefit of the group as a whole.

(b) State the tax consequences for the company of paying the dividend of £10,000.

(c) State the amount of any losses available to carry forward at 31 March 2020 for each company.

(d) State the due date of payment of any corporation tax payable.

10

Company Chargeable Gains

Learning Objectives

After studying this chapter you will understand that:

- How companies are taxed on the disposal of chargeable assets.
- The importance of, and conditions to be satisfied, for the substantial shareholdings exemption (SSE).
- The definition of a capital gains group and how to determine which companies are capital gains group members.
- The tax benefits of being in a capital gains group.
- The degrouping charge rules for capital gains group members that apply when a company leaves the group.

10.1 Chargeable Gains Liable to Corporation Tax

10.1.1 UK-resident Companies

UK-resident companies are liable to corporation tax in respect of all chargeable gains wherever they arise. As such, gains on disposal of foreign assets by a UK resident company are liable to UK corporation tax, although double tax relief may be available.

10.1.2 Non-resident Companies

A non-resident company is, generally, only liable to corporation tax if it carries on a trade in the UK through a permanent establishment. In addition, from 6 April 2020, non-resident companies will pay corporation tax on profits of UK property businesses, other UK property income and profits of loan relationships that the non-resident company is a party to for the purpose of the property business or generating the income. The chargeable gains which are assessable are those accruing on the disposal of assets situated in the UK used for the purposes of the trade of the permanent establishment.

Non-resident companies are also subject to tax on direct and indirect disposals of UK land and property properties under a special regime (but which are beyond the scope of this textbook).

10.2 Exemption from Tax on Disposal of Certain Shareholdings

There is an exemption from corporation tax for any gain arising when a company disposes of the whole or any part of a substantial shareholding in another trading company (or in the holding company of a trading group). This exemption is known as the substantial shareholdings exemption (SSE). When the conditions for the SSE are met, the exemption automatically applies, meaning any gains are exempt from corporation tax with any capital losses arising not relievable.

10.2.1 The Main Exemption

The SSE legislation is set out in Schedule 7AC TCGA 1992. It contains a main exemption and two secondary exemptions.

The main exemption is contained in Schedule 7AC paragraph 1. It states that a gain accruing to a company (the "holding company") on a disposal of shares in another company (the "subsidiary") is not a taxable gain if the requirements in relation to the substantial holding and the subsidiary company are satisfied.

Substantial Shareholding Requirement
The first requirement, in paragraph 1, in relation to the shareholding itself is that the holding company must have held a "substantial shareholding" in the subsidiary throughout a 12-month period in the six years before the disposal takes place.

The meaning of "substantial shareholding" in this context is set out in paragraph 8 and is a holding of shares in the subsidiary company by virtue of which the holding company:

1. holds at least 10% of the company's ordinary share capital;
2. is beneficially entitled to at least 10% of the profits available for distribution to equity holders of the company; and
3. would be beneficially entitled on a winding up to at least 10% of the assets of the company available for distribution to equity holders.

As only a 10% holding of shares is required, it is not technically correct to use the terms "holding company" and "subsidiary". The legislation uses the terms "the investing company" and "the company invested in". For ease of understanding, this section will continue to refer to holding companies and subsidiaries, but bear in mind that only a 10% shareholding, not a controlling one, is required to qualify for SSE.

Subsidiary Company Requirement
The first point to note is that there is no requirement for the subsidiary company to be UK resident. The key requirement is that the company being sold must have been a "qualifying company" throughout the 12 months prior to the disposal (paragraph 19). A "qualifying company" is a trading company or the holding company of a trading group or subgroup. The terms "trading company" and "trading group" require some consideration in this context. Paragraph 20 refers to a trading company as "a company carrying on trading activities whose activities do not include to a substantial extent activities other than trading activities". A "trading group", under paragraph 21, is a group:

> "(a) one or more of whose members carry on trading activities, and
> (b) the activities of whose members, taken together, do not include to a substantial extent activities other than trading activities".

The SSE will not be available if HMRC can show that there is a substantial element of non-trading activities in a company or group. "Substantial", for these purposes, is not defined in the legislation but is generally taken to be 20% and can relate to a percentage of turnover, assets or management time. This is the same test used for holdover relief and entrepreneurs' relief (see **Chapters 18** and **19**). Trading groups often assume that there will be no difficulty in falling below the 20% test when looking at non-trading activities. The problem is that HMRC's interpretation of "non-trading activities" may differ from that of the group or its advisors. Non-trading activities can include items such as the making of intercompany loans.

There are two instances where the company being sold must also be a qualifying company immediately **after the sale**:

1. where the share disposal is to a person connected to the investing company; or
2. when the trade has been transferred into a new company within the previous 12 months.

"Connected", for these purposes, takes the definition in section 1122 CTA 2010, which deals with companies under common control (greater than 50%).

There are two secondary exemptions in the SSE legislation; these are beyond the scope of this textbook.

Example 10.1
Holdco Ltd, an investment company, owns 100% of the shares in Tradeco Ltd, a qualifying trading company. Holdco Ltd is a holding company with no other investments and has held the shares for five years. Holdco sells the shares in Tradeco Ltd to an unconnected third party, realising a gain of £10 million.

As Holdco satisifies the substantial shareholding requirement and Tradeco Ltd is a trading company at the time of the disposal, the gain on the disposal of shares satisfies the requirements for the main exemption in paragraph 1 of Schedule 7AC TCGA 1992 and is thus exempt from corporation tax.

Example 10.2
Owner Ltd, a UK trading company, has owned 100% of Irish Ltd, a trading company resident in the RoI, for the last 10 years. Acquisition Ltd wishes to acquire Irish Ltd. This disposal by Owner Ltd will generate a profit of £5 million. Due to the availability of SSE, Owner Ltd will pay no corporation tax on this gain.

Conversely, if Owner Ltd incurred a capital loss on the disposal, this is not a qualifying capital loss for corporation tax purposes and is thus disregarded as a loss. As the company being sold is an Irish resident company, the Irish tax implications will need to be considered.

10.3 Method of Taxation

Where, for an accounting period, chargeable gains accrue to a company, the chargeable gain is calculated by comparing the gross sale proceeds, net of incidental costs of sale, with the allowable items of expenditure, to include the original cost of the asset (or the value at 31 March 1982 if held at that time and this is a higher amount), any enhancement expenditure and any incidental costs of acquisition.

As well as the allowable expenditure, a company may also deduct an "indexation allowance" against the allowable expenditure. This allowance is intended to reflect the "time value of money" associated with the allowable costs and is calculated by reference to the period of ownership up to the date of sale.

Indexation allowances for companies are frozen from 31 December 2017. Disposals of chargeable assets on or before this date still attract full indexation allowance; but for disposals on or after 1 January 2018, indexation allowance is only available on assets acquired before that date and is only calculated up to 31 December 2017 (see **Chapter 1, Section 1.9.2** for calculation of the allowance). Therefore, if a company acquires a chargeable asset on or after 1 January 2018, no indexation allowance will be available on its future disposal.

Note that when computing a company's chargeable gain, any **indexation allowance available cannot create or increase a loss**, i.e. the indexation allowance is limited to the amount required to reduce the gain to nil.

Example 10.3

X Ltd prepares accounts to 31 March each year. In the year ended 31 March 2020, the trading profit was £20,000. During that year, the company sold an asset for £17,000 which it had bought the previous year for £10,000. The indexation factor up to 31 December 2017 was a figure of 0.04. The company had a capital loss brought forward of £1,000.

X Ltd year ended 31 March 2020

	£	
Trading profit	20,000	
Chargeable gain (Note)	5,600	
Taxable total profits	25,600	
		£
£25,600 @ 19%		4,864
Note:		
Chargeable gain		
Proceeds		17,000
Cost	10,000	
Indexation (0.04 × £10,000)	400	
		(10,400)
Gain		6,600
Capital loss b/fwd		(1,000)
Chargeable gain		5,600

10.4 Capital Gains Group: Introduction

A company may be part of a group for capital gains purposes – a capital gains group. This can give important benefits to the companies within the group, namely that chargeable assets can be transferred from one group company to another without triggering a chargeable gain, i.e. on a no gain/no loss basis. There are several other benefits which are outlined later.

Companies are in a capital gains group where:

1. at each level, there is a 75% holding; and
2. the top company has an effective interest of at least 51% in the group companies.

The 75% definition is similar to the rules for group relief (see **Chapter 9**), but for capital gains group only 75% of the ordinary shares is needed and not 75% of distributable profits nor 75% of assets on a winding up.

The capital gains group regime also has slightly different rules for sub-subsidiaries. To be part of the group, the direct relationship must be at least 75%, but the indirect relationship need only be above 50%, i.e. at least 51% effective indirect control. In **Chapter 9** we saw that a company can be a member of more than one group for group relief of losses. However, a **company can only be a member of one capital gains group.**

The various reliefs available in a capital gains group can also apply to assets situated outside the UK and which are used in or for the purposes of a trade carried on in the UK **and** the company is a 75% subsidiary of a UK resident company.

Example 10.4

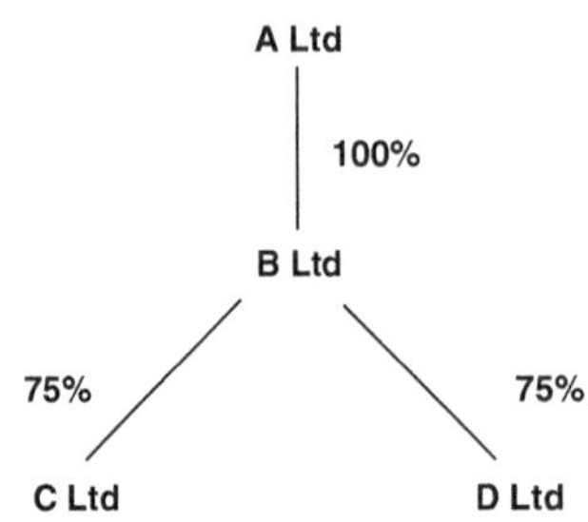

A, B, C and D form a capital gains group.

If A, C and D are UK resident and B is non-resident in the UK (and has no branch in the UK), A, B, C and D still form a capital gains group but the reliefs applying on transfer of assets between group members only apply to transfers between A, C and D. However, if B had a UK branch and if the asset **was** situated in the UK and used by the UK branch, then a transfer of the asset between B and A, C or D would qualify.

The distinction between a group for loss relief purposes and for capital gains purposes is that the top company **must have an effective** 75% direct or indirect interest for **group relief** purposes; whereas capital gains groups only require an effective 51% indirect interest, although direct relationships must be a minimum of 75%.

Example 10.5

X Ltd takes over 80% of the ordinary share capital of A Ltd. The new structure is as follows:

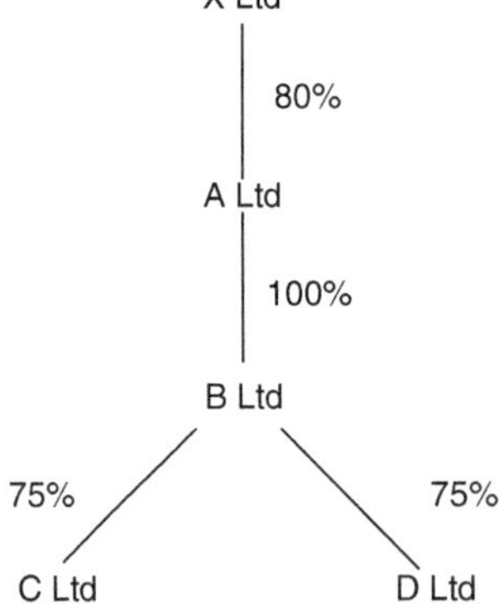

While X does not directly or indirectly own 75% of the ordinary share capital of C or D Ltd, all the companies X, A, B, C and D are members of the one capital gains group. This is because B, C and D are clearly 75% subsidiaries of A, and A itself is an effective 75% subsidiary of X. It should be noted, however, that all of the above companies do not form a single group for loss relief purposes, i.e. X, A, B, and A, B, C, D groups form separate groups for loss relief purposes, i.e. X is not common to both these groups.

A company can only be a member of one capital gains group. Where the conditions qualify so that it would appear that a company could be a member of two or more groups, it is the link to the principal company that determines to which group it belongs.

Example of group structures incorporating non-resident companies:

Example 10.6

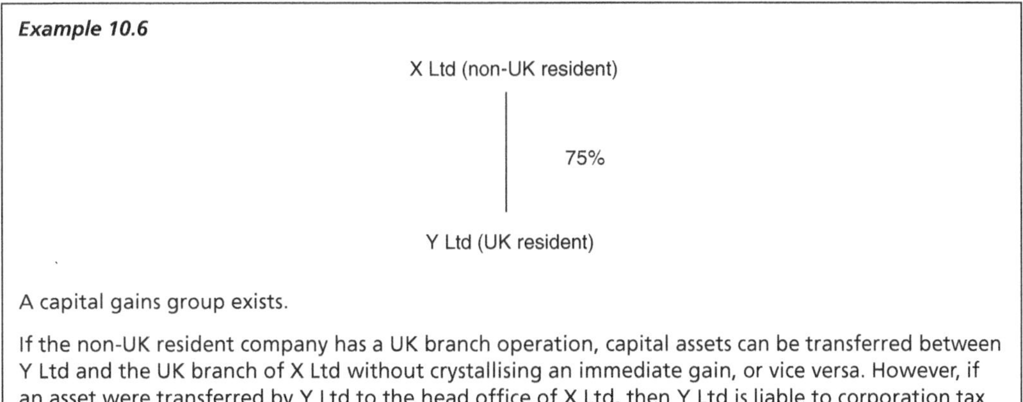

A capital gains group exists.

If the non-UK resident company has a UK branch operation, capital assets can be transferred between Y Ltd and the UK branch of X Ltd without crystallising an immediate gain, or vice versa. However, if an asset were transferred by Y Ltd to the head office of X Ltd, then Y Ltd is liable to corporation tax on its chargeable gain.

10.5 Disposal of Capital Assets within a Capital Gains Group

In general, a transfer of a chargeable asset from one member of the group to another is deemed to be for a consideration of such amount that neither a gain nor a loss accrues. This relief applies as a result of section 171 TCGA 1992.

The capital gains group is effectively treated as one taxpayer so that a chargeable gain does not arise until the asset is sold outside the group or the company holding the asset leaves the group.

Non-UK resident companies are included within a capital gains group and, provided there is no loss to HMRC, the no gain/no loss transfer is possible within a worldwide group of companies. For example, it may be possible to make a no gain/no loss transfer to a non-UK resident company with a branch or agency in the UK.

Example 10.7: UK-resident companies
X Ltd owns a building which it bought for £1 million, nine months ago. It disposes of it to its parent Y Ltd when it is worth £1.525 million. Indexation allowance is a figure of 0.225. Therefore, a gain of £0.3 million arose.

Normally this gain would be included in the profits of X Ltd. However, the section 171 rule ensures that the asset moves at no gain/no loss, i.e. its indexed cost of £1.225 million.

Consequently, X Ltd has no chargeable gain and Y Ltd's base cost is £1.225 million.

Relief for transfers of chargeable assets between capital gains group companies (UK to UK only) is granted automatically and is compulsory. Therefore an election is not required.

10.5.1 Capital Losses

As denoted in **Chapter 9**, capital losses cannot be included in a group relief surrender. However, under section 171A TCGA 1992, members of a capital gains group can elect for the chargeable gain or capital loss arising on disposal of an asset that is sold outside the group to be treated as if it had been transferred (either wholly or partially) between them immediately before its "outside" disposal. In this situation, the chargeable gain or allowable loss (either wholly or partially transferred) is deemed to belong to the transferee company.

A section 171A election must be made within two years of the end of the accounting period in which the disposal took place and can be for a percentage of the transaction if required. Partial transfers of gains or losses are therefore possible. Only current-year chargeable gains or capital losses can be transferred under this election.

The objective of this election is to ensure that capital losses or other losses arising in capital gains group companies fully, or partially, mitigate the gain arising, and that no company in the group is unnecessarily exposed to the instalment payment rules. This would be beneficial in circumstances where the transferee company had capital losses of its own (either carried forward or in the same period) which are unused and which would be available for offset against the deemed chargeable gain transferred under a section 171A election.

10.5.2 Pre-entry Losses

In the past, companies that anticipated a future gain on the disposal of an asset would acquire a company with capital losses forward. The asset with the gain would be transferred, before the sale, into the company with the losses forward so that the losses forward could be used to shelter the gain.

The term 'pre-entry losses' refers to losses accruing to the company on actual disposals of chargeable assets before entry to a group which triggered a capital loss. Anti-avoidance provisions prevent the use of pre-entry losses. While the provision ensures that these losses cannot be used subsequently by a group that had no previous commercial connection with the company when those losses accrued, that company will be allowed to use those losses itself in the same way that it could have had it never entered the group.

Pre-entry losses that actually accrued to the company before it joined the group can be set against:

1. gains on assets disposed of after entry but which were held by the company before entry;
2. a gain arising on the disposal of an asset that was acquired from a non-group member and which has been used for the purpose of the company's trade; or
3. gains on assets disposed of before joining the group.

Post-entry losses can be offset under the normal rules.

10.5.3 Rollover Relief

Provided certain conditions are fulfilled, a company may claim that a chargeable gain arising on the disposal of a business asset (the "old asset") may be "rolled over" against the cost of acquiring a replacement business asset (the "new asset").

In this scenario, the disposal of the old asset is deemed to give rise to neither a gain nor loss, and the cost of the new asset is reduced by the actual gain that would have arisen but for the rollover relief. In essence, the chargeable gain is "deferred" until such time as the new asset is disposed of (subject to the possibility of a further rollover claim being available).

Full rollover relief is only available provided **all of the disposal proceeds** (not just the chargeable gain) are applied in acquiring the new asset. Any proceeds not reinvested fall to be taxed immediately (provided the amount retained is less than the gain) and the cost of the new asset is reduced by the amount of the gain that was not immediately chargeable.

The conditions which must be satisfied in order for a company to make a rollover claim are:

1. both the old and new asset must be within one of the qualifying classes of assets but do not need to fall within the same category (see below);
2. the old asset must have been used only for trade purposes throughout the period of ownership and the new asset must be used only for trade purposes; and

3. the new asset must be acquired during the period beginning one year before and ending three years after the date of disposal of the old asset.

The classes of assets include, *inter alia*:

(a) land, buildings and fixed plant and machinery;
(b) ships, aircraft and hovercraft;
(c) satellites, space stations and spacecraft;

However, for companies (unlike individuals), the list does **not** include **goodwill** or **quotas** as these assets are incorporated within the intangible assets regime for companies. Rollover relief and group rollover for intangible fixed assets is dealt with in **Chapter 2**.

10.5.4 Holdover Relief

Where the new asset is a "depreciating asset" (an asset with an expected life of 60 years or less at the time of acquisition), the chargeable gain arising on the disposal of the old asset **cannot** be rolled over and is **not** deducted from the cost of the new asset. Instead, the chargeable gain is "held over" or "temporarily deferred" until it becomes chargeable (crystallises) on the earliest of the following three dates:

1. the date on which the new asset is disposed of;
2. the date on which the new asset ceases to be used in the trade; or
3. the 10th anniversary of the acquisition of the new asset.

The most common types of depreciating assets (which are also qualifying assets for rollover relief purposes) are fixed plant and machinery, and leases where the term of the lease is for 60 years or less. It should be noted that, if a company were to purchase a non-depreciating asset (within the relevant class) prior to the expiration of the earliest of the above three dates, then it could "convert" the temporary "held-over" gain into a "rolled-over" gain by making a claim to do so.

Rollover relief is also available within a capital gains group. If a group member disposes of an asset which is eligible for capital gains rollover (or indeed, holdover) relief, then it can treat all the group members as a single entity for claiming such relief (provided, of course, that all relevant conditions are met).

Thus, if other group members acquire a relevant asset within the qualifying period (one year before the disposal or three years afterwards) then the company making the disposal may match the acquisition for rollover/holdover relief purposes. For it to be effective, both the acquiring company and the disposing company must make the claim.

It should be noted that assets transferred intragroup on a no gain/no loss basis **are not available** to be matched for rollover/holdover relief purposes. See **Chapter 19** for more on rollover relief. Note that rollover relief in the context of a company is deducted **after** deducting any available indexation allowance.

10.6 Disposal of Capital Assets Outside the Group

If there is a disposal of an asset by a member of a group to a person outside the group, and the asset had been acquired by the company making the disposal from another group member, then the period of ownership for the purpose of calculating indexation allowance is arrived at **by reference to the length of time the asset had been owned by the group as a whole.** Of course, if the asset had originally been acquired prior to 31 March 1982, then either the original cost or the market value at that date will form the base cost for indexation purposes. Indexation will run from 1 April 1982 to the date of sale, but is only available up to 31 December 2017 for assets disposed of on or after that date.

Example 10.8

A Ltd and Y Ltd are UK resident members of a capital gains group. Both companies prepare accounts to 31 December each year. Y Ltd acquired an asset in 1973 at a cost of £10,000 and transferred it to A Ltd in August 1985. On 31 December 2019, A Ltd sold the asset to a non-group company for £200,000. The market value of the asset at 31 March 1982 was £60,000. Indexation factor is 1.80 up to 31 December 2017.

When the asset was disposed of by Y Ltd to A Ltd in 1985, no gain arose to Y Ltd (i.e. it transferred under the no gain/no loss rules).

A Ltd has a disposal in the year ended 31 December 2019 of an asset with a base cost of £60,000 (i.e. 31 March 1982 valuation as this is higher).

Computation of A Ltd's liability

	£	£
Proceeds		200,000
Base cost (market value at 31/03/1982)	60,000	
Indexed @ 1.80 (up to 31 December 2017 only)	108,000	
		(168,000)
Chargeable gain		32,000

10.7 Company Leaving Group: Anti-avoidance Measure

Where a company ceases to be a member of a group of companies within six years of an intragroup transfer, and at that time still owns that asset, a capital gain or loss may arise. This is known as a degrouping charge.

The chargeable gain is calculated by deeming that the asset was, in effect, sold and immediately reacquired by the company leaving the group at its market value at the time of its original acquisition from the other member of the group, i.e. **the gain (or loss) arising on the original transfer between the group members is triggered.** Indexation allowance is applied by reference to that date and not by reference to the date the company actually leaves the group. While the gain is calculated as at the date of the original intragroup transfer, it is not charged on the company leaving the group, but on the company selling the shares in the accounting period in which the company leaves the group. The cost of future disposals of the asset in question by the company leaving the group will, of course, be the market value attributed to the earlier transfer.

Rollover relief cannot be claimed on such degrouping gains.

Where a company leaves a group as a result of a disposal of shares by a group company, any degrouping charge is made by way of an adjustment to the consideration taken into account for calculating the gain or loss on the disposal of shares. A consequence of this is that any exemption or relief that may apply to the share disposal, such as the substantial shareholdings exemption, will also apply to the degrouping charge.

No chargeable gains degrouping charge is made in respect of an asset that has been transferred between two companies belonging to the same sub-group, if those companies leave the group together.

Section 171A TCGA 1992 (election to re-allocate gain or loss to another member of the group) can also apply to a standalone degrouping gain or loss if this has not been exempted by the SSE.

Example 10.9

Groups Ltd acquired a freehold property for £100,000 in 1991. In December 2013, when the market value of the property was £460,000 and indexation to date was £26,000, Groups Ltd transferred the property to it's 100% subsidiary, Just Ltd, for £375,000. Just Ltd leaves the group on 1 June 2019. Both companies prepare accounts to 31 July.

Calculate the chargeable gains arising in respect of the above transactions. Assume Groups Ltd cannot claim the substantial shareholdings exemption on the disposal of Just Ltd's shares.

Solution

2013: No chargeable gain arises as the transfer was to another group member on a no gain/no loss basis.

2019: Gain on Groups Ltd would be calculated as:

	£	£
Gross proceeds (market value)		460,000
Cost	100,000	
Indexation	26,000	
		126,000
Chargeable gain		334,000

This is chargeable on Groups Ltd in the year ended 31 July 2019. Note that £375,000 paid by Just Ltd is irrelevant; full market value must be used as the companies were connected at the date of the original transaction. The degrouping charge is added to the proceeds that Groups Ltd receives for the sale of Just Ltd's shares. As the substantial shareholdings exemption is not available, the degrouping chargeable gain is subject to corporation tax at 19%, being the corporation tax rate for the accounting period ended 31 July 2019.

Questions

Review Questions

(See Suggested Solutions to Review Questions at the end of this textbook.)

Question 10.1

It is April 2024 and a longstanding client comes into your office to discuss a proposed transaction. Paul Kelly is the managing director of Kelly Cars Group Limited, a UK company that acquired 100% of the shares in Kelly Luxury Cars GmbH in 2005. Kelly Luxury Cars GmbH is a German company specialising in sourcing and importing luxury cars from Europe for wealthy customers. Both companies have always been trading companies.

Kelly Cars Group Limited sold 95% of the shares of Kelly Luxury Cars GmbH on 25 June 2019 for a significant profit. The new owners of Kelly Luxury Cars GmbH converted the company to an investment company when they bought the shares.

Kelly Cars Group Limited held on to the remaining 5% of the shares for sentimental reasons. However, the company has now been approached by the same buyers and is in negotiations to sell the remaining 5% by the end of May 2024.

Requirement

Explain, with supporting analysis, whether the sale of the 95% shareholding in Kelly Luxury Cars GmbH in June 2019 qualified for the substantial shareholdings exemption (SSE). Advise whether the sale of the remaining 5% (for a profit) in May 2024 will qualify for SSE.

If the remaining 5% is to be sold at a loss, consider what recommendation you might make to the company.

Question 10.2

You are a tax senior in a mid-sized Belfast practice. One of the clients recently assigned to you is the Solar Group. Solar is a trading company that has four wholly-owned trading subsidiaries – Neptune Ltd, Venus Ltd, Saturn Ltd and Mercury Ltd. At a recent meeting with the managing director you discussed the group's tax affairs. The managing director is keen for the group's corporation tax affairs to be finalised as soon as possible and is anxious to know what the group's liability is for the year ended 31 March 2020. All companies in the group prepare accounts to 31 March and none paid tax in instalments in 2019.

During the year ended 31 March 2020, Solar and its subsidiaries had the following results:

- Solar made a trading profit of £67,550 and has unused capital losses carried forward from earlier years of £200,000.
- Neptune made a trading profit of £47,087. At 31 March 2017 it had trade losses available to carry forward of £75,000.
- Venus made a trading profit of £72,680 and also made a chargeable gain of £55,260. At 31 March 2019 it had capital losses to carry forward of £47,000.
- Saturn made a trading profit of £112,559, as adjusted for tax purposes, before deducting capital allowances. The capital allowances for the period are £29,766.
- Mercury made a trading loss of £9,236 before deducting capital allowances of £37,257. At 31 March 2017, the company had trade losses available to carry forward of £27,073.

You have been provided with the following additional information:

1. It is the intention to sell Saturn and an offer of £300,000 has been received from an interested party, Y Ltd. It is almost certain that this offer will be accepted within the next week. Y Ltd intends to inject additional funding into Saturn to assist them in purchasing additional freehold property and fixed plant and machinery and so expand Saturn's trade.

   The original cost of Solar's investment in Saturn in June 1997 was £55,000. Indexation allowance from 1997 to 31 December 2017 is 65%. The principal assets of Saturn are its freehold property and goodwill which has been created over a number of years. The property was originally bought by Solar in 1981 for £40,000 and transferred to Saturn in March 2015 when its value was £230,000.

   Its current value is £350,000 and, in March 1982, the property was worth £50,000. Indexation allowance from 1981–2015 is 100%, from 1982–2015 is 107% and from 1982 to 31 December 2017 is 122%.
2. Due to Neptune's continued expansion, it requires larger business premises. Solar therefore plans to transfer to Neptune a suitable freehold property that it no longer requires and which it currently rents out. If sold to an unconnected third party, a capital gain of £100,000 would arise.

   Neptune, in turn, proposes to sell the property it currently occupies outside the group. This property was acquired from Solar 10 years ago. X Ltd, an unconnected third party, has been identified as a possible purchaser. A capital gain of approximately £250,000 will be realised from the sale.
3. As part of the future marketing strategy of the group it has been decided to acquire a new company, Mars Ltd. Mars has significant trading losses, in excess of £500,000, which are proving attractive to the Solar Group. The board intends to focus on substantially different products aimed at new customer types and markets.

Requirement

The board of directors would like you to draft a report providing information on the following specific areas:

(a) The group's corporation tax liability for the year ended 31 March 2020, making use of all available claims and elections and advising on the due date for payment of any tax liabilities arising.

(b) Advice in relation to the tax implications of the proposed sale of shares in Saturn, in particular:
   (i) the amount of the capital gain arising in respect of the sale of Solar's shareholding in Saturn and whether the substantial shareholdings exemption will be available;
   (ii) any other tax implications arising from Saturn leaving the group.

(c) Advice in relation to the proposed transfer of the freehold property from Solar to Neptune and the sale by Neptune of its current property, in particular:
   (i) the tax implications arising out of the proposed transfer as part of Neptune's expansion plans;
   (ii) mitigating the gain arising on the sale of Neptune's property.

(d) Acquisition of Mars – advise the board on the availability for relief after acquisition of the trading losses that exist in this company.

11

Transfer Pricing

Learning Objectives

After studying this chapter you will understand:

- The aim of the transfer pricing rules.
- The situations in which the rules apply.
- Important exemptions in the legislation.
- How advance pricing agreements can be used to agree the arm's-length basis of transactions with HMRC.
- An overview of the methods adopted to establish an arm's length price.
- The administrative aspects of the rules.

11.1 Introduction

Transfer pricing often occurs in transactions between connected businesses where the price does not reflect the true commercial cost of the transaction. In other words, the transaction price is not at arm's length, i.e. the agreed price is not the same or similar to that which it would have been if the transaction had taken place between unrelated parties. This can give an unfair tax advantage to the connected parties, which the UK transfer pricing legislation seeks to prevent by adjusting the tax computation of the advantaged party.

The OECD publishes transfer pricing guidelines that set out different methods of calculating prices consistent with the arm's length principle. The UK's transfer pricing legislation, which is contained in the Taxation (International and Other Provisions) Act 2010, makes reference to these principles.

11.2 The Basic Rule

The basic rule is that where there is a non-arm's length transaction between two parties and either one of the parties or an individual connected to one of the parties was "directly or indirectly participating in the management, control or capital" of the other party then, for tax purposes, the transaction is considered to have been made at arm's length. This is sometimes referred to as the 'participation test' and seeks to remove any UK tax advantage.

Such transactions are not restricted to intercompany sales or purchases of goods/services. As a result, transfer pricing adjustments can be made in relation to common intercompany transactions such as management charges, royalty payments, corporate intangibles (e.g. patents) and loan relationships. The rules do not apply, however, to chargeable assets for capital gains tax purposes.

The rules also apply irrespective of the geographic location of the parties involved, meaning that transactions within the UK as well as cross-border transactions are caught. In reality, the rules impact less on transactions within the UK as the parties will usually pay the same rate of corporation tax. However, transfer pricing adjustments still need to be considered as any adjustments could result in a company being exposed to the instalment payment rules for corporation tax.

The transfer pricing rules only require adjustments to be made in the relevant tax calculations, i.e. the corporation tax computation and return. This means that the parties involved can charge what they wish in their financial statements, although financial reporting standards may require a related party disclosure.

11.2.1 Key Definitions

The key terms referred to in the transfer pricing rules are:

- direct participation – in the control of a company or a partnership;
- indirect participation – when a person has:
  - future rights to control;
  - rights are being exercised under their instruction or for their benefit; or
  - they are major participants in the company.
- major participants – two people in control of a company, each with at least 40% share of rights in the company.
- control – the power to direct the company by means of shareholdings (generally at least 51%), voting power or powers conferred by documents regulating the company. The participation test can therefore be applied to cases where one company controls another, or both companies are controlled by the same person(s). It can also apply in the case of joint ventures where the 40% test is met.
- connected persons – includes spouses/civil partners, siblings, lineal descendants (children, grandchildren, etc.). It also extends to relatives (siblings and lineal descendants) of spouses and spouses of relatives.

11.3 UK Tax Advantage

A transfer pricing adjustment is only made where, as a result of a non-arm's length transaction (or series of transactions), a UK tax advantage has been gained. This tax advantage is considered to have arisen if either:

1. a **lower** non-arm's length transaction price is taken into account in calculating the chargeable profits, i.e. taxable profits are reduced; or
2. a **higher** non-arm's length transaction price is taken into account in calculating any losses, i.e. a larger loss results or a loss is created.

Cross-border transactions, where one of the parties is not subject to UK tax, can often result in a UK tax advantage. However, as set out earlier, transactions within the UK can also result in a tax advantage.

11.4 Corresponding Adjustments

Non-arm's length transactions that result in a UK tax advantage mean that one party has reduced its UK tax liability, while the other may have paid more tax than they would have done if an arm's length price had been paid. If the disadvantaged party is also UK tax resident and has paid more UK income or corporation tax than it would otherwise have had, a claim can be made for the arm's length price to be used in computing its taxable profits. This adjustment is known as a 'corresponding' (or compensating) adjustment.

Claims for corresponding adjustments must be made to HMRC within two years after the potentially advantaged party has filed its relevant tax return showing the transfer pricing adjustment.

Example 11.1
X Ltd sells goods to its Y Ltd at a price of £250 per unit. The arm's length price would have been £380. During the accounting period ended 31 March 2020, X Ltd sold 10,000 of these items to Y Ltd.

A transfer pricing adjustment is made on the basis that the arm's length price was received. As a result, X Ltd's taxable income for corporation tax is increased by £1,300,000 (10,000 × £130) and any profit is increased (or a loss reduced or turned into a profit). X Ltd has gained a tax advantage as its profit was originally understated. Y Ltd is the disadvantaged party.

Y Ltd can adjust its allowable expenditure, increasing it by £1,300,000 to reflect the arm's length price. The difference in its calculation of taxable profits or losses is the corresponding adjustment, meaning either a lower profit (or a profit turned into a loss or a higher loss).

X Ltd is therefore taxed as if it had received £380 for each item and Y Ltd is taxed as if it had paid £380.

11.5 Exemptions

There are important exemptions in the legislation for dormant companies and small- and medium-sized enterprises (as defined).

11.5.1 Dormant Companies

From 1 April 2004, companies that were dormant, either for the whole of an accounting period that ends on 31 March 2004 or for the three months ending on 31 March 2004, are exempt from the transfer pricing requirements as long as they continue being dormant.

11.5.2 Small and Medium-sized Companies

In general, small or medium-sized enterprises are exempt from the transfer pricing rules. (There are exceptions to this rule, but these are beyond the scope of this textbook.) The rules follow the EU definition of small and medium-sized, namely:

- less than 250 employees, and either:
  - less than €50 million turnover; or
  - less than €43 million balance sheet total.

Note that this definition of SME differs to its definition for the purpose of the SME R&D tax relief regime (see **Chapter 2**).

11.6 Advance Pricing Agreements

Transfer pricing adjustments are part of the UK's corporation tax self-assessment regime. It is therefore each company's responsibility to ensure that all transfer pricing adjustments are made when calculating its corporation tax position for an accounting period. If the necessary adjustments are not made or are made incorrectly, this can result in interest on late payment or underpayment of corporation tax, and/or penalties for errors and omissions. To mitigate against this possibility, companies can enter into an advance pricing agreement (APA) with HMRC. APAs usually cover complex cross-border transactions.

An application for an APA must be made in writing to HMRC and should set out the transactions to be covered, the basis for needing a transfer pricing adjustment and how the company has calculated the arm's length price and proposes to deal with these transactions.

11.7 Transfer Pricing Methods

As noted at the outset, the UK legislation specifically refers to the OECD's guidelines when calculating prices in line with the arm's length principle. Two methods are proposed:

1. traditional transaction methods; and
2. transactional profit split methods

The OECD's guidelines also contain guidance on how to select the most appropriate transfer pricing method according to the circumstances of the case. The detail of these methods is beyond the scope of this textbook.

11.8 Administrative Issues

11.8.1 Record-keeping

It is the responsibility of the company to retain all records and documents relating to the transfer pricing, e.g. communications and agreements between parties, tax computations, adjustments and so on.

11.8.2 Penalties

If a company does not retain the appropriate records and documents, a penalty of up to £3,000 can be charged.

If the transfer prices are found to not be at arm's length and the company's behaviour is held to have been careless or deliberate in setting a non-arm's length price, a penalty can be charged for an incorrect return (see **Chapter 1**).

Example 11.2: HMRC example
A group of companies charge a service charge of 8% for services provided between them. HMRC determine that it should have been 12%–16%. The company cannot show that they considered whether 8% was arm's length, or there is documentation that states that 8% is arm's length without any supporting evidence. A penalty would arise.

Question

Review Question

(See Suggested Solution to Review Questions at the end of this textbook.)

Question 11.1

Shane Delaney has been in business for over 40 years running his 100%-owned company, Delaney Electrics (UK) Ltd (Delaney UK), which provides electrical engineering services to some major clients in the public and private sector. Delaney UK is not an SME under the EU definition for transfer pricing. Shane also holds 100% of the shares in an Irish resident trading company, Delaney Electrics (Ireland) Ltd (Delaney Ireland), which was set up to tender for Irish public sector contracts and which also provides electrical engineering consultancy services to clients of Delaney UK and Delaney Ireland.

The statement of profit or loss for Delaney UK, for the accounting period ended 31 March 2020, is outlined below.

Delaney UK had total trading income of £500,000 and property income of £67,000 in the 18-month accounting period ended 31 March 2019.

Shane has decided that on 31 March 2022, Delaney UK will cease to trade. As the business is being run down in the period up to its cessation, Delaney UK is projected to have the following results in the next two 12-month accounting periods:

Accounting period	**31 March 2021**	**31 March 2022**
Adjusted trading (loss)/profit	£ 60,000	(£ 1,792,000)
Property income	£ 75,000	-
Interest received	£ 70,000	-
Chargeable gains	£ 175,000	-

Delaney Electrics (UK) Ltd
Statement of Profit or Loss for the year ended 31 March 2020

	Note	**£**	**£**
Turnover			7,145,000
Cost of sales	1		(4,754,500)
Gross profit			2,390,500
Operating expenses:			
Wages and salaries	2	1,272,456	
Legal and professional fees	3	25,400	
Depreciation	1	155,250	
Amortisation	4	12,000	
Repairs and maintenance	5	34,222	
Insurance	6	25,780	
Rent and rates		145,000	
Audit fees		16,500	

Taxation compliance fees		15,450	
Bad debts	7	49,000	
Bank charges		2,150	
Sundry expenses	8	25,222	
			(1,778,430)
Other income and expenses:			
Rental income	9	40,000	
Dividend income	10	60,000	
Profit on disposal of patent	11	185,000	
Management charge	12	100,000	
Bank interest payable	13	(28,245)	
			356,755
Profit before tax			**968,825**

Notes:

1. Cost of sales includes depreciation of £25,000, which relates to plant and machinery bought under finance lease agreements.
2. Wages and salaries include a payment of £23,000 to a former manager of the company. £6,000 of this was a statutory redundancy payment, while £17,000 was an ex-gratia payment. The manager worked in a division of the company that closed in December 2019. He was the only employee of this division made redundant as he was not happy to move to another division of the company.
3. Legal and professional fees include:

Fees re. HMRC corporation tax enquiry (Note 8)	£3,559
Legal fees re. case against supplier for faulty goods	£12,500
Legal fees re. issue with tenants of leased commercial premises (Note 9)	£5,000

4. Company policy is to amortise goodwill over a 10-year period. The goodwill was originally acquired in 2016.
5. Repairs and maintenance include:
   (a) Repairs to plumbing and heating system in commercial premises costing £3,465 (see Note 9);
   (b) Extending the trading premises of the company – building new staff bathrooms, changing areas and showers costing £20,000.
6. Insurance includes:

Keyman insurance policy – the policy is in respect of Shane's wife who is not employed by the company	£6,200
Public liability insurance	£5,500
Insurance for leased-out commercial premises (see Note 9)	£2,375
Insurance for directors' motor vehicles owned by company	£3,300

7. At the end of the accounting period, the general provision for bad debts was £20,000 (31 March 2019: £30,000). The remainder of the bad debt provision is calculated in accordance with IFRS.
8. The following amounts are included within 'other expenses':
   (a) Penalties following the closure of the HMRC enquiry of £3,500. Corporation tax interest payable to HMRC following the closure of the enquiry of £2,500;
   (b) New division opening party and gifts totalling £2,045. The total cost of the new division opening party includes:
      - £500 for drinks and food for customers and suppliers;
      - £500 to a local celebrity to sing at the event
      - £1,045 in gifts of branded hoodies to suppliers and customers. Each branded gift cost £35.
   (c) Motor lease charges paid in respect of two BMW cars during the year ended 31 March 2020. The details of each lease are outlined below:

	Lease cost	**CO_2 emissions (g/km)**	**Date of lease**
BMW 5 Series	£5,500	108	1 October 2018
BMW 6 Series Coupe	£7,650	148	1 November 2017

9. Rental income is received in respect of the lease of commercial property to an unconnected company.
10. The dividend income was received from ordinary shares in an Irish company. Delaney UK is not a small company for the purpose of the dividend exemption rules.
11. The company sold patent rights used in its trade for £260,000 in December 2019; it had been bought for £150,000 in October 2011. By the time of their sale, these patent rights had been written down to £75,000. In July 2019 the company bought copyrights for use in its trade for £290,000.
12. The management income of £100,000 was received from Delaney Ireland for cross-referrals of clients from Delaney UK. The income did not take into account commission payable by Delaney Ireland to Delaney UK, which would have made the arm's length price £200,000.
13. The bank loan interest is payable on a bank overdraft used for working capital requirements of the company.
14. Capital allowances for the year ended 31 March 2020 are £92,324.

Requirement

(a) Calculate the taxable total profits, before any potential claim for loss relief, for Delaney Electrics (UK) Limited for the year ended 31 March 2020.
    Provide a brief explanation as to why an adjustment does or does not arise in calculating the total taxable profits in respect of **each** of the items referred to in Notes 1–13 (inclusive). Assume the company makes all beneficial claims and elections to mitigate or defer corporation tax where necessary.

(b) Using the projected results for 2021 and 2022, calculate the revised taxable total profits of Delaney Electrics (UK) Limited for the 2019–2021 accounting periods inclusive, and briefly explain how the projected trading loss arising in 2022 is used.

12

Taxation of Directors/Shareholders

Learning Objectives

After studying this chapter you will understand:

- The calculation of tax for company directors as a direct result of holding a directorship.
- The different ways of extracting cash from a company and the tax implications for both the company and the recipient.

12.1 Introduction

Many UK companies, particularly in Northern Ireland, are family-owned and managed. In family companies, the directors are also likely to be shareholders. As a consequence, directors of family companies often have control over their own remuneration packages and should consider the tax effects of such packages on both the company and on themselves.

Legislation is in place to prevent directors from arranging their remuneration in such a way as to avoid taxation. One example of this is in relation to National Insurance contributions (NICs). Class 1 NICs are calculated by reference to the earnings period. This means that an employee in receipt of a monthly salary has their NICs calculated for each month in isolation (in contrast to the calculation of their income tax liability, which is carried out on a cumulative basis).

Example 12.1

Rhonda's gross monthly salary for 2019/20 is £2,000. In March 2020, she receives a bonus of £5,000 on top of her normal salary. The primary Class 1 NICs are calculated as follows:

April 2019 – February 2020	£
Gross salary	2,000
Less: primary threshold	(719)
Earnings on which NICs are due	1,281
Class 1 NICs due @ 12%	154

Monthly NICs liability for the 11 months from April to February is, therefore, £154. So the total for the period is £154 × 11 = £1,694.

continued overleaf

March 2020

	£
Gross salary	2,000
Bonus	5,000
Total earnings for period	7,000
Class 1 NICs due (£4,167 – £719) @ 12%	414
Class 1 NICs due (£7,000 – £4,167) @ 2%	57
Total Class 1 NICs due	471

Rhonda's total annual NICs are therefore £1,694 + £471 = £2,165

As can be seen from this example, Rhonda's NIC liability in March 2020 is increased as the gross earnings for that period are in excess of the upper earnings limit for the month of £4,167. This is an area that could be exploited by directors with control over their remuneration – they could structure their salary in such a way as to utilise the upper earnings limit to restrict their exposure to primary Class 1 NICs.

For this reason, directors are subject to the **annual** earnings basis for the purposes of calculating their primary Class 1 NICs liability. This has the effect of calculating their NICs on a cumulative basis, so that they only benefit from the lower 2% rate of NICs when their total annual salary (including bonuses and other similar payments) exceeds the upper earnings limit.

Example 12.2
Using the same details as Example 12.1, this time assume Rhonda is a director and so subject to the annual earnings basis. The primary Class 1 NICs are calculated as follows:

April 2019 – March 2020

	£
Gross annual salary (£2,000 × 12)	24,000
Bonus in March 2020	5,000
Total annual earnings	29,000
Less: primary threshold	(8,632)
Earnings on which NICs are due	20,368
Class 1 NICs due @ 12%	2,444

Note: none of the earnings have been charged at 2% as the annual earnings are less than the annual upper earnings limit of £50,000. As a result, the total NICs charge for the year has been increased by £279.

12.2 Tax on Remuneration

As stated above, when a director who is also a shareholder of a company is planning their own remuneration strategy, they will want to consider the taxation impact on both the company and themselves. There is no point in saving £3,000 in income tax on profits extracted if the company is exposed to an additional corporation tax liability of £5,000 as a result.

The first consideration when developing a remuneration strategy is the level of profits to be extracted. It may be more tax-efficient to retain most of the profits within the company, where they will be subject to corporation tax at a maximum rate of 19%, rather than extracting them and exposing them to income tax at rates of up to 45% before any National Insurance cost is considered.

Income tax rates and bands are an annual tax and can be revised annually. Also, if profits are retained this will increase the value of the company, and so the value of the shareholdings in the company. This will increase any chargeable gain on the future disposal of those shares, but such a disposal may qualify for entrepreneurs' relief (see **Chapter 18**) and/or be exposed to lower CGT rates than if an extraction was made now, which could be taxed at up to 47% (45% income tax plus 2% NICs).

However, it will be the case that most directors will need to extract some level of profit to fund their living expenses; the rest of this section will consider the various ways in which this may be achieved.

12.2.1 Salary or Dividend

When profits are extracted by way of salary, NICs will be charged at the secondary rate (currently 13.8%) on the company and at the primary rate (currently 12%) on the recipient (2% on earnings in excess of the upper earnings limit). The recipient will also be exposed to income tax at up to 45% of the gross salary. The total cost of the salary, i.e. gross salary plus secondary NICs, will be an allowable deduction for corporation tax purposes.

When profits are extracted by way of dividends, no NICs are payable by either the company or the recipient. Income tax is restricted to a maximum of 38.1% after deducting the available level of the £2,000 dividend allowance that applies to the first £2,000 of dividend income received. However, dividends are not an allowable deduction for corporation tax purposes, as they must be paid out of the distributable reserves of the company.

Therefore, when determining the most tax-efficient method of profit extraction, the effect of corporation tax and NICs must be considered. As dividends are not deductible for corporation tax purposes, this means that they are not automatically more tax-efficient than salary payments.

Example 12.3

Rory is the director/shareholder of Mill Ltd. The company's taxable profit for the year ended 31 March 2020 is £600,000 and Rory would like to extract £50,000 by way of either a bonus or dividend. Rory's salary from the company is £150,000 in the 2019/20 tax year. (*Note:* no personal allowance is available to Rory as his income is in excess of £125,000). Rory receives no other dividends.

Extraction by way of bonus:

Mill Ltd		£	£
Profits			600,000
Less: remuneration (Note 1)			(50,000)
Taxable total profits (TTP)			550,000
Corporation tax:	£550,000 @ 19%		(104,500)
Profits after tax			445,500
Secondary NICs	£43,937 @ 13.8%	6,063	
Total tax charge		110,563	

continued overleaf

Rory			
Gross salary			43,937
Primary Class 1 NICs	£43,937 @ 2%	879	
Income tax	£43,937 @ 45%	19,772	
Total tax/NICs		20,651	(20,651)
Income after tax			23,286
Total tax		131,214	
Effective rate of tax	(£131,214/£600,000) × 100		21.87%
Extraction by way of dividend:			
Mill Ltd			
TTP			600,000
Corporation tax:	£600,000 @ 19%		(114,000)
Total tax charge			
Profits after tax			486,000
Profits after dividend	£486,000 − £50,000		436,000
Rory			
Gross dividend		50,000	
Less: dividend allowance		(2,000)	
Taxable dividend		48,000	
Income tax @ 38.1%		18,288	(18,288)
Income after tax			31,712
Total tax		132,288	

The effective rate of tax ((£132,288/£600,000) × 100) is 22.05%

Note:

1. This amount includes the gross salary of the director together with the employer's secondary NIC (13.8%). To calculate the gross salary, this needs to be divided by 113.8 and multiplied by 100. Therefore, £50,000 x 100/113.8, i.e. £43,937.

As can be seen in **Example 12.3**, because corporation tax is 19% and the rate of income tax is 38.1% for an additional rate taxpayer, the effective rate of tax between dividends and salary/bonus is very close, especially when dealing with an additional rate taxpayer.

Example 12.4

Thomas is the director/shareholder of Soap Ltd. The company's taxable profit for the year ended 31 March 2020 is £300,000 and Thomas would like to extract £40,000 by way of either a bonus or dividend. Thomas's salary from the company is £50,000 for the 2019/20 tax year and he receives no other dividends.

Extraction by way of bonus:

Soap Ltd		£	£
Profits			300,000
Less: remuneration			(40,000)
TTP			260,000
Corporation tax	£260,000 @ 19%	49,400	(49,400)
Profits after tax			210,600
Secondary NICs	£35,149 @ 13.8%	4,851	
Total tax charge		54,251	
Thomas			
Gross salary			35,149
Primary Class 1 NICs	£35,149 @ 2%	703	
Income tax	£35,149 @ 40%	14,060	
Total tax/NICs		14,763	(14,763)
Income after tax			20,386
Total tax		69,014	
Retained profits			228,386
Effective rate of tax	(£69,014/£300,000) × 100		23.00%

Extraction by way of dividend:

Soap Ltd			
TTP			300,000
Corporation tax	£300,000 @ 19%	57,000	(57,000)
Profits after tax			243,000
Profits after dividend	£243,000 – £40,000		203,000
Thomas			
Gross dividend		40,000	
Less: dividend allowance		(2,000)	
Taxable dividend		38,000	
Income tax @ 32.5%		12,350	(12,350)
Income after tax			27,650
Total tax		69,350	

The effective rate of tax ((£69,350/£300,000) × 100) is 23.12%.

As can be seen from the above examples, it is necessary to carry out detailed calculations to determine the most tax-efficient method. This is especially important where income straddles tax rate bands, where an individual may be exposed to the high-income child benefit charge, or where a loss of personal allowances is possible if income exceeds £100,000. The following should also be considered:

1. Dividends are not earnings and so the level of tax-relievable pension contributions that a director may make will be restricted if their remuneration is mainly in the form of dividends (contributions of up to £3,600 may be made irrespective of earnings). It may be possible to reduce the impact of this restriction on the growth of a pension pot by making a company contribution on behalf of the director. Indeed, this can be a very tax-efficient form of remuneration for directors/shareholders of family companies.
2. A small salary should always be paid to protect entitlement to contributions-related social security benefits, such as the state pension.
3. The company must have sufficient distributable reserves to cover any proposed dividends.
4. If the director is employed under an "explicit" employment contract then the national minimum and living wage must be considered.
5. The relevant paperwork for the dividend must be completed, including minutes of any meeting approving the dividend and any dividend vouchers. If a shareholder waives their entitlement, the dividend waiver document should also be prepared at that time.

12.2.2 Benefits in Kind

A limited company is a separate legal entity from its directors. This means that where a director meets personal expenditure with company funds, there will be a benefit in kind that will be charged to tax and NICs on the director as employment income. The taxation of benefits in kind is studied at CA Proficiency 1; however, there are certain items that tend to apply more specifically to company directors.

Where a company meets the personal expenses of a director, these are taxable expense payments. The payments should be included on the director's Form P11D and subject to income tax. Class 1 NICs will also be payable and should be collected through the payroll. The company will pay Class 1A NICs at 13.8%. The taxable amount may be reduced where there is legitimate business use.

Example 12.5

Cora is a director of Firefly Ltd and the company pays her home telephone bills. Cora is the subscriber. The total amount paid in 2019/20 was £800, including line rental of £100. Cora has determined that about 10% of the calls made from her home telephone were business calls relating to Firefly Ltd's trade (and has evidence for this). What is the PAYE/NICs treatment?

PAYE Income Tax

The full amount of line rental plus 90% of the cost of calls (i.e. the private portion) should be declared on form P11D. Income tax will therefore be charged on an amount of £730.

NICs

No Class 1A NICs are due as the company is meeting Cora's personal expenditure rather than providing a benefit. Class 1 NICs are however due and will be collected by putting an amount equal to the full line rental, plus 90% of the cost of calls through the payroll. The total amount on which Class 1 NICs are therefore due is £730.

Care should be taken to ensure that any company credit cards used by a director are not used for personal expenditure, as this would give rise to a taxable expense charge.

Assets transferred by the company to the director will give rise to a taxable benefit in kind, which should be reported on Form P11D. Such a transfer will **also** be subject to income tax and Class 1A NICs.

Certain payments or transfers made by a "close" company to a participator are, for income tax purposes, treated as distributions in the hands of the participator (see **Chapter 7**). When the participator is also a director or employee, such payments/transfers will instead be taxed as employment income.

> ***Example 12.6***
> Serenity Ltd is a family-owned and managed company. The shareholders are Neil (who has a shareholding of 40%), his sister Carol (who has a shareholding of 40%) and his brother David (who has a shareholding of 20%). Both Neil and Carol are directors in the company. David is not a director or employee of the company.
>
> Serenity Ltd pays the rent on each of the shareholders' houses. As Neil and Carol are directors of the company, they will be subject to an income tax charge based on the benefit in kind rules for the provision of living accommodation. The company is entitled to a corporation tax deduction for expenses treated as a benefit in kind.
>
> As David is not an employee of the company, the rent paid on his house will be taxed as a distribution in his hands under the rules relating to participators. The company is **not** entitled to a corporation tax deduction for expenses treated as a distribution.

12.2.3 Loans to Participators

Loans by a close company to a participator (including directors) can give rise to a potential charge on the company under section 455 CTA 2010 (see **Chapter 7**). The recipient, if a director, may also be treated as having received a beneficial loan under the benefit in kind rules, rather than a distribution, and taxed accordingly. It should be noted that such a loan can arise where a director's current account in the company becomes overdrawn. Even where no charge arises under section 455 CTA 2010 (e.g. where the overdrawn amount is repaid within nine months of the accounting year-end), there may still be a taxable benefit in kind.

Repayment of section 455 tax is only given for genuine repayments as opposed to instances where the loan is repaid and shortly there after drawn down again (see **Chapter 7**).

> ***Example 12.7***
> Peter is a full-time working director of Bap Ltd, in which he has a shareholding of 60%. Bap Ltd prepares its accounts to 31 December. On 6 May 2019, Peter purchased a painting for £15,000. As he had insufficient funds, he borrowed this amount from the company. On 5 March 2020, he repaid the £15,000 to the company.
>
> As the amount borrowed is repaid within nine months of the year end, there is no charge under section 455 CTA 2010.
>
> However, the loan is subject to the benefit in kind rules as it is "interest free and is more than £10,000", and Peter will be charged income tax on the cash equivalent on the loan. Bap Ltd will also have a Class 1A NICs liability in respect of the loan.

12.3 Pensions

Pension contributions can be a very tax-efficient form of remuneration for directors. They qualify for tax relief on personal contributions in the same way as other employees, but may also have the option of more significant employer contributions made by the company.

The tax relief available on pension contributions is covered at CAP 1, but it is worth mentioning here that a company contribution into a director's pension scheme is a deductible expense for corporation tax, provided it is wholly and exclusively for the purposes of the trade. Such contributions may also be subject to the corporation tax spreading provisions (see **Chapter 2**). When determining whether a company contribution is excessive (thereby failing the wholly and exclusively test), the complete remuneration package and pattern of profit extraction by the director will be taken into account.

As pension funds benefit from tax-free growth, extracting profits in this way can be a more tax-efficient method than taking a salary or dividend. However, it is only really useful for those who can afford to lock the profits into their pension pot until they retire. Also, it must be remembered that the funds eventually available to draw down from the pension will depend on the performance of the fund investments and may also be affected by changing legislation.

The annual allowance for pension contributions for an individual for the 2019/20 tax year is £40,000. However, the annual allowance for those earning above £150,000 is reduced on a tapering basis. An individual's annual allowance reduces by £1 for every £2 of income above £150,000, subject to a minimum annual allowance of £10,000. Therefore, individuals who earn more than £210,000, their annual allowance will reduce to £10,000 (i.e. £40,000 less £30,000, being £60,000/2). It is also possible, if certain conditions are met, to carry forward unused allowance from the previous three tax years to offset any excess in the current year.

The annual allowance limit is the maximum level at which an individual can benefit from tax relief. The contributions can be made by either the individual or their employer. Any contributions in excess of the available annual allowance limit are subject to income tax on the individual. Tax relief is available for gross personal contributions up to the higher of £3,600 or 100% of relevant earnings.

The lifetime allowance (the amount an individual can save in a pension scheme) is currently £1,055,000. An individual can protect their pension pot and keep a higher lifetime allowance, but by doing so they would not be able to make further pension contributions. Any pension pots that exceed the lifetime allowance are also subject to a tax charge. The rate of tax on pension savings above the relevant lifetime allowance depends on how the money is paid. The rates are as follows:

- 55% if the money is received as a lump sum; or
- 25% if the money is received any other way, e.g. pension payments or cash withdrawals.

12.4 Other Issues

12.4.1 Timing

It may be the case that the total remuneration payable to a director in respect of an accounting period will not be finally determined until the accounts have been prepared and the profits have been assessed. Also, remuneration may be credited to a director's loan account rather than being paid in cash.

For directors, the date of payment of remuneration for the purposes of PAYE/NICs will be the **earlier** of:

- the date the payment is made;
- the date the director becomes entitled to be paid;
- the date the payment is credited in the company accounts or records;
- the date the remuneration is fixed or determined.

In the case of profits extracted by way of dividend, the date of payment for the purposes of calculating the income tax charge is the date of the dividend as stated in the board minute declaring the dividend and the supporting documentation (i.e. tax voucher). It is important that this documentation is properly maintained, especially where a dividend is being credited to a director's current account rather than being paid out.

12.4.2 Limits on Remuneration

It should be remembered that remuneration, like any other trading expense, must be incurred wholly and exclusively for the purposes of the trade. HMRC may disallow a deduction for corporation tax purposes where they regard the remuneration as excessive.

12.4.3 Personal Liability

If PAYE/NICs are not properly deducted in respect of remuneration paid to a director, then the director may be personally liable to pay the tax if he knew of the failure to deduct or account for the tax.

Questions

Review Questions

(See Suggested Solutions to Review Questions at the end of this textbook.)

Question 12.1

To recognise the increased contribution by one of its directors, Clara, over the past year, a company has decided to reward her with an additional gross payment of £100,000 to be paid before the end of the current tax year 2019/20. Clara's gross salary for the year was £125,000.

Requirement

Calculate the tax implications to the company and Clara of making this payment, either as a bonus or as a dividend. Conclude which is more tax-efficient overall.

Question 12.2

It is March 2020 and you have just had a meeting with your clients, Mr and Mrs Andrews, who are both in their early fifties. At the meeting you discuss a number of issues. However, it is apparent that they would like some immediate advice in respect of the strategy for their remuneration by their company.

They each hold 50% of the shares in Andrews Transport Ltd (ATL) being 50 shares each and have done so since the company was incorporated in 1978.

The current total value of the company is £3 million. Annual pre-tax profits are in the region of £250,000. Most of the value of the company is in goodwill, current assets and motor vehicles, although there is also spare cash of £750,000. The cash has accumulated as no dividends have been paid by ATL over the years. Distributable reserves in ATL currently amount to over £1 million.

Currently Mr Andrews is paid £100,000 per annum by the company, and Mrs Andrews is not paid anything in respect of the secretarial services she provides to the company. Mr Andrews has been a full-time director of the company since 1978, while Mrs Andrews has never been an employee or director of ATL.

They have two children who are currently at university and who also work part time for the company. The children are not paid by the company, but are rewarded by Mr Andrews himself, who also pays their college expenses. Several years ago the company set up a Revenue-approved pension scheme to provide Mr Andrews with a pension. However, the actual contributions made to the scheme have been relatively low and the projected pension on his retirement is quite small.

Mrs Andrews has no company pension and Mr Andrews is concerned that his expected pension will not be sufficient to meet their needs.

Requirement

Draft a letter to Mr and Mrs Andrews dealing with the current remuneration structure and the various options for remunerating them from the company. In your letter include suggestions for potential savings. There is no requirement for detailed calculations.

Part Two

Capital Gains Tax

13

Introduction, General Principles and Administration

Learning Objectives

After studying this chapter you will understand:

- The application of the general principles for the computation of capital gains tax (CGT) liabilities.
- The payment of CGT and the filing of returns.
- How to identify chargeable and exempt assets for CGT purposes.
- How to determine and apply the appropriate treatment of capital losses.
- How to determine the appropriate treatment for assets passing on death.

Chartered Accountants Ireland's *Code of Ethics* applies to all aspects of a Chartered Accountant's professional life, including dealing with CGT issues. As outlined at the beginning of this book, further information regarding the principles in the *Code of Ethics* is set out in **Appendix 2**. **Appendix 3** of this book examines the distinction between tax planning, tax avoidance and tax evasion which can arise in relation to all taxes including capital gains tax.

13.1 Introduction

The Taxation of Chargeable Gains Act (TCGA) 1992, as amended by subsequent Finance Acts, contains the main provisions for the taxation of chargeable gains.

13.2 The Basic Charge to CGT

There are three basic elements that must exist before the provisions relating to the taxation of capital gains come into operation:

1. there must be a **chargeable disposal**,
2. of a **chargeable asset**,
3. by a **chargeable person**.

13.3 Disposal

In order for a liability to CGT to arise, a disposal of a chargeable asset must take place or must be deemed to take place. A disposal for these purposes will occur in each of the following situations:

- on the sale of an asset;
- on the sale of part of an asset (part disposal);
- on the gift of the whole or part of an asset;
- on the receipt of a capital sum resulting from the ownership of an asset, e.g. receipt of a capital sum in return for forfeiture or surrender of rights;
- on the receipt of a capital sum as consideration for use or exploitation of assets;
- on the transfer of an asset to a trust or a corporate body;
- on an exchange of assets in a barter transaction.

However, the sale of an asset in the course of a trade (for example, the sale of trading stock) is **not** a chargeable disposal since any gain arising is taxed as a trading profit.

In respect of **gifts**, the asset is treated as if it were sold for CGT purposes and the consideration is deemed to be its market value even though the transferor receives no consideration. Certain disposals are **exempt** from CGT including gifts to charities and gifts of national heritage property (subject to certain conditions). A list of exempt assets is included below.

As a general rule, CGT is not triggered on **death**. There is, therefore, no chargeable disposal on death, even though the deceased no longer owns the assets. Chargeable assets held on death are, however, revalued to their market value as at the date of death. The market value at the date of death (the probate value) becomes the base cost for the person inheriting the asset.

It is **important** to note that although transfers of assets between **husbands and wives** (and legally recognised civil partnerships) are chargeable disposals for CGT purposes, they are specifically deemed to occur at a value such that neither a chargeable gain nor an allowable loss occurs on the transfer (disposal), i.e. on a no gain/no loss basis.

A chargeable disposal occurs at the date of the unconditional contract or the date that the condition is satisfied on a conditional contract. A contract can be written or verbal. See **Section 13.9** for further details.

13.4 Chargeable Assets

Chargeable assets for CGT purposes include all forms of property, whether situated in the UK or not, including options, debts and foreign currency. The basic rule is that any capital asset of an individual or company is a chargeable asset unless it is specifically exempt from CGT or corporation tax on chargeable gains. Specifically included is an interest in property. As seen in previous chapters, a company generally calculates its chargeable gains on the same basis as individuals. However, a company is entitled to deduct indexation allowance up to 31 December 2017 where the asset was acquired before that date. In addition, there is no CGT annual exemption for companies and a company cannot claim entrepreneurs' relief.

Special rules for assets within the corporate intangibles regime and for loan relationships treat certain gains as income for corporation tax purposes rather than as chargeable gains.

The main **exempt assets** for CGT purposes include:

- motor cars;
- chattels (items of tangible movable property), which are disposed of for gross proceeds of £6,000 or less and where the cost is also £6,000 or less;

- wasting chattels, which are chattels with a predictable useful life of 50 years or less (unless used in the taxpayer's business and eligible for capital allowances);
- a taxpayer's principal private residence (subject to conditions);
- winnings from betting, lotteries and the pools;
- decorations for valour (unless purchased), life insurance policies (unless purchased from a third party);
- National Savings & Investment Certificates, Premium Bonds and ISAs;
- disposals of qualifying investments in Enterprise Investment Scheme or Seed Enterprise Investment Scheme companies and shares in a venture capital trust (provided certain conditions are met);
- gilt-edged securities (e.g. Treasury stock) and qualifying corporate bonds;
- foreign currency for private use abroad; and
- damages for personal or professional injury.

13.5 Chargeable Persons

CGT is charged on gains accruing (realised or deemed to be realised) by individuals, business partners, trustees and personal representatives of a deceased person. Companies are also chargeable persons, but are assessed to corporation tax on chargeable gains and not to CGT.

A person is chargeable to CGT in respect of worldwide chargeable gains accruing to them in the year of assessment if during any part of the tax year they are resident in the UK, even if they are not UK domiciled or deemed UK domiciled. This is known as the arising basis. Therefore CGT is not limited to gains on the disposal of UK assets. However, it should be noted that a UK resident and non-UK domiciled individual who is not deemed UK domiciled for UK CGT purposes can elect to choose the remittance basis of taxation (see **Chapter 14**) if it is not automatically available to them.

Persons who are not resident in the UK for a tax year are not subject to UK CGT unless they fall into one of three exceptions (for which see **Chapter 14, Section 14.7**).

A non-UK domiciled individual who is resident in the UK and who is not deemed UK domiciled for UK CGT purposes is subject to CGT on gains arising on non-UK assets, unless a claim is made for the remittance basis of taxation to apply or unless the remittance basis is automatically available (see **Chapter 14**). The broad effect of the remittance basis of taxation is to only tax non-UK gains if and when they are remitted to the UK.

13.6 Rate of Tax, Date of Payment and Returns

13.6.1 Rates of CGT

CGT is charged by reference to fiscal years of assessment for individuals, i. e. for relevant transactions within the tax year ending 5 April. Individuals must calculate their total taxable income to be able to apply the correct CGT rate. The calculation is as follows:

1. First, calculate taxable income by deducting any tax-free allowances and reliefs that are due.
2. Next, identify how much of the basic rate band is already being used against taxable income. The maximum basic rate band for 2019/20 is £37,500.
3. Allocate any remaining basic rate band, first against gains that qualify for entrepreneurs' relief or investors' relief (which are then charged at 10%).

4. Next, allocate any remaining basic rate band against other gains (these are charged at 10% or 18%). The legislation ensures that an individual can use any remaining basic rate band in the most tax-efficient way.
5. Any remaining gains above the basic rate band are charged at 20% or 28%.

Note that the 10% and 20% rates of CGT do not apply to gains made on the disposal of residential property where private residence relief (see **Chapter 16**) is not available. The rates for these gains are 18% for those in the basic rate band and 28% thereafter. A residential property for these purposes includes both UK and non-UK situs residential properties.

Trustees and personal representatives pay CGT at 20% on gains, regardless of the level of income. The 28% higher rate applies to residential property disposals.

Example 13.1
Julie's total taxable income in 2019/20, after deducting allowances and reliefs, is £31,715 and her capital gains, after tax-free allowance and reliefs, are £17,000. £5,000 of the gains qualify for entrepreneurs' relief. None of the gains relate to residential property.

The maximum basic rate band for 2019/20 is £37,500. Julie has used £31,715 of this amount against her income, so she has £5,785 remaining.

Julie then allocates £5,000 against the gains that qualify for entrepreneurs' relief, which are taxed at 10%.

She allocates the remaining £785 against her other gains, so these are taxed at 10%. The remaining £11,215 gains (£17,000 less £5,785) are taxed at 20%.

Companies pay corporation tax on their chargeable gains at the company's effective tax rate. For the financial year 2019 (which commenced on 1 April 2019) this is 19% for all companies; for FY 2020 the rate will be 17%.

13.6.2 Date of Payment

The UK self-assessment regime also applies to CGT. CGT due must be paid on or before 31 January following the end of the relevant tax year. For example, the CGT due on a chargeable gain or gains arising during 2019/20 falls due for payment on or before 31 January 2021. The payment of CGT does not impact on the following tax year's payments on account.

Example 13.2
An individual disposes of an asset in July 2019, giving rise to a chargeable gain of £10,000; and disposes of a second asset in November 2019, giving rise to a chargeable gain of £6,500. Neither is a disposal of residential property. The individual had a loss forward of £3,000 from the disposal of shares in 2018/19. The total taxable income for the year (after tax-free allowance and reliefs) was £19,500. CGT is payable by the individual as follows:

CGT rate computation

	£
Basic rate band 2019/20	37,500
Less: total taxable income	(19,500)
Remaining basic rate band	18,000

continued overleaf

Total taxable gains (i.e. chargeable gains after capital losses brought forward, annual exemption, etc.) are less than £18,000, so the CGT rate of 10% will be applied to all taxable gains.

CGT computation

	£
Chargeable gains	16,500
Less: capital losses from 2018/19 (see **Section 13.14**)	(3,000)
Less: CGT annual exemption (see **Section 13.7.3**)	(12,000)
Taxable gain	1,500
CGT @ 10%	150

CGT for 2019/20, payable on or before 31 January 2021, is £150.

13.6.3 Payment by Instalments

In a situation where the taxpayer receives the disposal proceeds in instalments over a period of 18 months or more, they may choose to make a claim to pay the CGT liability by way of interest-free instalments. The size and frequency of the instalments are at the discretion of HMRC, but the period over which they are paid must not exceed:

1. an eight-year period; **or**
2. the date on which the last instalment of the consideration is payable.

It is also possible for the taxpayer to elect to pay by instalments where gift relief is not available (see **Chapter 19**). This election for payment by instalment is not interest-free and interest will accrue on outstanding balances.

13.6.4 Returns

A return of chargeable gains must be made within the self-assessment income tax return filing deadline for individuals.

By way of reminder, the latest filing date for a personal tax return is:

- 31 October following the end of the tax year for paper returns; and
- 31 January following the end of the tax year for online returns.

Taxpayers are normally **not** required to complete the CGT pages of their tax return if **both** the following conditions are satisfied:

1. the total disposals proceeds from the tax year do not exceed four times the amount of the annual exemption (£48,000 for 2019/20); **and**
2. the total chargeable gains for the tax year do not exceed the annual exemption (£12,000 for 2019/20).

In this case, a statement to this effect, in lieu of the CGT pages, will suffice. For the purposes of these conditions, the total chargeable gains are before deduction of either current year capital losses or capital losses brought forward from previous years.

It should be noted that relief for capital losses cannot be claimed unless they are notified to HMRC within four years from the end of the tax year in which the losses were incurred. So if a loss is made in 2019/20, the deadline for claiming the loss (although not for claiming relief for the loss) is 5 April 2024.

As chargeable gains are reported to HMRC under self-assessment, the self-assessment regime equally applies to CGT. (Students are reminded that the detailed operation of this regime is cumulative knowledge previously covered on the CA Proficiency 1 course and is thus beyond the scope of this textbook. It is, however, potentially examinable material in the context of CGT at CA Proficiency 2. The material in this chapter is focused solely on the administrative aspects of the UK's CGT regime not previously covered at CA Proficiency 1.)

For direct and indirect disposals of UK residential property by non-residents, a special regime is in operation that requires the CGT on the transaction to be reported and paid within 30 days (see **Chapter 14, Section 14.13**).

From 6 April 2020, UK tax residents will also need to report and pay CGT on all residential property disposals within 30 days of the date of completion of the disposal (rather than the current deadline of 31 January following the end of the tax year in which the sale is made). The transaction must be reported to HMRC online using a specific form for the payment on account return, which should include a calculation of the projected tax liability.

The calculation of the CGT liability will, in some cases, require an estimate of the individual's income and other CGT transactions in order to complete the payment on account return and assess the relevant CGT rate. Individuals will also be required to report these disposals as part of their self-assessment return for the relevant tax year.

Any payment of CGT made will be offset against the individual's CGT and income tax liabilities for the relevant tax year when their self-assessment tax return is completed and submitted to HMRC.

These new reporting and payment requirements will not apply where the gain on the disposal is not chargeable to CGT. For example, this would include scenarios where:

- the gain is covered by private residence relief (see **Chapter 16**);
- the transaction is a gift between spouses on a no gain/no loss basis (see **Section 13.11.3**); or
- the UK CGT arising is covered by double tax relief or capital losses or a loss has arisen.

There are also penalties for non-compliance.

13.7 Computation of Gain or Loss

13.7.1 General

In summary, taxable gains are the net chargeable gains (after current-year capital losses) of the tax year reduced by unrelieved losses brought forward from previous years and the annual exemption.

The capital gain is the difference between:

1. the consideration for the disposal of the asset, or the deemed consideration (e.g. market value in the case of a gift or disposal between connected persons); and
2. the cost of acquisition of the asset or its market value if not acquired at arm's length (e.g. property acquired by way of inheritance or gift).

If any part of the sales consideration is taken into account in computing income tax or corporation tax profits or losses, it is excluded from the amount under 1 above. It therefore follows that expenditure that is allowable as a deduction from income tax or corporation tax profits, or which would be allowable if the asset had been employed as a fixed asset of a trade, is excluded from 2 above.

Allowable expenditure for CGT purposes includes:

1. The cost of acquiring (or providing) the asset and certain incidental costs of acquisition or disposal, e.g. agent's commission, stamp taxes (see **Chapters 28–31**), valuation costs, cost of transfer or conveyance, auctioneers', accountants' or solicitors' fees and advertising costs.
2. Expenditure incurred for the purposes of enhancing the value of the asset, which is reflected in the nature or state of the asset at the time of disposal, e.g. **improvements to property**. To be allowable, the expenditure must not have been abortive nor must its value have wasted away before the disposal of the asset. Expenditure incurred in establishing, preserving or defending an owner's title or interest in an asset is allowable within this definition. Enhancement expenditure does not include costs of repairs and maintenance, costs of insurance or capital grants expended out of public funds.

A typical CGT computation for an asset sold during 2019/20 might be as follows.

J. Jones – Capital Gains Tax Computation for 2019/20

	£	£
Sales proceeds (or market value)	X	
Less: incidental costs of sale	(X)	
		X
Deduct allowable costs:		
Original cost of asset	X	
Incidental costs of acquisition	X	
Enhancement expenditure	X	
		(X)
Gain		X
Deduct: relief available (if any – see **Chapters 16, 18** and **19**)		(X)
Deduct: capital losses (if any – see **Section 13.14**)		(X)
Deduct: annual exemption (see **Section 13.7.3**)		(X)
Taxable chargeable gain		X
CGT payable: taxable gain at 10%/18%/20%/28% (for individuals)		X

13.7.2 Indexation Allowance

As seen in earlier chapters, indexation allowance is available to increase the original cost of the asset, any incidental costs of acquisition and enhancement expenditure in line with inflation for companies, but only up to and including 31 December 2017 for assets bought before 31 December 2017 and sold on or after that date. Assets bought on or after 31 December 2017, therefore, attract no indexation allowance when sold.

13.7.3 Annual Exemption

Every individual is entitled to an annual exemption, which is available for offset against the "taxable" gains of the particular tax year. The annual exemption cannot be carried forward and thus any excess over the taxable gains is lost. Furthermore, the annual exemption cannot be transferred, e.g. between spouses or civil partners.

The annual exemption for 2019/20 is £12,000 (for 2018/19 it was £11,300).

The "taxable" gains are usually the chargeable gains accruing to the taxpayer for a year of assessment after deduction of allowable losses. Thus, allowable losses of the current year must be utilised against the chargeable gains arising in that year, even if this means that part or all of the annual exemption will be wasted. However, where capital losses are being carried forward or carried back (applicable only on death), these can be tailored so as not to waste any of the annual exemption. Current-year losses must be claimed in priority to losses brought forward. The offset of current-year losses cannot be tailored to protect the use of the annual exemption.

Both the annual exemption and losses should be used in the most beneficial way possible, i.e. set against any gains taxed at the higher CGT rate of 28%, followed by gains taxed at 20%, then gains taxed at 18% and finally against gains taxed at 10% (gains in the basic rate band or gains qualifying for entrepreneurs' relief (ER) or investors' relief (IR)). **However, losses that arise on the disposal of qualifying assets for ER/IR must be set off against ER/IR qualifying gains first.**

Individuals who claim the remittance basis of tax are not entitled to the CGT annual exemption. Only those individuals who are not required to make a formal claim for the remittance basis of tax may claim the annual exemption. See **Chapter 14** for further information on the remittance basis.

Companies are not entitled to the CGT annual exemption.

Example 13.3

Four taxpayers, John, Paul, George and Matthew, each make chargeable disposals during 2019/20. None of them have any capital losses brought forward from previous years. None of the gains relate to residential property. Calculate their CGT assessable chargeable gains for 2019/20.

(a) John had gains of £3,100 (30 June), £3,600 (15 September) and £5,150 (10 January) and a capital loss of £2,450 (5 May).

(b) Paul had gains of £10,600 (18 May), £3,600 (5 December) and capital losses of £1,000 (30 April) and £800 (1 February). He has £5,000 of his basic rate band remaining.

(c) George had a gain of £9,600 (5 August) and capital losses of £3,500 (30 November), £2,900 (12 December) and £8,200 (4 March).

(d) Matthew had gains of £6,300 (15 May), £8,600 (10 October) and £9,100 (8 February). He has £10,000 of his basic rate band remaining.

Solution

(a) John's "net" position is a net gain of £9,400. This is less than the annual exemption and thus he will have a CGT assessment of nil and the unused part of his annual allowance £2,600 (£12,000 – £9,400) is lost.

(b) Paul's "net" position is a net gain of £12,400. Deducting his annual exemption leaves a taxable gain of £400, which is within his surplus basic rate band. Therefore, CGT is payable for 2018/19 at 10% × £400 = £40.

(c) George's "net" position is a net loss of £5,000 and his CGT assessment for 2019/20 will be nil and all of his annual exemption will be lost. The capital loss will be carried forward and is available for offset against future capital gains.

(d) Matthew's "net" position is a gain of £12,000 (£24,000 – £12,000) after deducting the annual exemption. £10,000 of this will be taxed at 10% and £2,000 at 20%, resulting in a CGT liability of £1,400.

Example 13.4

Three taxpayers, George, Robert and Denis, have capital losses carried forward from previous years of £3,000, £4,000 and £5,000 respectively. All three had made chargeable gains of £15,100 and a capital loss of £1,400 during 2019/20. Calculate each of their CGT assessments for 2019/20. You can assume that each has used up their basic rate band in full before the gains are taken into account and that none of the gains relate to residential property.

Solution

Each has a "net" position for 2019/20 (prior to utilisation of their annual exemption and their individual capital losses brought forward) of £13,700. Each taxpayer needs only to utilise sufficient of his carried forward losses to reduce (where possible) the "net" gain to the level of the annual exemption.

In order to arrive at how much, if any, of the capital losses each taxpayer must use, one has to consider the position after deducting the annual exemption, **before** looking at losses forward. In each case, this would be a figure of £1,700 (£13,700 – £12,000).

Thus, George would use £1,700 of his carried forward capital losses of £3,000 and leave no taxable gain (after deduction of his annual exemption). He would carry forward the remaining £1,300 of his losses. His CGT assessment for 2019/20 is nil.

Robert would only utilise £1,700 of his capital losses brought forward (i.e. he leaves sufficient "net" gain to be covered by his annual exemption). He would then have capital losses to carry forward of £2,300 (£4,000 less £1,700 used in 2019/20). His CGT assessment for 2019/20 is nil.

Similarly, Denis would only utilise £1,700 of his brought forward losses and his carried forward capital losses would thus be £3,300 (£5,000 less £1,700 used in 2019/20). His CGT assessment for 2019/20 is nil.

Denis – CGT computation

	£
Chargeable gain	15,100
Less: current year capital losses	(1,400)
	13,700
Less: losses brought forward	(1,700)
	12,000
Less: annual exemption	(12,000)
Net chargeable gain	0
CGT	Nil
Memo of losses carried forward	5,000
Utilised 2019/20	(1,700)
Losses available for carry forward	3,300

Note differences in claiming relief for current year losses and losses carried forward.

13.7.4 Special Rules Relating to Allowable Deductions

As outlined above, expenditure that is allowable as a deduction when computing the quantum of the chargeable gain is:

1. The costs of acquiring (or providing) the asset, which includes certain incidental costs of acquisition wholly and exclusively incurred for the purposes of the acquisition (such as stamp duty, stamp duty land tax, fees, commission, valuation fees and professional services of estate agents, solicitors, surveyors, etc.) and advertising costs.

2. Enhancement costs for the asset and any costs of establishing, preserving or defending title to an asset.
3. Certain incidental costs of disposals. While the allowable incidental costs of disposal are generally similar to those for incidental costs of acquisition, specifically excluded are the costs associated with resolving valuation disputes with HMRC. As stated above, no deduction is allowable for expenditure which is allowable as a deduction in computing the profits or losses of a trade for income tax or corporation tax purposes.
4. Foreign gains – double taxation relief. Where a UK resident individual makes a capital gain on the disposal of a foreign asset and foreign tax is paid, relief can be claimed against the UK CGT liability.

   There are general provisions relating to the making of arrangements with governments of territories outside the UK for avoiding double taxation. The purpose of a double taxation agreement is primarily to avoid the incidence of double taxation by limiting the taxing rights of each contracting state.

   Relief for foreign tax suffered on gains that are chargeable to CGT (or corporation tax) in the UK may be obtained under the terms of a double taxation agreement between the UK and the relevant overseas territory. Under the terms of an agreement, it may be the case that the gain is only taxable in one of the contracting states (i.e. the state of residence or the state in which the gain arose). Where double taxation remains, i.e. where both states retain the right to tax the gain under the agreement, it is generally the case that the agreement will provide relief which, in the case of UK residents, invariably takes the form of a credit for the foreign tax against the UK tax liability on the profits or gains concerned.

   If the overseas territory does not have a double taxation agreement with the UK, the taxpayer can still avail of "unilateral relief". **Unilateral relief** is the lower of:

   (a) the UK tax on the foreign gain; or
   (b) the foreign tax suffered.

   Unilateral relief reduces the UK CGT charge.

   If there is no double taxation agreement and unilateral relief is not claimed then the foreign gain, net of foreign tax, is charged to UK CGT, i.e. the foreign tax is treated as an additional cost in CGT computation. This treatment may be appropriate if there is no UK tax to shelter, perhaps because the gain has been reduced by losses or other deferral reliefs.

   When calculating the CGT liability for a taxpayer where there are foreign gains, the annual exemption is allocated first against UK and foreign gains on which no double taxation or unilateral relief is being claimed, and then against gains on which relief is being claimed, beginning with the gain that has been subjected to the lowest effective rate of foreign tax.
5. Grants – No deduction is allowed in computing chargeable gains for any expenditure which has been met by the provision of government, public or local authority grants.

13.7.5 Part Disposal

As we have seen above, the partial disposal of an asset is a chargeable event for CGT purposes. Where a portion of an asset is sold, the sale proceeds are easily quantified but it is necessary to calculate **how much of the original cost of the asset is allowable as a deduction** in computing the chargeable gain or allowable loss arising on the part disposal.

For assets *other than shares* (see **Chapter 17**, **Section 17.1**), the legislation provides that this is calculated as being the proportion of the original cost of the asset which the value of the part being disposed of bears, at the time of disposal, to the market value of the whole asset. The formula is, therefore:

$$\text{Original Cost} \times \frac{A}{A + B}$$

where A is the amount of the "gross" proceeds/market value of the part disposal (i.e. before deducting incidental costs of disposal) and B is the market value of the portion of the asset which is retained. However, any expenditure incurred wholly in respect of a particular part of an asset should be treated as an allowable deduction in full for that part and not apportioned, e.g. selling costs which are wholly attributable to the part disposed of.

Example 13.5

Assume an asset cost £1,000 on 1 September 2004 and part of the asset was sold for £600 on 6 June 2019. The market value of the remainder of the asset was £700. The chargeable gain in respect of the disposal would be computed as follows (assuming that the annual exemption has been used elsewhere):

		£
Sales proceeds		600
Less: allowable cost:	$£1{,}000 \times \frac{600}{600+700}$	(462)
Chargeable gain		138

The base costs for onward disposal of the remaining part of the asset is:

	£
Original cost of asset	1,000
Less: cost of part disposal	(462)
Cost of remaining part	538

Example 13.6

A commercial investment property cost £10,000 on 10 April 1982. Part of the asset was sold on 10 November 2019 for £27,000. The market value of the remainder asset at that date was £50,000. The individual has other income in 2019/20 of £78,000.

Calculate the CGT liability.

		£
Proceeds		27,000
COST	$10{,}000 \times \frac{27{,}000}{27{,}000 + 50{,}000}$	(3,507)
		23,493
Annual exemption		(12,000)
		11,493

CGT payable is £11,493 × 20% = £2,299 (due by 31/01/2021)

Base cost of the remaining part for onward disposal is

	£
Original cost	10,000
Less: cost of part disposal	(3,507)
Cost of remaining part	6,493

"Small Disposal" Proceeds of Land

Where the proceeds for a part disposal of land are small compared with the value of the land held, then the taxpayer may claim not to be treated as having made a capital disposal, but instead deduct the proceeds from allowable expenditure on a subsequent disposal. This claim can only be made if:

1. the proceeds for the part disposal of land are not more than 20% of the entire holding of the land's market value **and** not more than £20,000; **and**
2. the net aggregate proceeds from the part disposal and any other disposals of land (including buildings) in the same tax year do not exceed £20,000.

The claim cannot be made if the allowable expenditure is less than the part disposal proceeds, i.e. a capital loss has arisen

Example 13.7

An individual bought five acres of land in October 2005 for £10,000 and sold one acre for £5,000 in November 2019. This was their only disposal in 2019/20. The market value of the land prior to sale is £40,000. The disposal costs were £500. What is the CGT position?

Can the taxpayer claim to be treated as if no disposal has been made?

The consideration is £5,000. This is less than 20% of the market value (20% of £40,000 = £8,000) and less than £20,000. As there have been no other disposals in 2018/19, the net aggregate proceeds of all land and buildings disposals are also less than £20,000. As all conditions are met, a claim for part disposal can be made.

Claim small disposal relief:	£
Base cost: cost of five acres	10,000
Deduct net proceeds of part disposal (£5,000–£500)	(4,500)
Allowable base cost of land retained	5,500

As a claim has been made, no disposal takes place at this time; therefore there is no taxable capital gain. Instead the base cost of the land is reduced by the net proceeds received and the reduced base cost is carried forward to be used in the CGT computation on any future sale of the remaining four acres of land.

13.7.6 Application of Market Value

Normally, where a disposal is at arm's length and the consideration is known in money terms, the consideration paid is accepted for CGT purposes. However, in certain circumstances, the market value of an asset is substituted for the actual consideration paid for the disposal. This will occur:

1. where there is a transaction between connected persons (see **Section 13.13.1** for the definition of connected persons).
2. where a disposal is not made at arm's length (e.g. a gift);
3. where the consideration is not valued in money terms or is a barter transaction;
4. where the asset is acquired or disposed of wholly or partly for a consideration that cannot be valued; or
5. where the asset is acquired by way of a distribution from a company in respect of shares in the company.

In all of the above scenarios, the market value is deemed to be the consideration for the purpose of determining the chargeable gain or allowable loss.

However, the market value rule is overridden when the asset is transferred between husband and wife and between civil partners. In such situations, the transfers are deemed to occur at a value such that there is neither a chargeable gain nor an allowable loss (i.e. on a no gain/no loss basis).

13.8 Specific Computational Rules

13.8.1 Enhancement Expenditure

Where enhancement expenditure has been incurred on an asset, the cost, and each subsequent item of enhancement expenditure, is treated as a separate asset for the purposes of CGT. The chargeable gain is calculated as the difference between the various items of expenditure, i.e. both original cost and enhancement expenditure, as adjusted, and the sale proceeds.

13.8.2 Valuation Rule for Quoted Shares and Unit Trusts

For CGT purposes, the method of valuation of shares, securities and strips is to use the middle figure (between the lowest and highest) of the closing prices of the day.

This rule applies equally for CGT, income tax and corporation tax purposes, but does not apply to inheritance tax (IHT). This means that there is a discrepancy in valuation methods between CGT and IHT. The value, for IHT purposes, is calculated as outlined at **Section 23.8**. For death estates, section 274 TCGA 1992 determines that where a value has been ascertained for IHT purposes, that value is to be used as the acquisition cost for CGT. This means that on death the valuations remain aligned.

13.9 Time of Disposal

The time of disposal for the purposes of CGT is generally determined by reference to the time a contract is made. Briefly, the rules for the following situations are:

1. In the case of an **unconditional contract**, the date of the contract is the relevant date, irrespective of the date of the conveyance or transfer of the asset (i.e. "the closing date" or "completion date" is not relevant).
2. In the case of a **conditional contract**, the time of the disposal for the purposes of CGT is the date on which the condition is satisfied.
3. In the case of **gifts**, the date of disposal is the date on which the property effectively passes, e.g. in the case of the gift of a chattel, the date that the chattel is delivered is the date of disposal for CGT purposes. This rule also applies to gifts into settlements.

13.10 Assets Situated Abroad

13.10.1 Location of Assets

The CGT legislation contains rules for determining the location of assets. For CGT, these rules are particularly relevant to an individual who is not UK domiciled, or deemed UK domiciled for UK CGT purposes, but who is UK resident. If such an individual makes a formal claim to the remittance basis or the remittance basis is automatically available, then they are only chargeable to UK CGT on chargeable gains accruing on the disposal of assets situated outside the UK (foreign assets) to the extent that the gains are remitted to this country. Chargeable gains on UK assets remain fully chargeable to UK CGT and are not subject to the remittance basis. See **Chapter 14** for more detail on the remittance basis of tax. Accordingly, it will be important for such an individual to establish that the gains were realised from the disposal of assets that were in fact situated outside the UK. The following particular rules apply:

1. Rights or interests in **immovable** or **tangible movable property** or **chattels** are situated where the property is situated.
2. In general, **debts** (secured or unsecured) are situated in the UK if the creditor (i.e. the person who owes the money) is resident in the UK. This is only really relevant to inheritance tax as debts owed to an individual are not a chargeable asset for UK CGT purposes.
3. **Shares or securities** issued by a government, governmental authority or municipal authority are situated in the country where that authority is established.
4. **Other registered shares and securities** are situated where they are registered and, if registered in more than one register, where the principal register is situated.
5. **A ship** or **aircraft** is situated in the UK if, and only if, the owner is resident in the UK.
6. **Goodwill** of a business is situated at the place where the trade, business or profession is carried on.
7. **Patents, trademarks** and **registered designs** are situated in the country where they are registered.
8. **Copyrights** and **licences** to use any copyrights, patents, trademarks or designs are situated in the UK if the rights derived from them are exercisable in the UK.

Note: the assets in categories 6–8 are treated instead under the corporate intangibles regime where they are disposed of by a company who acquired, enhanced or created the relevant asset on or after 1 April 2002 (see **Chapter 2, Section 2.5**).

The above rules for determining situs of assets also apply when considering where an asset is situated for IHT purposes.

13.11 Married Couples and Civil Partners

13.11.1 General

A husband and wife, or each member of a civil partnership, are separate "persons" for CGT purposes and their gains or losses are computed separately. (For the rest of this section references to "couple" or "spouse(s)" should be treated as referring also to civil partnerships and civil partner(s)). Losses made by one spouse cannot be transferred to the other spouse. Each spouse is responsible for making returns of their own gains, and for paying the CGT due on those gains. The residence status of each spouse is also considered individually to decide whether or not that person is chargeable to CGT.

13.11.2 Annual Exemption

Each person is entitled to their own annual exemption. For 2019/20, the annual exemption is £12,000 for individuals.

13.11.3 Disposal by One Spouse to the Other

A disposal of an asset from one spouse to the other does not give rise to a CGT liability where the spouses are living together. The asset is deemed to have passed from one to the other at a value which gives rise to a no gain/no loss position. On a subsequent disposal of the asset to a third party, there is a chargeable gain or allowable loss by reference to the whole period of ownership by both spouses. There is no requirement that the spouses should be living together throughout the tax year – it is sufficient for them to have lived together at some time in the year. In addition, it does not matter that one spouse is UK-resident and the other is not.

There is one exception to this important **no gain/no loss rule**, which is where the asset concerned forms part of the stock in trade of either spouse. In that case, there is a disposal and the consideration is always deemed to be the market value, regardless of the value agreed between the spouses.

13.11.4 Jointly Held Assets

Where a couple disposes of an asset that has been held in their joint names, any chargeable gain arising is apportioned between them in accordance with their respective beneficial interests in the asset at the time of the disposal. If the split of ownership between the spouses is clear, the respective gains should be reported to HMRC on the basis of that split. If the split of ownership is not clear, HMRC normally accepts that the spouses hold the asset in equal proportions.

13.12 Partnerships

An asset owned by all the partners is a "partnership asset". If not all the partners own an asset, then HMRC treat this as simply "other assets". Rollover relief may be available where a partner disposes of a qualifying asset (this is dealt with in **Chapter 19**). Where partners own assets personally, HMRC may allow rollover relief where the owner lets the assets to the partnership in which they are a partner, provided such assets are used for the partnership's business.

Dealings in partnership assets are treated as dealings by the individual partners and not by the firm. Each partner has to be considered to own a fractional share of each partnership asset, rather than an interest in the partnership as a whole. Chargeable gains or allowable losses accruing on the disposal of partnership assets are therefore apportioned among the partners in accordance with their capital profit-sharing ratio. An individual's share of a partnership's allowable capital loss may therefore be set-off against personal (non-partnership) gains, and vice versa. If a partnership makes a part disposal, then the part disposal rules are applied before the gain is divided among the partners.

Example 13.8

A and B are in partnership sharing profits and losses at 60% and 40% respectively. The capital sharing ratio is also 60 : 40. During 2019/20, the partnership disposed of a building which it had originally acquired for £30,000 in June 1984. It realised £100,000 on disposal.

Computation of gain	£
Sale proceeds	100,000
Deduct: cost	(30,000)
	70,000
Apportioned to A 60% × 70,000	42,000
Apportioned to B 40% × 70,000	28,000
	70,000

Each partner would be entitled to claim any personal capital losses against the above gains and, of course, each would be entitled to claim his or her annual exemption.

Partnership goodwill is a chargeable asset, and consequently a gain on the disposal by a partner of their share of a firm's goodwill is chargeable.

13.13 Connected Persons

13.13.1 Meaning of Connected Person

Where there is a transaction between "connected persons", the consideration is **deemed to be the open market value** (unless specifically overwritten, as in the case of spousal/civil partner transfers, etc.). Any consideration agreed between the connected persons is ignored for the purposes of computing chargeable gains or allowable losses. The following are connected persons:

1. **Relatives** Relatives include husband, wife, brother, sister, ancestor (e.g. parent, grandparent) and lineal descendants (e.g. child, grandchild) but **excludes** uncle, aunt, niece and nephew. However, transactions between spouses are potentially subject to the inter-spousal/civil partner no gain/no loss rule (see **Section 13.11.3**). In addition, the following are also treated as connected:
   (a) the spouse or civil partner of certain relatives of the individual; and
   (b) certain relatives of an individual's spouse or civil partner; and
   (c) the spouse or civil partner of certain relatives of the individual's spouse or civil partner.
2. **Trustees** A trustee of a settlement is connected with:
   (a) the settlor;
   (b) any person connected with the settlor; and
   (c) any company connected with the trust.
   A company will be deemed to be connected with the trust if, at any time during the year of assessment, it is a close company and the shareholders include the trustees of, or a beneficiary under, the settlement.
3. **Partners** A person is connected with any person with whom he is in partnership, and with the spouse or civil partner or a relative of any individual with whom he is in partnership. In this case, there is an exception to the market value rule in relation to the acquisition and disposal of partnership assets pursuant to bona fide commercial arrangements.
4. **Company** A company is connected with another person if that person has control of the company or if that person and the persons connected with him together have control of the company. Companies under common control are also connected persons.

13.13.2 Losses

Where a disposal to a connected person results in an allowable loss, that loss may only be set-off against chargeable gains on disposals to the same connected person.

13.13.3 Treatment of a Series of Transactions between Connected Persons

Where a person disposes of assets by means of a series of transactions to one or more connected person(s) (as defined in **Section 13.13.1**) through a series of linked transactions (rather than in one transaction), and:

- the aggregate market value of the asset acquired as a whole is greater than the combined total of their separate values when acquired singly; then
- all of the acquisitions are treated as if they were acquired in one single transaction for a consideration equal to their aggregate market value (when acquired in a single transaction); and

- that revised aggregate market value is then apportioned rateably to each transaction for the purposes of determining the consideration for which each disposal is deemed to have taken place.

Transactions are linked if they occur within six years of each other.

Example 13.9

George and Jimmy are brothers. George has three sets of rare antique Cuban stamps. He gifts them to Jimmy in three separate transactions as follows:

Date of gift		£
01/05/2017	Set 1 market value (on individual basis)	5,000
01/06/2018	Set 2 market value (on individual basis)	10,000
01/07/2019	Set 3 market value (on individual basis)	15,000
		30,000

The market value of the three sets, if disposed of together, is £40,000.

For the purpose of computing George's CGT liability (if any) on the disposals, the aggregate £40,000 market value will be apportioned rateably to the three transactions as follows:

	Revised consideration	£
Set 1:	$\frac{5,000}{30,000} \times 40,000$	6,667
Set 2:	$\frac{10,000}{30,000} \times 40,000$	13,333
Set 3:	$\frac{15,000}{30,000} \times 40,000$	20,000
		40,000

George's liability to CGT would then be computed by reference to the increased consideration for each of the three disposals separately. The non-wasting chattels rules would then be applied when calculating the CGT position on each transaction (see **Chapter 15**).

13.14 Losses

13.14.1 General

Losses are computed in the same manner as gains. An allowable loss may arise in certain circumstances, even where the asset is not disposed of, e.g. a loss arising from the value of an asset becoming negligible (see **Section 19.7**). Note that, when computing a company's chargeable gains position, **indexation allowance cannot create or increase a loss**, i.e. the indexation allowance is limited to the amount required to reduce the gain to nil. However the indexation allowance for companies is only available up to and including 31 December 2017 for assets bought before 1 January 2018 but sold on or after that date. Assets bought on or after 1 January 2018, therefore, attract no indexation allowance when sold.

Subject to certain specific exemptions, **allowable losses may not be carried back** prior to the year of assessment in which they are incurred. They may **not be set-off against other income**, except in certain situations (see later).

In general, a loss is an allowable loss if, had there been a gain on the disposal of the assets, the gain would have been a chargeable gain.

Current-year Capital Losses

Allowable losses arising must be set-off against chargeable gains accruing in the same year of assessment, insofar as this is possible, even if this wastes all or part of the annual exemption. Current-year capital losses may be set against gains in any way in order to maximise tax relief. This is subject to the caveat that losses on assets qualifying for entrepreneurs' relief (ER) must first be set-off against ER qualifying gains as part of the same qualifying disposal. To the extent that there is an unutilised balance, the capital losses unutilised must be carried forward and set-off against chargeable gains arising in subsequent years.

Capital Losses Carried Forward

As seen at **Section 13.7.3**, the taxpayer does not have to use all of the losses brought forward. The taxpayer may "restrict" the quantum of the brought forward loss (or not use it at all) in order to ensure that the full benefit of that year's annual exemption is preserved.

Note: good tax planning would be to reduce the chargeable gain with enough losses brought forward to bring the chargeable gain down to the level of the annual exemption, and then carry forward any excess capital losses.

Example 13.10
An individual has the following gains/losses for 2019/20:

		£
Asset 1	Gain	6,000
Asset 2	Gain	2,000
Asset 3	Loss	(4,000)
Asset 4	Gain	1,000

The individual also has allowable losses forward of £2,000 from 2018/19. Loss relief will be claimed as follows:

	£
Chargeable gains	9,000
Deduct: 2019/20 current-year capital losses	(4,000)
Brought forward losses not utilised (gain already covered by annual exemption)	5,000
Deduct: annual exemption	(5,000)
Net taxable gains after loss/annual exemption	nil

£7,000 of annual exemption is lost. Carry forward capital losses of £2,000 remain.

13.14.2 Carry-back of Losses

The general rule is that capital losses cannot be carried back to earlier years. An exception to this rule is made in the case of losses which accrue to an individual in the tax year in which they die. These losses may be carried back and set against gains of the three years of assessment preceding the year of assessment in which the individual died, with these losses set-off against the later years first.

As with capital losses carried forward, capital losses carried back are set against the net gains only to the extent that those net gains exceed the annual exemption for the year in which they arise.

> ***Example 13.11***
> Mr X dies on 31 August 2019. In the period 6 April to 31 August 2019, Mr X made disposals of assets and realised allowable losses of £15,000.
>
> The losses of £15,000 will first be available for set-off against any chargeable gains assessed on Mr X in 2019/20, with any residue against any chargeable gains in 2018/19, then against net gains in 2017/18 and, finally, against any net chargeable gains in the tax year 2016/17. Any overpaid tax will be repaid to his estate by HMRC.

> ***Example 13.12***
> Patricia died on 30 December 2019. She had made a capital loss of £8,500 in 2019/20 prior to her death. Patricia had net gains in the previous three years of £13,300 (2018/19), £8,800 (2017/18) and £11,200 (2016/17).
>
> Given that the annual exemption for each year was £11,700 (2018/19), £11,300 (2017/18) and £11,100 (2016/17) show the amount assessable to CGT for each tax year.
>
> *Solution*
>
> 2019/20: Losses in this tax year, so nil assessable and £12,000 of annual exemption is wasted.
>
> 2018/19: Net gains exceed the annual exemption of £11,700 by £1,600. Hence, only £1,600 of carried back losses will be utilised, leaving the excess of £6,900 available to carry back to earlier years.
>
> 2017/18: Gain of £8,800 can be covered by the annual exemption (£2,500 of which is wasted). No utilisation of carried back losses required.
>
> 2016/17: Net gain exceeds the then annual exemption of £11,100 by £100, so taxpayer can utilise loss of £100. The remainder of the carried back losses of £6,800 (£6,900 – £100) **cannot be relieved.**
>
> The assessable amounts for each of the years are thus NIL and the taxpayer's estate or personal representatives will be entitled to a repayment of the CGT already paid in the tax years 2016/17 and 2018/19.

13.14.3 Losses on Chattels

We will see in **Chapter 15** that, where a chargeable chattel is disposed of for gross proceeds of £6,000 or less and its original cost was also £6,000 or less, it is **exempt** from CGT. As it is exempt, a capital loss cannot therefore arise.

13.14.4 Losses between Connected Persons

Losses realised by a person on the disposal of an asset to another person with whom they are connected may **only** be set-off against any chargeable gains realised by them on the disposal of an asset to the **same connected person**. This is known as a 'clogged' capital loss.

13.14.5 General Restriction on Loss Relief

The following general rules apply in relation to relief for capital losses:

1. Losses may not be set-off against gains of an earlier year of assessment except in the case of losses accruing to an individual in the year of death.
2. Relief may not be given more than once in respect of any loss.
3. A loss accruing to a person who is not resident in the year of assessment is not an allowable loss for CGT purposes unless, if a gain had accrued instead of a loss on the disposal, the person would have been chargeable on the gain. Thus, in general, relief for capital losses

arising to non-resident persons is limited to losses incurred on the disposal of assets of a business carried on in the UK through a branch or agency (or permanent establishment in the case of a company).

4. Non-resident individuals directly or indirectly disposing of UK property are chargeable to CGT thereon. Should such a property be disposed off at a loss, the loss is ring-fenced for use against gains from other UK property disposals by them in the same tax year. Any unused losses are carried forward to use against UK property disposals in a later tax year. The rules for losses on the disposal of UK property by non-residents are outlined in **Chapter 14**.
5. There are special rules that apply to overseas losses of non-domiciles taxed under the remittance basis (see **Chapter 14**).

13.14.6 Personal Representatives

Personal representatives are treated as having the deceased's residence and domicile at the date of death. They are liable to CGT on any disposal made by them during the administration period of the estate. They are entitled to the annual exemption for the year of death and the following two years.

However, UK representatives of a non-resident deceased person are **not** chargeable to CGT. There are some exceptions to this rule, which are beyond the scope of this textbook.

13.14.7 Losses on Assets Qualifying for Capital Allowances

In general, expenditure allowable as a deduction in computing trading profits is not deductible in computing chargeable gains. There is no general exclusion of expenditure for which a "capital allowance" is made. However, if a capital loss accrues on the disposal of such an asset (e.g. machinery used in a business), it may be restricted with reference to any capital allowances claimed. This would have the effect of reducing the capital loss to nil, but it can never turn a loss into a gain. Where a gain arises on the disposal of such an asset, no account is taken of capital allowances claimed and the normal rules apply.

Example 13.13

Patricia purchased a machine used in her business for £115,000 on 6 April 2016. The machine was eligible for capital allowances (no first year allowances or annual investment allowances were claimed). She sold the machine in May 2019 for £65,000. Compute her chargeable gain/loss on this sale. The accounting date of the business is 31 March.

Solution

As capital allowances have been claimed on the cost of the asset, the capital loss arising of £50,000 is restricted by the capital allowances claimed. This is necessary as otherwise double tax relief would be obtained on the asset. Therefore, any loss arising on the sale of the asset will not be allowable for CGT purposes as it will have been effectively relieved already for income tax purposes.

Capital allowances after any balancing adjustment is £50,000 (£115,000 – £65,000).

To confirm:

	£	£
Cost	115,000	
Capital allowances claimed to date: 3 yrs (W1)	(51,593)	51,593
TWDV	63,407	
Entry in pool (lower of cost and proceeds)	(65,000)	
Balancing charge adjustment to pool in yr of sale	(1,593)	(1,593)
Total allowances claimed:		50,000

continued overleaf

CGT Computation

	£	
Gross proceeds	65,000	
Cost	(115,000)	
Gain/(Loss)	(50,000)	
Reduced by relief obtained for capital allowances against income tax	50,000	
Capital loss	0	
		Allowances
		£
W1: Purchase price	115,000	
Less: 18% WDA 2016/17	(20,700)	20,700
TWDV c/f to 2017/18	94,300	
Less: 18% WDA 2017/18	(16,974)	16,974
TWDV c/f to 2018/19	77,326	
Less: 18% WDA 2018/19	(13,919)	13,919
TWDV c/f to 2019/20	63,407	
Total capital allowances claimed		51,593

13.15 31 March 1982 Value

For disposals of assets acquired before 31 March 1982, the gain or loss arising is **always** calculated with reference to the market value as at 31 March 1982 (this is called rebasing).

Thus, all acquisition and enhancement costs incurred on or before 31 March 1982 are irrelevant for CGT purposes for individuals as they will be replaced by the asset's market value as at 31 March 1982.

It is important to note that this rule does **not apply** to companies. A company should always carry out two calculations of the chargeable gain – one using the 31 March 1982 value, and one using the original base cost. The lowest gain or highest capital loss is then chosen.

Questions

Review Questions

(See Suggested Solutions to Review Questions at the end of this textbook.)

Question 13.1

1. Maurice purchased a holiday home for £20,000 on 2 February 1987 and subsequently sold it on 30 November 2019 for £80,900. Incidental legal costs on purchase amounted to £600 and £750 on sale. Maurice's taxable income for the year, after all deductions and allowances, was £36,115.
2. Vincent bought shares in a plc in December 1971 for £800. He sold the shares for £9,800 on 30 April 2019. The market value of the shares on 31 March 1982 was £1,200. Vincent's taxable income for the year, after all deductions and allowances, was £22,465.

Requirement
Compute the CGT due or allowable losses in each case.

Note: assume that the individuals had no other realised gains or losses during the year or brought forward from previous years.

Question 13.2

1. James acquired a commercial property in July 1967 for £160,000. Additional capital expenditure was incurred as follows:

	£
July 1971	8,000
July 1995	10,000

James sold the property on 31 May 2019 for £650,900. The market value of the asset at 31 March 1982 was £230,000.

James had no other capital gains during 2019/20 and no capital losses brought forward. He had other taxable income in the year (after personal allowance and other reliefs) of £58,000.

Requirement
Compute the CGT payable by James.

2. Declan purchased a residential property, which he never lived in, on 6 April 1971 for £15,000. Additional expenditure was incurred as follows:

	£
Additional 5 June 1973	5,000
Additional 6 August 1984	20,000
Additional 1 February 2003	39,250

The market value of the property at 31 March 1982 was £55,000.

Declan sold the property for £400,900 on 1 July 2019.

Declan had no other capital gains during 2019/20 and no capital losses brought forward. He had other taxable income in the year (after personal allowance and other reliefs) of £32,500.

Requirement
Compute the CGT payable by Declan on the sale.

Question 13.3

Paulette owns a five-acre plot of land that she acquired as an investment in August 1995 for £18,000. On 25 March 2020, she sold two acres of it for £80,000, from which selling costs totalling £2,600 were deducted. The remaining three acres were valued at £145,000 on 25 March 2020.

Paulette had taxable income for 2019/20 of £30,715 and made no other disposals during the year.

Requirement
Calculate Paulette's capital gains tax liability for 2019/20 and state when the capital gains tax liability falls due for payment.

14

Territoriality Rules

Learning Objectives

After studying this chapter you will understand the UK's territoriality rules in the context of CGT and specifically:

- The application of the residence, domicile and deemed domicile rules for CGT purposes.
- The application of the rules on temporary non-residence.
- The application of the rules for non-residents directly or indirectly disposing of UK property.

14.1 Territoriality Rules

An individual's exposure to UK CGT generally depends on their residence and domicile status. The UK comprises Great Britain and Northern Ireland and includes its territorial waters. The Channel Isles and the Isle of Man are **not** part of the UK. Residence in the UK is assessed using the statutory residence test.

The terms "residence" and "domicile" have the same meaning for CGT as they have for income tax and inheritance tax. Note that there are differences between the definition of deemed domicile for CGT and income tax purposes compared to those for inheritance tax.

14.2 Residence

The statutory residence test (SRT) is intended to enable a taxpayer to receive a conclusive answer as to whether or not they are UK resident in any given tax year. The SRT determines an individual's liability to UK income tax, CGT and (in some cases) inheritance tax (where IHT-deemed domicile is relevant). There are three levels to the test:

1. an automatic overseas test;
2. an automatic residence test; and
3. a sufficient ties test.

Each test should be reviewed in turn and, if this does not conclude an individual's status, then it is necessary to review the next test. As soon as a conclusion is reached as to an individual's status, then there is no need to consider the remaining elements of the test.

For example, if the automatic overseas test is fulfilled, the individual will be classed as a non-UK resident. Otherwise it is necessary to progress through the two remaining tests and, if either one is satisfied, then the individual will be regarded as resident in the UK for tax purposes.

The test also distinguishes between "arrivers" and "leavers".

- Arrivers are individuals who have **not** been resident in the UK in any of the past three tax years.
- Leavers are individuals who have been resident in the UK for any of the past three tax years.

The SRT and its various tests were covered in detail on the CA Proficiency 1 course and should be revisited.

14.3 Domicile

Domicile is a tenuous concept as it has evolved through case law and is not legislatively defined. In broad terms, unlike residence, an individual can generally only have one domicile at any one time. An existing domicile is presumed to continue until it has been proved that a new domicile has been acquired. However, an individual can be deemed UK domiciled for CGT and income tax purposes (see **Section 14.4**). For deemed domicile in the context of inheritance tax, see **Chapter 21**, **Sections 21.3.1** and **21.3.2**.

An individual's domicile will depend on their specific circumstances. The concepts of domicile of origin, choice and dependency were covered in detail on the CA Proficiency 1 course and should be revisited.

14.4 Deemed Domicile

For UK CGT purposes (and income tax), there are two ways that an individual can be deemed UK domiciled for the tax year despite having a domicile of origin, choice or dependency elsewhere:

1. If the individual has been resident in the UK for at least 15 of the 20 tax years immediately before the relevant tax year. Such individuals, however, will not be deemed UK domiciled under this rule if:

   (a) the individual is not UK resident for the relevant tax year; and
   (b) there is no tax year beginning after 5 April 2017 and preceding the relevant tax year in which the individual was UK resident.

   Under this deemed domicile rule, deemed domiciled status is only shaken off if someone leaves the UK and there are at least six tax years as a non-UK resident in the 20 tax years before the relevant tax year. This is known as the long-term UK resident rule.

Example 14.1: Deemed domicile: long-term UK resident rule

Agi has a Polish domicile but works in the UK and is UK tax resident. She has lived and worked in the UK since 29 July 1996 but has always intended to return home to Poland.

She sells a Polish commercial investment property on 31 August 2019, triggering a significant gain, and does not remit any of the proceeds to the UK. Under her common law domicile, Agi would not be UK domiciled and so would be able to elect to use the remittance basis in 2019/20, thus escaping UK CGT on this disposal. However, the '15 out of 20' rule means that she is deemed to be domiciled in the UK for CGT purposes in 2019/20 and thus is taxed on the arising basis and is unable to avail of the remittance basis.

Agi can, of course, claim double tax relief for any CGT paid (or equivalent) in Poland against her UK CGT liability. She may also meet the conditions to rebase the base cost of the Polish commercial property to its 6 April 2017 market value, subject to the relevant conditions being met (see **Section 14.4.1**)

2. If the individual:

   (a) was born in the UK;
   (b) had a UK domicile of origin; and
   (c) was resident in the UK in the relevant tax year.

   This is known as the formerly domiciled resident rule.

If an individual is deemed UK domiciled under either of these rules, they are not able to claim the remittance basis (see **Section 14.8**).

> ***Example 14.2: Deemed CGT domicile – formerly domiciled resident rule***
> Shane was born in the UK and had a UK domicile of origin. In 2010 he emigrated to Australia, acquiring an Australian domicile of choice. Shane's employer seconded him to the UK on 6 April 2019 for one year. As a result, Shane is UK resident in 2019/20.
>
> On 30 January 2020, Shane sold shares in an Australian company. None of the proceeds were remitted to the UK.
>
> As Shane was born in the UK, has a UK domicile of origin and was UK resident in 2019/20, he is deemed UK domiciled for CGT purposes and thus is subject to UK CGT on the disposal of the Australian shares. Despite none of the proceeds being remitted, the remittance basis is not available to Shane. He can, of course, claim double tax relief for any CGT paid on the share disposal in Australia against his UK CGT liability.

14.4.1 Deemed Domicile – 6 April 2017 Rebasing

There are a number of transitional rules for individuals becoming deemed UK domiciled for CGT (or income tax) purposes from 2017/18, which are beyond the scope of this textbook. However, students should be aware of one important transitional rule. For CGT purposes only, individuals becoming deemed UK domiciled under category 1. above in 2017/18 may be able to 'rebase' the original base cost of their non-UK situs assets to the market value as at 6 April 2017 when calculating the gain or loss on the disposal of that asset. This is subject to the following conditions:

- the individual made a claim for the remittance basis and the remittance basis charge applied in relation to 2016/17 or an earlier year;
- the individual was resident in the UK in 2017/18;
- for 2017/18, and each subsequent year up to and including the year in which the disposal is made, the individual is deemed UK domiciled under the '15 out of 20' rule;
- the individual has not become domiciled in the UK;
- the asset was held on 5 April 2017;
- the disposal was made on or after 6 April 2017; and
- the asset was not situated in the UK at any time in the period from 16 March 2016 to 5 April 2017.

Rebasing can be considered on an asset-by-asset basis and, on disposal, an election can be made for rebasing not to apply to that asset. The main benefit of rebasing is that the base cost of the asset is uplifted to its market value at 6 April 2017, which may result in either a lower gain or higher capital loss.

14.5 Double Tax Relief

If an individual is UK resident and makes a gain on the disposal of a foreign asset that suffers foreign tax, then relief will be available in the UK against any UK CGT on the same disposal.

As discussed earlier, there are two forms of relief: reducing the net gain charged to UK CGT by the foreign tax paid and (the more widely used) credit relief, also known as unilateral relief. The form of relief available also depends on whether a double taxation treaty exists and, if so, what provisions are included therein. **Chapter 13, Section 13.7.4**, at point 4, sets this out in more detail.

14.6 Residence Condition is Met

14.6.1 UK Assets

A person is chargeable to UK CGT on gains arising on the disposal of UK assets if the residence condition is met in the year of assessment. The residence condition is, in the case of an individual, that the individual is resident in the UK under the SRT for the year in question. Losses arising on the disposal of such assets are allowable losses available for set-off (see **Chapter 13**).

14.6.2 Foreign Assets

A UK domiciled or deemed domiciled individual who is resident in the UK is chargeable to UK CGT on an arising basis on **worldwide** chargeable gains arising on the disposal of assets.

Therefore, an individual who is resident in the UK and is UK domiciled or deemed domiciled is taxable in the UK on gains arising anywhere in the world, regardless of whether or not the proceeds of any foreign asset disposals are remitted to the UK. Losses arising on the disposal of worldwide assets are again allowable losses available for set-off (see Chapter 13).

Please note below the special rules in relation to individuals with a foreign domicile and who are not deemed UK domicile. In essence, such individuals resident in the UK may, in certain instances, only be liable to UK CGT on foreign gains to the extent that the proceeds are remitted to the UK, i.e. be able to apply the remittance basis of tax. Such individuals will always be liable to UK CGT on gains arising in the UK. Where the remittance basis is not automatically available or is not elected for, the individual is assessable on foreign gains on an arising basis. See also the rules applying to overseas losses for individuals taxed under the remittance basis.

It is therefore important to determine if a gain is a UK gain or a foreign gain. **Chapter 13** sets out the CGT rules on location of assets.

14.6.3 Split-year Basis

If an individual is classed as UK resident then they are generally considered resident for the entire tax year, even if they arrived in or left the UK during the tax year. This means that all disposals of chargeable assets, irrespective of situs, are subject to UK CGT subject to the remittance basis rules for non-UK domiciled individuals (who are not deemed UK domiciled for UK CGT purposes).

However, if during a tax year an individual arrived in or left the UK, then the split-year residence rules may apply and they may be assessed only on gains arising after they arrived in the UK or before they left the UK, as applicable. Certain conditions have to be met, which are beyond the scope of this textbook.

In respect of the individual's non-resident part of the split year, the taxation rules for non-residents should also be considered (see **Section 14.7**).

14.7 Residence Condition is Not Met

The general rule is that an individual who is non-resident in the UK is not subject to UK CGT. There are, however, three exceptions to this rule that you should be aware of at CA Proficiency 2 level:

1. A non-resident person or company carrying on a business in the UK through a branch or agency (or permanent establishment in the case of a company) is chargeable to UK CGT (or corporation tax) on gains arising from assets in the UK that are used for the purposes of the UK business.
   Note: rollover relief may be available where the replacement asset is situated in the UK. (See **Chapter 19**.)
   There is also anti-avoidance legislation to deal with the situation where assets are transferred abroad before a disposal or where the branch or agency trade has ceased. In such situations, HMRC imputes a deemed disposal at market value at the relevant date.
2. Gains arising under anti-avoidance provisions for temporary non-residents (see **Section 14.12**).
3. Non-resident individuals directly or indirectly disposing of UK land or property are subject to UK CGT, despite being non-resident (see **Section 14.13**).

14.8 Non-UK Domiciles

Only certain non-domiciled individuals who are not deemed UK domiciled for UK CGT purposes are permitted to automatically avail of the generous remittance basis of taxation. The remittance basis means that a resident, non-domiciled individual who is not deemed UK domiciled for UK CGT purposes is taxable on foreign gains only to the extent that the proceeds are remitted (i.e. taken back) to the UK. UK gains are fully taxable irrespective of the remittance position.

Under the rules, there is a **basic assumption** that a resident but non-UK domiciled individual who is not deemed UK domiciled for UK CGT purposes is taxed on foreign chargeable gains on the arising basis of taxation **unless** they make a claim for the remittance basis of taxation to apply, or the remittance basis is automatically available (see **Section 14.8.1**).

Special rules apply where the individual is regarded as a long-term resident of the UK. Such individuals are required to pay a "remittance basis charge" in addition to any tax on sums remitted into the UK if they wish to claim the remittance basis of taxation in relation to their income and/or gains. This applies if they have been UK-resident for at least seven of the preceding nine tax years.

14.8.1 Remittance Basis of Taxation with No Claim Required

No formal claim is required for the remittance basis of taxation to be applied in three instances:

1. Where the unremitted income or gains arising overseas is less than £2,000. The £2,000 is the net unremitted income or gains for the year.

   > ***Example 14.3***
   > Pierre is UK resident but French domiciled. He has lived in the UK for the past 10 years and makes a capital gain in France of £120,000 (€145,000) in the tax year 2019/20. He has no other income or gains outside the UK and he remits £119,000 of the proceeds on the sale to the UK.
   >
   > Pierre will be taxed automatically on the remittance basis of taxation as his unremitted proceeds from the gain of £1,000 are less than £2,000.

2. Where:
   (a) the individual has no UK income or gains; and
   (b) no remittances of any foreign income or gains have been made; and
   (c) the individual has been resident in the UK for fewer than seven out of the preceding nine years or is under 18 years old.

> ***Example 14.4***
> Pierre's sister, Marie, is a student living in the UK since mid-2016. She is aged 21. She has no UK income or gains, but does have a small amount of French savings on which she receives interest. She has not made any remittances to the UK.
>
> Marie can have the benefit of the remittance basis of tax without having to make a formal claim as she meets conditions (a), (b) and (c).

3. Where:
   (a) the individual has no UK income or gains other than taxed investment income not exceeding £100; and
   (b) no remittances have been made; and
   (c) the individual has been resident in the UK for fewer than seven out of the preceding nine years, or is under 18 years old.

If either of the above three cases applies, the individual is still entitled to UK personal allowances (subject to the relevant conditions being met) and the CGT annual exemption.

14.8.2 Remittance Basis of Taxation with a Formal Claim Required

Where the remittance basis is not automatically available, a formal claim must be made. In such cases, certain allowances are withdrawn, including the CGT annual exemption (£12,000 for 2019/20) and any UK personal allowances.

14.9 Remittance Basis Charge

A non-domiciled individual who is not deemed UK domiciled for UK CGT purposes and who is over 18 years of age during the tax year may, if electing to use the remittance basis, also have to pay the remittance basis charge (RBC) in addition to full UK CGT on any UK gains and UK CGT only on foreign gains remitted. The RBC is payable if the individual is long-term UK resident, i.e. has been **resident in the UK for at least seven out of nine years immediately preceding the year of assessment**. Such individuals will only be able to use the remittance basis if they pay the RBC for the year. The RBC is not payable where the remittance basis is available without a formal claim being required.

A long-term UK resident non-domiciled individual (who is not deemed UK domiciled for UK CGT purposes) and who is not automatically entitled to the remittance basis has a choice as to whether they wish to be assessed on their foreign income and gains on the remittance basis of taxation, or on the arising basis of taxation. If they do not claim the remittance basis and so do not pay the RBC, or if they do claim but do not pay the applicable RBC, they will be assessed to UK tax on their worldwide income and gains on the arising basis.

A non-domiciled individual who is not UK deemed domiciled for CGT purposes and who arrived in the UK in 2012/13 (or earlier) will need to pay the RBC of £30,000 if they wish to have the benefit of the remittance basis of taxation in 2019/20.

In 2019/20, if the non-domiciled individual who is not deemed UK domiciled for UK CGT purposes arrived in the UK in 2007/08 (or earlier), the increased RBC of £60,000 will be payable as they will be have been UK resident for 12 of the previous 14 years immediately preceding the year of assessment, assuming the remittance basis of taxation is selected. The £30,000 or £60,000 charge is in addition to any tax due on the foreign income and gains remitted to the UK. Such individuals will also pay UK CGT on any UK gains arising as these remain taxable under the arising basis.

An individual with a foreign domicile who is not deemed UK domiciled for UK CGT purposes and who pays the £30,000 or £60,000 RBC is known as a "remittance basis user".

The RBC is a charge on **nominated unremitted income and gains** rather than a standalone charge. The foreign domiciled individual can nominate any amount of income or gains. The nominated amounts are then charged to tax as if they were taxed on an arising basis. They cannot be charged to tax again if they are subsequently remitted to the UK. Unremitted income and gains that the individual may have are deemed to be "remitted" **before** nominated income and gains.

If the RBC payment is paid directly to HMRC from an overseas account it is not treated as a remittance of tax and there is no UK liability on it. If the individual were to remit £30,000 or £60,000, to the UK **and** then use that money to pay the RBC, this latter remittance would be taxable in the UK.

The RBC is administered and collected through the self-assessment system and normal filing and payment dates apply. When considering whether the additional RBC charge is applicable, the individual will need to look back over the last 14 tax years, the 14th year being the tax year before the year of the potential claim.

It should also be noted that the RBC applies irrespective of whether the individual is resident in the UK for the whole of the year; there is no pro rata reduction for those coming to or leaving the UK part-way through a tax year, i.e. in situations where split year basis is available.

14.9.1 Summary: Claims for Remittance Basis

An individual who is UK resident and non-domiciled (and who is not deemed UK domiciled for UK CGT purposes) who wishes to pay tax under the remittance basis:

1. must make a claim to have access to the remittance basis, if not automatically entitled to it;
2. must have been resident in the UK for that tax year;
3. must pay the RBC if they are long-term UK resident (£30,000 if they have been resident in the UK for at least seven out of the preceding nine tax years, or £60,000 if resident in the UK for at least 12 out of the preceding 14 tax years);
4. will lose their UK personal allowances; and
5. will lose the UK CGT annual exemption.

The remittance basis is only available in respect of foreign chargeable gains (i.e. gains accruing on the disposal of assets situated outside the UK).

14.10 Overseas Losses of Foreign Domiciles

Losses on foreign assets are allowable losses if the individual is taxed on their worldwide gains on an arising basis, e.g. the individual is UK resident.

Where a foreign domiciled individual who is not deemed UK domiciled for UK CGT purposes claims the remittance basis of taxation and is not automatically entitled to it, relief for losses on foreign assets is only available if they make an election to do so.

This election must be made in the first year when the remittance basis is claimed, even if there are no foreign gains or losses realised in that year. If no election is made, foreign losses of that year and future tax years will **not be** allowable losses, even if the individual is later taxed on an arising basis (unless they accept that they are domiciled in the UK). The election must be submitted to HMRC within four years of the end of the tax year in question.

If an election has been made then, in a tax year in which the remittance basis applies, special ordering rules apply to determine how gains are to be relieved by losses. These are beyond the scope of this textbook.

14.11 Meaning of Remittances

HMRC guidance on what constitutes a remittance is very widely drawn and it would be very easy to inadvertently remit monies to the UK for these purposes. There are also a number of exemptions and a special relief for money remitted into the UK in order to acquire shares in, or make a loan to, a qualifying trading company (business investment relief). This was covered on the CA Proficiency 1 course.

14.12 Temporary Non-residents

A person who is a "temporary non-resident" may be chargeable to CGT on gains accruing during their period of absence from the UK, i.e. while non-UK resident. This is anti-avoidance legislation designed to cover the situation where the individual crystallises their unrealised gains whilst temporarily abroad (i.e. temporarily residing outside the UK). In the absence of this rule, the taxpayer could escape UK CGT by simply leaving the UK for a relatively short time and realising any gains on their chargeable assets during their period of non-UK residence.

In essence, where an individual has left the UK and subsequently returns, they are chargeable to CGT on gains arising during their absence on the disposal of assets they **owned prior to their departure** if:

- following a residence period (i.e. a full tax year or a split year) where the individual has a sole UK residence, one or more residence periods occur for which they do not have sole UK residence;
- in four or more of the seven tax years immediately preceding the year of departure the individual had either:
  - sole UK residence for the tax year; or
  - the year was a split year that included a residence period for which the individual had sole UK residence, and
- the period of non-residence is five years or less.

Note: this anti-avoidance rule does not therefore apply to assets acquired while non-UK resident.

The gains arising in their year of departure are taxable in that year under the normal rules; while the gains arising during their absence from the UK, under the temporary non-resident rules, are deemed to arise and be taxed in the tax year of their return to the UK, unless these are otherwise taxable under categories 1 and 3 in **Section 14.7**.

The individual will be able to claim the annual exemption for the year of departure and the year of return but, in general, will not be able to avail of annual exemptions during the period of non-residence unless these are otherwise taxable, under categories 1 and 3 in **Section 14.7**.

If, instead, losses are made during the period of non-residence, then these losses are allowable and will be set-off against the gains arising in the year of return, providing all of the above conditions for the temporary non-residence rule are met. If the gain has already been taxed in another country in the year that it arises and is then taxed in the UK in the year of return, relief for double taxation should be considered (see **Section 13.7.4**).

Therefore, if an individual who has always lived in the UK wishes to become non-resident to avoid paying UK CGT on assets owned at the date of departure, they must remain resident outside the UK for at least five years. However, consideration should also be given to whether the gain is already caught under categories 1 and 3 in **Section 14.7**.

Example 14.5
Richie Rich owns 40% of the shares in TeleUK Ltd. The shares cost him £200,000 in 2001/02. He lived in the UK from birth until he emigrated in October 2018. He sold the shares for £500,000 in December 2019 and realised a gain of £300,000.

During February 2019 he sold other shares making a loss of £10,000. He had also acquired these shares during 2001/02.

On 20 April 2021 he sold a UK commercial investment property, which he had acquired in December 2018, realising a gain of £100,000.

He returned to live in the UK in August 2023.

Solution

Date of departure: October 2018
Date of return: August 2023

As Richie Rich returned to the UK within five years the gains arising in the non-resident period on assets which were owned at the time of departure are taxable in the year of return.

	£
2019/20	300,000
2018/19	(10,000)
Total chargeable gains 2023/24	290,000

Note: the gain on the UK property in 2021/22 does not come into charge as it was acquired after Richie had left the UK and was disposed of during a tax year in which he was non-resident. Richie could have been advised to remain outside the UK until after October 2023, at which point the net gains of £290,000 would have escaped UK CGT.

14.13 Non-residents CGT on UK Land and Property

There are two special regimes that impose CGT on non-residents directly or indirectly disposing of UK land and property. These regimes together are known as the non-residents CGT (NRCGT) regime.

14.13.1 6 April 2015 – NRCGT on Disposals of UK Residential Property

Non-resident persons directly disposing of UK residential property interests on or after 6 April 2015 pay UK CGT on such disposals. UK commercial properties and indirect disposals are not caught by this legislation (however, see **Section 14.13.2**).

Definition of UK Residential Property Interest
A UK residential property interest is any interest in UK land or property that has consisted of or included a dwelling. However, this only applies to ownership periods on or after 6 April 2015.

In the legislation, a dwelling is "any property used or suitable for use as a dwelling, or in the process of being constructed or adapted for this use." Land that at any time is, or is intended to be, "occupied or enjoyed" as a garden or grounds (including any building or structure on it) is also taken to be part of the dwelling.

The legislation does include some specific exemptions from the definition of a dwelling, but these are beyond the scope of this textbook.

Definition of Non-resident Person

"Non-resident" is defined as not UK resident for tax purposes, depending on the category the non-resident "person" falls into. The legislation is widely drafted and applies to the following categories:

- non-resident individuals;
- personal representatives of non-residents who have died;
- any non-residents who are partners in a partnership.

The legislation also provides for an exemption from the legislation for certain institutional investors and for other categories of non-residents to be caught by the rules, which are beyond the scope of this textbook.

Calculation of NRCGT Gains and Losses

There are three possible approaches to the calculation. Non-resident persons can choose the most tax-efficient method for their particular circumstances, so each of the three calculations must be carried out to determine the most favourable approach to take.

Method 1 – Standard Default Approach

The standard approach for calculating the gain is to use the market value as at 5 April 2015, unless the property was acquired after 5 April 2015 but before 5 April 2019, in which case the property's market value at the date of its acquisition is used.

Step 1. Establish the value of the property as at 5 April 2015 (known as "rebasing").
Step 2. Calculate the difference between the value on 5 April 2015 and the value on the date the property is disposed of.
Step 3. Deduct any costs of improving the property incurred after 5 April 2015 and the legal cost of selling the property.

The following examples are taken from the HMRC guidance, *Capital Gains Tax for non-residents* (www.gov.uk).

Example 14.6: HMRC example of the standard default approach

Rebasing calculation – gain from 5 April 2015 to disposal:

Disposal proceeds	£1,250,000
Incidental disposal costs	£30,000
Net disposal proceeds	£1,220,000
Market value at 5 April 2015	£1,000,000
Enhancement costs	£0
Total cost	£1,000,000
Gain over period from 5 April 2015 market value	£220,000

An election can be made for the rebasing to 5 April 2015 not to apply. This then allows either method 2 or method 3 below to be used for calculating the gain/loss if either would result in a lower gain or a loss. See **Section 14.13.3** for more on this election.

Method 2 – Straight-line Time-apportionment Approach

A simple straight-line time apportionment of the whole gain made over the period the property was owned can be carried out instead, with only the element of the apportioned gain/loss falling after 6 April 2015 being taxable/relievable.

Example 14.7: HMRC example of straight-line time apportionment

Total ownership 65 months, period from 6 April 2015 to disposal was 14 months, 21.53% (14/65 × 100) of ownership relates to period from 6 April 2015 to disposal.

Disposal proceeds	£1,250,000
Incidental disposal costs	£30,000
Net disposal proceeds	£1,220,000
Acquisition cost	£750,000
Incidental costs of acquisition	£40,000
Enhancement costs	£0
Total acquisition cost	£790,000
Gain over entire period of ownership	£430,000
Time-apportioned post-5 April 2015 gain 21.53%	£92,579

Method 3 – Gain Over Whole Period of Ownership Calculation

The non-resident person can decide not to make an apportionment, particularly if they want to establish a capital loss on the property disposal. Further apportionments can also be made to reflect any non-residential use of the property.

Example 14.8: HMRC example of gain over whole period of ownership

Disposal proceeds	£1,250,000
Incidental disposal costs	£30,000
Net disposal proceeds	£1,220,000
Acquisition cost	£750,000
Incidental costs of acquisition	£40,000
Enhancement costs	£0
Total acquisition cost	£790,000
Gain over period of ownership	£430,000

Clearly, in the scenario used in **Examples 14.6** to **14.8**, the straight-line time-apportionment approach would be chosen by the non-resident person to calculate the gain/loss. Therefore this individual would be required to elect for rebasing to 5 April 2015 not to apply.

Rates and Exempt Amounts

The rates of CGT, and whether or not the annual exemption is available depends on what category the non-resident falls into (see above).

For individuals, individual partners in a partnership and personal representatives of a deceased non-resident, the following apply:

- Rate of CGT is 18% or 28%, depending on the level of other UK source income or chargeable gains in the tax year of disposal.
- CGT annual exempt amount available.

Note that the 18% rate is not available to the personal representatives of a deceased person. The CGT annual exempt amount is available to the personal representatives of a deceased person in the year of death and the following two tax years.

For the treatment of NRCGT losses, see **Section 14.13.3**.

14.13.2 6 April 2019 – NRCGT on Direct and Indirect Disposals of UK Land

Non-resident persons **directly or indirectly** disposing of UK land interests (including commercial property) on or after 6 April 2019 pay UK CGT on such disposals. This regime does not apply if the relevant disposal is already subject to UK CGT because the UK land disposed of was used in a UK branch or agency by the non-resident person (see **Section 14.7**).

The legislation also includes some specific exemptions from these rules and for certain non-residents; these are beyond the scope of this textbook.

Definition of Non-resident Person

"Non-resident" is defined as not UK resident for tax purposes and is identical to the definition set out in **Section 14.13.1** for direct disposals of UK residential property on or after 6 April 2015.

Indirect Disposals of UK Land

A non-resident person will be chargeable to UK CGT on indirect disposals where:

- the non-resident person disposes of an interest in a company (UK resident or non-UK resident); and
- that disposal is of an asset that derives at least 75% of its gross asset value from UK land; and
- the non-resident person making the disposal has a "substantial" indirect interest in the UK land (which broadly means they have an investment of at least 25% in the company being disposed of at any point in the **two years** prior to the disposal).

When establishing if the non-resident person has a "substantial" indirect interest, the rights and interests of persons who are connected with them must also be taken into account. For these purposes, a person is connected to:

- their spouse or civil partner;
- their lineal ancestor, e.g. siblings;
- their lineal descendant;
- the lineal ancestor or descendant of their spouse or civil partner.

However, a person is not automatically connected to their business partners or to the spouses or civil partners of business partners.

Effectively this measure treats the whole or part of the share disposal by the non-resident person as an indirect disposal of UK land subject to UK CGT. This means that entrepreneurs' relief, which is potentially available on certain disposals of shares in personal trading companies (see **Chapter 18**), is not available where the whole or part of the share disposal is treated as an indirect disposal of UK land under this regime.

> ***Example 14.9***
>
> Mark and Sarah (who are not connected with one another and are not married) are resident in Ireland. Together they own the entire share capital of an Irish resident company. Mark owns 80% of the shares and Sarah owns 20%. In June 2025, the company is sold for £2 million. At that time the company owned 20 acres of valuable commercial land in Belfast valued at £1.8million, which was acquired in June 2018.
>
> Mark makes a gain on the disposal of his shares of £1,520,000. Sarah makes a gain of £380,000.
>
> The disposal of Mark's shares is treated as an indirect disposal of UK land because:
>
> - he disposed of his interest in the company; and
> - more than 75% of the gross asset value of the company (in this case 90% – £1,800,000/£2,000,000) was derived from UK land; and
> - he held 80% of the company, which is a substantial investment.
>
> Sarah is not treated as having made an indirect disposal of UK land as she did not hold a substantial indirect investment (as her shareholding was below 25%). Mark and Sarah will also need to consider their Irish CGT position on this transaction.
>
> The calculation of the element of the chargeable gain of £1,520,000 treated as an indirect disposal of UK land by Mark is set out below.

Calculation of NRCGT Gains and Losses

The computational rules that follow apply to both direct and indirect disposals of UK land, as previously defined.

If the asset was acquired on or after 6 April 2019, the relevant gain or loss is calculated under normal principles.

If the asset was acquired before 6 April 2019, there are two possible approaches to the calculation. Again, the non-resident person can choose the most tax-efficient method for their particular circumstances, so both calculations must be carried out to determine the most favourable approach to take.

Method 1 – Standard Default Approach

The standard default approach for calculating the gain is to use the market value as at 5 April 2019 in place of the original base cost of the asset.

Step 1. Establish the value of the asset as at 5 April 2019 (known as "rebasing").

Step 2. Calculate the difference between the value on 5 April 2019 and the value on the date the asset is disposed of.

Step 3. Deduct any costs of improving the asset incurred after 5 April 2019 and any costs of selling the asset.

> ***Example 14.10: HMRC example of standard default approach***
>
> A non-resident person directly disposes of a UK commercial property that was acquired before 6 April 2019.
>
> Rebasing calculation – gain from 5 April 2019 to disposal:
>
> | | |
> |---|---:|
> | Disposal proceeds | £1,000,000 |
> | Incidental disposal costs | £50,000 |
> | Net disposal proceeds | £950,000 |
> | Market value at 5 April 2019 | £800,000 |
> | Enhancement costs | £0 |
> | Total cost | £800,000 |
> | Gain over period from 5 April 2019 market value | £150,000 |

Method 2 – Whole Period of Ownership Calculation
The non-resident person can elect not to rebase to the 5 April 2019 value, particularly if they want to establish a capital loss on the property disposal. In this case the whole period of ownership can be used to calculate gain/loss if either would result in a lower gain or a higher loss. (See **Section 14.13.3** for more on this election.)

However, if the election is made in respect of an indirect disposal of UK land any loss arising as a result of the election is not an allowable loss.

Example 14.11: HMRC example of whole period of ownership calculation

The details are the same as in **Example 14.10.**

Disposal proceeds	£1,000,000
Incidental disposal costs	£50,000
Net disposal proceeds	£950,000
Acquisition cost	£1,000,000
Incidental costs of acquisition	£10,000
Enhancement costs	£0
Total acquisition cost	£1,010,000
Loss over period of ownership	£60,000

Clearly, in the scenario used in **Examples 14.10** and **14.11**, the whole period of ownership calculation approach would be chosen by the non-resident person, which would result in a NRCGT loss (see **Section 14.13.3**). Therefore this individual would be required to elect for rebasing to 5 April 2019 not to apply.

Rates and Exempt Amounts
The following rules apply for direct disposals:

- Rate of CGT is 10% or 20% for non-residential land and property disposals and 18% or 28% for residential land disposals (depending on the level of other UK source income or chargeable gains in the tax year of disposal).
- CGT annual exempt amount is available.

For indirect disposals:

- Rate of CGT is 10% or 20% (depending on the level of other UK source income or chargeable gains in the tax year of disposal).
- CGT annual exempt amount is available.

Note that the 10% and 18% rates are not available to the personal representatives of a deceased person. The CGT annual exempt amount is available to the personal representatives of a deceased person in the year of death and the following two tax years.

14.13.3 NRCGT – General Points

Double Taxation
As the non-resident person is resident in another territory, it is likely that the transaction will also be taxed outside the UK. Where the gain is taxed in two territories, **double taxation relief is not**

available in the UK as the non-resident person is not UK resident. However, double taxation relief may be available in the overseas territory as double taxation agreements generally provide that tax paid by a non-resident in the source country will be credited against tax paid in the country of residence.

NRCGT Losses

Losses arising on NRCGT disposals can only be offset against NRCGT gains of the non-resident either in the tax year of disposal or in subsequent tax years. Where a non-resident individual dies, NRCGT losses can be claimed against NRCGT gains in the three tax years preceding death, setting the NRCGT losses against NRCGT gains in later years first.

If the non-resident person becomes UK resident, any unused NRCGT losses become general capital losses and are not ring-fenced. Likewise, if a UK resident becomes non-resident, any unused UK land or property capital losses become NRCGT losses and can only be set-off against future NRCGT gains.

These rules apply to NRGT losses under both of the NRCGT regimes set out in **Section 14.13**.

Administration

NRCGT disposals must be reported to HMRC within 30 days of completion of the property transaction, even if there is no NRCGT to pay. So, if the property was conveyed on 1 July 2019, the reporting deadline is 31 July 2019.

Each property liable to NRCGT must be notified **separately** to HMRC. Notification is made by completing a special online NRCGT return form, regardless of whether or not the non-resident person is registered with HMRC for UK tax through self-assessment.

Unless a non-UK resident person is within the UK self-assessment regime, the NRCGT return should include an assessment of any tax due. Payment of the NRCGT is due within 30 days.

If the non-resident person is already registered in the UK for self-assessment, they can defer the payment of their NRCGT liability and pay any NRCGT owed as part of their normal self-assessment the following 31 January after the tax year of disposal.

If the individual wishes to elect to not rebase to the relevant market value (at either 5 April 2015 (**Section 14.13.1**) or 5 April 2019 (**Section 14.13.2**), this election must be made in the non-resident's self-assessment return. If no election is made, the default rebasing rules apply.

An election is irrevocable if made in the non-resident's self-assessment return. If it is made in a return relating to the 30-day payment on account rules, the election may be withdrawn.

The normal self-assessment penalties apply if the non-resident person:

- reports the disposal late;
- submits the NRCGT online return late; or
- the payment deadline is missed.

A penalty will also arise if the information on the NRCGT online return form or the self-assessment return is inaccurate. The usual penalty regime for errors applies; and interest is payable as normal on any late or underpaid payments.

Principal Private Residence Relief

If the non-resident individual lived in the property as their main home, principal private residence relief (PPR) relief may apply to all or part of the gain on its disposal.

A non-UK resident will only receive PPR relief on a UK residential property disposal if:

- they, or their spouse/civil partner, were living in the UK for that tax year; or
- they, or their spouse/civil partner, stayed overnight at the property at least 90 times in the tax year (the 90-day rule).

If the property was only owned for part of the year, the 90 days are time apportioned in line with the period of ownership. If the 90-day rule is not met, the non-resident person will be counted as away from the property for that tax year. The normal rules for absence and lettings reliefs are unaffected (see **Chapter 16**).

Questions

Review Questions

(See Suggested Solutions to Review Questions at the end of this textbook.)

Question 14.1

Apply the statutory resident test to determine whether the following persons are or are not UK resident in the tax year 2019/20:

(a) Janet spends 10 days in the UK in 2019/20. She was previously resident in the UK in 2016/17.
(b) Paul comes to the UK in July 2019 and stays until March 2020, renting an apartment in Belfast. Paul was not resident in the UK in a previous tax year.
(c) In the tax year 2019/20, Victor works full time in Paris. He spends his summer holidays (three weeks of July 2019) in the UK, working five hours per day. He was resident in the UK in 2017/18.
(d) Christine comes to the UK in mid-November 2019. She buys a house in the UK on 1 February 2020, which she lives in as her home. This house is her only home and she stays in the UK for a number of years. Christine has never had an overseas home. She was not resident in the UK in a previous tax year.
(e) Terry spends 35 days in the UK in 2019/20. He was previously resident in the UK in 2015/16.
(f) Margaret comes to the UK on 22 November 2019 and begins full-time employment (eight hours per day) from 1 December 2019 to 30 November 2020. During that time she obtains holidays of 25 days.
(g) Ned loses his full-time job in the UK in March 2019. He remains unemployed in the UK and moves to Italy on 1 September 2019, and starts to work there full time the next day. He was resident in the UK in all previous tax years. He purchases an apartment in Italy shortly after he arrives, which he lives in as his home. Ned does not return to the UK during the remainder of 2019/20 and returns back to the UK permanently on 10 April 2020, when he starts a new full-time job. Ned does not have a home in the UK.

Question 14.2

You arrive into work on a Monday morning in mid-January to find the following email from a client, Jessica Arnold:

To: An Accountant
From: Jessica Arnold
Date: 10 January 2020 at 19.58pm
Subject: Help!

Dear An Accountant,

I'm hoping you remember me; I was a client of your practice some years ago before I emigrated to Brisbane, Australia, and I need help with some tax issues.

I'm back in Northern Ireland, briefly, for a month-long visit from Oz, where I moved to from Armagh in June 2016. I only went on a year-long secondment originally, but a week after arriving I met my husband, who was born here, and extended my stay indefinitely after getting married. We have just had our second child.

I'm here in Belfast for two weeks and we are hoping to move back permanently in early December of this year. We are hoping to have sold our flat in Australia by then, which we bought when we got married.

The plan is that the proceeds of that sale will help towards a down payment on a wee house in Holywood. Our estate agent is very positive and expects me to make a gain on the flat of around £80,000.

Another useful source of funds to help us start a life in Northern Ireland will be the proceeds from the sale of a painting I inherited from my favourite Aunt Delilah in January 2013. I got £750,000 for the painting at an auction last October. I couldn't believe it as the probate value had only been £520,000. Apparently the artist has a huge following in Oz!

I'm a bit worried, though, that these transactions may create UK tax issues for me. Can you advise?

Best wishes,
Jessica

Requirement
Assess whether the temporary non-residence rules for capital gains tax apply to the above transactions. What practical advice would you give Jessica?

Question 14.3

Sophia has been UK resident since 6 April 2006 but has a Belgian domicile of origin. She sold a foreign, residential investment property during 2019/20, resulting in a chargeable gain of £220,300 and remitted £25,000 of this to the UK during the year. Sophia is employed in the UK and has employment income of £90,000. She had no other sources of income during the tax year and paid no capital gains tax in Belgium.

Requirement
(a) Assess, with comparative calculations, if Sophia should make a claim to use the remittance basis in 2019/20 in respect of the above chargeable gain. Include calculations of the UK capital gains tax under each scenario and address any other relevant considerations.
(b) If Sophia had been UK resident since 6 April 2001, outline what difference this would make to her UK CGT position.

Question 14.4

It is February 2020. Catarine Martinique is financial director of a successful UK company and has telephoned you about a taxation matter she needs assistance on. Catarine was born in France but has lived and worked in the UK since 6 April 2006. Her only source of income is her £70,000 salary from her employer. Catarine did own an apartment in Paris but never generated any income from it and recently sold it (on 1 January 2020) for a profit of £472,300. No French tax is payable on the disposal due to several generous reliefs available in France. A month later Catarine transferred £240,000 from that disposal to her UK bank account to use as a down payment on a luxury holiday property near Lough Erne. The remaining £232,000 she intends to leave untouched in her French, high-interest savings account.

Requirement

Draft a letter to Catarine assessing, with comparative calculations, whether she should make a claim to use the remittance basis in 2019/20 in respect of the chargeable gain on the Parisian property.

A calculation of the CGT liability under each option is required, including any other relevant tax considerations. You should assume Catarine has made no other disposals in 2019/20 and that she is an additional rate taxpayer.

Question 14.5

It is April 2020 and you are a Tax Senior in a medium-sized practice based in Newry. Your client Annette Stewart has telephoned you about a taxation matter she needs assistance on. Annette has lived and worked in Australia since she left school at 18 and hasn't been back in the UK since she got married in Perth six years ago.

On 6 February 2020 Annette sold her holiday home in Lough Erne, Enniskillen for net proceeds of £650,000, she hasn't used it in six years and never lived in it. Annette bought the house on 6 December 2010 for £425,000. Annette read somewhere that the 5 April 2015 value of the property is important. The valuation she obtained established that the value at that date was £360,000.

Annette's only source of UK income is rental income on an investment property that uses up her basic rate band every year. She asks you to advise on any UK capital gains tax issues that arise in relation to this property. Annette doesn't need any advice on the Australian side of things as the transaction is exempt there.

Requirement

Draft a letter to Annette to address the following matters:

(a) Assess if a liability to UK capital gains tax arises on the disposal of the Lough Erne property by Annette.

(b) If Annette is liable to UK capital gains tax, calculate the chargeable gain arising using the most tax-efficient method. Calculate Annette's UK capital gains tax liability (if any) assuming she made no other disposals in 2019/20.

15

Chattels and Wasting Assets

Learning Objectives

After studying this chapter you will understand:

- The appropriate CGT treatment of wasting and non-wasting chattels.
- The appropriate CGT treatment of wasting assets (excluding leases).

15.1 Chattels

A chattel is an item of "tangible movable property". Movable is not defined in the legislation. If an asset is attached to land or any building, it is usually regarded as part of that land or building and, therefore, is not movable, so the chattel rules will not apply. As you will see below, a wasting chattel is an asset with a remaining life of less than 50 years and such assets are generally exempt from CGT. A non-wasting chattel has a remaining life of more than 50 years and is not generally exempt from CGT.

15.1.1 Non-wasting Chattels – Rules

There are three special rules to be aware of for non-wasting chattels:

1. **Exemption relief** If a non-wasting chattel is sold for gross proceeds of £6,000 or less and the original cost was £6,000 or less, then **any gain** will be exempt from CGT (even if capital allowances have been, or could have been, claimed). Any loss arising is not an allowable capital loss. This is a very practical relief and can prove to be very beneficial.

   The £6,000 limit relates to the gross proceeds, prior to the deduction of any incidental costs of sale such as commission costs, etc.

> ***Example 15.1***
> A work of art is bought for £1,000 and later sold for £3,500. The chargeable gain on disposal of £2,500 is exempt from CGT. There is no chargeable gain as the asset is a non-wasting chattel sold for less than £6,000 and its original cost was also less than £6,000, therefore the exemption rule applies.
>
> If the work of art had instead been bought for £3,500 and sold for £1,000, a loss of £2,500 would have arisen – however this loss would not be allowable.

2. **Restricted loss relief** If the disposal consideration is £6,000 or less and the base cost is more than £6,000, a loss arises and any such loss is restricted. In preparing the CGT computation, the actual proceeds are replaced by deemed proceeds of £6,000, which has the

effect of reducing the allowable capital loss. This rule cannot turn a loss into a gain, instead the loss would be reduced to nil and there is neither a gain nor a loss.

Example 15.2
Geraldine purchased an antique table in January 2006 for £9,700. She sells this table for gross proceeds of £5,800 in August 2019 (selling costs £200). Compute the allowable loss.

Solution
Since the gross proceeds are less than £6,000 and the original cost is more than £6,000, the gross proceeds are deemed to be £6,000 which restricts the capital loss.

	£
Gross proceeds – deemed to be £6,000	6,000
Less: disposal costs	(200)
Net proceeds	5,800
Cost	(9,700)
Allowable loss (restricted)	(3,900)

Without this rule, the loss would have been £4,100.
What would Angela's loss be if the gross sales proceeds had instead been £6,400?
In this instance, as both gross proceeds and cost exceed £6,000, none of the special rules at 1 or 2 (or 3 below) apply and Angela would have a capital loss as set out below.

	£
Gross proceeds	6,400
Less: disposal costs	(200)
Net proceeds	6,200
Cost	(9,700)
Allowable loss	(3,500)

3. **Marginal relief** Where the gross proceeds exceed £6,000 but the asset originally cost less than £6,000, an individual may be able to avail of "marginal relief" in that the chargeable gain is restricted to the **lower of**

   (a) the gain itself, and
   (b) 5/3rds of the excess of the gross disposal proceeds over £6,000 (5/3 × (gross proceeds – £6,000)).

Example 15.3
Angela purchased a watercolour painting in May 2006 for £5,250. She sold the painting in June 2019 for £5,940, having incurred commission costs of 10% of the selling price. Calculate her chargeable gain.

Solution

	£
Gross sale proceeds (£5,940 × 100/90)	6,600
Incidental costs of sale (commission at 10%)	(660)
	5,940
Cost	(5,250)
Chargeable gain	690

continued overleaf

Gain is the lower of:

(i) actual gain, £690 or

(ii) 5/3 × (£6,600 − £6,000) = £1,000

So the taxable gain is £690.

What would her gain have been if the cost in 2006 had been £4,600?

	£
Gross sale proceeds	6,600
Incidental costs of sale (commission at 10%)	(660)
	5,940
Cost	(4,600)
Chargeable gain	1,340

Gain is the lower of:

(i) actual gain of £1,340; or

(ii) 5/3 × (£6,600 − £6,000) = £1,000.

So the gain is restricted to £1,000.

15.1.2 Disposal as Part of a Set

Since the chattel exemption can be quite beneficial, taxpayers may try to abuse this relief by selling off parts of a set of chattels individually, with each sale being less than £6,000, thereby qualifying for the exemption. A set of chattels are chattels which are essentially similar and complementary, and where their value taken together would be greater than their total individual value, e.g. a set of four antique chairs, a set of two candlesticks, etc.

There is anti-avoidance legislation to counter this. Where a series of disposals of chattels forming part of a set are made **to the same person** (or persons acting in concert or persons connected with each other), HMRC treat the series of disposals as one single transaction. The three special rules described above apply to the set as a whole, so the gain will only be exempt if the total gross proceeds of the **set** are less than £6,000; otherwise, the marginal relief at rule 3 above applies.

Example 15.4

Sarah purchased a set of six chairs in May 2006 for £2,500. In April 2019, she sold two of the chairs to her sister for £3,000 and, in December 2019, she sold the remaining four chairs to this sister's husband for £4,600. This equates to market value for each chair. The entire market value of the set is no greater than the individual market value of each chair.

Solution

Without the anti-avoidance legislation, the taxpayer's disposals would each be exempt (being less than £6,000 as the cost is also less than £6,000). However, one must look at the entirety of the transaction as the set was sold to persons connected to each other.

	£
Gross proceeds (total of £3,000 + £4,600)	7,600
Cost	(2,500)
Gain	5,100

But the gain qualifies for marginal relief and is restricted to 5/3 × (£7,600 − £6,000), i.e. £2,667.

The overall taxable capital gain is, therefore, £2,667, which must be apportioned between the disposals as follows:

First disposal: 3,000/7,600 × £2,667 = £1,053

Second disposal: 4,600/7,600 × £2,667 = £1,614

15.2 Wasting Chattels

Chattels which have an effective useful life of 50 years or less are referred to as "wasting chattels" and are generally exempt from CGT, with the disposal normally giving rise to neither a chargeable gain nor an allowable loss. Wasting chattels include, for example, racehorses, leases with a useful life of less than 50 years and movable plant and machinery (however, see below). Plant and machinery are wasting chattels unless fixed to premises and immovable, in which case they are not chattels. Machinery includes motor vehicles (except cars, which are exempt under general rules), railway and traction engines, engine-powered boats, yachts, clocks and watches (even if antique).

As noted above, wasting chattels are generally exempt from CGT. Gains arising from the disposal of chattels used as plant or machinery, and where capital allowances could not be claimed, is one such case.

15.2.1 Wasting Chattels and Capital Allowances

There is an exception to the general rule that wasting chattels are exempt from CGT. Wasting chattels used in a business and eligible for capital allowances **are not exempt**. In this case, the wasting chattels are treated as non-wasting chattels and the normal chattel rules set out above in **section 15.1.1** should be considered. Therefore, the gain will only be exempt if the gross proceeds are less than £6,000 and the cost is also less than £6,000.

Thus a calculation of the potential chargeable gain/capital loss must be carried out under the normal chattel rules. One slight nuance is where a capital loss arises and the sales proceeds are actually less than the original cost. In this case, the allowable loss will be reduced by any capital allowances (including balancing adjustments) claimed. This effectively reduces the capital loss to nil and the result is a no gain/no loss disposal.

If gross proceeds are more than £6,000 and the original cost is less than £6,000, the subsequent chargeable gain may, as for non-wasting chattels, qualify for marginal relief and be restricted to the lower of the gain and 5/3rds of the excess over £6,000.

Example 15.5

Andrew purchased a machine used in his business for £5,200 in May 2010. The machine was eligible for capital allowances. He sold the machine in July 2019 for £7,900. Compute his chargeable gain on this sale.

Solution

The machine is a wasting chattel; however capital allowances have been claimed. Therefore, we apply the normal non-wasting chattel rules.

	£
Gross proceeds	7,900
Cost	(5,200)
Gain	2,700

The gain is not restricted to 5/3 × (£7,900 – £6,000), i.e £3,167 as this is higher.

Example 15.6

Louise purchased a machine used in her business for £125,000 in April 2014. The machine was eligible for capital allowances (no annual investment allowance (AIA) or first year allowance (FYA) were claimed). She sold the machine in May 2019 for £80,000. Compute her chargeable gain/loss on this sale. The accounting date of the business is 31 March.

Solution

Though the machine is a wasting chattel, capital allowances have been claimed so we must apply the non-wasting chattel rules. As capital allowances have been claimed on the cost of the asset, the loss arising is restricted by the capital allowances claimed. This is necessary as otherwise double tax relief would be obtained on the same asset. As such, any loss arising on the sale of the asset will not be allowable for CGT purposes, as it will have been effectively relieved for income tax purposes already.

Capital allowances after any balancing adjustment are £45,000 (£125,000 – £80,000).

To confirm:

	£	£
Cost	125,000	
Capital allowances claimed to date (W1)	(79,788)	79,788
TWDV	45,212	
Entry in pool (lower of cost and proceeds)	(80,000)	
Balancing adjustment in pool in year of sale	(34,788)	(34,788)
		45,000

CGT Computation:

Gross proceeds	80,000
Cost	(125,000)
Loss	(45,000)
Reduced by income tax relief claimed as capital allowances	45,000
Capital loss	0

Working 1 – Purchase price:	125,000	Allowances
Less: WDA @ 20% 2014/15	(25,000)	25,000
TWDV c/f to 2015/16	100,000	
Less: WDA @ 18% 2015/16	(18,000)	18,000
TWDV c/f to 2016/17	82,000	
Less: WDA @ 18% 2016/17	(14,760)	14,760
TWDV c/f to 2017/18	67,240	
Less: WDA @ 18% 2017/18	(12,103)	12,103
TWDV c/f to 2018/19	55,137	
Less: WDA @ 18% 2018/19	(9,925)	9,925
TWDV c/f to 2019/20	45,212	
Total capital allowances claimed		79,788

15.3 Wasting Assets (Not Chattels)

If a wasting asset is not a chattel, then it **is not** exempt from CGT. The main types of non-chattel wasting assets are intangible assets (as they are neither tangible nor movable), fixed plant and machinery (as it is not movable) or options and leases (as they are neither tangible nor movable). However, intangible assets acquired or created on or after 1 April 2002 and disposed of by companies are subject to the corporate intangibles regime (see **Chapter 2**).

As its name implies, the original cost of the asset "wastes away" over time. Generally, the allowable cost is reduced on a straight-line basis in proportion to the total length of ownership. The chargeable gain is calculated by comparing the disposal proceeds with the unexpired part of the asset's cost at the disposal date. Note that assets eligible for capital allowances and used throughout the period of ownership in a business do not have their allowable expenditure wasted away.

Example 15.7

Deborah acquired a 30-year patent for £24,000 in December 2010. In December 2019 she sold the patent for £41,000. Compute her chargeable gain.

Solution

The patent had 22 years unexpired life when Deborah sold it, having had a 30-year life when she acquired it.

	£
Sale proceeds	41,000
Allowable cost = 22/30 × £24,000	(17,600)
Gain	23,400

Note: the treatment of leases and options under the wasting assets rules is beyond the scope of this textbook.

Questions

Review Questions

(See Suggested Solutions to Review Questions at the end of this textbook.)

Question 15.1

Shauna Quinn made the following disposals in 2019/20:

1. A painting at auction for gross proceeds of £50,000 on 12 January 2020. The auctioneer's costs of sale were 1% of the gross proceeds. Shauna had inherited the painting from her great aunt Margaret on 31 March 1982. Its value at this time was £2,500.
2. An antique vase on 2 March 2020 for £4,000. This vase was purchased for £14,000 in May 2001.
3. A commercial unit on 2 March 2020 for £185,900. The unit was purchased by Shauna's husband on 1 August 2004 for £55,000. Darren transferred the unit to Shauna on 30 June 2018 when it was worth £75,000. The unit was let out to a local engineering company throughout the period

that it was owned by Shauna and Darren. On sale the legal fees were £2,250 and the estate agent's fee was £1,850.

4. Sale of four acres of land on 30 November 2019 for proceeds of £80,000. This was part of a 10-acre plot of land acquired as an investment by Shauna on 1 May 2002 for £40,000. The remaining six acres were valued at £48,000 on 30 November 2019.
5. Sale of her cherished vintage 1963 MGB Roadster car for £13,250 on 5 November 2019. Shauna bought the car in January 2003 for £11,250.

Requirement

Calculate Shauna's capital gains tax liability for the tax year 2019/20. Shauna's only other source of income for this tax year was employment income of £32,500. She has capital losses carried forward at the start of the year of £210,000.

Question 15.2

John Smith is a new client of your office, and at a recent meeting in July 2019 he was interested in a number of capital gains issues, as he owns several capital gains assets. However, he has never taken capital gains tax advice and therefore would like some general UK capital gains tax advice on what would happen if he sold a number of his assets. John is a wealthy man who earns in excess of £100,000 of income each year.

Requirement

Write a memo to John dealing with the following issues, with reference to the 2019/20 tax year:

(a) Rate of capital gains tax payable.
(b) Date that any capital gains tax will be due.
(c) How any significant capital gains are declared to HMRC.
(d) Amount of gains that can be realised in a tax year without a tax charge arising.
(e) John has heard that some countries give an "inflationary allowance" to deductible costs when a capital gains asset is sold. Clarify the position in the UK.
(f) What types of expenditure qualify as deductible from the sales proceeds received when he sells a capital asset?
(g) John thinks that he might have capital losses of about £15,000 carried forward from a sale of a painting many years ago. How can these capital losses be used?
(h) Would the answer to requirement (g) be different if the asset had been sold to his brother?
(i) John inherited a rental property from his grandmother on her death in February 2008, and wants to know what the capital gains base cost will be on a future sale.
(j) What would the capital gains base cost of the property have been in his hands if his grandmother had gifted it to him the day before she died?

16

Principal Private Residence and Lettings Relief

Learning Objectives

After studying this chapter you will understand:

- The application of principal private residence (PPR) relief.
- The application of lettings relief.

16.1 Principal Private Residence Relief

16.1.1 The Relief

Principal private residence (PPR) relief is one of the CGT reliefs that can potentially have an impact on the majority of individuals.

Provided certain conditions are met any gain on the disposal by an individual of their PPR is exempt. Note, this is an exemption relief and not a deferral relief. PPR relief is deducted from the chargeable gain arising on the disposal.

	£
Gain on property	X
Less: PPR relief	(X)
Chargeable gain	X

What is a PPR?
A PPR is an individual's only or main principal private residence. It includes:

1. a **dwelling house** or part of a dwelling house which is, or has been at any time during the period of ownership, an individual's only or main residence; and
2. **surrounding land**, which the individual has for their own occupation and enjoyment with that residence as its garden or grounds up to an area (inclusive of the site of the dwelling house) of half a hectare (approx 1.24 acres) or such larger area as, having regard to the size and character of the dwelling house, is required for the reasonable enjoyment of the property as a residence. If the house does not warrant grounds in excess of half a hectare, PPR relief will not apply to the excess grounds.

A dwelling house includes relevant buildings within the curtilage of the main house, e.g. garage, outhouses, etc. There is extensive case law on this area, which is beyond the scope of this textbook.

It is important to note that:

1. A taxpayer may have only one PPR at any given time.
2. It is not sufficient to simply own the property as the taxpayer must have occupied the property as a residence (i.e. not merely as temporary accommodation). Therefore, there must be a degree of permanency in the individual's occupation of the property.
3. As the relief prevents qualifying gains from becoming chargeable, it also prevents losses from being allowable. However, HMRC states that losses are not disallowed where a dwelling house is let as residential accommodation.
4. A married couple or civil partners who live together may only have one PPR between them.
5. If a taxpayer owns and actually resides in two (or more) properties, they must elect which of the properties is to be treated as their PPR (see **Section 16.3**).
6. Any residence owned by a UK or non-UK resident will only be capable of qualifying for PPR if it is located in a territory in which the individual, or their spouse/civil partner, is resident; or, where it is located in a different territory to their territory of residence, the individual meets the "day count test" in relation to the residence.
7. After a period of absence, a non-resident individual must meet the 90-day occupation test in respect of a property in order for the absence relief to apply to that property.
8. There is no PPR relief available where a property (or interest therein) was purchased with a view to resale to make a gain. This restriction also extends to expenditure subsequently incurred wholly or partly for the purposes of realising a gain on the disposal.
9. PPR relief is denied where there is a related claim to gift relief under section 260 TCGA 1992 (see **Chapter 19, Section 19.2**).

16.1.2 Full Exemption

A chargeable gain arising on the disposal of a PPR will be wholly exempt if the owner has occupied the whole of the residence throughout the entire period of ownership as their only or main residence.

Where the residence has been occupied for only part of the period, or only part of the property has been occupied as a residence (e.g. part has been used for business purposes), then the relief available is restricted.

16.1.3 Partial Exemption

If occupation of the PPR has been for only part of the period of ownership, the proportion of the gain which is exempt from CGT is given by the formula:

$$\frac{\text{Period of Occupation post-31 March 1982}}{\text{Total Period of Ownership post-31 March 1982}} \times \text{Total Gain}$$

Note: it is only the period of occupation and period of ownership since 31 March 1982 which is taken into account.

The above formula is further adjusted if only part of the property has been occupied as the owner's PPR (see below). For ease of calculation, the periods are normally calculated to the nearest month.

16.2 Deemed Periods of Occupation

For the purposes of determining the availability of the relief there are two types of periods of occupation:

(i) actual occupation where the individual resides in the property as their only or main residence; and
(ii) deemed occupation where the legislation treats periods of absence as periods of occupation for the purposes of the formula above.

Deemed periods of occupation include the following:

1. If an individual has resided in a property as their only or main residence at some point in time during the ownership period, then the **last 18 months will always be treated as a period of occupation**. This is the case even if during those last 18 months, the taxpayer has another property that has been elected as a new PPR, including occupation pre-31 March 1982. This is known as the final-period exemption.

   The final-period exemption is 36 months if, at the time of the disposal, one of the two following conditions is met:

   (a) the individual is a disabled person or a long-term resident in a care home and does not have any other relevant right in relation to a private residence.
   (b) the individual's spouse or civil partner is a disabled person or a long-term resident in a care home, and neither the individual nor the individual's spouse or partner has any other relevant right in relation to a private residence.

Example 16.1
Jane bought a house in April 1980 for £25,000. She lived in this property until she purchased a new home on 1 April 2016. She immediately moved into this new property and elected for it to be her PPR. Jane sold her former home on 31 December 2019 for £310,000. The 31 March 1982 value of the property was £70,000.

Solution
The total period of ownership (ignoring the period prior to 31 March 1982) is 37 years 9 months (453 months). Jane actually resided in the property for 34 years (again ignoring the period prior to 31 March 1982). The last 18 months are also deemed to be a period of residence (since she lived in the property as her PPR at some point). Thus her period of residence is 35 years and 6 months (426 months).

	£
Proceeds	310,000
Market value 1982	(70,000)
Gain	240,000
PPR exemption (426/453 × £240,000)	(225,695)
Chargeable gain (after PPR) (before AE)	14,305

Jane is effectively taxed on that proportion of the gain (27 months) when she was not residing in her former home and which did not relate to the last 18 months of deemed occupation. If Jane's annual exemption has not already been utilised in tax year 2019/20, then this will reduce the above chargeable gain to £2,305.

2. Certain other periods of absence are regarded as deemed periods of occupation provided that:

   (a) the taxpayer had no other exempt PPR at the time; and
   (b) there is a period of actual physical occupation both at some time before and after the period of absence. For these purposes, **deemed** occupation of the last 18 months **does not** count as actual occupation. It is not necessary for the periods of occupation to immediately precede and follow the periods of absence. It is enough that there was occupation at some time before and after periods of absence.

It is not possible to claim PPR on one property and also relief for another property for the same period under the absence relief rules, save for the last 18 months.

After a period of absence, a non-resident individual must meet the 90-day occupation test in order for the absence relief to apply to that property (see **Chapter 14**).

Hence, subject to (a) and (b) above, the **"deemed periods of occupation"** are:

(i) any period (or periods taken together) of absence, for **any reason,** up to a total of **36 months**;
(ii) **any periods of absence** during which the taxpayer is **working abroad**;* and
(iii) a total of up to **four years** of absence during which the taxpayer is **working elsewhere in the UK** (either employed or self-employed) such that they could not occupy their PPR.*

Note: these three periods of absence can apply cumulatively. In addition, it does not matter if the PPR was let during the period of absence.

* Legislation waives the requirement that the taxpayer must reside in the property at some time after the period of absence where their absence is work-related (i.e. (ii) and (iii) above) and they are unable to resume residence in their home because the terms of their employment require them to work elsewhere.

Example 16.2

John purchased a house in Omagh on 31 March 1995 for £45,000. He lived in this house as his PPR until 30 September 2002 when he went abroad to work for three years, returning to live in the house again on 1 October 2005. John's job meant that he had to move to Belfast on 1 April 2014 and he lived in rented accommodation from then on. John sold his former home in Omagh for £275,000 on 30 June 2019.

Compute the chargeable gain.

Solution

	£
Sale proceeds	275,000
Cost	(45,000)
Chargeable gain (before PPR)	230,000

continued overleaf

John's period of ownership of the house in Omagh is a total of 24 years 3 months (291 months) and can be broken down as follows:

Dates	Period	Residence	Absence	Actual Occupation	Deemed Occupation
01/04/1995 – 30/09/2002	90 mths	Actual		90	
01/10/2002 – 30/09/2005	36 mths	Working abroad			36
01/10/2005 – 31/03/2014	102 mths	Actual		102	
01/04/2014 – 30/06/2019	63 mths	Up to 48 mths working elsewhere in UK (by concession) plus the last 18 mths			63
Total	291 mths		0	192	99

Hence all of the gain is exempt.

	£
Gain as above	230,000
Less: PPR 291/291 × £230,000	(230,000)
Chargeable gain	0

Example 16.3

Celine bought a semi-detached house in Portrush on 1 March 1998 and lived in it from purchase. In March 1999, she relocated to Milton Keynes for employment, where she lived in an apartment which she leased until the end of February 2008. She returned to Portrush and lived in her house until the end of February 2012, at which point she moved to Belfast to reside with her mother. Celine never returned to the house after this date. She sold the house in Portrush on 28 February 2020, making a gain of £200,000.

What is the chargeable gain on the sale of the house?

Solution

Dates	Period	Residence	Absence	Actual Occupation	Deemed Occupation
Mar 1998 – Feb 1999	12 mths	Actual		12	
Mar 1999 – Feb 2008	108 mths	Working elsewhere in UK (36 deemed "any" reason and 48 deemed "employment elsewhere")	24		84
Mar 2008 – Feb 2012	48 mths	Actual		48	
Mar 2012 – Feb 2020	96 mths	Elsewhere in UK (last 18 deemed)	78		18
TOTAL	264 mths		102	60	102

	£
Gain	200,000
Less: PPR 162/264 × £200,000	(122,727)
Chargeable gain (before AE)	77,273

16.2.1 Delay in Moving In

There is a further relief where a taxpayer purchases land and builds a house on it but is unable to take up residence immediately (because he has still to sell his old home or is doing work on the new property). Provided the period from purchase to actually moving in does not exceed one year and is **immediately** followed by actual residence then this period will count as a period of residence.

16.3 More than One Residence

16.3.1 Election

Where a person has more than one residence (owned or rented), they may elect for one of the properties to be regarded as their main or sole residence by giving notice to HMRC within two years of commencing occupation of the second residence. It should be noted that, for the election to be valid, the individual must actually reside in both properties.

An election is not required if the second residence is being treated as a residence by means of the "delay in moving in rule" discussed above.

In the absence of an election, HMRC will impose a ruling as to which house is to be treated as the PPR of an individual with more than one residence.

For situations where the property is located in a different "territory" to that in which the taxpayer is resident, the availability of PPR is restricted for both non-UK residents with property in the UK and UK residents with property located in another country. Any residence owned by a UK or non-UK resident will only be capable of qualifying for PPR if it is located in a territory in which the individual, or their spouse/civil partner is resident; or, if where it is located is in a different territory, the individual meets the "day count test" in relation to the residence (see **Chapter 14**).

Example 16.4

Applying the facts of *Example 16.2* above, if John had purchased another property on 1 April 2014 when his job located him in Belfast and elected this new property to be his PPR from that date, would the CGT position differ?

Solution

If he had elected for his second new home to be his PPR then the 45 months from 1 April 2014 up to 31 December 2017 (the commencement of the last 18 months), **would not have been a deemed period of occupation**, as John was claiming another property as his PPR during that time. The last 18 months would still have qualified as deemed occupation as John lived in the house at some point as his PPR.

The chargeable gain would be as follows:

	£
Gain as above	230,000
Less: PPR 246/291 × £230,000	(194,433)
Chargeable gain (before AE)	35,567

16.4 Married Couples/Civil Partnerships

Where a husband and wife or civil partners live together, only one residence may qualify as the main residence for PPR. Where they each owned one property before the marriage/registration of the civil partnership, a new two-year period for electing which property is to be treated as their main residence commences on their marriage/registration.

On a marriage breakdown, provided one spouse disposes of their interest to the other spouse, the departing spouse will, by concession, be treated as continuing to be resident in the house for CGT purposes provided that they have not claimed another house as their PPR and the remaining spouse has continued to reside in the former matrimonial home.

Where a PPR passed from one spouse/civil partner to the other (e.g. on death) the recipient also inherits the previous spouse/civil partner's periods of ownership and occupation for PPR purposes. If the couple wish to elect a non-resident property as their PPR, this too will only be capable of qualifying for PPR if it is located in a territory in which the individual or their spouse/civil partner, is resident; or, if where it is located is in a different territory, the individual meets the "day count test" in relation to the residence (see **Chapter 14**).

An apportionment between business and residential use must be undertaken on a just and reasonable basis, e.g. number of rooms in use, floor area, etc. Each case is judged on its own merits and facts.

16.5 Business Use

As stated above, where part of a residence is used **exclusively** for business purposes throughout the period of ownership, PPR relief will not be available on the portion of the gain relating to this part of the property. Note that it is the use throughout that period of ownership which is considered and not just the use at the date of disposal. In addition, the last 18 months (36 months in some cases) of deemed occupation will not apply to this portion.

Example 16.5

Denise acquired a property in June 2010 and sold it in May 2019 making a gain of £350,000. The house contains seven rooms. From the date of purchase, four of the seven rooms in the property were used exclusively as Denise's main residence, one room was used partly for her hairdressing business and partly as her residence. The remaining two rooms were used wholly for her business. It is assumed that all the rooms are of equal size.

		Proportion used exclusively for business (2/7ths)	Remaining proportion (5/7ths)
	£	£	£
Chargeable gain	350,000	100,000	250,000
Deduct: PPR		(0)	(250,000)
Chargeable gain (annual exemption)		100,000	Nil

The total gain before annual exemption is £100,000. If a room is not used exclusively for business, then PPR should be available.

The part used for trade purposes may qualify for relief as the replacement of a business asset (see rollover relief in **Chapter 19**) or entrepreneurs' relief (see **Chapter 18**) if the conditions in each instance are met.

16.6 Lettings Relief

PPR relief is extended to a gain accruing, up to a certain limit, while the property is let to tenants as residential accommodation. This extended relief is known as "lettings relief". PPR relief should be deducted from the gain first and takes priority over lettings relief.

There are two main circumstances in which the letting exemption will apply, namely:

1. the property has been used entirely as a PPR during periods of occupation and is let out to tenants during periods of absence (where the absence is not a deemed period of occupation); or
2. part of the property has been used as a residence, whilst the other part has been let to tenants as residential accommodation (e.g. there are three floors of a property, with two floors used as the owner's residence and the top floor is let out to tenants). The absence from the let part cannot be deemed a period of occupation as the owner has another PPR at the same time (namely the rest of the property). However, the let part will qualify for the last 18 months (36 months in some cases) of deemed occupation if the let part formed part of the only or main residence at some point in time.

In relation to 1 and 2 above, the letting must have been for residential purposes only.

Lettings relief may be available to cover some or all of the gain which is not covered by PPR. Relief will normally be given where the let accommodation forms part of the owner's dwelling and the owner previously resided in the whole premises. It will not be available if the let accommodation is a dwelling which is entirely separate from the owner's residence.

Lettings relief is restricted to the **lower** of:

1. the gain accruing during the letting period (the letting part of the gain);
2. the part of the gain which is exempt under the PPR provisions (including deemed periods of occupation); or
3. £40,000.

Example 16.6

Christopher purchased a house on 1 June 1999 for £100,000 and occupied the entire house up to 1 July 2009 when he rented part of the top floor (comprising one-quarter of the house) to residential tenants. Christopher continued to reside in the remainder of the house. On 1 January 2020, he sold the house for £585,000. Compute the chargeable gain.

Dates	**Period**	**Residence**	**Let**	**Actual**	**Deemed**
01/06/1999 – 30/06/2009	121 mths	Actual		121	
01/07/2009 – 31/12/2019	126 mths	3/4 Actual		81	
		1/4 Let	27		
		Last 18 months			18
Total	247 mths		27	202	18

Solution

	£
Sales proceeds	585,000
Cost	(100,000)
Chargeable gain (prior to PPR exemption and letting relief)	485,000

The total period of ownership was 20 years 7 months (247 months). He resided in the whole property for 10 years 1 month (121 months) and the last 18 months, a total of 139 months. Christopher resided in three-quarters of the property for the remaining 108 months, so three-quarters of the gain arising in this period will also be exempt.

continued overleaf

Lettings relief will be available on any residue.

	£
Gain (as above)	485,000
Less: PPR exemption (202 + 18 = 220)	
220/247 × £485,000 (Note 2)	(431,984)
	53,016
Less: letting exemption – restricted (Note 1)	(40,000)
Net chargeable gain (before AE)	13,016

Note 1: Letting relief, being the lowest of:

(i) Gain during letting period:
27/247 × £485,000 = £53,016*
(ii) PPR relief £431,984
(iii) £40,000

*Gain during letting period could, alternatively, have been calculated as follows:

108/247 × £485,000 × 1/4 = £53,016

Note 2: PPR – could alternatively have been calculated as follows:

	£
139/247 × 485,000	272,935
108/247 × 485,000 × 3/4	159,049
Total	431,984

Where the letting consists of taking in a lodger who shares the taxpayer's living accommodation and has their meals with the family, HMRC does not consider that the taxpayer has ceased to occupy any part of the property as their only or main residence, therefore there is no restriction on the exemption. HMRC takes this view only where a taxpayer takes a single lodger into their home, not where a taxpayer runs a lodging house as a business. Where an individual lets a room under the "rent a room" scheme, PPR should still be available in full on the subsequent sale of the property.

Questions

Review Questions

(See Suggested Solutions to Review Questions at the end of this textbook.)

Question 16.1

James sold a house in the 2019/20 tax year and realised a gain, before any available reliefs, as follows:

Proceeds	£2,000,000
Original cost	(£1,200,000)
Gain arising	£800,000

James owned the house for a total of ten years. He lived in it for the first three years, and then let it for five years when he cycled across America. He returned to Northern Ireland to live in the house for the last year of ownership.

Requirement
Calculate, with appropriate explanations, the capital gains tax, if any, that is due for 2019/20. James has not made any other asset disposals in 2019/20, he is an additional rate taxpayer and it was the only house he owned in that ten years.

Question 16.2

Jack Bates, a widower with no children, is currently living in retirement in a rented apartment in Spain. His only investment in property to date is his residence in Belfast.

Jack has recently been offered a sum of £1.3 million for his Belfast property by developers who wish to incorporate the property into a large commercial development.

After acquiring the property on 1 September 1995 for its residential value of £65,000, Jack resided there until 1 January 2003, when he was transferred by his employer to their London office. During his period in London, Jack let his residence at a rental of £400 per month.

On 30 April 2011, Jack was transferred back to his employer's head office in Belfast, where he remained until his retirement on 31 January 2017. On 1 February 2017, Jack immediately moved away to live in Spain. While in Belfast between 2011 and 2017, Jack lived in his Belfast residence, but on retiring to Spain in 2017 this property has again been let.

Requirement
Write a letter to Jack outlining the following:

(a) How principal private residence relief operates and the consequences of absences from the property.
(b) The capital gains tax implications for Jack if he sells the Belfast property to the developer for £1.3 million on 1 July 2019, supported with a computation of the capital gains tax payable (if any). Jack is an additional rate taxpayer.

17

Shares

Learning Objectives

After studying this chapter you will understand:

- The application of the CGT rules for:
  - shares (including bonus issues and rights issues, but excluding other capital events such as scrip issues and the disposal of rights); and
  - employee share options, but excluding the employment-related securities legislation.

17.1 Introduction

Shares present special problems when attempting to compute gains or losses on disposal.

Where a taxpayer disposes of shares or securities in a company (hereafter referred to as "shares") which they have built up over a period of time, the calculation of the gain or loss arising on a disposal of some of the shares cannot be undertaken until one establishes the base cost of the shares being sold. The shares were purchased at different times at different costs. Thus, a set of share identification (**share matching**) rules are used to **match disposals with acquisitions**.

The share matching rules are only applied when there is a pot of shares of the same class in the same company.

Example 17.1
Joe bought the following shares in X Ltd:

1,000 in January 1995 for £2,000

1,000 in January 2006 for £8,000

If he sells, say, 1,200 shares today, how would his base cost be determined? To determine the chargeable gain, Joe needs to work out which shares out of the two original holdings were actually sold.

If Joe purchased 1,000 ordinary shares and 1,000 preference shares in X Ltd, then each would be dealt with separately and the share matching rules do not apply as each class of share is distinguishable.

17.1.1 The General Rule

The general rule is that disposals of shares are matched against acquisitions of the **same class** of shares in the **same company** in the following strict order:

1. Acquisitions made on the **same day** as the day of disposal.
2. Acquisitions made during the **following 30 days.** If there is more than one acquisition, then on a 'first in first out' (FIFO) basis – also known as the 'bed and breakfast' rule (see **Section 17.1.3**).

3. Shares forming the **share pool** "section 104 holding" – this holding will contain all the shares of the same class in the same company that were acquired before the date of the current disposal and which have not been matched at either 1. or 2. above.

Example 17.2
Jeremy had the following disposals and acquisitions of ordinary shares in Razor Plc:

Number of shares	Date	Acquisition/Sale
1,900	06/04/2018	Bought
800	09/09/2019	Bought
1,100	09/09/2019	Sold
180	30/09/2019	Bought
1,200	01/03/2020	Sold
950	23/03/2020	Bought

Set out how the disposals will be matched against the various acquisitions.

Solution
The disposal of 1,100 shares on 9 September 2019 is first matched with the 800 shares bought on the same day, leaving 300 shares to be matched. Then the residue is matched against the shares purchased within 30 days (180 shares) on 30 September 2019 (point 2 above), leaving 120 shares still to be matched. These 120 shares are finally matched against the section 104 holding (point 3 above), leaving a balance of 1,780 shares in this holding as at 9 September 2019.

Sold:	9 September 2019	1,100
Bought:	9 September 2019 – same-day rule	(800)
Bought:	30 September 2019 – 30-day rule	(180)
Bought	Share pool	(120) Leaves 1,780 in share pool

The disposal of the 1,200 shares on 1 March 2020 are first matched against the shares purchased within 30 days (as there were no shares bought on the same day), leaving a balance of 250 shares. Finally, these shares are matched against the section 104 holding (point 3 above), leaving a balance of 1,530 shares in this holding going forward.

Sold:	1 March 2020	1,200
Bought:	23 March 2020 – 30-day rule	(950)
Bought:	Share pool	(250) Leaves 1,530 in share pool

17.1.2 Section 104 Holding (TCGA 1992)

As seen in the previous paragraphs, the "section 104 holding" pooling arrangements eliminate the need to keep detailed records of the date and costs of each individual share acquisition. All that is required is to have a record of both the **number of shares** in the section 104 holding and the **total allowable expenditure,** i.e. the cost of the shares in the holding. The only potential modification required to the section 104 holding will be to replace the acquisition cost of shares purchased before 31 March 1982 with the market value of those shares as at that date, if the disposal is made by an individual. If the disposal is made by a company, remember that two calculations must be carried out (see **Chapter 13, Section 13.15**).

Example 17.3

Brian had made the following acquisitions over the years in Arnold Plc.

Number of shares	Cost £	Date
1,000	1,000	01/01/1978
3,200	5,600	01/01/1988
3,000	6,000	01/01/2004
2,400	7,200	01/01/2020
9,600	19,800	

The shares had a market value of £1.36 per share as at 31 March 1982 and Brian had made no disposals throughout the period.

Solution

The section 104 holding as at 1 January 2019 will be built up as follows:

Acquired	Number	Allowable Expenditure
01/01/1978	1,000	1,360 (MV)
01/01/1988	3,200	5,600
01/01/2004	3,000	6,000
01/01/2020	2,400	7,200
Section 104 holding as at 01/01/2020	9,600	20,160

Average price per share as at 1 January 2020 is £2.10.

All that is required to be carried forward is the holding of 9,600 and its associated costs of £20,160. This principle can be demonstrated by the following worked example.

Example 17.4

Following on from the last example, Brian sold 4,000 shares in Arnold Plc on 27 March 2020 for £11,000. He made no further acquisitions within the next 30 days. Calculate Brian's CGT liability for 2019/20. He has already fully utilised his basic rate band but has made no other chargeable disposals in the year.

Solution

Since there were no acquisitions on the same day or within 30 days of the sale on 27 March 2020, the sale is matched with the section 104 holding as follows:

		Allowable Expenditure £
Section 104 holding cost b/fwd	9,600 shares	20,160
Allowable expenditure: $£20{,}160 \times \frac{4{,}000}{9{,}600}$		(8,400)
Section 104 holding cost c/fwd	5,600 shares	11,760

Calculation of chargeable gain:	£
Proceeds	11,000
Allowable cost	(8,400)
Gain	2,600
Less: annual exemption	(2,600)
Assessable	nil

As can be can be seen in **Example 17.4** above, where a part disposal of shares takes place the legislation provides that this is calculated as being the proportion of the number of the shares being disposed of bears, at the time of disposal, to the number of shares as a whole. The formula is, therefore:

$$\text{Original cost} \times \frac{A}{(A+B)}$$

where A is the number of shares being sold, and B is the number of shares remaining.

Contrast this with the part disposal formula for other assets as set out in **Chapter 13, Section 13.7.5**.

17.1.3 Anti-avoidance – the "Bed & Breakfast" Rules

The requirement to match share disposals first with acquisitions on the same day, and then with acquisitions within 30 days, is an anti-avoidance measure. It is designed to prevent taxpayers benefiting from the creation of artificial losses and was introduced to remove the tax benefits of such transactions. The transactions involved are commonly referred to as "bed & breakfast" transactions. Typically, an individual would dispose of shares to trigger either a capital loss or a capital gain, but would acquire the shares back within a short timeframe as their long-term intention is to retain the shares.

Any gain was typically calculated so as to be sheltered by the annual exemption and the new shares would have a higher base cost for a future sale. Clearly, such a transaction was purely for tax reasons and not commercial reasons.

Example 17.5: Acquisition within 30 days of disposal

Harry owns 1,000 shares in X Ltd, which he originally purchased in 2005 at £5 each. On 30 December 2019, the shares are quoted at £1 each. Harry does not wish to sell his 1,000 shares as he believes they will rise in price in the future but, at the same time, he wishes to claim loss relief for the paper loss which he has suffered. He cannot do this unless he has a realisation, i.e. a disposal.

Accordingly, he arranges to sell his 1,000 shares at £1 each on 30 December 2019 on the understanding that his stockbroker will re-purchase 1,000 shares two or three days later. Harry will thereby realise a capital loss of £4,000 on the disposal which, in the absence of the anti-avoidance provisions, would be available to set-off against any gains in 2019/20. He will also still own 1,000 shares in X Ltd when he buys them back at a favourable price a few days later.

The legislation prevents this arrangement by providing that, as the disposal and reacquisition of the same class of shares takes place within 30 days, then the disposal is not matched with the acquisition in 2005 but is instead matched with the acquisition that takes either on the same day as, or within 30 days of, the sale, i.e. £1 per share. This greatly restricts, and may even eliminate, the capital losses arising. If the share price has not really altered in the short period between the sale and purchase, these rules mean that no gain or loss will be triggered.

17.2 Bonus Issues and Rights Issues

17.2.1 Bonus Issues (Scrip Issues)

For CGT purposes, a bonus issue is treated as a reorganisation of share capital. As its name implies, a bonus issue occurs when a company issues "free" shares to its existing shareholders, in direct proportion to their existing holding. So a "1 for 10" bonus issue would give each shareholder (of that class of share) one additional share for every 10 that they previously held **at no extra cost**; hence it is a reorganisation of the share capital.

All previous acquisitions fall within the section 104 holding, thus all that is required is to add the number of bonus issue shares to the carried forward share column and no cost to the carried forward allowable cost column – in essence, reducing the average value per share.

Example 17.6
In Example 17.4, Brian had a carried forward section 104 holding of 5,600 shares in Arnold Plc with an allowable cost of £11,760 as at 27 March 2020. If the company had made a "1 for 8" bonus issue on 6 June 2020, then the resultant section 104 holding would become:

	Number of shares	**Allowable Expenditure**
		£
Section 104 holding b/fwd	5,600	11,760
Bonus issue (06/06/2020)	700	nil
Section 104 holding c/fwd	6,300	11,760

Example 17.7
Rianna had made the following acquisitions in Games Plc.

Date	**Number of shares**	**Cost £**
01/01/1980	2,600	2,600
04/10/1986	1,000	2,000
11/09/2000	600	1,800
02/03/2004	1,800	4,200

The market value of the company's shares as at 31 March 1982 was £1.50 per share. On 1 July 2008, the company made a "1 for 6" bonus issue. Rianna sold 2,100 of her shares for £2.00 per share on 1 November 2019. She had no further acquisitions in the following 30 days. Calculate the chargeable gain arising on this latter sale, assuming that she has already utilised her annual exemption for 2019/20.

Solution
As the disposal on 1 November 2019 cannot be matched with any acquisition on the same day or the following 30 days, it must be matched with the section 104 holding.

Date	**Number of shares**	**Cost £**
01/01/1980	2,600	3,900 (MV)
04/10/1986	1,000	2,000
11/09/2000	600	1,800
02/03/2004	1,800	4,200
Section 104 holding b/fwd	6,000	11,900
01/07/2008 Bonus issue (1 for 6)	1,000	0
Section 104 holding as at 01/07/2008	7,000	11,900
01/11/2019 – sold 2,100 shares	(2,100)	
Allowable expenditure = 2,100/7,000 × £11,900		(3,570)
Section 104 holding as at 01/11/2019	4,900	8,330

continued overleaf

Chargeable gain:	
Proceeds (2,100 shares at £2 per share)	4,200
Allowable cost	(3,570)
Chargeable gain	630

Note: the average price of the section 104 holding after bonus issue on 1 July 2008 was £1.70 per share, being £11,900 divided by 7,000 shares.

17.2.2 Rights Issue

A rights issue occurs where a company offers its existing shareholders a right to buy extra shares at a price. Generally, the shares are offered in proportion to the existing shareholding and the price is usually set at a competitive rate compared to the open market value at that time. The company is offering shares at competitive rates to existing shareholders instead of going to the market for fresh capital investment.

A shareholder, having been offered the rights issue, will effectively have three options, namely:

1. to buy the shares being offered;
2. to not buy the shares, but instead sell the "rights" to buy the shares; or
3. do nothing and ignore the rights issue.

Depending on the option they choose, the CGT treatment will be different.

Option 1 – Buy the Shares

In this situation, the CGT treatment is similar to that for bonus issue shares except that the allowable cost column will have to incorporate the price paid for the shares.

Example 17.8

Continuing with the last example, let us assume that Games Plc had made a rights issue of "1 for 6" at a price of £1.40 on 1 July 2008 (instead of the bonus issue). If Rianna had purchased her entitlement to her shares, she would have purchased 1,000 shares at a cost of £1,400. In this situation, her section 104 holding would have become:

Date	**Number of shares**	**Cost £**
01/01/1980	2,600	3,900 (MV)
04/10/1986	1,000	2,000
11/09/2000	600	1,800
02/03/2004	1,800	4,200
Section 104 holding b/fwd	6,000	11,900
01/07/2008 rights issue (1 for 6) @£1.40/share	1,000	1,400
Section 104 holding as at 01/07/2008	7,000	13,300

Note: the average allowable cost per share is now £1.90 (£13,300/7,000).

Example 17.9
David had the following acquisitions of shares in Newbury Plc:

Date	Number of shares	Cost £
01/01/1977	2,000	2,000
04/01/1989	1,000	2,500
11/09/2000	600	1,800

The market value of the company's shares as at 31 March 1982 was £1.60 per share. On 1 September 2019, the company made a "1 for 9" rights issue at a price of £1.50 per share. David took up his shares. David sold 1,000 of his shares for £2.20 per share on 1 December 2019. He had no further acquisitions in the following 30 days. Calculate the chargeable gain arising on this latter sale, assuming that David had already utilised his annual exemption for 2019/20.

Solution
Once again, the disposal cannot be matched with same day or next 30-day acquisitions. Hence, the disposal must come from the section 104 holding.

Date	Number of shares	Cost £
01/01/1977	2,000	3,200 (MV)
04/10/1989	1,000	2,500
11/09/2000	600	1,800
Section 104 holding b/fwd	3,600	7,500
01/09/2019 rights issue (1 for 9) @ £1.50/share	400	600
Section 104 holding as at 01/09/2019	4,000	8,100
01/12/2019 – sold 1,000 shares	(1,000)	
Allowable expenditure = 1,000/4,000 × £8,100		(2,025)
Section 104 holding c/fwd at 01/12/2019	3,000	6,075
Chargeable gain:		
Proceeds (1,000 shares @ £2.20 per share)		2,200
Allowable cost		(2,025)
Chargeable gain		175

Option 2 – Sell the Rights to Buy the Shares
In this scenario, the taxpayer does not buy the shares but rather is selling the "right" or "option" to buy the shares. This process is known as "sale of rights nil paid", the tax treatment of which is beyond the scope of this textbook.

Option 3 – Ignore the Rights Issue
In this scenario, there will be no CGT implications as nothing has been bought or sold.

17.3 CGT Treatment of Employee Share Options

Share options are a common feature in the remuneration packages of company executives. They usually consist of the right to subscribe at a specified price for a specified number of shares in the employer company during a specified period of time. The income tax treatment of share options has been covered in the CA Proficiency 1 syllabus. Students will recall that a different tax treatment applies depending on whether the share option scheme is approved or unapproved.

17.3.1 Approved Share Option Schemes

There are a number of employee approved share option schemes, namely, the SAYE scheme, the Company Share Option Plan (CSOP) and Enterprise Management Incentives (EMI).

Broadly, the position can be summarised as follows:

- There is no income tax charge on the grant of the option.
- There is no income tax charge on the exercise of the option.
- The shares obtained on foot of the option are instead within the CGT regime and not the income tax regime, and have a base cost equal to the sum paid for them.

For each of the specific schemes, there are conditions to be met in order for the above tax treatments to be applied. **The specifics of each scheme are outside the scope of this course.**

Example 17.10
John works for ABC Plc. On 1 January 2007, he received options under the company's share option plan over 1,000 shares in the company exercisable at any time within the following five years at the market price of the shares at 1 January 2007. The option scheme was approved by HMRC. The market value of the shares as at 1 January 2007 was £10 per share. On 31 March 2008, John exercised his option and acquired the 1,000 shares for the sum of £10,000.

On 1 January 2020, John sold the shares for £30,000.

Because the share option scheme was approved by HMRC, and because there was no discount on the market value of the shares at the time of grant of the option, neither income tax nor CGT was chargeable at the time of grant or exercise of the option.

Accordingly, on 1 January 2020, John is treated as having a CGT disposal in respect of his shares. His base cost in that computation is £10,000. The sale proceeds are £30,000, so John has made a chargeable gain of £20,000.

17.3.2 Unapproved Share Option Schemes

Broadly, an employee is subject to income tax on the exercise of an unapproved share option and this is based upon the market value of the shares obtained, less the amount paid for the shares and less the amount (if any) which has been paid at the time of the granting of the option.

For CGT purposes, any amount which has been assessed to income tax must be taken into account in determining the CGT liability. An individual cannot be subject to tax twice on the same gain. Therefore, the base cost for CGT purposes will take into account the amount paid by the individual plus the amount which has been subject to income tax at the time of exercise/grant of the option.

A taxpayer acquired shares after exercising an option. The shares are later sold. The pro forma computation is:

Proceeds	X
Less: cost of shares on exercise	(X)
Less: charge to income tax on exercise and grant	(X)
Chargeable gain/loss	X

Example 17.11
Patrick is granted an option in 2012 by his employer, XYZ Plc, to subscribe for 1,000 £1 ordinary shares at a price of £1 each at any time in the following eight years. He is granted this right by reason of his employment at a time when the shares are valued at £3 each. Patrick exercised the option during December 2019 when the shares were worth £10 each.

There is no income tax suffered at the time of the granting of the option.

At the date of exercise Patrick is subject to income tax through the PAYE system on the uplift in the value of the shares, i.e. £10 less price paid of £1 = £9 per share. Specific employment income is £9 × 1,000 = £9,000.

CGT: Patrick's base cost of the shares is £10,000 (i.e. £1,000 actual cost + £9,000 subject to income tax). If Patrick sold the shares immediately for £10,000 on exercising his option, then he would have a no gain/no loss situation for CGT.

Questions

Review Questions

(See Suggested Solutions to Review Questions at the end of this textbook.)

Question 17.1

Mark had the following transactions in Magnet plc:

Purchase date		**No. of shares acquired**	**Cost**
			£
05/10/2001	Purchase	1,500	8,000
10/04/2004	Purchase	2,800	10,000
18/03/2006	Rights issue, 1 for 2 held @ £1.50 per share	2,150	3,225
Disposal date		**No. of shares**	**Proceeds**
			£
29/07/2019		2,500	30,000

Requirement
Assuming Mark is an additional rate tax payer, calculate his CGT liability in respect of the above disposal, assuming he has fully used his capital gains tax annual exemption, and state the due date for payment of the CGT.

18

Entrepreneurs' Relief and Investors' Relief

Learning Objectives

After studying this chapter you will understand:

- The operation of entrepreneurs' relief and its interaction with the other CGT reliefs.
- The operation of investors' relief.

18.1 Introduction

Entrepreneurs' relief (ER) is available in respect of gains on qualifying business disposals by individuals. The relief reduces the effective rate of CGT on such disposals to 10% (rather than the standard CGT rate of 20%), up to a lifetime limit of £10 million.

Note: on the whole, ER applies on the disposal of a business and not on the disposal of individual business assets (except in very limited circumstances).

18.2 What is a "Qualifying Business Disposal"?

For ER, any kind of disposal which gives rise to a chargeable gain will qualify for relief if the relevant conditions are met. Such disposals can include an outright sale, a gift, a transfer (e.g. at undervalue) and certain capital distributions, e.g. a distribution received from a company purchase of its own shares where the capital treatment is met and the relevant conditions for ER are satisfied (see **Chapter 20**).

A "qualifying business disposal" includes:

1. a "material" disposal of business assets; and
2. a disposal "associated" with a relevant "material" disposal.

Each of these two conditions are discussed in detail at **Section 18.5**. First, we will consider how ER works in principle.

18.3 How does ER Work?

ER applies so that any gain qualifying for the relief is simply charged to tax at 10%.

Example 18.1

During May 2019, Margaret sells her retail shop business for £650,000. The chargeable gains arising were £250,300, all of which qualifies for ER. Margaret had no other disposals in 2019/20.

Solution	£
Gains	250,300
Less: annual exemption	(12,000)
Taxable gain	238,300
CGT @ 10%	23,830

As noted above, there is a threshold limit for each individual on chargeable gains on which ER may be claimed. This is a lifetime limit.of £10 million. Therefore, an individual can claim ER on more than one occasion, provided the overall lifetime limit is not exceeded.

In determining the rate of CGT charged on other non-ER gains, gains qualifying for ER and investors' relief (see **Section 18.8**) are deemed to be set against any unused basic rate band before those other non-ER gains.

Example 18.2

Siobhan has previously used £5 million of her lifetime ER limit. In 2019/20, her taxable income, after all allowable deductions and the personal allowance, is £21,535. In May 2019, Siobhan realises a chargeable gain of £3 million on the disposal of a business. In December 2019, she sells another business, realising further chargeable gains of £7 million. Both disposals qualify for ER (subject to the lifetime limits). Siobhan has no allowable losses to set against these gains. None of the gains relate to residential property.

The £3 million gain realised in May 2019 is subject to the £10 million lifetime limit for ER, of which Siobhan has previously used £5 million. Consequently all of the gain will qualify for ER. The annual exemption will be used against the later gain as it is exposed to a higher rate of CGT.

Solution – May 2019 Disposal

	£
Gains	3,000,000
Less: annual exemption	–
Chargeable gain	3,000,000
CGT payable: £3 million (qualifying for ER) @ 10%	300,000

Only £2 million of the £7 million gain realised by Siobhan on the disposal of a further business in December is chargeable at the 10% rate of CGT. While Siobhan's taxable income is £15,965 below the basic rate band (£37,500 – £21,535), the £5 million of gains charged at 10% is taken into account in priority to other gains in determining whether total income and gains exceed the basic rate band. So the remaining £5 million gain, less the annual exemption, is charged at the higher rate of 20%, as none of the gain relates to residential property.

continued overleaf

Solution – December 2019 Disposal

	£
Gains	7,000,000
Less: annual exemption	(12,000)
Chargeable gain	6,988,000
CGT payable:	
£2m (qualifying for ER) @ 10%	200,000
£4,988,000 @ 20%	997,600
Total	1,197,600

It should be noted that the taxpayer can choose to offset the annual exemption in the most beneficial way. In this case, it is clearly more beneficial to use this against the element of the gain taxed at 20%.

18.4 Losses and ER

If a qualifying business disposal would be such that both chargeable gains and allowable losses are created, it is the "net qualifying gains" on which ER is given.

The annual exemption and losses on gains not qualifying for ER may be deducted from gains in whatever way is most beneficial, i.e. set against gains taxed at 28% in the first instance.

Example 18.3
Niall makes a chargeable gain of £900,000 in October 2019 which qualifies for ER. He makes further chargeable gains on the disposal of various quoted shares during 2019/20 of £260,900. Niall also has a current-year loss of £200,000 on the disposal of various quoted shares. The quoted shares do not qualify for ER or investors' relief (see **Section 18.8**). His taxable income for 2019/20, after all deductible tax reliefs and the personal allowance, is £27,500. Niall claims ER where possible.

	ER	**Non-ER**	**Total**
	£	£	£
Gains qualifying for ER	900,000		900,000
Other gains		260,900	260,900
Less: capital losses		(200,000)	(200,000)
Less: annual exemption		(12,000)	(12,000)
Taxable gains	900,000	48,900	948,900
CGT:			
Gain qualifying for ER @ 10%	90,000	–	90,000
£48,900 @ 20%	–	9,780	9,780
Total	90,000	9,780	99,780

Note that the gain qualifying for ER has used up the remaining £10,000 of the basic rate band when determining the CGT rate to be applied to other gains. Note also, that the capital losses and annual exemption are set against the gains not qualifying for ER, as this is the most tax-efficient utilisation.

18.5 Categories of Qualifying Business Disposals

18.5.1 Material Disposal of Business Assets

There are certain conditions which must be met for a gain to qualify for ER. The disposal must be "material", and be one of the following:

1. A disposal of the **whole or part of a business** (or a share in a partnership), as a going concern, which has been owned by the individual throughout the period of two years ending on the date of the disposal. The assets within this business must be used in the business, e.g. goodwill.

OR

2. A disposal of **one or more assets after the business has ceased** provided that:
   - the assets had been in use for the purposes of the business at the date of cessation;
   - the business was **owned** by the individual throughout the period of two years ending on the date of cessation; **and**
   - the **date of cessation** is within **three years** prior to the date of the disposal.

OR

3. A disposal of shares or securities in a company which has been the individual's **personal trading company** and of which the individual has been an employee or officer, and these conditions are met either:
   - throughout the period of two years ending on the date of the disposal, **or**
   - throughout the period of two years ending with the date on which the company ceases to be a trading company and that date is within the period of three years ending with the date of the disposal.

Under 1. and 2. above, it should be noted that ER is only given in respect of "relevant business assets". These are assets used for the purpose of the business and, hence, investments or shares will not qualify. A business under 1. above will qualify for ER if it is a trade, profession or vocation conducted on a commercial basis with a view to making a profit. This does not include property letting businesses (taxable as property income) but does include the business of commercial letting of furnished holiday accommodation (taxable as trading income) in the UK or the European Economic Area.

Under 3. above, an individual's "**personal trading company**" is a trading company in which the individual holds at least 5% of the company's ordinary shares **and** that holding also has an entitlement to at least 5% of the voting rights in the company in addition to entitling the holder to 5% of the company's distributable profits and 5% of the assets available to equity holders on a winding up. Note, this is a different definition to that of personal trading company under gift relief (see **Chapter 19**).

18.5.2 Associated Disposals

It may be the case that a person carries on a business through a company or partnership but personally owns some or all of the assets which that business uses (for example, the building which is used as the trading premises). The disposal of an asset owned personally by an individual may qualify for ER if it can be "associated" with a relevant "material" disposal. Three general conditions must be satisfied:

1. the individual must make a **"material"** disposal of either the whole or part (at least 5%) of their interest in the assets of a **partnership** or the **shares** in a company; and
2. the associated disposal is made as part of the **withdrawal** of the individual from participation in the business of the partnership or the company; and

3. the assets are **in use** in the business throughout the period of two years ending with the earlier of the dates of "material" disposal of business assets or the cessation of the business of the partnership or company.

> ***Example 18.4***
> A company director of X Ltd, who owns the factory premises from which the company operates its business, sells the premises at the same time as he sells his shares in the company; the sale of the premises may be treated as an associated disposal and so qualify for ER.

The "associated" disposal rule does not extend to disposals associated with a material disposal by a sole trader. It is also important to note that ER is restricted where the individual charges rent to the partnership or the company.

18.5.3 Disposals of Goodwill to Related Companies

ER is not available on most disposals of "the reputation and customer relationships associated with a business" (i.e. its goodwill) where the consideration received for the disposal is in the form of cash or debt. This measure sits alongside a measure that restricts a corporation tax deduction being obtained by a company when goodwill is acquired from a related party on incorporation (see **Chapter 2**).

Both measures are aimed primarily at incorporations whereby the proprietor(s) of a business sell it to a close company to which they are related in order to extract funds at what is, effectively, 10% rather than the normal rates of income tax and National Insurance contributions. As consideration in such incorporations is in the form of cash or debt, proprietors can draw this down tax-free from the company, having only paid a 10% rate of CGT upfront. The inability to claim ER on goodwill can therefore apply to incorporations where there is a sale of a business to a close company in which the previous owner of the sole trade or partnership will be a shareholder. Such gains are charged at the normal rates of CGT (subject to other reliefs being, potentially, available). A claim for ER, however, is still possible if the individual holds shares or voting rights in the acquiring company that are less than 5% of the company's total ordinary share capital or rights.

A close company, in this context, has its usual meaning (see **Chapter 6**). A related party takes the meaning in Part 8 CTA 2009, in particular section 835(5), where it is broadly defined as a participator or associate of a participator in a close company. This means anyone with a share or interest in the capital or income of the company, or their spouse/civil partner, parent/child or remoter, brother/sister or partner.

18.6 How to Claim ER

ER must be claimed by the individual on or before the first anniversary of 31 January following the end of the tax year in which the qualifying business disposal took place. For example, if the disposal took place during 2019/20, then the claim must be made by 31 January 2022.

18.7 Interaction with other CGT Reliefs

As discussed in **Chapter 19**, ER is applied after the following reliefs:

- Rollover relief – replacement of business assets relief (if claimed)
- Incorporation relief (if no election is made to disapply)
- Gift relief (if claimed).

Gains that are eligible for ER but which are instead deferred into EIS qualifying investments (known as EIS deferral relief – see **Section 19.4**) can benefit from ER when the gain is later realised (for instance, when the deferred frozen gain is triggered by the disposal of the EIS shares), subject to the normal conditions for ER applicable at the time of the first disposal.

In some instances, it may be preferable not to claim both ER and the reliefs above with a view to utilising the annual exemption and available losses.

Example 18.5

On 5 November 2019, Anita sold her pharmacy to her daughter Kerry. Anita owned has owned the pharmacy since 2010. The chargeable assets on disposal were goodwill and the freehold shop. Details are as follows:

	Cost £	Market Value £
Goodwill	Nil (the goodwill was not purchased)	100,000
Shop	40,000 (purchased January 2001)	150,000

Kerry paid Anita £40,000 for the goodwill and £60,000 for the shop.

Anita made a claim for ER, and Anita and Kerry made a joint election for gift relief. Anita made no other gains or losses in 2019/20 and has already fully utilised her basic rate band. This is Anita's first lifetime claim for ER.

Anita's CGT position:	£	£
Goodwill:		
Market value	100,000	
Less: cost	(0)	
Gain	100,000	
Less: gift relief	(60,000)	
Chargeable gain (excess proceeds rule)	40,000	40,000

Anita's CGT position:	£	£
Shop:		
Market value	150,000	
Less: cost	(40,000)	
Gain	110,000	
Less: gift relief	(90,000)	
Chargeable gain (excess proceeds rule)	20,000	20,000
Chargeable gains after gift relief		60,000
Less: annual exemption		(12,000)
Taxable gain		48,000
CGT @ 10%		4,800

continued overleaf

Kerry's base cost position:	£
Goodwill:	
Market value	100,000
Less: gift relief (joint election)	(60,000)
Revised base cost	40,000
Shop:	
Market value	150,000
Less: gift relief (joint election)	(90,000)
Revised base cost	60,000

Note: stamp duty land tax and inheritance tax should also be considered in such a transaction. No stamp duty land tax will arise on the goodwill as goodwill is not a stampable asset. Stamp duty land tax will not arise on the property as the consideration is £60,000, being less than the £150,000 zero-rate threshold for non-residential property.

18.8 Investors' Relief

Investors' relief is designed to provide a financial incentive for individuals to invest in unlisted trading companies over the long term where they are not connected with the company. Often a connection with the company is not appropriate or practical for outside investors.

The relief applies a 10% rate of CGT to gains on the disposal of qualifying shares in unlisted trading company held by individuals. Qualifying shares must be newly issued to the individual on or after 17 March 2016, and have been held for a period of at least three years starting from 6 April 2016. Gains that qualify for the relief are subject to a lifetime limit of £10 million (note that this limit is separate from the limit applying to ER).

The qualifying shares must:

- be new shares – they must have been acquired by the person making the disposal on a subscription for new consideration;
- have been issued by the company on or after 17 March 2016;
- be in an unlisted trading company or an unlisted holding company of a trading group.
- have been held continually for a period of three years before disposal, starting from 6 April 2016.

The claimant must be an individual, other than an employee or officer of the company. Unlike entrepreneurs' relief, there is no requirement to hold 5% of the shares or voting rights. The relief only applies to new shares issued for genuine commercial purposes; and it is restricted so that it does not apply to investors where those connected with the investor are officers or employees of the company.

However, a "relevant employee" can qualify for the relief, subject to all the remaining conditions being met. A "relevant employee" is one who becomes an unremunerated director of the company, or a connected company, following the subscription of qualifying shares. An unremunerated director must never have been previously involved with the issuing company and must not have previously received disqualifying payments. This is aimed at 'business angels' who may work closely with a company after their investment.

In addition, an individual who subsequently becomes an employee of the company more than 180 days after the shares are issued, where there was no reasonable prospect that they would become an employee at the time of the share issues, is also a "relevant employee".

In situations where the investor receives value in the period of one year before to three years after the date that the shares are issued, the shares become excluded and do not qualify for the relief. Any claim for investors' relief in respect of a disposal must be made on or before the first anniversary of the 31 January following the tax year in which the disposal is made.

Given the conditions for the relief, the earliest that a claim for investors' relief can be made is 6 April 2019, i.e. for disposals from the tax year 2019/20 onwards.

Questions

Review Questions

(See Suggested Solutions to Review Questions at the end of this textbook.)

In **Questions 18.1–18.9** (inclusive), calculate the effect of ER assuming that no earlier ER claim has ever been made and that the annual exemption and basic rate band are otherwise utilised.

Question 18.1

Anthony disposed of his trading business, which he had owned for five years, in May 2019, crystallising a gain of £900,000.

Question 18.2

Geraldine sold her trading business for £1.2 million in December 2019, having commenced to trade on 2 February 2018.

Question 18.3

Denis disposed of his trading business on September 2019, having owned it for 10 years. He received £11.5 million and made a gain of £10.3 million. He has made no previous claims for ER.

Question 18.4

Donald sold a residential property in January 2020 which he has let unfurnished to the same tenant since April 2006, crystallising a gain of £240,000.

Question 18.5

Brian ceased his trading business, which he had owned for 20 years, on 20 June 2019. Over the last five years Brian operated the business from three separate premises. He realised a gain of £360,000 on the sale of one property during August 2019 but made a loss of £90,000 on the sale of another business property during December 2019. In June 2020, he disposed of the remaining business property making a gain of £72,000. Assume the rules and the rates in 2020/21 are the same as the rules in 2019/20. He has made no previous claims for ER.

Question 18.6

Thomas owns 4% of a UK trading company and has owned these shares for the past three years. He sells the shares in March 2020, crystallising a gain of exactly £3 million. Thomas is an employee in the company throughout this time and is a higher-rate taxpayer.

Question 18.7

Terry sold his trading business in May 2018, realising gains of £630,000, having owned and operated this business for many years. In June 2018, Terry purchases a 10% share in a trading company and becomes a working director. He accepts an offer for sale in July 2020 for his shares, realising a gain of £10 million. Assume the rules and the rates in 2018/19 and 2020/21 are the same as the rules in 2019/20.

Question 18.8

Patricia ran a shoe shop for a number of years until she decided to cease trading on 30 April 2019. She did not sell the business but sold the premises in April 2020.

Question 18.9

Marie retires as a partner from her accountancy partnership on 30 June 2019. She realises capital gains on the disposal of her share of the trading premises of £150,000, and gains of £40,000 for the disposal of goodwill sold to an unconnected third party.

Question 18.10

You attend a meeting with your client, James Devlin, in April 2020. James has recently retired and on 15 March 2020 he sold his 40% shareholding in the company, Devlin Communications Ltd, an independent mobile phone shop, for £851,000. James had held these shares since the company was incorporated, when he subscribed for 1,000 £1 ordinary shares, which he paid for in full. James was appointed as a full-time director of the company on 1 April 2008.

James also owned a shop in Dungannon from which the company had always traded, having originally bought it as an investment on 1 April 2007 for £125,000. Devlin Communications Ltd started trading when it was incorporated on 1 April 2009 and from that date onward traded solely from the shop. James charged rent of £1,575 per month for the use of the shop from that date. A full commercial rent would have been £2,250 per month.

The shop was subsequently sold by James for £475,000 on 31 March 2020, as Devlin Communications Ltd was moving to larger premises and they no longer needed to rent the property.

Note: James is an additional rate taxpayer and the company is a trading company. The shares and Dungannon property are the only assets he has ever owned.

Requirement

Prepare a report to James dealing with the sale of the shares and the building that considers the following:

(a) The capital gains tax payable by James as a result of the above transactions. You should identify any potential claims/relief(s) James could avail of to reduce his chargeable gains on the disposals, state why the disposals qualify for any claims/reliefs you are proposing and outline the saving to be achieved.

(b) The due date for payment of the capital gains tax arising, together with the time limit(s) which apply to any claims/reliefs you consider available to mitigate the gain.

19

Capital Gains Tax Reliefs

Learning Objectives

After studying this chapter you will understand:

- How to determine and apply appropriate CGT reliefs, including:
  - relief for the transfer of a business to a company;
  - rollover relief for business assets; and
  - holdover/gift relief.
- The principles of relief for losses on shares in certain qualifying companies.
- How to determine the appropriate CGT reliefs available in relation to Enterprise Investment Scheme (EIS) and Seed Enterprise Investment Scheme (SEIS) shares.

19.1 Rollover Relief and Depreciating Assets

19.1.1 Rollover Relief

If an individual disposes of a business asset, a chargeable gain will crystallise. Where the individual reinvests the **proceeds** into a replacement asset within a fixed timeframe, they may make a claim to defer the CGT charge on the gain until a future date.

Rollover relief is relief for **the replacement of business assets** used in a trade. It is available for individuals as well as companies, but it cannot be claimed by an investment business.

Provided certain conditions are met, an individual may claim that a chargeable gain arising on the disposal of a business asset (the "old asset") may be "rolled over" against the cost of acquiring a replacement business asset (the "new asset").

In this scenario, the disposal of the old asset is deemed to give rise to neither a gain nor a loss and the cost of the new asset is reduced by the gain that would have arisen but for the "rollover" relief. In essence, the chargeable gain is "deferred" until such time as the new asset is disposed of (subject to the possibility of a further rollover claim being available).

A person who is resident in the UK can roll over a gain from the disposal of qualifying assets against the acquisition of new qualifying assets wherever they are situated. If all other conditions for relief are met, HMRC will not deny relief where a person has ceased to be resident in the UK when the new qualifying assets are acquired.

A person who is not UK resident but who is chargeable on gains from the disposal of qualifying assets of a branch or agency (or, in the case of a company, of a permanent establishment) in the UK can only roll over gains into the acquisition of further UK branch or agency assets.

The Relief

On a claim, full or partial relief is available depending on the circumstances. This relief is a deferral relief. The gain will therefore become taxable at some time in the future. In line with general CGT principles, as death does not trigger a CGT charge a gain rolled over is not triggered on death.

Full rollover relief is only available provided all of the disposal **proceeds** (not just the chargeable gain) are applied in acquiring the new asset.

Partial rollover relief is where any proceeds not reinvested fall to be taxed immediately. In this instance, the cost of the new asset is reduced by the amount of the gain that was not immediately chargeable.

No rollover relief is available where the amount retained (i.e. proceeds not reinvested) exceeds the chargeable gain.

The relief may be claimed by a person who carries on more than one trade, either consecutively or concurrently, on the basis that they are treated as a single trade. The relief is only available where the new assets are acquired by the same individual taxpayer who made the gain on the old assets.

The **conditions** that must be met before a rollover claim can be made are:

1. Both the old and the new asset must be within one of the specified classes of assets (see below). However, it is not necessary that they should both be within the same class.
2. The old asset must have been used only for trade purposes throughout the period of ownership and the new asset must be taken into and used immediately in the trade. However, see **Section 19.1.3** for rollover relief on mixed-use assets.
3. The new asset must be acquired during the specified period beginning 12 months before and ending 36 months after the date of disposal of the old asset.

The **class of assets** referred to above include:

- land, buildings and fixed plant and machinery;
- ships, hovercraft, aircraft, satellites, space stations and spacecraft;
- milk, potato and fish quotas and certain other EU quotas;
- goodwill (however, rollover relief is not available to companies making a disposal of tangible assets and then using the proceeds to acquire intangible fixed assets that fall within the corporate intangibles regime (see **Chapter 2**)).

Note: shares are not a qualifying asset for rollover relief as they cannot be used for the purposes of the trade.

It is generally accepted that it is the disposal consideration net of incidental costs of disposal of the old asset that should be compared with the total costs of acquisition, including incidental costs, of the new asset.

Example 19.1

On 1 January 2019, a farmer sells land for £40,000. The expenses of sale are £3,000. On 1 October 2018, the farmer buys land for use in the trade at a cost of £35,000 plus expenses of £4,000. For the purposes of a claim, the disposal consideration is £37,000 and the amount applied in acquiring new assets is £39,000. Full relief is therefore due as the full net proceeds have been reinvested.

Claims for Rollover Relief

Claims for the relief must be made within four years after the end of the tax year (or accounting period for companies) in which the later of the disposal of the old asset or the acquisition of the new asset took place. Where the disposal of the old asset takes place in 2019/20 and the acquisition of the new asset is made in 2020/21, the claim must be made on or before 5 April 2025.

It is possible to make provisional claims for rollover relief if it is intended that a purchase of a qualifying asset will take place within the specified period.

It may be preferred not to claim rollover relief on business assets where sufficient capital losses and annual exemption (individuals only) are available for claim.

Note: it is not possible to specify or tailor the amount of rollover relief to be claimed. Either full relief will be available where the full proceeds are reinvested, or partial relief in circumstances where the full proceeds have not been reinvested.

Example 19.2

On 1 July 2004, John Smith acquired freehold trade premises for £100,000. The business expanded and, during December 2019, new premises were acquired for £200,000 and the old premises were sold on 1 November 2019 for £160,000. John's full basic rate band is utilised against other income.

In the absence of a claim for rollover relief, there would be chargeable gains as follows:

Sale of old premises – without rollover relief	£
Disposal proceeds	160,000
Deduct: Allowable cost	(100,000)
Chargeable gain	60,000
Less: annual exemption	(12,000)
Taxable chargeable gain	48,000
CGT @ 20%	9,600

Note: John Smith cannot claim ER on the disposal of the trade premises, as he is not disposing of the trade itself.

Where rollover relief is claimed, the position is as follows:

Sale of old premises – with rollover relief	£
Disposal proceeds	160,000
Deduct: Allowable cost	(100,000)
Chargeable gain	60,000
Less: rollover relief	(60,000)
Taxable chargeable gain	0
Base cost of new asset:	
Purchase of new asset	
Cost	200,000
Deduct rollover relief	(60,000)
Revised base cost	140,000

Where rollover relief is claimed, John's annual exemption is wasted as his full rollover relief cannot be tailored, thus it is an "all or nothing" claim.

Example 19.3

Beth purchased a property for £80,000 in July 2002 for use in her business. In June 2019, she purchased another property for use in her business and two months later sold the original property for £175,000. Beth wishes to claim rollover relief on the sale of the original property. Compute her chargeable gain if the cost of the replacement property was respectively (assuming both the old and new asset are within the relevant class of assets):

(i) £190,000 (ii) £150,000 and (iii) £70,000

continued overleaf

The chargeable gain on the disposal of the original property is:

	£
Proceeds	175,000
Cost	(80,000)
Gain	95,000

The quantum of the gain which can be rolled over will depend on the amount reinvested:

1. If the new property was purchased for £190,000, all of the sale proceeds have been reinvested and, thus, all of the gain of £95,000 can be rolled over into the cost of the new asset. The base cost for CGT purposes of the new asset is £95,000 (being £190,000 – £95,000 (rolled over)). In essence, the gain of £95,000 is deferred until the new asset is sold (subject to any potential further rollover claim).
2. In this situation, £25,000 of the disposal proceeds have not been reinvested and thus become **immediately** chargeable. The residue of the gain, namely £70,000 (£95,000 – £25,000) can be rolled over into the cost of the new property and the CGT base cost of the new asset will be £80,000 (being £150,000 – £70,000 (rolled over)).
3. In this situation, the amount of the proceeds **not** reinvested is £105,000, which exceeds the actual chargeable gain of £95,000. Thus, all of the gain of £95,000 is immediately chargeable and rollover relief does not apply.

19.1.2 Companies and Rollover Relief

For companies (unlike individuals), the list of assets on which rollover relief can be claimed does **not** include **goodwill** or **quotas** if these assets are within the intangible fixed assets regime (see **Chapter 2**).

Rollover relief is also potentially available within a capital gains group of companies (see **Chapter 10**). If a capital gains group member disposes of an asset that is eligible for rollover relief, it can treat all the group members as a single entity for claiming such relief (provided, of course, that all the remaining conditions are met). Thus, if another group member acquires a relevant asset within the qualifying period (12 months before the disposal or 36 months afterwards), the company making the disposal may match the acquisition for rollover relief purposes. The acquiring company must be a member of the group at the time of acquisition and the disposing company must be a member of the group at the time of sale. However, there is no requirement for them both to be a member of the group at the same time.

For it to be effective, both the acquiring company and the disposing company must make a joint claim for the relief to apply.

It should be noted that assets transferred intragroup on a no gain/no loss basis *cannot* be matched for rollover relief purposes.

19.1.3 Mixed Use (Business and Non-business Use)

In order to qualify for full relief, the old asset must have been used only for the purposes of the business throughout the whole period of ownership and the new asset must, on acquisition, be taken into use and used only for business purposes. However, where this is not the case, then the business portion and non-business portion must be treated as separate assets. There are two situations in which partial relief may be given when these conditions are not met.

1. If the old asset was not wholly used for business purposes, it is treated as two separate assets in calculating the rollover relief. The disposal proceeds are apportioned between the business use and the non-business use. Only the part of the overall gain applicable to the business use qualifies for rollover relief.

A similar apportionment is made where the new asset not used wholly for business purposes. Any gain can only be rolled over into the expenditure arising on business use of the new asset. This scenario can therefore apply to the old asset, the new asset or to both.

2. If the claimant did not use the old asset for business purposes for the entire ownership period (excluding any period before 31 March 1982), the asset is treated as two separate assets in calculating the rollover relief. Expenditure on acquisition and disposal are apportioned between business use and non-business use. Only the part of the overall gain that relates to business use qualifies for rollover relief.

The apportionment is to be made on a just and reasonable basis.

Example 19.4

Richard Moss, trading in fireplace manufacturing, acquired a building on 1 November 1999 for £110,000. 40% of the building was used as business offices and the remainder was let on leases to unconnected parties. On 1 November 2019, the building was sold for £400,000 and a new building acquired for £500,000, of which 25% was used for business.

The calculation of the gain on the old building before rollover relief is:

	Total	**40% Business asset**	**60% Non-business asset**
	£	£	£
Disposal proceeds	400,000	160,000	240,000
Deduct: cost	(110,000)	(44,000)	(66,000)
Net gain	290,000	116,000	174,000

The business element in the new building is £125,000 (25% of £500,000); therefore, £35,000 of the proceeds of the £160,000 business disposal has not been reinvested. The amount not reinvested is less than the gain of £116,000; therefore, rollover relief is permitted for £81,000 of the gain. £35,000 is assessed to CGT immediately. The gain on the disposal chargeable to tax is:

	£
Gain on non-business asset	174,000
Gain on business asset: proceeds not reinvested	35,000
Chargeable gain	209,000

The deemed cost of the business element in the new building is £44,000 (£125,000 less gain rolled over of £81,000).

19.1.4 Interaction with Entrepreneurs' Relief

A taxpayer should consider if it would be more beneficial to claim ER or rollover relief or potentially both, where the relevant conditions for each are met. As set out in **Chapter 18**, ER is only available on the disposal of the whole or part of a business and not on the disposal of individual assets. Rollover relief is typically relevant where there is a sale of an individual business asset and the individual continues to carry on the business. If it is possible to claim both reliefs – an individual may wish to claim ER instead of rollover relief in order to crystallise a gain taxable at 10%, or to utilise capital losses and the CGT annual exemption.

If both reliefs are claimed, rollover relief applies before ER. This would apply, for example, where some proceeds have not been reinvested so that rollover relief does not cover the whole of the gain. In this case, ER will apply to the gain left after rollover relief has been applied. However, the gain must be a qualifying business disposal for ER.

19.1.5 Depreciating Assets

A depreciating asset is fixed plant and machinery not forming part of a building, or an asset that has a predictable useful life not exceeding 60 years from the time it is acquired. Another example of a depreciating asset is a short-term lease of 60 years or less.

Where the new replacement asset is a "depreciating asset", the chargeable gain arising on the disposal of the old asset **cannot** be rolled over and is **not** deducted from the base cost of the new asset. Instead, the chargeable gain is "frozen" or "temporarily parked" until it becomes chargeable (crystallises) on the **earliest** of the following three dates:

1. the date on which the new depreciating asset is disposed of;
2. the date on which the new depreciating asset ceases to be used in the trade; or
3. the tenth anniversary of the acquisition of the new depreciating asset.

If a taxpayer purchases a non-depreciating asset (within the relevant class – see **Section 19.1.1**) prior to the earliest of the above three dates expiring, then it could "convert" the temporarily "frozen" gain into a "rolled over" gain. This effectively widens the window of opportunity for the taxpayer to reinvest the original proceeds into the relevant class of assets.

In effect, the taxpayer can "park" the gain against the purchase of a depreciating asset until such time as a qualifying asset for rollover relief is purchased and a claim for the relief can be made.

Example 19.5

Michelle bought business premises in September 2007 for £115,000. She sold the premises for £150,000 on 1 October 2012. On 15 September 2012, she bought some fixed plant and machinery to use in her business costing £140,000. These were sold for £155,000 on 30 June 2019. What is Michelle's CGT liability?

The gain on the premises may be deferred by parking the gain against the purchase of the depreciating asset. Note that the gain on the premises is frozen; it is not rolled over into the cost of the depreciating asset. When the depreciating asset is sold, then as well as the gain on this sale being taxable, the gain on the frozen sale of the premises also crystallises.

2012/13 Sale of premises	£
Proceeds	150,000
Cost	(115,000)
Gain	35,000
Less: gain frozen on purchase of fixed P&M	(25,000)
Chargeable gain (proceeds not reinvested)	10,000

2019/20 Sale of fixed P&M	£
Proceeds	155,000
Cost	(140,000)
Gain	15,000

2019/20: Total gain chargeable on sale of fixed P&M	£
Gain on sale of fixed P&M	15,000
Crystallised gain	25,000
Total chargeable gain	40,000

19.2 Gift Relief/Holdover Relief

19.2.1 Section 165 Gift Relief – Business Assets

When a qualifying business asset is gifted for nil consideration, the transferor receives no proceeds from the transaction. For CGT purposes, the disposal is treated as a disposal at market value as the transaction is not at arm's length. This is the case even if the parties are unconnected. A chargeable gain will therefore crystallise, which means that the taxpayer, in the absence of any "gift relief", could find themselves in a difficult financial position, having to pay CGT in respect of the gift but not having received any proceeds with which to fund it. This is known as a 'dry' tax charge.

Section 165 gift relief is a form of deferral relief for business assets. Where a gain arises on a gift or a sale at an undervalue of a **business asset**, the gain may be "held over" until such time as the transferee disposes of the asset(s) concerned. Both the transferor and transferee must jointly elect for the gain on the gift to be held over. Where gift relief is claimed, the taxable capital gain is deferred by deducting the gain from the base cost of the asset in the hands of the transferee/recipient.

Example 19.6
A gifts an asset to B. The market value of the asset is £100,000 at the time of the gift. The chargeable gain on disposal of the asset is £40,000. A and B jointly elect to claim gift relief.

A has no CGT liability as the capital gain of £40,000 is reduced by the claim for gift relief. The base cost of this asset for B going forward is £60,000 (£100,000 – £40,000). B sells the asset for £130,000. B makes a gain of £70,000 (£130,000 – £60,000).

Claims must be made within four years from the end of the tax year of disposal, e.g. in respect of disposals made in 2019/20, claims must be made on or before 5 April 2024.

For the purposes of section 165 gift relief, gifts must be business assets. (Where section 260 gift relief applies (see **Section 19.2.7**), the asset does not have to be a business asset.) So what is a business asset for gift relief purposes? The gifted asset must be one of the following:

1. An asset used in the business carried on by the transferor or by the transferor's "**personal trading company**" (a trading company in which the transferor can exercise at least 5% of the voting rights). A holding company of a trading group also qualifies if the holding company is the transferor's personal company.
2. Shares/securities of trading companies or holding companies of trading groups where:
   (a) the shares are unlisted (i.e. not listed on a recognised stock exchange) (AIM listed shares are not listed shares for these purposes); or
   (b) the shares are in the transferor's **personal trading company** (provided the transferee is not a company).
3. Agricultural land and buildings used for a farming trade that would qualify for IHT agricultural property relief (see **Chapter 24**).

Note: the definition of "trading company" is the same for gift relief and ER. However, the definition of "personal trading company" is **not** the same for both reliefs (see **Chapter 18, Section 18.5.1**).

An individual may decide not to claim gift relief if the gain is such that it is covered by the annual exemption and/or capital losses.

19.2.2 Section 165 Gift Relief – Restricted Cases

There are two instances where gift relief will be restricted: sales at undervalue, and gifts of shares in a personal trading company.

Sales at Undervalue

Gift relief can also apply where qualifying assets are "sold" at an undervalue, i.e. for less than their market value. For example, transfers to a connected person may be at an undervalue. The rule in this instance is that the "excess proceeds", i.e. **the amount of the proceeds exceeding the original cost** of the asset, fall to be taxed immediately and only the residue is available to be "held over" and deferred.

Example 19.7

In December 2019, Gordon gifts a property (used in his business) to his son Tony when its market value is £210,000. The property was purchased in June 2000 by Gordon for £95,000. Gordon and Tony jointly elect for the chargeable gain to be "held over" under section 165. Calculate the quantum of gain which may be "held over" and indicate what effect, if any, there would be if the son were to pay £100,000 for the property.

Solution

(a) Outright gift

Chargeable gain for Gordon	£
Proceeds	210,000
Cost	(95,000)
Gain (available to be held over)	115,000
Less: gift relief	(115,000)
Chargeable gain	0

Tony's CGT base cost would thus be £95,000 (being the market value of £210,000 less held over gain of £115,000).

(b) Sale at an undervalue

If Tony paid £100,000 for the property, then the "excess proceeds" of £5,000 (the excess of the amount paid over the original cost) would become immediately chargeable and the held over gain would be reduced to £110,000 (being £115,000 less the £5,000 which is immediately chargeable). Tony's CGT base cost in this situation would be £100,000 (being the market value of £210,000 less the held over gain of £110,000). This makes sense as this is the financial cost to Tony of buying the property.

Chargeable gain for Gordon	£
Proceeds	210,000
Cost	(95,000)
Gain (available to be held over)	115,000
Less: gift relief	(110,000)
Chargeable gain	5,000

Gifts of Shares in a Personal Trading Company

If the gift is of shares in a **personal trading company**, and the company has any non-business chargeable assets (such as investments) at the date of the gift, the gain eligible for gift relief is restricted. Gift relief is only available on that part of the gain represented by the proportion of chargeable business assets (CBA) to total chargeable assets (CA).

$$\text{Qualifying gain} = \frac{\text{market value of CBA}}{\text{market value of CA}} \times \text{share gain}$$

Market values of the assets as per the statement of financial position at the date of the gift are used for these purposes.

CBAs are assets that are typically used in the business, e.g. goodwill, factory premises, plant and machinery, etc. However, goodwill will be neither a CBA nor a chargeable asset if it was acquired or created on or after 1 April 2002, as in those cases goodwill is treated as an intangible fixed asset under the corporate intangibles regime (see **Chapter 2**).

Chargeable assets are CBAs plus any non-business chargeable assets (e.g. investments). This would include, for example, rental properties and quoted shares held as investments. Stock, debtors and cash are not chargeable assets and do not form part of this calculation.

This restriction only applies to a section 165 gift relief claim and not on a section 260 claim (see **Section 19.2.7**)

Example 19.8

In December 2019, Gemma gave her daughter Lily shares in her personal company. The shares cost Gemma £40,000 when acquired in March 1995 and their market value is £300,000 in December 2019. The gain on the shares is £260,000. The company owned assets with the following values at December 2019:

	£
Freehold business offices	100,000
Plant and machinery (cost £50,000)*	30,000
Goodwill	80,000
Trade debtors	40,000
Cash	20,000
Shares held as investments	50,000
Sundry net assets (all non-chargeable)	30,000

* This comprises one single item of plant and machinery.

Chargeable assets and chargeable business assets are as follows:

	Chargeable assets	**Chargeable business assets**
	£	£
Freehold business offices	100,000	100,000
Plant and machinery	30,000	30,000
Shares held as investments	50,000	
Goodwill	80,000	80,000
	260,000	210,000

Gift relief is, therefore, restricted to the fraction 210,000/260,000.

	£
Gain on shares	260,000
Deduct: held over gain = £260,000 × 210,000/260,000	210,000
Chargeable gain	£50,000

The base cost of the shares now held by Lily is £90,000 (i.e. £300,000 less the £210,000 held over gain). In this example, goodwill is a chargeable asset as it was created before 1 April 2002.

19.2.3 Mixed Use (Business and Non-business Use)

As for rollover relief, gains on assets (other than shares) with mixed use must be apportioned, i.e.:

- an asset used partly for business and partly for non-business use; or
- an asset only used for business purposes for part of the ownership period.

Only the gain relating to the business portion may qualify for gift relief. It is therefore necessary to treat the business and non-business portions as separate assets.

The periods of non-trade use or partial trade use during the ownership period do not apply where the asset sold qualifies for agricultural property relief under IHT (see **Chapter 24**).

19.2.4 Anti-avoidance Rules

Gift relief is only available if the transferee is resident in the UK at the time of the gift.

If the transferee is an individual who becomes non-resident in the UK in any of the **six tax years following the year of the gift**, and before disposing of the asset transferred, then the gain held over is chargeable on them as if it arose immediately before they became non-resident in the UK.

19.2.5 Instalment Payments

For certain assets gifted where gift relief is not available (i.e. non-business assets), CGT may be payable in 10 equal annual instalments, if elected. The CGT instalment option is available for land and buildings, shares in unquoted companies (e.g. investment companies) and shares in quoted companies where the donor has control before the gift. Note, such instalments are interest-bearing. In certain circumstances, any outstanding CGT liability becomes due for payment if the asset is sold.

19.2.6 Interaction with Entrepreneurs' Relief

A taxpayer should consider if it would be more beneficial to claim ER or gift relief, or potentially both where the relevant conditions for each are met. This would only apply, for example, where some proceeds have been received, i.e. there has been a sale at undervalue. **Note**: where a gain is eligible for both gift relief and ER and a claim is made for both, gift relief is applied first. ER is only available on the disposal of the whole or part of a business and not on individual assets. Alternatively, it may be beneficial to claim neither in situations where the gain is covered by the annual exemption and/or losses.

19.2.7 Section 260 Gift Relief

Gift relief is also available on gifts which are immediately chargeable to inheritance tax (IHT) (section 260 TCGA 1992), e.g. most gifts into trusts. No joint election is required if the asset is gifted into a trust. In this instance, the asset does not have to be a business asset. NB: the transfer will be regarded as chargeable to IHT even if it falls within the IHT nil rate band, is covered by the IHT annual exemption or qualifies for an IHT relief such as business property relief. Claims must also be made within four years from the end of the tax year of disposal. This form of gift relief is available for all asset types.

19.3 Transfer of a Business to a Limited Company

Many individuals commence self-employment as a sole trader/partnership as to do so has relatively lower costs and more beneficial loss reliefs than corporate entities. As the business grows and expands, it may well be that the decision is made to incorporate and form a limited company. This will create a separate legal entity. This has become more prevalent in recent years due to the falling rate of corporation tax. The cessation of the sole trade/partnership business will result in adjustments in respect of capital allowances, income tax consequences and also potentially crystallise a CGT liability on the chargeable assets that are transferred to the limited company.

The implications of the incorporation of a sole trade business include the following:

- A cessation of the sole trade/partnership business for income tax purposes.
- The former proprietor/partner of the sole trade/partnership becomes an employee of the new company.
- Class 1 NICs will be payable by the company, whereas the sole trader will have been subject to Class 2 and Class 4 NICs.
- A disposal of the sole trade assets (including goodwill) for CGT purposes will arise on their transfer to the new company.
- The new company will be subject to corporation tax, whereas the sole trader will have been subject to income tax on the profits of the business.

As the business owner and their limited company (i.e. the company in which they are the majority shareholder) are separate legal entities, the transfer of business assets from a sole trade to a new company on incorporation is a chargeable event for CGT purposes. The transfer is deemed to take place at full market value as it is a transaction between connected parties. In the absence of any reliefs, the taxpayer would potentially incur a CGT liability without having received any monies for the transfer with which to fund the payment of the tax.

This is obviously an undesirable situation and would perhaps discourage individuals from incorporating their businesses, even where it makes very sound commercial sense. It is for this reason that "incorporation relief" is available where a sole trade or partnership business is transferred to a company in return for consideration, either wholly or partly, in the form of shares. Where all of the conditions for this relief are met it is applied **automatically**, without the need for the taxpayer to make a formal claim.

19.3.1 Incorporation Relief (section 162 TCGA 1992)

The **conditions** for incorporation relief are:

1. the sole trade business must be transferred as a going concern;
2. all of the assets (except cash) of the business must be transferred to the company;
3. the transferor must receive shares in the new company as consideration.

Full incorporation relief will be available where the only consideration for the transfer is shares.

Partial relief is available where only part of the consideration is in shares, in this case only part of the chargeable gain is held over. The held over gain is the ratio that the value of the shares bears to the total consideration (including any non-share consideration, such as loans or cash). This means that where cash or loan stock is provided as part consideration, then a percentage of the gain will be immediately taxable. Cash has the advantage that it can be left on a director's loan account and the director/shareholder can withdraw it, tax-free, from the company at any time.

Calculation of the Relief

Incorporation relief on gains arising is calculated as follows:

$$\text{Incorporation relief (i.e held-over gain)} = \frac{\text{Value of shares issued}}{\text{Total consideration}} \times \text{whole gain}$$

Incorporation relief is another form of deferral relief, as the **held over gain is deducted from the base cost of the shares received, i.e. the gain is deferred**. Note, it is the base cost of the shares that is reduced this time, not the assets transferred as with gift relief (under section 165 or section 260).

Sometimes it is preferable for the taxpayer that incorporation relief does not apply. The taxpayer therefore has the choice of opting out of this automatic relief and can elect that incorporation relief should not apply. Alternatively, the taxpayer could purposely ensure that the above conditions are not met, e.g. by not transferring all the assets into the company or not receiving any consideration in shares, so that incorporation relief will not apply. A taxpayer may prefer for incorporation relief not to apply where they have sufficient annual exemption and/or capital losses to cover any gain, and/or the rate of tax payable now is potentially less than what it may be in future years.

The deadline for electing to disapply section 162 relief is the first anniversary of the 31 January after the end of the tax year of incorporation. For example, if someone incorporates on 25 March 2020 , they must elect to disapply section 162 relief by 31 January 2022.

19.3.2 Transfer of Liabilities to the New Company

Where business liabilities (e.g. bank loans, trade creditors) are taken over by a company on the transfer of a business to that company, then ordinarily this is treated as paying non-share consideration to the former proprietor and the deferred gain would be only be due partial incorporation relief and reduced accordingly.

> ***Example 19.9***
> Market value of the assets was £1 million and incorporation included consideration in the form of shares and trade creditors taken over of £100,000. Total value of consideration is £1 million. Share value is £900,000 (£1 million – £100,000 = £900,000 of shares) as trade creditors are treated as consideration other than shares (same as cash consideration). Full incorporation relief would not be allowed as the deferral would be diluted by the formula:
>
> 900,000/1,000,000 (total value of shares/total value of the consideration).

However, by concession, HMRC do not treat such liabilities as part of the consideration for the transfer if the other conditions of section 162 TCGA 1992 are satisfied. This means that there is no restriction and full rollover relief is still available even if the sole trade's trade creditors are taken over by the company. Relief is also not precluded by the fact that some or all of the liabilities of the business are not taken over by the company.

> ***Example 19.10***
> Following on from the example above, assuming all other conditions are met, the concession says that full incorporation relief would be permitted as the total value of shares equals the total value of the consideration (900,000/900,000).
>
> It should be noted that the concession only applies in establishing whether the relief is available. It has no bearing in determining the net cost of the shares.
>
> If, by contrast, liabilities which are not business liabilities (e.g. a personal income tax bill) are taken over by the company, these are treated as consideration other than in the form of shares, so that an immediate CGT charge arises on part of the gain.

> ***Example 19.11***
> Michael's brother Martin commenced business as a pipe laying civil engineer on 1 January 1997. On 31 December 2019, he transfers his business to MMH Pipes Ltd in consideration for the issue of 20,000 shares of £1 each fully paid in that company, and £65,000 in cash. The value of the 20,000 shares is £450,000.
>
> *continued overleaf*

At the date of transfer, the balance sheet of the business was as follows:

		£
Assets:	Premises	150,000
	Plant and machinery	12,000
	Stock	20,000
	Debtors	40,000
	Goodwill	200,000
		422,000
Liabilities:	Trade creditors	75,000
	Capital and reserves	347,000
		422,000

On 31 December 2019, the assets and liabilities of the business are as follows:

	Chargeable gains	**Market value 31 Dec 2019**
	£	£
Premises	50,000	200,000
Plant and machinery*	–	15,000
Stock	–	25,000
Debtors	–	50,000
Goodwill	100,000	300,000
	150,000	590,000
Less: liabilities: trade creditors		(75,000)
	150,000	515,000

* No single item cost more than £6,000, or had a market value more than £6,000, on 31 December 2019.

All assets and liabilities are taken over by the new company MMH Pipes Ltd.

The market value of the assets is £515,000. The cash received is £65,000. Therefore, applying the HMRC concession, the shares are worth £450,000.

The chargeable gains arising on the disposal of the business to MMH Pipes Ltd are as follows:

		£
Total chargeable gains		150,000
Incorporation relief:	$\frac{450,000}{515,000} \times 150,000$	(131,068)
Gains chargeable in 2019/20 before annual exemption		18,932

The allowable base cost of the shares is £450,000 less £131,068 = £318,932. Plant and machinery is a wasting chattel, however, as it is used in a trade and capital allowances could have been claimed, it is treated under the non-wasting chattels rules. In this case, as both the proceeds for each item and the cost of each did not exceed £6,000, the transaction is exempt under rule 1 (see **Chapter 15**).

19.3.3 Gift Relief or Incorporation Relief?

If incorporation relief does not apply (or is not desirable), then the option of claiming gift relief on chargeable business assets such as goodwill, business premises, etc., is still available. Transferring all the assets of the business, including property, into the company could have high tax costs, e.g. stamp duty land tax and a potential double tax charge on the subsequent disposal of the property by the company (i.e. corporation tax on the chargeable gain within the company and then tax on the individual on the future extraction of the net proceeds). The use of gift relief under section 165 TCGA 1992 gives greater flexibility than incorporation relief under section 162, by allowing capital gains planning to be dealt with on an asset-by-asset basis. The main disadvantage of gift relief is that the base cost of the assets in the hands of the transferee company is the former sole trader's original base cost, rather than their market value at the date of transfer (i.e. under gift relief the base cost = market value less held over gain). Where incorporation relief is claimed, the base cost of assets transferred to the company is their market value at the date of transfer. It is the base cost of the shares that is reduced in value by any held over gain.

Example 19.12

Michael commenced business on 1 July 2000. On 1 October 2019, he transferred the business, comprising the assets set out below, to Comptech Ltd in consideration for the issue of 10,000 shares of £1 each fully paid in that company and £20,000 in cash. The value of the 10,000 shares was £140,000. The value of the assets transferred was £160,000 at the time of the transfer.

At the date of transfer, the balance sheet of the business was as follows:

		£
Assets:	Premises	25,000
	Plant and machinery	10,000
	Stock	6,000
		41,000
Liabilities:	Capital and reserves	41,000

	Chargeable gains	**Market value 1 Oct 2019**
	£	£
Premises	80,000	105,000
Plant and machinery*	–	7,000
Stock	–	8,000
Goodwill	40,000	40,000
	120,000	160,000

* No single item cost more than £6,000, nor had a market value of more than £6,000 on 1 October 2019.

The market value of the assets is £160,000. The cash received is £20,000; therefore, the shares are worth £140,000.

		£
Total chargeable gains		120,000
Incorporation relief:	$\frac{140,000}{160,000} \times 120,000$	(105,000)
Gain chargeable in 2019/20 before annual exemption		15,000

Note: The goodwill has no base cost as it was not acquired. Plant and machinery is a wasting chattel, however, as it is used in a trade and capital allowances could have been claimed, it is treated under the non-wasting chattels rules. In this case, as both the proceeds for each item and the cost of each did not exceed £6,000 then the transaction is exempt under rule 1 (see **Chapter 15**).

continued overleaf

On 1 January 2020, Michael sold the whole of his shareholding in Comptech Ltd for £220,000. His chargeable gain is computed as follows:

		£
Proceeds		220,000
Deduct: cost of acquisition	140,000	
Less: incorporation relief claimed	(105,000)	
		(35,000)
Chargeable gain before annual exemption		185,000

19.3.4 *Interaction with Entrepreneurs' Relief*

Since incorporation usually involves the disposal of all or part of a business, ER can usually also be claimed on incorporation. Incorporation relief is applied in priority to claiming ER. As noted above, it is possible to elect not to avail of incorporation relief.

If both reliefs are claimed, ER will be applied to any gain remaining after incorporation relief, e.g. where consideration is not wholly in the form of shares. However, it should be noted that there are restrictions on claiming ER in respect of goodwill gains arising on incorporation (see **Section 18.5.3**).

19.4 Enterprise Investment Scheme Shares – CGT Reliefs

The Enterprise Investment Scheme (EIS) aims to incentivise investments into qualifying companies. The EIS regime provides income tax and CGT reliefs for qualifying individual investors who subscribe in cash for qualifying new shares in qualifying companies. This section examines the two CGT reliefs potentially available for EIS shares. (The income tax relief for EIS investments and the conditions for a qualifying company, qualifying shares and a qualifying investor were covered in detail on the CA Proficiency 1 course and should be revisited.)

19.4.1 *EIS Deferral Relief*

As seen earlier, a chargeable gain is capable of being deferred in certain circumstances (transfers of business to a limited company, gifts of assets, rollover/holdover relief, etc.). For the aforementioned reliefs to be available, the assets broadly have to qualify as business assets. However, reinvestment into new EIS shares can give rise to a relief available for any type of capital gain, not just gains on the disposal of business assets.

A "deferral" of the gain is possible on **any** gain where an amount of money equal to the **gain** is used to subscribe for eligible new shares under the rules of the EIS. It should be noted that it is not necessary to reinvest the whole proceeds – all that is required is to **reinvest the gain**.

While it is possible for the taxpayer to also obtain income tax relief on a subscription for EIS shares, this is not a pre-condition in order to obtain CGT EIS deferral relief. Also the taxpayer can choose to restrict the amount of relief being claimed where this is beneficial (say to leave sufficient gains to utilise their annual exemption, capital losses etc.). Importantly, unlike income tax EIS relief, EIS CGT deferral relief has no cap.

In summary, the amount deferred is the lower of:

- the gain;
- the amount invested in EIS shares; or
- the amount specified in the claim.

The subscription for EIS shares must take place in the period starting 12 months before or ending 36 months after the date that the chargeable disposal has taken place. In addition, the taxpayer must be UK resident.

The effect of the relief is to 'freeze' the gain. **Note:** the base cost of the new shares is **not** reduced by the deferred gain.

The deferred gain becomes chargeable on:

1. the disposal of the EIS shares (although the taxpayer would have the option to defer again by subscribing for further EIS shares);
2. the taxpayer becoming non-resident within three years of the issue of the shares; or
3. the shares ceasing to be eligible.

A claim for EIS deferral relief must be made before the fifth anniversary of 31 January following the tax year in which the EIS shares were issued.

19.4.2 *Disposals of EIS Shares*

A gain on the sale of EIS shares is exempt from CGT if the following conditions are met:

1. the shares are held for three years from the date of issue, and
2. income tax relief was obtained on the original subscription for the shares.

A loss on EIS shares is always allowable but is restricted by the amount of income tax relief given and not withdrawn. EIS capital losses also qualify as a loss on disposal of shares in accordance with the provisions set out at **Section 19.6**. However, such a loss is not subject to the cap that applies for certain income tax reliefs.

19.4.3 *Interaction with Entrepreneurs' Relief*

Gains that are eligible for ER but which are instead deferred into EIS qualifying investments can still benefit from ER when the gain becomes chargeable later (in one of the three circumstances outlined in **Section 19.4.1**), subject to the normal conditions for ER applicable at the time of the first disposal.

19.5 Seed Enterprise Investment Scheme Shares – CGT Reliefs

The Seed Enterprise Investment Scheme (SEIS) operates in a similar manner to the EIS but is instead targeted at qualifying individual investors who subscribe in cash for qualifying new shares in new, qualifying SEIS companies. This section examines the two CGT reliefs potentially available for SEIS shares. (The income tax relief for SEIS investments and the conditions for a qualifying SEIS company, qualifying SEIS shares and a qualifying SEIS investor were covered in detail on the CA Proficiency 1 course and should be revisited.)

19.5.1 SEIS Reinvestment Relief

SEIS reinvestment relief exempts gains on disposals of assets reinvested into new, qualifying SEIS shares from CGT. The relief is restricted to 50% of the gains reinvested, up to a maximum of £50,000. This differs from EIS deferral relief because that relief is a deferral relief only; whereas reinvestment into SEIS shares is an exemption relief.

SEIS reinvestment relief must be matched with the year in which SEIS income tax relief is obtained. So, if SEIS income tax relief is treated as carried back to the previous tax year, SEIS reinvestment relief will only be available in that year.

In summary, the amount of the available SEIS expenditure that is exempted from CGT is the lower of:

- the gain;
- the amount reinvested on which SEIS income tax relief is claimed; or
- the amount specified in the claim.

As the maximum amount on which SEIS income tax relief can be claimed is £100,000 per tax year, the maximum available expenditure is £100,000. The maximum gain that can be treated as exempt is therefore £50,000.

As SEIS reinvestment relief only provides 50% relief of the gain up to a maximum of £50,000, the balance of the unrelieved gain may then qualify for EIS deferral relief.

Two notable differences exist between EIS deferral relief and SEIS reinvestment relief:

1. While it is possible for the taxpayer to obtain income tax relief on a subscription for EIS shares, this is not a pre-condition in order to obtain EIS deferral relief. However, SEIS reinvestment relief cannot be obtained unless the conditions are met for SEIS income tax relief to be claimed and it is claimed. This is because SEIS reinvestment relief is a CGT exemption relief, whereas EIS CGT deferral relief simply defers the gain to a later point in time.
2. SEIS reinvestment relief is capped at 50% of the gain up to a maximum of £50,000, whereas there is no upper limit on EIS deferral relief.

Claims must be made before the fifth anniversary of 31 January following the tax year in which the SEIS shares were issued.

Example 19.13

Catherine sells an asset in June 2019 for £200,000 and realises a chargeable gain (before exemption) of £80,000.

If Catherine makes qualifying investments of at least £80,000 in SEIS shares in 2019/20, and all other conditions are met, then £40,000 of the gain will be completely free from CGT (being 50% of the gain). She does not need to invest the whole £200,000 sale proceeds in order to get full exemption.

If Catherine makes qualifying investments of only £20,000 in SEIS shares in 2019/20, £10,000 of her gain will be exempt from CGT (provided all conditions are met) and she will be liable to CGT on a chargeable gain of £70,000 on the disposal of the asset in June 2018.

The remaining £70,000 chargeable gain will still be eligible for any other CGT reliefs that are available, and allowable losses and the CGT annual exempt amount can be set-off against it in the normal way. It should also be noted that Catherine may also be able to claim EIS deferral relief on the remaining £70,000 of the gain, subject to the necessary conditions being met.

19.5.2 Disposals of SEIS Shares

A gain on the sale of SEIS shares is exempt from CGT if the following conditions are met:

1. the shares are held for three years from the date of issue; and
2. income tax relief was obtained on the subscription for the shares.

A loss on SEIS shares is always allowable but is restricted by the amount of income tax relief given and not withdrawn. SEIS capital losses also qualify as a loss on disposal of shares in accordance with the provisions set out at **Section 19.6**. Such a loss is not subject to the cap that applies for certain income tax reliefs.

19.5.3 Interaction with Entrepreneurs' Relief

SEIS reinvestment relief exempts the gain, and so takes priority over ER. ER may be available on any unrelieved amounts remaining.

19.6 Losses on Disposals of Certain Shares

As a general rule, capital losses are restricted for set-off against capital gains only. The only exception to this is in relation to share loss relief, where, in certain circumstances, allowable capital losses on shares in unlisted trading companies are eligible for income tax relief as an alternative to CGT relief. These provisions can be found in Chapter 6 ITA 2007, section 131 onwards.

This relief can prove very valuable as it can provide relief for the capital loss against income, which might otherwise be taxed at 45% (if the individual was an additional rate taxpayer), compared to the maximum 28% CGT saving available by setting the loss against a chargeable gain on a residential property disposal.

19.6.1 The Relief

Where an individual incurs an allowable loss on the disposal of qualifying shares, they may claim to set that loss against their total income for:

- the year in which the loss was incurred, and/or
- the preceding year.

Relief is only allowed in respect of a disposal of shares where the shares were originally acquired by way of **subscription** for money or money's worth. This is distinct from shares purchased from others or acquired by gift or inheritance.

The taxpayer may therefore be able to reduce their income tax liability where they have allowable capital losses available following:

1. a disposal of shares at arm's length;
2. a distribution in a liquidation; or
3. on a claim that the shares have become of negligible value (see **Section 19.7**).

The year the losses are available for tax relief will depend upon the date of disposal or, if the loss arises from a claim for negligible value, on the date the claim is made and the deemed disposal date chosen by the claimant.

19.6.2 Method of Relief

Relief may only be claimed for the full amount of the loss (partial claims cannot be made). Hence it is not possible to restrict the loss relief claim for the year to the amount required to reduce the taxpayer's income to the level of personal allowances or reliefs, or to maximise relief at the additional rate or higher rate of income tax.

Losses arising on shares in a qualifying trading company that are neither EIS nor SEIS shares are subject to the individual's cap (that applies to certain income tax reliefs) for that tax year. This was covered on the CA Proficiency 1 course and should be revisited.

A capital loss for which relief is given against income is not also available for relief under the CGT provisions. The balance of the unused capital losses, if any, can be deducted from chargeable gains in the normal way.

Example 19.14
Mr Bloggs subscribed £20,000 in 1997 for shares in a company making seating. The business failed in July 2019, with the shares becoming worthless. Mr Bloggs made a negligible value claim in respect of the shares in August 2019 and claimed an allowable capital loss of £20,000 for 2019/20 from the deemed disposal of shares.

If all conditions for the relief are met, Mr Bloggs may claim to set the allowable capital loss on the shares either against chargeable gains in the normal way, or against his total income for 2019/20 or 2018/19, subject to his overall cap on income tax reliefs in each of those tax years.

This relief has to be claimed within one year of 31 January following the end of the tax year in which the loss was made. Thus, an allowable loss in 2019/20 has to be claimed on or before 31 January 2022. The claim must specify the year for which relief is claimed. Where a claim is to be made for both years, then it is necessary to specify which year takes priority.

19.6.3 What are "Qualifying Shares"?

"Qualifying shares" must either be:

- shares that already qualify for EIS/SEIS relief, although these reliefs need not be claimed; or
- ordinary shares in a qualifying trading company.

There are strict conditions as to what a qualifying trading company is, although these conditions are similar to those of a qualifying company under the EIS/SEIS regimes. **The detailed provisions of the definition of qualifying trading company and this relief are outside the scope of this textbook.**

19.7 Negligible Value Claims

Where an asset becomes worthless, a negligible value claim may be made to crystallise a capital loss. Where a claim is made, a disposal is deemed to take place and the asset is immediately reacquired for consideration equal to the value specified in the claim. The effect of a claim is to trigger a capital loss, even though a disposal has not actually taken place.

19.7.1 Method of Relief

Ordinarily, a capital loss cannot be carried back against gains in earlier periods. However, in this instance, the capital loss that arises can be claimed in that year, or in either of the two preceding tax years provided that the asset was of negligible value in the relevant year also. Once allocated to a year, it is treated as a capital loss for that year.

There is no requirement to make a claim within a specified time of the asset having become of negligible value.

If the value of the asset subsequently increases in value, the subsequent gain (as compared with the capital loss arising on its negligible value) is not chargeable until the asset is actually disposed of.

Negligible value relief therefore triggers a capital loss on an unrealised asset, which can be used in the usual way. However, note the interaction with the provisions under section 574 loss relief (see **Section 19.6**) where it is possible (if the conditions are met) for negligible value losses on qualifying shares to be converted into a loss that can be set against income for income tax purposes.

Questions

Review Questions

(See Suggested Solutions to Review Questions at the end of this textbook.)

Question 19.1

Sarah owns 10% of the shares in Rathdiner Limited, which she purchased in December 1996 for £50,000. Sarah has worked in this company since its commencement. She gave the shares to her 22-year-old daughter Emily as a gift on 1 February 2020.

The market value of Rathdiner Limited as at 1 February 2020 is £1,050,000, as below:

	Market values
	£
Goodwill	410,000
Land and buildings	470,000
Plant and machinery *	2,500
Motor vehicle	4,000
Debtors	40,000
Stock	3,000
Cash	500
Rental property	120,000
Total	1,050,000

* The cost of each individual item of plant and machinery is less than £6,000 and no individual item has a market value in excess of this amount.

Requirement

(a) Calculate the capital gain arising to Sarah if she jointly claims gift/holdover relief under section 165 TCGA 1992 with her daughter.

(b) What is the base cost for Emily once a claim is made under (a)?
(c) Calculate the capital gain arising to Sarah if she and her daughter do not claim gift/holdover relief.
(d) Under (c), what would be the base cost for Emily?

Question 19.2

It is mid-November 2019 and you are working on the file of your client, Áine Taylor, who runs a manufacturing business as a sole trader. The factory used in the business was acquired in November 1998 for £500,000, but due to recent growth in orders is now too small to cope with demand, even though the business has been working night shifts as well as day shifts.

Áine has therefore been considering her options and has decided to sell the factory and move to new premises. An offer of £1,500,000 was accepted from a local property developer for the existing factory on 8 November 2019.

She has recently been to see you to discuss her options. She is open to whether the business will lease new factory premises or purchase new factory premises. Furthermore, she has recently been approached by a friend to invest in her company, Shoe Manufacturer Ltd, which needs some additional cash to fund expansion into a new market. Áine is very keen to ensure that she takes advantage of any available reliefs to reduce/defer any tax liability arising on sale of the factory.

Áine has not made any other capital disposals in the 2019/20 tax year and is an additional rate taxpayer. For the purposes of the question, assume that entrepreneurs' relief is **not** available.

Requirement

Write a letter to Áine that covers the following topics:

(a) Calculate the tax payable on sale of the factory, state the date that the tax is due and the type of tax that is payable.
(b) Explain rollover relief and how it could be used to defer any tax payable on the sale of the factory.
(c) Explain how an investment in Shoe Manufacturer Ltd could be used to defer any tax payable on the sale of the factory. Assume that Shoe Manufacturer Ltd is a "qualifying company" for the purposes of relevant relief and that it is not a new company.

20

Acquisition by a Company of its Own Shares

Learning Objectives

After studying this chapter you will understand:

- The tax rules relating to a company's purchase of its own shares, including:
  - knowledge of the income tax treatment; and
  - the conditions for CGT treatment to apply.

20.1 Overview

A company may be legally able to buy back its own shares. A company might do this if a shareholder wishes to dispose of shares and the other shareholder(s) do not want to, or cannot afford to, buy the shares and want to ensure the shares are not sold to an unknown third party. The purchase of shares by a company is governed by companies legislation in the UK.

For tax purposes, a company purchase of its own shares is treated as either an income distribution or a capital disposal as the shareholder, whose shares are being bought back, is disposing of them.

20.2 Income Distribution – Dividend Treatment

In the absence of any relieving provisions, where an individual sells shares back to the original company for more than the original subscribed share capital (i.e. nominal value), any excess is treated as an income distribution for tax purposes

As a result, the recipient is treated in the same way as a recipient of ordinary dividends under the income tax rules (as covered in CA Proficiency 1). The dividend (distribution) is treated as income when calculating the shareholder's income tax liability, after deduction of the £2,000 dividend allowance, if available. The £2,000 dividend allowance is deducted against the first £2,000 of dividend income. Any dividends received over the £2,000 dividend allowance are taxed at the following rates:

- 7.5% on dividend income within the basic rate band;
- 32.5% on dividend income within the higher rate band; and
- 38.1% on dividend income within the additional rate band.

However, the £2,000 tax-free allowance is deemed to use up £2,000 of the relevant income tax band. The individual will also have a CGT calculation to carry out as the disposal of shares is also a chargeable disposal of a chargeable asset. However, the same "profit" cannot be taxed twice under tax legislation and, as the distribution is taxed under the income distribution route, any chargeable gain arising is reduced by the amount subject to income tax as a distribution. If the shares were subscribed for at more than nominal value, a capital loss would arise. If shares were subscribed for at nominal value, a no gain/no loss position position would result.

Example 20.1

Philip and his brother set up ABC Limited in April 2008 for £1 per share nominal value. The issued share capital was 1,000 shares. The shareholding was split 50:50.

In September 2019, Philip decided to sell his shares back to the company for £1.75 per share. A market valuation of the company was undertaken. What is the tax treatment of Philip's disposal? Ignore the dividend allowance.

Income tax calculation – distribution

	£
Proceeds	875.00
Less: nominal value (500 x £1)	(500.00)
Excess distribution	375.00
Taxed as a dividend	375.00

CGT calculation

	£
Proceeds	875.00
Less: cost (500 x £1)	(500.00)
Capital gain	375.00
Less: amount subject to income tax as a distribution	(375.00)
Capital gain	0.00

If Philip originally subscribed for his shares at a price of £3 per share, the calculations would be as follows:

Income tax calculation

	£
Proceeds	875.00
Less: nominal value (500 x £1)	(500.00)
Excess distribution	375.00
Taxed as a dividend	375.00

CGT calculation

	£
Proceeds	875.00
Less: cost (500 x £3)	(1,500.00)
Capital loss	(625.00)
Less: amount subject to income tax as a distribution	(375.00)
Capital loss	(1,000.00)

Overall, Philip has realised a loss of £625, i.e. he bought 500 shares at £3 and sold them for £1.75. This has been reflected as an income distribution of £375 and a capital loss of £1,000.

20.3 Capital Disposal – CGT Treatment

Where certain **conditions** are met, the excess distribution noted above will be treated as a capital disposal subject to CGT, instead of an income distribution subject to income tax (in this case, only a capital gains calculation needs to be carried out rather than an income and a capital gains calculation as was the case above under **Section 20.2**). Once the conditions are met, the treatment of the transaction as capital is **automatic**.

The rules governing a capital distribution are found in section 1033 CTA 2010 and apply on two occasions:

1. Payments made by an **unquoted trading company or an unquoted holding company of a trading group** on the purchase or redemption of its own shares, provided certain conditions are met. For these purposes, shares dealt in on the Unlisted Securities Market or the Alternative Investment Market (AIM) are treated as unquoted.
2. Where the payments from the company are used by the shareholder wholly or mainly to discharge an IHT liability arising as a result of a death. The company must, in this instance, also be an unquoted trading company or an unquoted holding company of a trading group (see below).

20.3.1 Unquoted Companies

Where an unquoted trading company or an unquoted holding company of a trading group buys back its own shares from a UK shareholder in order to benefit its trade, the payment made to the shareholder is, subject to certain conditions being met, not to be treated as an income distribution but instead will be a capital disposal falling under the CGT provisions. Therefore, the purchase of shares by the company will be treated as a disposal of shares by the shareholder and normal CGT rules will apply.

For the purposes of this legislation, a company is classed as a trading company if it is "wholly or mainly" trading, i.e. trading activities constitute at least 51%. This is a different test to the trading company test for entrepreneurs' relief (see **Chapter 18**), gift relief (see **Chapter 19**) and the substantial shareholdings exemption (see **Chapter 10**). The trading company test for the purpose of these reliefs requires non-trading activity to be less than 20%.

Conditions for CGT Treatment

The following conditions must **all** be met in order for CGT treatment to apply to the buy back of shares by such a company:

1. The trade must not consist of dealing in shares, securities, land or futures.
2. The main objective of the repurchase must **not** be one of avoidance of tax. It must be for bona fide commercial reasons.
3. The repurchase must be wholly or mainly for the benefit of the trade. The "benefit to the trade test" will be satisfied where any of the following apply:

   (a) a dissident or disruptive shareholder is bought out;
   (b) the proprietor wishes to retire to make way for new management;
   (c) an outside investor who provided equity wishes to withdraw his investment; or
   (d) a shareholder dies and his personal representatives do not wish to retain his shares.

   Note: this list is not exhaustive.
4. There are also various conditions that must be satisfied by the vendor:

   (a) They must be resident in the UK when the shares are bought back. This ensures that the vendor is within the charge to UK CGT.

(b) The vendor (or their spouse) must have owned the shares throughout a **five-year period** ending with the date of the buy-back. The period of ownership of a spouse living with a vendor at the date of the buy-back is aggregated with that of the vendor. (Five years is reduced to three years if acquired on death and the ownership of the deceased can also be taken into account.)

(c) Where the vendor's shareholding (and that of their **associates**) in a company is not fully purchased, redeemed or repaid, then the vendor and his associates must as a result of the purchase have their interest in the company's share capital substantially reduced, i.e. reduced to 75% or less of their interest before the disposal. This test is considered in two ways, first looking at the shareholding, and secondly looking at their share in the profits of the company. Associates include spouses, minor children, controlled companies, trustees and beneficiaries and, if the company is a member of a group, then the whole group is treated as one for these purposes.

(d) After the transaction, the vendor **must not** be connected with the company or any company in the same 51% group.

For these purposes, a person is "connected" with a company if they directly or indirectly possess, or are entitled to acquire, more than 30% of the ordinary share capital, the issued share capital and loan capital, the voting rights of the company or the assets for distribution on a winding up.

Any shares repurchased by the company are usually cancelled and not re-issued.

Example 20.2

Karen owns 1,500 shares in Winddrops Ltd, a UK unquoted trading company which has issued share capital of 5,000 shares. If all other conditions are met, can the buyback be treated as a capital disposal if the company buys back 400 shares from Karen?

Solution

	Winddrops Ltd Total Shareholding	**Karen's Shareholding**
Pre-repurchase	5,000	1,500
Repurchased and cancelled	(400)	(400)
Post-repurchase	4,600	1,100

Karen originally held 1,500 shares (out of the issued share capital of 5,000 shares) which amounted to a 30% interest in Winddrops Ltd. After the repurchase, this dropped to 1,100 shares (out of the reduced issued share capital of 4,600 shares) which is a 23.9% shareholding. Karen's shareholding has dropped by 6.1%, which amounts to a decrease of 20.3% (6.1%/30%). This is not enough to meet the test at 4(c) above as the repurchase must reduce her shareholding by at least 25%. The transaction would therefore be treated as an income distribution.

Assuming all other conditions were met, if the company had repurchased 484 shares the repurchase would be a capital distribution and CGT rules would apply. Karen's interest has to reduce by at least 25%; therefore, her 1,500 shares must be reduced to 1,016 shares or less.

	Winddrops Ltd Total Shareholding	**Karen's Shareholding**
Pre-repurchase	5,000	1,500
Repurchased and cancelled	(484)	(484)
Post-repurchase	4,516	1,016

Karen's interest of 1,016 shares amounts to a shareholding of 22.5% in the company which means that Karen's interest has dropped by 25% (30% × 75% = 22.5%).

Example 20.3

Doyle Books Ltd has an issued share capital of 100,000 £1 ordinary shares, of which Emmett holds 20,000 shares (i.e. a 20% shareholding). If Emmett sells 5,000 shares to Doyle Books Ltd, the company's issued share capital is reduced for tax purposes to 95,000 shares, of which Emmett holds 15,000, a fraction of 15/95ths or 15.79% shareholding.

	Doyle Books Ltd Issued Share Capital	**Emmett's Shareholding**	**%**
Pre-repurchase	100,000	20,000	20%
Repurchased and cancelled	(5,000)	(5,000)	
Post-repurchase	95,000	15,000	15.79%

Thus, although Emmett has sold 25% of his original holding, Emmett's percentage holding has been reduced by only 21% ((20% – 15.79%)/20%), and the buyback will not qualify for CGT treatment and it will be treated as an income distribution.

To achieve a reduction of 25%, Emmett would need to sell 5,890 shares.

	Doyle Books Ltd Issued Share Capital	**Emmett's Shareholding**	**%**
Pre-repurchase	100,000	20,000	20%
Repurchased and cancelled	(5,890)	(5,890)	
Post-repurchase	94,110	14,110	15%

Note: remember that the vendor must not be connected with the company or group company after the sale, i.e. the vendor and the vendor's associates must not, after the sale of the shares, be entitled to more than 30% of the capital, voting rights or assets on a winding up of the company. In addition, where the vendor maintains a shareholding in the company that is not small (i.e. more than 5%), it can be difficult to demonstrate that the "trade benefit" condition has been met.

20.3.2 Payments for Inheritance Tax

As noted above, where the whole of the payment (apart from any amount used to pay CGT arising) is applied by the recipient in discharging a liability for inheritance tax (IHT) charged on a death, and where it is so applied within a period of two years after the death, and the IHT so paid could not otherwise have been paid without undue hardship, then the payment may be treated as a capital disposal and CGT will apply. In this instance, there is no requirement to meet certain of the conditions as set out above, i.e. the benefit of trade test and the vendor conditions test; however, the company must be an unquoted trading company or an unquoted holding company of a trading group.

20.4 Other Aspects

20.4.1 Clearance Procedure

An advance clearance procedure is available under section 1044 CTA 2010, whereby the company can set out the precise reasons for the buy back and provide HMRC with all relevant information to enable them to determine if all of the conditions for the CGT treatment are met. HMRC have 30 days to reply to the clearance application. It is recommended that this clearance procedure is used.

20.4.2 HMRC Notification

After the company makes the payment to the shareholder it must file a return to HMRC within 60 days, giving details of the payment and the circumstances surrounding it and, in particular, justifying the application of the CGT treatment to the transaction. The return must be made even if HMRC have confirmed that the capital treatment will apply to the payment under the advance clearance procedure.

20.4.3 Other Issues

There is no corporation tax deduction for the company, irrespective of whether the repurchase is treated as an income distribution or as a capital disposal. This also applies to any expenses incurred in buying back the shares.

Where a company acquires any of its shares (by purchase, bonus issue or otherwise), it is not treated for tax purposes as acquiring an asset. As a result of acquiring or holding the shares the company is not treated as being a member of itself, hence the shares are cancelled.

The company will pay 0.5% stamp duty on the consideration paid for the acquisition of the shares (see **Chapter 28**). No reliefs are available to reduce or remove the resulting stamp duty charge, which must be paid within 30 days of the transaction.

The CGT treatment is generally more beneficial than the income tax treatment, due to the comparatively low CGT rates of 10% and 20% when shares are sold (compared to the maximum income tax rate of 38.1% on a distribution).

Careful consideration should always be given to determining the most tax-efficient treatment for the individual. However, it is likely to be the case that the CGT treatment will be preferred if the 10% rate of CGT applies or where ER can be claimed, or where the taxpayer is an additional rate taxpayer.

If the CGT treatment is not the most tax-efficient route (if, say, the income distribution route would tax the transaction at 7.5%, i.e. the basic rate of dividend tax), then it may be necessary to break one of the conditions for capital treatment, given that this is automatic if all the relevant conditions are satisfied.

Example 20.4

Harry and Peter, two UK resident individuals and additional rate taxpayers, set up Super Friends Ltd in 1992 to sell electronic equipment. Harry owns 80% of the shares, while Peter owns 20%. The company has been very profitable and now has revenue reserves of £2 million. Harry believes that the success of the company is due totally to his efforts. He believes that Peter does not really contribute to the success of the company and is more interested in his golf handicap. There have been a number of acrimonious board meetings and, as a result, Harry has decided to buy Peter out. Peter is happy to dispose of his shares provided that he receives £1 million (being the market value of his shareholding) and pays the least amount of tax on the disposal.

If Harry were to buy the shares, he would need £1 million of funds. As Harry does not have that amount of cash, he would have to either borrow the money (which would have to be repaid) or get money from the company (on which he would be liable to income tax, e.g. salary or dividend, etc.).

If Super Friends Ltd bought back the shares from Peter, then Harry would own all the shares, without having to find the cash to actually buy the shares. Peter will be liable to income tax on the cash received from Super Friends Ltd in excess of the amount he contributed for the shares. However, if he satisfies the conditions, he will be liable to CGT on the gain, and not income tax.

continued overleaf

Checklist of conditions:

1	Trading company?	Yes
2	Will the acquisition benefit the trade?	Yes, there is disagreement between shareholders
3	Is the main purpose of the buy-back the avoidance of tax?	No, genuine exit of a shareholder from the business
4	Is Peter resident in the UK in 2018/19?	Yes
5	Has Peter owned the shares for five years?	Yes
6	Is Peter selling all his shares, or at least substantially reducing his shareholding?	Yes, he is selling all his shares
7	Confirm Peter is not connected with Super Friends Ltd after the disposal?	Yes, confirmed

As all the conditions have been satisfied, Peter will be liable to CGT on the disposal of the shares to Super Friends Ltd.

As Peter is disposing of shares in his personal trading company, he should be able to avail of ER and thus pay CGT at a maximum of £100,000 (assuming his annual exemption is otherwise utilised), i.e. at a rate of 10%.

Note: the cost of the shares was not provided but would obviously be deducted from the proceeds before applying the 10% ER rate. This compares with the figure of £381,000 (38.1%, ignoring the dividend allowance) that he would have had to pay if he had received the £1 million as an income distribution (as his marginal income tax rate is 45% and again ignoring the original subscription price paid for the shares).

Question

Review Question

(See Suggested Solutions to Review Questions at the end of this textbook.)

Question 20.1

Andrew Jameson is 63 years old and is a 75% shareholder in Andrewstones Limited, an unquoted trading company. He has lived and worked in the UK all his life. His 30-year-old son, John, holds the remaining 25% shareholding. Andrew is considering retiring from the business to make way for new blood and thus give his son control of the company. His son does not have the cash to buy his shareholding and does not wish to enter into a claim for gift relief. Therefore the most suitable option is for the company to buy back Andrew's shares as he does not want the shares to go outside the family. It is confirmed that the company has adequate distributable reserves and cash to do so.

Andrew's original investment in the company shares was £75,000 in £1 ordinary shares when the company was incorporated in 1991. There was no share premium account. Andrew has been an employee and director of the company throughout this period. The firm has recently valued Andrew's shares at £35 each.

Requirement
Write a letter to Andrew in December 2019 setting out the following:

(a) The conditions that must be met in order for the proceeds received from a company acquiring its own shares to be treated as a share disposal for capital gains tax purposes.
(b) Assess whether the conditions are met and, if so, calculate Andrew's capital gains tax liability claiming any available reliefs.
(c) The consequences for Andrew if the conditions for capital treatment are not met. Include a calculation of the tax due.
(d) Outline the stamp duty consequences of the share buy-back, when any liability falls due for payment and who is responsible for payment of the liability.

Note: Andrew is UK resident for tax and has other income each year in the region of £200,000 and receives dividends annually in excess of £10,000.

Question 20.2

It is early March 2020. Peter Maddley, a relatively new client of your practice, called you a few weeks back in early February with some bad news. One of his fellow directors in Maddon Engineering Limited ("Maddon"), Aaron Donaldson, was tragically killed in a car crash.

Peter and his two friends, Aaron and Jeremy, set up Maddon, a successful engineering company, when they left university in the early 1990s. In 1991 each of them subscribed for 10,000 £1 ordinary shares each.

Peter, Aaron and Jeremy were full-time directors of the company until Aaron's untimely death. Just before his death, Aaron gifted his shares to his wife Sarah. However, Sarah does not wish to keep the shares now as they remind her of Aaron. Therefore, under the terms of the shareholder's agreement that was entered into when the company started, Maddon is going to buy back all of Sarah's shares for £150 a share on 4 April 2020.

Sarah is also a client of your practice. She has advised you that the transaction will only proceed if the "capital treatment" can be obtained. No one remembers what this actually means as the agreement was made so long ago. Sarah has done some research and would like to know what difference it would make if the 'income' treatment was adopted instead.

Sarah has also been in contact with you separately about her late husband's estate. She mentioned to you that in December 2016 Aaron set up a discretionary trust using £500,000 in cash from the sale of a property in California, USA. All UK and US capital gains tax liabilities on the sale of the property have been paid. However, no inheritance tax was paid at the time as the solicitor involved stated that it was not an issue and Aaron had no other transactions in his lifetime.

Sarah has asked you whether this is now required to be included in Aaron's death estate because "it was set up using cash that the tax has been paid on". She also suggested that, if it is required to be included, she would like to think you would be willing to turn a blind eye and forget she ever told you about this as she thinks HMRC have no way of finding out about it. In any case, she tells you Aaron would have delegated responsibility for paying any inheritance tax arising to the trust.

All parties are UK tax resident and additional rate taxpayers. Maddon should be treated as a trading company with no investment assets on its statement of financial position. Sarah should be treated as not owning any other shares aside from those gifted to her by her late husband, Aaron.

Note to students: part (b) of this question should be attempted after you have completed the chapters on inheritance tax and stamp taxes (**Chapters 21–31**).

Requirements

(a) Draft a letter to Peter, Jeremy and Sarah to include:
   (i) An explanation, together with calculations, of how Sarah will be taxed on the repurchase of the inherited shares. Include a comparison between the income and capital treatments and detail the conditions that must be met for capital treatment to be available for the share buy-back. Assess if the capital treatment will be available for this transaction and calculate the tax payable as a result of your assessment.
   (ii) A calculation of the stamp duty payable (if any) on the share buy-back and outline who is responsible for payment of the liability (if any).

(b) Write a briefing note for the partner to discuss with Sarah on the following matters:
   (i) Comment on the availability of business property relief for the shares in Maddon held by Aaron at the date of his death. Calculate the value of the shares to be included in Aaron's death estate after any relief that may be available.
   (ii) Discuss the lifetime inheritance tax (IHT) implications of setting up the trust and support your analysis with calculations. Advise on the due date for payment of any lifetime IHT. Consider whether the transaction is required to be included in Aaron's death estate and calculate the amount of IHT payable (if any) on death.
   (iii) Outline what action you would take in relation to Sarah's suggestion that, if the lifetime gift is to be included in Aaron's estate, you should leave it out entirely.

Part Three

Inheritance Tax

21

Introduction to Inheritance Tax

Learning Objectives

After studying this chapter you will understand:

- The meaning of "gift" and "inheritance".
- The application of the domicile and deemed domicile rules for inheritance tax.

Chartered Accountants Ireland's *Code of Ethics* applies to all aspects of a Chartered Accountant's professional life, including dealing with inheritance tax issues. As outlined at the beginning of this book, further information regarding the principles in the *Code of Ethics* is set out in **Appendix 2**.

In addition, **Appendix 3** examines the distinction between tax planning, tax avoidance and tax evasion, which can arise in relation to all taxes, including inheritance tax.

21.1 Introduction

The bulk of inheritance tax (IHT) legislation is contained in the Inheritance Tax Act 1984 (IHTA 1984). The legislation has been relatively unchanged since then, with the majority of changes coming in the form of anti-avoidance measures being introduced to tackle abuse and IHT avoidance.

All legislative references in this part are to the IHTA 1984 unless otherwise stated.

21.2 Meaning of Gift and Inheritance

21.2.1 Meaning of "Gift", "Inheritance", "Transfer of Value" and "Related Property"

Section 1 IHTA 1984 states that IHT is charged "on the value transferred by a chargeable transfer". The value transferred by an individual is measured using the loss to the donor principle. The amount that is subject to IHT is basically the value of the donor's estate before the gift, less the value of the donor's estate after the gift, i.e. the transfer of value. Generally, assets will potentially be subject to IHT unless they are classed as excluded property (see **Chapter 23, Section 23.8**).

One important point to note, particularly in relation to gifts of shares, is that the value received by the donee may not necessarily equate to the value transferred from the donor.

When measuring the loss to the donor, it is necessary to include the value of any related property. However the property should only be valued using its related property rule if this produces a higher value for IHT purposes.

Related property includes that owned by an individual's spouse/civil partner, plus any assets owned by a charity or held on trust for charitable purposes that were transferred by the donor/spouse, and which is either still held by the charity or held on trust for charitable purposes or was held at any time in the last five years.

Example 21.1: Calculation of transfer of value including related property

Tinky owns 6,000 shares in Spartan Ltd. Tinky's husband and her brother each own 2,000 shares in Spartan Ltd. The company has 10,000 shares in issue.

Tinky wants to give 2,000 shares to her son Po, and would like to know what value would be relevant for IHT.

0–50% shareholding	£10 a share
51%–74% shareholding	£15 a share
75%–100% shareholding	£20 a share

Value transferred for inheritance tax purposes:

	£
Before (6,000/8,000)* £20 × 8,000	120,000
After (4,000/6,000)* £15 × 6,000	(60,000)
Value transferred	60,000

* The shares owned by Tinky's husband must be included to determine the relevant share price as these are related property. Tinky is then treated as owning a proportion of the enlarged shareholding.

Note: assuming Tinky does not make a claim for gift relief under section 165 TCGA 1992 (see **Chapter 19**), for CGT purposes Po's base cost is only 2,000 × £10 = £20,000, being the market value of a stand-alone 20% shareholding!

'Inheritance' is not defined in IHTA 1984, but its common law meaning is the passing on of property following the death of an individual. Where the deceased has written a will, the recipients of property are generally referred to as beneficiaries, legatees or devisees.

When an individual dies, whether it be intestate (i.e. not having left a will) or having left a will, the person is treated as making a transfer of value equal to the value of their estate for IHT purposes on death – but one must not forget that IHT can also arise during their lifetime.

A liability to IHT can arise in the following circumstances:

- making a chargeable lifetime gift,
- on a lifetime gift (both chargeable lifetime transfers and potentially exempt transfers) following the death of the donor within seven years of the date of the gift, and
- on the value of the deceased's estate following death.

"Gift" is defined in section 42, which effectively says that a gift is any instance where property has been transferred from one person to another and the value of the donor's estate has been reduced as a result of the gift.

The scope of IHT is further restricted by stating that a gift must include a "gratuitous intent" on the part of the donor for the transfer of value to potentially fall within the charge to IHT. This allows for some important exceptions from the scope of IHT as follows:

- **Genuine "arm's length" transactions between parties (section 10)** If market value has been received for the transfer of any property, then there will be no loss of value to the estate to the donor.
  A 'bad bargain' does not in itself mean that a transaction has been carried out on a non-arm's length basis. However, if the parties are connected then there would need to be clear commercial evidence to support the price agreed.
- **Maintenance of an individual's family (section 11)** In this case, the value of the donor's estate will be reduced but there is no associated "gratuitous intent". Examples would be the payment of school fees for a child, paying for medical or specialist care for a dependent relative or for the maintenance of an ex-spouse following divorce.

There are a number of other exceptions, which are beyond the scope of this textbook.

21.3 Domicile Rules for IHT

IHT in the UK is subject to territorial limits. The UK does not seek to tax a transfer where neither the transferor nor the property transferred has a sufficient connection with the UK. Hence, it is important to consider both the domicile of the person and where the asset is located (situs).

Under UK law, every individual has a domicile, and an individual cannot have more than one domicile at a time unless they are classed as deemed UK domiciled (see **Sections 21.3.1–21.3.2**). Individuals who are either domiciled or deemed domiciled in the UK (for IHT purposes) are liable to IHT on their **worldwide estate**, wherever the assets are situated.

Individuals who are not domiciled or not deemed domiciled in the UK for IHT purposes are only liable to UK IHT to the extent that their assets are situated in the UK. They may also be subject to IHT on UK residential property owned indirectly by them (e.g. via a company or partnership) or by the trustees of trusts that they have created. See **Chapter 23**, **Section 23.8** for more details. To the extent that non-UK domiciled individuals hold non-UK property, this is **excluded property** for UK IHT purposes.

An individual's domicile will depend on their specific circumstances. The concepts of domicile of origin, choice and dependency were covered in detail on the CA Proficiency 1 course and should be revisited.

An individual's residence status for tax purposes (as determined by the statutory residence test from 6 April 2013) is largely insignificant for the purposes of IHT (but see **Section 21.3.1**).

21.3.1 Deemed UK Domicile

There are four ways that an individual can be deemed UK domiciled for IHT purposes:

1. If the individual:
   - has been resident in the UK for at least 15 of the 20 tax years immediately before the relevant tax year; and
   - the individual was UK resident in at least one of the four tax years ending with the relevant tax year.
2. For three years after they cease to be UK domiciled.

3. If the individual:
   - was born in the UK and the UK is also their domicile of origin;
   - has acquired another non-UK domicile of choice;
   - was resident in the UK in the relevant tax year; and
   - was resident in the UK for at least one of the two tax years immediately preceding that tax year.

   This is known as "formerly domiciled resident".

   Where the settlor of property in a trust is not UK domiciled at the time the settlement is made, the property will not be excluded property at any time in the tax year if the settlor is a formerly domiciled resident in that tax year. This means that the trust property is not excluded property and is therefore subject to UK IHT. As a result, trusts established when non-UK domiciled are not protected from UK IHT while the settlor is formerly domiciled resident.
4. The individual elects to be deemed UK domiciled under the non-domicile spousal election provisions (see **Section 21.3.2**).

An individual who is deemed UK domiciled for IHT purposes under one of these four categories is subject to UK IHT on the worldwide basis.

Example 21.2: Relationship between domicile and UK IHT

Ronaldo is Portuguese domiciled (and not UK deemed domiciled for IHT purposes) and owns a £7.5 million mansion in Cheshire. He also owns a £3 million apartment in Madrid. As he is non-UK-domiciled, he will only be subject to IHT in respect of the Cheshire mansion. The apartment in Madrid is not subject to UK IHT as it is excluded property.

However, should Ronaldo become UK-domiciled or acquire a deemed UK domicile through any of the four ways that this can be achieved, then the worldwide estate of Ronaldo will fall within the UK IHT net and the Madrid mansion would no longer be excluded property.

As long as Ronaldo is not UK domiciled or deemed UK domiciled, his estate cannot claim tax relief in the UK for any IHT paid (or equivalent) in any other country in respect of the Cheshire mansion.

Example 21.3: Deemed domicile: three-year rule

Paula has a UK domicile of origin and lives in England. She retires from work and decides that she wants to live for the rest of her life in Spain. She goes to Spain and takes a Spanish domicile of choice on 31 January 2017. She dies on 1 January 2020 still living in Spain.

Because of the deemed domicile "three-year rule" she is deemed domiciled in the UK at her death and her worldwide estate is chargeable to IHT. Her estate can claim tax relief for any IHT paid (or equivalent) in any other country.

If Paula had died after 31 January 2020 she would not meet the three-year rule and only UK situs assets contained in her estate would be subject to UK IHT.

Example 21.4: Deemed domicile: long-term UK resident rule

Bronislaw has a Polish domicile of origin although he works in the UK and is UK tax resident. He has lived and worked in the UK since 2 February 1997, but he has always intended to return home to Poland. He starts to feel ill and returns home to Poland to be with his family on 2 February 2018, and unfortunately dies on 2 February 2019.

Because of his common law domicile his worldwide estate would not be chargeable to IHT. However, the "15 out of 20" tax year deemed domicile rule means that he is deemed to be domiciled in the UK at his death and his entire worldwide estate is chargeable to IHT. His estate can claim tax relief for any IHT paid (or equivalent) in any other country.

Example 21.5: Deemed domicile: "formerly domiciled resident" rule
Steven was born in the UK and had a UK domicile of origin. In 2005 he acquired a Canadian domicile of choice when he emigrated to Canada to marry his long-term Canadian partner. Steven's employer seconded him to the UK on 6 April 2019 for a two-year period. As a result, Steven is UK resident in each of the tax years 2019/20 and 2020/21. On 31 March 2021, Steven was tragically killed in an accident crossing the street.

As Steven was born in the UK, has a UK domicile of origin, was resident in the UK in 2020/21 and was resident in the UK for at least one of the two tax years immediately preceding 2020/21 (being 2019/20), he is deemed UK domiciled at the date of his death and his entire worldwide estate is chargeable to IHT. His estate can claim tax relief for any IHT paid (or equivalent) in any other country.

21.3.2 Deemed Domicile: Election by Non-UK Domiciled Spouse or Civil Partner

Provisions within IHTA 1984 allow a person not domiciled in the UK but who is, or has been, married to/in a civil partnership with a UK domiciled person or deemed UK domiciled person (for IHT purposes) to elect to be treated as UK domiciled. This election applies for IHT purposes only. All references to "spouse" or "spousal" hereafter should be taken to include civil partners/civil partnerships.

If a transfer of value has already been made as a result of the death of the UK spouse, the election can be made by the surviving spouse within two years of that death. Where the election is not made, the spousal non-domicile exemption is £325,000 (see **Chapter 22**).

A person can make an election provided that during the period of seven years ending with the date on which the election is made/the date of death, the person had a spouse who was UK domiciled. At the time the election is made, the person making the election does not need to be married or in a civil partnership or resident in the UK.

Once an election is made, it cannot be revoked, although it is possible for the election to cease to have effect (see later).

In all cases, an election must be made by the non-domiciled person or their personal representative(s) in writing and sent to HMRC, and it must contain the date from which the election is to take effect.

This election operates independently from the main IHT-deemed domicile provisions outlined previously. Someone who has elected to be treated as domiciled in the UK may, whilst the election is in force, become deemed domiciled in the UK by meeting the relevant conditions outlined in **Section 21.3.1**.

When an election is made, the person making the election will be treated as domiciled in the UK for all IHT purposes from the date stated in the election, meaning that they are subject to UK IHT on the worldwide basis with double tax relief available for IHT (or equivalent) paid in any other country. Whether to make an election and the date it is take effect from requires careful consideration as it could mean that a transfer that did not give rise to a charge at the time is was made because it was excluded property, proves to be chargeable.

If a person has elected to be domiciled in the UK and as a consequence of that election an earlier disposition now gives rise to a transfer of value, clearly it would be not be reasonable for the original due dates for delivery of the IHT account and its payment to be satisfied.

Section 267B(8) provides that the due date for the delivery of such an account is 12 months from the end of the month in which the election is made. For the payment of the relevant tax and to establish the date from which interest is charged, the transfer is treated as if it was made at the date of the election.

Example 21.6: Deemed domicile – spousal election

Susan is domiciled in the UK and transfers property worth £2m in 2019 to her spouse, Rocco. This is Susan's only lifetime transfer. Rocco is not domiciled in the UK nor is he deemed domiciled for IHT purposes. Subsequently, in 2021, Rocco transfers some Italian shares to the trustees of an offshore trust. Susan dies in 2023. At the time of the 2019 lifetime transfer, the value transferred is exempt to the extent of £325,000 and a potentially exempt transfer (PET) to the extent of £1,675,000. Following Susan's death, the failed PET is chargeable and after deducting the nil rate band, £1,350,000 is subject to tax.

Rocco's transfer in 2021 was a transfer of excluded property. Following Susan's death, Rocco has the choice of electing to be treated as domiciled in the UK. If he does so, the gift from Susan in 2019 will become fully exempt as a transfer where both spouses are domiciled in the UK. However, Rocco will then be treated as domiciled in the UK from 2019 for all IHT purposes. This means that his transfer to the trustees in 2021 is no longer one of excluded property and will be subject to IHT. As a transfer to a trust, it will be immediately chargeable to tax, though reliefs should be considered in addition to double tax relief, if applicable.

Rocco will need to consider all the consequences of making an election.

Questions

Review Questions

(See Suggested Solution to Review Questions at the end of this textbook.)

Question 21.1

Grey Properties Ltd, an investment company, has 100,000 issued £1 ordinary shares. The shares are valued as follows:

76%–100% = £35 per share
51%–75% = £25 per share
26%–50% = £14 per share
25% or less = £8 per share

Mr Grey owns 50,000 shares and his wife owns 28,000. He makes a gift of 30,000 shares to his daughter Anne.

Requirement

(a) Calculate the transfer of value made by Mr Grey for inheritance tax purposes.
(b) What is the base cost of the shares for Anne for CGT purposes, assuming no reliefs are claimed?
(c) If Mr Grey were to die in 38 months' time, explain the IHT implications of the gift (calculations are not required). Assume the company is an investment company.

Question 21.2

On the occasion of their wedding in 2005, Walter gave his daughter Stephanie and his new son-in-law Martin a unique set of six antique chairs as a wedding gift. Stephanie received four and Martin received two. Stephanie's son James is an avid antique fan, so in December 2019 she gave one of her chairs to him when he turned 21.

The value of the chairs at the date of the gift was as follows:

	£
1 chair	50,000
2 chairs	110,000
3 chairs	250,000
4 chairs	375,000
5 chairs	500,000
6 chairs	800,000

Requirement
Calculate Stephanie's transfer of value for IHT purposes.

Question 21.3

Which of the following transactions are treated as a transfer of value for IHT purposes? Give explanations for your answers.

(a) Gift of shares in a family company to a daughter.
(b) Sale of a painting to a local art dealer.
(c) Payment of a daughter's school fees.
(d) Purchase of a Lamborghini from a local car dealership.
(e) Gift of an investment property to a family trust.

Question 21.4

Three wealthy clients of your practice, Zelda, Willem and Cerys, have valuable assets located both in the UK and overseas. They are currently considering transferring these into a UK resident discretionary trust in February 2020. Details are as follows:

(a) Zelda has been living and working in the UK since July 2005. Before that she lived in Hong Kong where she was born and which is her domicile of origin. Her parents are both non-UK domiciled. Zelda has not and does not intend to make the UK her domicile of choice.
(b) Willem, who was German domiciled, settled in the UK many years ago and has taken all necessary steps to make the UK his domicile of choice.
(c) Cerys was born in and brought up in the UK by her UK-domiciled parents. Cerys was resident in Ireland until she returned to the UK in 2012. In November 2018 she emigrated to Canada and, having broken all ties with the UK, has become non-UK domiciled.

Requirement
Briefly explain whether each of the above clients will be subject to inheritance tax on the transfers of their UK and overseas assets to a UK discretionary trust in March 2020.

Question 21.5

Pauline died aged 52 from a long illness on 29 July 2019, leaving her whole estate (comprising her London home and a property in Italy) to her only daughter, Penny. Pauline had never married and was born in, and always lived in, the UK. Penny too was born in, and lived in, the UK. For several years while her mother had been ill, Penny lived and cared for her mother at the family home in London, which Pauline owned when she died.

Penny now plans to fulfil a lifetime ambition to emigrate to Australia and cut off all ties with the UK, as she has no living relatives left and all of her close friends have emigrated to Sydney over the last 10 years. She has no intention of ever returning to the UK and plans to leave before the end of 2020.

Her mother's death has got Penny thinking about her own mortality and she has recently spoken to a solicitor, who mentioned the concept of "domicile" and "deemed domicile" for inheritance tax.

Requirement

Explain the concept of "domicile" and "deemed domicile" in the context of Penny's circumstances. How do these concepts affect her inheritance tax position both before and after her planned emigration?

22

Exemptions

Learning Objectives

After studying this chapter you will understand:

- The main exemptions from IHT, including:
  - inter-spouse transfers;
  - gifts in consideration of marriage;
  - miscellaneous other exemptions available for lifetime transfers of value; and
  - the annual exemption limit for lifetime transfers of value.

There are a number of exemptions from the scope of IHT. The main conditions to be met in relation to each of the main exemptions are considered in turn below.

22.1 Inter-spouse Transfers (section 18)

Transfers to a UK domiciled/deemed UK domiciled (for IHT purposes) spouses either during lifetime or on death are completely exempt from IHT.

Where the donor is UK domiciled but the spouse/civil partner is non-UK-domiciled, the first £325,000 of the transfer only is exempt from IHT, unless the non-UK domiciled recipient is deemed UK domiciled for IHT (see **Chapter 21, Section 21.3.1**). The reason for this is to prevent a UK domiciled person transferring their assets to a non-UK domiciled spouse, effectively taking the assets outside of the UK IHT net by virtue of the excluded property rules.

In addition, under an election regime, non-UK-domiciled individuals can, in certain circumstances, elect to be treated as UK-domiciled solely for IHT purposes. See **Chapter 21, Section 21.3.2** for the detailed conditions of this measure. A non-UK-domiciled individual can also become deemed domiciled in the UK under the rules for deemed domicile (see **Section 21.3.1**).

22.2 Small Gifts (section 20)

Lifetime gifts of up to £250 per donee may be made in any one tax year and be completely exempt from IHT. If a gift exceeds £250, then the whole amount is treated as a transfer of value (although it may be covered by some of the other lifetime exemptions), and not merely the excess over £250.

22.3 Normal Expenditure Out of Income (section 21)

A lifetime gift will not be treated as a transfer of value if the donor can evidence that it represents "normal expenditure out of income". This means that the expenditure must be of a habitual nature, year on year. The gift will be treated as being made out of income if the individual can show that they are left with sufficient income to maintain their normal standard of living. Examples would include the regular payment of life assurance premiums, school tuition fees or regular birthday/Christmas presents.

22.4 Gifts in Consideration of Marriage/Civil Partnership (section 22)

Lifetime gifts on the occasion of a marriage/civil partnership are also exempt up to certain limits. The gift must be made, or promised, on or shortly before the date of the wedding or civil partnership ceremony. The limit depends on the relationship between the donor and donee. The limits are as follows:

£5,000	–	From a parent
£2,500	–	From a grandparent or remoter ancestor (or between the persons getting married)
£1,000	–	From any other person

These exemptions apply per marriage/civil partnership and not per donee. Any excess over the exempt limit is treated as a transfer of value, again subject to deduction of other lifetime exemptions. Note the difference between this and the small gifts exemption – the gift on marriage exemption is not an 'all or nothing' exemption and only the excess over the relevant limit is a potential transfer of value for IHT.

22.5 Gifts to Charities or Registered Clubs (section 23)

Gifts to charities or registered clubs, whether during lifetime or on death, are wholly exempt if certain conditions are met. The charity must be a "qualifying" charity established in the UK, EU or another specified country in the EEA (i.e. Iceland and Norway).

22.6 Gifts to Political Parties (section 24)

Gifts to political parties, whether during lifetime or on death, are wholly exempt if one of two conditions are met. To qualify for exemption, the party must have obtained, at the last general election, either two members elected to the House of Commons or one member and not less than 150,000 votes were given to candidates who were members of that party.

22.7 Maintenance Funds and Gifts to Housing Associations (section 24A and section 27)

Gifts to maintenance funds, whether during lifetime or on death, are wholly exempt if the funds are to be used for the maintenance, repair or preservation of historic buildings.

Gifts of UK land to housing associations are similarly exempt, whether during lifetime or on death. The gift must be made to a registered housing association.

22.8 Gifts for National Purposes (section 25)

Gifts to some national institutions such as museums, universities and the National Trust are wholly exempt, whether made during lifetime or on death.

22.9 Annual Exemption (section 19)

The annual exemption reduces the value of lifetime transfers of value. The annual exemption is £3,000 per tax year, and must be used against gifts in the chronological order in which they are made in the tax year.

Any unused annual exemption for a tax year may be carried forward for **one year only**. The current period annual exemption must be used first before taking relief for any unused brought forward exemption from the prior year.

Where two or more transfers of value are made on the same day, the annual exemption should be apportioned between the transfers in proportion to the value transferred.

There are a number of other exemptions, but these are beyond the scope of this textbook.

Questions

Review Questions

(See Suggested Solution to Review Questions at the end of this textbook.)

Question 22.1

Sean, who is domiciled in the UK, transfers property worth £1.5 million in July 2019 to his spouse, Gita, who is not domiciled in the UK and who he married in 2012. Gita has never been UK resident or domiciled and is not deemed UK domiciled (for IHT purposes). In January 2021, Gita transfers some German shares valued at £200,000 to the trustees of a non-resident trust. The trust does not own any UK residential property. Sean dies in June 2022.

Requirement

What are the IHT consequences of the gift in July 2019? Would you advise Gita to elect to be treated as UK domiciled for IHT at the time of her husband's death in 2022? Assume the nil rate band remains at £325,000 at all times.

Question 22.2

Annette, who is UK domiciled and has made no previous transfers, made the following gifts in 2019/20:

- 20 September 2019 – a plot of land, with a market value of £80,000, to her daughter Ana as a present for her forthcoming wedding.
- 20 December 2019 – cash gifts totalling £5,000 to her five grandchildren. Annette saved this cash from her surplus income over the year. She always gives her grandchildren cash as Christmas presents.
- 20 January 2020 – shares in an investment company, worth £380,000, to her husband Stefan, who is non-UK domiciled and is not deemed UK domiciled (for IHT purposes).

Requirement

Briefly explain the availability and amount of any immediate inheritance tax exemptions (ignoring potential exemption) in relation to each of the above gifts.

23

Calculation of IHT Liabilities for Dispositions in Lifetime and on Death

Learning Objectives

After studying this chapter you will understand:

- The computation of IHT liabilities and the scope of the charge, including, *inter alia*:
  - potentially exempt transfers;
  - chargeable lifetime transfers;
  - the death estate;
  - the nil rate band and the residence nil rate band;
  - rates of IHT, including when the 36% rate is available;
  - excluded property rules; and
  - valuation rules.

23.1 Potentially Exempt Transfers

A potentially exempt transfer (PET) is a lifetime transfer made by an individual that will become fully exempt from IHT if the donor (i.e. the individual) survives seven years from the date of the gift. Therefore, a PET will only become a chargeable transfer if the donor dies within seven years of making the gift. This is referred to as a 'failed PET' and becomes potentially subject to IHT. If the donor dies between three and seven years after the date of the gift, then taper relief may be applied to reduce any IHT charge. PETs can also arise where an individual makes a gift to certain special types of trusts (these are beyond the scope of this textbook).

All gifts between individuals are PETs for IHT purposes. However, if the donor gives an asset away at any time but keeps an interest in it, e.g. a property in which they continue to reside rent-free, then the gift will be a PET **and** will also be a gift with reservation of benefit (see **Chapter 25**).

23.2 Chargeable Lifetime Transfers

Any transfer of value that is neither exempt nor a PET is a chargeable lifetime transfer (CLT). This includes gifts to most trusts (except certain special trust types and gifts to and from companies. Some trusts attract special tax treatment, which is beyond the scope of this textbook.

CLTs are the only occasion that can give rise to an IHT charge during the lifetime of a donor. IHT is effectively a cumulative tax and has a nil rate band (£325,000 in 2019/20) applicable for cumulative transfers up to this limit. Therefore, IHT only becomes payable once chargeable transfers over a seven-year period exceed this threshold. The relevant nil rate band to consider is that applicable to the tax year in which the CLT is made.

Note that PETs do not affect the lifetime IHT payable, save to the extent that they use up annual exemptions that could otherwise be set against CLTs. This is because annual exemptions are used in the chronological order in which lifetime gifts are made.

The rate of IHT on any CLT in excess of the nil rate band is 20%, i.e. half the 40% rate applied to transfers on death.

If the donor agrees to pay any IHT due on a CLT, then this must be grossed-up by 20/80ths (or 25%) as the tax paid will also represent a loss in value to the donor's estate.

In order to gross-up a lifetime gift, first deduct any available annual exemption(s) and any other exemptions from the value transferred. Any available nil rate band is then deducted to arrive at the net transfer. This is the amount that must be grossed-up.

By law, the primary responsibility to pay IHT rests with the donor. Therefore, if the donor does not expressly delegate this responsibility to the recipient of the gift, one must assume that the donor will pay the IHT. Where this is the case, the gross gift is the value transferred (after deducting any exemptions/reliefs, **but before** deducting the available nil rate band) plus the IHT paid by the donor. It is this value that is included in the seven-year cumulation period calculation. A key principle of calculating the IHT position on a CLT, therefore, is to look back seven years for any previous CLTs that have already used part of the current CLTs nil rate band.

Example 23.1: IHT treatment of lifetime gifts

Barry gave his daughter a house on the occasion of her marriage on 12 June 2019. The house was valued at £125,000. In the previous month he gave his son £2,000, and a Celtic artifact to the National Museum that was valued at £25,000. These are the first lifetime gifts Barry has ever made.

In August 2019, Barry settled £450,000 into a discretionary trust for the benefit of his grandchildren. Barry decided to pay any IHT that fell due personally.

The gift to his son is a PET, but it uses up part of the the annual exemption for 2019/20; the gift to the museum is exempt for IHT purposes.

The gift to his daughter is also a PET. Both PETs will be subject to IHT if Barry dies within seven years. The transfer of value is:

	£
Loss to donor's estate	125,000
Less: marriage exemption	(5,000)
Less: annual exemption 2019/20 (£2,000 used up)	(1,000)
Less: annual exemption 2018/19	(3,000)
PET	116,000

The gift to the trust is a CLT and an IHT charge will arise, applied at the lifetime rate. There are no annual exemptions available but the full nil rate band is available as there have been no CLTs in the previous seven years.

	£
Transfer to trust	450,000
Less: nil rate band	(325,000)
Chargeable transfer	125,000

The net transfer must be grossed up for the loss to Barry's estate caused by him paying the IHT himself.

	£
(£125,000 × 20/80) + £125,000	156,250
IHT due @ 20%	31,250
Gross transfer (£450,000 plus £31,250)	481,250

The gross gift is important for the purposes of the seven-year accumulation.

23.3 Implications for IHT on Death

When an individual dies, there are three types of transfer which are chargeable to IHT:

1. PETs made within the seven years prior to death (sometimes known as 'failed PETs').
2. CLTs made by the deceased in the seven years prior to death.
3. The transfer of the estate itself on death. i.e assets to which the deceased was beneficially entitled to at the date of death.

23.4 PETs becoming Chargeable and Additional IHT on Lifetime CLTs

23.4.1 PETs becoming Chargeable on Death

When calculating any IHT due on a PET made within the seven years prior to death, it is first necessary to consider all CLTs made in the **seven years before the date of the PET**. The cumulative total of all such CLTs are deducted from the relevant nil rate band (that is, using the nil rate band applicable to the tax year of death) to arrive at the residual amount that will be available to set against the PET, which has now become a chargeable transfer because it has failed.

There is a further measure of relief (known as taper relief) given on any IHT that crystallises on a death occurring within seven years of the date of the PET. This reduces the IHT **and not** the failed PET. The longer the period between the date of gift and the date of death, the greater the rate of relief:

Time between the date the gift was made and the date of death	Taper relief percentage applied to the IHT due
Less than 3 years	Nil
3–4 years	20%
4–5 years	40%
5–6 years	60%
6–7 years	80%

23.4.2 Additional IHT on CLTs at Death

Where a CLT is made within the seven years prior to the date of death, all or part of which has been charged at the 20% rate, additional IHT may be payable on death. If no lifetime IHT had arisen on the CLT within the seven years prior to the date of death, IHT may still arise on death. This is because the IHT charge on CLTs in the seven years prior to death is recalculated at the date of death, using the full scale rate (i.e. 40%) and the nil rate band applicable at that date. The recalculation takes into account:

- other CLTs and PETs within seven years before the date of the CLT (PETs in the seven years before the CLT may not be failed PETs themselves, thus their only impact may be to use annual exemptions); and
- any failed PETs falling in the seven years before death.

The nil rate band in the year of death is used against CLTs and failed PETs in the previous seven years in strict date order.

The 36% rate of IHT is only available on the deceased's death estate (see **Section 23.7**).

Taper relief is also available on any IHT that becomes payable on death in respect of a CLT made within the last seven years. Credit is also given for any lifetime IHT paid in respect of the CLT **after** taper relief has been deducted. Note that the credit for lifetime IHT paid may reduce the IHT payable on death to £nil but **cannot** result in a refund becoming due.

Example 23.2: Taper relief for lifetime gift between three and seven years of death

Mark made the following lifetime gifts before his death on 25 April 2019:

		£
March 2007	Gift to discretionary trust	132,000
August 2012	Gift to his brother	280,000

Calculate the lifetime tax and any tax payable by Mark's brother as a consequence of his death.

Solution

(i) March 2007 – CLT

	£
Gift to discretionary trust	132,000
Less: annual exemption 2006/07	(3,000)
Less: annual exemption 2005/06	(3,000)
CLT	126,000

No lifetime IHT due as below £285,000 (the then nil rate band)

(ii) August 2012 – PET

	£
Gift to brother	280,000
Less: annual exemption 2012/13	(3,000)
Less: annual exemption 2011/12	(3,000)
PET	274,000

No lifetime tax due as a PET.

(iii) On death, any transfers occurring within the previous seven years become chargeable.

Only the PET to the brother was made within seven years prior to the date of death. However, when calculating the IHT now due on that PET, we need to take into account the effect of the CLT that was made within the seven years prior to the date of the PET.

	£	£
PET		274,000
Nil rate band at death	325,000	
Less: CLT within seven years	(126,000)	
Nil rate band available to set against PET		(199,000)
Taxable on death		75,000
IHT @ 40%		30,000
Less: taper relief (six to seven years = 80%)		(24,000)
IHT due		6,000

23.5 IHT on Estate on Death

On death, the deceased is treated as having made a final transfer of the whole of their estate. The tax charged depends on the value of the estate (ignoring any "excluded property" – see **Section 23.8**), and the effect of any CLTs and PETs made within the seven years prior to the date of death (which will utilise the nil rate band at death first). The nil rate band applying to the tax year in which the death occurs that is not used by PETs or CLTs in the seven years prior to death will be available to reduce the value of the estate chargeable to IHT. Any unused NRB can be transferred to the estate of a surviving spouse/civil partner (see **Chapter 24, Section 24.4.1**).

Any gifts out of the death estate that are exempt transfers (e.g. gift to a spouse or gifts to a qualifying charity) are also left out of account in determining the value of the estate chargeable on death to IHT.

Important points to note in valuing the death estate:

- Only assets to which the deceased was beneficially entitled are included in the death estate. For example, if the deceased was a beneficiary of an interest in possession trust then the trust forms part of the estate and is included, whereas the proceeds of a life assurance policy where the deceased was not the beneficiary is left out of account. Note also, in relation to life assurance policies, the value to be brought into account in the estate of the beneficiary if they pre-decease the life assured individual is the open market value of the policy and not the policy surrender value.
- Assets should be valued at open market value, i.e. the value between a willing buyer and a willing seller (subject to special valuation rules for certain assets, which are discussed at **Section 23.9**).
- Excluded property is left out of account, e.g. overseas assets of a non-UK domiciled individual that do not indirectly relate to UK residential property.
- Debts and liabilities are deductible from the estate if they are owed by the deceased at the date of death. Where a debt is secured on a particular asset, it is deducted from the value of that asset, whereas other debts are deducted from the estate generally. Deductible debts include debts for goods or services, income tax or CGT; gambling debts are not deductible.
- Reasonable funeral costs, including the cost of a tombstone, funeral clothes and mourning expenses are allowable.
- Executor costs of administering the estate are generally not deductible.
- The cost of administering or realising overseas assets is allowable but is limited to 5% of the asset value.

Any IHT payable on the death estate is borne by the executors and paid out of the estate. The person(s) who ultimately bears the IHT on the death estate depends on whether bequests made are 'tax-bearing' or 'tax-free'. The phrase "tax-free" does not mean that the assets are not charged to IHT, but refers to the fact that the recipient is to receive the asset and someone else will effectively bear the IHT.

Recipients of specific gifts of non-UK assets bear the IHT unless an expression is made to the contrary in the deceased's will. Unless otherwise stated, specific gifts of UK assets out of the estate are tax-free gifts and any IHT due is to be borne out of the residue of the estate. The residue of the estate is what is left over after all specific bequests have been taken into account. It is normal practice to have a residuary beneficiary who is entitled to the residue of the estate.

The residue of the estate is, therefore, calculated after all tax-free bequests have been made. The tax on the residue of the estate is also effectively borne by the residuary legatee where the beneficiary is chargeable. This will not be the case, however, where the residuary beneficiary is non-chargeable, e.g. the residuary beneficiary is a charity or trust, or where the spouse/civil partner exemption is available.

One specific scenario requires consideration in relation to the **residue of an estate**. This is where the deceased makes tax-free specific legacies and the residue of the estate is wholly exempt.

In this case the tax-free gift must be grossed up by adding the death rate of IHT, i.e. by 40/60. The IHT is then computed on this gross gift and the IHT is borne out of the residue of the estate.

Note that no IHT is payable on the exempt residue; the residue available for the exempt residuary beneficiary is only being reduced by the tax payable on the tax-free specific legacy.

The total IHT borne by an estate over the total chargeable assets of the estate is a percentage, referred to as the "estate rate".

Example 23.3

Jennifer dies on 31 August 2019 leaving an estate valued at £825,000. Included in this is a UK investment property valued at £425,000, which she never lived in and leaves to her daughter. Jennifer leaves the residue of the estate to her husband. Jennifer made no lifetime transfers.

The IHT arising on Jennifer's estate is as follows:

	£
Estate on death	825,000
Less: transfer to husband – exempt	(400,000)
Transfer to daughter – chargeable	425,000
Less: nil rate band	(325,000)
Taxable estate	100,000
IHT grossed up × 40/60	66,667

Jennifer's gift to her daughter is a specific legacy, hence her daughter is deemed to receive the gift of the property plus the IHT thereon, which requires the gift to be grossed up using the 40% rate on death (i.e. × 40/100 – 40).

The gross gift to her daughter, including the IHT, is £100,000 plus £66,667 = £166,667. To check, the IHT of £66,667 should be 40% of £166,667, which it is.

Jennifer's death estate is distributed as follows:

	£
Property – to her daughter	425,000
IHT thereon – to HMRC	66,667
Remainder to residuary legatee – husband	333,333
Total estate	825,000

In this example the residuary legatee is exempt; however, the residuary legatee bears the IHT on the specific legacy to Jennifer's daughter as this is a gift of UK property and as such is tax-free.

Note that no IHT is payable by Jennifer's husband on the exempt residue; the residue available to him is only being reduced by the tax payable on the tax-free specific legacy of the property to her daughter.

23.6 Main Residence Nil Rate Band

The residence nil rate band (RNRB) is available for interests in a residential property, which has been the deceased's residence at some point, and which is included in their estate and left to one or more direct descendants on death. A direct descendant is a child (including a step-child, adopted child or foster child) of the deceased and their lineal descendants (e.g. grandchildren). The qualifying residential interest is limited to one residential property, but personal representatives can nominate which residential property should qualify if there is more than one in the estate.

The value of the RNRB for an estate is the lower of the net value of the interest in the residential property (after deducting any liabilities, such as a mortgage) or the maximum amount of the RNRB, depending on the tax year of death. The applicable value of the RNRB should be deducted before the nil rate band.

The RNRB is available for qualifying transfers on death on or after 6 April 2017. It reduces the tax payable by an estate on death only. Therefore it is not available to reduce IHT payable on lifetime transfers that are chargeable as a result of death because of the seven-year look-back rule, either for failed PETs or CLTs.

Any unused RNRB can also be transferred to the estate of a surviving spouse/civil partner where that spouse/civil partner dies on or after 6 April 2017, irrespective of when the first spouse/civil partner died (see **Chapter 24, Section 24.4.2**).

The maximum level of the RNRB is being phased in as follows:

- 2017/2018 – £100,000
- 2018/2019 – £125,000
- 2019/2020 – £150,000
- 2020/2021 – £175,000

The legislation also includes a tapered withdrawal of the RNRB for estates with a net value of more than £2 million. If the net value of the estate (defined as after deduction of any liabilities but before reliefs and exemptions) is above £2 million, then for every £2 over the £2 million threshold, £1 of the RNRB is withdrawn.

Example 23.4

John dies on 29 June 2020 leaving an estate worth £1 million, including the home he owned and lived in all his life. At the date of his death, his home is worth £435,000. He leaves the home to his daughter, Zoe, and the remainder of his estate to his wife, Margot. John made no lifetime gifts.

John's inheritance tax position is as follows:

	£
Estate	1,000,000
Less: exempt legacy to spouse	(565,000)
	435,000
Less: residence nil rate band 2020/21	175,000
Less: nil rate band 2020/21	260,000
Chargeable estate	Nil

£65,000 of John's NRB has not been used. This represents 20% of his NRB, which can be transferred to his wife's estate on her death.

The RNRB rules also provide that, where part of the RNRB might be lost because the deceased downsized to a less valuable residence before their death or ceased to own a residence on or after 8 July 2015, the "lost" part will still be available provided the deceased left that smaller residence, or assets of an equivalent value, to direct descendants. The "lost" part reinstated is known as the additional RNRB. However, the total amount available cannot exceed the maximum RNRB in the tax year of death.

The qualifying conditions for the additional RNRB are broadly the same as those for the RNRB. These are as follows:

- the individual dies on or after 6 April 2017;
- the property disposed of must have been owned by the individual and it would have qualified for the RNRB had the individual retained it;
- less valuable property, or other assets of an equivalent value if the property has been disposed of, are in the deceased's estate; and
- less valuable property, and any other assets of an equivalent value, are inherited by the individual's direct descendants on that person's death.

23.7 36% Rate of Inheritance Tax

A reduced rate of IHT is available on death estates where a minimum level of legacy has been left by the deceased to a qualifying charity. 'Charity' has the normal meaning for IHT purposes, and includes registered community amateur sports clubs and organisations in the European Economic Area that are recognised by HMRC as being a charity for tax purposes. The 36% reduced rate of IHT only applies to charges that arise on death. The actual legacy to charity remains exempt from IHT and, subject to meeting the qualifying conditions, the rate of IHT payable in respect of the remainder of the estate is reduced from 40% to 36%.

In order to qualify for the reduced rate, at least 10% of the net value of the estate must be left to the charity. For the purposes of the 36% rate, the net value of the estate is the sum of all the assets after deducting any debts, liabilities, reliefs, exemptions and the nil rate band, but **excluding** relief for the charitable legacy itself.

Example 23.5

Hugo died on 30 April 2019 leaving an estate valued at £600,000 after the deduction of liabilities. He leaves £35,000 to the National Trust in his will.

	£
Estate (net of liabilities)	600,000
Less: nil rate band	(325,000)
Baseline amount	275,000
Baseline amount @10%	27,500

Legacy qualifies as it exceeds 10% of baseline amount.

Inheritance tax payable:

Baseline amount from above	275,000
Less: exempt gift to National Trust	(35,000)
Taxable estate	240,000
Inheritance tax @ 36%	86,400

Example 23.6

John died on 31 August 2019 leaving an estate valued at £850,000 after deduction of liabilities. He leaves £65,000 to the NSPCC in his will. His only lifetime gift was a gift of £250,000 cash to his daughter in July 2013. Because this gift had been made less than seven years before he died it must be taken into account in working out the IHT payable on his estate.

July 2013 – PET

	£
Gift to daughter	250,000
Less: annual exemption 2013/14	(3,000)
Less: annual exemption 2012/13	(3,000)
PET	244,000

continued overleaf

	£	£
Estate (net of liabilities)		850,000
Less: nil rate band	325,000	
PET	(244,000)	
Available nil rate band		(81,000)
Baseline amount		769,000
Baseline amount @ 10%		76,900

The legacy does not qualify as it is less than 10% of the baseline amount.

Inheritance tax payable:

	£
Baseline amount (from above)	769,000
Less: gift to NSPCC	(65,000)
Taxable estate	704,000
IHT @ 40%	281,600

Can anything be done to take advantage of the 36% rate?

The beneficiaries of this estate could choose to increase the charitable donation by another £11,900 by making an "Instrument of Variation" (see **Chapter 27**) so that the 10% baseline amount test is passed. This would mean IHT could be paid at the 36% reduced rate resulting in IHT of £249,156 ((£769,000 − £76,900) × 36%) rather than £281,600. This is a tax saving of £32,444, which will cover the additional payment to charity.

23.8 Excluded Property

The term "excluded property" is a technical term used to refer to certain types of property that are, subject to certain conditions, outside the scope of IHT. The most common examples of excluded property are:

1. Property situated outside the UK, where the person beneficially entitled to the property is domiciled outside the UK and is not deemed UK domiciled for IHT purposes.
2. Settled property, where the settlor was domiciled outside the UK when the settlement was made. However, such settled property will not be excluded property if the settlor is a "formerly domiciled resident" in that tax year (see **Section 21.1.2**, point 4).

Property will not be excluded if it is UK residential property owned indirectly (e.g. via a company or partnership) by the non-UK domiciled individual (who is not deemed UK domiciled for IHT purposes), or by the trustees of trusts that they have created. Such property is not excluded property and thus IHT may arise for the non-UK domicile.

The calculation of the value of property that is not excluded property under this rule is the extent to which the open market value of an interest in either:

- a foreign close company (same definition as for corporation tax, see **Chapter 6**), or
- a foreign partnership,

is directly or indirectly attributable to the value of UK residential property.

For these purposes, UK residential property is defined as an interest in UK land that consists of or includes a dwelling, and replicates the definition under the non-UK resident capital gains regime (see **Chapter 14, Section 14.13**).

The property will remain excluded property if:

1. the value of the interest in the close company is less than 5% of the total value; or
2. the value of the interest in the partnership is less than 5% of the total value.

In determining whether the 'less than 5%' test is met, the value of the person's interest is increased by the value of any connected person's interest in the close company or partnership.

Example 23.7

Claude has been UK resident since July 2013. His domicile of origin is France where he was also born. Claude made a gift of a property in Bordeaux to his daughter Elaine in July 2014. He made no use of the property after the date of the gift. Claude became UK domiciled in January 2015 and died in March 2020.

As Claude was not UK domiciled/deemed domiciled at the date of the transfer, the property is excluded from IHT and consequently there is no PET in July 2014 and the property is not included in valuing Claude's death estate in March 2020. In addition, the property is not a UK residential property in which he holds an indirect interest, it thus remains an excluded property.

Example 23.8

Leon and his two friends (no relation), Saoirse and Peter, are domiciled and resident in Ireland where they were born and have always lived and worked. Together they own the entire share capital of an Irish resident company currently valued at £2 million. Leon owns 51% of the shares, Peter owns 45% and Saoirse owns the remaining 4%.

The company owns a valuable freehold property in London, which currently has an open market value of £1 million.

On 20 June 2020, while attending a business conference, Peter and Saoirse are both killed in an accident.

Despite being a non-UK domicile, the value of Peter's shares in the non-resident company is not wholly excluded property – 50% (£1 million/£2 million) of the value of his 45% shareholding is indirectly derived from UK residential property. Therefore £450,000 of the £900,000 value of his shares (£2 million × 45%) will fall within his death estate and is potentially subject to IHT, subject to any available reliefs or exemptions. As Peter was not UK domiciled or deemed UK domiciled for IHT purposes, double tax relief would not be available in the UK for any IHT (or equivalent) that Peter may be required to pay in Ireland.

The entire value of Saoirse's 4% shareholding is excluded property as she holds less than 5% in the foreign close company, despite 50% of the value of her shares being attributed to UK residential property.

If Leon and Saoirse were married or in a civil partnership, the attribution of Leon's 51% shareholding would mean that she would fail the less than 5% test and £40,000 (50% of the value of her 4% shareholding (£2 million × 4%)) would fall within her death estate and be potentially subject to IHT, subject to any available reliefs or exemptions.

Again, as Saoirse is not UK domiciled or deemed UK domiciled for IHT purposes, double tax relief would not be available in the UK for any IHT (or equivalent) that Saoirse may be required to pay in Ireland.

23.9 Valuation of Certain Assets

23.9.1 Quoted Shares and Unit Trusts

The process for valuing quoted shares is relatively straightforward: the stock exchange official closing price for the shares on the date of transfer is used. If a range of closing prices is provided, then the lower of the two values is used. The first is calculated using the 'quarter up' rule – meaning that the lowest closing price is taken and added to a quarter of the difference between the lowest and highest closing price. The second value is the average of the highest and lowest normal marked bargains recorded on that day. The price used for the valuation of the quoted shares is the lower of these two values.

The process for valuing unit trusts is to take the lower of the two prices provided by the fund managers for the relevant date, i.e. the date of transfer.

Example 23.9: Valuation of quoted shares and unit trusts

Blake has the following assets in his death estate:

100,000 shares in Aviva Plc

6,000 units in the Meridian Unit Trust

On the day Blake died, the *Financial Times* reported Aviva Plc's bid price as 23p, an offer price of 35p with marked bargains at 24p, 29p, and a special marked bargain at 33p.

The fund managers of Meridian Unit Trust provided the following information for the date of death:

Bid price 117p

Offer price 121p

The assets will be valued as follows in the death estate:

Aviva Plc shares at the lower of the quarter up rule and the average of highest and lowest marked bargains (ignoring any special bargains):

Quarter up = (23 + (35 − 23) × ¼) = 26

Average of normal bargains = (24 + 29)/2 = 26.50

So value of Aviva shares = 100,000 × 26p = £26,000

Units in Meridian using the lower of the two prices: 6,000 × 117p = £7,020

23.9.2 Unquoted Shares

Unquoted shares, by their very nature, do not have a readily ascertainable market value. It is therefore necessary to agree a value for unquoted shares with the Share Valuation Division of HMRC. It is important to note that the value of unquoted shares usually increases disproportionately as the number of shares held increases. This is due to the fact that the ability to influence and, eventually, to control decisions made by the company increases at certain percentage holdings in the company. For example, at:

- less than 20%
- 51% or more
- more than 75%
- more than 90%
- 100% total ownership.

The relevant price to be used is given in examples and questions in this textbook and it is necessary to consider how the value is affected by the percentage of the shareholding held by the donor's related property, in addition to the loss in value to the donor as a result of reducing their shareholding. The related property value should be used only if it produces a higher price (see **Chapter 21, Section 21.2.1**).

23.9.3 Life Insurance Policies

Lifetime transfers of life insurance policies are valued at the greater of the surrender value or the premiums paid. If someone takes out a policy on their own life and has it written in trust for the benefit of someone else, then each premium payment is a transfer of value and will be a PET unless it falls within an exemption (e.g. small gifts or normal expenditure out of income or the annual exemption).

When the life-assured individual dies, the proceeds of the policy is payable to the person who owns the policy or to some other person specified under its terms. The maturity value of a policy taken out by the deceased on his own life will be included in his estate. If a policy has been assigned to another person during the deceased's lifetime, this is treated as a lifetime transfer.

23.9.4 Jointly Owned Property

Where a property is owned jointly by a married couple/civil partners, the value of the property is equivalent to the proportion of ownership to the total value of the asset. So, if two spouses each own 50% of a property worth £200,000, then that property would have a value of £100,000 for each of them.

Where the joint owners are not married or in a civil partnership, then it is possible to make a deduction from the proportionate value based on the ownership percentage of between 5–15%. For the purposes of this textbook, assume a deduction of 10%. Using the example above, the value for each of the owners if not married would be £90,000 (i.e. £100,000 less 10%). The reason for this deduction is that the property must be valued on a standalone basis and a purchaser is less likely to buy a share in an asset that is part-owned by a third party.

23.9.5 Joint Tenants versus Tenants in Common

It is important to appreciate the distinction in holding property as joint tenants or as tenants in common. Property held by joint tenants automatically reverts to the fellow joint tenant (under the law of survivorship) whereas tenants in common can each gift their part of the property as they see fit. Joint tenants are always treated as having a joint and equal share to the whole property, whereas ownership between tenants in common does not have to be split equally.

Example 23.10: IHT treatment of death estate with prior lifetime gifts

Greg died on 19 October 2019 and left his estate of £750,000 to be divided equally between his wife and two children.

His only lifetime gift had been when he settled £350,000 into a discretionary trust in December 2012. Greg paid the IHT due on the gift so that the full value of the gift was available for the purposes of the trust's objectives.

continued overleaf

Calculate the IHT payable on the death of Greg.

Solution

(i) CLT (in lifetime)

	£
Gift to discretionary trust	350,000
Less: annual exemption 2012/13	(3,000)
Less: annual exemption 2011/12	(3,000)
CLT	344,000
Less: nil rate band for 2012/13	(325,000)
Taxable transfer	19,000
IHT on grossed-up transfer £19,000 + (19,000 × (20/80))	23,750
IHT @ 20%	4,750

CLT for cumulation = £344,000 + £4,750 = £348,750

(ii) Additional tax due on CLT at death

	£
CLT	348,750
Less: nil rate band for 2019/20	(325,000)
Taxable transfer	23,750
IHT @ 40%	9,500
Less: taper relief at 80% (six to seven years)	(7,600)
IHT due	1,900
Less: tax paid on lifetime gift	(4,750)
IHT due on CLT at death	NIL

No refund can be obtained of lifetime tax paid on CLT.

(iii) Tax on death estate

		£
Death estate		750,000
Less: exempt transfer (one-third to spouse)		(250,000)
Chargeable estate		500,000
Nil rate band 2019/20	325,000	
Less: CLTs within seven years	(348,750)	
Remaining nil rate band		NIL
Taxable estate		500,000
IHT @ 40%		200,000

23.10 Pro Forma Computation to Calculate the Value of the Death Estate

Death estate of Mr X who died on …

	£	£	£
Stocks and shares			X
Insurance policy proceeds			X
Personal chattels			X
Cash (including accrued interest net of tax)			X
Accrued income from interest in possession trusts (net of tax), etc…			X
			X
Less:			
Debts due from deceased estate		(X)	
Funeral expenses		(X)	(X)
			X
UK property	X		
Less: mortgage	(X)	X	
Foreign property	X		
Less: mortgage	(X)		
Less: expenses of realisation (max. 5%)	(X)	X	X
Net estate			X
Gifts with reservation			X
Chargeable estate			X

All workings for reliefs, valuation calculations, etc. (e.g. business property relief (BPR), agricultural property relief (APR), post-mortem relief, etc.) should be shown as separate workings and referenced to the pro forma computation with supporting explanations provided.

Questions

Review Questions

(See Suggested Solutions to Review Questions at the end of this textbook.)

Question 23.1

Fredrick gave £400,000 in cash to a discretionary trust on 6 April 2016. This was his first gift of any kind.

Requirement

What inheritance tax is due, and on whom does the liability fall? Would any additional inheritance tax be due on the gift if Fredrick died on 10 April 2019 without making any further gifts? If so, how much?

24

Reliefs

Learning Objectives

After studying this chapter you will understand:

- The application of appropriate IHT reliefs, including, *inter alia*
  - business property relief;
  - agricultural property relief;
  - quick succession relief;
  - post-mortem relief;
  - transfer of unused nil rate band;
  - transfer of unused residence nil rate band; and
  - fall in value of gift before death.

24.1 Business Property Relief (sections 103–114)

Business property relief (BPR) is available to reduce the amount chargeable to IHT on certain business assets for both lifetime and death transfers. The relief is given before annual exemptions in the case of lifetime transfers so that these are not unnecessarily wasted.

BPR on lifetime transfers is calculated as follows:

	£
Value transferred	X
Less: **BPR @ 50%/100%**	(X)
	X
Less: annual exemptions	(X)
Transfer	X

If an individual dies and their estate includes relevant business property, BPR is also given as a deduction in the estate when calculating death tax.

There is no need to claim the relief if it is due, as it is given automatically if the relevant conditions are satisfied. The assets transferred must be **relevant business property** for BPR to be available. The relief is therefore only generally available on the transfer of a business or an interest in a business/partnership and is not available on the transfer of a single business asset.

The following are relevant business property together with the applicable rate of BPR:

1. A business or an interest in a business.	100%
2. Shares in an unquoted trading company (no minimum holding).	100%
3. Securities (loan stock) in an unquoted company where the company is controlled by the donor (i.e. where the donor holds more than 50% of the voting shares).	100%
4. Shares and securities in a quoted company where the donor controls the company (i.e. more than 50% of the voting rights). It is very unusual for an individual to hold more than 50% of the shares of a quoted company, so in the majority of cases quoted shares will **not** qualify for BPR.	50%
5. Any land or building, machinery or plant owned outside the business which, for the two years before the transfer, was used wholly or mainly for the purposes of a business carried on by a company of which the transferor then had control or by a partnership of which the individual then was a partner.	50%
6. Land, buildings, plant and machinery owned outside of the business, where they are used in the donor's business and held in a trust that the donor has a right to benefit from (as a beneficiary of an interest in possession trust).	50%

AIM-listed shares are treated as unquoted for the purposes of BPR.

BPR is not available if:

- The business or company is involved primarily in dealing in shares, land or buildings, or in the making or holding investments.
- The business is not carried on with a view to making a profit.
- The business is the subject of a binding contract for sale, unless that sale is to a company that will continue the business, and the sale is made wholly or mainly in consideration of shares in the acquiring company (i.e. an incorporation or company reconstruction).

24.1.1 Ownership

General Rule

The general rule is that property is not relevant business property for the purposes of BPR unless it has been held for a minimum of two years at the date of the lifetime or death transfer. Generally, if the property has not been held for this minimum period, then no BPR is due.

Exceptions to the General Rule

There are a number of exceptions to the two-year general rule for specific circumstances.

1. Where the transfer occurs between spouses on death – if the transferor became entitled to the property on the death of a spouse or civil partner, then relief is available for any period during which the deceased spouse or civil partner also owned it. This has the effect of aggregating the period of ownership between spouses/civil partners where there has been a transfer on death and allows BPR where the combined ownership period meets the two-year test (section 108).

Example 24.1
James owns 20% of the shares in Driver Ltd, an unquoted trading company, and has done so since 1 April 2015. James died on 1 April 2019, leaving his entire estate to his wife Jane. On 1 December 2019, Jane gifted the Driver Ltd shares to a discretionary trust when the shares were worth £400,000.

Even though the two-year ownership period is not met, BPR is still available on the CLT of the shares to the discretionary trust. Although Jane only owned the relevant business property in Driver Ltd for eight months, when this ownership period is combined with the ownership period of her husband, the combined ownership period meets the two-year test because Jane became entitled to the Driver Ltd shares on the death of her spouse.

However, section 108 allows the periods to be aggregated only if the donor and the donee are married, **and** the transfer by the donor to the donee was made on death. This is the only time that the ownership period of the donor and the donee can be added together.

2. Where there are successive transfers in a two-year period – if the transferred property was acquired by way of an earlier transfer within the two-year period, then relief will still be available if the following conditions are met:

    (a) The earlier transfer qualified for BPR.
    (b) The earlier transfer was made to the current transferor or spouse or civil partner.
    (c) At least one of the transfers was made on a death.
    (d) The property would, apart from the two-year rule, qualify for BPR.

Example 24.2: BPR and successive transfers
Brian received 60% of the shares in Zee Ltd, a qualifying unquoted company, under the will of Charles, who died on 1 December 2018 and had held the shares for 20 years. The 60% holding attracted 100% business property relief on Charles's death estate.

On 1 February 2020, Brian transfers the 60% holding in Zee Ltd to a discretionary trust.

In this instance, rule 2 applies as:

(a) The earlier transfer from Charles to Brian qualified for BPR.

(b) The earlier transfer was made to the current transferor, Brian.

(c) At least one of the transfers was made on a death, being the earlier transfer from Charles to Brian.

(d) Except for the two-year test, the property would qualify for BPR.

BPR is therefore still available on this CLT.

3. Where old business property is sold and replaced with new business property – if "old" relevant business property is sold by the owner and replaced within three years by "new" relevant business property **before** the transfer, then it will satisfy the two-year ownership period if, when taken together with the property it has replaced (and indeed the property it in turn replaced, and so on), it has been owned by the transferor for at least two years during the five years immediately before the current transfer, provided each item in the chain would have been relevant business property (apart from the length of ownership) if the transfer had been made immediately before it was replaced. However, BPR on the replacement asset cannot exceed the BPR that would have been available on the original asset. In addition, only the relevant proportion of the proceeds from the sale of the first business property reinvested in the replacement business property will qualify.

Example 24.3: BPR and replacement property
On 1 March 2018, Sarah sold her shareholding (which she had held for 10 years) in Brandon Ltd, a qualifying unquoted company. On 1 February 2019, using the total proceeds from the sale of these shares, she bought a holding of shares in Tritan Ltd, another qualifying unquoted trading company.

Sarah died on 1 October 2019.

Business property relief is still available on the Tritan Ltd shares included in Sarah's death estate even though the two-year period is not met. Although she only owned the replacement business property in Tritan Ltd for eight months, when this ownership period is combined with the ownership period of her Brandon Ltd shares, the combined ownership period is two years out of the previous five. Sarah also purchased the replacement business property within three years.

If Sarah had only reinvested 50% of the proceeds from the sale of her Brandon Ltd shares in the Tritan Ltd shares, then only 50% business property relief would be available.

24.1.2 Excepted Assets

The BPR available on shares is restricted where the company holds "**excepted assets**" on its statement of financial position.

An excepted asset is one not used for business purposes throughout the two-year period preceding a transfer, or is not intended to be used in the future for the purposes of the business (i.e. a trading business or trading activity). Items that are held for investment purposes, e.g. investment properties and share investments, are excepted assets for BPR purposes, as are assets used wholly or mainly for the personal benefit of the transferor or a person connected with the transferor. A large cash deposit held for investment purposes and not required for future use in the business would also be classed as an excepted asset.

BPR is restricted to that proportion of the total assets of a company that the relevant business assets represent, i.e.:

$$\text{Transfer qualifying for BPR} = \text{Gift} \times \frac{\text{Total assets} - \text{Excepted assets}}{\text{Total assets}}$$

Example 24.4: BPR and shares
Jack owned all of the shares in Gravy Ltd, an unlisted company mainly engaged in a catering trade, since 2001. He died on 4 August 2019 and left the shares, worth £620,000, to his nephew Willis. He has held the shares for a number of years and the statement of financial position of the company is as follows:

	£
Factory	350,000
Plant	75,000
Investments	45,000
Quoted shares	15,000
Net assets	485,000

As the investments and the quoted shares are excepted assets, BPR relief is calculated as follows, assuming that the balance of the value relates to the trading goodwill:

100% × £620,000 × ((£620,000 – £45,000 – £15,000)/£620,000) = £560,000 BPR available

It should be noted that if the excepted assets represent more than 50% of the total assets, HMRC may deny BPR on the grounds that the business is mainly an investment business. This is on the basis that the business must be wholly (i.e. 100%) or mainly (i.e. at least 51%) carrying on a business that is not an investment business and is not of the type excluded.

24.1.3 BPR on Lifetime Gifts Following Death

Chargeable Lifetime Transfers

Where BPR is given on a chargeable lifetime transfer (CLT) of value, it is not always the case that the relief continues to be available where the donor dies within seven years of the gift. In certain circumstances, normally where the donee has either sold or given away the business property, the relief may be withdrawn. The relief will also be withdrawn if the property no longer qualifies as business property.

The relief will **not be** withdrawn if the business property has been sold but has been replaced by other qualifying business property. As set out earlier, the replacement business property must be purchased within three years of the disposal of the old business property and the whole of the original proceeds of sale of the old property must be reinvested.

Where BPR is withdrawn, it increases the tax payable by the donee as a consequence of the donor's death within seven years of the gift. It does not alter the IHT position at the point of the actual lifetime transfer. Similarly, it does not affect the calculation of the donor's cumulative lifetime transfers for the purposes of using up the nil rate band available at the date of death, i.e. BPR remains available on the original CLT.

Potentially Exempt Transfers

There can be no withdrawal of BPR on a potentially exempt transfers (PETs) as there is no lifetime tax charge on a PET, hence BPR will not have been claimed.

If a PET becomes chargeable as a result of the death of the donor within seven years of the date of the PET, then BPR will be a consideration.

If the donee still owns the business property at the date of death, then BPR may be available if the other conditions were met at the date of the gift. If the donee has sold the business property before the death of the donor, then no BPR will be available to reduce the IHT charge, unless the proceeds of the sale have been reinvested into replacement business property. If the property no longer qualifies as relevant business property at the date of death, then BPR will not be available. An example would be on the transfer of unquoted shares in a company that become listed on a stock exchange before the date of death.

Example 24.5

Barney gave his shares in an unquoted trading company to his sister Eileen in July 2013 when they were worth £400,000. This was his only lifetime gift. Eileen sold the shares on 1 July 2014 and used the proceeds to buy a holiday home in Florida. Barney died in September 2019.

Calculate the IHT payable by Eileen in respect of the shares on the death of Barney.

	£
Gift in July 2013	400,000
Less: annual exemption 2013/14	(3,000)
Less: annual exemption 2012/13	(3,000)
	394,000

continued overleaf

Less: nil rate band applying at date of death	(325,000)
Chargeable to IHT	69,000
IHT @ 40%	27,600
Less: taper relief (80% 6–7 years)	(22,080)
IHT payable	5,520

BPR cannot be claimed as the property no longer qualified at the date of Barney's death (because Eileen had disposed of it and not replaced it with relevant business property at Barney's date of death). As the original gift was a PET and no lifetime tax was due, the annual exemptions are not displaced by the BPR that might otherwise have been available.

24.2 Agricultural Property Relief (sections 115–124C)

Agricultural property relief (APR) works in a similar manner to BPR. It is available for gifts of farmland and farm buildings (including farmhouses) during lifetime or on death. Farm machinery and farm animals are not qualifiying APR assets; however these may qualify instead for BPR. The relief is given before the annual exemptions but before BPR is applied for lifetime transfers. For assets that qualify for both reliefs, APR again takes precedence over BPR.

APR on lifetime transfers is calculated as follows:

	£
Value transferred	X
Less: **APR @ 50%/100%**	(X)
	X
Less: BPR	(X)
	X
Less: annual exemptions	(X)
Transfer	X

If an individual dies and their estate includes agricultural property, APR is also given as a deduction in the estate when calculating death tax. The relief is also automatic and no formal claim is required.

APR is available where the farm is situated in the UK, Channel Islands, Isle of Man or the European Economic Area (i.e. all EU countries plus Norway, Iceland and Liechtenstein).

The relief is available to shelter the **agricultural** value of the property which is **normally less than its market value or development value**. The agricultural value is the value of the land on the basis that it can only be used for farming.

The relief is available to a farmer who owns farmland and uses it in a farming business, or to a landowner who lets the land to a farmer who uses it for farming purposes.

APR is given at the rate of 100% of the agricultural value of the land, except in one very precise circumstance. APR is given at the rate of 50% where the land is let to a farmer and the lease was signed before 1 September 1995 and there is still more than two years left to run on the lease. If any of these conditions are not met, then 100% APR is due.

24.2.1 Ownership

Generally, the land must be owned for the two years immediately preceding the transfer for APR to be available. This is increased to seven years where the land is let to a farmer.

As with BPR, if the land is sold and replaced by other qualifying land, then the combined period of ownership must be at least two out of the last five years for APR to be available. Where the land is let, the relevant period is seven out of the last 10 years.

The BPR rule that allows ownership periods to be aggregated where property passes from one spouse to another on death, similarly applies for APR purposes. Likewise, APR is also available in respect of successive transfers (see **Section 24.4.1**).

Where a farmer runs a farming business, BPR may be available to cover any market value not otherwise covered by APR. This is often the case where the farmland has clear development value.

APR is also available to the controlling shareholder in a company that owns agricultural land. The relief is calculated with reference to the percentage of the agricultural value of the land to the total value of the company. BPR should then be considered in relation to the remaining value.

APR is also available for farmhouses/farm cottages as long as they are of an appropriate character in relation to the property. The occupation of the property must be in connection with the farming business and it should be normal for the land to include a dwelling of the type concerned.

The rules on withdrawal of BPR following the death of the donor noted above are also applicable to APR lifetime transfers falling into the death estate.

Example 24.6: APR

The Viscount of Antrim owns a significant holding of farmland, which he lets to a local farmer who uses it mainly for growing potatoes. The lease on the property was granted in 1985 for a term of 40 years.

In June 2016 he gave his daughter, Lady Penelope, 150 acres on the occasion of her marriage. The land had a market value of £2,400,000 and an agricultural value of £2,250,000.

The Viscount died in October 2019 and had made no other gifts in the seven years preceding his death.

Calculate the IHT payable by Lady Penelope on the Viscount's death on the basis that she still holds the land.

	£
Gift	2,400,000
Less: APR @ 50% (£2.25m × 50%)	(1,125,000)
	1,275,000
Less: marriage exemption	(5,000)
Less: annual exemption 2016/17	(3,000)
Less: annual exemption 2015/16	(3,000)
PET	1,264,000
Less: nil rate band at death	(325,000)
Taxable transfer	939,000
IHT @ 40%	375,600
Less: taper relief (3 to 4 years = 20%)	(75,120)
IHT payable	300,480

Note:

The APR was 50% in this example as:

- it was tenanted land;
- the lease was granted pre-1 September 1995; and
- the lease still had more than two years left to run.

24.3 Quick Succession Relief (section 141)

Quick succession relief (QSR) is intended to alleviate situations where the same assets are subject to IHT twice within a relatively short period of time (five years). Where a donee dies after their estate has been increased by a chargeable transfer, tax may be due on the increased estate and may have already been charged on the earlier transfer. Where the death of the donee occurs within five years of the earlier transfer, QSR may be claimed. QSR is available for a transfer on death or for a PET that becomes chargeable due to the death of the original donor within seven years of the earlier transfer. If the time period is less than one year, 100% QSR will be available and this reduces by 20% for each additional year that passes between the date of the first and second death.

Years between transfer and death	Percentage relief
Up to 1 year	100%
More than 1 but no more than 2	80%
More than 2 but not more than 3	60%
More than 3 but not more than 4	40%
More than 4 but not more than 5	20%

The formula for calculating the available QSR is as follows:

$$\frac{\text{Previous transfer net of tax}}{\text{Previous gross transfer}} \times \text{Tax paid on previous transfer} \times \text{QSR \%}$$

The reason for the "tax paid on previous transfer" part of the formula is to take account of whether the gift had to bear its own tax or whether it was "tax-free". Unless specified to the contrary, gifts of UK assets do not bear their own tax whilst gifts of non-UK assets do bear their own tax. Where gifts do not bear their own tax, any IHT due is paid out of the residue of the estate (see **Chapter 23, Section 23.5**).

It is also important to note that QSR is available even if the donee has sold or disposed of the asset prior to death. This is because QSR is available if an individual's estate has been increased by a chargeable transfer in any of the five preceding years.

Example 24.7

Frank died on 3 April 2017 and left his entire estate valued at £554,000 to his cousin Vinny. Frank had made a gift of £126,000 to his best friend in the month before he died.

Vinny died in July 2019 leaving an estate of £625,000.

Step 1: Calculate the IHT due on Frank's estate

	£
Death estate	554,000
Less: nil rate band (Note)	(205,000)
Net taxable estate	349,000
IHT due @ 40%	139,600

Note: Nil-rate band

Lifetime gift	126,000
Less: annual exemption 2016/17	(3,000)
annual exemption 2015/16	(3,000)
	120,000

continued overleaf

Nil rate band	325,000
Utilised	(120,000)
Available	205,000

Step 2: Calculate the IHT due on Vinny's estate

	£
Death estate	625,000
Less: nil rate band	(325,000)
Chargeable estate	300,000
IHT @ 40%	120,000
Less: QSR: $\frac{£414{,}400^*}{£414{,}400 + £139{,}600} \times 139{,}600 \times 60\%$	(62,654)
IHT due	57,346

*Being £554,000 − £139,600.

Vinny received the value of Frank's estate less the IHT due on this. The increase to his own estate as a result of the transfer is therefore the net of these amounts.

24.4 Reliefs for Surviving Spouse of a Deceased Person

24.4.1 Transfer of Unused Nil Rate Band

This relief works by allowing the surviving spouse/civil partner to claim any unused nil rate band (NRB) of their deceased spouse/civil partner. It is available to all survivors of a marriage or civil partnership, no matter when the first partner died.

The NRB that is available to the surviving spouse or civil partner on their death will be increased by the proportion of the NRB unused on the first death. The amount of the NRB that can be transferred is not reduced by the value of exempt transfers made on the death of the first spouse.

Example 24.8: Transfer of unused nil rate band
Jackie died when her chargeable estate was £150,000 and the NRB was £300,000. She left her entire estate to her son. Her estate did not include a residence.

Jackie's husband has just died and his chargeable estate is £560,000. His son wants to know what NRB will be available in respect of his father's estate as the father had not made any transfers in the last seven years. His estate did not include a residence.

The NRB for 2019/20 is £325,000 and this is uplifted by 50% (i.e. the proportion of the NRB not used by Jackie at her death) to £487,500. The husband's estate will potentially be liable to IHT on the excess over the extended NRB of £72,500 (£560,000 – £487,500).

24.4.2 Transfer of Unused Residence Nil Rate Band

Any unused residence nil rate band (RNRB) can also be transferred to the estate of a surviving spouse/civil partner where that spouse/civil partner dies on or after 6 April 2017, irrespective of when the first spouse/civil partner died.

A claim must be made on the death of the surviving spouse/civil partner to transfer any unused proportion of the first spouse's/civil partner's RNRB on their death, in the same way that the existing unused nil rate band of a spouse/civil partner can be transferred.

Where the family home has been left to the spouse or civil partner on the first death at any time before 6 April 2017, an additional RNRB of £100,000 is available to the estate of the surviving spouse (subject to the tapering rules where the estate is worth more than £2 million (see **Chapter 23, Section 23.6**)).

Where the first death is on or after 6 April 2017, the transferable allowance is calculated as the unused percentage of the RNRB available to the first spouse or civil partner.

> ***Example 24.9: Transfer of unused residence nil rate band***
> Shane died on 15 September 2016 when his estate was £250,000 (which included his home). Shane left his entire estate to his wife, Denise, and he made no lifetime transfers.
>
> Denise died on 31 December 2019 with a chargeable estate of £1,000,000, including her home. She left her entire estate to her daughter. Denise made no lifetime transfers.
>
> Denise's daughter wants to know what nil rate bands are available in respect of her mother's estate.
>
> The NRB for 2019/20 is £325,000 and is uplifted by 100% (i.e. the proportion of the nil rate band not used by Shane at his death) to £650,000. Denise was also entitled to the RNRB in 2019/20 of £150,000. As Shane died before 6 April 2017 and he left his residence to his wife, a further £100,000 RNRB is also available on Denise's death.
>
> Denise's estate will, potentially, be liable to IHT on the excess over the available nil rate bands of £100,000 (£1,000,000 – £650,000 – £250,000).

24.5 Fall in Value of Gift Before Death (section 131)

An IHT relief is available, known as a "section 131 claim", where the value of an asset has fallen between the date of the original gift and the date of death of the donor. The claim reduces the further tax payable by a donee on a lifetime gift that comes into charge on the death of the donor within seven years. It is possible to make this claim if the donee no longer owns the property. In this case, the fall in value relief is determined by reference to the proceeds received for the disposal rather than the current market value at death. Relief is given by reducing the lifetime transfer by an amount equal to the fall in value, and it should be noted that this relief is calculated by reference to the loss in value to the donee, not by reference to the loss in value to the donor (which is used to calculate the value transferred by the donor).

> ***Example 24.10: Fall in value relief***
> Ryan gave a painting to Sandra in January 2014. It was part of a set of two paintings which together were worth £750,000. Each painting on its own was worth £200,000 both before and after the gift. Ryan made no other lifetime gifts.
>
> Ryan died in November 2019. At that date, the painting given to Sandra was only worth £80,000 as it had been damaged. Therefore, the value of the asset has gone down between the date of gift and the date of the donor's death.
>
> The painting will be valued as follows in calculating any IHT due on death.

	£
Value of two paintings before transfer	750,000
Value of one painting after transfer	(200,000)
Value transferred by donor	550,000
Less: annual exemptions for 2013/14 and 2012/13	(6,000)

continued overleaf

Less: fall in value relief (£200,000 – £80,000)	(120,000)
Chargeable on death	424,000
Less: NRB	(325,000)
Chargeable to IHT	99,000

The fall in value claim only affects the additional tax now payable by Sandra (on the failed PET) as a result of Ryan's death. It does not affect the value of the PET for accumulation purposes for Ryan. Therefore, the original PET (after annual exemptions) of £544,000 remains for the purposes of the seven year accumulation period. So for example, for the purposes of calculating the IHT on Ryan's death estate, when determining how much of the NRB at death is reduced by the chargeable transfers in the past seven years, the gift in 2014 would have a chargeable value of £544,000 not £424,000.

24.6 Post-mortem Relief

The general rule that IHT is calculated on the value of the death estate at the date of death is relaxed in certain circumstances. It may be possible to substitute a lower value for certain assets if they are sold after the date of death and realise a lower value than that which applied at the date of death. There are three common cases where this IHT relief can apply and the conditions and bases of valuation are considered below.

24.6.1 Sale of Quoted Shares/Securities within 12 Months of Death (section 179)

If the proceeds realised on the sale of quoted shares or securities within 12 months of the date of death of the donor are lower than the value included in their estate, it is possible to make a claim to substitute the lower value for the purposes of calculating the IHT due on the estate.

When calculating the claim that may be made, it is a requirement to determine the net effect of all disposals of such assets that take place within 12 months of the death. Thus any relevant assets sold for an amount higher than the value included in the estate valuation will reduce the benefit of making the post-mortem claim.

There is an important planning point here, in that it may be possible to delay sales that would achieve a higher sales price until after 12 months from the date of death, this would maximise the value of any claim.

Obviously, if the relevant sales that took place within 12 months of death would produce a higher value than originally included in the death estate, then no claim should be made.

In evaluating the possible benefit of making a claim, it is the gross sales figures that are compared to the original probate value included in the death estate.

There is also an anti-avoidance measure that must be considered. This is designed to stop shares being sold to realise post-mortem relief and then immediately reinvesting the proceeds (whether into the same shares/securities or not). The anti-avoidance legislation restricts the loss in value that can be claimed where there are any investments purchased between the date of death and the end of two months from the last sale of relevant assets within the 12-month period from the date of death. Where this restriction applies, the restriction is calculated as:

$$\text{Loss} \times \frac{\text{Amount invested}}{\text{Total gross proceeds}}$$

Example 24.11: Post-mortem relief – quoted shares
Darina died on 12 August 2019 and left her estate of £725,000 to her three children. The estate included shares in AIG plc, valued at £50,000.

The executors sold the shares in September 2019, realising proceeds of £12,250 after deducting sales costs of £250. In November 2019, the executors purchased £10,000 of shares in Centrica plc.

Calculate any post-mortem relief available.

	£
Probate value	50,000
Less: gross proceeds	(12,500)
Loss	37,500
Less: restriction	
$\frac{10,000}{12,500} \times £37,500$	(30,000)
Section 179 claim	7,500

Therefore the shares would be included in the death estate at a value of £42,500 (£50,000 – £7,500).

24.6.2 Sale of Land or Buildings within Three Years of Death (section 191)

This relief works in a similar fashion to that for sales of quoted shares, etc. but with a few significant differences. The time period is three years from the date of death rather than one. The aggregation of profits and losses rule still applies but is modified in that it also includes sales that take place at a loss in the **fourth** year after death (sales at a profit in the fourth year are completely ignored).

When calculating the relief, differences in value between the date of death and the date of sale are ignored if they are less than the lower of £1,000 or 5% of the probate value.

A similar anti-avoidance rule on reinvestment also applies and covers the period from death to four months after the last sale in the three-year period. The relevant formula for calculating the restriction is:

$$\text{Loss} \times \frac{\text{Amount invested}}{\text{Total gross proceeds}}$$

Example 24.12: Post-mortem relief – land and buildings
Justin's death estate included the following assets at the date of his death on 5 May 2019:

	£
House in Bristol	165,000
Cottage in Donegal	185,000
Apartment in Benidorm	95,000

In administering Justin's estate the following transactions took place:

- Sold house in Bristol on 12 August 2019 for £160,000
- Sold cottage in Donegal on 9 September 2019 for £164,500
- Sold apartment in Benidorm on 3 December 2019 for £94,500
- Bought farmland in Fermanagh for £35,000 on 2 February 2020

continued overleaf

Calculate any post-mortem relief that may be due.

The losses on the Bristol and Donegal properties are relevant to the section 191 claim. The loss of £500 on disposal of Benidorm must be ignored as it is below the lower of £1,000 and 5% of probate value.

The effect of ignoring the Benidorm disposal is that the last relevant sale took place on 9 September 2019 and only purchases taking place between death and four months from 9 September 2019 are relevant for restricting the claim. Therefore, the purchase of farmland in Fermanagh will not restrict the post-mortem relief.

The section 191 loss claim is £25,500, i.e. (£165,000 – £160,000) + (£185,000 – £164,500). Therefore the properties would be included in the death estate at a value of £160,000 and £164,500 for the Bristol and Donegal properties, respectively.

24.6.3 Sale of Related Property to an Unconnected Party within Three Years of Death (section 176)

A claim for this relief will be possible where the death estate included related property which is sold within three years of death to an unconnected party for a value less than that included in the death estate. This relief works differently from the other post-mortem reliefs referred to above in that the relief is obtained by substituting the standalone value applicable at the date of death (rather than by reference to the proceeds received at the date of disposal), i.e the higher related property value is not included in the death estate.

Example 24.13: Post-mortem relief – related property
Rosie died on 3 May 2019 and her death estate included 40% of the shares in Arkle Investments Ltd, a property investment company. Her husband owns a further 30% of the shares in the company. At the date of death, a 40% shareholding is worth £250,000, while a 70% holding is worth £525,000.

As no BPR is due because the activity of the company is an excluded activity, the shares were included in the death estate as 40/70 × £525,000 = £300,000.

The executors sold Rosie's shares for £280,000 six months after her death to a third party.

Calculate any post-mortem relief due.

All the conditions necessary to qualify for post-mortem relief have been satisfied as:

- the asset was related property in the death estate as the related property value was higher;
- it has been sold to an unconnected third party within three years of death; and
- the proceeds realised (£280,000) are less than the amount included in the death estate (£300,000).

The relief is claimed by substituting the standalone value of £250,000 (note that this is not the sale price of £280,000!) for the original related property value of £300,000. Therefore, relief of £50,000 is effectively obtained.

Questions

Review Questions

(See Suggested Solution to Review Questions at the end of this textbook.)

Question 24.1

Relief from inheritance tax is available on relevant business property.

Requirement

(a) What is "relevant business property"?
(b) What types of business do not qualify for this relief?
(c) What is the nature of the relief and at what rates is it given?

Question 24.2

Relief from inheritance tax is also available for agricultural property.

Requirement

(a) Under what circumstances is a transferor entitled to inheritance tax relief when transferring agricultural property and what is the nature of the relief?
(b) Is the relief available to a transferor of shares or debentures in a farming company?

Question 24.3

Chris Adams is a wealthy individual whose grandmother died on 13 November 2019. His grandmother was born, and always lived, in the UK. Chris is an executor of her estate, and of the discretionary trust noted below, and is keen to finalise the inheritance tax issues associated with her death as soon as possible.

Chris realises that he does not have the necessary knowledge to calculate the inheritance tax that is due and does not want to miss out on any relief which could be claimed to reduce the IHT liability and so increase the funds available to the beneficiaries of his grandmother's will.

Chris has given you the following information:

1. His grandmother gave £500,000 to a discretionary trust in June 2016, and paid any IHT due. He can't find the papers showing how much inheritance tax was paid.
2. Chris had been given the family home by his grandmother in May 2018, when it was worth £600,000.
3. His grandmother owned three rental properties on the Lisburn Road, Belfast. He has obtained an independent valuation of the three properties which indicates that the value at the date of death was £560,000. However, as his grandmother's will states that the properties are to be sold and the proceeds divided between her four grandchildren, he placed them on the market in February 2020. At this point the estate agent recommended an asking price of £550,000, but due to the state of the property market, the highest offer received to date (which Chris has just accepted) is £525,000.
4. His grandmother had credit card debt of £15,000 at the date of her death.
5. She owed £50,000 to Bank of Ireland, secured on her collection of art. The loan was used by her to travel all around the country and display her art at various exhibitions and will be repaid from her estate. The art is worth £250,000.

6. His grandmother owned a holiday home in Iceland worth £78,000.
7. At the date of death she had cash of £250,000 in a UK bank account and cash of £40,000 in an account in the Isle of Man.
8. Chris has incurred the following costs in his role as executor, which have been paid for out of his grandmother's estate: solicitor's fees of £5,000 in administering the estate, £2,000 on a headstone, £550 on mourning clothes for his family for the funeral and £14,500 in obtaining probate on the holiday home his grandmother owned in Iceland.

Requirement

(a) Calculate the inheritance tax due as a result of the death of Chris's grandmother.
(b) State who has to pay any additional inheritance tax due on the lifetime gifts.

Question 24.4

You work in the trusts and estates division of a local mid-sized practice. Your client, Fionn O'Shea, died on 31 March 2020. During your review of Fionn's tax file, you note that, during his lifetime, he had made the following gifts:

1. £9,000 to his son Shay on the occasion of his marriage on 10 March 2014.
2. £300,000 to a discretionary trust on 28 December 2014. You note that the trustees agreed to pay any tax due.
3. 100,000 Angel Bank plc £1 ordinary shares valued at £175,000 to the same discretionary trust on 25 November 2015. Again, the trustees agreed to pay any tax due. The shares had fallen in value to £75,000 at the date of Fionn's death.

Fionn also owned the following assets when he died: his home valued at £225,000, cash and investments valued totalling £85,000 and chattels valued at £15,000.

Fionn was also the life tenant of a qualifying interest in possession trust created by his brother's will following his death in 1988. The value of the trust fund at Fionn's death was £276,000.

Fionn was married to Alanna, who died in 2015 with no assets. He never remarried and left his estate to his son.

Requirement
Prepare a memo to the partner in your practice dealing with the following:

(a) Calculation of the lifetime inheritance tax payable, if any, in respect of the lifetime gifts.
(b) Calculation of the inheritance tax due on Fionn's death estate, making any appropriate claims or reliefs available to reduce the liability arising (if any).

Question 24.5

James Quinn died on 20 November 2019. His brother Andrew predeceased him on 31 March 2016, leaving his entire estate, valued at £575,000, to James. The month before Andrew died, Andrew made a gift of £156,000 to their only sister Laura.

At the time of his death, James's estate was valued at £1.5 million, including the assets left to him by Andrew in 2016. James left his estate to his favourite nephew.

Requirement
Calculate the inheritance tax payable due to James's death, making any appropriate claims or reliefs available to reduce the liability arising (if any). Assume James made no lifetime gifts. Outline the rationale for any claims or reliefs.

Question 24.6

It is 18 June 2019 and you are meeting Alexander Johnston, a new client of your office. Alexander's wife died earlier this year on 14 February and all of her estate passed to him. Shocked at her sudden death, it has made him think about the large number of assets he owns and the gifts he has made, and the inheritance tax that might be payable on them.

Alexander has requested a calculation of the amount of inheritance tax that would be payable if he died today as a prelude to considering what inheritance tax planning could be implemented to reduce any liabilities that might arise. He provides you with the following information:

1. He has cash of £82,000 in a French bank account. He owes £10,000 in credit card debt.
2. He owns a house that he inherited from his brother in August 2016. This house was a specific gift of UK property left to him in his brother's will. His brother's estate paid inheritance tax of £75,000 that related to the value of the property in the death estate. The property had cost his brother £340,000 and was worth £525,000 at the date of his brother's death. The property is currently worth £590,000.
3. He owns 6,000 of the 10,000 shares in issue in AJ Ltd, an unquoted trading company. The following share values are relevant:

	£
Value – 40% interest in the company	275,000
Value – 60% interest in the company	625,000
Value – 100% interest in the company	1,400,000

4. He gave his son £220,000 cash in May 2015.
5. He owns an investment property in Stranmillis which is worth £280,000. However, due to the recent fall in property prices, the outstanding mortgage on the property is £290,000. The bank has a charge over his general assets.
6. He owns a ski chalet in Switzerland. The property is worth £120,000 and it is estimated that the cost of obtaining probate of the chalet would be £12,000.
7. He gifted his Aston Martin DB9 to his son in May 2016 when it was worth £65,000. He and his son both work in the same office block in Belfast and his son lives in Bangor. As Alexander lives in Holywood, his son picks him up in the DB9 three days a week and gives him a lift to work. The Aston Martin is currently worth £90,000.

Requirement

Prepare a report to Alexander dealing with the following:

(a) Calculate the inheritance tax that would be payable on his death if he were to die today. Claim all available reliefs.

(b) Outline the due date for payment of any inheritance tax arising, and advise what date the inheritance tax return would need to be filed with HMRC.

Question 24.7

Portia di Rossi died on 29 July 2019. She is survived by her four children and six grandchildren.

During her life, Portia was always very generous. She turned 80 in October 2013 and, every Christmas from then on, she gave £200 to each of her grandchildren. For Christmas 2013 only, she also gave £4,500 to each of her children. When her godson was married on 19 March 2015, Portia gave him £6,000. She made no gifts of any sort in any tax years prior to 2013/14.

A sum of £25,000 was donated by her in July 2014 to an American charity established in New York for fire-fighters injured in 9/11 as her brother was a long-time resident of New York and had been rescued from the street that day by a passing fire crew.

Keen to also provide for her children, five months before her death, in February 2019, Portia gifted £380,000 cash to create a discretionary trust which she established for her children. Portia made it clear at that time that any tax that arose on the gift was to be taken care of by the trustees.

At the time of her death, Portia owned the following assets:

1. Her home in Armagh, valued at £725,000 for probate purposes, but sold after her death in December 2019 for £645,000.
2. The contents of the Armagh house, valued at £48,500.
3. A villa in Portugal, valued at £225,000.
4. 18,000 shares in Belfast Ceramics Plc. The closing bid and offer prices quoted in the Stock Exchange Daily Official List for the company at the date of death were £2.72 and £2.76. The shares were sold six months later for £1.45 each. Portia did not hold a controlling interest in this company.
5. 3,500 shares in British Meats Plc. The closing bid and offer prices quoted in the Stock Exchange Daily Official List for the company at the date of death were £12.35 and £12.95. The shares were sold three months later for £13.60 each. Portia did not hold a controlling interest in this company.
6. 390 of the 1,000 issued shares in Italiana Wine SA, a successful Italian trading company established by Portia's son, Paolo, which produces wine in Sicily mainly for the export market. Paolo owns the remaining 610 shares. Portia acquired the shares in January 2014. The shareholding is estimated to have a value of £180,000.
7. £69,000 in bank and building society accounts in Belfast.
8. £228,000 in a Guernsey bank account.

For tax purposes, Portia was domiciled in the UK at the time of her death.

Requirement

Calculate the IHT payable as a result of Portia's death, split between amounts payable in respect of her estate on death, and the amount(s), if any, payable on death in respect of Portia's lifetime gifts. Explain your treatment of each item and claim any reliefs possible to minimise tax which may be due.

25

Interaction between IHT and CGT

Learning Objectives

After studying this chapter you will understand:

- The interaction between IHT and CGT.
- The IHT treatment of "gifts with reservation of benefit".

25.1 Overview of IHT and CGT Interaction

IHT and CGT are very different taxes, each with their own exemptions and reliefs and different methods of calculating the value of the asset and the tax due. So, having dealt with the rules of each of them separately, it can seem like a step too far to deal with both of them in respect of the same transaction. However, once it is appreciated that the taxes should be addressed one at a time (and not simultaneously), it becomes clear that all that is necessary is a clear knowledge of the rules together with an orderly approach to the situation in question.

Always try to deal with the CGT and IHT implications of a transaction separately before considering any interaction elements. Strictly, it does not matter which of the taxes is addressed first, but it is likely to be helpful to consider IHT initially as its implications may be useful when considering whether or not gift holdover relief for CGT is available under section 260 TCGA 1992.

Overall, there will only be a true interaction in three circumstances:

1. Where there is potentially an immediate charge to IHT in lifetime on the transaction (i.e. because the transaction is a CLT), meaning section 260 TCGA 1992 "gift relief" will be available to relieve any CGT that arises on the transaction.
2. In circumstances where the donee pays the IHT on a gift. This will also form part of the base cost of the asset for CGT purposes on a later disposal by them.
3. The market value of the asset at the date of death, for IHT purposes, becomes the legatee's base cost for CGT. This is despite there being no CGT implications if a donee receives an asset from the deceased's death estate. In other words, the legatee receives the uplift to market value CGT-free.

25.2 Explanation of the Interaction of IHT and CGT

A gift can have both IHT and CGT consequences at the same time. The base cost for CGT purposes of a lifetime gift in the hands of the donee (for both PETs and CLTs) is the market value at the date of transfer unless gift relief is claimed. Remember also that the value of the transaction may be different for IHT purposes under the loss to the donor rule. The donor will be subject to CGT if the gift is a chargeable asset for CGT purposes. Any tax charge will be based on the market value of the asset at the date of gift. This will be the case unless the asset is exempt from CGT or if it is possible to make a holdover election under section 165 (mainly for business assets) or section 260 TCGA 1992 (see **Chapter 19**, **Section 19.2**). It may be possible to make a section 260 TCGA 1992 claim if the transfer is immediately chargeable to IHT, e.g. on a gift into a trust. The claim can be made even if the IHT charge is at 0%, i.e. within the nil rate band, or covered by a relief. Section 260 gift relief can be used on any type of asset, including non-business assets, so is a useful relief in situations where section 165 gift relief is not available or is restricted (for example where the transaction is a gift of shares that would otherwise be restricted by virtue of the level of chargeable non-business assets on the statement of financial position of the company).

If both section 165 and section 260 reliefs are potentially available, section 260 has priority. In most instances, gift relief is a joint claim to be made by the donor and the donee. This is not the case when the donee is a trust and section 260 relief applies. Therefore if the settlor transfers assets to a trust and wishes to defer the gain under section 260, the claim will be made by the settlor only and the consent of the trustees is not required. As we saw earlier, a gift relief claim must be made within four years after the end of the tax year in which the assets were transferred. Therefore, for gifts in 2019/20, a gift relief claim must be made no later than 5 April 2024.

Where there is a gift of an asset and it is possible to make a CGT holdover election, the base cost for the recipient becomes the market value at the date of transfer less the amount of gift relief claimed. The effect of this is that the gain is effectively passed on to the donee.

When an asset has been acquired following the death of the donor, the probate value becomes the CGT base cost. This can be particularly valuable where 100% BPR or APR is available. There will be no IHT due on a transfer on death and the donee will receive the property at its current market value.

Where post-mortem relief is claimed, this lower value becomes the CGT base cost rather than the original probate value.

Example 25.1

Jonathan Williamson is 70 years old and a widower. He has one child, his son Peter, to whom he intends to leave the whole of his estate on his death. Both Jonathan and Peter were born in the UK and have always lived and worked here.

Peter is currently planning to buy a house and so Jonathan would like to make a lifetime gift to him of one of his assets to fund the property purchase. Peter needs around £425,000 after deducting any tax payable, either by himself or his father. He will sell whatever gift he receives from his father immediately in order to buy the house

Jonathan owns two assets valued at £425,000 (see below) and would like advice on which he should gift (and why), factoring in all the relevant tax consequences. He would also like to know if he is better to gift the assets now or wait to pass them on to his son in his will.

1. 15,000 shares in Williamson Holidays Ltd

This is an unquoted trading company. Jonathan currently owns 30,000 shares in the company, representing a 75% holding. The 15,000 shares have an estimated market value of £425,000 and they cost him £325,000 in 2013.

The company owns a plot of land that it holds as an investment. The land comprises 6% of the value of its total assets and 10% of the value of its chargeable assets.

continued overleaf

2. A sailing boat known as "William and Son"
The boat is also worth £425,000 but cost £200,000 in June 2008. Jonathan took it on as project and spent a further £125,000 the next year installing a more powerful engine and satellite navigation equipment.

The tax implications of the two proposed gifts are considered below.

Gift of shares
(a) CGT implications

Lifetime gift
Jonathan would make a capital gain by reference to the deemed sales proceeds equal to the market value of the shares – i.e. a gain of £100,000 (£425,000 – £325,000) as Peter is a connected party under section 286 TCGA 1992.

Jonathan owns more than 5% of Williamson Holidays Ltd and has owned the shares for more than 12 months. In addition, Williamson Holidays Ltd is a trading company. However, entrepreneurs' relief will only be available if Jonathan is a director or employee of the company in the two years prior to the gift of the shares to his son.

Gift holdover relief would also be available as the shares are unquoted and Williamson Holidays Ltd is a trading company. However, the relief would be restricted to 90% only because the company owns chargeable non-business assets (the plot of land held as an investment comprises 10% of the company's chargeable assets).

If Jonathan is an employee of Williamson Holidays Ltd, gift holdover relief should not be claimed unless Peter has significant capital losses to use because gift holdover will create a sizeable gain for Peter when he sells the shares immediately after receiving them.

Entrepreneurs' relief is a better option. Jonathan's gain of £100,000 would be reduced by any available annual exempt amount; assuming he has none remaining, the maximum capital gains tax would be £10,000 (£100,000 × 10%). Peter's base cost in the shares would be their market value at the time of the gift being £425,000. Accordingly, there would be no gain on the immediate sale of the shares by Peter following the gift, as his sales proceeds would equal his base cost, assuming he can sell them immediately for the same price. This would mean that Peter would have a clear £425,000 of cash available for the property purchase.

If Jonathan is not an employee of Williamson Holidays Ltd, he and Peter can claim gift holdover relief as both could then benefit from their CGT annual exemption. Jonathan would make a maximum gain of £10,000 (£100,000 × 10%) due to the non-business chargeable assets, which would then be reduced by any available annual exempt amount.

The maximum CGT liability for Jonathan would be £2,000 (£10,000 × 20% maximum) depending on the level of his income and the existence of any other capital gains. The remainder of the gain of £90,000 would be held over and would reduce Peter's base cost of the shares to £335,000 (£425,000 − £90,000).

Accordingly, Peter's gain on an onward immediate sale for £425,000 would be £90,000 (£425,000 − £335,000) as reduced by any available annual exempt amount. The maximum CGT liability would be £18,000 (£90,000 × 20%). The total CGT due would be a maximum of £20,000 between Jonathan and Peter (£2,000 + £18,000). Peter would only have £408,000 to fund the property purchase.

Gift via Jonathan's will
Gifts on death are exempt from CGT. Hence Peter's base cost would be the market value of the shares at the time of death. However he would not be able to fund the property purchase at the time he wants to and would be forced to wait, assuming he has no other way of funding the purchase.

(b) IHT implications

Lifetime gift
The gift would be a potentially exempt transfer that would only be subject to IHT if Jonathan were to die within seven years. If the gift became chargeable, business property relief would not be available as Peter would not own the shares at the time of Jonathan's death and he would not have replaced the shares with equivalent business property.

continued overleaf

In addition, Jonathan will still hold 15,000 shares in Williamson Holidays Ltd. Accordingly, the value of the transfer for IHT would be calculated under the loss to the donor principle representing the fall in value of Jonathan's estate at the time of the gift. This is likely to differ from the market value of the shares gifted as Jonathan's holding would be reduced from 75% to 37.5%, such that he would no longer control the company.

The fall in value in Jonathan's estate would be reduced by any available annual exemptions. If Jonathan dies, IHT would then be due on the excess of this amount over the nil rate band at the date of death (as reduced by any chargeable transfers in the seven years prior to the gift of the shares). Taper relief would be available if Jonathan were to survive the gift by at least three years. The maximum IHT liability would be 40% of the fall in value.

Gift via Jonathan's will
100% business property relief would be available on the non-excepted assets. Accordingly, only 6% of the value of the shares as at the time of death would be subject to IHT (on the assumption that the proportion of the company's assets held in the form of investments has not changed).

The shares would be included in Jonathan's death estate. The excess of the death estate over the available nil rate band (as reduced by any chargeable transfers in the seven years prior to death) would be subject to IHT at 40%. The maximum liability would be 2.4% (6% × 40%) of the value of the shares.

Gift of sailing boat
(a) CGT implications

Lifetime gift or via Jonathan's will
The sailing boat is a wasting chattel (tangible, moveable property with a useful life of no more than 50 years) and, as such, is an exempt asset for the purposes of capital gains tax. So Peter would have £425,000 cash in hand from the sale. Gifting the boat via his will would result in the same outcome, however, Peter's ownership would be delayed and he would not have the cash to fund the property purchase when he needs it.

(b) IHT implications

Lifetime gift
The gift would be a potentially exempt transfer and would only be subject to IHT if Jonathan were to die within seven years. IHT would be due on the excess of the value of the sailing boat at the time of the gift (as reduced by any available annual exemptions) over the available nil rate band at death (as reduced by any chargeable transfers in the seven years prior to the gift). Taper relief would be available if Jonathan were to survive the gift by at least three years.

Gift via Jonathan's will
The sailing boat would be included in Jonathan's death estate at its value on death. The excess of the death estate over the available nil-rate band (as reduced by any chargeable transfers in the seven years prior to death) would be subject to IHT at 40%.

Recommendation
It is clear that, purely from a tax point of view, Jonathan should give Peter the sailing boat rather than the shares.

There will be no tax at the time of the gift, either CGT or IHT. In addition, there will be no tax at the time of death, provided Jonathan survives the gift by seven years. Even if Jonathan were to die within seven years of the gift, the amount of IHT due on death is likely to be less than the amount due if the sailing boat were held by Jonathan until death due to the availability of taper relief. Before concluding on this, it would be necessary to consider the chargeable transfers made by Jonathan during the seven years prior to the proposed gift and the likelihood of the sailing boat increasing or falling in value.

The situation regarding a gift of the shares is not so straightforward. A lifetime gift will result in a CGT liability of up to £20,000. There is also the possibility of an IHT liability of 40% of the fall in value of Jonathan's estate if Jonathan were to die within three years of the gift. However, there would be no IHT liability if he were to survive the gift by at least seven years.

continued overleaf

Retaining the shares until death would avoid the CGT liability, but would guarantee an IHT liability up to a maximum of 2.4% of the value of the shares. Accordingly, a lifetime gift of the shares would be a gamble by Jonathan. If he were to survive the gift by seven years, the total tax due would be CGT of either £10,000 or £20,000, depending on whether or not he is an employee of Williamson Holidays Ltd (and the availability of entrepreneurs' relief). If he were to die within three years of the gift, the total tax due is likely to be considerable due to the IHT payable. His alternative is to hold on to the shares and pay a relatively small amount of IHT out of his death estate. Finally, Jonathan could be advised that an insurance policy could be taken out on his life in order to satisfy any future IHT liability arising in respect of a lifetime gift.

The following general conclusions can be drawn from the above.

1. IHT – assets that are subject to IHT but not CGT (i.e. those that are exempt from CGT) can be planned for by reference to IHT only. From an IHT point of view, it is advantageous to give away assets as soon as possible as this opens up the possibility of surviving the gift by seven years or, failing that, the possibility of taper relief. It is particularly important to gift assets that are expected to increase in value as the value on which IHT is calculated is frozen at the time of the gift.

2. IHT – care must be taken when advising on assets that qualify for business property relief or agricultural property relief due to the need for the recipient to hold the assets until the death of the donor in order for the relief to be available on the donor's death. If it is clear from the facts that the recipient intends to sell the assets gifted, there is likely to be a significant difference between the IHT due on death within seven years of the lifetime gift and that due on the asset when comprised within the death estate.

3. CGT – it is not always advantageous to claim gift holdover relief. Also, the relief is not always available; in particular, unless the gift is to a trust, the assets must qualify for the relief.

25.3 Consideration of the Impact of "Gifts with Reservation"

The "gifts with reservation" (GWR) rules were introduced as an anti-avoidance measure to prevent individuals gifting assets but continuing to derive some benefit from those assets after the gift had been made. Without the rules, the assets could fall outside the taxable estate if the donor survived seven years from the date of making the PET, even where they continue to derive a benefit from the assets.

The rules operate by treating the asset as continuing to form part of the donor's estate for IHT purposes, i.e. the gift is ignored. The most common asset to be affected by this legislation is the main residence of the donor, where it is gifted to someone (e.g. the donor's son or daughter) but the donor continues to derive a benefit from the property by continuing to live there.

The anti-avoidance legislation does not apply where the donor pays full market value for the use of the property gifted or if the donor is virtually excluded from benefiting from the property.

If a donor makes a GWR and dies within seven years, there is a potential double charge, with tax becoming due both on the original lifetime gift of the property (being a 'failed PET') and on the property being included in the death estate as a consequence of the reservation of benefit. HMRC acknowledges that there could be a double charge and deals with the matter by requiring two IHT computations – one showing the tax charge on the original PET, and one showing the tax charge if the asset is included in the death estate. Rather than imposing a double IHT charge, HMRC accepts the computation that produces the higher IHT charge, including taking into consideration the availability of the residence nil rate band/unused spouse's residence nil rate on the GWR (not available on the failed PET). In carrying out this comparison, credit for any tax previously paid on a lifetime transfer is limited to the amount of tax payable on the death in respect of the GWR property.

The residence nil rate band, which came into operation for deaths on or after 6 April 2017 (see **Chapter 23, Section 23.6**), will be available against a single residence that is part of the deceased's estate on death, whether owned directly by the deceased, or to which they are beneficially entitled through a qualifying interest in possession or a GWR (see **Chapter 23, Section 23.6**), subject to the remaining conditions for accessing the residence nil rate band being met.

Example 25.2: Gift with reservation (GWR)

Luke gave his daughter his holiday cottage in Portrush in January 2006. Luke continued to spend three months of each year in the cottage between the date of the gift and his death in July 2019. This is a GWR and the value of the property at the date of his death will be included in Luke's death estate for IHT purposes, even though the original PET succeeded. Luke will be entitled to deduct the applicable residence nil rate band in the tax year of his death against the GWR.

NB: The value of the property in January 2006 is his daughter's base cost for CGT purposes.

Example 25.3: GWR double charge calculation

In July 2013, Anne gives a holiday home worth £450,000 (after annual exemptions) to her daughter, Betty, but continues to use the home on a regular basis. Anne's husband is still alive. The PET that arises at that time is also a GWR for IHT.

Anne dies in June 2019, having continued to use the holiday home up the date of her death.

At the date of her death it is worth £550,000, and is therefore treated as part of her estate under the GWR rules. Her remaining death estate is valued at £600,000. Anne made no other lifetime gifts.

Two calculations are required – one on the basis of only including the GWR, and one on the basis of only including the failed PET. HMRC take the calculation that produces the highest liability.

First calculation

Ignore the lifetime charge and charge the holiday home as part of Anne's death estate.

July 2013 – gift ignored, tax nil

June 2019 – tax on death estate, as follows:

	£
Holiday home	550,000
Remaining estate	600,000
Chargeable estate	1,150,000
Less: residence NRB	(150,000)
Less: NRB	(325,000)
Chargeable	675,000
IHT @ 40%	270,000

Total tax is therefore £270,000.

Second calculation

Charge the lifetime gift and ignore the holiday home as part of the death estate.

continued overleaf

July 2013 – tax on £450,000 gift, as follows:

	£
Holiday home	450,000
Less: NRB	(325,000)
Chargeable	125,000
IHT @ 40%	50,000

June 2019 – tax on death estate, as follows:

	£
Remaining estate	600,000
Chargeable estate	600,000
IHT @ 40%	240,000

Total tax is therefore £290,000 (£50,000 on the failed PET and £240,000 on the death estate).

The second calculation results in the greater amount of tax being payable; IHT is therefore charged on the basis of the second calculation, with the value of the GWR being reduced to nil.

It is possible to release a GWR before death by relinquishing any benefit retained. However, this is treated as a deemed PET at the date of the release of the benefit (and at the value at the date of release). As this is a deemed PET it is not possible to claim the annual exemption(s) against it. To avoid the double IHT charge on the original gift and the subsequent release of the benefit, HMRC again accepts the IHT computation that produces the higher IHT liability.

Questions

Review Questions

(See Suggested Solution to Review Questions at the end of this textbook.)

Question 25.1

Sean has gathered substantial wealth in his lifetime and is considering disposing some of it to his son, Shay. He is considering gifting his home to Shay but continuing to live in the house until his death. Sadly, Sean has recently been diagnosed with a terminal illness and his life expectancy is no more than three years. Sean has lived in the house all his life. He would not intend to pay any rent to Shay.

Requirement

Briefly explain the capital gains tax and inheritance tax implications of this proposal.

26

Administration of IHT

Learning Objectives

After studying this chapter you will understand:

- The administrative procedures around IHT.
- The deadlines for payment of IHT and the filing of IHT returns.
- The penalties and interest charges for late payment, late filing and errors in IHT returns.

26.1 Payment of IHT on Lifetime Gifts

Primary responsibility for the payment of any IHT due on lifetime gifts rests with the donor. The donor may delegate responsibility for payment of IHT to the donee. Where a donor makes a chargeable lifetime gift and does not delegate the responsibility for payment to the donee, the gift must be grossed up for the IHT that the donor has paid (see **Chapter 23**, **Section 23.2**). The reason for this is that the donor's estate has also been reduced by the IHT due.

The actual gift, in the hand's of the donee, is deemed to be net of any IHT due (see **Chapter 23** for the tax treatment of chargeable lifetime transfers and potentially exempt transfers). The due date for payment of the relevant IHT and filing of the relevant return is six months from the end of the month in which the transfer is made.

26.2 Payment of IHT on Lifetime Gifts Following Death within Seven Years

The due date for payment of IHT on a CLT or a failed PET is six months from the end of the month in which the death occurs.

26.3 Payment of IHT on Death Estate

The due date for payment of IHT on the death estate is payable on the earlier of:

1. six months from the end of the month in which the transfer takes place on death, or
2. the date of delivery of the IHT400 return.

Interest will accrue for any IHT paid late (with the exception that no interest will accrue for the first six months if the IHT400 is filed before the six-month date).

26.4 IHT Instalments

26.4.1 General Conditions

Any IHT payable on certain qualifying assets (referred to as qualifying property) may be paid in instalments if a claim is made to HMRC. If a claim is made, the IHT is payable in 10 equal instalments with the first instalment falling due on the normal due date.

No claim for the instalment option may be made if the donor agrees to pay any IHT due on the lifetime gift. Furthermore, if there is IHT due in respect of a lifetime gift that becomes payable following the death of the donor, the instalment option will only be available if the donee still owns the asset. The only exception to this rule is that, where the donee has sold business property that does not qualify for full BPR and reinvests the proceeds in acquiring replacement business property, then the right to pay IHT in instalments is preserved.

26.4.2 Interest Position

Depending on the type of property transferred, the instalments may be either 'interest-bearing' or 'interest-free'. As the name suggests, interest-free instalments are more attractive as interest only accrues from each instalment date if the IHT is paid after this date, whereas interest accrues from the normal due date for interest-bearing instalments. For interest-bearing instalments an interest charge is added at each instalment date based on the balance of unpaid IHT at the time.

Generally, the interest-free instalment option is available for transfers of land qualifying for APR, shares in trading companies and for a business or partnership share.

26.4.3 Qualifying Property

Qualifying property for the purposes of paying IHT by instalments is restricted to land or buildings, certain shareholdings, and a business or partnership share.

The instalment option is available in respect of all land and buildings, wherever situated. Generally, if BPR is available the instalment option is not relevant to the transfer of a business or partnership share. However, it may be relevant where the minimum period of ownership test has not been satisfied for BPR.

26.4.4 Cases where Instalments may Apply

The rules to determine whether or not shares are qualifying property are considered below. There are four cases in which the instalment option may be available:

1. Quoted or unquoted shareholdings that gave the owner control of a company (and, for this purpose, related property is also taken into account to determine whether the company is under control of the donor) are qualifying property.
2. Unquoted shares where the IHT payable on their transfer represents more than 20% of the total IHT payable on the estate.
3. Unquoted shares with a value for IHT purposes of greater than £20,000 and which represent at least 10% of the voting rights of the company.

OR

4. Unquoted shares where the executors have insufficient funds with which to settle the IHT due (known as a hardship claim). This is a subjective test and is normally only considered as a last resort if cases 1. to 3. above are not viable.

Whether the instalments are interest-free or interest-bearing will depend on whether the shares are in a trading company as noted above.

> ***Example 26.1: Payments***
> Frank left his home in his will to his nephew, Rick, following his death on 2 February 2019. £25,000 of IHT was payable.
>
> Explain the IHT payments to be made and advise what will happen if the house is sold in December 2019.
>
> The IHT may be paid in 10 equal interest-bearing instalments commencing 31 August 2019. Ten instalments of £2,500 may be paid and interest will be due on the unpaid balance of IHT due at each instalment date.
>
> If the house is sold in December 2019, the balance of IHT plus any accrued interest becomes immediately due.

26.5 Filing of Returns

The filing date of the IHT100 for lifetime gifts is six months from the end of the month in which the transfer is made.

An IHT400 should be filed by the executors of the estate for any CLT and failed PETs together with details of the death estate within 12 months from the end of the month in which the death occurs. The executors may also include details of any GWR but there is no statutory obligation to do so.

There are provisions which allow for small estates, referred to as "excepted estates", to be exempted from the obligation to file an IHT400.

26.6 Penalties

The late filing penalty regime is:

- an initial £100 penalty;
- if the account is more than six months late, the penalty is £200;
- if the account is more than 12 months late the penalty increases to a maximum of £3,000;
- if the actual tax liability is less than these figures, the penalty cannot be more than the amount of the tax due.

Errors in IHT returns are subject to the same penalty regime that applies to other taxes (see **Chapter 1, Section 1.12.4**).

Questions

Review Questions

(See Suggested Solution to Review Questions at the end of this textbook.)

Question 26.1

Please refer to question 24.4 (Fionn O'Shea) in Chapter 24.

Requirement

In relation to the gift made on 25 November 2015:

(a) What is the due date for payment of IHT on this lifetime CLT and filing of the relevant IHT 100?
(b) If there had been additional IHT payable on death in respect of that gift, what would the due date have been?
(c) Assuming the executors of the estate deliver the IHT 400 on 29 July 2020, on what date is payment of IHT on Fionn's death estate due? What is the due date for filing an IHT400?

Question 26.2

Trevor Smyth inherited Smyth Farm from his father in 1993. In 1992, Trevor's father granted a 40-year tenancy over the whole of the farm to the family-owned company, Smyth Farms Ltd, which has carried on a mixed farming business there ever since.

In 2010 Trevor gave cash of £226,000 to a discretionary trust for his children, David and Sarah, and he was totally excluded from any benefit. In 2013 Trevor bought Windy Farm and Primrose Farmhouse. At the same time, he retired from any active part in the farm business in order to live in Primrose Farmhouse with his long-term partner, Eileen, whom he married in 2015.

On 14 June 2015, as an engagement present for Eileen, Trevor transferred Primrose Farmhouse into his and Eileen's joint names. At that time Primrose Farmhouse was worth £900,000. Valuers have advised that a half share owned by either party should be discounted by 15%.

Trevor died on 1 January 2020. At the time of his death his assets were:

1. His half share as beneficial joint tenant of Primrose Farmhouse – the whole was valued at £1,000,000.
2. Smyth Farm valued at £1,900,000, of which £700,000 is the value of the farmhouse and £300,000 is the value of Smyth Farm Stables (see below).
3. Windy Farm valued at £950,000.
4. 50% of the shares in Smyth Farms Ltd valued at £425,000.
5. Personal bank accounts and investments (net of funeral expenses and other debts owing at death) worth a total of £240,000.
6. A collection of shotguns and other shooting equipment with a value of £48,000.

Smyth Farm Stables, which comprises a riding school, stables, and some 30 acres used for horse grazing, was released from the agricultural tenancy some years ago. Sarah has since run Smyth Farm Stables as a riding school and horse livery business and paid her father rent.

The rest of Smyth Farm (comprising the farmhouse, farmland and a number of farm buildings used for storage and for shelter of farm animals) has remained within the tenancy granted in 1990 and has continued to be used for the Smyth Farms Ltd farming business. Since his father's move to

Primrose Farmhouse, David has lived at the farmhouse on Smyth Farm, from where he has run Smyth Farms Ltd.

The executors' valuer has advised that HMRC is likely to successfully argue that, although the market value of the farmhouse at Smyth Farm is £700,000, its agricultural value is £600,000, but that the agricultural value of the rest of Smyth Farm is equal to its market value.

Windy Farm, which comprises only agricultural land and does not include any buildings, has also been occupied and farmed by Smyth Farms Ltd since Trevor's purchase. In this case there is no formal tenancy agreement. The valuer has advised that its agricultural value is the same as its market value.

Requirement

Calculate the inheritance tax payable as a result of Trevor's death, with comments explaining reliefs or exemptions available, if any.

27

Other Sundry Matters

Learning Objectives

After studying this chapter you will understand:

- The IHT treatment of gifts from companies.
- The impact of deeds of disclaimer/variations.
- Overseas aspects of IHT.

27.1 IHT Treatment of Gifts from Companies

Where a close company (as defined in **Chapter 6**) makes a transfer of value, that value may be apportioned among the participators according to their interests in the company and treated as a transfer of value by each individual for the purposes of IHT.

There is no apportionment of any value that is treated as the participator's income, for the purposes of corporation tax or income tax. There is also no charge in respect of excluded property, i.e. an amount that would be apportioned to a non-UK domiciled individual and which is attributable to property outside the UK. There is also no apportionment to shareholders who hold 5% or less of the company.

Any transfers of value caught by this legislation are treated as an immediate chargeable lifetime transfer (CLT) and not as a potentially exempt transfer (PET). As they are "deemed" transfers, the lifetime exemptions are generally not available. However, the legislation specifically provides that the annual exemption is available against such transfers, as is the spousal exemption to the extent that the estate of the spouse/civil partner is increased.

A change in the rights or number of shares held by a participator in a close company will also be considered to be a transfer of value. This is a deemed disposition and will also be treated as an immediate CLT and not as a PET. As the transfer is a deemed disposition rather than a deemed transfer of value, all the exemptions are available against the resulting transfer of value.

Example 27.1

Delta Ltd has an issued share capital of 100 shares, Richard owns 60 shares and Sean owns 40.

60 shares are issued to Richard's daughter and 40 to Sean's son.

Richard now has 60 shares out of 200 and has lost control of the company. Sean now has a "non-influential" 20% holding compared to his "influential" 40% holding. The values of both Richard and Sean's shareholding in the company have substantially diminished and each has made a transfer of value.

27.2 Double Tax Relief for Overseas Taxes Suffered

Relief for any overseas IHT is generally given under the provisions of a tax treaty, or more commonly by way of unilateral relief. Double tax relief is most commonly available where a UK domiciled/deemed UK domiciled individual dies owning foreign property.

Unilateral relief is available in the UK for the overseas tax suffered, and will be given as the lower of the overseas tax payable or the UK IHT due on the foreign asset. For this purpose it will be necessary to calculate the "estate rate" to determine the UK IHT payable in respect of the foreign asset. Any unrelieved foreign tax is effectively wasted.

27.3 Deed of Disclaimer/Variation

If a beneficiary is entitled to receive assets on the death of the donor, the potential recipient is under no legal obligation to accept the gift. Instead, the beneficiary may disclaim the gift. If this is done by way of formal written deed, the asset passes to the residuary beneficiary of the estate.

The potential beneficiary must have received no benefit from the property before it is disclaimed. For example, if the potential recipient has received some dividend income from shares, then the gift cannot be disclaimed

If the potential recipient would prefer the gift to pass to a nominated person or some other body, then they may use a deed of variation to achieve this objective.

If a valid deed is made, the gift is treated as passing directly from the original donor to the revised beneficiary for IHT purposes. The original potential donor is not treated as having made a transfer of value for IHT purposes.

In order to make a valid deed of disclaimer/variation, all of the following conditions must be made:

- it must be made in writing, normally in the form of a deed;
- it must be signed by the person making the variation/disclaimer;
- it should include a statement that section 142 IHTA 1984 and section 62 TCGA 1992 apply to the variation/disclaimer; and
- it must be made within two years from the date of death of the original donor.

Normally, no consent is required to enter into a disclaimer/variation; the only exception is where the amount of IHT payable by the estate is increased by the disclaimer/variation.

Deeds of variation and disclaimer are very useful post-death planning tools. They can be used to derive the maximum benefit from any unused spousal NRBs. This is now less important with the surviving spouse's ability to transfer unused NRBs.

They are also useful for transferring bequests to the surviving spouse for later transfer as a PET. For example, where the entire estate would be immediately chargeable and the surviving spouse may survive for more than seven years (or three to benefit from taper relief).

They can also be useful in circumstances where an exempt charitable legacy has been insufficient to meet the 10% limit for accessing the 36% rate of IHT. In some situations, a deed to vary the legacy to meet the limit should be considered where the IHT saved more than covers the additional charitable legacy.

Questions

Review Questions

(See Suggested Solution to Review Questions at the end of this textbook.)

Question 27.1

You recently meet with the client of a new company you act for. Stewart Desmond is the sole shareholder of Desmond Engineering Limited and he wishes to discuss the tax implications of a transaction he is contemplating. He acquired his 100% shareholding in 1995 at a cost of £10,000. The company has a 31 March 2020 period-end. The following is an extract of the discussion:

"As you know, the company has a plot of land that I would like to take out of the company in order to sell it on to an interested third party. The sale should be concluded by the end of April 2019. I recently obtained an independent valuation of the property in the amount of £625,000, but I would like to transfer the warehouse out of the company to myself for £350,000. The company only paid £100,000 for the plot in June 2001."

Requirement

Outline the corporation tax, inheritance tax and capital gains tax implications of the above proposed transaction.

Part Four

Stamp Taxes and VAT on Property

28

Introduction and General Principles

Learning Objectives

After studying this chapter you will understand:

- The application of the general principles regarding the scope of stamp duty and the rate of stamp duty.

Chartered Accountants Ireland's *Code of Ethics* applies to all aspects of a Chartered Accountant's professional life, including dealing with stamp taxes and VAT on property issues. As outlined at the beginning of this book, further information regarding the principles in the *Code of Ethics* is set out in **Appendix 2**.

In addition, **Appendix 3** examines the distinction between tax planning, tax avoidance and tax evasion, which can arise in relation to all taxes, including the various stamp taxes and VAT on property matters covered in Chapters 28–32.

28.1 Background

Stamp duty, stamp duty land tax (SDLT) and stamp duty reserve tax (SDRT) are the liability of the purchaser or acquirer of the asset.

28.2 Charges to Stamp Duty

Stamp duty applies to transfers of stock/shares and marketable securities that are transferred by a stock transfer form. Stamp duty is charged on instruments, i.e. written documents.

The transfer of shares, stocks or marketable securities is charged to stamp duty at 0.5% of the consideration, unless the transaction falls within one of the specific exemptions mentioned below. This duty is rounded up to the nearest £5.

The purchase of shares, stocks or marketable securities for a consideration of £1,000 or less is not subject to stamp duty and the purchaser does not have to notify HMRC of the transaction. If the purchase is for more than £1,000, the purchaser will have to send HMRC the stock transfer form for stamping and pay the appropriate stamp duty.

> ***Example 28.1***
> On 31 July 2019, Steven purchases his brother, Paul's, shares in their family trading company for £75,000.
>
> As this is above the £1,000 consideration threshold Steven will pay stamp duty of £375 (£75,000 × 0.5%) on the share acquisition.

28.3 Exemptions

The exemptions from stamp duty are primarily for transfers where there is no consideration; these include:

1. gifts;
2. divorce arrangements or dissolution of civil partnership;
3. property (or shares in property) or shares acquired through a will or variation of a will;
4. changes in trustees;
5. property (or shares in property) or shares acquired on entering into marriage or a civil partnership acquired from a spouse or civil partner; and
6. government securities and most company loan stock.

Sales of government securities and most company loan stock are exempt from stamp duty.

> ***Example 28.2***
> If, in Example 28.1, Paul gifted his shareholding to Steven, what would the stamp duty consequences be?
>
> *Solution*
>
> Steven would not be subject a stamp duty charge as the shares were gifted to him; this is one of the exemptions from stamp duty. However, the CGT and IHT consequences of the gift should be addressed.

28.4 Administration

Stamp duty is payable by the purchaser. A document must be stamped within 30 days of its execution, or within 30 days of being brought into the UK if it was executed outside the UK (and it does not relate to UK shares). Penalties can be imposed for late submission as follows:

Length of delay	**Amount of penalty**
Documents late by up to 12 months	10% of the duty, capped at £300
Documents late by 12 to 24 months	20% of the duty
Documents late by more than 24 months	30% of the duty

The late submission penalties apply in addition to any stamp duty due. The minimum penalty charge is £20, rounded down to the nearest multiple of £5. A penalty will not be levied by HMRC where it is less than £20.

HMRC will only cancel a late submission penalty if there is a "reasonable excuse" for submitting the documents late. HMRC will also not accept a personal reason for the delay if that reason did not prevent the taxpayer from dealing with other matters.

The civil penalty regime that applies for incorrect returns also applies to the various stamp taxes, including stamp duty.

This penalty regime focuses on the behaviour of the taxpayer. For example a company is deemed to be acting through its directors and officers. Where a company or taxpayer has made a mistake in a stamp taxes return submitted to HMRC, but has taken reasonable care in the preparation of that return, no penalty will be applied.

As stamp duty, SDRT and SDLT are considered to be "duties", rather than "taxes", and much of the legislation requires a knowledge of UK law (e.g. land law for SDLT), it is advisable for a solicitor or a stamp taxes specialist to be involved in preparing the necessary returns.

The categories of behaviour where penalties will be imposed are:

1. careless (failure to take reasonable care);
2. deliberate but not concealed (the inaccuracy is deliberate but there are no arrangements to conceal it); and
3. deliberate and concealed (the inaccuracy is deliberate and there are arrangements to conceal it).

Once HMRC has categorised the behaviour of the taxpayer, the potential lost revenue (PLR) will be computed. The penalty imposed is based on a percentage of the PLR. The PLR is the additional amount of tax due or payable as a result of correcting the inaccuracy.

However, HMRC may apply reductions to the proposed penalty where the taxpayer has disclosed the inaccuracy. Disclosure is split into two types (unprompted and prompted), with greater reductions being given where the taxpayer makes a disclosure which has not been prompted by HMRC.

A disclosure is unprompted if it is made at a time when the person making it has no reason to believe that HMRC has discovered or is about to discover the inaccuracy e.g. HMRC have not already opened an enquiry.

The ranges of percentage penalties that are applied by HMRC to the PLR are based on the behaviour of the taxpayer and the extent of the disclosure. These are detailed in **Chapter 1**. A taxpayer has the right to appeal against any stamp taxes (including stamp duty) penalty that they disagree with. They must do this in writing within 30 days of receiving the formal adjudication notice.

If paid late, interest is chargeable from 30 days after the date of execution, whether or not the document was executed in the UK. From 21 August 2018, interest is charged at a rate of 3.25% per annum for each day, or part day, that the payment is late.

Example 28.3
Taking **Example 28.1**, when is the stamp duty liability payable by Steven due for payment?

Steven acquired the shares on 31 July 2019. Therefore the document transferring the shares and the stamp duty thereon (£375) must be submitted for stamping within 30 days, i.e. by 30 August 2019, to avoid a late filing penalty and interest.

28.5 Consideration

The consideration subject to duty is any money or money's worth provided by the purchaser. Where the payment of the consideration is subject to a contingency, it is assumed that the contingency is satisfied. However, any contingency that would result in a reduction of the consideration is assumed not to occur. Where the consideration cannot be ascertained at the time of the transaction, it must be estimated. For example, the shares in a company may be sold for a fixed amount plus a contingent amount (typically based on the company reaching certain financial targets in the periods after the sale). At the time of the sale, the purchaser of the shares will be required to pay stamp duty at 0.5% on the fixed consideration plus the best estimate of the amount of the contingent consideration.

Any changes to the consideration caused by future events must be notified to HMRC, and duty will be paid or repaid as appropriate.

> ***Example 28.4***
> Again, using Example 28.1, assume that Steven pays his brother £75,000 for the shares plus a contingent amount of an additional £75,000 payable in five years' time if the turnover of the company exceeds £10 million per annum for a continuous period of at least two years.
>
> As this is still above the £1,000 consideration threshold, Steven will pay stamp duty of £375 (£75,000 × 0.5%) on the share acquisition. However, Steven would also be required to pay stamp duty on the best estimate of the amount of the contingent consideration – an additional stamp duty liability of £375 on the basis of the £75,000 contingent payment.
>
> The total stamp duty of £750 would be due within 30 days. Should the contingent payment not be fulfilled, then any changes to the consideration as a result of future events should be notified to HMRC and the additional duty would be repaid as appropriate.

Questions

Review Questions

Questions on the material covered in Chapter 28 are included at the end of **Chapter 30**.

29

Stamp Duty Reserve Tax

Learning Objectives

After studying this chapter you will understand:

- The liability to, and payment of, stamp duty reserve tax.

29.1 General Principles

Stamp duty reserve tax (SDRT) is a transaction tax, charged on "agreements to transfer chargeable securities", unlike stamp duty which is charged upon documents. This would generally be in situations where the stock/shares or marketable securities are acquired through the stock market or a stockbroker.

SDRT thus applies to paperless share transactions (including electronic transactions) instead of stamp duty and applies to agreements to transfer chargeable securities for consideration in money or money's worth.

29.2 Items Liable to SDRT

SDRT is payable on paperless transactions when a person buys:

1. shares in a UK company;
2. shares in a foreign company with a share register in the UK;
3. an option to buy shares.

For transactions on or after 30 March 2014, SDRT is not payable on shares acquired via UK unit trust schemes and UK open-ended investment companies. Since 28 April 2014, SDRT and stamp duty is not payable on shares in companies admitted to trading on recognised growth markets (e.g. AIM), provided the shares are not also listed on a recognised stock exchange.

29.3 Rate Charged

SDRT is charged at 0.5% of the amount or value of the consideration for the sale. The tax charge arises on the date the agreement is made or becomes unconditional.

Once again, the sale of government securities and most company loan stock is exempt as are paperless transactions covered by one of the exemptions set out in **Chapter 28, Section 28.3**.

> ***Example 29.1***
> Steven trades on the stock exchange and holds an account online. All transactions are paperless and all could have been made through CREST (see **Section 29.4**). On 31 August 2019 he buys shares in three companies as follows:
>
> Grow Limited – a company quoted (only) on the Alternative Investment Market – shares cost £100,000
> Indelt Limited – a Germany company with a UK share register – shares cost £200,000
> Partek Limited – a UK unquoted company – shares cost £5,000
>
> The SDRT consideration for each transaction is:
>
> Grow Limited – as these shares are quoted on AIM, no SDRT is payable as it was abolished from 28 April 2015.
> Indelt Limited – although this is a foreign company, SDRT is payable as the company has a UK share register. SDRT of £1,000 arises (£200,000 × 0.5%).
> Partek Limited – SDRT of £25 arises (£5,000 × 0.5%).

29.4 Payment of SDRT

Many paperless share transactions that SDRT arises on are carried out electronically through CREST, the electronic settlement and registration system administered by Euroclear. CREST automatically deducts the SDRT and sends it to HMRC. CREST is then paid by the stockbroker who bills the individual for the SDRT and their own fees.

If the transaction occurs "off-market" (e.g. shares transferred outside of CREST and held by a nominee like a bank), a stockbroker deals with this type of transaction and pays the SDRT direct to HMRC.

However, if the individual deals with it themselves, they must notify HMRC about the transaction and make the SDRT payment.

29.5 Deadline for Notifying and Paying HMRC

If someone makes a trade "off-market", i.e. not through CREST, HMRC must be notified in writing. If the payment could have been made through CREST but was not, the deadline for both the payment and the notice is 14 days from the date of the trade.

If the payment could not have been made through CREST, the deadline is the 7th day of the month after the calendar month in which the agreement took place.
For example, if shares or units are bought on 18 April, the purchaser must notify HMRC and pay the SDRT on or before 7 May.

If payment is not made by the due date, interest will arise from the date the SDRT was due until the date when it is paid. Penalties may also apply, as detailed in **Chapter 28**.

> ***Example 29.2***
> From Example 29.1, when is the SDRT liability payable by Steven due for payment?
>
> As the shares in Indelt Limited and Partek Limited could have been bought through CREST, to avoid a late filing penalty and interest the due date for payment and written notice is 14 days from the date of the trade, i.e. by 14 September 2019.

Questions

Review Questions

Questions on the material covered in Chapter 29 are included at the end of **Chapter 30**.

30

Stamp Duty Land Tax

Learning Objectives

After studying this chapter you will understand:

- The operation of stamp duty land tax (SDLT), including:
  - when SDLT is chargeable;
  - the rates of SDLT applicable to different property types and acquisitions (freehold or leasehold);
  - the treatment of lease premiums;
  - stamp duty/SDLT group relief; and
  - the interaction of SDLT with VAT on property.

30.1 General Principles and Background

Stamp duty land tax (SDLT) is a modern transaction tax on land transactions involving any estate, interest, right or power in or over land in the UK (with the exception of land and property in Scotland and Wales, which have their own devolved regimes). It should be noted that documents evidencing land transactions and chargeable to SDLT are not physically stamped.

30.2 What and Who is Chargeable

SDLT applies to land transactions and is payable by the purchaser. An acquisition can take the form of the creation, surrender, release or variation of a "chargeable interest".

A "chargeable interest" means:

1. an estate, interest, right or power in or over land or property in England or Northern Ireland; or
2. the benefit of an obligation, restriction or condition affecting the value of any such estate, interest, right or power, other than an "exempt interest".

The "chargeable consideration", for the purpose of SDLT, comprises anything given for the transaction that is money or money's worth, of which cash is by far the most common form. However, chargeable consideration can also be non-monetary, such as:

1. the release or assumption of a debt;
2. works or services; and
3. the transfer of other property.

As a general rule, any non-monetary consideration should be valued at its market value, unless otherwise provided.

30.3 Exemptions

Certain interests in land are exempt interests and as a result are not chargeable to SDLT. The following land transactions are exempt:

1. Transactions where there is no chargeable consideration, except where there is a gift to a connected company (although SDLT group relief may be available in company-to-company situations).
2. Certain transactions following a person's death (variations of a will or intestacy within two years of death, for no consideration).
3. Certain transactions on the ending of a marriage or a civil partnership (divorce, annulment or judicial separation) or on the entering into a marriage or civil partnership.
4. Transfers to charities if the land is to be used for charitable purposes.
5. The grant of a lease by a registered social landlord in certain specific situations.
6. Changes in trustees.

Example 30.1
Steven and his wife divorce on 29 December 2019. In the divorce agreement they agree that she will live in the family home for the foreseeable future and it will be under her sole ownership. The family home is valued at £750,000. Steven will live in their London flat, which will be under his ownership. The flat is worth £850,000.

What is the SDLT consideration?

Solution
No SDLT is payable on either transaction, despite each being an acquisition of land and property by Steven and his wife. This is because a transaction is exempt from SDLT for couples divorcing, separating or dissolving a civil partnership where they agree either to split the property and land between them or the property is split under the terms of a court order.

30.4 When SDLT is Chargeable

The fact that a purchaser enters into a contract for a land transaction does not automatically crystallise a liability to SDLT.

Generally, a contract governing a land transaction that is to be completed by a conveyance will be chargeable on completion. However, where such a contract is "substantially performed" before it is formally completed, the contract is treated as if it were itself the transaction provided for in the contract. In this case, the date of substantial performance is the effective date.

Broadly, substantial performance is the point at which:

1. any payment of rent is made;
2. payment of most of the consideration other than rent is made; or
3. the purchaser is entitled to possession of the subject matter of the transaction.

30.5 The Charge to SDLT

The charge to SDLT depends on whether the land in question is entirely residential or if it is wholly or partly non-residential; and by the amount of the chargeable consideration, the amount being rounded down to the nearest pound.

A mixed use property is one that incorporates both residential and non-residential elements. Non-residential property includes:

- commercial property such as shops or offices;
- agricultural land;
- forests;
- any other land or property which is not used as a dwelling;
- six or more residential properties bought in a single transaction.

30.5.1 Residential Rates

The rates of SDLT for residential land transactions are:

Chargeable consideration	SDLT rate
Up to £125,000	Zero
The next £125,000 (the portion from £125,001 to £250,000)	2%
The next £675,000 (the portion from £250,001 to £925,000)	5%
The next £575,000 (the portion from £925,001 to £1.5 million)	10%
The remaining amount (the portion above £1.5 million)	12%

A flat 15% rate of SDLT applies if the purchase is of a high-value residential property, costing £500,000 or more, by a company (or by a partnership including a company) or collective investment scheme enveloping the property. There are a number of reliefs available from this 15% rate, aimed at genuine business acquisitions, but these are beyond the scope of this textbook.

From 22 November 2017, a relief for first-time buyers is available if certain conditions are met (see **Section 30.5.2**).

Example 30.2
Paula and her partner exchange contracts for the purchase of a house for £375,000 on 5 December 2019, with completion expected in March 2020.

The SDLT on the property is calculated as:

Charge	Amount
0% on the first £125,000 (a)	£0
2% on the next £125,000 (b)	£2,500
5% on the final £125,000 (c)	£6,250
Total SDLT (a + b + c)	£8,750

> ***Example 30.3***
> Using Example 30.1, if instead Steven's wife agreed to buy him out of his share of the family home at a cost of £450,000 and this was not under the terms of a court order, a SDLT liability would arise as follows:
>
> The SDLT on the property is calculated as:

Charge	Amount £
0% on the first £125,000	0
2% on the next £125,000	2,500
5% on the final £200,000	10,000
Total SDLT	12,500

30.5.2 First-time Buyers Relief

First-time buyers purchasing a residential property for £500,000 or less can avail of first-time buyers relief, provided that they intend to occupy the property as their only or main residence and the transaction takes place on or after 22 November 2017.

Where the purchase price is £300,000 or less, no SDLT will be due. Where the purchase price is over £300,000 but does not exceed £500,000, SDLT is due at 5% on the 'slice' above £300,000.

30.5.3 Higher Rates for Purchases of Additional Residential Property

The rates for each 'slice' in **Section 30.5.1** are each subject to an additional 3% surcharge where the property is classed as an additional residential property acquisition. Broadly, the acquisition will be treated as an additional residential property acquisition where someone acquires a residential property (or a part of one) for £40,000 or more and the following apply:

- it is not the only residential property worth £40,000 or more owned (or part-owned) anywhere in the world;
- the person has not sold or given away their previous main home; and
- no one else has a lease on the additional property, which has more than 21 years left to run.

The rates of SDLT for additional residential property transactions are therefore:

Chargeable consideration	SDLT rate
Up to £125,000	3%
The next £125,000 (the portion from £125,001 to £250,000)	5%
The next £675,000 (the portion from £250,001 to £925,000)	8%
The next £575,000 (the portion from £925,001 to £1.5 million)	13%
The remaining amount (the portion above £1.5 million)	15%

Note that the 15% rate of SDLT that applies to purchases of high-value residential property costing £500,000 or more by a company (or by a partnership including a company) or collective investment scheme enveloping the property is not subject to the higher rates, i.e. the rate for such properties remains a flat rate of 15% and not 18%.

There are different rules for determining whether a property acquisition is an additional residential property acquisition depending on whether the purchaser is an individual or a company. There are also special rules for joint purchasers, married couples and civil partners. These rules are beyond the scope of this textbook.

30.5.4 Non-Residential/Mixed Use Rates

The rates of SDLT for non-residential and mixed use land transactions are:

Chargeable consideration	SDLT rate
Up to £150,000	Zero
The next £100,000 (the portion from £150,001 to £250,000)	2%
The remaining amount (the portion above £250,000)	5%

Example 30.4

A buyer exchanges contracts for the purchase of a commercial property for £375,000 on 5 April 2019, with completion expected in June 2019.

The SDLT on the property is calculated as follows:

Charge	Amount £
0% on the first £150,0000	0
2% on the next £100,000	2,000
5% on the final £125,000	6,250
Total SDLT	8,250

30.5.5 SDLT Rules for Bulk Purchases

Relief from SDLT for purchasers of residential property acquiring interests in more than one dwelling may be available. Where the relief is claimed, the rate of SDLT is determined not by the aggregate consideration but instead by the mean consideration (i.e. by the aggregate consideration divided by the number of dwellings), subject to a minimum rate of 1% overall.

The relief may be claimed in respect of a transaction that is a "relevant transaction", defined as either:

1. a transaction, the main subject matter of which includes interests in more than one dwelling; or
2. a transaction which is one of a number of linked transactions, the main subject matter of which includes interests in at least one dwelling and where one or more transactions linked to it includes interests in at least one other dwelling.

Example 30.5

Paula purchases the freehold of a new block of five flats for £1 million.

The transaction is a relevant transaction for the purposes of the new relief as it involves the acquisition of more than one dwelling – i.e. the five flats. Therefore, the freehold is treated as if it were interests in the individual dwellings and the chargeable consideration is divided by the number of dwellings to give a chargeable consideration of £200,000 per flat.

The amount of SDLT payable on £200,000 is £1,500 (0% of £125,000 + 2% of £75,000). £1,500 × 5 = £7,500. But this is less than 1% of £1 million (£10,000), so the amount of SDLT payable is £10,000.

30.5.6 Interaction with VAT on Property

If output VAT is required to be charged on a commercial property, the purchaser of that commercial property will pay SDLT on the total consideration, including VAT, i.e. SDLT arises on the VAT-inclusive price (see **Chapter 32** for more detail.)

30.6 Lease Premiums

When someone buys a leasehold property, the SDLT they have to pay depends on whether it is an existing lease or a new one. If it is an existing lease (an "assigned lease"), they only have to pay SDLT on the purchase price as if they'd bought a freehold property. The same rates, thresholds and conditions for deciding whether to complete an SDLT return also apply.

How SDLT is calculated on the grant of a new lease depends on the "premium" (the lump sum paid to buy a new lease), the rent payable under the lease, and whether it is a residential or non-residential lease.

30.6.1 Residential Property

SDLT on the premium paid for a lease of residential property is charged using the rates table in **Section 30.5.1**. The amount of any rental payments is not taken into account in determining the amount of tax payable on the premium. However, if the net present value (NPV) of the rent is more than the residential property SDLT threshold of £125,000, the buyer must pay SDLT on the rent as well as on the premium. In this case, the tax is calculated at a flat rate of 1% on the amount of the net present value that exceeds the SDLT threshold.

For example, if the NPV of the rent under a lease is £180,000 then the amount of the NPV that is over the £125,000 threshold is £55,000. SDLT has to be paid on this £55,000 at the rate of 1%. This is added to the amount of SDLT that is due on the premium.

Example 30.6

Parker Limited leases a residential property building for 15 years signing the lease on 15 September 2019. A premium of £190,000 is payable with the annual rent £20,000 per annum. The NPV of the rent is £250,000.

Calculate the SDLT arising and state the due date for payment.

Solution

SDLT arises on both the premium element of the lease and the rental element. The SDLT on the property is calculated as follows:

Charge	**Amount £**
Premium element:	
0% on the first £125,000	0
2% on the next £65,000	1,300
Rental element:	
£125,000 (£250,000 – £125,000) @ 1%	1,250
Total SDLT	2,550

This falls due for filing and payment 14 days later on 29 September 2019.

30.6.2 Non-residential Property

For non-residential properties, the amount of SDLT due when someone buys a new non-residential lease depends on the amounts of the premium and rent they pay under the lease.

The buyer pays SDLT on the premium at the same rate as they would pay on the purchase price of a freehold non-residential property using the rates table in **Section 30.5.3**, which means they will only have to pay SDLT if the premium is more than the £150,000 non-residential threshold.

Also, in respect of non-residential property, the lease rental payable during the term of a lease will also be charged to SDLT to the extent that the NPV of the rental exceeds the thresholds using the rates table in **Section 30.5.3**. The rate of charge is 1% of the excess above the threshold. A 2% rate for leasehold rent transactions applies where the NPV is above £5 million. Therefore rent transactions with a NPV between £150,001 and £5 million will pay 1% on that amount, with any amounts above £5 million charged at 2%.

Example 30.7

Assume the same facts as in Example 30.6, except that Parker Limited leases a commercial building. Calculate the SDLT arising.

Solution

SDLT arises on both the premium element of the lease and the rental element as follows:

Premium element:	
0% on the first £150,000	0
2% on the next £40,000	800
Rental element:	
£100,000 (£250,000–£150,000) @ 1%	£1,000
Total SDLT	£1,800

This falls due for filing and payment 14 days later on 29 September 2019.

30.7 Notification Threshold

The purchaser only needs to file a SDLT return when:

- buying a freehold property for £40,000 or more;
- buying a new or assigned lease of seven years or more, where the premium is £40,000 or more and the annual rent is £1,000 or more;
- buying a new or assigned lease of less than seven years, where the amount paid is more than the residential/non-residential SDLT thresholds.

30.8 Stamp Duty/SDLT Group Relief

There is potential relief from SDLT where land and buildings are transferred within a group of companies (or bodies corporate), provided certain conditions are met. This relief allows groups to move property for commercial reasons without having to consider the SDLT implications. The two group companies do not necessarily have to be resident in the UK, though there may be corporation tax consequences for the transaction. Group relief for stamp duty is also available where the inter-group transfer is of stocks, shares or marketable securities.

If the purchaser and vendor of a chargeable interest are companies and, at the effective date of the transaction, they are both members of the same group, relief from stamp duty/SDLT (which would otherwise be payable on the market value of the shares, land or property being transferred) may be claimed by the purchaser. This is so that stamp duty/SDLT is not paid on transfers within groups. The purchasing company **may** choose to pay the tax **by not claiming** the relief. However, stamp duty/SDLT group relief is not available if the transaction is not effected for honest commercial reasons or the transaction forms part of arrangements of which the main purpose, or one of the main purposes, is the avoidance of tax. 'Tax' here means SDLT, stamp duty, income tax, corporation tax and CGT.

For the purposes of this relief, companies are members of the same group if one is the 75% subsidiary of the other or both are 75% subsidiaries of a third company. One company, B, is the 75% subsidiary of another company, A, if company A satisfies the following conditions:

1. it is the beneficial owner (either directly or through another company) of not less than 75% of the ordinary share capital of company B;
2. it is beneficially entitled to not less than 75% of the profits available for distribution to equity holders of company B; and
3. it would be beneficially entitled to not less than 75% of any assets of company B available for distribution to its equity holders on a winding up.

30.8.1 Restrictions on Availability of Stamp Duty/SDLT Group Relief

Where the purchasing company (purchaser) and selling company (vendor) are in the same group (as defined above), **no** group relief will be available to the purchaser in three situations, which are as follows:

1. Where arrangements are in existence which would mean that a person/persons, could obtain control of the purchaser **but** not the vendor. This restriction operates where the arrangements are in existence at the effective date of the land transaction. The arrangements must be such that a person/persons, could obtain control of the purchaser on/after the effective date of the transaction. It does not matter whether the arrangements are actually used to transfer control.
2. Where a non-group member, or person, is to provide/receive, directly/indirectly, all or part of the consideration for the transaction, and this is done in connection with, or in pursuance of, an arrangement.
3. Where, in connection with, or in pursuance of, an arrangement or arrangements, the purchaser ceases (or could cease) to be in the same group as the vendor, i.e. the 75% condition is no longer met.

30.8.2 Withdrawal of SDLT Group Relief

A new land transaction return should be submitted if the purchaser ceases to be a member of the same group as the vendor either:

1. before the end of a period of three years beginning with the effective date of the relevant land transaction; or
2. in pursuance of, or in connection with, arrangements made before the end of a period of three years beginning with the effective date of the relevant land transaction.

The term "arrangements" includes any scheme, agreement or understanding, whether or not legally enforceable, e.g. a memorandum of understanding.

This effectively results in withdrawal of the previous SDLT group relief.

For the withdrawal of the relief to be considered at the time the purchaser ceases to be a member of the same group and SDLT group relief was previously claimed, the purchaser must hold either:

1. the chargeable interest that was acquired under the relevant transaction; **or**
2. a chargeable interest derived from the chargeable interest acquired under the relevant transaction; **and**
3. the chargeable interest has not subsequently been acquired at market value by means of a chargeable transaction where group relief was available **but** not claimed.

Where group relief from SDLT has been claimed on a land transaction, any subsequent withdrawal of the relief must be reported by the purchaser on a new land transaction return.

While there is no clawback of stamp duty group relief on shares, this relief is denied in the first place if at the time of the transfer, arrangements are in existence which mean that any other person can gain control of the transferee company, i.e. there are arrangements for the transferee company to leave the group (see **Section 30.8.1**).

Questions

Review Questions (Chapters 28–30)

(See Suggested Solutions to Review Questions at the end of this textbook.)

Question 30.1

A client, Mr Symon Cawell, has been involved in a number of transactions and approaches you in February 2020 for advice. Details of the transactions are as follows:

Transaction 1 (11 October 2019) Symon took on a newly executed lease on commercial property in a prime area with a premium payable of £575,000, and a net present value of the rent payable of £185,000.

Transaction 2 (31 October 2019) Symon's oldest son married in December having purchased a property on 31 October costing £225,000, in which he and his wife are living. It is their first home and they do not own any other residential properties.

Transaction 3 (12 December 2019) Symon purchased government securities valued at £325,000.

Transaction 4 (1 January 2020) Symon recently lent £1,750,000 interest-free to a friend's internet advertising company. The company is now proceeding with a reorganisation and, in order to settle the debt, Symon agreed to receive, as consideration for the debt, 1,750,000 10p shares issued by the company in full satisfaction of the original loan.

Transaction 5 (12 January 2020) Symon gifted shares in his trading company worth £565,000 to his only daughter who works alongside him and has helped him grow the business.

Transaction 6 (28 February 2020) Symon's youngest daughter is due to start university later this year. Symon has bought a second residential property near the university for her to live in at a cost of £182,000. Symon's own residence is worth £250,000.

Requirement

In letter format to Mr Cawell, calculate the amount of stamp duty/SDLT arising on each transaction (if any). Provide explanations for your analysis.

Question 30.2

Armour Ltd owns 77.5% of Brent Ltd, and 82% of Destiny Ltd. Brent Ltd owns 51% of Gaston Ltd.

On 1 September 2019, Armour Ltd sold the freehold of two warehouses, one for £750,000 to Destiny Ltd, and one for £120,000 to Gaston Ltd.

On 1 January 2020, Armour Ltd sold 8% of its shares in Destiny Ltd to an unconnected third party. As of that date, both Destiny Ltd and Gaston Ltd continued to own the freeholds of the warehouses and to occupy them.

Requirement
Explain the SDLT implications of these transactions, together with supporting calculations where necessary.

Question 30.3

Owen owns a commercial property that has an open market value of £350,000. There is an outstanding mortgage on the property of £50,000.

Requirement
Calculate the SDLT due if he sells it to his son for £200,000 (both with and without the outstanding mortgage) or sells it to his son for full market value and uses the proceeds to pay off the mortgage.

Question 30.4

Please refer to Chapter 10, Question 10.2.

Requirement
What are the SDLT land tax implications of transferring the freehold property from Solar to Neptune?

Question 30.5

Apple Ltd owns 77.5% of Banana Ltd, and 85% of Date Ltd. Banana Ltd owns 51% of Grape Ltd. On 1 July 2019, Apple Ltd sold the freehold of two warehouses, one for £750,000 to Date Ltd, and one for £120,000 to Grape Ltd. Both Date Ltd and Grape Ltd continue to own the freeholds and remain in occupation of the warehouses.

Requirement
Explain the SDLT implications of these transactions and calculate any SDLT payable.

31

Administration of SDLT

Learning Objectives

After studying this chapter you will understand:

- The payment of SDLT, including penalties and interest.
- The filing of SDLT returns.

31.1 Duty to Deliver Land Transaction Return Form

The relevant legislation requires that, for every notifiable transaction completed or effectively completed, a land transaction return form (LTR) SDLT1 must be delivered to HMRC within 14 days of the effective date of the transaction. If SDLT is due on a transaction, the payment deadline is the same as for the return, i.e. within 14 days of the effective date.

Interest is chargeable on unpaid tax from the relevant date until the date of payment at the current rate of 3.25% per annum for each day or part day the payment is late. As discussed in **Chapter 1** and **Chapter 28**, the civil penalty regime applies to stamp duty, SDLT and SDRT.

A return is also required for all notifiable transactions even where there is no SDLT to pay or where a relief is being claimed, e.g. group relief (see **Chapter 30, Section 30.8**).

31.2 Who is Chargeable?

The purchaser is responsible for submission of the SDLT return and payment of the SDLT due.

If there are joint purchasers, only a single SDLT return is required and this can be completed by any one of them. However, **each** purchaser must sign the declaration. If the purchaser is a partnership, the declaration must be signed by all of the partners or by a representative of the partnership nominated to HMRC.

Where there are joint purchasers, they are jointly liable for payment of the tax although that obligation can be discharged by any one of them.

31.3 Penalties

31.3.1 Flat-rate Penalties

A purchaser who fails to deliver the SDLT return by the filing date is liable to:

1. a flat-rate penalty of £100 if the LTR is delivered within three months after the filing date, or
2. £200 in any other case.

31.3.2 Tax-geared Penalties

A purchaser who is required to deliver a LTR in respect of a chargeable transaction and fails to do so within 12 months of the filing date is liable to a tax-geared penalty.

The penalty is an amount not exceeding the amount of tax chargeable in respect of the transaction (and this is in addition to the above flat-rate penalty).

Often the most appropriate way of encouraging the submission of a late LTR is for HMRC to make a determination. HMRC may also choose this option where it considers that a purchaser, from other information that it holds, should have made a LTR and the filing date has passed. In this situation, if the purchaser does not comply with the notice of determination within the specified period, HMRC may ask the Tax Tribunal to impose a daily penalty.

The SDLT regime gives purchasers clearly defined obligations and, accordingly, HMRC have clearly defined powers to ensure compliance with these obligations. SDLT is a 'process now–check later' regime, similar to self-assessment. The 'check later' aspect is supported by enquiry and information powers. The compliance checks regime, and the various powers available to HMRC as a result, apply equally to the various stamp taxes (see **Chapter 1, Section 1.11.7**).

Questions

Review Questions

(See Suggested Solution to Review Questions at the end of this textbook.)

Question 31.1

Adam purchased his first house on 31 October 2019 for £150,000, funded by a bank mortgage of £120,000 and a deposit of £30,000. Adam does not intend to live in the property and plans to rent it out.

Requirement

(a) What SDLT was due and why?
(b) What is the threshold of chargeable consideration above which a SDLT return is required for a residential property transaction?
(c) On the basis that Adam's purchase completed on 31 October 2019, on what date is the associated SDLT return and payment due for filing?

Question 31.2

Please refer to Chapter 18, Question 18.10.

Requirement

Calculate the SDLT payable on the sale of the Dungannon building. State who is responsible for this liability, the due date for payment of any liability that may arise and the filing date of the relevant return.

Question 31.3

Shaun is due to undertake the following transactions on 30 April 2019:

- Purchase of shares in Apple plc, a British company, for £950.
- Purchase of shares in Peaches plc, a British company, for £6,725.
- Purchase of shares in Blackberry SA, an Italian company, for £1,600.

Shaun is old-fashioned. He likes to complete as much as possible on paper, so he will not use the electronic share trading systems and will therefore use hard copy share transfer forms for his purchases.

Requirement
Calculate the stamp duty due on the above transactions, providing explanations for your calculations. State the due date for payment of any liability that may arise and the filing date of the relevant stamp duty return.

Question 31.4

Outline the stamp duty payable (if any) on the following:

(a) A transfer of UK unlisted shares worth £90,000 on the divorce of husband to wife.
(b) A sale of shares in a UK unlisted company for £524,000 to a registered UK charity.
(c) A sale of shares in a UK unlisted company for £150,000 between unconnected individuals.
(d) A sale of UK shares worth £895 between unconnected parties.
(e) A sale of shares in a UK unlisted company for £60,000 in cash and an agreement to waive £20,000 debt owed by the seller to the purchaser.

32

VAT on Property

Learning Objectives

After studying this chapter you will understand:

- The VAT treatment of the supply of land and buildings in the UK.
- The 'option to tax' election, which converts an exempt supply of commercial land and buildings to the standard rate of VAT.
- The interaction of VAT with of stamp duty land tax.

32.1 Introduction

The final chapter of this section moves away from stamp taxes to introduce the basic principles associated with VAT on property, a particularly complex area of tax legislation. The relevant legislation that establishes the VAT treatment of property is the Value Added Tax Act 1994 (VATA 1994), while several HM Revenue & Custom's *VAT Notices* set out the treatment of VAT on property in more detail.

32.2 The Basic Rule

VAT on property is a complex and specialised area of tax law and expert advice should always be sought before a transaction is completed. The basic rule is that transactions in land may be taxable supplies (i.e. subject to VAT at zero-rate (0%), reduced rate (5%) or standard rate (20%)) or exempt supplies (no VAT is chargeable). Reduced rate supplies of property are beyond the scope of this text and are not addressed further.

Note that the word 'supplies' includes an outright sale or the grant of a lease in relation to the property. In respect of the grant of a lease, the lease must be a long lease, which is defined as one being for a period of more than 21 years.

The VAT classification of a property supply is important because, for the supplier, it not only dictates if output VAT is chargeable on the supply and at what rate (0%, 5% or 20%) but also if they are able to reclaim input VAT incurred on any purchases or expenses incurred by them that relate to that supply. For any taxable supplies of property, output VAT must be charged at the appropriate rate. Input VAT, however, can be recovered on any purchases used to make that taxable supply but only where VAT is charged at 0%, 5% or 20%. For exempt supplies of property, no output VAT is charged, and there can be no recovery of any input VAT on related purchases or expenses.

32.1.1 Zero-rated Supplies

The following are the main categories of zero-rated supplies of property:

1. the construction or renovation of new dwellings or buildings for **residential** purposes;
2. the construction or renovation of new dwellings or buildings for **charitable** purposes;
3. the sale of, or grant of a lease in, new dwellings or buildings for **residential** purposes;
4. the sale of, or grant of a lease in, new dwellings or buildings for **charitable** purposes;
5. the sale of, or grant of a lease in, non-residential buildings converted to residential use.

Note, this is not an exhaustive list.

32.1.2 Standard-rated Supplies

The following are the main categories of standard-rated supplies of property:

1. the construction or renovation of commercial buildings;
2. the sale of the freehold of a "new" commercial building ("new" is less than three years old);
3. the sale of the freehold of a commercial building that has not yet been completed;
4. the provision of accommodation in a hotel, inn, boarding house or similar establishment of sleeping accommodation.

Note, this is not an exhaustive list.

It is important to appreciate that the lease of a commercial property is **not** within the list of standard-rated items. Consequently, any premium and/or rental income in respect of a commercial property will be an exempt supply, unless an option to tax has been excercised.

32.1.3 Exempt Supplies

Group 1 Schedule 9 VATA 1994 sets out those supplies of land and buildings that are exempt from VAT. The following are the main categories of exempt supplies of property:

1. the sale of the freehold of a commercial building which is not "new" (unless an 'option to tax' has been made, see **Section 32.3**);
2. the grant of a lease in a commercial building, including the grant of a lease in a "new" commercial building (unless an 'option to tax' has been made, see **Section 32.3**);
3. supplies of residential property that are not standard-rated, e.g. the sale of an old dwelling used for residential or charitable purposes.

This list is not exhaustive. It should be noted, therefore, that if a property supply is neither standard-rated nor zero-rated its supply will be exempt.

As previously outlined, where an exempt supply is made (and in the absence of an 'option to tax') any VAT suffered on costs relating to that supply are non-deductible. For example, an individual purchases a commercial unit for £500,000, on which VAT of £100,000 was charged by the vendor, with the intention of leasing the unit out to a tenant. If the landlord does not opt to tax the lease, they will not be able to recover the VAT charged on the purchase (£100,000). Such an individual may therefore become partially exempt as a result of their decision to lease commercial property (which has not been opted to tax) to a tenant. **Partially exempt businesses were covered on the CA Proficiency 1 course and are not reproduced here.**

32.3 Option to Tax – Commercial Buildings

Exempt supplies of land and buildings often cause problems because any input tax related to that exempt supply is irrecoverable, unless the partial exemption *de minimis* test applies. However, owners of property may elect to treat sales and leases of land and **commercial** buildings as taxable instead of exempt. This election is known as the 'option to tax'. There are certain specific circumstances in which the option can be revoked.

The option to tax replaces an exempt supply with a standard-rated supply, which means that any related input tax can be recovered in full by its owner because the supply being made is now a taxable supply. Once the option is made, it will **apply to all future supplies** that are then made in respect of that building by that taxable person. Thus, if a landlord makes the option to tax, this will affect all supplies relating to that building, e.g. rent charged to existing tenants, any premium or rent charged on a subsequent lease, any proceeds from the sale of the freehold, etc.

The owner must become registered for VAT (if not already registered) in order to make the option to tax. Once an option to tax has been made, it has to be notified to HMRC within 30 days of being made.

The option is made on a **building-by-building basis**. This means that if an owner of several different buildings wants to make an option to tax, they can choose to do so for some buildings and not others – it is entirely at their discretion. The option to tax may be revoked on a particular property under certain conditions, called the "cooling-off" provisions. The option to tax can be revoked in the following three situations:

1. **within the first six months** after making it, provided that no supplies have been made that are affected by the option. Any input tax repayable as a result of the change from taxable to exempt supplies will need to be repaid.
2. Where no interest has been held in the property for over six years the option to tax will automatically lapse.
3. The option can be revoked **20 years after it was made**.

There are some supplies that an option to tax does not affect and which remain exempt, even though the option has been exercised on the property in question. These include:

- dwellings – any grant in relation to a building, or part of a building, designed, adapted or intended for use as a dwelling or for a relevant residential purpose. The most common example would be a shop with a flat above it where an option to tax would make any rent from the shop standard-rated but any rent from the flat would remain exempt.
- Buildings for conversion into dwellings, etc. – when a business sells its commercial property, any option to tax can be disapplied if the buyer confirms their intent to convert the building into dwellings or relevant residential purposes.
- Charitable use – a supply in relation to a building intended for use solely for a relevant charitable purpose, other than as an office.

To sum up, the option to tax is therefore a useful planning tool – it can change the status of a supply in such a way that a trader is protected from suffering irrecoverable input tax.

32.4 Interaction with Stamp Duty Land Tax

If output VAT is required to be charged on a commercial property, the purchaser of that commercial property will pay stamp duty land tax (SDLT) on the total consideration, **including** VAT, i.e. SDLT arises on the VAT-inclusive price.

Example 32.1

On 31 July 2019, Devenish Limited bought a commercial property that was built in June 2017. The company agreed to pay £625,000 for the property. As the property is less than three years old it is "new" and 20% standard rate VAT is chargeable by the vendor. The total consideration is therefore £750,000 (£625,000 + (20% × £625,000)). The SDLT liability of Devenish Limited arises on the VAT-inclusive price and is as follows:

	£
0–£150,000 @ 0%	0
Next £100,000 @ 2%	2,000
Remaining £500,000 @ 5%	25,000
Total SDLT	27,000

Devenish Limited will pay an extra £6,250 (£125,000 output VAT × 5%) in SDLT as a result of the output VAT charged because the property is new.

Questions

Review Questions

(See Suggested Solutions to Review Questions at the end of this textbook.)

Question 32.1

Assume today's date is 31 December 2019. Classify the following property supplies as standard-rated, zero-rated or exempt. Provide explanations for your answer.

(a) The sale of the freehold of an office block constructed in November 2017.
(b) The grant of a 99-year lease in a brand new factory.
(c) The sale of the freehold of a factory first constructed in January 2015.

Question 32.2

Assume today's date is 31 December 2019. Classify the following property supplies as standard-rated, zero-rated or exempt. Provide explanations for your answer.

(a) A factory owner grants a 30-year lease over half his factory to another business that will be using the space for its partially exempt business. The factory was first constructed in June 2017.
(b) A property development company sells the freehold of a 25-year-old house it bought in a part-exchange deal with a customer.
(c) A property investment company sells the freehold of an office block first constructed in August 2017.
(d) A property investment company sells the freehold of an office block first constructed in August 2016 and which has been opted to tax.

Question 32.3

EyeSpy Ltd runs a chain of opticians in different towns across Northern Ireland. The company is partially exempt for VAT and in the year ending 31 March 2020 its partial exemption recovery percentage was 70%.

In January 2019, the company expanded to a new location in Enniskillen and bought an office building for £450,000 excluding VAT, if any. The office building was built in June 2017.

Requirement

Explain if EyeSpy Ltd incurred VAT on the building and, if so, calculate how much it is able to recover.

Question 32.4

Consider each of these supplies and decide whether or not the option to tax would be effective on the supply. Provide explanations for your answer.

(a) Sale of commercial land.
(b) Sale of a 75-year-old terraced house.
(c) Lease of a 15-year-old factory.
(d) Freehold sale of a two-year-old office block.
(e) 99-year lease of a one-year-old shop.

Question 32.5

Decide whether each of the different supplies below is standard-rated, zero-rated or exempt. If a supply is exempt, outline whether an option to tax can be made in respect of that supply. Provide explanations for your answer.

(a) Freehold sale of two-year-old factory.
(b) Grant of a 30-year lease in a brand new office block.
(c) A farmer rents out a plot of land to another farmer.
(d) A landlord leases out four floors of a building to an insurance company tenant (making exempt supplies).
(e) A landlord leases out a flat in a brand new luxury residential development for five years to an individual using it for their business.

Question 32.6

Paul James owns an office block in Belfast, which is currently let out to two tenants, an insurance company (making exempt supplies) and a firm of accountants (making taxable supplies). The building needs some renovation, costing £800,000 plus VAT.

Requirement

(a) Explain the VAT treatment and implications of renovating the property for Paul.
(b) What would be the VAT implications, for both Paul and his tenants, if Paul were to opt to tax the property?

Question 32.7

Spidey Enterprises Ltd sold a commercial property built in July 2015 to Iron Man Developments Ltd for £1,250,000. The company had opted to tax the property in May 2018.

Requirement
Explain if Iron Man Developments Ltd incurred VAT on the building. Calculate how much stamp duty land tax the company paid on the acquisition of the building.

Appendices

Appendix 1

Taxation Reference Material for Tax Year 2019/20 (Finance Act 2019)

Table of Contents

Income Tax Rates*

	Rate%
Starting rate for non-dividend savings income up to £5,000	0
First £37,500	20 (Basic rate)
£37,501–£150,000	40 (Higher rate)
Over £150,000	45 (Additional rate)
Basic rate for dividends	7.5
Higher rate for dividends	32.5
Additional rate for dividends	38.1

Income Tax Allowances*

	£
Personal allowance (1)	12,500
Income limit for personal allowance (1)	100,000
Marriage allowance (2)	1,250
Blind person's allowance	2,450
Dividend allowance (3)	2,000
Personal savings allowance (4):	
Basic rate taxpayers	1,000
Higher rate taxpayers	500
Property allowance (5)	1,000
Trading allowance (5)	1,000

* The rates and allowances in Scotland and Wales may differ.

(1) All individuals are entitled to the same personal allowance, regardless of the individuals' date of birth. This allowance is subject to the £100,000 income limit, which applies regardless of the individual's date of birth. The individual's personal allowance is reduced where their income is above this limit. The allowance is reduced by £1 for every £2 above the limit.

(2) A spouse or civil partner who is not liable to income tax; or not liable at the higher or additional rate, can claim to transfer this amount of their personal allowance to their spouse or civil partner. The recipient must not be liable to income tax at the higher or additional rate. The relief for this allowance is given at 20%.

(3) The dividend allowance means that individuals do not have to pay tax on the first £2,000 (2018/19: £2,000) of dividend income they receive.

(4) The personal savings allowance means that basic rate taxpayers do not have to pay tax on the first £1,000 of savings income they receive and higher rate taxpayers will not have tax to pay on their first £500 of savings income.

(5) The first £1,000 of trading income is not subject to income tax. The trading allowance also applies to certain miscellaneous income from providing assets or services. A £1,000 allowance is also available for property income.

Income Tax – Car Benefits Charges

Car Benefit Percentage

The relevant base level of CO_2 emissions is 95 grams per kilometre (g/km).

The percentage rates applying to petrol cars with CO_2 emissions up to 95g/km:

50g/km or less	16%
51–75g/km	19%
76–94g/km	22%
95g/km	23%

For each 5g/km that a car is above 95g/km, an additional 1% is added to the percentage rate.

For diesel cars, a 4% diesel supplement is added. Diesel cars that meet the Real Driving Emissions test are exempt from the diesel supplement.

The maximum percentage charge is 37%.

Fuel Benefit Charge

The same percentage figure used to calculate the car benefit charge, as above, is used to calculate the fuel benefit charge. The relevant percentage figure is multiplied by £24,100 for 2019/20 (£23,400 in 2018/19).

Income Tax – Van Benefits Charges

Van benefit	£3,430
Fuel benefit	£655

The charges will not apply if a "restricted private use condition" is met throughout the year.
The van benefit charge for zero-emission vans is 60% of the main rate in 2019/20 (2018/19: 40%).

Capital Allowances

	2018/19 %	2019/20 %
Main pool (Note 1)	18	18
Motor cars – CO_2 emissions:		
< 50g/km	100	100
51–110g/km (Note 1)	18	18
> 110g/km (Note 1)	8	6
New and unused zero-emission goods vehicles	100	100
Special rate pool (long-life assets and integral features within a building) (Note 1)	8	6
Research and development	100	100
Energy-saving and environmentally beneficial assets	100	100

Notes:

1. Allowances are given on a writing down allowance reducing balance basis.
2. For the two years from 1 January 2019 there is a 100% annual investment allowance on the first £1,000,0000 tranche per annum of capital expenditure incurred per group of companies or related entities on plant and machinery, including long-life assets and integral features but excluding cars. The limit was £200,000 prior to 1 January 2019.

3. From 29 October 2018 a new structures and buildings allowance of 2% per annum is available for certain expenditure on physical construction works entered into on or after that date.

Authorised Mileage Allowance Rates

Use of own vehicle:

Vehicle	Flat rate per mile with simplified expenses
Cars and goods vehicles – first 10,000 miles	45p
Cars and goods vehicles – after 10,000 miles	25p
Motorcycles (all miles)	24p
Bicycles (all miles)	20p

Use of company car (rates from 1 June 2019):

Engine size	Petrol	LPG
1400cc or less	12p	8p
1401cc to 2000cc	15p	9p
Over 2000cc	22p	14p

Engine size	Diesel
1600cc or less	10p
1601cc to 2000cc	12p
Over 2000cc	14p

National Insurance Contributions

		£
Lower earnings limit:	Weekly Monthly Yearly	118 512 6,136
Upper earnings limit:	Weekly Monthly Yearly	962 4,167 50,000
Primary threshold (employee):	Weekly Monthly Yearly	166 719 8,632
Secondary threshold (employer):	Weekly Monthly Yearly	166 719 8,632
Upper secondary threshold (under 21) (employer):	Weekly Monthly Yearly	962 4,167 50,000
Upper secondary threshold (apprentice under 25) (employer):	Weekly Monthly Yearly	962 4,167 50,000

Employee's Contributions

- Rate:
  - on weekly earnings between £166 and £962 — 12%
  - on weekly earnings above £962 — 2%
- Married woman's reduced rate:
  - on weekly earnings between £166 and £962 — 5.85%
  - on weekly earnings above £962 — 2%

Employer's Contributions

- Rate:
  - on weekly earnings over £166 — 13.8%
- Employer's allowance — £3,000

Other Classes

Classes 1A and 1B	13.8%
Class 2:	
Self-employed per week	£3.00
Small earnings exception	£6,365
Class 3:	
Voluntary per week	£15.00
Class 4:	
Self-employment (rate on profits):	
on annual profits between £8,632 and £50,000	9%
on annual profits above £50,000	2%

Beneficial Loans

Official rate of interest is 2.5%

HMRC Late Payment and Repayment Interest Rates

The current late payment and repayment interest rates applied to income tax, National Insurance, VAT, corporation tax* and inheritance tax are:

Underpayments:	late payment interest rate – 3.25%
Overpayments:	repayment interest rate – 0.5%

*Only applies to companies not paying corporation tax in instalments.

Pension Scheme Limits 2019/20

Annual allowance	£40,000*
Lifetime allowance	£1,055,000
Maximum contribution without earnings	£3,600
Lifetime allowance charge – if excess drawn as cash	55%
Lifetime allowance charge – if excess drawn as income	25%
Annual allowance charge on excess – linked to individual's marginal tax rate	20%/40%/45%

* The annual allowance for those earning above £150,000 is reduced on a tapering basis. For every £2 of income above £150,000, an individual's annual allowance will reduce by £1 but is not reduced below £10,000.

Individual Savings Accounts (ISAs)

Overall annual investment limit: 2019/20 £20,000
(split any way between cash and stocks/shares)

The annual limit on a Lifetime ISA is £4,368.

Tax Credits

	2019/20
	£ per year (unless stated)
Working Tax Credit	
Basic element	1,960
Couple and lone parent element	2,010
30-hour element	810
Disabled worker element	3,165
Severe disability element	1,365
Childcare Element of Working Tax Credit	
Maximum eligible cost for one child	£175 per week
Maximum eligible cost for two or more children	£300 per week
Percentage of eligible costs covered	70%
Child Tax Credit	
Family element	545
Child element	2,780
Disabled child element	3,355
Severely disabled child element	1,360
Income Thresholds and Withdrawal Rates	
First income threshold	6,420
First withdrawal rate	41%
First threshold for those entitled to child tax credit	16,105
Only income rise disregard	2,500
Income fall disregard	2,500

Sufficient Ties Table – Statutory Residence Test

Days spent in the UK	Arrivers	Leavers
Fewer than 16 days	Always non-resident	Always non-resident
16–45 days	Always non-resident	Resident if at least 4 ties apply
46–90 days	Resident if 4 ties apply	Resident if at least 3 ties apply
91–120 days	Resident if at least 3 ties apply	Resident if at least 2 ties apply
121–182 days	Resident if at least 2 ties apply	Resident if at least 1 tie applies
183 days or more	Always resident	Always resident

Simplified Expenses

Motor Expenses

Vehicle	Flat rate per mile
Cars and goods vehicles:	
first 10,000 miles	45p
after 10,000 miles	25p
Motorcycles	24p

Working from Home

Hours of business use per month	Flat rate per month
25 to 50	£10
51 to 100	£18
101 and more	£26

Living at Business Premises

Number of people	Flat rate per month
1	£350
2	£500
3+	£650

Other Reliefs

Rent-a-Room limit		£7,500
Venture Capital Trust	Rate at 30%	Max. £200,000
Enterprise Investment Scheme	Rate at 30%	Max. £1,000,000
Seed Enterprise Investment Scheme	Rate at 50%	Max. £100,000
Remittance basis charge	Resident in UK in 7 or more of previous 9 years. Resident in UK in 12 or more of previous 14 years.	Annual amount of £30,000 Annual amount of £60,000

Cap on Certain Income Tax Reliefs
Unless otherwise restricted, reliefs are capped at the higher of:

1. £50,000; or
2. 25% of the individuals adjusted net income.

High-income Child Benefit Charge
Where income is between £50,000 and £60,000, the charge is 1% of the amount of child benefit received for every £100 of income over £50,000.

Value-Added Tax

Registration/Deregistration Limit	Annual Value of
Taxable Supplies	
Registration limit from 1 April 2019	£85,000
Registration limit from 1 April 2018	£85,000
Registration limit from 1 April 2017	£85,000
Deregistration limit from 1 April 2019	£83,000
Deregistration limit from 1 April 2018	£83,000
Deregistration limit from 1 April 2017	£83,000

Standard rate..20.0%
Reduced rate..5.0%
Zero rate...0.0%

Exempt Supplies

These include the following types of items: insurance, postal services, finance, education, health and welfare and professional subscriptions.

Zero-rated Supplies

These include the following types of items: food, water and sewage services, books, construction and sale of new buildings for a relevant charitable purpose transport, charities, children's clothing and international services.

Reduced Rate

These include the following types of items: supplies of domestic fuel or power, installation of energy-saving materials for residential purposes and children's car seats.

Standard-rated Supplies

Applies to all supplies of goods and services by taxable persons that are not exempt or specifically liable at 0% or 5%. Includes goods such as adult clothing and footwear, office equipment and stationery, drinks and certain foods.

Corporation Tax

	Main rate
1 April 2016–31 March 2017	20%
1 April 2017–31 March 2018	19%
1 April 2018–31 March 2019	19%
1 April 2019–31 March 2020	19%
1 April 2020–31 March 2021	17%

EU SME Definition for R&D Tax Relief

The company must have fewer than 500 staff and either:

1. less than €100 million turnover; or
2. balance sheet total less than €86 million.

Capital Gains Tax (Individuals)

Annual exemption for individuals..£12,000
Annual exemption for trustees..£6,000

Rates

The following rates apply to gains (except for residential land and property gains – see below)

10% for basic rate taxpayers
20% for higher rate/additional rate taxpayers
10% for gains qualifying for entrepreneurs' relief and investors' relief up to the lifetime cap (see below)

Gains on residential property disposals are taxed at 18% for basic rate taxpayers and 28% for higher rate/additional rate taxpayers.

Entrepreneurs' Relief Lifetime Cap

Gains qualifying for entrepreneurs' relief are subject to a lifetime limit of £10 million.

Investors' Relief Lifetime Cap

Gains qualifying for investors' relief are subject to a lifetime limit of £10 million.

Non-resident Capital Gains Tax on Direct Disposals of UK Land and Property

The following rates apply (except for residential land and property gains – see below):

10% for individual basic rate taxpayers
20% for individual higher rate taxpayers
20% for personal representatives of someone who has died who is non-resident

Gains on residential land and property are taxed at 18% for basic rate taxpayers, 28% for higher rate/additional rate taxpayers and 28% for personal representatives of someone who has died.

Non-resident Capital Gains Tax on Indirect Disposals of UK Land and Property

The following rates apply:

10% for individual basic rate taxpayers
20% for individual higher rate taxpayers
20% for personal representatives of someone who has died who is non-resident

Stamp Duty

The rate of stamp duty is 0.5% on amounts in excess of £ 1,000.

Stamp Duty Reserve Tax

The rate of stamp duty reserve tax is 0.5%.

Stamp Duty Land Tax

Residential Rates

The residential rates for stamp duty land tax (SDLT) on purchases and lease premiums are:

Chargeable consideration	Percentage
Up to £125,000	0%
The next £125,000 (the portion from £125,001 to £250,000)	2%
The next £675,000 (the portion from £250,001 to £925,000)	5%
The next £575,000 (the portion from £925,001 to £1.5 million)	10%
The remaining amount (the portion above £1.5 million)	12%

The above rates are each increased by 3% where the property is classed as an additional residential property acquisition.

A higher rate of 15% SDLT applies if the purchase is of a high-value residential property costing £500,000 or more by a company (or by a partnership including a company) or collective investment scheme enveloping the property.

Non-Residential/Mixed Use Rates

The non-residential and mixed use rates for stamp duty land tax (SDLT) on purchases and lease premiums are:

Chargeable consideration	Percentage
Up to £150,000	0%
The next £100,000 (the portion from £150,001 to £250,000)	2%
The remaining amount (the portion above £250,000)	5%

New Leases – SDLT on Lease Rentals

Rate	Net Present Value of Rent	
	Residential	**Non-residential**
Zero	Up to £125,000	Up to £150,000
1%	Excess over £125,000	£125,001–£5 million
2%	N/A	Over £5 million

Inheritance Tax

Rates

Lifetime	20%
Death*	40%

* 36% where 10% or more of the net estate is left to charity.

Nil Rate Bands

Tax Year	Nil Rate Band £
2007/08	0–300,000
2008/09	0–312,000
2009/10	0–325,000
2010/11	0–325,000
2011/12	0–325,000
2012/13	0–325,000
2013/14	0–325,000
2014/15	0–325,000
2015/16	0–325,000
2016/17	0–325,000
2017/18	0–325,000
2018/19	0–325,000
2019/20	0–325,000

Main Residence Nil Rate Bands

Tax Year	Main Residence Nil Rate Band
2017/18	£100,000
2018/19	£125,000
2019/20	£150,000
2020/21	£175,000

Taper Relief

Period before death:

3 years or less	0%
3–4 years	20%
4–5 years	40%
5–6 years	60%
6–7 years	80%

Quick Succession Relief

Period between earlier transfer and death:

1 year or less	100%
1–2 years	80%
2–3 years	60%
3–4 years	40%
4–5 years	20%

UK Retail Price Indices (as adjusted to base 100 in January 1987)

	1982	1983	1984	1985	1986	1987	1988	1989	1990	1991	1992	1993	1994	1995	1996	1997	1998	1999	2000
January	-	82.6	86.8	91.2	96.2	100.0	103.3	111.0	119.5	130.2	135.6	137.9	141.3	146.3	150.2	154.4	159.5	163.4	166.6
February	-	83.0	87.2	91.9	96.6	100.4	103.7	111.8	120.2	130.9	136.3	138.8	142.1	146.9	150.9	155.0	160.3	163.7	167.5
March	79.4	83.1	87.5	92.8	96.7	100.6	104.1	112.3	121.4	131.4	136.7	139.3	142.5	147.5	151.5	155.4	160.8	164.4	168.4
April	81.0	84.3	88.6	94.8	97.7	101.8	105.8	114.3	125.1	133.1	138.8	140.6	144.2	149.0	152.6	156.3	162.6	165.2	170.1
May	81.6	84.6	89.0	95.2	97.8	101.9	106.2	115.0	126.2	133.5	139.3	141.1	144.7	149.6	152.9	156.9	163.5	165.6	170.7
June	81.9	84.8	89.2	95.4	97.8	101.9	106.6	115.4	126.7	134.1	139.3	141.0	144.7	149.8	153.0	157.5	163.4	165.6	171.1
July	81.9	85.3	89.1	95.2	97.5	101.8	106.7	115.5	126.8	133.8	138.8	140.7	144.0	149.1	152.4	157.5	163.0	165.1	170.5
August	81.9	85.7	89.9	95.5	97.8	102.4	107.9	115.8	128.1	134.1	138.9	141.3	144.7	149.9	153.1	158.5	163.7	165.5	170.5
September	81.9	86.1	90.1	95.4	98.3	102.4	108.4	116.6	129.3	134.6	139.4	141.9	145.0	150.6	153.8	159.3	164.4	166.2	171.7
October	82.3	86.4	90.7	95.6	98.5	102.9	109.5	117.5	130.3	135.1	139.9	141.8	145.2	149.8	153.8	159.5	164.5	166.5	171.6
November	82.7	86.7	91.0	95.9	99.3	103.4	110.0	118.5	130.0	135.6	139.7	141.6	145.3	149.8	153.9	159.6	164.4	166.7	172.1
December	82.5	86.9	90.9	96.0	99.6	103.3	110.3	118.8	129.9	135.7	139.2	141.9	146.0	150.7	154.4	160.0	164.4	167.3	172.2

	2001	2002	2003	2004	2005	2006	2007	2008	2009	2010	2011	2012	2013	2014	2015	2016	2017
January	171.1	173.3	178.4	183.1	188.9	193.4	201.6	209.8	210.1	217.9	229.0	238.0	245.8	252.6	255.4	258.8	265.5
February	172.0	173.8	179.3	183.8	189.6	194.2	203.1	211.4	211.4	219.2	231.3	239.9	247.6	254.2	256.7	260.0	268.4
March	172.2	174.5	179.9	184.6	190.5	195.0	204.4	212.1	211.3	220.7	232.5	240.8	248.7	254.8	257.1	261.1	269.3
April	173.1	175.7	181.2	185.7	191.6	196.5	205.4	214.0	211.5	222.8	234.4	242.1	249.5	255.7	258.0	261.4	270.6
May	174.2	176.2	181.5	186.5	192.0	197.7	206.2	215.1	212.8	223.6	235.2	242.4	250.0	255.9	258.5	262.1	271.7
June	174.4	176.2	181.3	186.8	192.2	198.5	207.3	216.8	213.4	224.1	235.2	241.8	249.7	256.3	258.9	263.1	272.3
July	173.3	175.9	181.3	186.8	192.2	198.5	206.1	216.5	213.4	223.6	234.7	242.1	249.7	256.0	258.6	263.4	272.9
August	174.0	176.4	181.6	187.4	192.6	199.2	207.3	217.2	214.4	224.5	236.1	243.0	251.0	257.0	259.8	264.4	274.7
September	174.6	177.6	182.5	188.1	193.1	200.1	208.0	218.4	215.3	225.3	237.9	244.2	251.9	257.6	259.6	264.9	275.1
October	174.3	177.9	182.6	188.6	193.3	200.4	208.9	217.7	216.0	225.8	238.0	245.6	251.9	257.7	259.5	264.8	275.3
November	173.6	178.2	182.7	189.0	193.3	201.1	209.7	216.0	216.6	226.8	238.5	245.6	252.1	257.1	259.8	265.5	275.8
December	173.4	178.5	183.5	189.9	194.1	202.7	210.9	212.9	218.0	228.4	239.4	246.8	253.4	257.5	260.6	267.1	278.1

Chartered Accountants Ireland *Code of Ethics*

Under Chartered Accountants Ireland's *Code of Ethics*, a Chartered Accountant shall comply with the following fundamental principles:

1. **Integrity** – to be straightforward and honest in all professional and business relationships.
2. **Objectivity** – to not allow bias, conflict of interest or undue influence of others to override professional or business judgements.
3. **Professional Competence and Due Care** – to maintain professional knowledge and skill at the level required to ensure that a client or employer receives competent professional services based on current developments in practice, legislation and techniques, and act diligently and in accordance with applicable technical and professional standards.
4. **Confidentiality** – to respect the confidentiality of information acquired as a result of professional and business relationships and, therefore, not disclose any such information to third parties without proper and specific authority, unless there is a legal or professional right or duty to disclose, nor use the information for the personal advantage of the Chartered Accountant or third parties.
5. **Professional Behaviour** – to comply with relevant laws and regulations and avoid any action that discredits the profession.

The Institute's "Five Fundamental Principles, Five Practical Steps" is a useful resource for members and students and is available at www.charteredaccountants.ie. As a Chartered Accountant, you will have to ensure that your dealings with the tax aspects of your professional life are also in compliance with these fundamental principles. You may be asked to define or list the principles and also must be able to identify where these ethical issues arise and how you would deal with them.

Examples of situations that could arise where these principles are challenged in the context of tax are outlined below:

Example 2.1

You are working in the Tax Department of ABC & Co and your manager is Jack Wilson. He comes over to your desk after his meeting with Peter Foley. He gives you all the papers that Peter has left with him. He asks you to draft Peter's tax return. You know who Peter is as you are now living in a house that your friend Ann leased from Peter. As you complete the return, you note that there is no information regarding property income. What should you do?

Action

As a person with integrity, you should explain to your manager that your friend Ann has leased a property from Peter and that he has forgotten to send details of his property income and expenses. As Peter sent the information to Jack, it is appropriate for Jack to contact Peter for details regarding property income and related expenses.

Example 2.2
You are working in the tax department of the Irish subsidiary of a US-owned multinational. You are preparing the corporation tax computation, including the R&D tax credit due. You have not received some information from your colleagues dealing with R&D and cannot finalise the claim for R&D tax credit until you receive this information. Your manager is under pressure and tells you to just file the claim on the basis of what will maximise the claim. He says, "It is self-assessment, and the chance of this ever being audited or enquired into is zero." What should you do?

Action
You should act in a professional and objective manner. This means that you cannot do as your manager wants. You should explain to him that you will contact the person in R&D again and finalise the claim as quickly as possible.

Example 2.3
Anna O'Shea, financial controller of Great Client Ltd, rings you regarding a VAT issue. You have great respect for Anna and are delighted that she is ringing you directly instead of your manager. She says that it is a very straightforward query. However, as you listen to her, you realise that you are pretty sure of the answer but would need to check a point before answering. What should you do?

Action
Where you do not know the answer, it is professionally competent to explain that you need to check a point before you give an answer. If you like, you can explain which aspect you need to check. Your client will appreciate you acting professionally rather than giving incorrect information or advice.

Example 2.4
The phone rings, and it is Darren O'Brien, your best friend, who works for Just-do-it Ltd. After discussing the match you both watched on the television last night, Darren explains why he is ringing you. He has heard that Success Ltd, a client of your tax department, has made R&D tax credit claims. Therefore, you must have details regarding its R&D. Darren's relationship with his boss is not great at present, and he knows that if he could get certain data about Success Ltd, his relationship with his boss would improve. He explains that he does not want any financial information, just some small details regarding R&D. What should you do?

Action
You should not give him the information. No matter how good a friend he is, it is unethical to give confidential information about your client to him.

Example 2.5
It is the Friday morning before a bank holiday weekend, and you are due to travel from Dublin to west Cork after work for the weekend. Your manager has been on annual leave for the last week. He left you work to do for the week, including researching a tax issue for a client. He had advised you that you were to have an answer to the issue by the time he returned, no matter how long it took. It actually took you a very short time and you have it all documented for him.

Your friend who is travelling with you asks if you could leave at 11am to beat the traffic and have a longer weekend. You have no annual leave left, so you cannot take leave. You know that if you leave, nobody will notice, but you have to complete a timesheet. Your friend reminds you that the research for the client could have taken a lot longer and that you could code the five hours to the client. What should you do?

Action
It would constitute unprofessional behaviour and would show a lack of integrity if you were to charge your client for those five hours.

Tax Planning, Tax Avoidance and Tax Evasion

The global financial and economic crash of 2008 and the ensuing worldwide recession led to a fall in tax collected by many governments and moved tax and tax transparency higher up the agenda. Recent global developments and initiatives have further increased the focus and attention of governments and the wider public on both tax avoidance and evasion of taxes. The revelations in the Paradise Papers and the Panama Papers, the EU's state aid decision against Ireland and Apple Inc., coupled with the 'tax-shaming' of many multinational brand names and famous people has led to tax, and tax ethics, appearing in media headlines almost on a daily basis. As a result, a number of international and domestic initiatives have dramatically changed the tax planning and tax compliance landscape and brought tax transparency to the fore in many businesses and boardrooms.

The tax liability of an individual, partnership, trust or company can be reduced by tax planning, tax avoidance or tax evasion. Although the overriding objective of each is to reduce the taxpayer's tax bill, the method each adopts to do so is different. Each is also vastly different from an ethical and technical perspective.

Tax receipts are used to fund public services such as education, hospitals and roads. Individuals and businesses in a country benefit from these services directly and indirectly and it is therefore seen as a social and ethical responsibility for them to pay their fair share of taxes. Evading or avoiding paying your taxes is viewed as unacceptable as a result.

Tax Planning

Tax planning is used by taxpayers to reduce their tax bill by making use of provisions within domestic tax legislation. For example, any company with good tax governance will seek to minimise its tax liability by using the tools and mechanisms – allowances, deductions, reliefs and exemptions for example – made available to them by the government.

Planning can also take the form of simple decisions, such as delaying sales when a fall in the rate of corporation tax is expected so that the company pays a lower rate of corporation tax on its taxable profits. Or a taxpayer may consider what type of assets to buy to maximise capital allowances. Any tax planning decision should work, not just from a tax planning and legislative perspective, but it should also be commercially feasible.

The UK government accepts that all taxpayers are entitled to organise their affairs in such a way as to mitigate their tax liability – as long as they do so within the law and within the spirit in which Parliament intended when setting the law. Tax planning is both legally and ethically acceptable.

Tax Avoidance

Tax avoidance is often viewed as a grey area because it is regularly confused with tax planning. Tax avoidance is the use of loopholes within tax legislation to reduce the taxpayer's tax liability. Although tax avoidance may seem similar to tax planning, as the taxpayer is using tax law to reduce their overall tax burden, the taxpayer is using tax legislation in a way not intended, or anticipated, by Parliament.

In 2004, the UK government launched the Disclosure of Tax Avoidance Schemes (DOTAS) regime, which covers most taxes in the UK including income tax, National Insurance, VAT, capital gains tax, corporation tax, inheritance tax and stamp duty land tax. DOTAS was designed to provide early information to HMRC about tax avoidance schemes that had been developed and the users of those schemes.

The regime has been amended a number of times to ensure it remains up to date and that it identifies tax avoidance schemes as the tax avoidance market changes. The DOTAS regime requires schemes that contain certain 'hallmarks' of tax avoidance to be notified to HMRC. HMRC then take action to close down the scheme, usually by legislation as part of the annual Budget process.

The users of such schemes are also required to notify HMRC that they have used a particular scheme by including the scheme notification number on the relevant tax return or submission made to HMRC. HMRC will thereafter pursue the scheme user by opening an enquiry that challenges the avoidance scheme.

Avoidance behaviour is also challenged by the UK's General Anti-Abuse Rule (GAAR), which took effect from 17 July 2013 and is intended to counteract "tax advantages arising from tax arrangements that are abusive" and applies across a number of taxes.

Tax arrangements exist where obtaining a tax advantage is "one of the main purposes". To date, the opinions given by the GAAR advisory panel have all been in HMRC's favour. The GAAR counteracts the abusive behaviour and in effect reverses the tax saving.

The *Ramsay* principle (or doctrine) refers to an approach to statutory interpretation developed by the courts in cases involving tax avoidance. It began with the landmark decision by the House of Lords in *W. T. Ramsay Ltd. v. Inland Revenue Commissioners* (1981). The *Ramsay* principle can be summarised as:

1. look at the legislation – what did Parliament intend when it chose those words?
2. look at the particular facts of the transaction – should an individual transaction be considered in a wider context?
3. in light of 1. and 2., how does the law apply to these facts?

While tax avoidance is arguably legal, it is generally viewed as ethically unacceptable behaviour. Tax avoidance behaviour that is successfully challenged by HMRC will lead to the original tax saving being paid, in addition to penalties and interest on the error. The error will generally fall into the deliberate behaviour without concealment category (see **Chapter 1, Section 1.10.6**).

Tax Evasion

At the extreme end of the spectrum is tax evasion. Tax evasion involves breaking the law deliberately and either not paying any of the taxes that fall due or underpaying the taxes that fall due when the law clearly states that they must be paid. Tax evaders intend to deliberately break rules surrounding their tax position in order to avoid paying the correct amount of tax they owe.

A tax evader illegally reduces their tax burden, either by a misrepresentation to HMRC or by not filing tax returns at all, thereby concealing the true state of their tax affairs. Tax evasion can include onshore (within the UK) and offshore deliberate behaviour.

Examples of tax evasion include, *inter alia*:

- failure to file a tax return and pay the relevant tax arising;
- failure to declare the correct income;
- deliberately inflating expenses, which reduces taxable profits or increases a loss;
- hiding taxable assets;
- wrongly claiming a tax refund or repayment by being dishonest;
- not telling HMRC about a source of income;
- not operating a PAYE scheme for employees/pensioners;
- not registering for VAT when required to do so; and
- deliberate submission of incorrect or false information.

In all cases the Exchequer suffers a loss of tax. This is known as tax fraud. Tax evasion, and the tax fraud that flows from this behavior, is a criminal offence prosecutable by HMRC. It is viewed as ethically unacceptable behaviour. The error will generally fall into the deliberate behaviour with concealment category (see **Chapter 1, Section 1.10.6**).

As Chartered Accountants, we must be cognisant of the activities of clients and potential clients, particularly in cases of both avoidance and evasion.

Suggested Solutions to Review Questions

Chapter 1

Question 1.1

If the new company is incorporated in the UK, it will be UK resident. If it is incorporated overseas, and if the central management and control of the company is exercised in the UK, it will also be UK resident. The central management and control of a company is exercised where the highest level of control is exercised, i.e. major not operational decisions. Therefore, as Peter and Angela will make all the strategic decisions in the UK, the new company will be UK resident.

A company which has not received a company tax return or notice to file must tell HMRC if it becomes chargeable to tax within 12 months from the end of the relevant accounting period. Penalties can arise for failure to notify and these are chargeable on a behaviour basis.

Question 1.2

Venus Ltd

Venus Ltd will pay in instalments for the year ended 31 December 2020, if it:

- was "large" in the previous year (31 December 2019); and
- it is "large" in the current year – year ended 31 December 2020.

Year ended 31 December 2019

In year ended 31 December 2019 Venus had two related 51% group companies during the period. Saturn Limited was not an associate because it was not under the control of Venus (as the shareholding is only 40%). So the upper relevant maximum amount of £1.5 million is divided by three, i.e. £500,000. Therefore Venus Ltd was "large" in the previous period as its augmented profits were £550,000.

Year ended 31 December 2020

In order to determine whether the company is "large" for 2020, the £1.5 million upper relevant maximum amount must be divided by the number of related 51% group companies at the end of the previous accounting period.

Venus Limited, once again, had two related 51% group companies in the year to 31 December 2019. The upper relevant maximum amount was, again, £500,000 (£1.5 million divided by three). Therefore the company, having augmented profits of £505,000, is a "large" company for instalments purposes. This is because we are required to include the £80,000 dividend expected to be received from Saturn Ltd, which is a non-group company, so this dividend is franked investment income. The £80,000 dividend is added to the TTP of £425,000 to give augmented profits of £505,000. Venus Limited may have the opportunity to waive part of its dividend entitlement so that its augmented profits are below £500,000 and it is not exposed to instalment payments.

Energy Ltd
Where the company has a short period of account the limits are pro-rated. As profits are expected to exceed £1,125,000 (£1.5 million × 9/12) it looks like Energy Ltd is required to pay in instalments for the nine months ending 31 December 2020, as its projected profits are £1,200,000.

However, it was not a large company in the year ended 31 March 2020, and therefore because projected profits are not expected to exceed £10 million × 9/12 (£7,500,000) in the nine months to 31 December 2020, instalment payments are not required.

Chapter 2

Question 2.1

TELESTAR LTD
Corporation Tax Computation for the 12-month Accounting Period Ended 31 March 2020

		£	£
	Profit (pre-tax)		117,000
Add:	Depreciation	15,389	
	Motor expenses (Note 1)	–	
	Entertainment (Note 2)	1,050	
	Finance lease depreciation (Note 3)	–	
	Legal fees (Note 4)	2,400	18,839
			135,839
Less:	Grant for extension of premises (Note 5)	10,000	
	Employment grant (Note 6)	–	
	Patent royalty (Note 7)	1,600	
	Dividends from UK company (Note 8)	1,300	
	Profit on sale of van (Note 9)	1,000	
	Profit on sale of shares (Note 10)	3,000	
	Bank deposit interest (Note 11)	600	
	Capital allowances	7,272	(24,772)
	Trading income		111,067
Loan relationships – bank interest (gross)			600
Miscellaneous income			2,000
Patent royalty (gross) $= 1{,}600 \times \frac{100}{80}$			
Chargeable gain (Note 12)			1,632
Taxable total profits (TTP)			**115,299**

Corporation tax payable:	
£115,299 @ 19%	21,906.81
Less: income tax suffered on patent royalty £2,000 @ 20%	(400.00)
Corporation tax payable	21,506.81

Corporation tax is due on or before 1 January 2021 as the company is not "large" for instalment purposes, it's augmented profits being less than £1,500,000.

Notes

1. It is assumed that motor expenses are wholly allowable, therefore there is no add-back.
2. Entertainment costs are disallowed as follows:

	£
Christmas gifts for suppliers	150
Entertainment costs incurred by MD	350
General customer entertainment	550
	1,050

   Costs incurred for benefit of staff, i.e. Christmas party and prizes, are deductible.
3. As depreciation on finance lease assets is deductible, no adjustment is required.
4. Legal fees are of a capital nature and, therefore, are disallowed.
5. Grant for extension of premises is a capital receipt and is not liable to corporation tax.
6. Employment grant is taxable as a revenue receipt relating to the trade.
7. Patent royalty is not taxable as trading income as it relates to non-trading activities. The gross amount is taxable as miscellaneous income. However, the income tax suffered can be set-off against the corporation tax chargeable. As **only** the net amount (i.e. the amount after deduction of standard rate income tax) has been credited in the statement of comprehensive income, then this is the correct amount to deduct. Had the patent royalty income have been received from trading activities the gross amount would have been taxable as part of trading income under the intangible fixed assets regime.
8. The dividend from the UK company is exempt from corporation tax under the exemption in section 931B CTA 2009 as Telestar Ltd is a small company.
9. Profit on sale of van is a capital profit and not a trading receipt and so is adjusted through capital allowances.
10. Profit on sale of shares is a capital profit and not a trading receipt and so it is taxable as a chargeable asset (see Note 12).
11. Bank deposit interest is taxable as income from a non-trading loan relationship.
12. Chargeable gain:

	£	£
Proceeds		6,000
Cost	3,000	
Indexation	1,368	
Indexed cost		(4,368)
Chargeable gain		1,632

Note: SSE is not available as the company did not own at least 10% of the shares in Video Plc.

Question 2.2

Zaco Ltd Corporation Tax Computation Year Ended 30 September 2019

		£	£
Profit per accounts			379,900
Add:	Disallowed repairs	5,200	
	Disallowed professional fees	300	
	Political donations	750	
	Entertainment	600	
	Depreciation	13,000	19,850
			399,750
Less:	Dividends (Note 2)	3,600	
	Profit on sale of fixed assets	15,200	
	Bank interest receivable	1,200	
	Property income	4,300	(24,300)
			375,450
Less:	Capital allowances		(9,846)
Tax-adjusted trading profits			365,604
Loan relationships			1,200
Property income			4,300
Add:	Chargeable gains (Note 1)		Nil
Taxable total profits (TTP)			**371,104**
Corporation tax payable:			
£371,104 @ 19%			70,509.76

Zaco Ltd is not "large" for instalment purposes as its augmented profits are less than £1,500,000. Therefore the corporation tax liability is due on or before 1 July 2020.

Notes

1. Chargeable gain on sale of building	£	£
Proceeds		215,200
Cost	200,000	
Indexation (£200,000 × 0.035)	7,000	(207,000)
Gain		8,200
Less: capital loss forward (restricted)		(8,200)
Chargeable gain		NIL
Capital loss carried forward		(1,800)

2. The foreign dividend is exempt from UK tax; therefore no credit is available for the withholding tax suffered.

Question 2.3

Alpha Ltd Corporation Tax Computation Year Ended 31 March 2020

		£	£
Profit per accounts			424,605
Add:			
	Repairs	15,000	
	Insurance	350	
	Loss on sale of investments	600	
	Legal expenses	2,000	
	Depreciation	13,260	
	Subscriptions (Note 1)	1,815	
	Motor expenses (Note 2)	3,169	
	Sundry (Note 3)	2,201	
	Entertainment	1,191	
			39,586
			464,191
Less:			
	UK dividends	4,500	
	Royalties received	2,500	
	Gain on sale of fixed assets (Note 4)	1,000	
	Amortisation of grant	240	
	Interest on tax overpaid	475	
	Rents received	6,000	
	Deposit interest	1,500	
			(16,215)
			447,976
Capital allowance			(26,006)
Trading income for period			421,970
Less: loss carried forward – section 45 CTA 2010			(20,000)
			401,970
Net credit from loan relationships (£475 + £1,500)			1,975
Miscellaneous income: Patent royalties (including tax of £625)			3,125

Property income:		
Gross rents	6,000	
Less: Insurance		(350)
Net property income		5,650
Taxable total profits (TTP)		412,720

Corporation tax payable @ 19% = £78,417 and is due on or before 1 January 2021 (as the company is not "large" for instalment purposes, it's augmented profits being less than £500,000 (£1,500,000/3)).

Notes

1. Subscriptions

	£
	–
Political	1,815
	1,815

2. Motor expenses

Leasing charges: disallowable £21,126 × 15%*	3,169

* As the CO_2 emissions exceed 130g/km, the limit which applies for leases entered into on or before 1 April 2018.

3. Sundry

Interest on late payment of VAT	1,630
Parking fines	30
Gifts to customers	541
	2,201

4. Profit on sale – excluded from calculation of taxable total profits.
5. Property income of £1,000 received on sub-letting to a tenant on a short-term basis is treated as trading income under section 44 CTA 2009 – see **Section 1.7.4**.
6. The capital loss of £189 carried forward from 31 March 2019 remains unused and is increased by a further capital loss of £600 on the share disposal. This is because the share disposal does not qualify for the substantial shareholdings exemption. The total capital loss carried forward is therefore £789.

Question 2.4

To: Finance director
From: Financial controller
Re: Proposed claim for tax relief on qualifying Research & Development (R&D) expenditure

I refer to our recent meeting in relation to my review of the draft corporation tax computation which identified that no claim for R&D expenditure has been included therein.

By way of background and as requested, relief in the UK is available for capital R&D through the capital allowances regime; and for revenue R&D through the various tax regimes available for qualifying R&D expenditure.

Revenue expenditure
The enhanced tax relief for revenue R&D can only be claimed on "relevant" R&D, i.e. R&D is related to the trade carried on by the company. As the work carried out by the R&D department directly relates to the trade of Comtech, this condition of the regime is not an issue.

Qualifying R&D expenditure
While the definition of R&D follows that in UK GAAP and IAS 38 *Intangible Assets*, HMRC recommends that the Department of Business Innovation and Skills guidance tests must be applied. In essence, a project will qualify as an R&D project if it is carried on in the field of science or technology and is undertaken to extend knowledge and to address scientific or technology uncertainties. The projects of our R&D department clearly qualify in this regard.

There are two regimes in the UK – one for the SME sector (giving a further 130% tax deduction on qualifying revenue expenditure offering total overall relief of 230%); and the large company regime, which provides for a taxable 12% R&D expenditure credit on qualifying expenditure.

Under both regimes, the expenditure must *inter alia* meet the following conditions:

1. must not be capital in nature;
2. must be attributable to relevant R&D that is either directly undertaken by the company or on its behalf; and
3. must be incurred on qualifying costs.

The qualifying expenditure must be such that it would have been allowable as a deduction in computing the taxable profits of a trade carried on by the company. The tax relief is claimed as an adjustment to the trading income computation. The expenditure on which I propose to submit a claim on behalf of Comtech Limited meets all of the above conditions.

Under the SME scheme, where a company claims SME R&D tax relief and has a trading loss in the accounting period, the company can choose to surrender the loss for a cash payment of 14.5% of the loss for the chargeable period.

An SME may also make a claim under the large companies rules if it fails to meet the specific criteria for that regime, but in so doing will be restricted to the limits for such companies.

Tax saving
See Appendix 1 for my calculations of the reliefs available to Comtech Limited for qualifying expenditure in the 2020 period. Overall, a corporation tax saving of £73,818.23 is available to the company.

I would be pleased to meet with you to discuss this claim in more detail and would also suggest we conduct a review to establish if Comtech Limited would still be within time to submit claims for any prior periods. I suggest we implement procedures to easily capture R&D costs in future periods given the significant cash flow benefits and savings available. Please also note that a claim for the year to 31 March 2019 would be possible until 31 March 2021. I would suggest that this is reviewed as soon as possible given the upcoming deadline for making the claim.

APPENDIX 1

COMTECH LIMITED

Claim for R&D relief for the accounting period ended 31 March 2020

Qualifying revenue expenditure:

	£
Gross wages	212,567
Redundancy payments (Note 1)	0
Employer's NIC	27,209
Pension scheme contributions	15,000
Company car benefit in kind (Note 1)	0
Consumable items	22,425
Power, water and fuel	8,762
Software	4,933
Rates (Note 1)	0
Sub-contracted costs (Note 2)	7,963
	298,859
Enhanced R&D deduction (Note 3)	388,517

Amended corporation tax computation:

	£
Taxable total profits (TTP) before R&D claimed	1,828,925
Enhanced R&D deduction	(388,517)
Amended taxable total profits	1,440,408
Tax payable:	
TTP @ 19%	273,677.52
Tax saved as a result of the R&D claims above:	
Draft tax liability on TTP of £1,828,925 @ 19%	347,495.75
Amended liability	273,677.52
Tax saving	73,818.23

Notes

1. Redundancy payments, non-cash benefits in kind (in this case, company car benefits) and rates do not qualify for the enhanced R&D deduction.
2. Sub-contracted costs payable to a non-connected third party are a qualifying cost. As the amount that qualifies must be restricted to 65%, the calculation is as follows: £12,250 × 65% = £7,963.

3. The amount of relief the company is entitled to claim will depend on whether it is classed as a small company, which attracts 230%, or a large company, which attracts a taxable 12% RDEC under the R&D regime.
   SME is defined in accordance with the EU guidelines as follows:
   A company meeting either the turnover requirement of €100 million or the balance sheet total of €86 million plus the headcount limit for employees of fewer than 500.
   As the company has a turnover of £34.6 million and 55 employees, it meets the EU definition of an SME and thus qualifies for the SME R&D regime, giving an additional 130% tax deduction on qualifying expenditure.

Question 2.5

The tax computation of Investco Ltd for the accounting period ended 31 March 2020 will be as follows:

	£	£
Surplus non-trade loan relationship credits		3,000
Property income		12,000
Chargeable gain		5,000
Total taxable gross income		20,000
Less: expenses of management:		
Shareholder meeting costs	2,240	
Directors' remuneration (Note 2)	12,000	
Office rent	3,000	
Repairs	500	
Total management expenses		(17,740)
Taxable total profits		2,260
Corporation tax @ 19%		429

Notes

1. The company is not subject to corporation tax on the dividend as it is a small company under the dividend exemption rules.
2. The full amount will be deductible, provided that the directors can demonstrate that the amount charged is reasonable for the work carried out. This is not necessarily a measure against the company's income, but is more likely to be considered in the context of the director's activities, e.g. the director may spend significant time monitoring the company's shareholdings in listed companies.
3. Appraisal costs would be deductible if they were in respect of an overall appraisal of the market; however, when a specific target is identified, any appraisal costs associated with a decision to go ahead with the acquisition would no longer be allowable. In this case, the appraisal costs do not qualify as management expenses but as a cost of acquiring an asset.

Question 2.6

Anytown Tax Advisors
Anytown

Mr Paul Morrisey
Classic Engineering Consultancy Ltd

11 July 2021

Dear Paul,

Amended corporation tax computation – 31 March 2020

Further to your recent instructions, I have set out below the information and advice you requested.

I have enclosed with this letter the amended corporation tax computation for the accounting period ended 31 March 2020.

In summary, there were a number of errors identified in the computation. Including those identified on Appendix 1, the corporation tax rate originally applied to the adjusted trading profits was also not correct – the rate was 19% for the 2019 financial year, which corresponds with the company's accounting period ended 31 March 2020. Despite the company's taxable profits being in excess of £1,500,000 in 2020, quarterly instalments were not required because it would appear that this was the first period where taxable profits exceeded £1,500,000, and, as they did not exceed £10,000,000, quarterly instalments were not required in 2020. Therefore the corporation tax liability was due on 1 January 2021.

Unfortunately, the corporation tax liability for 2020 has been underpaid by £10,384.68. This is net of a refund of section 455 tax on the loan to you of £50,000, which was written off in the period. It is not correct that the company can obtain a deduction for this write-off if it forgoes the section 455 refund which is due.

As a result of this, interest of 3.25% per annum for late payment is payable from the original due date of 1 January 2021. This will be due on the full amount of £22,884.68, i.e. before the £12,500 refund, as this is subject to the company making a claim and cannot be netted-off.

The company is also likely to be subject to a penalty as a result of the underpayment. The penalty will fall into the "careless" category as the company did not deliberately seek to underpay (the computation had been prepared by an accountant). Penalties in the careless category can be mitigated to 0% if an unprompted disclosure is made. However, because HMRC have already opened an enquiry into the 2020 period, the company cannot avail of the 0% category and thus the penalty will be either 15% for a prompted disclosure (£3,432.70) or, if the company does not make a prompted disclosure, 30% (£6,865.40).

In light of the potential to mitigate the penalty by some 15%, i.e. £3,432,70, we would recommend a full disclosure is made to HMRC as soon as possible. This can be done either by letter or by amending the 2020 corporation tax return. It would be preferable to do so by amending the 2020 corporation tax return as that is how the section 455 refund claim should be made.

The net underpaid tax of £10,384.68 should also be paid at the same time. The letter submitting the amended return should clearly outline all adjustments and note that the company wishes to offset the £12,500 refund against the underpaid liability for 2020. Paying the underpaid tax at the same time that the amended return is submitted also has the benefit of 'stopping the interest clock'.

You should also note that a £100 late filing penalty will also arise – it is irrelevant that this is the first time the company has filed a late corporation tax return.

If we can be of further assistance in this regard, or if you have any questions, please do not hesitate to contact me.

Yours sincerely,
Any Accountant

CLASSIC ENGINEERING CONSULTANCY LTD

Amended corporation tax computation for the accounting period ended 31 March 2020

	Workings	**£**	**£**
Adjusted trading profit per original computation			1,598,328
Less: profit on sale of machine	W1		(22,800)
Add:			
Disallowed repairs and renewals	W2	50,400	
Disallowed legal fees	W3	13,225	
Depreciation	W4	28,289	
Disallowed motor expenses	W5	400	
Disallowed travel expenses	W6	900	
Loan to Paul written off	W7	50,000	
			143,214
Amended adjusted profit			1,718,772

Corporation tax payable:

	£
Revised corporation tax payable @ 19%	326,566.68
Corporation tax per original computation submitted	303,682.00
Underpayment	**22,884.68**
Section 455 refund due – £50,000 @ 25%	(12,500.00)
Net underpayment	**10,384.68**

Workings

W1 These were added back instead of being deducted, hence we need to deduct twice.

W2 The building extension costs of £50,400 are capital in nature and should have been added back in the original computation.

W3 The planning appeal fees of £11,725 are also capital in nature and should have been added back.

The personal tax enquiry fees paid for by the company are a personal expense of Paul's and as such are not deductible and should be added back. As the company is a close company this has an additional implication – these will either be treated as a distribution in Paul's hands. If he is an employee of the company he will be taxed on this as a benefit in kind, though the company would be entitled to a deduction for the expense.

W4 Depreciation on the assets under hire purchase is also disallowable.

W5 The parking fines incurred by Paul of £400 are disallowed.

No add-back needed of contract hire on car costs as the CO_2g/km is < 110g/km, the limit for contracts taken out on or after 6 April 2018.

W6 Add back meals with potential new suppliers/customers.

W7 The loan to Paul written off, amounting to £50,000, is not allowable and must be added back. This has a number of other implications. The company has paid section 455 tax in relation to this in the amount of £12,500. The company can reclaim this tax from HMRC – it can do so nine months and one day after the end of the accounting period in which the loan is repaid or written off, i.e. on or after 1 January 2021. Additionally, Paul will be taxed on the loan write-off as a distribution in his own hands at an effective rate of 38.1% as he is an additional rate taxpayer. It is not correct that the company can get relief on the loan write-off if it forgoes repayment of the section 455 tax. If Paul is an employee or director of the company, he will also be taxed on the write-off as employment income instead, with **no** corporation tax deduction available to the company.

All other items in the computation submitted appear correct.

Chapter 3

Question 3.1

	£
Profit	96,000
Add: depreciation	5,000
Trade profit	101,000
UK property business	17,000
Total profits	118,000
Less: qualifying charitable donation	(8,000)
Taxable total profits	110,000

Question 3.2

Credits	£
Interest received	15,000
Loan written off by bank	20,000
	35,000
Less:	
Debits	
Legal fees incurred re: loan write-off	(1,500)
Net loan relationship credit	33,500

Question 3.3

(a) A loan relationship is any transaction for the borrowing or lending of money in relation to a money debt. Loan relationships cover all loans made both by and to the company. These will either be trading or non-trading.

(b) Examples include: bank overdrafts and loans, mortgages, employee loans, interest on underpaid and overpaid corporation tax, corporate bonds, interest on savings.
(c) All non-trading debits and credits, calculated in line with generally accepted accounting principles, are aggregated separately and the overall debit or credit is included in the corporation tax computation. Trading debits are deductible in calculating trading profits. Excess non-trading credits are taxable and included in the calculation of total taxable profits. Non-trade debits are relievable in various ways.

Question 3.4

Non-trade interest received:	£
Bank deposit interest	6,233
Bond held with local council	775
	7,008
Less:	
Non-trade interest paid:	
Mortgage on rental property	(3,178)
Bank loan for shares	(555)
	–
Net non-trade loan relationship credit	3,275

All of the remaining sources of interest received and paid are trade-related.

Question 3.5

Interest on corporation tax paid late is allowable as a non-trading loan relationship debit, therefore it should be added back to the adjustment of trading profits and relieved later as a non-trade debit.

The loan to buy equipment is for a trading purpose and so interest is allowable as a deduction against trading income on an accruals basis, i.e. £2,200 is deductible.

The mortgage interest is an allowable trading deduction.

Question 3.6

	£
Debenture interest receivable	7,000
Bank overdraft interest payable (trading related)	–
Property loan interest (2/4 × £12,000)	(6,000)
Incidental costs of loan finance (2/4 × £2,500)	(1,250)
Non-trading loan relationship debit	(250)

This can be offset against total profits of the same accounting period or carried back and set against surplus non-trading loan relationship credits for the previous twelve months. Alternatively it can be carried forward against non-trading profits of future accounting periods or group relieved, if the company is part of a group-relief group.

Chapter 4

Question 4.1

Enya Limited

31/03/2017	£
Trading income	600,000
Net credit from loan relationships	100,000
Property income	50,000
Taxable total profits	750,000

31/03/2018	
Trading income	700,000
Net credit from loan relationships	50,000
Property loss	(40,000)
Taxable total profits	710,000
Less: section 37(3)(b) claim	(710,000)
Taxable total profits	Nil

31/03/2019	
Trading income	–
Net credit from loan relationships	100,000
Property income	60,000
Total profits	160,000
Less: section 37(3)(a) claim	(160,000)
Taxable total profits	Nil

31/03/2020	
Trading income	100,000
Net credit from loan relationships	35,000
Property income	80,000
Total profits	215,000
Less: section 45A claim (see Loss Memo)	(215,000)
Taxable total profits	–

Loss Memo

	£
Relevant trading loss for y/e 31/03/2019	1,300,000
Utilised by way of section 37(3)(a) against y/e 31/03/2019	(160,000)
Utilised by way of section 37(3)(b) against y/e 31/03/2018	(710,000)
Utilised by way of section 45A against y/e 31/03/2020	(215,000)
Loss carried forward at 31/03/2020	215,000

continued overleaf

Section 45A claims are subject to the restriction rule. However, the company's deductions allowance for losses carried forward is £5 million, meaning 100% relief is available for these losses against total profits.

Question 4.2

Hells Bells Ltd
Year ended 31 March 2020

	£
Trading income	167,000
Property income	4,000
Net credit from loan relationships	10,000
Total profits	181,000
Less: section 37(3)(b) claim	(174,000)
Taxable total profits	7,000
Tax payable £7,000 @ 19%	1,330

9 months ended 31 December 2020

Trading income	–
Property income (Note 1)	(4,000)
Net credit from loan relationships	20,000
Chargeable gains (Note 2)	–
Total profits	16,000
Less: section 37(3)(a) claim	(16,000)
Taxable total profits	Nil

Notes

1. Property income – A property loss must be set against other profits in the current accounting period.
2. Chargeable gains

	£
Gain	10,000
Less: capital loss forward	(19,000)
Loss forward	(9,000)

Loss Memo

	£
Relevant trading loss for p/e 31/12/2020	190,000
Utilised by way of section 37(3)(a) p/e 31/12/2020	(16,000)
Utilised by way of section 37(3)(b) y/e 31/03/2020	(174,000)
Loss forward to 2021	Nil

Question 4.3

Monk Ltd
Year ended 31 March 2021

	£
Trading income	–
Net credit from loan relationships	30,000
Property income	20,000
Chargeable gain	126,000
Taxable profits	176,000
Less: section 37(3)(a) claim	(176,000)
Taxable total profits	Nil

Year ended 31 March 2020

	£	£
Trading income	360,000	
Less: capital allowances	(20,000)	340,000
Less: section 45 – loss carried forward *		(20,000)
Trading income		320,000
Net credit from loan relationships		5,000
Property income		15,000
Chargeable gain		12,000
Taxable profits		352,000
Less: section 37(3)(b) claim		(224,000)
Taxable total profits		128,000
Tax:		
£128,000 @ 19%		24,320

Loss Memo

	£
Relevant trading loss for y/e 31/03/2021 (£310,000 + £90,000)	400,000
Utilised by way of section 37(3)(a) against y/e 31/03/2021	(176,000)
Utilised by way of section 37(3)(b) against y/e 31/03/2020	(224,000)
Loss forward to 2022	Nil

* Section 45 claims are subject to the restriction rule. However, the company's deductions allowance for losses carried forward is £5 million, meaning 100% relief is available for these losses.

Chapter 5

Question 5.1

The dividend is exempt from corporation tax as Ice Sculptors Ireland Limited can be controlled by Ice Sculptors Limited and therefore (as we have no further information to the contrary) the dividend falls with section 931E CTA 09 as an exempt distribution from a controlled company. Therefore the dividend receipt is not taxable and thus no double taxation relief is available for the 10% withholding tax deducted at source.

Question 5.2

The general rule is that dividends paid by a UK company to another UK company out of post-tax profits are exempt from further taxation. The rule also includes dividends paid by a UK or overseas company to a company or branch within the charge to UK corporation tax, so that dividends received are exempt if the conditions for the exemption are met. In general, dividends that fall to be taxed as trading profits, profits of a UK property business or insurance company profits will always fall outside the dividend exemption.

The dividend exemption rules and how they work depend on whether the recipient company is a "small company" or a "large company", but companies can always elect for exempt dividends to be taxable on a receipt-by-receipt basis. This can sometimes reduce the rate of withholding tax under double taxation treaties and may be beneficial if the recipient company has tax losses.

Currently, the definition of a small company is as follows:

- has no more than 50 employees; and
- has an annual turnover of less than €10 million; or
- gross assets of less than €10 million.

All companies that are not "small companies" are "large companies" for the purposes of the dividend exemption.

The small company exemption applies to dividends received where:

- the payer is resident in the UK or a qualifying territory. These are countries with which the UK has a comprehensive double taxation treaty and contain a non-discrimination clause; and
- the dividend is not interest which has been re-categorised as a distribution, and
- the dividend has not been allowed as a deduction from taxable profits outside the UK; and
- the general anti-avoidance rule that the distribution is not part of a scheme of tax avoidance is met.

The large company exemption applies to dividends that fall in to one of five classes, is not re-categorised interest and where no deduction is allowed outside the UK.

The five classes of exempt dividend are:

1. Where the recipient controls the payer (subject to detailed rules).
2. Distributions in respect of non-redeemable ordinary shares.
3. Distributions in respect of portfolio holdings (broadly where the recipient controls less than 10% of the payer).
4. Distributions from transactions not designed to reduce tax.
5. Dividends from shares accounted for as liabilities.

Question 5.3

The following transactions are classed as distributions by a company:

- Dividends paid by a company.
- Any distribution of assets in respect of shares, except any part of which represents a repayment of capital.
- A bonus issue subsequent to a repayment of share capital.
- Interest payments in excess of a normal commercial rate of return.

- Redemption of bonus securities or redeemable shares.
- Certain expenses incurred by a close company where the participator is neither an employee nor a director.
- Sale of assets by a company at undervalue, or purchase of assets by a company at overvalue from a shareholder, again, where the participator is neither an employee nor a director.

Question 5.4

The dividend is exempt from corporation tax as Dragger GmbH qualifies as a small company as it has less than 50 employees and gross assets of less than £10 million therefore (as we have no further information to the contrary) the dividend falls with section 931B CTA 2009 as an exempt distribution from a small company. Therefore the dividend receipt is not taxable and no double taxation relief is available for the 20% withholding tax deducted at source.

Chapter 6

Question 6.1

The trustees of A's settlement are associates of Mrs A by virtue of section 448(1) CTA 2010 and their rights and powers may be attributed to Mrs A, who therefore controls the company. Company X is therefore a close company as it is under the control of Mrs A, being five or fewer participators.

Question 6.2

Control by voting rights is determined under section 450(3) CTA 2010.

The associates of A are:

- his wife and his brother; and
- the trustees of A's settlement (section 448(1) CTA 2010).

The rights and powers attributable to A are:

- the rights and powers of his associates (section 451(4) CTA 2010); and
- the rights and powers of Company X (section 451(4) CTA 2010).

As a total of 510 votes are thus possessed by A or attributable to him, the company is a close company controlled by one person.

Question 6.3

Control – the rights in the shares held by Company Z in Company Y may be attributed to F, who controls that company (section 451(4) CTA 2010).

F is an associate of E but the rights attributed to F cannot be further attributed to E (section 451(4) CTA 2010).

No group of five participators or fewer can control Company Y, nor do the director/participators control it, and nor would the winding up test be of assistance here.

Therefore company Y is not a close company.

Chapter 7

Question 7.1

(a) Tax law provides that the company must account for tax as if the loan were a net annual payment after deduction of tax. If the loan amounted to £8,000 in the accounts to 31 March 2020, the company must self-assess tax liabilities in respect of any loans and this can mean that it will have to pay tax to HMRC equal to 32.5% of the outstanding loan made during the accounting period, i.e. £2,600. This will be the case where the loan remains unpaid and has not been released or written off within nine months and one day following the end of the relevant accounting period (the effective due date for payment of corporation tax for all but large companies).

If and when the loan is repaid, the company may claim a refund of £2,600. Exemption from this tax charge is, however, available:

- where the business of the company is or includes the lending of money and the loan is made in the ordinary course of that business, or
- where a debt is incurred for the supply of goods or services in the ordinary course of the business of the close company, unless the credit given exceeds six months or is longer than the period normally given to the company's customers, or
- the borrower satisfies the following conditions:
  - total loans to borrower or spouse do not exceed £15,000, and
  - the borrower works full-time for the close company or any of its associated companies (companies under common control), and
  - the borrower and/or his or her associates is not the beneficial owner of or able to control more than 5% of the ordinary shares of the company.

(b) Corporation tax liability – year ended 31/03/2020

	£
Taxable total profits: £133,000 @ 19%	25,270

Corporation tax payable on or before 1 January 2021.

Question 7.2

(a) Corporation tax computation for year ended 31/03/2020

		£	£
Net profit per accounts			32,900
Add:	Depreciation	15,000	
	Disallowed sundry (Note 1)	800	15,800
			48,700
Less:	Interest	8,500	
	Capital grants	1,500	(10,000)
			38,700
Less:	capital allowances		(4,000)
Trading income			34,700

continued overleaf

Net credit from loan relationships	8,500
Taxable total profits	43,200
Corporation tax payable	
£43,200 @ 19%	8,208

(b) Specific Items
Note 1. The expense payment is treated as a "distribution" in the hands of Y's brother and added back in the trading income computation.

Question 7.3

Corporation Tax Computation for y/e 31/03/2020

		£	£
Net profit per accounts			1,870,000
Add: Entertainment	W1	11,900	
Depreciation		100,000	
Loss on sale of plant		20,000	
			131,900
Less:			
Profit on sale of building		1,480,000	
Rents		200,000	(1,680,000)
			321,900
Capital allowances			(50,000)
Trading income			271,900
Trading losses forward – section 45 CTA 2010*			(210,000)
			61,900
Property income	W2		181,000
			242,900
Chargeable gain	W3		1,377,000
Taxable total profits			1,619,900
Corporation tax:			
£1,619,900 @ 19%			307,781
Tax on loan £550,000 @ 32.5%**			178,750

* Section 45A claims are subject to the restriction rule. However, the company's deductions allowance for losses carried forward is £5 million, meaning 100% relief is available for these losses.
** If the loan is not repaid within nine months and one day of the year end.

Workings

1. Entertainment disallowed	£
Entertaining customers	6,000
Entertaining suppliers	5,000
Christmas gifts for suppliers	900
	11,900

2. Property income

	£	
Portion of premium subject to corporation tax: £50,000 × (50−19)/50	31,000	
Property income (£200,000 − £50,000)	150,000	
Property income	181,000	

3. Chargeable gain

		£
Sale of building		
Proceeds from building		1,500,000
Legal fees		(18,000)
		1,482,000
Market value at 31/3/1982	50,000	
Indexation: 1.10	55,000	(105,000)
Gain		1,377,000

Question 7.4

Servisco Ltd Corporation Tax Computation year ended 31 March 2020

	£
Trading income	430,000
Less: loss forward under section 45*	(9,000)
	421,000
Net credits from loan relationships	50,000
Property income	100,000
	571,000
Chargeable gains	86,400
Taxable total profits	657,400
Corporation tax	
£657,400 @ 19%	124,906

* Section 45 claims are subject to the restriction rule. However, the company's deductions allowance for losses carried forward is £5 million, meaning 100% relief is available for these losses.

Servisco Ltd's dividend income would be exempt from UK corporation tax.

Question 7.5

Machinery Ltd Corporation Tax Computation year ended 31 March 2020

	£	£
Net profit from trading		626,700
Add: depreciation	59,790	
Loan interest treated as a distribution (Note 1)	2,731	62,521
		689,221
Less: capital allowances		(10,700)
Trading income		678,521

continued overleaf

Net credits from loan relationships	10,000
Property income	50,000
Taxable total profits	738,521
Corporation tax payable:	
£738,521 @ 19%	140,318.99

Note:

1. Loans from directors (and/or associates) with material interest.

	Loan £	Interest paid £	Interest at 6%	Deemed distribution
V. Duffy	4,000	600	240	360
Mrs J. Duffy	5,000	600	300	300
Trustees	5,000	750	300	450
Executors	5,000	750	300	450
D. O'Connell	5,000	750	300	450
L.T. Smith	10,000	1,321	600	721
	34,000	4,771	2,040	2,731

Neither Louise or Paul Hare are classed as having received excessive interest as each of their interest rates is 6% or less.

Question 7.6

Tax Advisors Ltd

Corporation Tax Computation for the year ended 31 March 2020

	£
Trading income	100,000
Net credits from loan relationships	100,000
Total profits	200,000
Qualifying charitable donations	(60,000)
Taxable total profits	140,000

Total corporation tax payable is £140,000 @ 19% = £26,600.

Chapter 8

Question 8.1

Controlled Foreign Companies (CFC) Rules

The CFC rules apply to prevent international groups of companies from generating and retaining profits in low-tax jurisdictions. Where the rules come into play, the profits of CFCs are apportioned back to the UK and charged to tax at a rate equal to the main rate of corporation tax with credit for any foreign tax already paid on those profits.

The rules apply to the accounting period beginning 1 July 2019 and ending 30 June 2020, which is the period in which the joint venture was undertaken.

The purpose of the rules is to target the CFC charge so that it is not applied to profits arising from genuine foreign economic activities or where there has been no artificial diversion of UK profits.

The CFC regime applies to companies resident outside the UK that are controlled by UK residents.

Control for these purposes includes the scenario where a foreign company (MedAssist Ltd) is controlled by two persons together, one of whom is a UK resident company (Medtech Ltd) that holds at least 40% of the interests, rights and powers in the foreign company (MedAssist) and the other of whom is not UK resident (Medservices SA) and holds at least 40% but not more than 55% of the interest rights and powers in the foreign company (MedAssist). These conditions are both met as Medtech holds 48% of the shares and Medservices SA holds 52% of the shares in MedAssist Ltd.

Under section 371AA TIOPA 2010, **any** controlled foreign company is a CFC. Chapter 2 of Part 9A TIOPA 2010 sets out the steps for determining if a CFC charge arises now that it is established that MedAssist is a CFC.

There is a CFC charge only if the following apply:

- the CFC has "chargeable profits";
- none of the CFC exemptions apply; and
- there is a UK "interest holder" that is not exempt and holds an interest of at least 25%.

As the investment in MedAssist meets the last of these (Medtech holds a 48% interest), it is therefore necessary to consider if it meets either one of the CFC exemptions or if it has "chargeable profits".

A CFC's chargeable profits are the part of its profits that pass through the "CFC charge gateway". The gateway is a series of definitions of profits that may fall within the CFC regime. So while MedAssist may be profitable, it may not have chargeable profits.

We do not have enough information regarding the profits of MedAssist to determine whether it has chargeable profits. To determine if it has chargeable profits, we would need sight of MedAssist's most recent accounts and tax computation to be able to conclude on this, and information on projected future activities and results.

However, even if MedAssist does have chargeable profits it may still meet one of the exemptions under the legislation removing the CFC charge completely.

There are a number of entity level exemptions which, if they apply, will exempt all the profits of MedAssist from the CFC charge. These are:

1. *Exempt period (for foreign companies becoming CFCs for the first time)*
   This applies for the first 12 months after MedAssist comes under UK control by Medtech, provided any necessary restructuring is undertaken to ensure no CFC charge arises in the subsequent accounting period. This would be available for the accounting period 30 June 2020 only. It is only a potential exemption and is dependent on there being no CFC charge or one of the other entity level exemptions being met in all subsequent accounting periods after 30 June 2020.
2. *Excluded territories (for CFCs resident in certain territories, subject to conditions)*
   MedAssist is resident in Cyprus – this is not on the list of excluded countries.
3. *Low profits (for CFCs with low levels of profit)*
   Applies if the total accounting or taxable profits of the CFC are < £50,000, or if total accounting or taxable profits are < £500,000 and non-trading income therein is < £50,000. We do not have the information to determine if this would be the case in relation to MedAssist.

4. *Low profit margin (for CFCs whose profit is no more than 10% of operating expenditure)* Again, we do not have the information to determine if this is the case.
5. *Tax exemption (for CFCs that pay at least 75% of the tax they would have paid in the UK)* The Cypriot corporate tax rate of 10% is well below 75% of the current main rate in the UK of 19% (i.e. 14.25%), so MedAssist will be subject to a lower level of taxation. Therefore this exemption would not be met.

The exemptions that may be met in relation to MedAssist are exemptions 1, 3 and 4. First we would recommend that exemptions 3 and 4 are considered to determine if these exemptions will be met in subsequent accounting periods. If it is the case that these are unlikely to be met, then consideration will need to be given to exemption 1 and to whether any action can be taken to remove the CFC charge. This action, however, would need to be taken before 12 months has expired (i.e. by 30 June 2020 at the latest), otherwise the exempt period exemption will not apply to the first period.

Even if one of these exemptions cannot be met, it may still be the case that MedAssist does not have chargeable profits and for this reason it will be important to provide the accounting information and projections requested to establish this as soon as possible.

With careful planning, before the 12-month period ended 30 June 2020 is up, it should be possible to ensure a CFC charge does not arise. It would therefore be reasonable at this stage to expect that the CFC rules will not therefore apply to MedAssist for the 12-month period from July 2019, but further analysis is required to confirm this point definitively.

Question 8.2

(a) Under section 371AA of the Taxation (International and Other Provisions) Act 2010, **any** controlled foreign company is a CFC. The CFC regime applies to companies resident outside the UK that are controlled by UK residents. The rules define what is meant by UK control, including by reference to accounting standards.

A company will be a CFC if it meets all of the following conditions:

- it is resident outside the UK; and
- it is controlled by persons resident in the UK.

Control for these purposes includes the scenario where a foreign company (Black Widow Co.) is controlled by two persons together, one of whom is a UK resident company (Hulk Ltd) that holds at least 40% of the interests, rights and powers in the foreign company (Black Widow Co.) and the other of whom is not UK resident (Hawk Eye Srl) and holds at least 40% but not more than 55% of the interest rights and powers. This test is met.

Therefore Black Widow Co. is a CFC as it is resident outside the UK and is controlled by persons resident in the UK, under the 40% control test. It meets the 40% control test as Hulk Ltd holds more than 40% (46%) of its shares and Hawk Eye Srl holds more than 40% but less than 55% of the shares (54%). This particular test is designed to catch joint venture situations such as this.

(b) A CFC charge is levied because Black Widow Co. is a CFC, it does not meet any of the CFC exemptions and 75% of its profits pass through the trading profits gateway test as 75% of its profits have been artificially diverted from the UK. A CFC charge is therefore imposed on Hulk Ltd.

The CFC charge levied on Hulk Ltd is calculated as follows:

	£
Chargeable profits of Black Widow Co. (£1,500,000 × 75%)	1,125,000
Chargeable profits attributable to Hulk Ltd. (£1,125,000 × 46%)	517,500
UK corporation tax (£517,500 × 19%)	98,325
Less creditable tax (£150,000 × 75% × 46%)	(51,750)
CFC charge	46,575

The above CFC charge is required to be reported to HMRC by Hulk Ltd on its corporation tax return form CT600 for the accounting period ended 31 March 2020. In addition, the company must also complete and submit supplementary corporation tax return for CT600B – Controlled Foreign Companies.

Question 8.3

Anytown Tax Advisors
Anytown

Stephanie Adams
Finance Director
Shed-It Ltd
Any Road
Newry

Dear Stephanie,

With reference to your telephone call I outline below the matters raised by you, as follows:

1. The corporation tax implications of the potential expansion of Shed-It Ltd into the Republic of Ireland, together with other relevant tax considerations.
2. The controlled foreign company (CFC) rules, which can apply where a UK company controls a non-resident company or a non-resident branch operation.
3. A calculation of the CFC charge payable by Shed-It Ltd in respect of the CFC, Shed-It Cyprus Inc.

1. Proposed expansion into the Republic of Ireland

The company is considering expanding its trading activities into the Republic of Ireland and is looking at establishing either a branch of Shed-It Ltd or a wholly owned Irish subsidiary company, Shed-It (Ireland) Ltd.

The corporation tax and other relevant tax considerations of each option are addressed below.

(a) Branch operation

A UK resident company is subject to corporation tax on its worldwide profits. Therefore should the activities of the Irish operation be structured through a branch of the existing company, the profits of the Irish branch will be subject to UK corporation tax at the rate of 19%.

The profits of the Irish branch will also be subject to Irish corporation tax at 12.5%. Double taxation relief (DTR) would be available in respect of the Irish corporation tax suffered, up to a maximum of the equivalent UK corporation tax liability. DTR is limited to the lower of the UK corporation tax paid or the Irish corporation tax paid. In this case, full relief would be obtained for the 12.5% Irish corporation tax as this would be lower than the 19% UK rate. An additional

6.5% UK corporation tax (19% – 12.5%) would be paid by Shed-It Ltd on any Irish profits arising.

Shed-It Ltd can make a permanent irrevocable election that the results from its overseas branches are exempt from UK corporation tax, this would mean that corporation tax would only be payable in Ireland on any branch profits – saving corporation tax of 6.5%. However, any branch losses would not be relievable in the UK as a result.

Shed-It Ltd should also consider if the CFC rules could apply (see 2. below) as these are equally applicable to branch operations where a foreign branch exemption election has been entered into.

In a situation where the branch is loss-making and a branch exemption has not been entered into, any losses of the Irish branch are relievable against UK profits and vice versa. In this scenario, Irish losses would attract relief in Ireland at 12.5% but an additional 6.5% (19% – 12.5%) UK corporation tax relief would be achieved against any UK trading profits.

As the initial activities are projected to be loss-making it would be recommended that Shed-It Ltd does not enter into a branch exemption election, allowing it to enable the Irish losses to be relieved in the UK. An election could then be considered once the branch is projected to make profits; any election should be made in advance of the beginning of the accounting period in which profits are projected.

(b) Subsidiary operation

The profits of a non-UK resident subsidiary of a UK resident parent should not be subject to UK corporation tax, but they will be subject to Irish corporation tax at 12.5%. However Shed-It Ltd should consider if the CFC rules could apply (see 2. below) to the activities of Shed-It (Ireland) Ltd.

Shed-It Ltd will not be subject to UK corporation tax on any dividends it receives from Shed-It (Ireland) Ltd as it is likely to meet the distribution exemption rules either as a small company or as a distribution from a controlled company.

Any losses sustained by the Irish subsidiary will not be available for group relief in the UK under the normal rules. However, UK legislation does provide for relief under the specific rules that apply for EEA/EU group relief, subject to certain conditions being met.

While an overseas subsidiary will increase the number of related 51% group companies for UK corporation tax purposes, this is not relevant to Shed-It Ltd as it does not pay corporation tax in instalments.

Should Shed-It Ltd sell the shares in Shed-It Ltd in the future, this would potentially benefit from the substantial shareholdings exemption, subject to the relevant conditions being met. The sale of a branch operation by Shed-It Ltd would not benefit from this exemption.

2. Controlled foreign company (CFC) rules

The CFC rules apply to prevent international groups of companies from generating and retaining profits in low tax jurisdictions. Where the rules come into play, the apportioned chargeable profits of CFCs are taxed on any UK resident company with an interest of 25% or more in the CFC, brought into that company's corporation tax computation and taxed at a rate equal to the main rate of corporation tax. The CFC charge is reduced by a credit for any foreign tax attributable to the apportioned chargeable profits.

As previously mentioned, the rules are also extended to permanent establishments where an election has been made to be treated as an exempt foreign branch.

The purpose of the rules is to target the CFC charge so that it is not applied to profits arising from genuine foreign economic activities, or where there has been no artificial diversion of UK profits.

The CFC regime applies to companies resident outside the UK that are controlled by UK residents. The rules define what is meant by UK control, including by reference to accounting standards. Under section 371AA Taxation (International and Other Provisions) Act 2010 (TIOPA 2010), any controlled foreign company is a CFC. A CFC is a company which is resident overseas but controlled by persons (including companies) in the UK as follows:

- the overseas company is more than 50% controlled by persons (including companies) in the UK; or
- the overseas company is at least 40% owned by a UK person (which may be a company), but is not more than 55% owned by a non-UK resident person (which may be a company).

Chapter 2 of Part 9A TIOPA 2010 sets out the steps for determining if a CFC charge arises. There is a CFC charge only if the following apply:

1. the CFC has "chargeable profits";
2. none of the CFC exemptions apply; and
3. there is a UK "interest holder" that is not exempt and that (together with connected companies) holds an interest of at least 25%.

Once it is established that a foreign resident company is a CFC, it is then necessary to consider if it meets either one of the CFC exemptions or if it has chargeable profits.

A CFC's chargeable profits are the part of its profits that pass through the "CFC charge gateway". The gateway is a series of definitions of profits that may fall within the CFC regime. So, while the CFC may be profitable, it may not have chargeable profits. However, even if the CFC does have chargeable profits it may still meet one of the exemptions under the legislation removing it from the CFC charge completely.

There are a number of "entity level" exemptions which, if they apply, will exempt all the profits from the CFC charge. These are:

1. Exempt period exemption (for foreign companies becoming CFCs for the first time)
   This applies for the first 12 months after a CFC comes under UK control provided any necessary restructuring is undertaken to ensure no CFC charge arises in the subsequent accounting period.
2. Excluded territories exemption (for CFCs resident in certain territories, subject to conditions).
3. Low profits exemption (for CFCs with low levels of profit).
   This applies if the total accounting or taxable profits of the CFC are less than £50,000; or if total accounting or taxable profits are less than £500,000, and of that non-trading income is less than £50,000.
4. Low profit margin exemption (for CFCs whose profit is no more than 10% of operating expenditure).
5. Tax exemption (for CFCs that pay at least 75% of the tax they would have paid in the UK).

The Irish corporate tax rate of 12.5% is well below 75% of the equivalent UK rate of 19%, i.e. 14.25%, so this exemption would not be met in relation to an Irish CFC such as Shed-It (Ireland) Ltd.

Even if one of these exemptions cannot be met it may still be the case that the CFC does not have chargeable profits. A number of gateway tests define the profits which are considered to have been artificially diverted from the UK and which therefore fall within the scope of the regime. An overseas company can rely on several safe harbours (e.g. by proving a commercial business exists in another jurisdiction) to show that profits are outside the scope of the regime

3. Calculation of CFC charge

Corporation tax of £61,241 is payable by Shed-It Ltd in respect of the CFC charge on its share of Shed-It Cyprus Inc.'s chargeable profits for the accounting period ended 31 March 2020 (see calculation attached).

As Shed-It Ltd is not required to pay corporation tax in quarterly instalments, this will be due for payment nine months and one day after the end of the 2020 accounting period, i.e. 1 January 2021. This CFC charge should be reported to HMRC on supplementary corporation tax return form CT600B.

I trust this information is useful, please contact me to discuss should anything be unclear.

Yours sincerely,

A.N. Accountant

SHED-IT LIMITED

Calculation of CFC charge for the year ended 31 March 2020

	£
Taxable profits	1,822,650
Chargeable under CFC legislation (60%)	1,093,590
Apportioned to Shed-It Ltd (56%)	612,410
CFC charge:	
UK corporation tax on Shed-It Ltd apportionment @ 19%	116,358
Less: creditable foreign tax	
£612,410 @ 10%	(61,241)
CFC charge payable	55,117

Question 8.4

With an irrevocable election, no charge to UK tax arises on the foreign branch profits. The computation is as follows:

Corporation tax computation: year ended 31 March 2020

	£
Trading profits	1,400,000
Corporation tax @ 19%	266,000

£79,412 (£450,000 × 100/85 – £450,000) withholding tax was paid on the exempt foreign income and this will not be relievable in the UK due to the election. However, tax of 4% has been saved on the foreign branch profits.

Without an irrevocable election, the computation would be as follows:

Corporation tax computation: year ended 31 March 2020

	£	£
Trading profits		1,400,000
Foreign income:		
$\frac{£450{,}000 \times 100}{85}$		529,412
Taxable total profits		1,929,412
Corporation tax @ 19%		366,588
Less: DTR – lower of:		
Foreign tax	79,412	
or		
UK tax on foreign income: £529,412 @ 19%	100,588	
		(79,412)
Corporation tax due		287,176

Chapter 9

Question 9.1

Corporation Tax Computation Period Ended 31 March 2020 – Z Ltd

	£
Trading income	NIL
Net credit from loan relationships	20,000
Total profits	20,000
Loss (under section 37(3)(a))	(20,000)
Taxable total profits	NIL

Corporation Tax Computation Period Ended 31 March 2020 – B Ltd

	£
Trading income	170,000
Deduct: losses forward under section 45	(16,000)
	154,000
Net credit from loan relationships	4,000
Property income	20,000
Total profits	178,000
Deduct: group relief surrendered by Z Ltd	(76,000)
Taxable total profits	102,000
Corporation tax £102,000 @ 19%	19,380
Loss memo	
Loss	96,000
Used against other income of current year	(20,000)
Surrendered under section 99 CTA 2010	(76,000)
Loss available	Nil

Question 9.2

A Ltd – Corporation Tax Computation Period to 31 March 2020

	£
Net credit from loan relationships	1,000
Property income	20,000
	21,000
Loss set-off	(21,000)
Taxable total profits	NIL

B Ltd – Corporation Tax Computation Period to 31 March 2020

	£
Trading income	56,000
Net credit from loan relationships	2,000
Property income	25,000
	83,000
Less: group loss surrendered by A Ltd	(69,000)
Taxable total profits	14,000
Corporation tax £14,000 @ 19%	2,660

C Ltd – Corporation Tax Computation Period to 31 March 2020

	£
Trading income	48,000
Less: losses forward	(26,000)
	22,000
Net credit from loan relationships	3,000
Property income	2,000
Taxable total profits	27,000
Corporation tax £27,000 @ 19%	5,130
Loss memo of A Ltd	
Trading losses brought forward	4,000
Loss – current year	90,000
Used against other income of current year	(21,000)
Claim section 99 balance of loss to B Ltd	(69,000)
Loss available to carry forward*	4,000

*The brought-forward trading loss of £4,000 can only be carried forward to set against future profits of the same trade as this is a trading loss pre-1 April 2017. Alternatively, part of the current-year loss of A Ltd could instead have been surrendered to C Ltd to reduce its total trading income to nil, or all of the losses could have been surrendered without utilising £21,000 against current year first.

Note that, as each company is paying corporation tax at 19%, alternative group relief solutions would yield similar results.

Question 9.3

	Queen Ltd	Rook Ltd	Pawn Ltd
	£	£	£
Profit/loss per accounts	199,313	(80,586)	(2,030)
Disallow:			
Depreciation	12,000	16,000	10,000
Entertainment	1,350	1,650	1,200
Interest (Note 1)	400	–	10,720
	213,063	(62,936)	19,890
Capital allowances	(7,375)	(5,627)	(3,000)
	205,688	(68,563)	16,890
Trading losses brought forward			(16,890)
	205,688	(68,563)	–
Net credit/(deficit) from loan relationships (Note 2)	23,846		(10,720)
	229,534	(68,563)	(10,720)
Group relief re. trading losses carried forward	(63,110)		
Group relief re. LR deficit	(10,720)		10,720
Group relief re. current-period trading losses (Note 3)	(68,563)	68,563	–
Taxable total profits	87,141	NIL	NIL

Corporation tax payable:

	£
Pawn Ltd	Nil
Rook Ltd	Nil
Queen Ltd	Nil

Taxable total profits = £ 87,141 @ 19% = £16,556.79 payable on or before 1 January 2021 (as none of the companies are paying corporation tax in instalments).

Notes:

1. The PAYE interest is not tax deductible.
2. The interest payable by Pawn Ltd is for a non-trading purpose and is, therefore, deductible as a loan relationship, rather than a trading expense. This deficit can be group-relieved to Queen Ltd.
3. The trading loss of Rook Ltd is available via group relief to be offset against the trading income of Queen Ltd.
4. It is assumed that the dividend received from the French company qualifies for one of the exemptions and is not therefore taxable.
5. The group has an overall deductions allowance of £5 million that can be used in any way. Hence there is no restriction in the use of the losses carried forward by any company as the total is below £5 million.

Chapter 10

Question 10.1

Sale in June 2019
The conditions to qualify for substantial shareholding exemption (SSE) are as follows:

Shareholding requirements

- The holding must have been substantial (i.e. at least 10%). This condition was met as at that time the holding was 100%.
- The substantial shareholding must have been held throughout a 12-month period in the six years before disposal. This conditions was also met as the shares have been held since 2005.

Investee condition

- Must have been a sole trading company or member of a trading group in the qualifying period (generally 12 months before disposal).

This condition was met as Kelly Luxury Cars GmbH was a trading company at the time of the disposal. As the disposal is not to a connected person, it does not matter that the company will be an investment company after the sale. Therefore SSE was available and the entire gain in June 2019 was exempt, saving corporation tax at the main rate of 19%. It should also be noted that the substantial shareholding does not have to be held in a UK resident company, so the German residence of the company is not an issue. There may also be foreign tax payable in Germany on the disposal and any tax thereon would not be available for double taxation relief in the UK as the gain is entirely exempt in the UK.

Proposed sale in May 2024
The 5% shareholding appears not to meet the substantial shareholding test as it is less than the 10% requirement.

However, as long as the 10% requirement is met throughout a 12-month period in the six years prior to the proposed disposal, then the disposal will qualify.

Hence the 5% disposal in May 2024 will also qualify for SSE, because in the six-year period prior to this (i.e. from 1 June 2018 to 31 May 2024) there was a 12-month period where the company held at least 10% of the shares in the subsidiary (i.e. it held 100% of the shares from 26 June 2018 until 25 June 2019).

If the remaining 5% shares are to be sold at a loss, no capital loss will arise as the loss is also subject to SSE.

We would recommend delaying the transaction until after May 2025, when the substantial shareholding requirement required for SSE will not be meet and a capital loss will crystallise, which can be used by the company against any current period chargeable gains or carried forward to be utilised in the future (carry back is not possible).

Question 10.2

REPORT TO THE BOARD OF DIRECTORS

Solar Group Corporation Tax Position – Accounting Period Ended 31 March 2020

Introduction

(a) The group's corporation tax liability for the year ended 31 March 2020 is £35,110 and is payable to HMRC by 1 January 2021. None of the companies in the group have taxable total profits in 2020 in excess of £300,000 (£1,500,000/5), hence corporation tax was not due on an instalment basis. The computation of the group's corporation tax liability for the year ended 31 March 2020 is included below.

(b) (i) The calculation of the chargeable gain on the disposal of Solar's investment in Saturn is included below. The gain after indexation allowance is £335,750. Ordinarily, Solar would have been assessed to tax on this gain at the main rate of corporation tax, being 19%.

However, under the substantial shareholdings exemption (SSE) legislation, there is an exemption from tax on gains and losses made by companies on the disposal of shares. There are a number of conditions that must be satisfied to qualify for the relief.

The main exemption will apply where a company makes a disposal of all or part of a substantial shareholding of shares in a trading company or member of a trading group. For this purpose, substantial means at least 10% of the ordinary shares of the company concerned, together with an entitlement to at least 10% of:

- the profits available for distribution to equity holders; and
- the assets available to equity holders in a winding up.

Trading company means a company carrying on trading activities whose activities do not include, to a substantial extent, activities other than trading activities. Substantial in this context is not defined, although in common with other tax reliefs, 20% is typically taken as the benchmark. The shares must have been held for a continuous 12-month period in the previous six years prior to the disposal.

Based on the above, Solar would appear to satisfy the conditions so that the gain on the sale of the shares in Saturn will be exempt from corporation tax on the potential capital gain arising of £335,750.

(ii) *Degrouping charge*

The calculation of the chargeable gain arising from the transfer of the property from Solar to Saturn, as a result of Saturn leaving the group is included below. When Saturn ceases to be subsidiary of Solar, it will be deemed to have sold the freehold property acquired from Solar at the date it was originally acquired from that company (i.e. March 2015). The deemed sale proceeds will be the market value at that time.

A gain of £126,500 will be deemed to have been made by Solar in March 2015 under TCGA 1992 section 179 (referred to as a degrouping charge) by virtue of the fact that where a company leaves a group and has, within the six years ending at the time, acquired an asset from another group member, the company leaving is treated as having sold the asset when it was acquired from the other group member at its market value at that time and immediately reacquired it.

Although computed as if the asset had been disposed of in March 2015, the gain is regarded as arising at the start of the accounting period in which Saturn leaves the group and would ordinarily be charged corporation tax at the rate applicable to that accounting period.

Under the legislation, where a degrouping event takes place, the degrouping charge arising is treated as deemed proceeds on the disposal of the relevant shares for calculating the gain or loss on the disposal of the shares. A consequence of this is that SSE is also available on the degrouping charge, meaning both the chargeable gain on the share sale and on the £126,500 degrouping charge are fully exempt from corporation tax.

(c) (i) *Proposed property transfer*

The proposed transfer of the property from Solar to Neptune will not give rise to a chargeable gain arising for Solar even though the sale to an independent third party would result in a capital gain of £100,000 by virtue of the fact that Neptune is a wholly-owned subsidiary of Solar and assets transferred between both companies are treated as transferred on a no gain, no loss basis under section 171 TCGA 1992 (i.e. no gain will be deemed to have arisen).

Corporation tax on the capital gain will therefore be deferred until such time as the asset is sold outside the group or if Neptune leaves the groups within six years, subject to the rules for degrouping charges.

(ii) *Sale of Neptune property*

The disposal of the property currently occupied by Neptune will be a disposal outside the group giving rise to a chargeable gain in Neptune. To mitigate the gain arising, advantage can be taken of TCGA 1992 section 171A. Neptune can jointly elect with Solar, within two years of the disposal, that the property is deemed to be transferred on a no gain, no loss basis to Solar with Solar being deemed to make the disposal. This enables the group to use the £200,000 capital losses of Solar against the capital gains of Neptune without having to physically transfer ownership of the asset intragroup before making the disposal outside the group.

Alternatively, if advantage of capital loss relief available from say Solar is not taken, the chargeable gain may be rolled over or held over against a qualifying acquisition by Neptune or a qualifying acquisition by another group company. The usual 12 months before and three years after rules relating to rollover relief would apply.

(d) *Acquisition of Mars*

The group should be aware that anti-avoidance legislation is in place to prevent companies buying other companies and taking advantage of existing trading losses. These provisions disallow the carrying forward of trading losses incurred before a substantial change in ownership of the company's shares. The disallowance will apply if there is a change in the ownership of the company and either:

- there is a major change in the nature or conduct of trade carried on by the company within five years (beginning no more than three years before the change in ownership); or
- at any time after the change in ownership, the scale of activities of the trade carried on by the company has become small or negligible.

Given that the board of directors intends to make significant changes to the products sold, customers and markets, it is possible that (b) above would apply and the £500,000 losses would not be available to carry forward. These would be effectively wasted. We would recommend that the exact changes proposed are reviewed in more detail, taking into account HMRC guidance in this area before a decision to purchase Mars is made, as the availability of these losses should be factored in to the price paid for the company. We would also stress that even if the acquisition of Mars does not fall foul of this specific anti-avoidance rule, if there is any suggestion that the Mars acquisition is being undertaken to access these losses, then relief will also be denied. If this anti-avoidance rule does not apply, note that pre-acquisition losses cannot be group-relieved until a five-year period has elapsed.

SOLAR GROUP

Computation of corporation tax liability year ended 31 March 2020

	Solar	**Neptune**	**Venus**	**Saturn**	**Mercury**
	£	£	£	£	£
Trading profits	67,550	47,087	72,680	82,793	0
Chargeable gains			8,260		
Current year loss offset		(47,087)			
Profits before group relief	67,550	0	80,940	82,793	0
Less: group relief	(2,760)	0	(20,940)	(22,793)	0
Taxable total profits	64,790	0	60,000	60,000	0
Corporation tax @ 19%	12,310		11,400	11,400	**Total £35,110**

Workings

Working 1: Trading profits – Saturn

	£
Profits before capital allowances	112,559
Capital allowances	(29,766)
	82,793

Working 2: Trading loss – Neptune

	£
Loss b/f	75,000
Current year offset	(47,087)
Loss c/f	27,913

Neptune's trading loss is pre-1 April 2017 and can only be offset against future trading profits from the same trade. The group has a £5 million deductions allowance to utilise losses carried forward – the amount to be potentially offset is below the allowance and so can be fully used.

Working 3: Loss memorandum – Mercury

	£
Adjusted loss	46,493
Group relief:	
Solar	(2,760)
Venus	(20,940)
Saturn	(22,793)
Remaining	Nil

Working 4: Capital gain – Venus

The capital gain of Venus (£55,260) will be reduced by capital losses brought forward (£47,000), leaving an amount assessable to corporation tax of £8,260. (Note that treating the capital gain in Venus as reallocated to Solar under the rules for chargeable gains relating to groups of companies would have been correct also. It does not matter how the losses are group relieved as each company is paying corporation tax at 19%.)

SOLAR GROUP

Chargeable gain on sale of Solar's shares in Saturn

	£
Proceeds	300,000
Deemed proceeds: degrouping charge	126,500
Cost	(55,000)
Gain before indexation allowance	371,500
Indexation allowance: £55,000 @ 65%	(35,750)
	335,750

Chargeable gain arising on property transferred to Saturn as a result of Saturn leaving the group within six years – degrouping charge

	£
Deemed proceeds – March 2015	230,000
March 1982 market value	(50,000)
Gain before indexation allowance	180,000
Indexation allowance: £50,000 @ 107%	(53,500)
Gain after indexation allowance	126,500

Chapter 11

Question 11.1

(a)

DELANEY ELECTRICS (UK) LIMITED

Corporation Tax Computation for Accounting Period Ended 31 March 2020

	Notes	£	£
Profit/(loss) before tax			968,825
Add back:			
Depreciation		155,250	
Amortisation	4	12,000	

Legal and professional fees	3	3,559	
Repairs and maintenance	5	20,000	
Insurance	6	6,200	
Corporation tax penalty and interest	8(a)	6,000	
Customer entertaining	8(b)	1,000	
Leased car restriction	8(c)	1,148	
Management charge – transfer pricing adjustment	12	100,000	
			305,157
Deduct:			
Movement in general provision for bad debts	7		(10,000)
Rental profit	9		(29,160)
Dividend income	10		(60,000)
Profit on disposal of patent rights	11		(110,000)
Capital allowances			(92,324)
Adjusted trading profit			972,498
Taxable Total Profits:			
Trading profits			972,498
Property business profits	9		29,160
Total profits			1,001,658
Less: surplus NTLRD	8(a)		(2,500)
Taxable total profits			999,158

Notes:

1. Depreciation on finance-leased assets is deductible for corporation tax.
2. Statutory redundancy payments are always deductible. The ex gratia payment of £17,000 is also allowable, as this does not bring the total payment of £23,000 to more than four times the statutory amount (£6,000 × 4 = £24,000).
3. Legal fees in relation to the HMRC corporation tax enquiry are not tax deductible as the enquiry outcome was not in the company's favour and thus the cost is not wholly and exclusively for the purposes of the trade of the company. Legal fees re. the case against the supplier are wholly and exclusively for the purposes of the trade and so are deductible. Legal fees re. issue with tenants of leased property are not trading expenses but expenses of the rental business. The required adjustment is taken account of in the rental profit deduction line in the computation.
4. As the goodwill was acquired after 8 July 2015 but before 1 April 2019, the company is not entitled to a deduction for the £12,000 amortised in the period.
5. Repairs of the leased-out commercial premises are not trading expenses but expenses of the rental business. The required adjustment is taken account of in the rental profit deduction line

in the computation. The extension to the trading premises is capital and not revenue and must be added back, but it should be considered if any of the expenditure qualifies for capital allowances.

6. As the keyman policy is not wholly and exclusively for the purposes of the trade, the premiums must be added back. Insurance in respect of the rented portion of the property is not a trading expense but a rental expense. The required adjustment is taken account of in the rental profit deduction line in the computation. Public liability and directors' leased car insurance are incurred wholly and exclusively for the purpose of the trade and are thus tax deductible.
7. Increase in bad debt provision calculated in accordance with IFRS is tax deductible. However, the general provision has decreased by £10,000 and as this would have been added back previously a deduction is available.
8. Sundry expenses:
   (a) Penalties and interest in relation to the HMRC enquiry are not wholly and exclusively for the purpose of the trade and thus not deductible for trade purposes. However, the corporation tax interest is allowed later as a non-trade debit.
   (b) Drinks, food and entertainment at the party is entertaining customers and suppliers and is therefore disallowed.
   The branded top is allowed for corporation tax as each:
   - individually cost under £50; and
   - bears the business name, logo or a clear advertisement; and
   - does not consist of food, drink or tobacco.

   (c) A restriction is applied to the cost of leased cars where CO_2 emissions are > 130g/km for leases entered into between April 2013 and April 2018. The limit is 110g/km from April 2018.
   The restriction re. the BMW 6 Series is £7,650 × 15% = £1,148
9. Rental profit

	£
Rental income	40,000
Less expenses:	
Professional fees	(5,000)
Repairs and maintenance – rented building	(3,465)
Insurance – rented building	(2,375)
Rental profit	29,160

10. As the company is not small under the dividend exemption rules, the dividend income is exempt from corporation tax as it was received in respect of ordinary shares.
11. Under the corporate intangibles regime, the profit on the sale of patent rights would usually be taxed as trading income. However, as the entire proceeds on the sale of intangible fixed assets (patent rights) have been reinvested in other intangible fixed assets (copyrights) for use in the trade within a three-year period after the disposal, £110,000 (£260,000 – £150,000) can be rolled over/deferred until sale of the new copyrights. Therefore only £75,000 (£150,000 – 75,000) is taxed as trading income now and the remaining £110,000 profit is deducted.

12. As the arm's length price is £200,000 an additional amount of £100,000 arises under the transfer pricing rules because Delaney UK has received a tax advantage and Delaney UK and Delaney Ireland are under common control.
13. Bank interest payable in relation to an overdraft to fund working capital requirements is trading in nature and therefore a deductible expense in the calculation of trading profits.

(b) Corporation tax – loss in 2022

The company will cease to trade in the 2022 accounting period and is projected to make a trading loss of £1,792,000 that will be extinguished on cessation of the trade as it has no current-year income in 2022 to offset it against, and it is not possible to carry the loss forward as there will be no future profits (and no future trade).

Under the terminal loss relief rules, the trading loss of the final 12 months of the trade in 2022 can be carried back against the total profits of the previous three years. Losses are relieved first against total profits of the year ended 31 March 2021, followed by the year ended 31 March 2020 and then against 12 of the 18 months results for the accounting period ended 31 March 2019.

The table below summarises how Delaney (UK) may claim terminal loss relief to reduce its taxable total profits for the years ended 31 March 2019–2021 inclusive.

		Accounting Periods	
	31 March 2021	**31 March 2020**	**18 months ended 31 March 2019**
	£	£	£
Trading profit	60,000		500,000
Property income	75,000		67,000
Surplus NTLRC	70,000		
Chargeable gains	175,000		
Taxable total profits	380,000	999,158	567,000
Less: terminal loss relief	(380,000)	(999,158)	(378,000)
Revised taxable total profits	Nil	Nil	189,000

Loss Memo

	£
Loss y/e 31/03/22	1,792,000
Less: terminal loss relief against	
31 March 2021	(380,000)
31 March 2020	(999,158)
12 months ended 31 March 2019 (£567,000 × 12/18)	(378,000)
Unused – extinguished on cessation	34,842

Chapter 12

Question 12.1

Salary versus Dividend

Scenario 1 – Company perspective

Payment of a gross bonus of £100,000	£
Bonus	100,000
Add: employer's NIC @ 13.8%	13,800
	113,800
Less: corporation tax saved @ 19%	21,622
Cash cost to the company	92,178

Payment of a gross dividend of £100,000

The payment of a dividend by a company is from after-tax profits. Therefore there is no further tax cost or saving on the payment of dividend and the cash cost to the company is £100,000.

Scenario 2 – Tax position of Clara

Receipt of a gross bonus of £100,000			£
Bonus			100,000
Less: income tax:	£25,000 @ 40%		10,000
	£75,000 @ 45%		33,750
Employee's NICs @ 2%			2,000
Net cash received by Clara			54,250
Receipt of a gross dividend of £100,000			
Gross dividend			100,000
Income tax	£2,000 @ 0%	£0	
	£23,000* @ 32.5%	£7,475	
	£75,000 @ 38.1%	£28,575	
			36,050
Net cash received by Clara			63,950

* Gross remuneration £125,000, therefore £25,000 left of higher rate band. However, when Clara receives a dividend, £2,000 of the dividend she receives is deemed to use up £2,000 of her remaining £25,000 higher rate band, hence only £23,000 is available against the £100,000 dividend.

Overall

Dividend	£
Cost to the company	100,000
Tax cost to the company	–
Net receipt by Clara	(63,950)
Net cost	36,050
Bonus	
Cost to the company	100,000
Tax cost to the company	13,800
Tax saved on the bonus	(21,622)
Net receipt by Clara	(54,250)
Net cost	37,928

Payment of a dividend is more tax-efficient by £1,878.

Question 12.2

Mr and Mrs Andrews
Andrews Transport Limited
Any Road
Any Town
15 March 2020

Dear Mr and Mrs Andrews,

Remuneration Strategy

Further to our meeting of last week, please find attached my analysis of the current remuneration structure of Andrews Transport Limited ("ATL") and my proposed changes to it under the following headings:

- Salary
- Dividends
- Pension planning
- Recommendations

When planning to benefit from tax-free payments in the future, it is important to bear in mind that that tax law can change and impact the rules and benefits in these areas.

When you have considered the opportunities outlined in the attached, please contact me so that we can decide how you will proceed with implementing any changes.

Changes to the remuneration structure of ATL – improving tax efficiency

1. *Salary Payments*
   - At present you, Mr Andrews, are the sole member of your family to be paid a salary by ATL, despite the fact that Mrs Andrews and the Andrews children also work in the business.
   - At present you receive a salary of £100,000 per annum from ATL. As Mrs Andrews does not receive a salary from the company, you can only avail of one personal allowance and one basic rate band of £37,500. I would recommend considering making salary payments to Mrs Andrews and possibly reducing your own salary. Making salary payments to Mrs Andrews will allow you to avail of another personal allowance and another basic rate band of up to £37,500.
   - I also recommend making salary payments to your children to reward them for their part-time work in the business. Payments up to the personal allowance of £12,500 in 2019/20 would represent tax-efficient remuneration for your children. But you must be aware of national minimum wage legislation and that details of the salary should be reported to HMRC under Real Time Information. The National Insurance implications should also be addressed.
   - ATL could receive a corporation tax deduction at 19% for the gross salary payments plus employer's NIC to both Mrs Andrews and your children.

2 *Dividends*
   - As shareholders in ATL, both you and Mrs Andrews are entitled to receive dividend payments from the company. Assuming that both of you are receiving the maximum salary payments possible from ATL, you will be liable to income tax at 32.5% on the dividend received from ATL (or 38.1% if your taxable income was greater than £150,000). You are

also each entitled to a £2,000 dividend allowance, meaning the first £2,000 of dividend income is tax-free.

- Unlike with salary extraction, there is no NIC on dividend payments.
- ATL will not receive a corporation tax deduction for the dividends paid to you.
- Dividends tend to be more tax efficient than salary/bonus, but there are other non-tax considerations to be addressed.

3 *Pension Planning*

- I would also recommend increasing the pension contributions to your pension fund. This could be done by you or ATL. The funding by you personally could be up to the level of your salary. You can contribute up to £40,000 per year to your pension scheme (known as your 'annual allowance') and receive tax relief on the contribution. The annual allowance for those earning above £150,000 reduces on a tapering basis so that it reduces to £10,000 for those earning above £210,000. For every £2 of income above £150,000, an individual's annual allowance reduces by £1.
- It may also be possible to use any unused annual allowance from the past three financial years. This is likely to be relevant in your case as only low pensions contributions have been made to date through your company pension. It is possible to contribute more than the allowance but no tax relief will be given on the contributions and you may be subject to the annual allowance charge.
- Alternatively, ATL could make the contribution. If this is done, then this limit does not apply. The limit on the contributions by the company is the funding required to pay your pension, subject to an overall fund limit of approximately £1.055 million.
- As your pension is underfunded, there should not be an issue of a limit on the contributions that ATL can make. Your pension advisor could advise regarding this pension issue. ATL should get a corporation tax deduction for the contributions it makes to your occupational pension fund (subject to the spreading provisions). Also, contributions are only deductible if paid.
- In addition, the pension scheme is exempt from income tax and capital gains tax in respect of assets held in the fund.
- On retirement you can take a tax-free lump sum from the pension fund equal to 25% of the pension fund. Withdrawals from the pension scheme are taxed as emoluments and are subject to tax at your marginal rate.
- An associated benefit of the pension contributions is that they extract cash out of the company to you/your pension fund. This should prove to be tax efficient for you from a capital gains tax perspective if you wish to sell the business in the future, as the company's available cash will have been extracted by you at a minimum tax cost and the value for CGT purposes on a sale will reflect the value of the business and assets only and therefore could qualify in full for entrepreneurs' relief.

5 *Recommendations*

- There are opportunities for you to save tax by rewarding yourself and your family adequately for the work that you do for the company. ATL should pay your two children for their work. This will lead to a saving for you as you will not need to fund them because of their earnings from ATL, i.e. instead of you funding them from income taxed at 40% they will fund themselves from income not taxed if kept within their personal allowances.
- Mrs Andrews should be paid for the work she does for ATL. This will allow her to use the full basic rate band and possibly benefit from termination payment relief at a later time.

- Consideration needs to be given to whether dividends should be paid.
- Consideration should be given to increasing your salary to maximise any pension contributions. If a large pension contribution is envisaged, it would be more tax efficient for ATL to make the payment rather than you personally.

Chapter 13

Question 13.1

1. Maurice – CGT Computation 2019/20

	£	£
Sale proceeds		80,900
Incidental costs of disposal		(750)
Net proceeds		80,150
Deduct:		
Base cost	20,000	
Costs of acquisition	600	
		(20,600)
Chargeable gain		59,550
Less: annual exemption		(12,000)
Taxable gain		47,550
CGT liability:		
£37,500 − £36,115 = £1,385 @ 18%		249.30
£47,550 − £1,385 = £46,165 @ 28%		12,926.20
Total		13,175.50

As the holiday home is residential property, the gain does not attract the 10% or 20% rate of CGT.

2. Vincent – CGT Computation 2019/20

	£	£
Sale proceeds		9,800
Deduct: allowable cost		
Market value at 31 March 1982	1,200	
		(1,200)
Chargeable gain		8,600
Less: annual exemption		(8,600)
Taxable gain		Nil

£3,400 of annual exemption is wasted.

Question 13.2

1. James – CGT Computation 2019/20

	£	£
Sale proceeds		650,900
Deduct: allowable costs:		
Market value at 31 March 1982	230,000	
Enhancement expenditure – July 1994	10,000	
		(240,000)
Chargeable gain		410,900
Less: annual exemption		(12,000)
Taxable gain		398,900
CGT @ 20%		79,780

Note: the gain is taxable at 20% as the level of James's taxable income for 2019/20 exceeded the basic rate band threshold and the asset disposed of is not residential property.

2. Declan – CGT Computation 2019/20

	£	£
Sale proceeds		400,900
Deduct: allowable costs:		
MV 31 March 1982	55,000	
Expenditure August 1984	20,000	
Expenditure February 2003	39,250	(114,250)
Chargeable gain		286,650
Deduct: annual exemption		(12,000)
Taxable gain		274,650
CGT @ 18% of £5,000 (i.e. £37,500 – £32,500)		900
CGT @ 28% of £269,650 (i.e. £274,650 – £5,000)		75,502
Total CGT payable on 31 January 2021		76,402

Question 13.3

Capital Gains Tax Computation 2019/20

	£
Sale proceeds	80,000
Less: selling costs	(2,600)
	77,400
Less: cost	
$\frac{80{,}000}{80{,}000 + 145{,}000} \times £18{,}000$	(6,400)
Chargeable gain	71,000
Less: annual exempt amount	(12,000)
Taxable gain	59,000
Taxable as follows:	£
£37,500 − £30,715 = £6,785 @ 10%	679
£59,000 − £6,785 = £52,215 @ 20%	10,443
CGT liability	**11,122**

The above liability falls due for payment on 31 January 2021. The base cost of the remaining land is £11,600 for any future disposal. The disposal does not qualify as a small part disposal of land as the various conditions are not met.

Chapter 14

Question 14.1

(a) Janet is not resident in 2019/20 as she meets an automatic overseas test, in that she was resident in one or more of the previous three tax years and visits the UK for fewer than 16 days in the current tax year.

(b) Paul is resident in 2019/20 as he does not meet an automatic overseas test but does meet an automatic UK test in that he is present in the UK for at least 183 days in the tax year.

(c) Victor is not resident in 2019/20 as he meets an automatic overseas test, in that he works full time overseas and visits the UK for fewer than 91 days, with the number of days in the tax year on which he works for more than three hours in the UK being less than 31.

(d) Christine is resident in 2019/20 as she does not meet an automatic overseas test but does meet an automatic UK test, in that she has a home in the UK for more than 90 consecutive days (of which at least 30 days fall in the tax year), more than 30 days are spent there in the tax year and she has no home overseas.

(e) Terry is not resident in 2019/20 as he meets an automatic overseas test, in that he was non-resident in all of the previous three tax years and visits the UK for fewer than 46 days in the current tax year.

(f) Margaret is resident in 2019/20 as she does not meet an automatic overseas test but does meet an automatic UK test. This is because:
   - she carries out full-time work in the UK for a period of 365 days, with no significant break (i.e. at least 31 days) and all or part of that 365-day period falls within the tax year;
   - more than 75% of the total number of days in the 365-day period when more than three hours per day are worked in the UK; and
   - at least one day in the tax year is a day on which she works more than three hours in the UK.

   Margaret may be entitled to split-year basis in her year of arrival to the UK (2019/20) and the year of departure (2020/21).

(g) As Ned does not meet any of the automatic overseas tests or any of the automatic UK tests, residence will depend upon the number of UK ties that the he has and the number of days spent in the UK.

   Ned is resident in the UK in the tax year 2019/20 by meeting the sufficient ties test in that:
   - he spent between 121 and 182 days in the UK; and
   - he has a sufficient UK tie (90-day tie), having spent more than 90 days in the UK in one or both of the previous two tax years.

   As a leaver, Ned only required one tie to be resident in 2019/20.

Question 14.2

Jessica states that she left the UK in June 2016 and intends to return by December 2020.

As Jessica had always lived in the UK before June 2016, she would have been resident in the UK for four out of the seven tax years prior to the tax year of departure. This means that, unless she remains outside of the UK for a period of more than five complete years commencing from her date of departure, she will be treated as if she had remained resident in the UK for CGT purposes under section 10A TCGA 1992.

The period between June 2016 and December 2020 includes only four complete years.

If Jessica returns when she intends to later this year, she will be charged to UK CGT on the gain made on the disposal of the painting she inherited from her aunt in 2013. She will be treated as if the gain arose in the 2020/21 tax year and the CGT will be payable by 31 January 2022. The CGT liability could be as high as £46,000 ((£750,000 – £520,000) × 20%, assuming the current rates of CGT remain the same), though the CGT annual exemption will be available in the year of her return. Jessica will be responsible for advising HMRC of the gain by either contacting the self-assessment helpline or completing and submitting a form SA1 and submitting her 2020/21 tax return by 31 January 2022.

These rules do not apply to assets acquired whilst overseas, so the gain on the disposal of the Australian flat will not be caught under section 10A TCGA 1992. However, if Jessica were to become tax resident in the UK before she disposes of the flat, the gain will fall within the UK CGT net though principal private residence relief may be available under section 222 TCGA 1992. The "90-day" test would have to be met in relation to the Australian property. Jessica could avoid this and a CGT liability on the painting sold during her time in Australia by simply delaying her return to the UK until after June 2021, at which point she will have been non-resident for more than five complete years.

Question 14.3

(a)

Capital gains tax position under the arising basis

	£
Foreign chargeable gain	220,300
Less: annual exempt amount	(12,000)
Chargeable gain	208,300
CGT @ 28%	58,324

Under the arising basis of taxation, an individual who is UK resident is taxed on the arising basis on their worldwide income, hence Sophia would be taxable on the foreign chargeable gains in full in addition to her employment income.

Capital gains tax position under the remittance basis

	£
Remitted foreign chargeable gain	25,000
CGT @ 28%	7,000
Remittance basis charge	60,000
Total CGT	67,000
Additional income tax on employment income	5,000
Overall tax bill under remittance basis	72,000

As Sophia is not UK domiciled, she can elect to be taxed on the remittance basis. However, as she is a long-term UK resident (resident in more than 12 out of the last 14 tax years), she is required to pay £60,000 as a remittance basis charge. Under the remittance basis, Sophia loses entitlement to both the capital gains tax annual exempt amount and the £12,500 personal allowance for 2019/20 (resulting in additional income tax of £5,000 (i.e. £12,500 × 40%)). Therefore it would be more beneficial for Sophia to be taxed on the arising basis as the tax payable would be £13,676 lower.

(b) If Sophia was UK resident since 6 April 2001, in 2019/20 she will have been UK resident for 15 of the previous 20 tax years. She would therefore be deemed UK domiciled for UK CGT purposes and would only be taxable under the arising basis. The remittance basis would not be available. As calculated above, the UK CGT arising would be £58,324.

Question 14.4

Anytown Tax Advisors
Anytown

Catarine Martinique
Anyplace
Anytown

Dear Catarine,

Capital gains tax
This letter addresses the issues requested and is based on the information provided to us.

First, you are UK resident in 2019/20 under the statutory residence test as you meet the first automatic UK test, i.e. you are present in the UK for 183 days, you also do not meet any of the automatic overseas tests. As you are UK resident you are automatically taxed on the arising basis in respect of the foreign capital gain. A calculation of this is included below. CGT under the arising basis amounts to £128,884.

As you are French domiciled, and not deemed UK domiciled for UK CGT purposes, you can elect instead to be taxed on the remittance basis in 2019/20. This would mean only the £240,000 of the foreign gain remitted to the UK would be subject to UK capital gains tax (CGT). However, you would forgo both your UK personal allowance and UK CGT annual exemption in 2019/20 as a result.

As you are also classed as long-term UK resident, you would also be required to pay the £60,000 remittance basis charge having been resident in the UK for 12 out of the 14 tax years prior to 2019/20. A calculation of CGT under the remittance basis is also included below. Overall a CGT liability of £127,200 would arise in addition to additional income tax of £5,625 as a result of the lost personal allowance.

Consequently, you should not elect to be taxed on the remittance basis as you would pay additional UK tax of £3,941. Under the arising basis you will be free to remit the remaining proceeds to the UK at your leisure.

I look forward to discussing the above matters in more detail when we next meet, please give me a call at your convenience to arrange a meeting.

Yours sincerely,

A.N. Accountant

Catarine – 2019/20 arising basis of taxation

Capital gains tax

	£
Gain on Parisian apartment	472,300
Less: annual exemption	(12,000)
Taxable gain	460,300
Capital gains tax @ 28%	128,884

Catarine – 2019/20 remittance basis of taxation

Capital gains tax

	£
Remitted gain on Parisian apartment	240,000
Less: annual exemption	(Nil)
Taxable gain	240,000
Capital gains tax @ 28%	67,200
Remittance basis charge	60,000
Capital gains tax liability	127,200
Plus additional income tax	
£12,500 @ 45%	5,625
Total tax payable	132,825

Question 14.5

Anytown Tax Advisors
Newry

Annette Stewart
Anyplace,
Anytown

Dear Annette,

This letter addresses the UK capital gains tax position of the Lough Erne property disposal by you and is based on the information provided to us.

Broadly, an individual who is UK tax resident is taxed on the arising basis of taxation, which would mean that the disposal of the Lough Erne property would be subject to UK capital gains tax (CGT) of up to 28% on any chargeable gain arising.

Under Section 2(1) TCGA 1992, residence in the UK drives chargeability to UK CGT. Therefore we first need to establish if you are UK resident for tax purposes in 2019/20, the tax year of the disposal.

As you live in the US and have not been in the UK for six years it is likely that you will meet the second of the automatic overseas tests (non-resident in all of the previous three tax years and spends fewer than 46 days the UK in current tax year) and are thus not UK resident in 2019/20. Therefore, on first review, it would appear that you are not subject to UK CGT on this disposal.

However, a non-resident person disposing of UK residential property is subject to UK CGT. Thus this disposal by you as a non-resident person is caught, the Lough Erne property clearly being residential.

There are three possible approaches to the NRCGT calculation. Non-resident persons are free to choose whatever is the most tax-efficient calculation for them. The different methods of calculation are outlined below.

Method 2 would result in the lowest NRCGT gain, of £118,643. Clearly, this method should be chosen to report the gain. After the 2019/20 CGT annual exemption of £12,000 is deducted, the remaining gain of £106,643 is taxable at 28% as you use up all of your basic rate band every year. The resultant CGT liability is therefore £29,860.04.

I look forward to discussing the above matter in more detail when we next meet. Please give me a call at your convenience to arrange a meeting.

Yours sincerely,

A. N. Accountant

CHARGEABLE GAINS CALCULATIONS

Method 1 – rebasing

	£
Net proceeds	650,000
Less: market value at 5 April 2015	(360,000)
NRCGT chargeable gain	290,000

Method 2 – straight-line time apportionment

	£
Net proceeds	650,000
Less: cost	(425,000)
NRCGT gain over period of ownership	225,000

continued overleaf

Time-apportioned post-5 April 2015 gain @ 52.73%*	118,643

* Total ownership is 110 months, period from 6 April 2015 to disposal was 58 months, 52.73% (58/110 × 100) of ownership relates to period from 6 April 2015 to disposal on 6 February 2020.

Method 3 – calculation over whole period of ownership

	£
Net proceeds	650,000
Less: cost	(425,000)
NRCGT gain over period of ownership	225,000

Chapter 15

Question 15.1

Shauna Quinn – CGT 2019/20

	Painting	Vase	Shop	Land	Total
	£	£	£	£	£
Chargeable gains	47,000	0	126,800	55,000	228,800
Capital losses current year					(8,000)
Capital losses c/fwd					(208,800)
Net chargeable gains					12,000
Annual exemption					(12,000)
Chargeable gains					Nil

	£
Capital losses b/fwd	210,000
Used against 2019/20 gains	208,800
Capital losses c/fwd	1,200

Workings

1. Painting – as proceeds are more than £6,000 and cost is less than £6,000, the gain is the lower of:

   (i) the actual gain; or
   (ii) 5/3 of the gross proceeds.

   Actual gain is:

	£
Proceeds	50,000
Less: costs of sale	(500)
Net proceeds of sale	49,500
Less: cost	(2,500)
Chargeable gain	47,000

   5/3 of gross proceeds = 5/3 × (£50,000 − £6,000) = £73,333.

   Therefore the gain is £47,000.

2. Antique vase

	£
Proceeds:	4,000
Deem gross proceeds to be £6,000	6,000
Less: costs	(14,000)
Loss	(8,000)

3. Freehold shop – the transfer from Darren to Shauna is a no gain/no loss transfer. The base cost for Shauna is therefore £55,000. The value of the unit at the date of the transfer is irrelevant.

	£
Proceeds	185,900
Less: costs of sale: Legal fees	(2,250)
Estate agents fee	(1,850)
Net proceeds of sale	181,800
Less: cost	(55,000)
Gain	126,800

4. Land

	£
Proceeds	80,000
Less: costs	
$£40,000 \times \frac{80,000}{80,000 + 48,000}$	(25,000)
Gain	55,000

The small disposal rules do not apply.

5. Car – exempt from capital gains tax.

6. Capital losses – the current-year capital losses must be used in their entirety against any available current-year gains and in priority to any capital losses carried forward. However, the capital losses carried forward can be tailored in how they are used so as not to waste any of Shauna's annual exempt amount. Only £208,800 of the capital losses carried forward are used and Shauna will have capital losses carried forward to 2020/21 of £1,200.

Question 15.2

MEMO

From: An Accountant
To: John Smith
Date: 3 July 2019
Subject: Outline of UK capital gains tax system

As discussed in our recent meeting, I have outlined below the basic principles of the UK capital gains tax system. Please do not hesitate to contact me if you have any queries in relation to this memo.

(a) Capital gains tax is payable in the UK at a flat rate of 10% on chargeable gains in the available basic rate band (£37,500 in 2019/20) with 20% charged on gains in excess of the basic rate band. Note that gains on residential property are taxed at 18% within the basic rate band and 28% thereafter. A rate of 10% is also available on any gains qualifying for entrepreneurs' relief, e.g. sale of shares in a personal trading company up to the lifetime limit per individual of £10 million, or investors' relief (qualifying gains on or after 6 April 2019 only). As you have income in excess of £100,000, any chargeable gains would be taxed at 20% subject to the availability of entrepreneurs' relief or other reliefs that might apply.

(b) Any capital gains tax due for the year ended 5 April 2020 will be due for payment by 31 January 2021.

(c) The capital gains should be declared to HMRC by filing in the relevant sections in your self-assessment tax return for the 2019/20 tax year.

(d) Each individual has an annual exempt amount for each tax year which can be set against gains in that year. For 2019/20 the annual exempt amount is £12,000. This can be set against gains arising in the most beneficial way, i.e. against gains arising at 28% first, followed by gains at 20%, then those at 18% and finally against gains at 10% (including those qualifying for entrepreneurs' relief and investors' relief, which are also taxable at 10%).

(e) Indexation allowance is generally not available to individuals. Note that companies still receive indexation on capital assets they sell from the month of acquisition to the month of sale, but up to 31 December 2017 only.

(f) The following types of expenditure qualify as deductible for capital gains purposes:
- Consideration given wholly and exclusively for acquisition of the asset.
- Incidental costs of acquisition and incidental costs of disposal. These are limited to stamp taxes and professional fees directly related to the acquisition and/or sale.
- Expenditure incurred on enhancing the value of the asset that is reflected in the state and nature of the asset at the date of sale and expenditure in preserving or defending title to the asset.

(g) Unused capital losses are carried forward to set against capital gains arising in future periods. They cannot be carried back, except on death. However, as the capital losses will be used in periods after the period in which they arose, they can be partially set against gains arising to bring them down to the level of the annual exemption so that this is not wasted (rather than being used to reduce the gain to below the annual exemption or £Nil).

(h) If the asset had been sold to your brother, this would be a sale to a connected person. Therefore the capital loss would be 'ring-fenced' and could only be used against a capital gain arising on a sale of a capital asset to your brother either in the same tax year that the loss arose or in a future tax year. Such a loss could therefore not be used against general gains on sale of capital assets.

(i) The capital gains base cost of the rental property will be the probate value of the property. This is likely to be the market value of the property at the date of your grandmother's death.

(j) As you are 'connected' with your grandmother under the capital gains tax legislation, then the gift of the property to you would be deemed to occur at the market value of the property at the date of gift – which would then be your capital gains base cost. Gift relief under section 165 TCGA 1992 would not be possible as the gift of rental property is not a business asset. The gift before death would also have IHT consequences. At the time of the gift, it will be classed as a potentially exempt transfer. However, if your grandmother died the next day (which is within seven years), the gift (after deducting any available annual exemptions) would fall within her death estate potentially liable to IHT at 40%. Section 260 TCGA 1992 gift relief, which is available on non-business assets, would not be available here as the gift was not immediately chargeable to IHT in your grandmother's lifetime.

Chapter 16

Question 16.1

The house will have been James's principal private residence (PPR) as it was the only house he owned when he purchased it and he lived in it as a residence on acquisition.

Therefore the periods of qualifying ownership for PPR exemption are as follows:

- First three years (actual occupation).
- Last 18 months (always treated as a period of ownership).
- Years 4, 5 and 6.

These years qualify because there was actual occupation both before and after the period of absence, and the legislation contains a deemed period of occupation to cover three years of absence for any purpose.

The three years of deemed occupation are available even though the house was let in the period of absence. Thus, 7.5 years of ownership count as occupation and 2.5 years do not. The gain subject to tax is therefore £800,000 × 2.5/10 = £200,000.

However, as the property was let for residential purposes, letting relief is available to further reduce the chargeable gain that arises.

The letting relief is the **lower** of:

- gain arising in the letting period – this is £200,000;
- gain exempt under the PPR provisions – this is £600,000; or
- £40,000.

Thus, an additional £40,000 of the gain is exempt. The tax due is then calculated as follows:

	£
Gain after PPR relief	200,000
Less: lettings relief	(40,000)
	160,000
Less: annual exemption	(12,000)
Chargeable gain	148,000
Capital gains tax @ 28%	41,440

Question 16.2

Mr Jack Bates
Your Place
Your Town
Spain

24 June 2019

Dear Jack,
Further to our recent conversation, I have set out below responses to your queries regarding capital gains tax in relation to your UK property.

Principal private residence (PPR) relief

The general rule is that a gain on the disposal of an individual's only or main residence is exempt from capital gains tax. Grounds of up to half a hectare (approx. 1.24 acres) including the dwelling house, or larger areas that are appropriate to the size of the house, also qualify for the relief.

Full exemption applies where the owner has occupied the house throughout his entire period of ownership. Where occupation of the house has been only for part of the period of ownership, the exempt part of the gain is the proportion given by the following formula:

$$\frac{\text{Period of ownership post-31/03/1982}}{\text{Total period of ownership post-31/03/1982}} \times \text{Chargeable gain}$$

Where there is a delay of up to a year in taking up residence of a property (e.g. complicated sale, house built, redecorations, etc.) then the period of non-residence will count as a period of residence. Providing a property has been an individual's only or main residence at some time during his total ownership (whether before or after 31 March 1982), the last 18 months automatically count as a period of residence (this is 36 months in some specific cases).

Certain other absences also count as residence, if preceded and followed (not necessarily immediately before and after) by a period of actual residence and provided that relief is not being claimed for another main residence during the absence. These are:

- Up to three years for any reason.
- Any absence throughout which the individual is employed abroad.
- A total of up to four years of absence during which the taxpayer is working elsewhere in the UK (either employed or self-employed) such that they could not occupy their PPR.

There is further relief for owner-occupiers who, at any time during their period of ownership, have let all or part of the property as residential accommodation. This is known as "lettings relief". Lettings relief is restricted to the lower of:

- the gain accruing during the letting period;
- the part of the total gain that is exempt under the PPR provisions (including deemed periods of occupation); or
- £40,000.

CGT consequences of potential sale

I attach the capital gains tax calculation associated with the proposed sale of your Belfast property. You will note from same that the potential capital gain arising on disposal is £64,591, which would be taxed at 28% as you are an additional rate taxpayer.

Should you have any further queries in connection with the above, please do not hesitate to contact me.

Yours sincerely,
ABC & Co.
Chartered Accountants

Jack Bates

Sale of apartment

	£
Sale proceeds – July 2019	1,300,000
Cost	(65,000)
	1,235,000
Less:	
Exempt element of gain:	
259/286 × £1,235,000	(1,118,409)
Lettings relief:	(40,000)
Lower of £40,000	
Exempt gain of £1,118,409; and	
Letting gain:	
27/286 × £1,235,000 = £116,591	
Chargeable gain	76,591
Annual exemption	(12,000)
	64,591
CGT thereon @ 28%	18,085

Workings

Total duration of ownership:

01/09/1995–01/07/2019 – 286 months being as follows:

	Months	
01/09/1995–01/01/2003	88	
01/01/2003–30/04/2011	100	Letting
30/04/2011–31/01/2017	69	
31/01/2017–01/07/2019	29	Letting
	286	

Exempt proportion:	
Owner occupied	88 months
Deemed owner occupied	48 months (max.) + 3 years for any reason
Owner occupied	69 months
Last 18 months deemed	18 months
Total exempt portion	259 months

Chapter 17

Question 17.1

	£
Sales proceeds re: 2,500 shares	30,000
Cost: 2,500/6,450 × £21,225	(8,227)
Taxable gain	21,773
CGT @ 20%	4,354.60
Due for payment on 31 January 2021	

Note: as the disposal cannot be matched with any acquisition on the same day or the following 30 days, it must be matched with the section 104 holding, which is as follows:

Date		No. of shares acquired	Cost £
5/10/2001	Purchase	1,500	8,000
10/4/2004	Purchase	2,800	10,000
18/3/2006	Rights issue, 1 for 2 held at £1.50 per share	2,150	3,225
Section 104 holding		6,450	21,225

The average allowable cost per share is therefore £3.29.

Chapter 18

Question 18.1

	£
Meets Condition (1)	
Gain	900,000
CGT payable @ 10%	90,000

Question 18.2

ER not available – Condition (1) is not met, as she did not own business for at least two years prior to the disposal. The gain arising will be taxed at 20%.

Question 18.3

	£
Meets Condition (1)	
Gain	10,300,000
CGT:	
£10,000,000 @ 10%	1,000,000
£300,000 @ 20%	60,000
Total CGT	1,060,000

Note: gain exceeds lifetime limit of £10 million.

Question 18.4

ER not available – Condition (1) is not met as it is not a qualifying business, i.e. not a trade, profession or vocation. A letting of unfurnished property is not a furnished holiday let; therefore, it is a property letting under rental provisions and is not a trade. The gain arising of £240,000 will be subject to CGT at 28%; the liability will be £67,200.

Question 18.5

Meets Condition (2)	£
Net qualifying gain (£360,000 – £90,000) 2019/20	270,000
CGT @ 10%	27,000

Gain (on subsequent disposal) 2020/21	£
Condition (2) is met	72,000
CGT @ 10%	7,200

Question 18.6

ER not available as Condition (3) is not met. Must have at least a 5% interest. The gain arising of £3 million will be subject to CGT at a rate of 20%, resulting in a liability of £60,000.

Question 18.7

Meets Condition (1)	£
Gain	630,000
CGT @ 10% (2018/19)	63,000
Gain on second disposal (2020/21)	10,000,000
CGT @ 10% on £9,370,000 (i.e. £10m – £630,000 = £9,370,000)	937,000
CGT @ 20% on £630,000 (i.e. excess over lifetime allowance)	126,000
Total CGT 2020/21	1,063,000

Question 18.8

No chargeable gains arise on cessation as there is no disposal at that time. The actual disposal will qualify for ER as Patricia meets the criteria of Condition (2). If Patricia sold the property after 30 April 2022 instead, then no ER would be available.

Question 18.9

Meets Condition (1)	£
Gain	190,000
CGT @ 10%	19,000

Question 18.10

Report to James Devlin – Tax Implications of Recent Transactions

April 2020

Introduction

This report outlines the tax consequences of the disposal of both your shares in Devlin Communications Ltd and the Dungannon property. Both transactions constitute chargeable gains; therefore we have also considered reliefs available and outlined our recommendation that capital gains tax entrepreneurs' relief (ER) is claimed as this is available on both transactions (although only partially available on the Dungannon property disposal). ER reduces the rate of capital gains tax from the maximum rate for businesses from 20% to 10% and applies on a 'lifetime cap' of £10 million for qualifying gains. Your full lifetime limit of £10 million is available as these are the only assets you have ever owned.

Details of the timing of tax payments and of available elections and detailed calculations are also included.

Devlin Communications Ltd share disposal

To qualify for ER on a disposal of shares in a trading company or holding company of a trading group, the company must be your 'personal company', which means that you must be an officer or employee and must hold a 'material interest' of at least 5% of the ordinary share capital and voting rights in addition to holding 5% of the company's distributable profits and 5% of the assets on a winding up. These conditions must be fulfilled for a period of two years prior to the disposal.

You appear to meet all of these conditions as the company is a trading company, you were a director at the time of the disposal, you held 40% of the shares and you did so for a period of over two years prior to disposal. Therefore entrepreneurs' relief is available on this transaction.

Dungannon property disposal

ER is also available for the disposal of an asset owned personally by an individual if it can be 'associated' with a relevant 'material disposal'. Three conditions must be satisfied:

1. The individual makes a 'material disposal' of either the whole or part of their interest in the assets of a partnership or the shares in a company. Your disposal of your entire shareholding in Devlin Communications Ltd fulfils this condition.
2. The associated disposal is made as part of the withdrawal of the individual from participation in the partnership or the company. This condition is also clearly fulfilled as the Dungannon property disposal is tied into the share disposal.
3. The assets are in use in the business for two years ending with the earlier date of material disposal of (in this case) the shares in Devlin Communications Ltd. As the property was used and rented by Devlin Communications Ltd since 2009, this condition is also met.

4. The 5% condition is also met as you have disposed of your entire 40% shareholding in Devlin Communications Limited.

Therefore ER is available, however the amount of ER is restricted because the shop was not used throughout its entire period of ownership by Devlin Communications Limited, and is further restricted because a rent was payable by Devlin Communications Ltd – see Notes 2 and 3 of the calculation for further explanation.

Conclusion

As noted above, we recommend that ER is claimed. This represents a saving of £93,884 (i.e. (£1,200,000 – £12,000) × 20% less £143,716). You should note that ER is not automatic and must be claimed by the first anniversary of the 31 January following the tax year in which the gain arose. As both transactions happened in the 2019/20 tax year, the claims for ER on each must both be made by 31 January 2022.

The capital gains tax that arises on the gains, which totals £143,716, must be paid on or before 31 January following the end of the relevant tax year. Therefore the liability must be paid by 31 January 2021.

James Devlin

CGT position

	Shares	**Shop**
	£	£
Proceeds	851,000	475,000
Less: cost	(1,000)	(125,000)
Gains before relief	850,000	350,000
Less: gains on shop not eligible for ER £350,000 × 2/13 ths (Note 2)		(53,846)
		296,154
Less: restriction to ER for rent charged £296,154 × 70% (Note 3)		207,308
Gains eligible for entrepreneurs' relief	850,000	88,846
Total eligible gains (£850,000 + £88,846)	938,846	
Total gains not eligible for ER	261,154	
	1,200,000	
Less: annual exemption (Note 1)	(12,000)	
Chargeable gains	1,188,000	
Capital gains tax liability:	£	
£938,846 @ 10%	93,885	
£249,154 @ 20%	49,831	
Total CGT liability	143,716	

Notes

1. The annual exemption should be set against the gain subject to the highest tax (i.e. the gain not qualifying for ER (20%), rather than those qualifying for gains (i.e. 10%). This reduces the non-qualifying gains to £249,154.
2. The shop was only used in the business for 11 out of the 13 years of James' ownership. Therefore only 11/13ths of the gain on this associated disposal will qualify for entrepreneurs' relief and 2/13ths will not.
3. James received rent on the shop, which represented 70% of the market rent (£1,575/£2,250). Therefore the gain eligible for entrepreneurs' relief is further restricted by 70%.

Chapter 19

Question 19.1

This is Sarah's personal company as she owns at least 5% of the company and its voting rights. The assets are broken down between chargeable business assets and chargeable assets as follows:

	Market value @ 01/02/2019	**Chargeable business assets**	**Chargeable assets**
	£	**£**	**£**
Goodwill	410,000	410,000	410,000
Land and buildings	470,000	470,000	470,000
Plant and machinery	2,500	Exempt	Exempt
MV	4,000	Exempt	Exempt
Debtors	40,000	n/a	n/a
Stock	3,000	n/a	n/a
Cash	500	n/a	n/a
Rental property	120,000	n/a	120,000
	1,050,000	880,000	1,000,000

(a)

		£
Proceeds – deemed		
Proceeds		1,050,000
Less: cost		(50,000)
Gain		1,000,000
Less: gift relief	$1,000,000 \times \frac{880,000}{1,000,000}$	(880,000)
Taxable gain		120,000
Annual exemption		(12,000)
		108,000

(b) Base cost for Emily under (a):

	£
Market value	1,050,000
Less: gift relief	880,000
Base cost	170,000

(c)

	£
Gain	1,000,000
Annual exemption	(12,000)
Taxable gain	988,000

(d) Base cost for Emily under (c):

	£
Base cost = Market value	1,050,000

Question 19.2

Áine Taylor
Belfast

26 November 2019

Dear Áine,
I refer to our recent meeting in relation to the proposed factory disposal. I have outlined the information requested below:

(a) Tax due

UK capital gains tax will be payable on the sale of the factory. The calculation below indicates that, in the absence of suitable reliefs, capital gains tax of £197,600 will be payable.

As you are trading as a sole trader, this tax will be payable by you personally. As the disposal will be made in the 2019/20 tax year, the capital gains tax will be payable on or before 31 January 2021. As you are an additional rate taxpayer, the rate of capital gains tax is 20% before any reliefs. This is calculated as follows

	£
Proceeds	1,500,000
Less: base cost	(500,000)
Taxable gain	1,000,000
Less: annual exemption	(12,000)
Taxable gain	988,000
Tax @ 20%	197,600

(b) Rollover relief

Rollover relief is available when a sole trader such as yourself sells a capital asset which is in their trade and uses the sales proceeds to acquire one of a number of specified assets that is immediately brought into use in the trade.

Qualifying assets include:

- Land and buildings.
- Goodwill.
- Fixed plant and machinery.
- Ships, aircraft, hovercraft, satellites, space stations, spacecraft, milk/potato/fish/ewe quotas, suckler cow premiums and payment entitlements under the agricultural subsidy Basic Payment Scheme.

However, the asset acquired does not have to be the same as the asset sold.

Rollover relief is only available if the new asset is acquired in the period twelve months before and three years after the date the factory is sold. If you are unsure when the new investment will be made, as long as it is within the three years from disposal (i.e. by 8 November 2022) a provisional claim for relief can be made. In addition, it would be recommended that you review expenditure in the year prior to disposal (i.e. from 9 November 2018 to 8 November 2019) to check if any qualifying spend was incurred in that period.

In order for full rollover relief to be available, the entire proceeds of sale of the first asset must be reinvested in the second asset.

If all of the proceeds on the sale of the factory (i.e. £1,500,000) are not fully reinvested, a gain equal to the lower of:

- the full gain (i.e. £1,000,000); or
- the cash retained

is left chargeable. If the amount of cash retained exceeds £1,000,000, then no rollover relief may be claimed. So for every £1 of cash that is not reinvested (up to £1,000,000 not reinvested), £1 of the gain is subject to capital gains tax. Therefore, rollover relief will only be available in respect of every pound reinvested over £1,000,000.

The gain rolled over reduces the capital gains base cost of the new asset by the amount of that gain.

Rollover relief must be claimed in writing to HMRC within four years after the **later** of:

- the end of the tax year in which *disposal of the old asset* took place (i.e. by 5 April 2024); or
- the end of the tax year in which *acquisition of the new asset* took place.

In your case, if reinvestment did not occur until 8 November 2022, the date for the claim for relief would be 5 April 2027. The earliest date a claim would be due will always be 5 April 2024 even if you had reinvested in sufficient qualifying assets in the period 9 November 2018–8 November 2019.

You should note that holdover relief is another form of deferral relief that may be available should you decide instead to lease property instead of purchasing a freehold investment.

(c) Enterprise Investment Scheme relief

On the basis that Shoe Manufacturer Ltd is a qualifying company, it may be possible to claim Enterprise Investment Scheme (EIS) deferral relief on the gain on disposal of the factory if you subscribe for shares in this company.

Relief given under EIS deferral is the lower of:

- the gain itself (i.e. £1,000,000);
- the amount specified in the claim (compared to rollover relief which cannot be tailored); or
- the amount subscribed for new shares in the EIS company.

This is a significant difference from rollover relief as only £1,000,000 would need to be subscribed for shares in the company for the capital gains tax on the gain to be fully deferred. Under rollover relief, the entire £1,500,000 would need to be reinvested to fully rollover the gain.

However, whereas rollover relief reduces the base cost of the new asset, under EIS relief the capital gain is merely deferred and will crystallise when certain specified events occur (normally on the sale of the shares). Rollover relief does significantly reduce the base cost of the new asset when disposed of in future, unless it is again replaced with a further qualifying asset.

Again, the relief will only be available if the shares are subscribed for within the period 12 months before to three years after the date the factory is sold.

EIS deferral relief must be claimed in writing to HMRC within five years from the tax filing deadline for the tax year in which the shares were issued. So if you reinvested £1,000,000 in Shoe Manufacturers Ltd shares in 2019/20, the claim should be made on or before 31 January 2026.

There are also a number of other valuable reliefs available under the EIS, including income tax relief at 30% on the initial investment (assuming you will not hold 30% or more of the shares) and capital gains tax relief on their eventual disposal if they are held for a minimum three-year period.

I hope this is helpful. However, if you have any queries please give me a call.

Yours sincerely,

A.N. Accountant

Chapter 20

Question 20.1

Mr Andrew Jameson
Andrewstones Limited

11 December 2019

Dear Andrew,
As requested, we have set out below the tax consequences of the proposed purchase by the company of your shares in Andrewstones Ltd.

(a) Conditions for capital gains treatment

If the following conditions are met, the share buy-back of an unquoted trading company (which Andrewstones Ltd is) will be treated as a capital transaction taxable as a capital gain on you. We have also assessed whether, in the case of the proposed transaction, each of the conditions below is met:

- *Wholly or mainly for the benefit of the trade and not in the course of a scheme whose main purpose is the avoidance of tax.*
  In Statement of Practice 2/82, HMRC accepts the circumstances in which the trade benefit test will be met. The company's sole or main purpose in making the payment must be to benefit a trade carried on by it or by its 75% subsidiary. If the purpose is to ensure that an unwilling shareholder who wishes to end his association with the company does not sell his shares to someone who might not be acceptable to the other shareholders, the purchase will normally be regarded as benefiting the company's trade. Included within the examples of unwilling shareholders are a controlling shareholder who is retiring as a director and wishes to make way for

new management. Therefore the trade benefit test should be met in this case. In addition, there is no suggestion that the transaction is being undertaken for a tax avoidance motive.

- *Vendor must be UK resident when the shares are bought back.*
  You have always been UK resident and there is no suggestion that this will change in any respect, hence this condition will be met.
- *Vendor must have owned the shares for the preceding five years (three years if acquired on death).*
  You have held the shares since 1991, clearly satisfying the five-year ownership test.
- *Must make a substantial reduction in shareholding: after-sale vendor and associate's interest must be reduced to 75% or less of interest before disposal.*
  You are disposing of 100% of your shareholding and thus clearly meet this condition. We do not count your son John's 25% shareholding as the shareholding of an associate in this case because John is not a minor.
- *After the transaction the vendor must not be connected with the company (or any company in the same 51% group). Connected means one can control more than 30% of the ordinary share capital, issued share capital and loan capital or voting rights in the company or is entitled to 30% of the assets of the company if it were to be wound up.*
  You will no longer hold any shares in the company, hence this condition will be met.

OR

- *If the buy-back facilitates the payment of an IHT charge within two years of the death of the individual whose death gave rise to the liability crystallizing.*
  This does not apply in this case.

On the basis of the above, it would appear that each of the necessary conditions are met in order to obtain capital treatment. However, please be advised that it is possible to obtain HMRC advance clearance that capital treatment will apply to the transaction. We would recommend that this clearance procedure is availed of to provide more certainty given the significant tax saving to be achieved (£253,800 capital gains tax versus £971,550 income tax distribution ignoring the dividend allowance).

(b) Anticipated CGT liability

It is expected that entrepreneurs' relief is available to reduce the rate of CGT on the gain from 20% to 10% because you have disposed of a 75% shareholding in a personal trading company. The company is a trading company and you have held a shareholding of more than 5% for a two-year period (75% shareholding since 1991). You also meet the director/officer condition, thereby enabling a 10% rate of CGT. We are not aware of you having used your lifetime limit for entrepreneurs' relief and assume the full lifetime limit of £10 million is available. On this basis, you will have CGT liability of £253,800. The full calculation is given below.

	£
Proceeds: 75,000 × £35	2,625,000
Less: original cost	(75,000)
	2,550,000
Less: annual exemption	(12,000)
Chargeable gain	2,538,000
CGT @ 10%	253,800

(c) Consequences if capital treatment is not obtained

If capital treatment is not obtained, any payment the company makes in respect of its shares will be treated as an income distribution (i.e. a dividend), apart from the amount that represents repayment of the nominal value of the shares.

We understand that you originally subscribed £75,000 for 75,000 £1 shares in 1991. As such, if the company paid you £2,625,000 in exchange for these shares and capital gains tax treatment was not obtained, then you would be treated as in receipt of a cash dividend of £2,550,000. As you are an additional rate taxpayer (because your income is over £150,000), tax of £971,550 (dividend additional rate of 38.1%; your £2,000 dividend allowance is assumed to have already been used by the £10,000 dividends you receive annually from other sources) would be payable. No capital gain/allowable loss arises on the £75,000 that is treated as the repayment of the nominal value of the shares as this would already have been taxed under the income tax rules as a distribution.

(d) Stamp duty

Please also be aware that the company (Andrewstones Limited) will be subject to stamp duty tax on the share buy-back in the amount of £13,125, being 0.5% of the £2,625,000 proceeds that the company will pay for the shares. There is a 30-day time limit after execution (when the share transfer documents are dated and signed by all parties) for getting the document stamped and paying the required stamp duty. If the share transfer document is not presented to the Stamp Office until after 30 days from the date the transaction is executed, then a late filing penalty and interest may be charged.

I hope the above is helpful, however if you have any questions, please do not hesitate to contact us.

Yours sincerely,

A.N. Accountant

Question 20.2

(a)

The Directors and Mrs Sarah Donaldson
Maddon Engineering Limited

11 March 2020

Gentlemen and Mrs Donaldson,

Re: Company buy-back of shares

First, may I once again extend my condolences on the recent death of Aaron.

I refer to our recent discussions in relation to the forthcoming share buyback by Maddon Engineering Limited ("Maddon"). You also requested information explaining the tax treatment, together with an explanation (with associated calculations) of how Sarah will be taxed and whether the capital treatment is available.

Tax legislation specifies that if the consideration payable by Maddon for the shares exceeds the amount of capital originally subscribed for them, the excess will constitute an income distribution unless the capital treatment applies. In this case, the consideration for the shares clearly exceeds the original consideration, as Maddon will be paying £1,500,000 to Sarah for the shares (10,000 shares

× £150 per share). As Sarah received the shares from her husband, her base cost is the original base cost when Aaron bought them and not their market value.

From Sarah's perspective, the buy-back is a taxable disposal. Essentially there are two possible tax treatments i.e. taxable as a capital gain or taxable as an income distribution. Calculations for each treatment are outlined below. As and as you can see the capital treatment is more favourable due to the lower rate of tax – 20% compared to an effective rate of 38.1% under the income treatment.

The remainder of this letter therefore assesses whether the capital treatment is available as Sarah has indicated the transaction will not proceed unless this is available.

Share buy-back – capital treatment

The capital treatment only applies where:

- *The repurchase is by an unquoted trading company whose trade does not consist of dealing in shares, securities, land or futures.*
  Maddon is a trading company, therefore this condition is met.
- *The repurchase is wholly or mainly for the benefit of the trade.*
  Sarah does not wish to retain the shares she received from Aaron just before his death – HMRC is likely to accept this scenario as meeting the wholly or mainly for the benefit of the trade test.
- *The shares must be bought back from a UK resident vendor who has held the shares for at least five years (three years if acquired on a death).*
  On 4 April 2020, Sarah will not have held the shares for three years; however Aaron's ownership period can also be taken into account. As he acquired the shares in the 1990s, this test is clearly met. Sarah is also UK resident; therefore the residence test is also met.
- *The vendor must, as a result of the buy-back, reduce his or her interest in the company by at least 25%.*
  Sarah is disposing of the entire shareholding, hence this condition is met.
- *The vendor must not be connected with the company following the buy-back. The vendor will be treated as connected with the company if they either possess, or are entitled to possess, more than 30% of the issued ordinary share capital, loan capital, or voting power, or are entitled to receive more than 30 % of the assets on a winding up of the company.*
  Sarah will no longer be connected with the company as she will hold no shares after the transaction is completed, therefore this condition is met.
- *The share buy-back is not undertaken solely for tax avoidance reasons.*
  There does not appear to be any tax avoidance motive and hence this condition appears to be fulfilled.

Based on all of the above, the capital treatment will be available for the transaction and will provide a tax saving for Sarah of £271,328. More certainty can be obtained by applying to HMRC in advance for clearance.

Stamp duty

Please also be aware that the company, Maddon Engineering Limited, will be subject to stamp duty on the share buyback in the amount of £7,500, being 0.5% of the £1,500,000 proceeds that the company will pay for the shares. If the buy-back occurs on 4 April 2020, the stamp duty payment and filing deadline will be 4 May 2020.

If you have any further questions, do not hesitate to contact me.

Yours sincerely,

A.N. Accountant

Calculation of CGT /income tax liability re: share buy-back

Income treatment

	£
Amount received on share buy-back (10,000 × £150)	1,500,000
Less: original subscription price	(10,000)
Gross dividend received	1,490,000
Gross dividend	1,490,000
Less: dividend allowance	(2,000)
Taxable dividend credit	1,488,000
Income tax due at 38.1%*	**566,928**

*Sarah is an additional rate taxpayer so the dividend additional rate applies.

Under the income treatment, Sarah will also have a capital gains disposal as follows:

CGT calculation

	£
Proceeds	1,500,000
Less: cost	(10,000)
Capital gain	1,490,000
Less: amount subject to income tax as a distribution	(1,490,000)
Chargeable gain	Nil

Capital treatment

Sale proceeds (10,000 × £150)	1,500,000
Less: cost	(10,000)
Chargeable gain	1,490,000
Less: annual exemption (2019/20)	(12,000)
Taxable gain	1,478,000
CGT payable @ 20%	**295,600**

Sarah is not an employee or director, therefore entrepreneurs' relief is not available to reduce the gain arising.

(b) Briefing note

To: Any Partner
From: A.N. Accountant
Date: 25 March 2020
Subject: Shares in Maddon Engineering Limited

Further to my recent conversations with Sarah, this briefing note addresses the IHT and ethical implications in respect of the chargeable lifetime transfer.

1. Availability of BPR for the Maddon shares

BPR will be available at the rate of 100% on the 10,000 shares held by Aaron at the date of his death. This is due to the fact that they qualify as shares in an unquoted trading company. There is no minimum holding requirement, so the fact that Aaron only held one-third of the shares has no impact. As the shares have been held since the 1990s, the two-year holding period requirement is also met. BPR is also fully available as there are no excepted assets on Maddon's statement of financial position.

However, even if BPR was not available it should be noted that no inheritance tax (IHT) liability would arise as the shares are being transferred to Sarah on Aaron's death and are thus fully exempt from IHT under the spousal exemption.

The value of the shares to be included in Aaron's estate is therefore calculated as follows:

10,000 shares × £150 per share	£1,500,000
Less: 100% business property relief	(£1,500,000)
Value in death estate	£NIL

2. IHT and ethical implications re. the chargeable lifetime transfer

The transfer of cash to the discretionary trust comes within the relevant property regime and IHT should have been paid thereon in lifetime as follows:

Lifetime IHT

December 2016	£	£
Gift to discretionary trust		500,000
Annual exemption – 2016/17		(3,000)
Annual exemption – 2015/16		(3,000)
Chargeable lifetime transfer		494,000
Inheritance tax threshold – 2016/17	325,000	
Less: cumulative chargeable transfers in the previous seven years	0	
Available inheritance tax threshold	325,000	
Less: nil rate band		(325,000)
Chargeable lifetime transfer		169,000
Lifetime IHT thereon @ 20%		33,800

On lifetime transfers, the primary liability for payment lies with the donor (unless the donee agrees to pay tax), though Andrew would have delegated responsibility of this to the trust. In such a scenario the lifetime IHT is 25%.

As the gift was made in December 2016, the liability was due for payment on or before 30 June 2017. Interest and penalties will arise for failure to pay this liability.

The gift is also required to be included in Aaron's death estate as it was made in the previous seven years. IHT arises as follows:

Death estate		
December 2016		£
Gift to discretionary trust		500,000
Annual exemption – 2016/17		(3,000)
Annual exemption – 2015/16		(3,000)
		494,000
Inheritance tax threshold – 2019/20	325,000	
Less: cumulative chargeable transfers in the previous seven years	Nil	
Less: available inheritance tax threshold		(325,000)
		169,000
Inheritance tax:		
£169,000 @ 40%		67,600
Taper relief @ 20%		(13,520)
Lifetime tax paid		(33,800)
Additional IHT payable on death		20,280

Please note that Sarah has suggested that if the transfer to the trust fails to be included in Aaron's estate, she would like us to turn a blind eye to this as she believes HMRC have no way of finding out about this. On the basis of the foregoing, the transfer to the trust is required to be included**.** As you know, it would be unethical to omit this from the inheritance tax return and, under the *Code of Ethics* of Chartered Accountants Ireland, we cannot do as Sarah wishes.

Could I suggest that when we next meet we agree how best to approach this with Sarah. I would also suggest that we take the opportunity to discuss with Sarah the importance of ensuring that the inheritance tax return is complete and the potential penalties that could arise for failure to include all relevant items.

Chapter 21

Question 21.1

(a) The transfer of value made by Mr Grey for IHT under the related property rules is calculated as follows:

Value of shares before transfer (78,000 × £35) × 50,000/78,000	£1,750,000
Value of shares after transfer (48,000 × £14) × 20,000/48,000	£(280,000)
Value transferred	£1,470,000

The unrelated value should be used if this produces a higher figure. In this case the unrelated value is lower and is calculated as follows:

Value of shares before transfer 50,000 × £14	£700,000
Value of shares after transfer 20,000 × £8	£160,000
Value transferred	£540,000

Thus the transfer of value for inheritance tax is £1,470,000.

(b) Anne has received the shares by way of gift from her father. Anne is treated as a connected person under section 286 TCGA 1992, hence Anne's base cost of the shares in Grey Properties Ltd is deemed to be their open market value. On the basis of receiving a 30% shareholding which is valued at £14 per share, Anne has a base cost for capital gains tax of £420,000 (30,000 shares × £14). A claim for gift relief is not possible as the company is an investment company.

(c) If Mr Grey dies within 38 months, the gift valued at £1,470,000 (which was originally a PET) after deduction of exemptions will fall within his death estate as he has survived less than seven years. However, taper relief of 20% would be available.

Question 21.2

In cases where assets (other than shares) are owned jointly by husband and wife, and one spouse makes a transfer of value for inheritance tax purposes, the value transferred is calculated as below.

	£
Value before transfer:	
£800,000 × [£375,000/(£375,000 + £110,000)] (Note 1)	618,557
Value after transfer:	
£500,000 × [£250,000/(250,000 + £110,000)] (Note 2)	(347,222)
Transfer of value	271,335

Note 1:
Six chairs are worth £800,000, Stephanie has four of these.
Four chairs are worth £375,000.
Martin's two chairs are worth £110,000.

Note 2:
Five chairs are worth £500,000. Stephanie has three of these.
Three chairs are worth £250,000.
Martin's two chairs are worth £110,000.
The unrelated value of one chair is £50,000, which is lower; hence the related value is used for IHT purposes.

Question 21.3

(a) Gift of shares in family company to daughter
Yes, this is a transfer of value because it is a gift. The transaction would also have capital gains tax implications as a transaction with a connected person. Gift relief may be available.

(b) Sale of a painting to a local art dealer
No, this would not be a transfer of value because it is a genuine arm's length transaction between the parties, there is no gratuitous intent and there is no loss to the original donor as cash has replaced the asset.

(c) Payment of daughter's school fees
No, this would not be a transfer of value. While the donor's estate would be reduced, there is no associated gratuitous intent as this constitute's maintenance of the individual's family.

(d) Purchase of Lamborghini from a local car dealership
No, this would not be a transfer of value because it is a genuine arm's length transaction between the parties and there is no loss to the original donor as a car has replaced the money paid for it.

(e) Gift of an investment property to a family trust
Yes, this is a transfer of value because it is a gift. The transaction would also have capital gains tax implications.

Question 21.4

(a) Zelda's domicile of origin is outside the UK. As she has not been resident in the UK for at least 15 of the 20 tax years immediately before the relevant tax year, being 2019/20 (she has been UK resident for 14 tax years (2005/06 to 2018/19)), she remains non-UK domiciled and is only subject to inheritance tax on a transfer of her UK assets.

(b) Willem has acquired a UK domicile of choice and is therefore subject to inheritance tax on transfer of both his UK and overseas assets.

(c) Cerys is no longer UK domiciled but she remains UK deemed domicile for three years after changing her domicile status in November 2018 and is therefore subject to inheritance tax on transfer of both her UK and overseas assets. It may be advisable to delay transferring her foreign assets into the UK resident trust until after November 2021, at which point she will be not be deemed UK domiciled. However, at that point Cerys would still be subject to IHT on the transfer of any UK assets. It should be noted that should Cerys become deemed UK domiciled for IHT purposes under the formerly domiciled resident provisions, trust property is not excluded property at any time in the relevant tax year.

Question 21.5

Currently Penny's domicile is a domicile of origin in the United Kingdom, as an individual acquires their mother's domicile at birth where their parents are unmarried. This means that should Penny die before she leaves the UK, she will be UK domiciled for IHT purposes at that time and subject to inheritance tax on all her worldwide assets, including the London property and the Italian property inherited from her mother. This would also apply to any gifts in lifetime. This is the most robust form of domicile and can only be displaced by acquiring a domicile of choice.

Penny plans to emigrate to Australia before the end of 2020; she plans to cut off all remaining ties with the UK. This is suggestive that Penny intends to acquire a domicile of choice in Australia by being both physically present there **and** sufficiently evidencing the intention of staying there permanently. There will be a heavy burden of proof on Penny to demonstrate to HMRC that she has displaced her domicile of origin in the UK with a domicile of choice in Australia.

This is because if Penny is not UK domiciled she will only be subject to UK IHT on her UK assets (including the London property if she still owns it at the time) with relief available for any inheritance tax she might pay on her UK assets in Australia. However, the deemed domicile rules are also relevant. These mean that any individual previously UK domiciled will be considered to be UK domiciled for UK IHT purposes (only) for three years after they cease to be UK domiciled. So if Penny permanently leaves the UK for her new domicile of choice in Australia in December 2020, she will remain UK deemed domicile for IHT until December 2023. Once again, all of her worldwide assets will be caught.

In addition, where a non-UK domiciled individual has been resident in the UK for 15 of the previous 20 tax years immediately before the relevant tax year and the individual was UK resident in at least one of the four tax years ending with the relevant tax year, deemed domicile will again apply. At the point that Penny becomes non-UK domiciled in December 2023, she will only have been non-UK resident for three complete tax years (2023/24, 2022/23 and 2021/22 as in 2020/21 she will have been UK resident until the date of her departure), meaning she will have been UK resident for 15 of the previous 20 years of assessment and she was UK resident in 2020–21, one of the four tax years ending with 2023–2024. Penny remains deemed domicile under this rule until 5 April 2025. Four complete tax years of non-residence are therefore required to shake off deemed domicile. Thereafter, Penny will be non-UK domiciled for IHT purposes and only subject to UK IHT on any UK situs property with credit available for any IHT she may also pay on those assets in Australia.

Should Penny become resident in the UK after acquiring her domicile of choice in Australia, she is also at the risk of becoming deemed domicile under the formerly domiciled resident rule. This would catch her worldwide assets and the assets of any non-UK trust established while she is non-UK domiciled.

Chapter 22

Question 22.1

At the time of the transfer by Sean in July 2019, the value transferred of £1,500,000 is exempt to the extent of £325,000 only as Gita is non-UK domiciled and a PET to the extent of £1,175,000. Sean dies less than seven years later in June 2022, meaning the failed PET is chargeable and, after deducting the nil rate band, £850,000 is subject to tax. No taper relief is available because Sean died less than three years after the original gift.

The £200,000 transfer by Gita in January 2021 was a transfer of excluded property under section 6(1) IHTA 1984 by a non-UK domiciled individual holding non-UK property. Following Sean's death, Gita has the choice of electing to be treated as deemed domiciled in the UK. If she does so, the gift from Sean in 2019 will become fully exempt as a transfer where both spouses are domiciled in the UK. This would result in an IHT saving of £340,000 (£850,000 × 40%).

However, Gita will then be treated as deemed domiciled in the UK from 2019 for all IHT purposes. This means that the £200,000 transfer to the trustees would no longer be one of excluded property and will be subject to UK IHT. As a transfer to a trust, it will be immediately chargeable to tax as a chargeable lifetime transfer at the date of the deemed spousal election. The relevant IHT return will be due for filing within 12 months from the end of the month of the election and the IHT payment due (if any) within six months of the end of the month of the election. However, it will be fully covered by the nil rate band.

It seems that an election would be worthwhile given the tax saving of £340,000, however Gita will need to consider all the consequences of making an election in the context of her entire asset portfolio.

Question 22.2

- The land valued at £80,000 gifted to her daughter Ana is reduced to £69,000 by applying the marriage exemption of £5,000 for a marriage gift to a child and annual exemptions of £3,000 for each of 2018/19 and 2019/20.

- The gifts to her grandchildren are likely to be fully exempt as 'normal expenditure out of income', as they are habitual, paid out of surplus income and presumably Annette is able to maintain her usual standard of living.
- The first £325,000 of the gift from Annette to Stefan is exempt as it is from a UK domiciled to a non-UK domiciled spouse. Stefan may wish to consider electing to be deemed domicile as £55,000 constitutes a transfer of value by his wife.

Chapter 23

Question 23.1

Lifetime IHT arises as follows:

	£
Cash gift – April 2016	400,000
Less: annual exemption:	
2016/17	(3,000)
2015/16	(3,000)
Net gift	394,000
Less: 2016/17 NRB	(325,000)
Chargeable transfer	69,000

Primary responsibility for any lifetime IHT rests with the donor unless Frederick specifically requests as a term of the gift that the donee bears the IHT. Thus IHT due in lifetime is 20/80 × £69,000 = £17,250.

Should Frederick die on 10 April 2019, additional IHT falls due on the gift on death as follows:

	£
Net gift including lifetime tax	411,250
Less: 2019/20 NRB	(325,000)
	86,250
IHT @ 40%	34,500
Less: taper relief (3–4 years) @ 20%	(6,900)
	27,600
Less: lifetime IHT paid	(17,250)
Additional IHT on death	10,350

Chapter 24

Question 24.1

(a) Relevant business property means:
  (i) A sole trader's business, or a partnership share, including professions and vocations.
  (ii) Unquoted securities of a company which, together with any unquoted shares of the company (including related property in both instances), give the transferor control immediately before the transfer.

   (iii) Any unquoted shares in a company.
   (iv) Quoted shares and/or securities of a company that, together with any related property, give the transferor control immediately before the transfer.
   (v) Any land or building, machinery or plant owned outside the business which, for the two years before the transfer, was used wholly or mainly for the purposes of a business carried on by a company of which the transferor then had control or by a partnership of which the individual then was a partner.
   (vi) Any land, buildings, machinery or plant that, immediately before the transfer, were used wholly or mainly for the purposes of a business carried on by the transferor and were settled property in which he was then beneficially entitled to an interest in possession.

   Shares on the Alternative Investment Market (AIM) are treated as unquoted.

(b) A business, or an interest in a business, or shares in or securities of a company, are not relevant business property if the business, or as the case may be, the business of the company, consists wholly or mainly of:
   (i) Dealing in securities, stocks or shares (except for market makers and discount houses).
   (ii) Dealing in land or buildings.
   (iii) Making or holding investments.

(c) The relief applies to transfers of value in lifetime or on death, the value attributable to relevant business property being reduced by 100% in respect of (a) (i) to (iii) above and 50% in respect of (a) (iv) to (vi).

Question 24.2

(a) Agricultural property relief is available on the transfer of agricultural property. This includes agricultural land or pasture; woodland and any building used in the intensive rearing of livestock or fish if the occupation of the woodland or building is ancillary to that of the agricultural land or pasture; and also such cottages, farm buildings and farmhouses occupied with the agricultural land as are of a character appropriate to the property.

   The provisions for agricultural property relief are very similar to the rules for business property relief, in that the agricultural value is reduced by 100%. Agricultural property relief is given at the rate of 50% where the land is let to a farmer and the lease was signed before 1 September 1995 and there is still more than two years left to run on the lease. If any of these conditions are not met, then 100% relief is due. Where a farmer runs a farming business, business property relief may be available to cover any market value not otherwise covered by agricultural property relief. Therefore agricultural property relief should be applied first.

(b) Agricultural property relief is available on the transfer of shares or debentures in a farming company, provided that the holding gave the transferor control of the company immediately before the transfer and the agricultural property forms part of the company's assets. Relief is given only on that part of the value of the holding that reflects the agricultural value of the underlying property. The rate of relief is 100%.

   Business property relief is available on the non-agricultural value of a holding where the relevant conditions are satisfied at 100% on holdings in unquoted farming companies and at 50% on quoted controlling holdings.

Question 24.3

Transfer to Discretionary Trust

Tax due on gift in June 2016

	£
Gift	500,000
Less: two annual exemptions (2016/17 and 2015/16)	(6,000)
Less: nil rate band for 2016/17	(325,000)
Taxable	169,000
Taxable @ 25% (as grandmother paid the tax due to presumption in law)	42,250
Total value transferred as a result of gift	536,250

Additional tax now due on death

	£
Initial transfer of value	536,250
Less: nil rate band for 2019/20	(325,000)
Chargeable on death	211,250
Inheritance tax due @ 40%	84,500
Less: taper relief (20% as 3–4 years between gift and death)	(16,900)
Tax due	67,600
Less: lifetime tax paid	(42,250)
Tax now due	25,350

Payable by trustees of estate

Gift of family home is now a failed PET and is chargeable to IHT

	£
Value of gift	600,000
Less: two annual exemptions of £3,000 (2018/19 and 2017/18)	(6,000)
Value now chargeable (no nil rate band remains)	594,000
Inheritance tax due @ 40%	237,600

Payable by Chris personally

The residence nil rate band is not available as this is a lifetime and not a death transfer.

Death Estate

	£	£
Rental properties (Note 1)		525,000
Cash – UK bank account		250,000
Cash – IoM bank account		40,000
Art	250,000	

continued overleaf

Less: associated debt (Note 2)	(50,000)	
		200,000
Holiday home in Iceland	78,000	
Less: allowable probate costs (max. 5% so restricted)	(3,900)	
		74,100
Total		1,089,100
Less debts of estate		(15,000)
Less: funeral costs – headstone		(2,000)
Less: funeral costs – clothes		(550)
Death estate		1,071,550
Inheritance tax due @ 40%		428,620

Nil rate band all used by lifetime gifts.

Costs incurred by executors in administering the estate and in respect of obtaining probate are not allowable.

Notes

1. As the buildings will have been sold by the executors within three years of death and the sales price is lower than market value at the date of death by more than 5% of that value and £1,000, the sales price can be used in the death estate.
2. The loan secured against the art collection is deductible in full.

Question 24.4

MEMO

To: Any Partner
From: A.N. Accountant
Date: 30 April 2020
Subject: Fionn O'Shea estate

This briefing note deals with the following matters:

(a) Calculating the lifetime inheritance tax (IHT) payable for lifetime gifts.
(b) Calculating the inheritance tax due on Fionn's death estate, making any appropriate claims or reliefs available to reduce the liability arising.

Each of these matters is considered in turn below.

(a) Lifetime IHT on gifts

10 March 2014 – gift to Shay

	£	£
Gift to Shay		9,000
Marriage exemption		(5,000)
Annual exemption – 2013/14		(3,000)
Annual exemption – 2012/13		(1,000)
		NIL

No inheritance tax due.

28 December 2014 – gift to a discretionary trust

		£
Gift to discretionary trust		300,000
Annual exemption – 2014/15		(3,000)
Annual exemption – 2013/14 (already used)		0
Chargeable lifetime transfer		297,000
Inheritance tax threshold – 2014/15	325,000	
Less: cumulative chargeable transfers in the previous seven years	0	
Available inheritance tax threshold	325,000	
Less: nil rate band		(297,000)
		NIL

No inheritance tax due.

25 November 2015 – gift to a discretionary trust

		£
Gift to discretionary trust		175,000
Annual exemption – 2015/16		(3,000)
Annual exemption – 2014/15 (already used)		0
Chargeable lifetime transfer		172,000
Inheritance tax threshold – 2015/16	325,000	
Less: cumulative chargeable transfers in the previous seven years	(297,000)	
Less: available inheritance tax threshold		(28,000)
Amount liable to inheritance tax		144,000
£144,000 @ 20%		28,800

BPR is not available on the gift of shares to the discretionary trust as it is assumed that the holding was less than 51% and was thus not a controlling interest.

(b) Death Estate

10 March 2014 – gift to Shay

Exempt transfer due to marriage exemption and annual exemptions.

No inheritance tax due.

28 December 2014 – gift to a discretionary trust

		£
Chargeable lifetime transfer		297,000
Inheritance tax threshold – 2019/20	325,000	
Less: cumulative chargeable transfers in the previous seven years	NIL	
Less: available nil rate band		(297,000)
		NIL

No inheritance tax due.

25 November 2015 – gift to a discretionary trust

		£
Gift to discretionary trust – fall in value relief applied*		75,000
Annual exemption – 2015/16		(3,000)
Annual exemption – 2014/15		0
Revised chargeable lifetime transfer		72,000
Inheritance tax threshold – 2019/20	325,000	
Less: cumulative chargeable transfers in the previous seven years	(297,000)	
Less: available inheritance tax threshold		(28,000)
Amount liable to inheritance tax		44,000
£44,000 @ 40%		17,600
Less: taper relief 40% (4–5 years)		(7,040)
Less: lifetime tax paid		(28,800)
Additional IHT payable on death		NIL

* When death tax is payable on a gift because the transferor has died, but the value of the gift has fallen between the date the gift was originally made and the date of death, then a claim may be made to have death tax charged on the reduced value of the gift.

31 March 2020 – death estate		£
Main residence		225,000
Cash and investments		85,000
Chattels		15,000
Value of interest in possession trust		276,000
Gross value		601,000
Inheritance tax threshold – 2019/20	325,000	
Less: cumulative chargeable transfers in the previous seven years		
Chargeable lifetime transfer – 28/12/2014	(297,000)	
Chargeable lifetime transfer – 25/11/2015	(172,000)*	
Available inheritance tax threshold		NIL
Amount liable to inheritance tax		601,000
Less: claim to use wife's NRB		(325,000)
		276,000
Inheritance tax payable £276,000 @ 40%		110,400

* Where a lifetime gift has fallen in value, relief is only available against IHT payable in respect of the gift itself. The reduced value does not get cumulated or carried forward to the death estate. The original transfer value is still included in the death estate calculations for the purpose of calculating the available nil rate band.

Question 24.5

IHT due on Andrew's death estate:

	£
Death estate	575,000
Less: remaining NRB*	(175,000)
Taxable estate	400,000
IHT @ 40%	160,000

NRB*:	
Lifetime gift	156,000
Annual exemption 2015/16	(3,000)
Annual exemption 2014/15	(3,000)
	150,000
NRB	325,000
Utilised	(150,000)
Remaining NRB	175,000

James's death estate	£
Value of death estate	1,500,000
Less: NRB	(325,000)
Chargeable estate	1,175,000
IHT payable @ 40%	470,000
Less: quick succession relief	
$\frac{415{,}000^*}{415{,}000 + 160{,}000} \times £160{,}000 \times 40\%$	(46,191)
IHT due	423,809

* Estate of £575,000 − IHT £160,000 = £415,000.

Question 24.6

Report to Alexander Johnston – Inheritance Tax

June 2019

Introduction

This report outlines the inheritance tax (IHT) consequences if you were, unfortunately, to die on today's date (18 June 2019) on the basis of your current wealth, assets and various gifts made.

IHT of £132,625 would arise on your estate based on the information provided to us. Detailed calculations are outlined below.

The due date for payment of IHT is six months from the end of the month of death or, if earlier, the date the IHT return is filed. Using 18 June 2019 as a reference point for these calculations would leave the IHT liability due for payment on or before 31 December 2019. The relevant inheritance tax return would be due for filing 12 months from the end of the month of death, i.e. 30 June 2020.

Conclusion

As this work is a prelude to IHT planning, please read the information herein carefully and we will be in touch to arrange a time to meet to discuss in more detail and to consider any queries you may have.

Calculation of potential inheritance tax liability – assumed date of death 18 June 2019

Potential Death Estate

	£	£
House inherited from brother		590,000
Cash		82,000
Shares in AJ Ltd	625,000	
Less: available BPR		
(100% for unquoted shares in a trading company)	(625,000)	
Investment property	280,000	
Less: associated debt	(280,000)	–
Chalet in France	120,000	
Less: allowable probate costs – 5%	(6,000)	–
		114,000
Aston Martin (Note 1)		90,000
Total		876,000
Less: debts of estate		(10,000)
Less: nil rate band (Note 3)		(436,000)
Death estate		430,000
Inheritance tax @ 40%		172,000
Less: quick succession relief (Note 2)		(39,375)
Inheritance tax due		132,625

Notes:

1. Aston Martin is a gift with reservation. Therefore the higher of the value at the date of gift and the value at the date of death is included in the death estate.

2. Quick succession relief is available, calculated as:

   IHT paid on previous transfer × relevant % × (increase in donee's estate as a result of first transfer / (increase in donee's estate as a result of first transfer + IHT paid on thereon))

   $$\text{i.e. } £75{,}000 \times 60\% \times \frac{£525{,}000}{£525{,}000 + £75{,}000}$$

   = £39,375

3. Calculation of available nil rate band:

	£
Nil rate band at death	325,000
Less: gifts in previous 7 years (cash to son)	(214,000)
Available own nil rate band	111,000
Nil rate band from wife's death	325,000
Total available nil rate band	436,000

The gift of cash to Alexander's son in May 2015 was a PET, however, as Alexander hypothetically dies within 7 years on 18 June 2019, this is chargeable as follows:

	£
Gift of cash	220,000
Less: annual exemption	
2015/16	(3,000)
2014/15	(3,000)
	214,000

Question 24.7

Portia di Rossi – Inheritance tax calculations 2019/20

Lifetime Gifts

Portia has made a number of lifetime gifts which need to be assessed from an IHT perspective to establish tax payable in lifetime and potential additional IHT payable thereon on death.

None of the gifts qualify as a PET as Portia died less than seven years after making the earliest transfer of value.

The following failed PETs and CLTs arise during Portia's lifetime:

2013/14 Tax year	£	£
Failed PET – Gifts to children	18,000	
Less:		
Annual exemption 2013/14	(3,000)	
B/f annual exemption 2012/13	(3,000)	
		12,000*

continued overleaf

2014/15 Tax year		
Failed PET – Gift to USA charity	25,000	
Wedding gift to godson	6,000	
	31,000	
Less:		
Annual exemption 2014/15	(3,000)	
Marriage exemption	(1,000)	
		27,000*
2018/19 Tax year		
Discretionary trust	380,000	
Less:		
Annual exemption 2018/19	(3,000)	
Annual exemption 2017/18	(3,000)	
		374,000
Total chargeable		413,000

* No tax in lifetime as it was then a PET nor on death as both are covered by the IHT NRB.

Tax payable on death by trustees of discretionary trust

	£	
Value liable to tax		374,000
NRB at death	325,000	
Utilised by PETs now chargeable on death	(39,000)	
		(286,000)
Liable on death		88,000
IHT thereon @ 40% on death		35,200
Less: IHT @ 20% paid on CLT of £49,000 (CLT £374,000 less NRB £325,000)		(9,800)
Additional IHT on death		25,400

IHT treatment of assets at date of death

Calculation of taxable estate on death

	Notes	£
Armagh house	2	645,000
House contents	2	48,500
Villa in Portugal	3	225,000
Belfast Ceramics Plc shares – 18,000 × £1.45	4	26,100
British Meats Plc shares – 3,500 × £13.60	4	47,600

continued overleaf

Belfast bank accounts			69,000
Guernsey bank account	3		228,000
Italiana Wine SA shares	5	180,000	
Less: business property relief	5	(180,000)	
Nil			0
Taxable estate			1,289,200

IHT payable by Portia's executors on her estate at death:

As Portia's £325,000 NRB has been exhausted by lifetime transfers, the whole of the taxable estate is chargeable to IHT at 40%, being £515,680.

Notes

1. Lifetime Gifts
   The annual Christmas gifts to Portia's grandchildren are covered by the £250 small gifts exemption and are therefore exempt from IHT.
   As only gifts to EU charities are exempt from IHT, the gift to the US charity is not exempt.
   The first £1,000 of the gift to her godson is exempt as a gift in consideration of marriage, with the remainder being a transfer of value.

2. House in Armagh
   The property was sold for less than its probate value. Under post-mortem relief, where an interest in land is sold within four years of the date of death, a claim may be made that the sale price is treated as the date of death value for IHT purposes. The sale value has been included in the estate tax calculation on the basis that such a claim would be made. The value of the contents of Portia's Armagh house also falls into her estate.

3. Overseas assets
   As Portia died domiciled in the UK, her worldwide assets are liable to UK IHT. Therefore, both the Portuguese villa and the Guernsey bank account are part of her estate on death.

4. Quoted shares
   Post-mortem relief also allows, where quoted shares are sold within 12 months of the date of death for less than their probate value, a claim to be made to substitute the gross sale price for the probate value.
   However, the change in value of all investments sold within 12 months of death must be taken into account.
   The Belfast Ceramics Plc shares were sold at a loss, whereas the British Meats Plc share sale produced a gain.
   Overall, as a claim would be beneficial, the actual sale proceeds after death have been included in the calculation, on the basis that a claim would be made.

5. Company assets
   Business property relief (BPR) is not limited to UK situated business property.
   Since Portia held shares in an unquoted trading company and meets the two-year ownership test (having acquired the shares in 2014), BPR is available in respect of these shares.

Chapter 25

Question 25.1

Capital Gains Tax

As Shay is Sean's son, he is treated as a connected party under section 286 TCGA 1992, hence market value is imposed on any transactions between them that are gifts or at undervalue.

The gift of his residence is a deemed disposal at market value for capital gains tax purposes. However, as Sean has lived in the property all his life, the entire gain will be exempt by virtue of principle private residence relief.

Inheritance Tax

The gift of his house will be treated as a gift with reservation of benefit, and as such is treated as follows:

(i) as a PET at the time of the gift (using the valuation at the time of the gift); and
(ii) as part of Sean's death estate (using the valuation at the time of death) because it is assumed Sean will die within seven years of making the gift.

This results in a potential double charge should Sean die within seven years of the gift. HMRC will select the treatment giving rise to the higher total tax payable and will require two computations as denoted above. When calculating the inheritance tax arising under the GWR rules, Sean will be able to claim the available residence nil rate band in the year of death together with any residence nil rate band unused by his spouse/civil partner. This, however, is not available when calculating inheritance tax on the failed PET.

Chapter 26

Question 26.1

(a) The due date for payment of the lifetime IHT and the filing of the IHT 100 is six months from the end of the month in which the transfer takes place (i.e. 31 May 2016).
(b) The due date for additional IHT payable on the lifetime gift as a result of Fionn's death on 31 March 2020 is six months from the end of the month in which death occurs (i.e. 30 September 2020).
(c) Payment of IHT on the death estate is due on the earlier of:
    - six months from the end of month in which the transfer takes place, assuming this occurs on 31 March 2020 (i.e. 30 September 2020); or
    - the date of delivery of the IHT400 return (i.e. 29 July 2020).

In this case IHT on the death estate is due on 29 July 2020. The due date for filing the IHT400 for any CLTs, failed PETS and details of the death estate is within 12 months from the end of the month of death (i.e. 31 March 2021).

Question 26.2

Calculation of IHT on failed PET to Eileen – 14 June 2015

No spouse exemption is available despite the subsequent marriage.
The value is the loss to the donor which will be more than half of the total value of £900,000.
Peter's 50% retained is worth less than 50% of the whole. Using a 15% discount the value is £382,500

	£	
Value of PET (loss to estate)	517,500	
Less: annual exemptions 2015/16 and 2014/15	(6,000)	
Net chargeable transfer	511,500	
Available nil rate band (Note 1)	(105,000)	
Taxable amount	406,500	
		£
Tax @ 40%		162,600
Less: taper relief at 40% (gift more than 4 but less than 5 years before)		(65,040)
Tax payable		97,560

Note:

1. The chargeable transfer in 2010 (less £6,000 for two annual exemptions) used £220,000 of the nil rate band, so the nil rate band for calculating IHT on the failed PET reduced from £325,000 to £105,000.

Tax on estate at death – 1 January 2020

	£
Bank accounts, investments, etc. net	240,000
Shotguns, etc.	48,000
Smyth Farm	1,900,000
Windy Farm	950,000
Smyth Farm Ltd shares	425,000
Total	3,563,000
Less: agricultural relief and business property relief (Note 2)	(1,175,000)
Total value of estate net of reliefs	2,388,000
Less: nil rate band (nil due to all used by failed PET in 2015)	Nil
Net taxable value	2,388,000
Inheritance tax @ 40%	£955,200

Notes:

1. The half share of Primrose Farmhouse passing to Eileen, as the surviving beneficial joint tenant, is exempt by virtue of the spouse exemption. Thus it is ignored.
2. Business property and agricultural property relief

   Business property relief (BPR)

   Total value of Smyth Farm Ltd shares (seemingly a trading company, so 100% BPR available) is £425,000.

   Agricultural property relief (APR)

   Windy Farm: no APR available as Trevor has never occupied it for farming – seven years of ownership would have been needed for APR to apply.

Smyth Farm:

- No APR available for stables (£300,000) as they are not occupied for agriculture.
- APR is only available on £600,000 (agricultural value) of £700,000 (market value) of the farmhouse.
- As the tenancy is prior to 1995 and has more than two years left to run, APR is only available on 50% of £1,500,000 (£1,900,000 less £300,000 for stables and £100,000 of farmhouse value) i.e. £750,000.

Total value of reliefs £1,175,000.

Chapter 27

Question 27.1

There are several tax consequences of the proposed transfer of the warehouse from the company at undervalue.

Corporation tax

The transfer of the plot of land from the company to Stewart is a disposal of a chargeable asset; any gains arising on the disposal are liable to corporation tax for the company. Stewart is connected to the company under section 286 TCGA 1992 as he controls the company through his ownership of the majority of the company's share capital. As a result, section 18 TCGA 1992 imposes market value on any capital transaction between Stewart and the company. The market value imposed by section 18 forms the base cost for any future disposal by Stewart of the warehouse.

The corporation tax payable by the company will be as follows:

	£
Deemed proceeds – market value	625,000
Less: original base cost	(100,000)
Indexation allowance*:	
$\frac{278.1-174.4}{174.4} \times 100{,}000$	(59,500)
Chargeable gain	465,500
Corporation tax thereon @ 19%	88,445

*Indexation factor up to 31 December 2017 used.

Close company implications

Furthermore, there are, potentially, both IHT and CGT implications if the transaction is proceeded with as a transfer at undervalue. The company is a close company under section 439 CTA 2010 as it is controlled by five or fewer participators as Stewart holds 100% of the shares.

CGT

The provisions of section 125 TCGA 1992 mean that a transfer at undervalue by a close company can result in the reduction in the base cost of the company's shares for its shareholders by the amount by which the asset is undervalued, thereby reducing the base cost Stewart can use in the calculation of CGT arising on a future disposal of the his shares in the company.

However, section 125(4) TCGA 1992 provides an exception from this legislation in several cases, including where the transferee is a participator, or an associate of a participator, in the company and an amount equal to the undervalue amount is treated as a distribution or a capital distribution; or in cases where the transferee is an employee of the company and an amount equal to the undervalue amount is treated as the employee's employment income.

In these circumstances, it is likely that the transfer at undervalue would be treated as an income distribution under section 385(1) ITTOIA 2005, unless Stewart is an employee. This works by treating the amount by which the asset is undervalued as a dividend liable to income tax. Therefore, if Stewart only pays £350,000 to the company for the land plot, he will be treated as receiving a dividend of £275,000. A distribution of this size would be subject to income tax at an effective rate of 38.1%, resulting in an income tax liability of £104,775 (ignoring the £2,000 tax-free dividend allowance).

IHT
There are also potential IHT implications to consider. Sections 94–102 IHTA 1984 contain anti-avoidance rules applying to transfers of value (e.g. sales at undervalue) by close companies. The transfer of value is apportioned between the close company's participators for IHT purposes. In Stewart's case, the entire transfer of value of £275,000 would be apportioned to Stewart for IHT purposes as he holds 100% of the shares.

Assuming Stewart made no other transfers of value in the same tax year, or in the previous seven years, the entire amount would be covered by his nil rate band (£325,000) and annual exemption (£3,000 plus a potential £3,000 from the previous tax year if it remains unused). Though there would be no IHT payable in lifetime, this chargeable lifetime transfer could affect the level of IHT on Stewart's death estate if he died within seven years. However, as it is likely that the transfer at under-value would be treated as an income distribution under section 385(1) ITTOIA 2005, unless Stewart is an employee, no CLT will arise for IHT purposes.

Chapter 30

Question 30.1

Private and Confidential
Mr Symon Cawell,
Grove House,
2 Maybury,
Belfast

1 March 2020

Dear Symon,

First, may I start by thanking you for your time at our recent meeting.

You asked me to consider the stamp duty implications of the various transactions, to which please see below.

Stamp duty on transactions

Rental of property
Stamp duty land tax (SDLT) is chargeable on the premium at the rates applicable for non-residential property. This is calculated as follows:

	£
£0–£150,000 @ 0%	0
Next £100,000 @ 2%	2,000
Remaining £325,000 @ 5%	16,250
Total SDLT payable on premium	18,250

However, SDLT is also chargeable on 1% of the net present value of the rent exceeding £150,000. The SDLT on the rent is, therefore, 1% of £35,000 which comes to £350. Therefore, the total SDLT payable amounts to £18,600.

Purchase of house by son
No SDLT is payable as first-time buyer's relief is available because the consideration is less than £300,000 and they intend to live in the property as their only or main residence.

Sale of Government securities
No stamp duty arises on this purchase as the purchase of Government securities and loan stock is an exempt transaction.

Shares received in satisfaction of debt
You received shares worth £175,000 in lieu of repayment of the loan originally provided. Consideration subject to stamp duty is any money or money's worth provided by the purchaser. Therefore, the loan provided constitutes consideration and is thus chargeable to stamp duty as being consideration for the purchase of shares at a rate of 0.5% which comes to £875.

Gift of shares to daughter
No stamp duty arises on this as it is a gift for no consideration.

Purchase of property for daughter
As you are not replacing your main residence with this acquisition and your main residence is worth more than £40,000, this will be classed as an additional residential property acquisition. A 3% surcharge applies to each 'slice' of the consideration, thus SDLT is payable as follows:

	£
£0–£125,000 @ 3%	3,750
Remaining £57,000 @ 5%	2,850
Total SDLT payable	6,600

Should you require anything further, do not hesitate to contact me.

Yours sincerely,

An Accountant

Question 30.2

For the purpose of claiming group relief for SDLT on the transfer of the two warehouses by Armour Ltd, Armour's ownership of Destiny Ltd was 82% at the time of the transaction and thus no SDLT was payable on the sale of the warehouse to Destiny Ltd for £750,000 due to SDLT group relief. However, within a three-year period, and by 1 January 2020, Destiny is no longer a member of the group as Armour's ownership has fallen to 74%. As this is below the 75% ownership threshold, group relief will be withdrawn. SDLT of £27,000 is now payable (being the total of the first £150,000 at 0%, plus the next £100,000 at 2% and the remaining £500,000 at 5%).

Gaston Ltd did not qualify for group relief for SDLT purposes at the time it acquired the warehouse from Armour Ltd as its ownership by Armour Limited is less than 75%. However, as the chargeable consideration of £120,000 is below the non-residential threshold of £150,000, no SDLT is payable.

Question 30.3

If it is sold for £200,000 after the mortgage is paid off, the consideration is £200,000. The SDLT on the property is 0% on the first £125,000 and 2% on the next £75,000. Therefore the charge is £1,500. If it is sold for £200,000 with the son taking over the mortgage, the consideration is £250,000 (as assumption of a debt is viewed as consideration). The SDLT on the property is 0% on the first £125,000 and 2% on the next £125,000. Therefore the charge is £2,500.

The sale for £350,000 means consideration is £350,000. The SDLT on the property is 0% on the first £125,000, 2% on the next £125,000 and 5% on the next £100,000. Therefore, the charge is £7,500. The mortgage is not taken on by his son and so has no impact on the SDLT due.

Question 30.4

Assets subject to stamp duty land tax (SDLT), typically land and property, can be transferred between 75% group companies without any stamp duty liability, provided the transfer is not part of arrangements for the transferee company to leave the group or consideration for the transfer is not being provided directly or indirectly by a third party.

In this situation, no SDLT liability will arise. However, relief from SDLT will be withdrawn if Neptune was to leave the group within three years of the execution of the instrument of transfer while still holding an interest in the freehold property. Relief would also be withdrawn if Solar's ownership of Neptune fell below 75%.

Question 30.5

Apple, Banana, and Date form a group for SDLT group relief purposes, as Banana and Date meet the 75% subsidiary test. The sale to Date Ltd was eligible for SDLT relief and one condition for that relief is that Date Ltd must remain within the SDLT group for three years after buying the warehouse.

Grape Ltd was never in the same SDLT Group as Apple Ltd, but no SDLT was due as the consideration is less than £150,000.

Chapter 31

Question 31.1

(a) First-time buyer's relief is not available as Adam does not intend to live in the house as his only or main residence. The chargeable consideration is £150,000; it is irrelevant that a £30,000 deposit was paid first followed by the balance of £120,000.This is subject to SDLT at 0% on the first £125,000 and 2% on the next £25,000. Therefore SDLT of £500 is due.
(b) A SDLT return is required if the chargeable consideration is more £40,000.
(c) The SDLT return and payment are both due 14 days after completion (i.e. 14 November 2019).

Question 31.2

Stamp duty land tax (SDLT) will be payable by the purchaser of the Dungannon Property in the amount of £13,250 (being the total of the first £150,000 at 0%, plus the next £100,000 at 2% and the remaining £225,000 at 5%). There is a 14-day time limit after execution for getting the document stamped and paying the required stamp duty. Therefore, as the transaction occurred on 31 March 2020, the SDLT and associated return must be presented to HMRC by 14 April 2020, otherwise a penalty and interest may be charged. The SDLT is a liability of the purchaser and not the vendor of thte property.

Question 31.3

Apple
As the amount being paid for the shares is below the "nil duty rate" of £1,000, no stamp duty is payable.

Peaches
As the amount being paid for the shares is above the "nil duty rate" of £1,000, the rate of stamp duty payable on the purchase of the shares is 0.5%.

Therefore, the stamp duty payable is 0.5% of £6,725 = £33.62. Stamp duty is rounded up to the nearest £5, so the actual amount payable is £35.

There is a 30-day time limit after execution (when the share transfer documents are dated and signed) for getting the document stamped and paying the required stamp duty.

Therefore, assuming the Peaches transaction proceeds on 30 April 2019, the share transfer document must be presented to HMRC by 30 May 2019 with the correct duty payment of £35 to avoid a penalty and interest being charged.

Blackberry
There is no duty payable on foreign shares, so the stamp duty here is nil.

Question 31.4

(a) A transfer of UK unlisted shares worth £90,000 on divorce from husband to wife is exempt from stamp duty.
(b) A sale of shares in a UK listed company for £524,000 to a registered UK charity is exempt from stamp duty (subject to being adjudicated).
(c) A sale of shares in a UK unlisted company for £150,000 between unconnected individuals is stampable at 0.5% × £150,000 = £750.
(d) A sale of UK shares worth £895 between unconnected parties does not attract a stamp duty liability because the consideration is less than £1,000.
(e) A sale of shares in a UK unlisted company for £60,000 in cash and an agreement to waive £20,000 of debt owed by seller to purchaser attracts stamp duty at 0.5% on £80,000, being £400, as the debt waiver counts towards consideration.

Chapter 32

Question 32.1

(a) The sale of the freehold of an office block constructed in November 2017 is the sale of a new commercial property (under three years old) therefore this is a standard-rated supply on which 20% output VAT must be charged.
(b) The grant of a 99-year lease in a brand new factory is the grant of a lease. This is not a standard-rated supply and because it is commercial property it is therefore an exempt supply as the option to tax has not been elected for.

(c) The sale of the freehold of a factory first constructed in January 2015 is the sale of a commercial property that is not new and is therefore an exempt supply as the option to tax has not been elected for.

Question 32.2

(a) A factory is a commercial property and the word "lease" means it is an exempt supply as the option to tax has not been elected for.
(b) Some domestic property is zero-rated, i.e. residential property that is brand new and is being sold by the constructor – this property does not meet either of these criteria, therefore it is not a zero-rated supply. It cannot be standard-rated as it is not commercial property, therefore it is an exempt supply.
(c) As this is a sale of a new commercial freehold, it is standard-rated and 20% output VAT must be charged.
(d) As this is the sale of a commercial freehold that has been opted to tax, despite the property not being new, this is a standard-rated supply and 20% output VAT must be charged.

Question 32.3

As the building is a new commercial building less than three years old, the sale of the building will have been standard-rated. VAT charged thereon would have been £90,000 (£450,000 × 20%).

As EyeSpy Ltd is partially exempt, it would have been entitled to recover input tax of £63,000 (£90,000 × 70%) in the year ending 31 March 2020.

Question 32.4

(a) The sale of land is an exempt supply and the option to tax can be made on this supply.
(b) The sale of a 75-year-old terraced house is an exempt supply, but it is a dwelling and residential building rather than a commercial building, so the option to tax can be made but will not be effective.
(c) The lease of a 15-year-old factory is an exempt supply – because it is a commercial building, the option to tax can be made.
(d) The freehold sale of a two-year-old office block – the sale of a new, commercial freehold is a standard-rated supply. It is therefore not exempt so the option to tax is not relevant.
(e) A 99-year lease on a one-year-old shop – this is not the sale of a new commercial freehold, so it is an exempt supply. The option to tax can therefore be made.

Question 32.5

(a) The freehold sale of a two-year-old factory is freehold, new and commercial and hence a standard-rated supply. An option to tax could be made but would not have any effect.
(b) The grant of a 30-year lease in a brand new office block is an exempt supply. As it is an exempt supply of a commercial building, the option to tax will be effective.
(c) A farmer rents out a plot of land to another farmer. This is not residential so it is not zero-rated. It is not the sale of new commercial property and is thus not standard-rated. Therefore this must be an exempt supply. The option to tax can be made because it can be effective over an exempt supply of any sort of land.
(d) A landlord leases out four floors of a building to an insurance company – it is a lease, it is a commercial building so it is an exempt supply. The exempt supply of a commercial building

means the option to tax can be made and effective. It does not matter that the tenant is making exempt supplies. The option will mean standard-rate VAT at 20% will be charged on any supplies in relation to this property, including rents. As the tenant is exempt they will not be able to recover the related input VAT.

(e) This is a lease of residential property, so it is an exempt supply. It does not matter that the tenant is using the property for business purposes. Zero-rating does not apply as no major interest has been granted. The option to tax is not effective over a domestic property.

Question 32.6

(a) Renovating and building services are standard-rated supplies, so VAT will be charged to Mr Jones on these costs.

(b) Since Mr James is letting-out a commercial property, he is making exempt supplies. Because he leases the building out to tenants and hence makes an exempt supply, the input tax on the renovation costs will relate to the exempt supply of that office block and will be irrecoverable. If Mr James were to opt to tax the building, he would then be making a taxable supply. Thus, when the renovation occurs, the input tax he pays will relate to a taxable supply and hence will be recoverable in full.

The option to tax means that any future supply he makes in connection with the office block will be a standard-rated supply. The next time he sends an invoice for rent to his tenants, he will have to add 20% VAT on top. For the tenants, they will receive an invoice for rent that has gone up by 20%.

One of those tenants is an accountant making fully taxable supplies. Therefore, the extra 20% is input tax for the accountant and because the accountant makes taxable supplies, the input tax charged on the rent is recoverable in full. The most that the accountant tenant will 'suffer' from the 20% increase is a cash-flow disadvantage.

The other tenant is an insurance company, which makes exempt supplies. When the rent goes up by 20% that increase is input tax, which is irrecoverable as it relates to exempt supplies. This will be a direct cost to the insurance company.

When the landlord makes an option to tax, he does not have to seek permission from the tenants before doing so. However, the landlord should check the lease agreement because some lease agreements do not allow the rent to be increased (even by VAT). In such cases, the irrecoverable VAT must be met out of the landlord's rental profits. If the lease agreement is silent, the landlord can make an option to tax without any permission being given by the tenants.

Question 32.7

Even though the property is not less than three years old it has been opted to tax by its owner, therefore 20% standard-rate VAT of £250,000 (£1,250,000 × 20%) is chargeable by the vendor, Spidey Enterprises Ltd. The total consideration is therefore £1,500,000 (£1,250,000 + (20% × £1,250,000)). The SDLT liability of Iron Man Developments Ltd that arises on the VAT-inclusive price is as follows:

	£
0–£150,000 @ 0%	0
Next £100,000 @ 2%	2,000
Remaining £1,250,000 @ 5%	62,500
Total SDLT	64,500

Index

THANKS FOR JOINING US

We hope that you are finding your course of study with Chartered Accountants Ireland a rewarding experience. We know you've got the will to succeed and are willing to put in the extra effort. You may well know like-minded people in your network who are interested in a career in business, finance or accountancy and are currently assessing their study options. As a current student, your endorsement matters greatly in helping them decide on a career in Chartered Accountancy.

HOW CAN YOU HELP?

If you have an opportunity to explain to a friend or colleague why you chose Chartered Accountancy as your professional qualification, please do so.

Anyone interested in the profession can visit www.charteredaccountants.ie/prospective-students where they'll find lots of information and advice on starting out.

Like us on Facebook, follow us on Twitter.

Email us at info@charteredaccountants.ie

We can all help in promoting Chartered Accountancy, and the next generation to secure their success, and in doing so strengthen our qualification and community. We really appreciate your support.